THE RULING CLASS

Dilexi justitiam, quaesivi veritatem

THE
RULING CLASS

(*Elementi di Scienza Politica*)

by
GAETANO MOSCA

TRANSLATION BY
HANNAH D. KAHN

EDITED AND REVISED, WITH AN INTRODUCTION, BY
ARTHUR LIVINGSTON

FIRST EDITION

McGRAW-HILL BOOK COMPANY, INC.
NEW YORK AND LONDON
1939

THE MAPLE PRESS COMPANY, YORK, PA.

CONTENTS

v

INTRODUCTION

I. TAINE AND MOSCA: THE *Teorica*

Gaetano Mosca's theory of the ruling class was evolved in its first form during the years 1878–1881, while Mosca was a student under Angelo Messedaglia at the University of Palermo. It occurred to him at that time to generalize the method which Taine had used in the *Ancien régime*. There, it will be remembered, Taine sought the origins of the French Revolution in the decadence of the groups of people that had ruled France during the golden age of the old monarchy, a class which he considered and analyzed under three headings, the crown, the clergy and the nobility.

The first thought of the student Mosca was that perhaps any society might be analyzed the way Taine had analyzed monarchical France; and his second was that, in view of the vogue that doctrines of majority rule had had in the nineteenth century, he had hit upon a most fertile and suggestive hypothesis. If one looks closely at any country, be it commonly known as a monarchy, a tyranny, a republic or what one will, one inevitably finds that actual power is wielded never by one person, the monarch or head of the state, nor yet by the whole community of citizens, but by a particular group of people which is always fairly small in numbers as compared with the total population. Taine had shown, also, that the traits of the brilliant French civilization of the age of the Great King were the traits less of the French people at large than of the same French aristocracy and, in fact, seemed to be connected with the special conditions under which that aristocracy had functioned during the seventeenth and eighteenth centuries. That principle, too, could be generalized into the thesis that the dominant traits of the civilization of a given society during a given period will be the traits of the group of people who govern it (politicians, rulers).

Today Mosca is eighty years old; but at no time in the course of his long life has he ever been quite able to forget the thrill of discovery that he experienced away back in the seventies as he found himself in possession of what he thought to be a golden key to the arcana of human history. To tell the truth, the originality of his discovery has not seldom been a subject of dispute among his colleagues and competitors; and during the fifty years that have intervened since those days, many writers have busied themselves compiling lists of thinkers who have explicitly noted a fact which has always been perfectly apparent to everybody, *viz.*, that in all human groups at all times there are the few who rule and the many who are ruled.

The maxim that there is nothing new under the sun is a very true maxim; that is to say, it covers about half the truth, which is a great deal of truth for a maxim to cover. All human beings who have lived on earth have lived, by and large, on the same earth. They have all beheld, at least out of the corners of their eyes, the same realities; they have all experienced the same emotions; they have all thought, we may imagine, the same thoughts. But what the history of human civilization shows is the unending variety with which individuals evaluate the various things that everybody sees. Probably no human being since Adam has been without an approximate knowledge of the law of gravity; but no one till Galileo's day thought of centering his whole attention upon the falling object and making it the pivot of a scientific revolution. No human being since the day of Cain and Abel has been unaware that people preach moral principles and then use such power as they have often, if not always, without regard to moral principles. Yet no one before Machiavelli ever thought of taking that fact and founding upon it a scientific politics which would eliminate ethical considerations. I believe Croce has said it somewhere: The originality of thinkers lies not always in their seeing things that nobody else has ever seen, but often in the stress they give now to this commonplace and now to that. I consider it useful to make this little digression for the benefit of an ever-lengthening roster of source hunters who spend their time drawing literary and scientific parallels without considering questions of stress or the uses that men of genius make of commonplaces. The medieval Venetians or the ancient Romans were so much in possession of the concept of class and of the concept of ruling classes that they devised meticulous legislation to cover class relations and even the movement of social atoms from class to class. All the same, no Venetian and no Roman ever formulated Mosca's theory of the ruling class. Class is a visible external fact of everyday life in Europe, and few European writers have been able to discuss social problems at any great length without eventually encountering the fact of class, of class struggle, of class circulation, in some form or other. None of them, however, not Guicciardini, not Marx, not Taine, made the use of the fact of class that Mosca made. And conversely, one may say the same of those who have paralleled or utilized Mosca—of Michels, of Sorel, of Pareto.

Why do individual thinkers come to stress certain relations and facts which everybody observes and takes for granted? Usually these problems of personal evolution are beyond recovery by history. We shall never know why Voltaire became a mocking skeptic while his brother remained a pious "enthusiast." We know, indeed, that, in periods of intense and free cultural activity, if a certain number of intellectuals are placed in one general environment in the presence of the same general problems, certain numbers of them will evolve the same solutions. This fact is ordinarily taken account of in the remark that at certain periods certain concepts, certain manners of thinking, seem to be "in the air." Sorel developed the concept of the political myth in the first decade of the twentieth century. Mosca had developed his concept of the "political formula" twenty years before. Sorel was not a methodical scholar. He knew nothing of Mosca. Evidently the concept was "in the air." For two generations before Mosca's time, socialism had been emphasizing the conflict of classes, and in Italy in particular the educated classes had become explicitly aware of their duties and responsibilities as "leading" or "directing" classes (*classi dirigenti*). One should not be surprised, therefore, at such evident parallels as exist between Mosca and many other thinkers before him or after him.

While the details of individual evolution most often remain undiscoverable, apart from individual memoirs or confessions which are themselves not too trustworthy in such regards, one is usually able to note certain general environmental circumstances that seem to influence individual choices of stress in certain directions. When we find Mosca in possession of Taine in 1878, we should not forget that Mosca was an Italian while Taine was a Frenchman. I find it very French in Taine that he should never have been interested in the general bearings of the method that he was using. So true is this that, as he proceeds to rear his intellectual structure about the old regime, he is continually led into the fallacy of assigning particular causes (associated with the fact of the exclusion of the French aristocracy from their feudal functions) to phenomena that are general and world-wide—preciosity, for instance, rationality, politeness, display, all of which recur in times and places where ruling classes are situated far otherwise than was the French aristocracy of the golden age. I find it also very French in Taine that he should never free himself, in the *Origines*, from the preoccupation with good citizenship. Aspiring indeed to a stern and rigorous historical method, Taine can think of history only as at the service of certain high moral ideals.

Mosca instead was an Italian, to whom the analytical method of thinking came naturally. He leaped upon Taine's method as a tool for straight thinking and sought to be, and, to a surprising extent in one still so young, succeeded in being "objective." I find that very Italian. Italians do easily and as a matter of course what other human beings do rarely, if at all, and then only with great effort and after hard and sustained discipline: they think by processes of distinction. While the rest of the world is hunting for ways to show that the true is good and the good true, and that both are beautiful, the Italians are busy keeping virtue, truth and beauty separate and in the heart as well as in the mind. Perhaps that is the great Italian "contribution to civilization," which Italian nationalists are always trying to discover.

One may as well add that Mosca is a Sicilian (born at Palermo in 1858). That too is a determining factor in his individuality which Americans especially should bear in mind. Americans as a rule stand at an opposite pole to the run of Sicilians in their manner of approaching life through thought. Americans are impatient of theory and suspicious of philosophies and general principles. We study history and almost never the philosophy of history. Few American lawyers will have anything to do with the philosophy of law. Let an American show a definite propensity for theoretical generalizing and he will be barred from public life as an impractical menace. It is amazing, on the other hand, with what a dearth of theoretical discipline certain famous Americans can get along through life and go far. To that deficiency we partly owe the reputation for ignorance and naïveté that we enjoy, as a nation, in a more sophisticated Europe. The level of theory in the United States is much lower than the level of theory on the Continent. The Continent in its turn is, on the whole, in the rear of Italy in this respect, and the great Italian theoreticians tend to be southerners. In a charming "confession" with which he prefaced the 1884 edition of the *Teorica*, Mosca tells of his great interest as a boy in history and boasts of his retentive memory. But what strikes one in Mosca, the historian, is the fact that history has no meaning whatever to him until it has become general principle, uniformity, philosophy. So it was with Vico and Bruno, and so it is with Croce— all men of the Italian South.

Two other determinations, one professional, the other Sicilian, have perhaps a more direct bearing upon Mosca's development of the vision he owed in the first instance to Taine. In the *Teorica* of 1884, Mosca kept strictly to problems of government, and that interest is paramount even in the *Elements*. This narrowing of his field is all the more striking as one contrasts the uses to which the concept of class, or of the ruling class, has been put by thinkers all the way from Marx to Pareto. The reason undoubtedly is that Mosca began life as a student of constitutional law and of political theories. He became an unsalaried lecturer on those subjects, first at Palermo (1881–1886), then at Rome (1887–1895). From Rome he went on to be a professor of constitutional law at Turin (1895–1923), returning to Rome (1923–1931) as professor of political theories. Now it is clear that government proper is only one phase of social life, while the implications of the theory of the ruling class as Taine had applied that theory in the sixties and as Mosca had conceived it in 1881, lead out into society as a whole and beckon toward a general sociology. Mosca was never to follow them in that direction beyond the limits reached in the *Elements*.

Perhaps in a spirit of professional specialization, perhaps for practical reasons, he always kept turning backward and inward upon the strictly constitutional or political problem, leaving some of his richest and most suggestive ideas in the form of hints, assertions, or casual observations, but at any rate undeveloped.

Sicilian again one may call the political bent which Mosca's placid biography shows. Not all Sicilians are politicians, but when a Sicilian is a politician he is a good one. The Sicilian takes to politics as a duck to water. North Italians, too, of course, have been seen in Italian public life. But they make a great to-do about it. They shout and wave their arms from soap-boxes, they fill the newspapers with their publicities, their polemics, their marches on Rome, they fight libel suits and duels; and finally they get into the government, only to be upset, as likely as not, at the next turn of the wheel. The Sicilian, instead, simply takes the train and goes to Rome, where a coach-in-four is waiting to drive him to what Carducci called "the summit of the Capitol." That, more or less, was Mosca's experience in public life. Editor of the journal of the Chamber of Deputies from 1887 to 1895 (a bureaucratic post—it maintained him during his unpaid lectureship at the university), he became a deputy himself in 1908, and sat with the Liberal Conservatives during two legislatures till 1918 (those included the war years), serving also as under-secretary for the Colonies under the Salandra ministry (1914–1916). And there he was, in 1918, senator for life by the usual royal appointment, and all without any great clamor, any boisterous quarrels or exposures, without even any particular public fame. Prezzolini and Papini tried to publicize Mosca in 1903–1904—"to valorize him as a public asset," as the language went in those days. Prezzolini made a second effort in his *Voce* series in 1912 (see *Il nuovo nazionalismo*). One need mention this aspect of Mosca's career, always eminent yet never prominent, simply as reinforcing the mental attitudes that inclined him to leave his work permanently in a somewhat embryonic form, and even to subordinate it, in some few respects, to the outlook of a political party.

The Italian and Sicilian background, the professional outlook, the political talent, which are revealed by this forward look from Mosca's student days, help us to understand the developments that Mosca gave to his theory of the ruling class in the years

1881–1883.   At that time he was in possession of three or four
simple concepts which he thought he could use for the construction of an outline history of the rise of the modern state.   Contrary to theories of majority rule, he perceived, societies are
always ruled by minorities, by oligarchies.   The current classification of governments, therefore—Aristotle's (monarchies, aristocracies, democracies), Montesquieu's (absolutisms, limited
monarchies, republics), Spencer's (militant and industrial
states)—could be dispensed with in favor of a classification of
oligarchies.   Essaying this classification, Mosca distinguished a
number of types: military and priestly aristocracies, hereditary
aristocracies, aristocracies of landowners, aristocracies of liquid
wealth (money), aristocracies of merit (allowing, that is, free
access to power to all elements in society and notably to people
of the poorer classes).   Now the various political theories that
have prevailed in history—"chosen people" theories based on
conceptions of race or family, divine-right theories or theories of
popular sovereignty—by no means reflect the realities underlying
this classification.   Mosca, therefore, went on to develop his
theory of the "political formula."   There is always a ruling
minority, but such minorities never stop at the brute fact of
holding power.   They justify their rule by theories or principles
which are in turn based on beliefs or ethical systems which are
accepted by those who are ruled.   These "political formulas"
contain very little that could be described as "truth," but they
should not be regarded as deliberate deceptions or mystifications
on the part of scheming rulers.   They express, rather, a deep
need in human nature whereby the human being more readily
defers to abstract universal principles than to the will of individual human beings.

Mature in 1881, these ideas were formulated in the *Teorica
dei governi e governo parlamentare*, which was complete in 1883 and
published in 1884 (2d ed., 1925).   In spite of its age and the
writings of Mosca that have followed it, this book still has its
interest and its points of originality.   Eleven years later, 1895,
Mosca completed and published his *Elements* (*Elementi di
scienza politica*, 1896).

As compared with the *Teorica*, the *Elements* presents the theory
of the ruling class in more rounded form, along with a series of
new concepts that are exceedingly suggestive.

II. The Concept of History

In the *Elements,* in line with an outstanding preoccupation of European scholarship during the nineties, Mosca confronts the problem of constructing a political science (which he prefers to keep distinct from sociology). The content of that science will be the discovery of the constant tendencies or laws that determine the behavior of the human masses (page 1) and regulate the organization of political authority (page 3). These tendencies or laws can be discovered only from a study of "social facts," which in turn can be found only in the history of the various nations (page 41): "It is to the historical method that we must return."

Actually, Mosca's practice is better than this incomplete statement would indicate. He will of course take the facts about society from any source or method that can supply them, only so they are facts—from economics, from anthropology, from psychology, or any similar science. He does explicitly reject for the politico-social field any absolute or exclusive acceptance of climatic or north-and-south theories, anthropological theories based on the observation of primitive societies (the question of size is important), the economic interpretation of history (it is too unilateral), doctrines of racial superiorities and inferiorities (many different races have had their moments of splendor), and evolutionary theories (they fail to account for the rhythmical movement of human progress—biological evolution would require continuous improvement). However, apart from some keen remarks (as, for instance, those on the limitations of the experimental method or on the applicability of science to the control of social living), the main interest in this statement of the problem of scientific sociology lies in the fact that it undoubtedly influenced the penetrating and altogether novel discussion of the same problem in Pareto's *Trattato* (chap. I), which, in turn, is the final enlargement of an essay by Pareto written in 1897.

The interest of Mosca's view comes out if we consider it not from the standpoint of social science, but from that of historical science. Now if one were to say that this view is new and original, a host of scholars would appear with no end of citations to show that Mosca says nothing that has not been known to everyone since the days of Herodotus. Historians have always felt more or less vaguely that their work ought somehow to enrich human experience, that one can, after all, learn something from the fact that billions of human beings have lived out their lives on earth before us. Historians as metaphysical and theological as Bonald have always contended that history confirmed their arbitrary creeds. On the other hand a very respectable list of authorities could be quoted to show that history can teach us nothing; that life is always new; that where there is a will there is a way; that no impulse of the present need be checked in the light of analogies from the past. If one examines the present outlook of historical science in the United States, one observes a considerable variety of attitudes and practices. Of the routine and elementary task of the historian, the construction of the historical record, there is general awareness, and one notes many distinguished performances in this field. As to the meaning of the record, its utility—why "to know all about Poussin" is any more important than to know how many cigarette butts are thrown daily on the subway stairs—the greatest bewilderment prevails. There is the anecdotic interest in history, the sentimental titillation that comes from reliving exciting episodes in the past or retraversing the lives of unusual or successful individuals (the common rule in literary or free-lance productions). There is the propaganda history, where the writer is meticulous about the accuracy of the record and even makes contributions to it, but then feels it necessary to give the record an apparent meaning by saucing it with reflections which amount to saying, "I am a pacifist"; "I am a socialist"; "I am a Catholic"; and so on. There is the pseudo-scientific or semi-artistic history where the record is again accurate and fairly complete, but where the writer gives it an arbitrary meaning by organizing the facts around more or less unconscious sentimental attitudes borrowed from his environment, now ethical, now romantic, now optimistic, now (if the author is unusually intelligent) ironical or cynical. Finally, there is the Robinsonian history, the most scientific of these various types, where the past is taken as the explanation of the present, and, to a certain extent, the present is taken as the explanation of the past, but where the matter of choosing ideals is regularly left hazy and doubtful.

Into this atmosphere Mosca's conception of history should come as a clarifying breeze. The record of human experience is now from three to ten thousand years old. It is probable that during that time human nature has been able to make a fairly complete revelation of its general traits, its basic tendencies and laws. What are those tendencies, those laws? It is the business of the historian to tell us, and history is a mere amusement, a purposeless activity, unless its record is made to contribute to knowledge of tendencies and laws. To complete this theory a remark or two may be necessary. The construction of the historical record, the determination of facts in their sequence, motives or causes is a research by itself. In itself it has no purpose and envisages no utility. It has its own methods, its own technique, which reign sovereign over the research. As regards what can be learned from history, it is clear that the latter can supply only the general forms of human behavior—the specific situation will always be new, without exact precedent or analogy in the past.

Mosca feels that history is probably better able to tell us what not to do than what to do in the given case. But, really, it always remains a question of tendencies, of psychological, social forces which man may conceivably learn to master some day, the way he has learned, and marvelously learned, to master and utilize the material forces of nature. At any rate, Mosca's conception of history suggests the proper attitude to take toward his various theses. "Human societies are always governed by minorities"; "Rapid class circulation is essential to progress"; "Human societies are organized around collective illusions"; "Level of civilization corresponds to grade of juridical defense"; "Human societies show a tendency to progress toward higher and higher levels of civilization"; "Over-bureaucratization facilitates revolution." These and the others like them would be so many tentative statements of general laws. They are subject to objective scientific criticism, emendation, refutation.

III. Social Forces and Balance of Social Forces

The concept of social forces was already present in Mosca's early *Teorica*. In the *Elements* it is amplified, and its implications are more fully perceived.

A "social force" is any human activity or perquisite that has a social significance—money, land, military prowess, religion, education, manual labor, science—anything. The concept derives from the necessity of defining and classifying ruling classes. A man rules or a group of men rules when the man or the group is able to control the social forces that, at the given moment in the given society, are essential to the possession and retention of power.

Implicit in the theory of the ruling class is the law (I like to call it "Mosca's law") that "type and level of civilization vary as ruling classes vary." Ruling classes will vary in respect to the number and grade of the social forces which they control, tolerate, stimulate or create. The internal stability of a regime can be measured by the ratio between the number and strength of the social forces that it controls or conciliates, in a word, represents, and the number and strength of the social forces that it fails to represent and has against it. Progressive, and one might even say "successful," regimes regularly create social forces which they find it difficult to absorb; governments often fall because of their virtues, not their defects (a drastic emendation to Taine and to ethical interpretations of history in general). Struggle is one of the continuous and never-failing aspects of human life. Social forces, therefore, regularly manifest themselves in aspirations to power. Soldiers want to rule, and they are a hard group to control since they hold the guns and know best how to use them. Money wants to rule and it is hard to control money because most people succumb to the glamour and influence of wealth. Priests want to rule, and they have the weight of the ignorant masses and the majesty of the mysteries of life in their favor. Scientists want to rule, and, from Plato to Comte and from Comte to Scott, they have dreamed of dictators who will establish their technocracies and their "rules of the best." Labor wants to rule and would rule did it not always encounter the law of the ruling class and fall into the hands of its leaders. Public officeholders want to rule, and they might easily do so for they already sit in the seats of power.

When we have Mosca safely ensconced among the immortals, a mystery will confront the historian of social theories: Why, having reached this point in his meditations, did Mosca not throw his political research away and set out to write a sociology?

The answer will probably be found in the professional and temperamental determinations to which we have alluded. Mosca was thinking primarily of the political aspects of society and could never wholly divest himself of that interest.

Montesquieu had supplied him, already in his student days, with the concept of balance—with Montesquieu it was a balance of powers, of which the American constitution was eventually to supply an impressive example. Mosca transfers the concept to social forces.

In certain cases we see social forces that do succeed in usurping power, and one symptom of the usurpation is their imposition by force of the political formula that they happen to hold as an absolute principle to which everyone must bow and which everyone must believe or pretend to believe. That means tyranny, and it also means a reduction in the number of active social forces and, therefore, a drop in level of civilization. In other cases we see, for example, military power checked and balanced by money or by religion; or money, perhaps, checked and balanced by taxation imposed by land; or an obstreperous religious hierarchy checked and balanced now by superstitious sects which grow up within itself, now by coalitions of external forces of enlightenment. At certain moments—they are the heavenly interludes in history—we see fairly stable balances of forces where nearly everyone can do as he pleases and have his say so that the whole infinite potentialities of human nature burst into bloom.

IV. Juridical Defense: the Importance of Political Organization

This beneficent balance is attained, Mosca decides, at times and in peoples where it has become law, where, that is, the aggressiveness of social forces, or of the individuals who embody them, is checked, not by the sheer manifestation of force applied case by case, but by habit, custom, acquiescence, morals, institution and constitution—in a word (his word), juridical defense (government by law with due process). Contrary to Marxist, evolutionary and other materialistic or sociological interpretations of history, Mosca holds that the problem of political organization is paramount. If ruling classes can be appraised by noting the number and grade of social forces which they recognize, the governments which various ruling classes manage can be appraised by the grade of juridical defense which they provide. This Mosca seems sometimes to regard as very largely a technical problem of government.   A blossoming Mohammedan civilization first became stationary and then declined because the caliphs failed to solve the problem of the army.   The armies in the provinces followed their generals, the generals became independent and arbitrary despots; social forces contracted in numbers and then languished.   There is no reason to assume that the evolution of the Mohammedan peoples was any more predetermined than that of the Christian peoples.   The fact is that at certain moments in their history they, or rather their ruling classes, must have made wrong political decisions that headed them toward decline instead of toward higher levels of civilization.   In the case of the Mohammedan world one mistake, according to Mosca's system, would have been the failure to separate church and state, since that separation he regards as one of the basic essentials for a proper balance of social forces.

A high grade of juridical defense depends also, Mosca contends, upon a sufficient division of wealth to allow of the existence in fairly large numbers of people of moderate means; in fact, the numbers of such people will probably supply the gauge for measuring the effectiveness and stability of the balance of social forces.   The presence of a strong middle class in a society means that education is discovering and utilizing the resources of talent which, quite independently of race and heredity, are forever developing in the human masses at large (resources which backward societies somehow fail to use; that is why they are backward).   It also means that the ruling classes always have available materials with which to restock and replenish themselves as their own personnels deteriorate under pressure of the multiple forces that are always edging aristocracies toward decline. Middle classes represent the variety and the intensity of a society's activities and the maximum variety in types of wealth and in distribution of wealth.   Standing apart from the daily clash of the more powerful interests, they are the great repositories of independent opinion and disinterested public spirit.   One hardly need say it: In developing these postulates and their many corollaries, Mosca has written the classic of Italian conservatism, which functioned as an influential minority in Italy's political life just before the war.

But supposing we bring these arguments back to the strictly objective plane. We have spoken of "mistakes" and of choices as though the lawgivers of Mosca, like those of Rousseau or of the many writers who antedated the rise of deterministic theories, were free agents who could do with society just as they pleased. Suppose it be conceded that the separation of church and state and a distribution of wealth that allows the existence of a strong middle class are essential in a society if it is to attain a high level of civilization. How is science to obtain the recognition and application of those "laws" in the face of the religious interests which will in all pious enthusiasm continue to strive for uniformity of dogma and for control of education and the state, and in the face of the greed of human beings, who will go madly on amassing great fortunes and then using them to acquire power and dominion? Mosca leaves us no hope except in the enlightened statesmanship of those who wield power over the nations. Instructive in this connection is the distinction he draws between the politician and the statesman, the former being the man who is skilled in the mere art of obtaining power and holding it, whereas the latter is the man who knows how to manipulate the blind instincts of the human masses in the direction of conformity with the laws of man's social nature, much as the navigator manipulates the brute forces of tide and wind to the advantage of his ship and its passengers. Mosca has little confidence in the inborn good sense of the masses and despairs of ever bringing any great number of people to a rational and scientific view of public problems. History shows not a few ruling classes, on the other hand, the Venetian and English aristocracies, for instance, which have been able to lay interests and sentiments aside to a very considerable extent and to govern scientifically and objectively.

V. Standing Armies

Ampler consideration of the problem of juridical defense leads Mosca to one of the most brilliant and original investigations in the *Elements*. From the standpoint of struggle, military power is the best equipped of all social forces to assert itself and claim dominion. Why then is the military dictatorship not the normal form of human government? The peoples of the western world have for some generations now been familiar with systems where armies and navies are rigidly subject to civil authorities, and they are wont to regard the military rebellion as something exceptional and monstrous. Actually the human beings who have lived on this earth in security from the brutal rule of the soldier are so few in number, on the background of the whole of human history, as hardly to count. The military tyranny in some form or other is in fact the common rule in human society; and even in the best-ordered societies, as we are only too easily able to observe after the experience of the nineteenth and twentieth centuries in Europe, any serious disturbance of an established order of a nonmilitary type is likely to result in a reversion to the military dictatorship. The process by which the modern civilized nations have escaped from this grievous law of man's social nature Mosca rightly regards as one of the most interesting in history. Paradoxically enough, and contrarily to the modes of thinking of those liberals who dream of total disarmaments, Mosca finds the solution of the secret in the growth of the standing army.

Croce, somewhere in the *Ethics*, classifies human beings into four types, corresponding to the stresses of the four "forms of the spirit" which he makes basic in his system: the artist, the scientist, the statesman, the saint. That classification overlooks the adventurer, the warrior, the man who instinctively resorts to violence in his relations with his fellow men and prefers dangerous living to any other mode of existence. The antics of this individual on the stage of history are so conspicuous and withal so fascinating that a virtual revolution in historical method has been required in order to win some attention from the thoughtful for the types whom Croce recognizes. Give the adventurer a good brain, a good education, a supply of genius and an historical opportunity, and he becomes a Napoleon or an Alexander. Give him a great ideal and he becomes a Garibaldi. Give him a chance and he becomes a Mussolini. Give him a job and he becomes a soldier and a general. Ignore him and he becomes the gangster and the outlaw. A believer in final causes might soundly assert that the man of violence was invented by a wise Creator as a sort of catalyzer for human progress. The adventurer is never in the majority. The majority of human beings prefer peaceful orderly existences, and, when they dream, they dream of heavens where there is only light and music and no sorrow or toil, where the lion lies down with the lamb, where manna falls now from the sky and now from the government, where, in short, we are free from the competition of our neighbors and from the wearying struggle of life. Eras of prosperity are continually recurring in human history when the dream of security and idleness seems almost realizable; then, just as regularly, the man of violence comes along and sets the wheels to grinding again. So in our day, the citizens of the prosperous democracies had referred the movement of history to the social workers and the lawyers at Geneva in order to settle back in the night clubs to enjoy the nobility of their peaceful sentiments and the dividends of science. But a Hitler, a Mussolini, a Japanese general rises and tells them that to win or retain the right to drink and dance and be self-complacent they have to get out and fight.

On the other hand, the man of violence is not much more than that. The world that he creates is a pretty wretched affair. Give him the power and he regularly enslaves the rest of men, leaving them only the bare means of subsistence. Quite regularly he stultifies thought into hypocrisy and flattery, and the stimulating lift of organized public spirit he replaces with some form of mob fanaticism.

Mosca conceives of the standing army as a device automatically arrived at by the modern world for disciplining, canalizing and making socially productive the combative elements in the peoples. In loosely organized societies, violence concentrates around a large number of different focuses and differing interests, and the anarchy of the Middle Ages and of feudal societies at large results. In our own day, in Russia, Italy, Germany, Spain, we have seen that as soon as the stability of a society wavers power recreates itself in small centers, and periods of rule by local gangs ensue for greater or lesser lengths of time. The standing army, instead, tapers up to control by the state and therefore becomes part and parcel of the social order. Strong enough to enable the state to master local or sporadic manifestations of violence, it is itself under the direct control of all those mighty social forces which create and maintain the state itself. Recent history again confirms this conception of the status and objective role of the standing army. The national army of our time is an organism of incalculable might. The human forces which it embraces, the weapons and other material agencies of which it disposes, are incredibly powerful. Yet we have seen two revolutions take place in great and highly civilized countries in the face of the army and against the army. Certain observers of the rise of Fascism and National Socialism in Italy and in Germany looked to the loyally monarchical or republican armies to crush those movements, and undoubtedly they could have with a mere show of force. But the submersion of the German and Italian armies in the established order was complete, and, lacking the impulse from the apex of civil authority, they did not move. Not only that: Once new rulers were established in the seats of power, the armies responded obediently to their new orders.

What is the secret of the amazing subordination of the armies of the West? Mosca finds the answer in the aristocratic character, so to say, of the army, first in the fact that there is a wide and absolute *social* distinction between private and officer, and second that the corps of officers, which comes from the ruling class, reflects the balance of multiple and varied social forces which are recognized by and within that class. The logical implications of this theory are well worth pondering. If the theory be regarded as sound, steps toward the democratization of armies—the policy of Mr. Hore-Belisha, for instance—are mistaken steps which in the end lead toward military dictatorships; for any considerable democratization of armies would make them *active* social forces reflecting all the vicissitudes of social conflict and, therefore, *preponderant* social forces. On the other hand, army officers have to be completely eliminated from political life proper. When army officers figure actively and ex officio in political councils, they are certain eventually to dominate those councils and replace the civil authority—the seemingly incurable cancer of the Spanish world, for an example.

VI. SOCIAL TYPE AND POLITICAL FORMULA

The concept of social type is basic in Mosca's thought, and, since the phenomenon of the social grouping is one of the facts that the historian encounters at the most superficial glance at society, there is nothing remarkable in that. An elementary

discussion of what Mosca calls social type is already present in
Machiavelli.   Mosca's analysis of the elements that constitute
the greater social groupings was complete in the nineties.   It is
interesting that at that early date he was discounting race as a
factor in the sense of nationality and emphasizing the greater
importance of the myth of race.   But he was also, with remarkable insight, foreseeing an intensification of nationalisms in the
twentieth century as a sort of compensation for the decline of
faith in the world religions which, under the pressure of experimental science, were losing their utility as cohesive forces in
society.   Quite original and too much neglected, I believe, is
Mosca's conception of the modern sense of nationality as a
product of the world religions, to the extent that those religions,
with their doctrines that transcend race and nationality, came to
embrace the most diverse groups within the same social type
and so inclined those groups to coalesce individually around
political formulas of a nonreligious character.   That doctrine
throws light upon the conflict of church and state in the Middle
Ages in the West, a conflict that was essential to the growth of
secular civilization which rescued Europe from the fossilization
that settled upon the Mohammedan and eastern worlds.   In
this regard Mosca, one may say, has formulated rather than
prosecuted the research into the complicated interplay of group
instincts within each separate society.   His conclusions, at any
rate, are susceptible of almost indefinite elaboration.

The methodological advantages of Mosca's concept of social
type are very considerable.   In the first place it points the way
to sound scientific solutions of conflicts that cannot be solved by
ethical methods.   For instance, the United States prohibits
the immigration of Asiatics.   Whenever our diplomats go
prattling about democratic principles or even Christian principles
they expose themselves to devastating rejoinder from the Japanese diplomats, who can quite properly observe that democratic
or Christian principles would require unlimited Asiatic immigration.   It is well to note, therefore, that the questions at issue
are not questions of democratic theory or Christian ethics, but
questions of social type, which latter are always settled either
by force or by accommodation and reconciliation of apparent
interests.

To complete our examination of conscience we might go on and ask what, then, we are to do with our democratic principles and our Christian ethics? The answer is that these latter are formulas which have a very limited scientific validity and function as guides of conduct within strictly limited fields. What those limits shall be, just how and where they shall be drawn, are problems for statesmen, not for pastors or for professors of ethics. Our civilization subsists only so long as our social type subsists. Whether or not certain social types "ought" to vanish in the interests of civilization is a cosmic question that could be answered only by some neutral divinity looking at our planet from afar off. What we know is that social types good and bad insist on existing and that the measure of that insistence is a measure of force (or of accommodation as a substitute for force). So it is with any conflict between a universal ethical ideal and the instincts and the interests of social type.

The extent to which political formulas of universal pretension are serviceable for specific groups is an interesting and important one which the events of our time have raised to a critical prominence. Hitler's Germany seems to have concluded that a national myth in which only Germans can believe is of stronger cohesive potency than universal myths such as Christianity, democracy or socialism. Apparent to the eye is the advantage of ease of enforcement, in that such a myth makes a direct appeal to group instincts without mitigations or attenuations from rationality. But equally apparent are the disadvantages. Strictly national myths, like the "chosen people" myths of the Jews or Greeks, tend to sharpen international antagonisms unduly. Hitler is building up the same universal detestation that the pan-Germanism of the first decade of the century aroused. Such myths, besides, have in the past been effective only on very low planes of civilization where they have had very few social forces to fuse or coordinate. One may wonder whether German civilization will not in the end be oversimplified by the long inculcation of an exclusively national myth.

Fascist Italy is working on the theory that the universal myth can be subordinated to the national myth (subjugation of church to state) and then used as a channel of influence upon the countries that accept or tolerate it. Says Mussolini (to Pro-

fessor Starkie, *The Waveless Plain*, page 397): "The Latin
tradition of Imperial Rome is represented by Catholicism. . . .
There are in the world over 400,000,000 men [i.e., human beings]
who look towards Rome from all parts of the earth. That is a
source of pride for us Italians." Soviet Russia is using a universal political formula, communism, and explicitly claims
leadership over the minorities which accept the myth in other
countries. The myth intrinsically has considerable potency, as
resting on powerful combative sentiments (hatred of the poor
for the rich), reinforced by humanitarian sentiments of aversion
to suffering (poverty can be abolished). In this sense it has its
analogies with early democratic theory, which rested on those
same sentiments. It is less fortunate than democratic theory in
respect of the sentiments of property. These it openly flouts,
whereas democratic theory takes full advantage of them. It is
curious that Russian nationalism has grown in intensity under
the communist political formula much as the western nationalisms grew up inside the Christian and democratic formulas.
However, all such formulas are absolute and strive to achieve
uniformity of acceptance. When their universal character is
taken too seriously, believed, that is, with too great ardor, they
suck the life blood from the social type, either by absorbing too
much of the type's combative energy or by oversimplifying its
structure and so lowering its civilization level.

Mosca's concept of social type has another methodological
advantage in that it supplies the general form and, therefore,
emphasizes the common nature of many varied phenomena.
Two men see each other at a distance in Hong Kong. They
meet in Cairo, and the fact that they had seen each other at a
distance in Hong Kong constitutes a bond between them that
justifies closer contacts. They form thereby an embryonic
social type, which rests upon a single, inconsequential fact.
At another extreme we find millions of people bound together
by millions of ties, memories, interests, common experiences.
It is the same phenomenon but with a differing inner structure.
Mosca's concept of the social type supplies a tool for severing
the common from the differing elements. It stops, however, one
step short of Pareto's concept of group-persistence—persistence
of relations between persons and things, which would be an
hypothesis for investigating the basic psychological phenomena

involved in human associations of whatever type. Parties, sects, religions, movements, nations, states, are still often regarded as separate phenomena. "Nationalism began with the French Revolution," writes an American historian. Actually nationalism began with Adam, in the sense that it rests upon a fundamental law of human nature, which can be seen at work in thousands of other manifestations.

Mosca repeatedly emphasizes the historical utility of the social type as coordinating a multiplicity of wills and efforts for the achievement of common ends. On that basis it can be seen that history will be a play of two contrary forces, a trend toward unity and expansion, and a trend toward diversity and concentration. The Abyssinians, the Armenians and the Californians are Christians, and humanity surely profits in many ways from that advance toward world solidarity—group and even class isolation seem regularly to be elements in social fossilization and decline. On the other hand, the world has profited even more from particularity of social type—the existence of separate and powerful groups, all on the offensive and on the defensive, each struggling first for independence and then for domination, each living in a fever heat of life and death struggle in which the talents and moral traits of its individual members are stimulated and utilized to the utmost. Even within particular types a very considerable play of subtypes is an advantage, as implying multiplicity of social forces. This is just the reverse of the doctrine of Bossuet who viewed multiplicity of social types (or rather of political formulas) as disastrous. Bossuet wanted Europe to fossilize at the level of the Council of Trent. The prosperity, rising civilization level and world dominion of the Protestant countries after Bossuet's time refute his thesis. Obviously questions of proportion are involved: The social type must be large enough and compact enough in structure to survive in the struggle of types; it must be diversified enough, that is, tolerant enough, to utilize all its social forces and increase their number. The western world today threatens to fly to pieces from the violence of its antagonisms. It would gain by a little more unity which a hackneyed democratic formula, with its disastrous doctrine of minority determinations, seems unable to supply. The eastern world would surely gain, as it is in fact gaining, from more diversity. The great civilizing force in Asia at present is nationalism.

In dealing with the relations between social type and political formula, Mosca halts on the brink of a great research. The external manifestation of the existence of a type, at least of the larger types, will be the acceptance of a given formula. Does the type create the formula or the formula the type? Mosca answers quite soundly with a theory of interdependence: The type partly creates the formula in that the latter is usually a dogma put forward by some seer or prophet—now Mahomet, now Rousseau, now Marx—in response to certain "demands" of the given era. Once the formula exists and is accepted, it helps powerfully in molding the type by formulating maxims and precepts to which individuals more or less necessarily and successfully conform. The formula normally contains a large amount of nonsense mixed in with a certain small amount of verifiable truth. Observing the same facts Bentham considered in some detail the specific case where politicians talk the nonsense involved in the formula for the purpose of swaying mobs (scientifically, one should say, for the purpose of utilizing the social type for a given purpose). Making this difficulty the center of a research and centering all his interest upon it, Pareto evolved his epoch-making theory of residues and derivations.

VII. LEVEL OF CIVILIZATION

Mosca is one of the few (if any) political theorists to take level of civilization frankly and squarely as a criterion of evaluation. In not a few passages in the *Elements* he seems to assume that the desirability of high levels of civilization is self-evident, and that would be a very venial departure from the objective standpoint that he strives to maintain in his work. As a matter of fact relatively few people care very much about level of civilization—the great majority are interested in achieving some ideal—communism, democracy, peace, "happiness," "spirituality," "the salutary captivity of the faith," to quote Monsignor Moreau —regardless of the level at which civilization will find itself when those ideals are achieved or as a result of the effort to achieve them. The "nostalgie de la boue" is an organized human sentiment that snipes at the outposts of every free society when it is not slinking into the inner fortress under the guise of idealism and love of "higher things."

But subjective or metaphysical as this preference on Mosca's part may be, the concept of level of civilization nevertheless contributes, almost more than anything else, to maintaining the objective attitude in the *Elements*. It is a criterion that is definable to a high grade of approximation as multiplicity of activities; grade or quality of achievement in each; size and stability of social cohesion and, therefore, offensive and defensive power; standard of living and distribution of wealth; control of nature and utilization of that control; and so on—so on even to the "higher things" themselves. (Why be so disheartened over the number of our airplanes, telephones or bathtubs, when in addition to them we are producing humanists, neo-Thomists and even saints in fair abundance?)

The methodological advantages of the concept are enormous: and prime among them is the need which the concept creates, and the analytical method which it supplies, for viewing the given historical phenomenon or appraising the given proposal in the light of the total social picture. The literature of science and the literature of opinion suffer continually from their very virtues of specialization. In restricting the field of fact with which they deal they often develop unilateral methodologies which end by establishing arbitrary relations between facts. If we consider the Christian unity, so called, of the Middle Ages and linger on the metaphysical or logical implications of medieval political formulas, we may get a very distorted view of the importance of Christian unity or even of unity itself. Any consideration of the general level of civilization in the Middle Ages would certainly correct that view. So, for that school of writers which magnifies Greek thought and art as though those were manifestations of a heavenly state which mankind has lost forever. So, for those orientalists who propound the sublimities of the wisdom of the East without remembering that the eastern peoples have for ages been a sort of herring on which the sharks of the world, domestic and foreign, have feasted at their will and leisure. So, also, for those who regard literature, the arts, and philosophy as the distinctive representatives of level of culture. It is certain that arts, letters and metaphysical thinking can flourish among limited numbers of individuals in civilizations of very low level. It is also certain that when any great proportion of a nation's energies are devoted to arts, letters and metaphysics, its cultural level will decline.   To be sure, it is just as certain that no highly diversified and intensely cultivated civilization will fail to show eminence in those activities.

Level of civilization is a dynamic, not a static, level, and in no civilization are all activities at the same level, or even at a level where they can automatically meet all the needs of the given historical moment.   The ancient world needed more physical science than it possessed, if it was to perpetuate its achievements in the political and social fields.   As Mosca points out, the great political upheaval at the end of the eighteenth century became more drastic through a lag in historical science.   Napoleon's empire collapsed for the reason, among others, that transportation was in arrears both of industry and of military science—the steamboat and the railroad came a generation too late for the united Europe of which Napoleon dreamed.   In our own time one may wonder whether the economic and social sciences will have attained a level to meet the great crises which our highly geared civilization periodically produces.   One clings the more willingly to Mosca's concept of level of civilization in that, on a subjective plane, it is optimistic as to man's future on earth. In spite of the tremendous forces of inner expansion and dis-gregation that are continually rocking the societies of our day, Mosca very soundly feels that, in view of the scientific and moral resources that our time has at its disposal, the man of the present is far better placed than any of his historical predecessors have been to deal with the destructive material, social and psychological influences that have wrecked civilization so many times in the past and are threatening to wreck our own.

VIII. Democracy and Representative System

Mosca's theory of the ruling class enters a third stage of development with the 1923 edition of the *Elementi*, which was enlarged by a "second part" (chaps. XII to XVII of the present translation).   This second part contains a tentative history of the theory of the ruling class.[1]   It contains an outline of the

[1] The first clear formulation of the theory Mosca recognizes in Saint-Simon. However, consideration of stress, as proposed above (§1), would probably minimize Saint-Simon's importance in this regard; whereas the role of Taine, especially in its direct bearing on Mosca's own theory, might have been enlarged upon.

rise of the modern state from the standpoint of types of ruling classes and types of political organization. Interesting here especially is the essay on the rise of the bourgeoisie and the origins of the French Revolution. As for the classification of governments, which in Mosca's earlier works had been reduced to two types, the feudal and the bureaucratic, Mosca now tries out another order of distinctions—autocratic and liberal principles, democratic and aristocratic tendencies. This discussion gives him occasion to add some interestingly objective reflections on class or social circulation in its bearing on the prosperity and decadence of nations.

But the most significant portions of the "second part" are a clarification, and first of all in Mosca's own mind, of the import of the criticism of democracy that he had made in the past and his impassioned appeal for a restoration of the representative system in Europe.

Mosca was on safe ground in asserting that great human masses can be organized and utilized for the attainment of specific purposes only by uniting them around some formula that will contain a large measure of illusion. He was also right in asserting that one element in that fact is the further fact that human beings more readily defer to abstract principles that seem to have an abiding validity than to the will of individual persons, which not seldom functions capriciously, may be valid only case by case, and, in any event, may shock the self-respect of the plain man who has a right to feel that he is being overridden by brute force. But in this regard all systems of political metaphysic are in the same boat: The "will of God," the "will of the people," "the sovereign will of the State," the "dictatorship of the proletariat," are one as mythical as the other. Perhaps of the lot, the least mythical is the will of the people, if by it one agree to mean that resultant of sentimental pressures, beliefs, habits, prejudices, temperaments (the general will of Rousseau or MacIver), on which common action can be based, and almost always is based, in tyrannies as well as in republics. In refuting a metaphysical thesis, one may be left in a metaphysical position oneself if one attaches any great importance to the refutation, on the assumption that political action must be based on formulas that are "true." Mosca is well aware of that. He repeatedly emphasizes the fact that the historic role of Christianity is there, whatever the scientific soundness of its dogmas.   More directly to the point he urges that statesmen should beware of trying to enforce all the apparent implications of metaphysical formulas. The Church would not last a week if it tried to live up to its doctrine of poverty. No democracy would endure if it followed the "will" of the ignorant peace-loving masses instead of the aggressive leadership of the enlightened few. So, he argues in the *Teorica* and again in the *Elements*, the mere fact that universal suffrage follows from the premise of majority rule or the will of the people is in itself no recommendation for universal suffrage as a practical measure. Other considerations of a utilitarian character have to be introduced. Democratic metaphysics would require that the voting of budgetary expenditure be in the hands of the people's representatives, of Congress, let us say. In practice, it might easily be more satisfactory to have the budget in the hands of a responsible minister or president than in the hands of an irresponsible Congress. At least the sense of responsibility will be more active and effective in one conspicuous individual than in six hundred less conspicuous individuals.

But in spite of this very considerable consistency and objectivity, Mosca, in the *Teorica* and in Part I of the *Elements*, was undoubtedly swayed by certain prejudices of nationality, region and party and so lapsed into metaphysical errors. It is an error to argue that a limited suffrage is any sounder, theoretically, than universal suffrage (an error arising in sentiments of liberal conservatism). It is an error to argue that the history of a social system which is based on universal suffrage will necessarily follow the apparent logical implications of the theory of majority rule. Between the publication of the second and the third editions of the *Elements* the political equilibrium was upset in Europe—in Russia, in Italy, in Germany and Austria. In none of those cases did the upset occur because of the application of universal suffrage and the growth of the demagoguery required for governing by universal suffrage. The Fascist and communist regimes have come into being and have governed in joyous indifference to universal suffrage. The upset in Italy in particular did not come either from socialism or from the church. It came from those public-spirited young men whom Mosca was inclined to laud for their attacks on socialism, and those young men were working on a myth, not of democracy, but of nationalism. Far more fortunate were Mosca's prophecies when he stuck close to his theory of social forces and foresaw, in Russia, all the anarchy and horror that would follow from the attempt to establish communism by force, and in Italy all the consequences of the establishment of a single absolute formula to which absolute adherence would be forcibly required—and the end is not yet.

On the basis of the *Teorica* and the first form of the *Elements* it was easy to classify Mosca among those many Italian writers who have combatted the theory of democracy. The democratic system always had a stronger hold on the Italian head than on the Italian heart. Strong in all classes in Italy was the sense of social subordination (the sense of equality is more characteristic of France and the Protestant countries). Especially in rural Italy and on the Italian latifundia one still encounters many of the phenomena of class dependence that went with the older feudal world and, as Stendhal in his day perceived with a homesick yearning for old times, were not without their charm. The Italian intellectual and upper classes never embraced democracy wholeheartedly. They never applied the theory of mass education with any real conviction. One may therefore explain the antidemocratic intonation of Mosca's earlier works as partly a matter of fashion and partly a matter of youth. Democratic theory was generally accepted—it was original, therefore, to attack it. Democracy was unpopular, especially in south Italy. One was therefore swimming with the current in overstressing the corruption and inefficiency of parliamentary politicians and in waving the menace of socialism in the face of those who were eager to strengthen popular education and extend the suffrage.

All the same, the defense of the representative system in the second part of the *Elements* is not a mere case of the "jitters of '22," nor is it exactly a palinode. It is a bona fide return to the implications of Mosca's theory of social forces, freed of metaphysical divagations. "A maturer contemplation of history" has convinced Mosca that, of all forms of political organization, the representative system has shown itself capable of embracing the largest social units at incredibly high levels of civilization; and that, as compared with competing systems today, it gives promise of allowing freest play to increasing numbers of social forces and of providing more readily for that rapid social circulation which is essential to the stability of ruling classes and to reinforcing culture with tradition.

IX. MOSCA AND PARETO

This translation edition of the *Elements* of Mosca was planned in 1923 as part of an enterprise for making the monuments of Italian Machiavellian thought available to English-speaking scholars. Normally it should have appeared, and but for difficulties associated with the crisis of '29 would have appeared, in advance of my American edition of Pareto's *Trattato*. That order of publication would have preserved the chronological sequence of the two works in their native language and given a more satisfactory inception to the problems of relationship that very evidently arise between them. As it is, we find ourselves confronted today with polemics which are echoes of polemics of thirty years ago; and there is already a line of Italian or Italo-American writers who, somewhat tardily to tell the truth, discover Mosca in order to diminish Pareto, while there are again a few who disparage Mosca for the greater glory of Pareto. As a matter of fact, a question of indebtedness first raised by Mosca (1902, 1907) has been attenuated to a question of "unrecognized priority" (Luigi Einaudi, 1934, Sereno, Megaro, Salvemini, 1938); but both those questions, from any scientific standpoint, can be regarded only as irrelevant.[1]

There is no dialectical or historical connection between Pareto's theory of the élite and Mosca's theory of the ruling class. On the dialectical side, Mosca's theory of the ruling class derives from a criticism of the doctrine of majority rule and is, as we have seen, a generalization of the method of Taine. Pareto's theory of the élite derives from a study of the relations of distribution of wealth to class differentiations in society and aims specifically at a correction of Ammon. On the historical side, Pareto had not seen Mosca's *Teorica* as late as 1906 (see *Manuale*, §97, 3). The publication of his *Cours* (1896, 1897) was contemporaneous with that of Mosca's *Elementi* to a matter of days and the work

---

[1] For the literature of this quarrel see Renzo Sereno, "The Anti-Aristotelianism of Gaetno Mosca and Its Fate," *Journal of Ethics*, July 1938, to which add Gaudence Megaro, *Mussolini in the Making*, Boston-New York, 1938, p. 116, and Gaetano Salvemini, review of Megaro, *Nation*, July, 1938.

must therefore have been written some months before the *Elementi* appeared.[1] Now the *Cours* contains the concept of the élite in virtually the form that it was to have in Chaps. XII and XIII of Pareto's *Trattato* (1916, 1923). As Pareto developed his theory in the course of the years (*Applicazione*, 1900, *Systèmes*, 1902), he began to cross positions of Mosca, without mention of Mosca's works. When he quotes Mosca it is in regard to other matter than the theory of the ruling class or the political formula. The reason for this silence is not certain—it was certainly not malice. In his sarcastic rejoinder to Mosca in the *Manuale* Pareto implies that Mosca's views were either obvious or else accounted for in earlier literature. That is an unhappy contention if one considers the point of stress alluded to above (§1). Mosca was the one writer to have given the concept of the ruling class the importance that the concept of élite has in Pareto's *Systèmes*. On the other hand, the specific points of contact between Mosca's theories and Pareto's are of a minor significance and have no bearing on the originality or intrinsic interest of Pareto's use of the concept of the élite. The "moral" question, therefore, can easily be overworked, and has in fact been overworked; for any harm that may have been done to Mosca by Pareto's silence has long since been undone by historical criticism.

With the questions of indebtedness and priority thus disposed of, we are in a position to consider the relations between the theories of Mosca and Pareto from another standpoint. It is a case of two authors who start with one same method, the historical, and in the same objective spirit to prosecute two researches that run parallel to each other in many respects and pass many of the same landmarks. But similar as they are in method and spirit the two researches are vastly different in range and magnitude. Pareto's research, based on an analysis of the social equilibrium, leads out to a comprehensive view of all society and results in a monument of gigantic architectural proportions—the

---

[1] The *Elementi*, dated 1896, appeared "late in 1895." Deposit of the copyright volume is noted in the *Bollettino* of Feb. 29, 1896. The preface of Vol. I of Pareto's *Cours* is dated January, 1896; Vol. II, dated 1897, is announced as received by the *Journal des économistes* in its November number, 1896. There was therefore no interval of consequence between the writing of Vol. I and that of Vol. II.

Trattato, which is a culture and a manner of living rather than a book. In such a research the problems of political organization that Mosca sets out to solve are mere details, yet in solving them Mosca has to take account of many of the facts that are basic in Pareto's larger structure; and he does take account of them in the form of observations, asides, intuitions, remarks that delight and astound for their shrewdness and profoundness.

Mosca, for a few examples, perceives that the concept of cause, as it was used by the older historians and is still used by many moderns, is inadequate—that the historical cause is often partly effect and the historical effect also partly cause. But with Mosca this perception remains a literary finesse. With Pareto it becomes a problem that requires and in a measure attains scientific formulation. And let there be no talk of priorities or plagiarisms, for Pareto could have derived the concept of interdependence from Spencer as well as from Mosca. It is very likely to occur to anyone who ponders history at all deeply and so is called upon to decide to what extent Rousseau, for instance, was a product or expression of his times and to what extent he influenced and shaped his times. So again Mosca sees that political formulas are invalid as "truth" but yet somehow determine the exterior aspects, at least, of whole civilizations, of social types that are immensely populous. But that perception remains as a coloring of good-natured scepticism in the *Elements*. Pareto wrestles with it, instead, as a scientific problem, and the solution of it gives rise, on the one hand, to his theory of the role of the nonlogical in human society and human history, and, on the other, to his epoch-making classification of "derivations." And again let there be no talk of priorities or plagiarisms, for Pareto could just as well descend from Bentham, if he were not, in this as in every other respect, the child of his own genius. Mosca perceives that membership in the ruling class has a relation to human traits and he lingers, again in a mood of half-mirthful skepticism, on the traits that bring one "success in life." He fails to perceive, meantime, that that problem has an intimate bearing on the problem of the scientific classification of ruling classes toward which he was working. In Pareto the same perception leads to a masterly study of the belief that virtue has its rewards, and, further, to his now celebrated classification of ruling classes as "combinationist" or "abstractionist" (promoters-believers). Mosca perceives that the manner in which ruling classes renew their membership has a vital significance for the prosperity of nations. That again is a shrewd intuition. In Pareto it becomes scientific hypothesis in a theory of social cycles, where social circulation is considered as one, merely, of the factors that determine social movement and where the problem of its relation to those other factors is formulated.

All of this leads one to suspect that the real influence of Mosca on Pareto was of the type that one normally notes in the history of the sciences. By 1898, or thereabouts, Mosca's masterpiece was known to Pareto, and he could only be responsive to its various stresses. After the *Elements*, with its ruling class theory, Pareto was unlikely to overlook the fact that in the social equilibrium ruling-class traits far outweigh majority traits. After Mosca's stress on the humanitarian decadence of aristocracies it was unlikely that Pareto would overlook that same type of decadence. So for the doctrine of social crystallization or for the discussion of types of history, of the role of facts in scientific method, of the roles of force and propaganda in society, of theories of revolution and revolt. The anti-Paretans, in general, make a mistake in limiting the question of Pareto's indebtedness to Mosca to consideration of the concept of the ruling class. Really, and in the *Trattato* especially, Pareto holds in view all the major positions of Mosca, just as he holds in view the positions of dozens of other writers. The *Elements* are one of the foils that he uses to give a polemical development to some of his discussions. Characteristic here would be Pareto's criticism (*Trattato*, 2566, note 3) of Taine's theory that ruling classes succumb because of neglecting their "duties" (a theory that Taine may have taken over from Tocqueville). One element in that painstaking refutation may easily have been the fact that Mosca takes over Taine's theory, ethical fallacies included, and makes it basic in his theory of the decline of ruling classes. In the same way one might compare Mosca's utilization of Salvian of Marseilles (on Roman morals) or Martin del Rio with the use that Pareto makes of those same authors.

X. On Translating Mosca

This translation edition of Mosca's *Elements* has aimed at a readable, organic presentation of Mosca's thought, quite apart from systematic literalism or any mechanical reproduction of the various devices by which Mosca adapted a text written in 1895 to the movement of science and history and to his own intellectual evolution. The Italian edition of 1923 shows two books moving side by side, one as text, the other as notes, with a third book added as a tail that is sometimes inclined to wag the dog. This irregularity of 'composition has been smoothed out by incorporating the notes in the text at points where they fit organically, by breaking up the once ponderous Chapter X into two, by numbering the chapters consecutively and by some slight rearrangement of material. For instance, the criticism of Comte and Spencer has been moved from Chapter VI, where it hung loose in space, to Chapter III where it logically belonged. That discussion, moreover, seemed to be an independent article written during Spencer's lifetime under the shadow of the master's overpowering prestige. It has been rewritten to conform with the spirit of the book as a whole and, it is hoped, with some little gain in clarity.

A half-century's time has of course borne heavily upon the critical apparatus of the old *Elements* of 1895 and upon certain discussions which Mosca retained as late as 1923. Mosca himself has insisted on deleting the study of the Roman question from the American edition. In the spirit of that revision the editor has further deleted from the notes a number of antiquated bibliographies, several debates dealing with socialist metaphysics as propounded in the nineties by Labriola and others, and in general all notes that seemed for one reason or another to have lost interest. That such suppressions have been relatively few bespeaks, in the editor's opinion, the classic soundness of Mosca's text as it first appeared in 1895 or as he left it in 1923.

In Mosca's early days parliamentary eloquence in Italy still remembered its Ciceronian origins in a slow-moving periodic sentence that piled modifiers on modifiers, dependent clauses on dependent clause. Mosca was still close enough to that style to wield it with force, clarity and elegance. No one in America has been able to make it seem probable since Henry James or W. C. Brownell—one might almost say, since Melville. Miss Kahn did wonders, in the editor's opinion, in transferring Mosca's period into English; but the editor finally decided to replace it with a more analytical paragraph, taking the risks of mistaking "slants" that such a method of translation often involves. As against the literalists, the editor will confess that he has always tried to live up to the three requisites in the translator that were once proclaimed by Joel Spingarn, the first being courage, the second courage, and the third courage.

In this translation edition, Mosca's term "political class" is regularly rendered by the more usual English expression "ruling class," on the basis of the permission extended in the *Elements* (chap. II, §1). It should never be forgotten, of course, that these two terms, which are interchangable in Mosca, function, subject to his definition of the political or ruling class, as the group of people who actually and directly participate in government or influence it. Mosca's "ruling class," therefore, covers a narrower field than Pareto's élite (the sum of outstanding talents) or the Marxian "ruling class" (the employer or property-holding class and its appendages, political or social). One might illustrate with the case of the American professor. Under some administrations he is in Mosca's ruling class, as one can establish by giving an ear to the general clamor of disapproval. Under other administrations he is not in Mosca's ruling class—and the clamor is just as great but elsewhere directed. In Marxian theory he would always be a member of the ruling class, even if ignored in town and hen pecked at home, and for Pareto always a member of the élite.

The editor is indebted to Senator Mosca for reading proof of this English edition and to many friends for assistance at one time or another in the furtherance of this enterprise: to Giuseppe Prezzolini, for a first personal contact with Senator Mosca in 1922; to Irene di Robilant and Gaudence Megaro, for the performance of a number of personal errands to Senator Mosca in Italy; finally to Mario Einaudi, who first interested the present publishers in the Mosca enterprise and who also made a number of much-appreciated suggestions on the proofs.

ARTHUR LIVINGSTON.

NEW YORK,
December, 1938.

THE RULING CLASS

CHAPTER I

POLITICAL SCIENCE

1. During centuries past it has many times occurred to thinkers to consider the hypothesis that the social phenomena unwinding before their gaze might not be mere products of chance, nor yet expressions of some supernatural, omnipotent will, but rather effects of constant psychological tendencies determining the behavior of the human masses. Even in Aristotle's early day an effort was made to discover the laws that govern the operation of such tendencies and their manner of functioning, and the science devoted to that purpose was called "politics."

During the sixteenth and seventeenth centuries many writers, particularly in Italy, applied themselves to "politics."[1] Yet they—beginning with Machiavelli, the most famous of them all—were less concerned with determining constant trends in human societies than with the arts by which an individual, or a class of individuals, might succeed in achieving supreme power in a given society and in thwarting the efforts of other individuals or groups to supplant them.

Those are two different things, substantially, though there may be points of contact between them, as an analogy will serve to show. Political economy studies the constant laws or tendencies that govern the production and distribution of wealth in human societies; but that science is by no means the same as the art of amassing wealth and keeping it. A very competent economist may be incapable of making a fortune; and a banker or a business-man may acquire some understanding from knowledge of economic laws but does not need to master them, and may, in fact, get along very well in his business even in utter ignorance of them.[2]

[1] Ferrari, *Corso sugli scrittori politici italiani*.

[2] On the distinction between politics as the art of governing (*Staatskunst*) and politics as the science of government (*Staatswissenschaft*), see Holtzendorff,

1

2. In our day the science founded by Aristotle has been sub-divided and specialized, so that we have not so much a science of politics as a group of political sciences. That is not all. Efforts have been made to synthesize and coordinate the results of such sciences, and this has given rise to the science of sociology. In interpreting legislation, or otherwise commenting upon public enactments, jurists and writers on public law are almost always carried on into investigations of the general tendencies that have inspired legislation. Historians, too, in telling the story of human vicissitudes, have frequently sought to deduce from a study of historical events the laws that regulate and determine them. That was the case with Polybius and Tacitus, among the ancients, with Guicciardini in the sixteenth century, with Macaulay and Taine in the century just past. Philosophers, theologians, jurists—all thinkers, in short, who, directly or indirectly, have written with a view to improving human society and have, therefore, examined the laws that regulate its organization—may be considered, under one aspect or another, to have been dealing with problems of political science. It turns out that a good half of the field of human thought, an immense portion of the intellectual effort that man has devoted to delving into his past, probing his future, analyzing his own moral and social nature, may be looked upon as devoted to political science.

Among the political or social sciences one branch, so far, has attained such scientific maturity that through the abundance and the accuracy of its results it has left all the others far behind. We are thinking of political economy.

Toward the end of the eighteenth century a number of men of great ability segregated the phenomena involved in the produc-tion and distribution of wealth from the mass of other social phenomena and, considering them apart from other data, suc-ceeded in determining many of the constant psychological laws or tendencies that they obey. This method of separating economic phenomena from other aspects of social activity, along with the habit that has grown up of considering them as inde-pendent of the other phenomena that affect the organization of political institutions, undoubtedly accounts for the rapid progress that political economy has made; but at the same time it may be

---

Prinzipien der Politik, chaps. I–II. We touch on this matter again below, chap. VIII, §1.

held chiefly responsible for the fact that certain postulates of the science of economics are still open to controversy. If, therefore, political economy could manage to coordinate its own observations with what has been learned of other phases of human psychology, it might be able to make further and perhaps decisive progress.

During the last thirty or forty years there has been a tendency to explain all political events in human history on the basis of economic considerations. In our opinion, this point of view is too one-sided and too exclusive. There are social and political phenomena (for example, the rise and spread of the great religions, the renascence of certain ancient nationalities, the establishment of certain powerful military monarchies) which cannot be explained solely by variations in the distribution of wealth, or by the conflict between capital and labor or between fixed and circulating capital.

However, the tendencies that regulate the organization of political authority cannot be studied without taking into account the results that political economy, a sister science of more precocious growth, has already obtained. To study the tendencies mentioned is the aim of the present work. We call this study "political science." We have chosen that designation because it was the first to be used in the history of human thought, because it has not yet fallen into disuse and because the term "sociology," which many writers have adopted since the day of Auguste Comte, still has no precise and sharply defined meaning (in common usage it covers all the social sciences, among them economics and criminology, rather than the science directly concerned with the study of the phenomena that are more specially and properly designated as "political").[1]

3. A science is always built up on a system of observations which have been made with particular care and by appropriate methods on a given order of phenomena and which have been so coordinated as to disclose incontrovertible truths which would not have been discovered by the ordinary observation of the plain man.

---

[1] The term "political science" has been used, among other writers, by Holtzendorff, Bluntschli, Donnat, Scolari, Brougham, Sheldon Amos, De Parieu and Pollock.

The mathematical sciences furnish the simplest and readiest illustration of the development of the truly scientific procedure. In mathematics the axiom is the fruit of an observation that is accessible to everybody, and its truth is apparent even to the eyes of the plain man. Stating a number of axioms and coordinating them, we get proofs for the simpler theorems. Then, still further coordinating the truths derived from such theorems with the truths of the axioms, we get proofs for new and more difficult theorems, the truth of which could be neither guessed nor proved by any one untrained in the mathematical sciences. The procedure in physics and the other natural sciences is quite the same, but in them the method begins to be complicated by new elements. To coordinate a number of simple observations often will not suffice to provide a demonstration of a truth that we may call "composite"—in other words, not apparent at first glance. In the majority of cases something corresponding to the axiom in mathematics is obtained only through experiment or prolonged observation, both of which have their value when they are conducted by special and accurate methods and by individuals who have been properly trained in such methods. In the early days of the various sciences the sound procedure was almost always found as the result of lucky hypotheses, which were eventually substantiated by experiments and observations of fact and which in their turn explained many other observations, many other facts. A long period of empiricism, of imperfect or erroneous methods of observation, of mistaken theories that have hampered the useful coordination of data on individual phenomena, has almost always preceded the strictly scientific period in the given science. So for many centuries astronomy and chemistry floundered about in the errors and follies of astrology and alchemy. Only after human minds had long labored over given orders of phenomena did a wealth of accumulated data, better methods, better material instruments of observation, and the insight and unflagging patience of mighty intellects finally succeed in producing those fortunate hypotheses that have made real science possible.

The mere use of observation and experience within a given order of phenomena does not of itself assure truly scientific results. Francis Bacon was mistaken as to the absolute capacity of the experimental method for discovering scientific truth, and many thinkers and writers in our day are harboring the same illusion. As is well known, Bacon compared the experimental method, which for that matter had been in use long before his day, to a compass, which will allow the hand unpracticed in drawing to trace perfect circles—in other words, to obtain accurate scientific results.[1] As a matter of fact, if observation and experience are to yield sound results the conditions that we have specified above are essential. Ill-used, and with mistaken scientific procedures, they lead to false discoveries, or may even lend a semblance of plausibility to downright nonsense. After all, astrology and alchemy were based on observation and experience, real or presumed; but the method of observation, or rather the point of view from which observations were conducted and coordinated, was profoundly mistaken. In his *Disquisitiones magicae* the notorious Martin Del Rio thought that he was relying on observations of fact in drawing his distinctions between love magic, hate magic and sleep-inducing magic and in revealing the wiles and ways of witches and sorcerers. Indeed he intended that his observations should help people to detect witches and sorcerers and guard against them. So economists before the day of Adam Smith thought that they were resting on observations of fact when they held that the wealth of a nation lay solely in its money and in the products of its soil; and Don Ferrante, the typical scientist of the seventeenth century, so effectively sketched by Manzoni,[2] was arguing from facts and experiences that were universally accepted in his time when he showed, by a reasoning which was faultlessly logical and positive as far as appearance went, that the bubonic plague could not possibly be contagious. He reasoned as follows: In *rerum natura* there is nothing but substance and accident. Contagion cannot be an accident because an accident cannot pass from one body to another. It cannot be a substance because substances are terreous, igneous, aqueous and aeriform. If contagion were a terreous substance, it would be visible; if aqueous, it would be

---

[1] Macaulay, "Lord Bacon" in *Critical and Historical Essays*, vol. II, p. 254 [The passage reads: "His philosophy resembled a compass or a rule which equalizes all hands, and enables the most unpractised person to draw a more correct circle or line than the best draftsmen can produce without such aid." And see *Novum organon*, Preface and I, 122.]

[2] *I promessi sposi*, chap. XXXVII.

wet; if igneous, it would burn; if aeriform, it would soar aloft to its proper sphere.

4. Even today political science has not yet entered upon its truly scientific period. Though a scholar may learn from it many things that escape the perception of the plain man, it does not seem to offer any body of incontrovertible truths that are accepted by all who are versed in its discipline, and much less to have acquired, so far, a trustworthy and universally accepted method of research. The causes of this situation are multiple, and for the present we cannot go into them. We may say simply that such causes are to be sought not so much in a lack of talent in the men who have pondered the subject of politics as in the great complexity of the phenomena involved in that subject and, especially, in the circumstance that, down to a few decades ago, it was virtually impossible to get accurate and complete information about the facts on which we are obliged to depend in trying to discover the constant laws or tendencies that determine the political organization of human societies.

However fragmentary or defective we may consider the various methods or systems of ideas that have so far been brought to bear upon the field of political science, it is none the less our duty to make a rapid survey of them. Some of them have been, as they are still, little more than philosophical, theological or rational justifications of certain types of political organization which have for centuries played, and in some cases are still playing, a significant role in human history. As we shall presently see, one of the most constant of human tendencies is the tendency to justify an existing form of government by some rational theory or some supernatural belief. We have accordingly had a so-called political science at the service of societies in which belief in the supernatural still holds sway over the minds of men and in which, therefore, the exercise of political power finds its explanation in the will of God (or of the gods); and we have had, as we still have, another political science which justifies that power by representing it to be a free and spontaneous expression of the will of the people, or of the majority of the individuals composing the given society.

Among all the various systems and methods of political observation, we must concern ourselves more especially with two, which are more objective and universal in character than the others and which have designedly set out to discover the laws that explain the existence of all the various forms of government that appear in the world. The first of these two methods makes the political differentiation of the various societies dependent upon variations in external environment, and more particularly in climate; the other correlates it primarily with the physical, and therefore psychological, differences between the various races of men. The first method lays primary stress on the criterion of physical environment; the other, upon the ethnological or somatic criterion. The two methods occupy such important places in the history of science and in contemporary science and are, as far as appearances go, so positive and experimental in character, that we cannot be excused from going into the matter of their actual scientific value.

5. From the days of Herodotus and Hippocrates down to the present century an enormous number of writers have assumed that climate has an influence on social phenomena in general and on political phenomena in particular. Many have tried to demonstrate that influence and have based whole scientific systems upon it. In the forefront among these stands Montesquieu, who insists most emphatically upon the preponderant influence of climate on the moral and political systems of nations. "The closer one gets to the countries of the south," he writes,[1] "the farther one seems to get from morality itself"; and he declares[2] that liberty is incompatible with warm countries and never flourishes where the orange grows. Other writers concede that civilization may have been born in the warm countries but nevertheless maintain that its center of gravity has continuously crept northward and that the countries that are best organized politically today are located in the north.[3]

Now to begin with, the climate of a country is not entirely a matter of latitude but depends also on such factors as elevation above sea level, exposure, prevailing winds, and so on. Not all of the physical environment, moreover, is dependent on climate,

---

[1] *Esprit des lois*, book XIV, chap. 2.

[2] *Ibid.*, book XVII.

[3] Mougeolle, *Statique des civilisations* and *Les problèmes de l'histoire;* and see Bluntschli, *Politik als Wissenschaft.*

in other words, on variations in temperature and rainfall. Other circumstances figure in it—for example, the greater or lesser population that a region may have, and consequently the degree of development its agriculture has attained and the kind of crops that are most commonly in use. The inhabitants of a sparsely populated and therefore pastoral or wooded territory live in a physical environment that is wholly different from that of people who inhabit a densely populated and therefore intensively cultivated territory.

It is undeniable, furthermore, that the influence that climate may have on the life of a people as a whole and on its political organization in particular must steadily diminish with the growth of its civilization. The vegetable kingdom is undoubtedly most at the mercy of atmospheric and telluric conditions in that plants, unless they are raised in hothouses, are almost wholly destitute of means of reaction or defense against external influences. Animals are somewhat better off, since self-defense and reaction are not altogether impossible for them. Primitive or even savage man is still better situated, for his means of defense are at least superior to those of the animals. Best situated of all is civilized man. He is so rich in resources that he feels but scant effects from changes in climate—and he is perfecting his resources and increasing their number from day to day.

Granting that premise, the following conception seems to us obvious and acceptable: that the first great civilizations arose in spots where nature offered the greatest and most numerous facilities, or the fewest and least serious obstacles; that, therefore, they flourished in broad valleys that were fairly mild in climate and well enough watered to permit easy cultivation of some sort of grain. A fair density of population is a condition that is almost indispensable to the rise of a civilization. Civilization is not possible where a hundred human beings are scattered over a thousand square miles of land. But if human beings are to live in large numbers in a relatively small area (say at least ten or twenty inhabitants per square mile), a grain culture is essential. In fact, we find that the rise of Chinese civilization was contemporaneous with, or subsequent to, the cultivation of rice. The Egyptian and Mesopotamian civilizations were based on wheat, barley and millet, and the aboriginal American civilizations on maize. In a few tropical countries certain fruits, such as the banana, or farinaceous roots such as manioc, may have taken the place of cereals.

This induction is corroborated by history, which shows early civilizations in the valleys of the Nile, the Euphrates, the Ganges, and the Yellow River, and on the Anáhuac plateau—lands which present all the physical conditions that we have mentioned. But once man has succeeded in so marshaling his forces as to tame nature in some exceptionally favorable spot, he can go on to master her in other places where she is more recalcitrant. In our day—with the exception of the polar regions, a few spots, possibly, about the equator, and certain areas where excessive aridness or the presence of malaria creates peculiarly unfavorable conditions—all the lands of the earth are, or can be made, capable of harboring civilized populations.

6. The principle that civilization always spreads from south to north, or rather from warm to cold areas, we regard as one of those oversimple formulas which attempt to explain extremely complicated phenomena by a single cause. It is based on a mere fragment of history—on the history of a single period in European civilization, and a history superficially studied at that. If one were to use this method in examining a map—a map of northern Germany, or of Siberia, let us say—one might deduce a law that all rivers flow from south to north, because that is true of those countries, which have highlands in the south and seas to the north. The rule might be reversed if one were studying southern Russia, while South America might furnish still a third law, namely, that rivers flow from west to east. The truth is that, with no reference whatever to latitude or longitude, rivers flow from high to low, from mountains or plateaus to seas or lakes. If one were to call lands offering the lesser resistance "lower" lands, one might say that the law that governs the expansion of civilization is the very same. The civilizing current flows indifferently from south to north and from north to south, but it flows by preference in the direction in which it encounters the least natural and social resistance—and by social resistance we mean the impact of other original civilizations developing in inverse directions.

Chinese civilization arose in the central provinces of the empire. It was shut in on the north by the barren and frigid plateaus of central Asia, while on the south it could flow not only into the southern provinces of China proper but into Indo-China as well. Hindu civilization, encountering the almost insurmountable chain of the Himalayas on the north, pressed from north to south, from northern India into the Deccan, and thence on to Ceylon and Java. Egyptian civilization crept northward until it met the powerful confederation of the Hittites, in other words the impact of another civilization, in northern Syria. On the other hand, it was in a position to expand more extensively to the south, and it in fact ascended the Nile from Memphis to Thebes and from Thebes to Meroë. It now seems certain that the earliest dynasties flourished at Tanis and Memphis, that Thebes came into prominence only after the invasion of the Shepherd kings and that Ethiopia was civilized by the Egyptians and did not become an independent realm until a very late date.

Heir to the ancient cultures of Mesopotamia, Persian civilization spread from east to west—in the direction in which it encountered fewest natural obstacles—until it collided with Greek civilization. Greco-Roman civilization embraced the whole basin of the Mediterranean. Arrested to the south by impassable deserts and toward the east by Oriental civilization in the form of the Parthian empire and then of the Persian, it spread northward until it came to the swamps and forests, at the time almost impassable, of northern Germany and Scotland. Mohammedan civilization was barred on the south by sea and desert and so was impelled towards the northwest. During the Middle Ages, European civilization was checked on the south by Arab civilization, which wrested the entire southern portion of the Mediterranean basin from it. It moved northward, accordingly, absorbing Scotland, northern Germany, Scandinavia and Poland. Today the civilization of Europe is stretching out in all directions, wherever there are sparsely populated lands that are easy to colonize, or decadent nations that are waiting for a conqueror.

The center of a civilization, as the latter flows in one direction or another, seems to move in conformity with the law we have just stated. The countries that lie on the frontiers of a type of human civilization are not as a rule the ones that are most advanced in it. When European civilization embraced the whole Mediterranean basin, Greece proper and southern Italy were the hub of the civilized world, and they were the most vigorous, the most cultured, the most prosperous countries in it. When they became the most advanced outposts of civilization facing the Mohammedan world, they declined. In a given country, conditions being equal, the most civilized and prosperous district seems almost always to be the one that has the readiest means of communication with the lands that constitute the hearth, or radiation center, of the civilization to which the country itself belongs. As long as Sicily was part of the Hellenic world, which had its center to the east of Sicily, the most prosperous and highly civilized section of the island was the east coast.[1] During the Arab period western Sicily was the most cultured, prosperous and thickly populated, being closest to Africa, whence Mohammedan civilization was radiating.[2] Today the greatest population and wealth are concentrated on the north coast of the island, facing northern Europe.

7. It is also, in our opinion, a very rash hypothesis to ascribe a superior morality to the peoples of the north as compared with the peoples of the south. Morality results from such complex qualities of mind and spirit, and the external circumstances within which human life unfolds play such a large part in positive or negative expressions of morality, that to determine whether a single individual is *potentially* more moral than another is in itself not a little difficult. Difficult indeed is that same judgment with respect to two societies, two human masses composed of many individuals. Statistical data on this subject cannot tell everything—often they fail even to tell enough. Personal impressions are almost always too subjective—on the whole they are less trustworthy than statistics. Generally speaking, it is the unfamiliar form of immorality that makes the greater impression, and so we are prone to judge people of another country as worse than people of our own. Moreover, we are commonly given to considering as less moral than others the country in which we came first or most thoroughly to know and appraise certain vices and frailties which, really, are common to all men.

[1] Beloch, "La popolazione della Sicilia antica" and see: *Die Bevölkerung der Griechisch-Römischen Welt*, chap. VII, pp. 261–305.

[2] Amari, *Storia dei Musulmani in Sicilia.*

The vice most commonly attributed to southerners is lust, whereas northerners are more generally charged with drunkenness. And yet it may be observed that Congo negroes become more disgracefully drunk than Russian peasants or Swedish laborers; and as for lust, it appears that folkways and the type of social organization that each people creates for itself as the result of a sequence of historical circumstances exert a profounder influence upon it than does climate. Before his conversion to Christianity, St. Vladimir (the czar who was canonized and became the patron saint of all the Russias) had more women in his harem than the caliph Harun-al-Rashid ever did. Ivan the Terrible emulated and outstripped in cruelty and lust Nero, Heliogabalus and the bloodiest sultans of the East. In our day there is perhaps more prostitution in London, Paris and Vienna than there ever was in ancient Babylon and Delhi. In present-day Europe, Germany leads in the number of sex crimes, and then follow, in descending order, Belgium, France, Austria and Hungary. Italy stands near the bottom of the list, and Spain comes last of all.[1]

Many criminologists assume a predominance of crimes of violence, or offenses against the person, in the south, whereas they credit the north with a larger quota of offenses against property.[2] But Tarde and Colajanni have shown conclusively that such relations as have been sought between climate and type of crime are rather to be ascribed to differences in social conditions such as may be encountered in various districts in a given country.[3] It is true that in the United States, France and Italy crimes of violence regularly prevail in the south, while the northern parts of those countries show a relatively higher frequency of crimes against property. But as Tarde himself well points out, in all those countries the southern districts are poorer in facilities of communication, are farther removed from the great industrial cities and from the centers of present-day civilization, than are the northern regions; and it is to be expected that violent forms of crime should predominate, irrespective of climate, in less advanced regions, and that crimes requiring skill and shrewdness should be more common in better educated ones. This, in fact,

[1] Colajanni, La sociologia criminale, vol. II, chap. 7.
[2] Maury, Lombroso, Ferri, Puglia.
[3] Tarde, La Criminalité comparée, chap. IV.

would seem to be the most adequate explanation of the phenomenon. The French departments that show the highest figures for
crimes of violence (Ardèche and Lozère, in the eastern Pyrenees)
lie, to be sure, in the south of France, but they are relatively cold
regions because of the mountainous nature of the country. In
Italy the Basilicata furnishes one of the highest percentages of
crimes of violence, but it is a mountainous district and relatively
cold—the peaks of the Matese, the Gargano and the Sila are snow-
covered for most of the year as are the highlands that bear certain
Sicilian towns notorious for enterprises involving blood and
brigandage.[1]

8. Going on to the strictly political aspect of the question, we
may note that before we can decide whether southerners are
unfitted for liberty we must come to an understanding as to
the exact meaning of the term "liberty." If we assume that
the freest country is the country where the rights of the governed
are best protected against arbitrary caprice and tyranny on the
part of rulers, we must agree that political institutions that are
regarded as superior from that point of view have flourished both
in cold countries and in very temperate countries, such as Greece
and Rome. Vice versa, systems of government based on the
arbitrary will of rulers may be found in such very cold countries
as Russia. The constitutional form of government had no more
vigorous beginnings in foggy England than it had in Aragon,
Castile and Sicily. If Montesquieu had extended his travels a
little farther south he would have found, in Sicily, a political
order under which, even in his day, the royal authority was much
more limited than it was in France.[2] Granting that in our time
the various representative systems may be regarded as the least
imperfect forms of government, we find them in force in northern
and southern Europe equally, and, outside of Europe, they
probably function as well in chilly Canada as they do at the Cape
of Good Hope, where the climate, if not actually hot, is certainly
very mild.

The reason why southerners should be less well fitted for free
and enlightened forms of government can only be this: that they

[1] For other examples, see Colajanni, *La sociologia criminale*, vol. II, chap. 7.

[2] On the importance and extensive development of the old Sicilian constitution
see the two classic treatises by Gregorio, *Introduzione allo studio del diritto
pubblico siciliano* and *Considerazioni sulla storia di Sicilia*.

are possessed of less physical, and especially less moral and intellectual, vitality. It is, in fact, very commonly believed that in view of a superior energy, which expresses itself in industriousness, in war, in learning, northerners are destined always to be conquerors of the ineffectual southerners. But that view is even more superficial and contrary to fact than the ones we have just refuted. Actually, civilizations which arose and developed in hot or very mild climates have left behind them monuments that attest an advanced culture and an untold capacity for labor which are all the more astonishing in that the peoples in question did not have at their disposal the machines that today multiply man's resources a hundredfold. The capacity of a people for hard work seems to depend not so much on climate as on habits that are in large part determined by the vicissitudes of its history. In general, habits of application and industry are shown by peoples of very ancient civilization who have long since attained the agricultural level and have, moreover, long enjoyed tolerable political systems that assure the working man of at least some fraction of the fruits of his toil. On the other hand, peoples that have relapsed into a partial barbarism, or barbarous and semibarbarous peoples that are accustomed to live to some extent by war and thieving, are usually indolent and sluggish apart from activities relating to fighting or hunting. In just such terms did Tacitus describe the ancient Germans. In our time the North American Indians and the Kalmuks of Asia are exceedingly lazy, though the former once lived, as the latter still live, in very cold countries. The Chinese of the southern provinces are a hardworking people, and the Egyptian fellah can toil with the utmost endurance. The absence of large-scale industry in the southernmost parts of Europe has created and continues to sustain the impression that their inhabitants are indolent workers, but anyone who knows these peoples well knows how little, on the whole, that reputation is deserved. Sicily may be taken as an example. That island, with an area of about 20,000 square miles, supports a population of over four million—in other words, about 180 people per square mile. There are no large industries and no great abundance of capital. The soil, largely mountainous, is rich in sunshine but poor in water. If a population is to live with any degree of comfort at all under such conditions, the soil must be tilled with untiring effort and with a certain amount of technical proficiency.

If we assume that military superiority is a test of greater energy, it is hard indeed to decide whether northerners have defeated and conquered southerners more often than southerners have defeated and conquered northerners. The Egyptians were southerners, and in their heyday they swept in triumph over Asia as far as the mountains of Armenia. The Assyrian warriors lived in the mildest of climates, yet, however much we may deplore their brutality, we cannot but marvel at their indomitable energy in war. The Greeks were southerners, but they managed to conquer all western Asia, and by force of arms, colonization, commerce and intellectual superiority they Hellenized the entire eastern portion of the Mediterranean basin and a considerable part of the basin of the Black Sea. The Romans, too, were southerners, and their legions overran the plains of Dacia, penetrated the inaccessible forests of Germany, and pursued the Picts and Caledonians into the deepest recesses of their bleak, wild mountains. The Italians of the Middle Ages were southerners, and they wrought miracles in war, industry and commerce. Southerners, too, were the Spaniards of the sixteenth century, those glamorous conquistadores who in less than half a century explored, overran and conquered most of the Americas. The Franco-Norman followers of William the Conqueror were southerners, as compared with the English, yet in a few years' time they were able almost entirely to dispossess the inhabitants of southern Great Britain and to drive the Angles, at the point of the sword, back to the old Roman wall. The Arabs were southerners in an absolute sense, yet in less than a century they imposed their conquest, and with their conquest their language, their religion and their civilization, upon as generous a portion of the world as the modern Anglo-Saxons have conquered and colonized in the course of many centuries.

9. Differences in social organization depending on land configuration or topography may be considered as secondary to those due to variations in climate, though they may perhaps be more important. Whether a country is more or less level or more or less mountainous, whether it is situated on the great highways of communication or remote from them, are factors that exert a far greater influence on its history than a few degrees more or less of mean temperature. The importance of such factors must not

be exaggerated, however, to the point of making an inexorable law of them. Topographical features that are favorable under certain historical conditions may become very unfavorable under others, and vice versa. When all Europe was still in the Bronze and the early Iron Age, Greece found herself in an amazingly favorable situation for achieving leadership in her corner of the world, since she was better placed than any other country for absorbing infiltrations from Egyptian and Asiatic civilizations. But in modern times, down to the cutting of the isthmus of Suez, Greece was one of the least favorably situated of the countries of Europe, since she lay remote from the center of European culture and from the great highways of transatlantic and East Indian commerce.

Another widespread opinion in such matters is that mountaineers are usually superior to lowlanders and are destined almost always to conquer them. Certainly more can be said for that theory than for the ascription of marked superiority to peoples of the north. It may be questionable whether a cold climate is more salubrious than a temperate or warm climate, but it seems to be established that highlands are almost always more healthful than lowlands—and better health implies stronger physical constitution and therefore greater energy. But great energy is not always combined with strength of social structure, upon which, after all, decision as to whether a people is to rule or to be ruled depends. Now a sound political organism that unites and directs the energies of great masses of people arises and maintains itself more readily on plains than in mountainous countries. In fact we see, in Turkey and the Near East, that though the Circassian, Kurdish and Albanian mountaineers have frequently attained importance as individuals, and though bands of them in the service of bordering countries have often become forces to be reckoned with and feared, yet Albania, Circassia and Kurdistan have never, in historic times, become nuclei of great independent empires. On the contrary, they have always been drawn into the orbits of the great political organisms that touched their borders.[1] The Swiss, too, have had great importance as individuals and as corps of mercenaries, but Switzerland as

---

[1] Saladin was a Kurd. Mehemet Ali, the first khedive of Egypt, was an Albanian. The famous Mameluke beys, who ruled in Egypt for many centuries, were Circassians.

a nation has never weighed perceptibly in the political scales of
Europe.

History shows, in general, that if intrepid bands of mountaineers have often devastated, rather than conquered, lowlands, still
more often have the organized armies of lowlanders crushed the
disconnected efforts of highlanders and reduced them to permanent submission.   The Romans conquered the Samnites,
while the Samnites were able to defeat the Romans only in an
occasional battle.   Bands of the Scottish highlanders did now
and then overrun northern England and ravage it, but the lowland English more often defeated mountainous Scotland and
ended by conquering it, taming its warlike impulses and assimilating it completely.   For that matter, lowland peoples are not
necessarily destitute of energy, or even poorly endowed with it.
One has only to think of the Dutch, the North Germans, the
Russians, the English, who are in large part inhabitants of very
low countries.

10. The method that ascribes the degree of progress and
civilization that a nation has attained and the type of political
organization that it has adopted to the race to which it belongs
is much less ancient than the method which views climate as the
arbiter of everything.   That could hardly be otherwise.   Anthropology and comparative philology, upon which the scientific
classification of the races of mankind is based, are very recent
sciences (Broca and Grimm lived in the nineteenth century),
whereas approximative information as to climatic differences was
available in the early day of Herodotus.   However, newcomer as
it may have been, the ethnological trend in the social sciences
has been correspondingly aggressive; and the last decades of the
nineteenth century witnessed an attempt to interpret all human
history on the basis of racial differences and racial influences.[1]
A distinction was drawn between superior races and inferior
races, the former being credited with civilization, morality and a
capacity for organizing themselves into great political units,
while for the latter was reserved the harsh but inevitable lot
either of vanishing before the encroachment of the higher races
or of being conquered and civilized by them.   At the most it was

---

[1] See, among others, Quatrefages, Gumplowicz, Lapouge and Hellwald.
Gobineau's *Essai sur l'inégalité des races humaines* appeared in 1853.

granted that they might go on living in independence, but without ever attaining the degree of culture and the flawless social and political organization that were proper to peoples of the privileged stocks.

Renan wrote that spiritual poetry, faith, liberty, honor, self-sacrifice appeared in the world only with the advent of the two great races which, in a sense, had fashioned humanity, the Aryan and the Semitic.[1] For Gobineau the central point of history is always located where the purest, strongest, most intelligent white group abides. Lapouge pushes the same doctrine to its extremest consequences. In his opinion not only is the race that is truly moral, truly superior in all things, the Aryan, but within the Aryan race itself those individuals excel who have kept the Aryan type in pure and uncontaminated forms—those who are tall, blond and dolichocephalic. Yet even among the nations that pass as Indo-Germanic, individuals of this type constitute only a small minority scattered about among a short, dark, brachycephalic majority. The true Aryans, therefore, are fairly numerous in England and North America. They begin to dwindle in numbers in Germany, being encountered there only in the upper classes. They are very rare in France and become a virtually unknown commodity in the countries of southern Europe. Morselli espouses Lapouge's thesis, maintaining the superiority of blond strains over dark, because the most highly civilized nations are those in which blonds prevail in numbers and within any given country the most highly civilized region or province is always the one where blonds are most numerous.[2]

Along with this school which maintains the innate and inevitable superiority of certain races there is another, which, without being in absolute opposition to it, is more directly linked with Darwin's theories, so widely applied to the social sciences during the second half of the past century. Spencer is the best-known writer of this second school, which has many followers. Without

----

[1] *Vie de Jésus*, chap. 1. In other works Renan speaks of the Semites in far from flattering terms.

[2] Granting all this for the sake of argument, it would still be necessary to show that in the past the dark races had never been more highly civilized or more powerful than the fair. If at any time they were, the present superiority of nations and provinces where fair hair is the commoner could well be due to other causes.

maintaining the inevitable and unbroken superiority of any one race over others, these scholars believe that all social progress has come about, and is still being made, by a process of organic, or superorganic, evolution, so-called. A continuous struggle, the struggle for existence, is always going on *within* every society. As a result, the stronger and better individuals, those who are best adapted to their environment, survive the weaker and less well adapted and propagate their kind in preference to the latter, passing on to their descendants as an inborn heritage the qualities, acquired by a slow process of education, which won them their victory. The same struggle goes on *between* societies themselves, and by it the more soundly constituted societies, those composed of the stronger individuals, conquer societies that are less advantageously endowed; the latter, driven to territories less favorable to human progress, are condemned to remain in a state of everlasting inferiority.

It is not hard to find a fundamental difference between these two theories. Even if the monogenistic theory, that all the races of mankind derive from a common stock, be granted, the fact still remains that differentiating traits are certainly very ancient and must have been fixed in ages extremely remote, when man had not yet emerged from his savage stage and was therefore more prone to feel the influence of the natural agencies with which he came into contact. The aboriginal American race had the physical traits it now has in a fairly remote prehistoric epoch. In very ancient Egyptian bas-reliefs, which go back some twenty centuries before our era, figures of Negroes, Semites and native Egyptians show the physical characteristics that still distinguish them. Keeping to the strictly ethnological theory, therefore, the higher races must already have possessed their traits of superiority at the dawn of history and have retained them practically unaltered; whereas the evolutionary theory proper implicitly or explicitly assumes that the struggle for existence has had its practical effects more recently. To that struggle it ascribes the rise and fall of the various nations and civilizations during the historic period.

11. Before the question of racial superiority or inferiority can be considered the value of the word "race" has to be determined, for it is used sometimes in a very broad, sometimes in a very

narrow, sense. We speak of white, yellow and black races to designate varieties of the human species that not only differ in language but present fairly important and fairly palpable anatomical differences. We speak of the Aryan and the Semitic races to indicate two subdivisions of the white race, which differ, to be sure, in language, but which present very striking physical resemblances. We also say the Latin, the Germanic, the Slavic races, designating by the same term three subdivisions of the Aryan branch of the white race. Though these "races" speak different languages, it can nevertheless be proved, philologically, that they are bound together by a common origin, while their physical differences are so slight that a member of one group can be mistaken for a member of another. Now in this case, as in all others, confusion in terminology leads to confusion in ideas. The fact of racial difference is pressed into service as much to explain certain diversities in civilization and political organization between whites and Negroes as to account for similar diversities between Latins, Germans and Slavs, whereas in the first case the ethnological coefficient may have a real significance and in the second, hardly any at all.

We must also bear in mind that in historic and prehistoric times race crossings and mixtures, particularly between closely related races, were frequent. In the latter case, since the physical differences between the crossed races are of scant importance, and not readily perceptible in any event, classification has been based upon philological affinities rather than upon anatomical traits. But the language criterion is anything but trustworthy and infallible. It may happen, and frequently does happen, that two groups which are closely related by blood speak languages that have only remote philological kinship, while peoples of different races may speak languages and dialects that are closely affiliated as to word roots and grammatical structure. However dubious that statement may seem at first glance, there are many examples that prove it and many historical situations that explain it. In general, conquered peoples who are less civilized than their conquerors adopt the laws, arts, culture and religion of the latter and often end by adopting their language.

The languages and civilizations of the Greeks and Romans enjoyed a marvelous expansion through their adoption by barbarous peoples.   In France the substratum of the population is still Cimbro-Celtic, but French is essentially a Neo-Latin language.   In Spain Basque blood probably predominates in the north.   In the south the admixture of Arabo-Berber blood must be very strong.   In Italy there are appreciable ethnic differences between Italians of the north and Italians of the south and the islands, but the various dialects are all essentially Neo-Latin. Leaving the sphere of Latin, we find that the fellahs, who are descendants of the ancient Egyptians, have forgotten the ancient tongue of Mizraim and adopted Arabic, which, moreover, has become general throughout 'Irak-'Arabi and Syria, and is becoming more and more the spoken language of the African Berbers. As for India, dialects of Sanskrit origin are spoken by populations which in skin color and facial features show a strong admixture, and perhaps even a predominance, of Dravidic blood.   In Silesia, Brandenburg, Pomerania and old Prussia, German is the language of populations that were partly Slavic or partly Lettish in origin.   In our own day, finally, the Celts of Ireland and northern Scotland are adopting English more and more.

These considerations are self-evident; yet people continue to make ethnographic classifications, especially of European peoples, with sole reference to philological criteria.   To tell the truth, it may be said in defense of this system that similarity of language, engendering as it does a freer interchange of ideas and feelings between certain peoples, tends to give them a far stronger resemblance in intellectual and moral type than customarily results from mere blood relationship.

Bearing all this in mind, it seems to us an established fact that the most primitive races, those which anthropologists call "lower"—the Fuegians, the Australians, the Bushmen, and so on—are physically and intellectually inferior to the others. Whether that inferiority is innate, whether it has always existed, or whether it is to be attributed to the barrenness of their habitats, to the meagerness of the resources that their surroundings offer and to the abject poverty resulting, is a question that it is neither easy nor essential for us to answer.   After all, these races represent only a very minute fraction of mankind, and that fraction is rapidly dwindling before the expansion of the white race, which is being followed in its turn, in many places, by an infiltration from the yellow race.   In strict justice we are obliged to recognize that the prosperity of the white and yellow races in localities where the aborigines barely managed to subsist has not been wholly due to the organic superiority which the former boastfully claim. The newcomers bring with them knowledge and material means which enable them to reap an ample livelihood from soils that of themselves would yield practically nothing. The Australian native for centuries upon centuries was content to track the kangaroo, bring down birds with his boomerang or, if worse came to worst, eat a lizard. But we must remember that he had no means of securing the seeds to grow grains or other edible plants, or the breeders for flocks of sheep, which the English colonists had at their disposal.

It is still harder to come to any decision as to the inferiority of the native American and the black races. Those races have from time immemorial held possession of far-flung territories in which powerful civilizations might have developed. In America, populous empires arose in Mexico, Peru and a few other regions. We cannot determine the degree of their culture with any exactness, since it was their misfortune to crumble before the onslaught of a few hundred Spanish adventurers. In Africa, the blacks have managed to organize fairly extensive political units at one time or another, for example, in Uganda; but not one among such states ever attained by itself a degree of culture that could be compared with that of the most ancient empires founded by the white races, or of the Chinese, Babylonian and ancient Egyptian empires, where the civilizing races were not black. It would seem, accordingly, that a certain inferiority might also be attributed prima facie to both the American Indians and the Negroes.

But when things have gone in a certain way, it is not always legitimate to assume that they necessarily and unfailingly had to go that way. It is doubtful whether man existed in the Tertiary period, but it has been scientifically proved that his antiquity goes back to the beginnings of the Quaternary period and that the age of man therefore has to be computed not in thousands of years but in hundreds and perhaps thousands of centuries. Now the races of man, as we noted above, must have been formed at a very remote epoch, and since such long periods are involved the fact that a race has attained a notable degree of culture thirty, forty, even fifty centuries before another is not an infallible proof of its organic superiority. External circumstances, often fortuitous—the discovery and utilization of a metal, which may happen more or less easily according to the region, the availability or absence of domesticable plants or animals—may accelerate or retard the progress of a civilization, or even alter its history. If the American Indians had known the use of iron—a hypothesis that is not in the least far-fetched, since they did know other metals, such as gold and copper—or if the Europeans had invented gunpowder two centuries later than they did, the Europeans would not so swiftly or so completely have destroyed the political organizations of the Indians. Nor should we forget that if a race that has attained a ripe civilization, on coming into contact with another race that is still in a state of barbarism, contributes to the latter a store of useful tools and knowledge, it nevertheless profoundly disturbs, if it does not altogether arrest, the spontaneous and original development of the primitive society.

Not only, in fact, have the whites almost everywhere wiped out or subjugated the American Indians. For centuries and centuries, now with alcohol, now with the slave trade, they have brutalized and impoverished the Negro race. We are obliged to agree, therefore, that European civilization has not only hindered but actually thwarted any effort toward progress that Negroes and Indians might have made of their own accord.

At various branches of the American Indian race, as well as at the Polynesians, the Australians and others of the less fortunate races of human beings, the charge has been leveled that they cannot survive contact with the white man but vanish rapidly before his advance. The truth is that the whites deprive the colored races of their means of livelihood before those races have time to accustom themselves to utilizing the new means of subsistence that are introduced by the whites. As a rule the hunting territories of the primitive tribes are invaded and the big game destroyed before the native can adapt himself to agriculture. Moreover the civilized races communicate their diseases to the less civilized, while the latter are unable to take advantage of the preventive or curative measures that scientific progress and long experience have taught to the whites. Tuberculosis, syphilis and smallpox would probably wreak as great havoc among us as they have wrought in certain primitive tribes if we tried to forestall and cure them exclusively with the means that the savages have at their disposal—no means at all, in other words.

Are Indians and Negroes on the whole inferior to whites as individuals? While most people would answer with a ready and emphatic yes, some few with equal promptness and resolve say no. As for us, we find it as hard to agree as to disagree in terms at all positive. Observers rarely fail to report, in strictly primitive groups of these races, individuals who are outstanding for qualities, now of mind, now of heart. Where the American aborigines have mingled with the whites and adopted their civilization, they have not failed to produce distinguished men in nearly all branches of human activity, and under identical conditions the Negroes can boast of a list of names almost as long. Nevertheless, one has to admit, as regards both these races, that the roster of conspicuous individuals is very brief as compared with the number of individuals who have been, and are, in a position to enjoy the advantages offered by civilized life. Some weight, however, has to be given to a remark that was made to Henry George by a scholarly Negro bishop,[1] that Negro school children do as well as white children and show themselves just as wide-awake and intelligent up to the age of ten or twelve; but as soon as they begin to realize that they belong to a race that is adjudged inferior, and that they can look forward to no better lot than that of cooks and porters, they lose interest in studying and lapse into apathy. In a great part of America colored people are generally regarded as inferior creatures, who must inevitably be relegated to the lowest social strata. Now if the disinherited classes among the whites bore on their faces the indelible stamp of social inferiority, it is certain that few individuals indeed among them would have the energy to raise themselves to a social position very much higher than the one to which they were born.

If some doubt may be raised as to the aptitude of Negroes and American Indians for the higher forms of civilization and political organization, all perplexity vanishes as regards the Aryans and the Semites, the Mongolian, or yellow, race and that dark Asiatic race which lives mixed with the Aryan stock in India and has fused with the yellow in southern China, in Indo-China and

[1] *Progress and Poverty*, book X, chap. II, p. 2.

perhaps in Japan. These races taken together make up more than three-fourths, and perhaps as much as four-fifths, of all mankind. We say nothing of the Polynesian race. It may well have superior capacities, but being scant in numbers and dispersed over small islands, it has not been able to create any great civilization.

The Chinese succeeded in founding a highly original civilization which has shown wondrous powers of survival and even more wondrous powers of expansion. Offshoots in large part of Chinese civilization are the cultures of Japan and Indo-China, and the Sumerian people which founded the earliest civilization in Babylonia seems to have belonged to a Turanian stock. The dark Asiatic race seems to have developed a very ancient civilization in Elam, or Susiana, and an autochthonous culture apparently existed in India before the coming of the Aryans. Egypt owes her civilization to a so-called sub-Semitic or Berber race, and Nineveh, Sidon, Jerusalem, Damascus and perhaps even Sardis belonged to the Semites. Reference to the more recent civilization of the Mohammedan Arabs seems to us superfluous.

12. While not holding to the absolute superiority or inferiority of any human race, many people believe that each race has special intellectual and moral qualities and that these necessarily correspond to certain types of social and political organization, from which the spirit, or, better, the peculiar "genius" of the race, will not permit it to depart.

Now, making all due allowances for the exaggerations that gain ready admission to discussions of this subject, and taking account at all times of the great fund of human traits that is present in all peoples in all ages, it cannot be denied that—not to say every race—every nation, every region, every city presents a certain special type that is not uniformly definite and clear-cut everywhere but which consists in a body of ideas, beliefs, opinions, sentiments, customs and prejudices, which are to each group of human beings what the lineaments of the face are to each individual.

This variation in type could safely be regarded as due to physical diversities, to racial variations, to the different blood that flows in the veins of each different nationality, did it not find its explanation in another fact, which is one of the best authenticated and most constant that observation of human nature affords. We refer to mimetism, to that great psychological force whereby every individual is wont to adopt the ideas, the beliefs, the sentiments that are most current in the environment in which he has grown up. Save for rare and rarely complete exceptions, a person thinks, judges and believes the way the society in which he lives thinks, judges and believes. We observe that aspect of things which is commonly noted by the persons about us, and the individual preferably develops those moral and intellectual attitudes which are most prevalent and most highly esteemed in the human environment in which he has been formed.

In fact, unity of moral and intellectual type is found to be very strong in groups of persons having nothing special in common as regards blood or race. The Catholic clergy will serve as an example. Scattered the world over, it always preserves a singular uniformity in its beliefs, its intellectual and moral attitudes and its customs. The phenomenon is most striking in the various religious orders. Well known is the remarkable resemblance of an Italian Jesuit to a French, German or English Jesuit. A strong resemblance exists, too, in the military type that is common to almost all the great European armies, and a fairly constant intellectual or moral type may further exist within separate regiments, in military academies and even in secular schools—anywhere, in short, where a special environment has somehow been established, a sort of psychological mold that shapes to its own contour any individual who happens to be cast into it.

We are not for the moment inquiring as to how the great national environments, and better still those great psychological currents that sometimes embrace a whole civilization or all the followers of a religion, have come into being, lived their lives and, often, vanished from the world scene. To launch out on such a study would involve retraversing the history of the whole civilized portion of mankind. But this much we can safely say: that historical circumstances peculiar to each of the great groups of mankind have in the main fashioned the special environments mentioned, and that new historical circumstances slowly modify, or even destroy, those environments. The role that blood relationship, that race, plays in the formation of the various moral and mental environments may, in certain cases at least, be slight and of difficult appraisal even when the ethnological factor seems at first glance to be preponderant.

Apt to this point would be the example of the Jews, who have been dispersed among other peoples yet for centuries upon centuries have wondrously preserved their national type. But we must not forget, either, that the children of Israel have always lived spiritually apart from the peoples among whom they dwelt, and therefore have always been in a special environment. As Leroy-Beaulieu well says,[1] the modern Jew is a product of the isolation in which he has for centuries been kept by the Torah, the Talmud and the ghetto. The progeny of Jewish families that are converted to Christianity or to Islamism rarely retain the characteristics of their ancestors for any length of time—for many generations, that is; and the unconverted Jew best preserves his special type in countries where he keeps most to himself. A Jew from Little Russia or Constantinople is much more Jewish than his coreligionists who have been born and bred in Italy or France, where the ghetto is now just a memory. Chinese immigrants in America take over white civilization in many respects, but their mental type remains unchanged, while the Chinese in California and some other states always keep to themselves in a Chinese environment. In European and Asiatic Turkey, Turks, Greeks, Armenians, Jews and Levantines live together in the same cities. They do not fuse nor are their races modified, for in spite of the fact that they live in material contact, they are spiritually separated, each group having its own special environment. The great tenacity with which the English national type maintains itself, as, compared with other nationalities of Europe, may be the result of the scant sociability that English settlers in foreign countries manifest toward natives, which inclines them to cluster together in a miniature British environment. Many cases might be mentioned where ethnic affinity between two peoples is a virtually negligible bond as compared with the ties that result from similarities in religion or from the fact of common histories and civilizations. Ethnologists have discovered that a Magyar is more closely related to a Chinese or a Turk than to a Frenchman or a German. But who would claim that he is morally and intellectually closer to the

[1] "Les Juifs et l'anti-sémitisme."

two former than to the two latter?   The Mohammedan Aryans
of Persia and Hindustan certainly have closer moral affinities
with the Arabs and Turks than with their European kinsmen;
and Jews long settled in western Europe certainly feel spiritually closer to the nations among whom they live than to the
Arabs, who are blood relatives but who have adopted Oriental
civilization.

The so-called genius of a race, therefore, has nothing predestined or inevitable about it, as some people are pleased to
imagine.   Even granting that the various "higher" races—in
other words races that are capable of creating original civilizations of their own—differ organically from each other, it is not
the sum of their organic differences that has *exclusively* or even
principally determined the differences in the social type that
they have adopted, but rather the differences in social contacts
and in the historical circumstances to which every nation, every
social organism—let alone every race—is fated to be subject.

13. The question of race would at this point be settled if
everyone were in agreement that the organic and psychological
changes by which a human race may be modified over an extensive period of history—for example, twenty or thirty centuries—
are hardly appreciable and virtually negligible.   But this is far
from being a generally accepted belief.   There is, in fact, a whole
school of historical thinking that is founded on quite different
postulates.   Applying Darwin's doctrines about the evolution
of species to the social sciences, this school holds that every
human group can make considerable organic improvements in
relatively brief periods of time, whence the possibility of political
and social betterment.

Now, without discussing or denying Darwin's theories about
the transformation of species, and even granting man's descent
from a hypothetical Anthropopithecus, one fact seems to us certain, undebatable and obvious at first glance: that the famous
struggle for existence, along with the natural selection that
follows from it, as described for plants, animals and savage man,
does not appear in human societies that have attained anything
higher than a very elementary stage of civilization.   The eager-
ness to find such a struggle in human societies is in part due to
the extraordinary success of the Darwinian hypothesis when

applied to the natural sciences. That success was bound to offer a strong temptation to systematic minds to extend the application of the hypothesis to other fields. But it is also due to a misapprehension, to a failure to distinguish between two facts that are basically different though apparently they have points of contact—and this confusion, too, is readily understandable in minds that are strongly predisposed in favor of the evolutionary theory. To put the situation in a few words, the struggle for *existence* has been confused with the struggle for *preeminence*, which is really a constant phenomenon that arises in all human societies, from the most highly civilized down to such as have barely issued from savagery.

In a struggle between two human societies, the victorious society as a rule fails to annihilate the vanquished society, but subjects it, assimilates it, imposes its own type of civilization upon it. In our day in Europe and America war has no other result than political hegemony for the nation that proves superior in a military sense, or perhaps the seizure of some bit of territory. But even in ancient times, when Greece was fighting Persia and Rome Carthage, the political organization, the national existence, of the vanquished peoples was sometimes destroyed, but individually, even in the worst cases, they were usually reduced to servitude rather than put to the sword. Cases like that of Saguntum and of Numantia, or like the taking of Tyre by Alexander the Great, or of Carthage by Scipio, have been at all periods of history altogether exceptional. The Assyrians in the ancient East and the Mongols in the Middle Ages were the peoples most given to the practice of systematically butchering the peoples they conquered. But even they used the practice rather as a means of frightening enemies into surrender than as an end in itself; and it cannot be said that a single people was ever exterminated root and branch by their frightful slaughters. As instances of complete destruction of peoples by conquerors the cases of the Tasmanians, the Australians and the American Indians are commonly mentioned. But actually those were primitive tribes with small populations scattered over large territories. They perished, or are perishing, chiefly because, as we have seen, agriculture and an encroaching civilization have reduced the supply of big game which was their principal means of subsistence. In a few regions where the Indians have been able to adapt themselves to a crude sort of agriculture, they have escaped destruction. In Mexico and Peru the natives were numerous at the time of the Spanish conquest because they had reached the agricultural stage. In spite of the slaughters committed by their Spanish conquerors they today form the great majority in Spanish American populations. In Algeria, too, a hard and bloody conquest by the French has not reduced the numerical strength of the natives.

If we consider, rather, the inner ferment that goes on within the body of every society, we see at once that the struggle for preeminence is far more conspicuous there than the struggle for existence. Competition between individuals of every social unit is focused upon higher position, wealth, authority, control of the means and instruments that enable a person to direct many human activities, many human wills, as he sees fit. The losers, who are of course the majority in that sort of struggle, are not devoured, destroyed or even kept from reproducing their kind, as is basically characteristic of the struggle for life. They merely enjoy fewer material satisfactions and, especially, less freedom and independence. On the whole, indeed, in civilized societies, far from being gradually eliminated by a process of natural selection so called, the lower classes are more prolific than the higher, and even in the lower classes every individual in the long run gets a loaf of bread and a mate, though the bread be more or less dark and hard-earned and the mate more or less unattractive or undesirable. The polygamy that is common in upper classes is the only point that might be cited in support of the principle of natural selection as applied to primitive and civilized societies. But even that argument is weak. Among human beings polygamy does not necessarily imply greater fertility. In fact, the preferably polygamous human societies have been the ones that have made least social progress. It would seem to follow, therefore, that natural selection has proved to be least effective in the cases where it has had freest play.

14. Then again, if the progress of a race or a nation depends primarily on organic improvement in the individuals who compose it, the world's story should present a far different plot from the one we know. The moral and intellectual, and therefore the

social, progress of every people should be *slower* and *more con-tinuous*. The law of natural selection combined with the law of heredity should carry each generation a step, but only a step, ahead of the preceding generation; and we should not, as is frequently the case in history, see a people take a great many steps forward, or sometimes a great many steps backward, in the course of two or three generations.

Examples of such rapid advances and giddy declines are so common as scarcely to require mention. A mere hundred and twenty years intervened between the day of Pisistratus and the day of Socrates; but during those years Hellenic art, Hellenic thought, Hellenic civilization made such measureless progress as to transform a nation of mediocre though ancient civilization into the Greece which traced the most glamorous, the most profound, the most unforgettable pages in the story of human progress. We do not mention the case of Rome because, to tell the truth, Hellenic influence played a large part in her meteoric passage from barbarism to civilization. The Italy of the Renaissance is chronologically only a little over a century removed from the Italy of Dante; but in that interval the artistic, moral and scientific ideal is transformed by an inner creative ferment of the nation and the man of the Middle Ages changes and is gone.

Compare, for a moment, the France of 1650 and the France of 1750. Still alive in the former are men who can remember St. Bartholomew's Eve. The religious wars, the Holy League, the falling of two kings under the assassin's dagger, are facts which have not yet acquired the mystery of ancientness—eyewitnesses of them cannot be rare. Anyone who has passed early youth may easily have been present at the taking of La Rochelle, the closing scene in the historic period referred to. Almost no one dares voice a doubt as to the existence of goblins and witches. A scant thirty-seven years have passed since the wife of Marshal d'Ancre was burned at the stake as a witch. A century later, Montesquieu is an old man, Voltaire and Rousseau are in their prime, the Encyclopedia, if not published, has already ripened in the intellectual world. As far as ideas, beliefs, customs, are concerned, the revolution of '89 may be considered virtually complete. But without wandering far afield for other examples, why not take the chief countries of present-day Europe— England, Germany, Italy, Spain? Certainly if the intellectual and spiritual revolution that has taken place in those countries in the course of the past century had had to depend on organic modifications in their populations, many dozens of generations at least would have been required.

In certain regions, which for special causes had lagged behind the general trend in Europe, the transformation has been more rapid and, especially, more profound. Anyone superficially familiar with the histories of Scotland and Sicily can make a ready comparison between social conditions in Scotland in 1748 and the status that country had attained in 1848, and between social conditions in Sicily in 1812 and conditions there today.[1]

On the other hand, examples of swift declines in nations or whole civilizations are far from rare. There is a very general inclination to charge these to destructive barbarian invasions, but this is to forget that before a civilized country can fall prey to barbarians it must have lapsed into a state of great exhaustion and disorganization, which in turn must be due to moral and political decay. Greater civilization almost always presupposes greater population and the possession of more potent and effective resources for offense and defense. China has twice been conquered by Mongols or Tatars, and India a number of times by Turks, Tatars and Afghans. But the Chinese and Hindu civilizations had already entered upon periods of decline at the time of such invasions.

That decline in civilized peoples is in certain cases spontaneous can be almost mathematically proved. All Orientalists know that the most ancient of all the Egyptian civilizations—the one that built the Nile canals, invented hieroglyphic writing and reared the great pyramids—fell to pieces of its own accord and vanished so completely that so far no one has been able to learn why. There were civil wars—that is all we know. Then came darkness and barbarism, from which, more than four centuries later, a new civilization just as spontaneously emerged. Says Lenormant:

Beginning with the civil disturbances in which Nit-agrit lost his life, Egyptian civilization enters upon a sudden eclipse that has so far remained unexplainable. Manetho counts 436 years between the end of the Sixth Dynasty and the beginning of the Eleventh. During that

[1] The rapid progress of the Scottish highlanders has been studied by Colajanni in *La sociologia criminale.*

period the monuments are absolutely silent.   It is as though Egypt had
been stricken from the roster of nations, and when civilization reappears
at the end of the long slumber it seems to begin without any tradition
from the past.[1]

As a matter of fact, Lenormant does not deny that foreign
invasions may have occurred during the period in question, but,
in any event, over and above the fact that there is no trace of
them in monuments and inscriptions, it is certain that they must
have followed, not preceded, the decline of the earlier Egyptian
civilization.

Babylonia, for many centuries a center of civilization, was not
destroyed by its conquerors—not by Cyrus, not by Darius, not
by Alexander.   It collapsed and disappeared from the world
scene by slow decay, by automatic dissolution.   The Roman
Empire in the West is said to have been destroyed by barbarians.
But anyone even moderately familiar with Roman history knows
that the barbarians killed a mere corpse, that the decline in art,
literature, wealth, public administration—in short, in all phases
of Roman civilization—had been tremendous between the days of
Marcus Aurelius and the days of Diocletian.   During this
period the barbarians made temporary raids into a few provinces,
to be sure, but they gained a foothold nowhere within the empire
and wrought no lasting harm.   A great invasion by the Goths
occurred under the Emperor Decius and was finally repulsed by
Claudius II.   It was, however, exceptional.   It laid waste the
eastern provinces of the empire, but Greco-Roman civilization
was to survive for many, many centuries in those very districts.
Without disturbances from any foreign invasion or other external
forces, the Spain of the second half of the seventeenth century
became a mere shadow of the country that a century earlier had
been the Spain of Charles V, and half a century earlier had had
a Cervantes, a Lope de Vega and a Quevedo.   This rapid decline
of the Iberian peninsula has been blamed on the expulsion of the
Moors, which occurred for the most part in 1609, under Philip
III.   But the expulsion of the Moors injured only a few provinces, notably parts of Valencia and Andalusia, and these were
the regions that suffered least in the general impoverishment of
Spain.   Portugal and Italy declined simultaneously with Spain,

[1] *Histoire ancienne de l'Orient*, vol. II, chap. II.

though to a less appreciable extent. Certainly they were not suffering from any expulsion of Moors.

The theory of organic and superorganic evolution with natural selection explains all such facts very badly, or rather not at all. Keeping to that theory, a more highly civilized people should be progressively purified and improved by the struggle for existence and should through heredity acquire over others an advantage, which, so far as one can see, it should not lose in the race of the nations across the centuries. What we see, instead, is a nation, or a group of peoples, now leaping forward with irresistible impetus, then collapsing or lagging wretchedly behind. One may note, to be sure, a certain progressive movement which, in spite of interruptions and gaps, thrusts mankind farther and farther forward, and the present civilization of the Aryan race is in fact superior to all preceding civilizations. But we must bear in mind that every new people that has the good fortune to become civilized has a shorter road to travel and expends infinitely less effort, because it inherits the *experience* and the *positive knowledge* of all the civilizations that have preceded it.

Certainly the Germans of Tacitus would never have succeeded in so few as eighteen centuries in forming such centers of culture as London, Berlin and New York if they had had to discover by themselves alphabetic writing, the fundamental principles of mathematics and all the immense store of knowledge that they gained from contact with the Greeks and Romans. Nor would Hellenic and Roman civilizations have made the progress they made without infiltrations from ancient Near Eastern civilizations, to which they in fact owed the alphabet and the rudiments of the exact sciences. Human civilization progresses by scientific rather than by organic inheritance. The descendants of a civilized people may stagnate or may even relapse into barbarism, but the learning of their fathers may fertilize the nascent civilization of uncouth hordes that happen to find themselves favorably placed for receiving such beneficent germs. The modern Anglo-Saxons are not descendants of the Romans or the Greeks, or of the Semites of Syria among whom the religion that has left so deep an imprint on the people of Great Britain and its colonies originated. They are not descendants of the Arabs to whom the world owes much of the physical and mathematical knowledge which the English and Americans of modern times have so wondrously applied and made productive. What they have inherited is not the blood but the scientific and psychological achievements of the peoples mentioned. At times a people rising anew to civilization may avail itself of the intellectual and spiritual activity of ancestors who have regressed from civilization after once attaining it. That was the case with the ancient Egyptians and with the Italians of the Renaissance; but that very fact, if we choose to scrutinize it carefully, furnishes one more argument against the theory that social progress depends on organic heredity.

Even the evolutionists recognize that other races attained civilization earlier than the Aryan race and earlier than the Germanic branch of that race in particular; but they add that those races declined or became stationary because they had aged —in other words, because they had exhausted all the intellectual and moral resources at their command. Really, this idea of the aging of races seems to us the product of a wholly specious analogy between the life of an individual and the life of a community. But, to keep to the facts as we see them, for the very reason that the members of a community continuously reproduce themselves and each new generation has all the vigor of youth, a whole society can hardly grow old in the same sense in which an individual grows old when his powers begin to fail.[1] So far as we know, furthermore, no organic difference has ever been found between the individuals in a progressing society and the individuals in a declining society.

Societies in decline grow old because of changes in their type of social structure. At such times religious beliefs, customs, prejudices, the traditions on which political and social institutions are grounded, grow old, or rather are gradually discredited. But these are all social elements, the changes in which come about through the interposition of new historical factors with which a people chances to come into contact, or even through a slow and automatic intellectual, moral and social evolution within the people itself. It is hazardous, therefore, very hazardous indeed, to assert that changes in the physical constitution of a race play any part in such things. It would be difficult to show that the brains of the Frenchmen of Voltaire's day were differently con-

---

[1] We borrow this remark from Henry George, *Progress and Poverty*, book X, chap. I, last page.

stituted from the brains of their great-grandfathers who committed the Massacre of St. Bartholomew and organized the League. It is very easy to show, on the other hand, that in a little over a century and a half the economic and political situation in France, and her intellectual atmosphere, had altered radically.

The belief that all non-Aryan civilizations—the Egyptian, the Babylonian, the ancient and modern Chinese—have been, and still are, uniformly stationary seems to us to be due to nothing less than an optical illusion arising from the fact that we view them from so far away. So it is with the mountains of Sicily, which, viewed from afar off under that limpid, transparent sky, look like lovely azure walls closing the horizon with a uniform perpendicularity, but which from close at hand look altogether otherwise, since each comprises its own particular little world of ascents, descents and irregularities of every kind. Chaldean and Egyptian monuments have shown with a positiveness that can no longer be questioned that there were ups and downs, periods of decline and periods of renascence and progress in goodly number both on the banks of the Nile and on the banks of the Euphrates and the Tigris.[1] As for China, its civilization has, to be sure, endured amazingly and without interruption for some thousands of years, but that is not saying that it was always the same. We know enough of Chinese history to be certain that the political and social organization of the Celestial Empire has undergone tremendous changes in the course of the centuries. China had her feudal period and, at least until very recently, she was ruled by a bureaucracy recruited by competitive examinations. Religion and property ownership have also undergone most varied vicissitudes in China.[2]

15. In his *Évolution de la morale*, Letourneau attributes progress in human societies to an organic process whereby a good action, which would be a useful action, leaves its mark on the brain and nerve centers of the individual who performs it. That mark, repeated over and over again, produces a tendency to reiterate the same act, and the tendency is in turn transmitted

[1] Lenormant, Maspero, Brugsch.
[2] Rousset, *À travers la Chine;* Mechnikov, *La civilisation et les grands fleuves historiques;* Élisée Réclus, *Nouvelle géographie universelle*, vol. VII.

to the individual's descendants. In the first place, one might ask why bad—in other words, harmful—actions should not leave similar marks; and in the second place, as regards useful acts, one might ask, useful to whom?   To the individual who performs them or to society?   The two utilities are only too separate and distinct, and it would seem necessary to have had very little experience of the world to maintain that an action that is useful to society is generally useful to the individual who performs it, and vice versa.   But suppose we let Letourneau speak for himself:

Just as phosphorescent bodies remember light, so the nerve cell remembers its intimate acts, but in ways that are infinitely more varied and persistent.   Every act that has been performed at the instance of a nerve cell leaves on the cell a sort of functional residue that thenceforward will facilitate repetitions of the act and sometimes provoke it. Such reiteration, in fact, will become easier and easier and in the end will take place spontaneously, automatically.   By that time the nerve cell has acquired an inclination, a habit, an instinct, a need.[1]

And again he says:

Nerve cells are essentially impregnation mechanisms.   Every current of molecular activity that runs through them leaves a more or less revivescent trace upon them.   By sufficient repetition these traces become organic, fixed, and are even transmitted by heredity, and each of them has a corresponding tendency, a corresponding inclination, which will manifest itself in due time and contribute to the formation of what is called character.   This general picture must be held in view if one would have any comprehension of the origin and evolution of morality.

Further pursuing the same idea he adds:

In their essential aspects ethics are utilitarian and progressive. However, once they have been formed, once they have been established in the nerve centers, moral or immoral inclinations fade as slowly as they have been clothed with flesh.   Often also they reappear atavistically, and in such cases one suddenly sees moral specimens from the Stone Age rising in the full midst of a relatively civilized society, or heroic types in the flower of a mercantile civilization.

These quotations should suffice to give a fairly accurate idea of the writer's basic conception.   They will further suffice to give a

[1] *Évolution de la morale*, chaps. II and XX.

fairly clear idea of the arguments of the whole school that bases its sociology on the anthropological sciences.

But however attractive, however daring, hypotheses may be, they are of value in science only when they are supported by experience, in other words, by demonstrations based on fact. We have no intention of discussing here the genuineness of the complicated organic process that we find set forth in Letourneau's book with such definiteness and assurance. But facts are always facts. They have the same scientific value whether they are derived from studies of nerve cells, or of the hair color and cranial measurements of this race or that, from observations of animal societies or from studies of human history. The only classification in order of importance that is permissible is a classification that distinguishes carefully ascertained facts—facts, for example, that have not been discovered and championed by the same men who have spun theories about them—from dubious, inadequately tested facts that have been colored by the preconceptions of the observer. Now all history amply shows that the progress of human societies does not follow the course that it would follow if the theories of the anthropological school were sound. Before we can accept these theories, therefore, they at least have to be qualified. It has to be admitted that the civilized human being, or the human being capable of civilization, who is certainly no newcomer on the face of the earth, has experienced in his nerve cells so many and such varied moral impressions that he is able to adopt the most disparate tendencies and habits, both those which lead a society toward intellectual, moral and political betterment and those which carry it toward decline and ruin.[1]

16. But so qualified, the anthropological theory has no practical value left. It does not, it cannot, tell us anything that we do not already know. It is more worth our while, therefore, to seek scientific results along some other road, however rough the

[1] See Fouillée, "La Psychologie des peuples et l'anthropologie." This article supports practically the same thesis that we put forward here, with more or less similar arguments. Fouillée writes: "Ethnic factors are not the only factors, nor the most important ones, that figure in a national character. Uniform education, similar training, common beliefs more than make up for differences in racial stock." Colajanni and Mechnikov also vigorously and brilliantly combat writers who are inclined to exaggerate the importance of race as a social factor.

going may be. The truth is that just as the study of climatic differences has never been able to supply a general law to explain the organization of human societies and the variety of type that such societies present, so too no satisfactory law has been found on the basis of racial diversities; nor is it possible to ascribe the progress or the ruin of nations to organic improvements or organic degenerations in races.

Anyone who has traveled a good deal ordinarily comes to the conclusion that underneath superficial differences in customs and habits human beings are psychologically very much alike the world over; and anyone who has read history at all deeply reaches a similar conclusion with regard to the various periods of human civilization. Dipping into the documents that tell us how people of other ages felt, thought and lived, we come always to the same conclusion: that they were very much like us.

Psychological resemblance is always stronger among peoples who have attained approximately similar levels of civilization than it is among peoples closer to each other chronologically and ethnically. In his manner of thinking a modern Italian or German is nearer to a Greek of the time of Plato and Aristotle than he is to a medieval ancestor of his own. The literatures of the different epochs bear the most emphatic testimony to that fact.

Such psychological resemblances, and the fact that the great races which constitute four-fifths of mankind have shown themselves capable of the most varied vicissitudes of progress and decline lead us to advance a hypothesis which follows also from the negative investigations we have so far been making. We are inclined to think that just as human beings, or at least the great human races, have a constant tendency toward social grouping, so too they have equally constant and powerful psychological tendencies which impel them onward toward ever higher levels of culture and social progress. Such tendencies, however, operate with more or less vigor, or may even be stifled, according as they find physical environments—complexes of circumstances that might be called "chance"—which are more or less favorable; and according also as they are more or less hampered by social environments, in other words by psychological tendencies equally universal and constant.[1]

[1] For proof that what we call "chance"—a chain of circumstances that escape human control and foresight—has its influence on the destinies of nations,

That, after all, is an organic process similar to what takes place
in the whole animal and vegetable world, though far more complicated. A plant has a strong tendency to spread and multiply.
The tendency may be seconded or thwarted by physical environment, in other words by conditions of water supply and climate,
by chance in the form of wind and birds which fertilize or scatter
its seeds, and then again by traits of the plant itself, the greater or
lesser resistance it offers to diseases that attack it. And a
similar process goes on in that branch of social activity which
has been so generally and so successfully studied—the production
of wealth. Wealth production has a tendency to increase unlim-
itedly, but the tendency is more or less hindered by physical
obstacles; it is to an extent hindered by chance; and it is hindered,
finally, by the ignorance, the consuming greed and the mental
attitudes of human beings.

Man neither creates nor destroys any of the forces of nature,
but he can study their manner of acting and their interplay and
turn them to his advantage. That is the procedure in agriculture, in navigation, in mechanics. By following it modern
science has been able to achieve almost miraculous results in
those fields of activity. The method surely cannot be different
when the social sciences are involved, and in fact it is the very
method that has already yielded fair results in political economy.
Yet we must not disguise the fact that in the social sciences in
general the difficulties to be overcome are enormously greater.
Not only does the greater complexity of psychological laws (or
constant tendencies) that are common to all human groups make
it harder to determine their operation, but it is easier to observe
the things that go on about us than it is to observe the things we
ourselves do. Man can much more easily study the phenomena
of physics, chemistry or botany than he can his own instincts
and his own passions. One should think of the "divers prejudices" which, according to Spencer, impede progress in the
social sciences. Certainly the student of political science has to
look objectively upon nationalities, religions, political parties,
political doctrines, treating them merely as phenomena of the

we need only reflect that in the past the fate of a nation has often hinged on the
outcome of a single battle (for example, Plataea, Zama, Jérez, Poitiers, Hastings)
and that, especially before wars came to be waged according to scientific principles, chance played a large part in the outcome of a battle.

human mind. But the precept is more easily given to others than applied by one's self. It must be confessed that the objectivity essential to the successful conduct of this type of observation will always be the privilege of the limited number of individuals who are endowed with special aptitudes and have undergone special intellectual training. But then, even granting that such individuals can attain scientific results, it is highly problematical whether they can succeed in using them to modify the political conduct of the great human societies. What happens in economics is instructive. Free trade is unanimously regarded by unprejudiced experts in that science as a good thing, yet the most highly civilized nations are today turning to the fiercest protectionism.

17. Whatever practical value political science may have in the future, progress in that field will be based upon the study of the facts of society, and those facts can be found only in the history of the various nations. In other words, if political science is to be grounded upon the observation and interpretation of the facts of political life, it is to the old historical method that we must return. To that method a number of objections, more or less serious, are being raised and we must briefly consider them.

It is said, in the first place, that any number of writers, from Aristotle down to Machiavelli, Montesquieu and the scholars of our own day, have used the historical method and that, though many of their incidental observations have been universally accepted as grounded upon fact and as truths scientifically acquired, no truly scientific system has as yet been found.

But what we have already said of the positive method in general may be said of the historical method in particular: that to yield good results it has to be properly applied. Now before it can be properly applied an indispensable requirement is a wide and accurate knowledge of history, and that was not within the reach of Aristotle or Machiavelli or Montesquieu, or of any other writer who lived earlier than a century ago. Great syntheses can be essayed only after a vast body of facts have been accumulated and verified by the scientific method. Historical information was of course not lacking in centuries past, but it bore almost exclusively upon isolated periods. Down to the beginning of the last century, Greco-Roman civilization and the history of the modern European nations were known perhaps after a fashion, but as for the past of the rest of the world nothing was available except the vaguest of legends and very untrustworthy traditions. Even within the limited portions of history just mentioned, such knowledge as was available was far from perfect. The critical sense was still undeveloped. There was none of that patient documentary research, of that minute and attentive interpretation of inscriptions, which has not only drawn the general lines of the acts of great historical characters more accurately and clearly but has revealed details of social custom and political and administrative organization in the different peoples which are of far greater interest to the study of political science than the personal feats of great warriors and rulers.

Exact knowledge of physical geography, ethnology and comparative philology, which shed light on the origins and blood ties of nations; prehistory, which has revealed the ancientness of the human species and of certain civilizations; the interpretation of hieroglyphic, cuneiform and ancient Hindu alphabets, which has unveiled the mysteries of Oriental civilizations now extinct— all these were conquests of the nineteenth century. During the same century the mists that enveloped the history of China, Japan and other nations of the Far East were at least partially cleared away and the records of ancient American civilizations were in part discovered, in part more accurately studied. Finally during that century comparative statistical studies first came into general use, facilitating knowledge of conditions among faraway peoples. There can be no doubt about it: where the student of the social sciences could once only guess, he now has the means to *observe* and the instruments and the materials to *demonstrate*.

Aristotle had but a very imperfect knowledge of the history of the great Asiatic monarchies. His information was probably limited to what Herodotus and Xenophon had written and to what he had been able to learn from Alexander's veterans, who had little understanding of the countries they conquered. The only political type he knew was the Greek city-state of the fourth and fifth centuries before our era. He could have learned little or nothing that was accurate about the rest of the world. Under those circumstances his *Politics* is an extraordinary intellectual feat, and his classification of governments into monarchies, aristocracies and democracies (a classification that might now be judged superficial and incomplete) was certainly the very best that the human mind could contrive in his day.

The only model for the state that Machiavelli had directly before him was the Italian commune of the late fifteenth century, with its alternatives of tyranny and anarchy, where power was won or lost in a game of violence and trickery, with the winnings to him who was the better liar or delivered the last dagger thrust. We can understand how such a model must so have impressed his mind as to make him write his *Prince*. The fact that his information was confined almost exclusively to such Roman history as could be learned in his day and to the history of the great modern monarchies which had risen a little before his time explains his commentary on Livy, his histories and his letters. Montesquieu had no way of knowing the history of the Orient very much better than Aristotle, or that of Greece and Rome any more profoundly than Machiavelli. His wider knowledge of the institutions and history of France, England and Germany, coupled with his little knowledge of other countries, explains his theory that political liberty would be possible only in cold countries.

18. Another objection is made to the historical method. If it is no sounder than the above objection, it is certainly more alluring, so much so that in the eyes of many it may seem to be very serious, if not insuperable. It relates to the scant reliability of historical materials. It is commonly alleged that, for all of their many efforts, historians often fail to discover the truth: that it is often hard to determine with any exactness just how things which have happened in our own towns within the year actually came to pass; so that it is virtually impossible to obtain accounts that are worthy of belief when faraway times and places are concerned. No one forgets to point to contradictions between the different historians, to the lie they often give each other, to the passions by which they are commonly swayed— the conclusion being that no certain inferences, no real science, can be derived from facts which are always very dubious, always very imperfectly known.

It is not hard to answer such arguments. First of all, and incidentally, one might note that only when we have no interest in learning the truth, or no means of doing so, or when contrary interests are opposed to our doing so, do we fail to learn the exact truth about contemporary happenings. If no such obstacles are present, anyone who is willing to spend the time and the money required can always, by a more or less intensive inquiry, discover in the maze of varying versions, gossipings and hearsays just how a given event came to pass. As regards historical facts, the older they are the fainter becomes the clamor of the interests that aim to distort exact knowledge regarding them, and we take it for granted that the historian has patience enough and time enough to disentangle the truth concerning them.

Of far greater importance is a second observation that we must make in this connection. The historical facts which are and always will be shrouded in the greatest uncertainty are anecdotal, biographical facts, facts which may involve the vanity or profit of a man, a nation, a party. It is chiefly in regard to such facts that the passions of a writer may be the cause, be it unwittingly, of error. Fortunately that type of fact is of scant interest to the student of the political sciences. It makes little difference to him whether a battle has been won through the merit of one commander or lost through the fault of another, or whether a political assassination was more or less justifiable. On the other hand, there are facts that concern the social type and organization of the various peoples and the various epochs; and it is about such facts, which are of the greater interest to us, that historians, spontaneously and without bias, often tell the truth. At any rate, more enlightening than the historians are the documents themselves.

We shall probably never know just when Homer lived, in what city he was born, what episodes marked his life. These problems may have a certain interest for the critic or the scholar, who would like to know the most minute details about the life of the author of the *Iliad* and the *Odyssey*. They are of little interest to the political scientist, who is studying the psychological and social world that the great poet describes, a world which, however much the bard's fancy may have embellished it, must actually have existed in an age but slightly anterior to his time. No one will ever know the breed of Alcibiades' dog, the color of Alexander's horse, what the exact faults and merits of

Themistocles were, just how the speeches of Pericles were delivered, whether Agesilaus was lame in his right leg or his left. But it has been established beyond possibility of doubt that from the sixth to the fourth century before our era there existed in Hellas a certain type of political organization, the different varieties and peculiarities of which we already know well (and shall know even better as inscriptions and monuments that are gradually being found are studied), along with the details of its administrative, economic and military structure.

No one, probably, will ever know anything exact about the life of Cheops, the Egyptian king of the Fourth Dynasty, in spite of the great pyramid that he ordered raised as his tomb. No one will ever possess the biography of Ramses II, of the Nineteenth Dynasty, though Pentaur's poem in celebration of his victories, real or imaginary, still survives. But no one will doubt that thirty or forty centuries before our era there existed in the valley of the Nile an organized, civilized, very populous society, and that the human spirit must have made prodigious efforts of patience and originality to raise it from barbarism. No one can doubt that that society, ever changing with the revolving centuries, had religious beliefs and scientific information and, at times, an administrative and military organization so remarkable that it might almost be compared with those of the most highly civilized states of our own time.[1]

We may doubt whether Tiberius and Nero were the rascals that Tacitus said they were and whether the feeblemindedness of Claudius, the lasciviousness of Messalina, Caligula's passion for his horse, may not have been exaggerated. But we cannot deny that the Roman empire existed and that its emperors had a power to commit crimes and follies which would not have been tolerated in other epochs and in other types of political organization. Nor can we doubt that in the early centuries of our era a great civilization, embodied politically in a great state, embraced the whole Mediterranean basin. We already know well, and shall know better and better, the legislation and the highly perfected financial, administrative and military organization of that state. We may go so far as to assume that Sakya

---

[1] There were periods when public offices seem to have been awarded by examinations and when army officers were educated and trained in special military schools.

Muni was wholly a myth, that Jesus was never crucified or even that he never existed. But no one will ever deny the existence of Buddhism and Christianity, along with the dogmas and moral precepts on which they were founded; nor will anyone ever deny that since those two religions have spread abroad so widely and have so long endured they must satisfy emotions and psychological needs that are widely prevalent in the human masses.

19. In conclusion, then, while the anecdote and the biographical detail may have had their influence on the history of nations, they can be of little help in discovering the great psychological laws that are manifested in the lives of the nations. Such laws reveal their operation, rather, in administrative and judicial institutions, in religions, in all the moral and political customs of the various nations; and it is therefore upon these last categories of facts that we must concentrate our attention.

With regard to such facts, it seems to us difficult and scarcely worth our while to establish very rigid standards of preference. Any detail of information, be it historical or contemporary, which relates to the institutions of a people that is organized politically—a people, in other words, that has consolidated in fairly populous masses and attained a certain degree of civilization, of whatever type—may be very interesting. If any recommendation may be made in the matter, it is this: that we avoid deriving all our observations from a group of political organisms that belong to the same historical period or present the same, or not widely differing, types of civilization.

For example, if the only history we considered were that of the Greek states in the age of Pericles, we might be led to believe that the history of the world comes down to a struggle between Hellenism and barbarism, or between democracy and aristocracy (or better, between two oligarchies, the one of a more limited, the other of a more inclusive membership). If we thought only of Europe between the year 1500 and the year 1600, we might conclude that the whole movement of humanity during that period came down to a conflict between Catholicism and Protestantism, or between European and Mohammedan civilizations.

In his *First Principles* Spencer tried to forearm students of the social sciences against what he called "perversions of judgment" or "bias," against certain habits of the human mind whereby the observer views the facts of society from a subjective, one-sided and limited point of view that is inevitably productive of erroneous results. Now to eliminate that pitfall it is not enough to warn anyone likely to fall into it that the pitfall exists. His mind has to be trained in such a way as to avoid it. Awareness of political prejudice, national prejudice, religious or anti-religious prejudice, does not prevent an individual, when he comes to a practical application of the Spencerian theories, from falling into one or more such prejudices if he has been reared in the belief that the adoption of a given form of government is enough to regenerate mankind, that his nation is the first in the universe, that his religion is the only true one or that human progress consists in destroying all religion. The real safeguard against that type of error lies in knowing how to lift one's judgment above the beliefs and opinions which are current in one's time or peculiar to the social or national type to which one belongs. That—to go back to a point on which we have already touched—comes with the study of many social facts, with a broad and thorough knowledge of history, not, certainly, of the history of a single period or a single nation but—so far as we possibly can—the history of mankind as a whole.

20. In our day there prevails, or at least down to a very recent day there prevailed, in social research a tendency to give special attention to the simpler and more primitive political organizations. Some scholars go as far back as possible and scrupulously analyze animal societies, tracking down in bee-hives, anthills and the lairs of quadrupeds and quadrumanes the earliest origins of the social sentiments that find their complete expression in the great political organisms of men. The majority keep to the organizations of savage tribes, and all circumstances relating to such peoples are noted and recorded. The narratives of travelers who have lived among savages have so acquired special importance, and quotations from them fill modern volumes on sociology.

We do not say that such studies are useless—it is hard to find any application of the human intelligence that is completely unfruitful. But certainly they do not seem the best adapted to furnishing sound materials for the social sciences in general and for political science in particular. First of all, the narratives of travelers are as a rule more subjective, more contradictory, less trustworthy than the accounts of historians, and they are less subject to checking by documents and monuments. An individual who finds himself among people who belong to a very different civilization from the one to which he is accustomed generally views them from certain special points of view, and so may readily be misled. Herodotus was the greatest traveler of antiquity, and, as checking has now proved, he was a conscientious and far from superficial observer. Nevertheless, he reported many things incorrectly, for the sole reason that he was steeped in a Greek civilization and so was poorly equipped to interpret certain phenomena of Near Eastern civilization. If one could check the reports of modern travelers on authentic documents, as has occasionally been possible in the case of Herodotus, we do not believe that they would prove to be any more exact. If one is looking for light on the real social conditions of a given people, an authentic document such as the Laws of Manu, the fragments of the Twelve Tables or the Code of Rothari is worth much more than the reports of any number of modern travelers. We understand, however, that a traveler's account may prove very useful in providing illustration and comment for such documents. In the case of primitive peoples, of course, no documents whatever are available.

In the second place, social facts can be gathered only in a human society, and by society we mean not a small group of a few families but what is commonly called a nation, a people, a state. Psychological social forces cannot develop, and cannot find scope, except in large political organisms, in aggregates, that is, where numerous groups of human beings are brought together in a moral and political union. In the primitive group, in the tribe of fifty or a hundred individuals, the political problem hardly exists, and therefore cannot be studied.

Monarchy, for example, is easy enough to understand in a small tribe where the strongest and craftiest male readily imposes his will on a handful of comrades. But we must be in possession of very different elements before we can account for the establishment of such an institution in a society of millions of individuals, where a single man alone cannot force himself by physical strength upon all the others combined, and where, however crafty and energetic a man may be, he will readily find in the masses about him hundreds of individuals who, at least potentially, are as talented and resourceful as he. So again we can easily see how a few dozen or even a few hundred individuals living together, and holding apart in moral if not material isolation from the rest of the world, should come to present a definite oneness of mental type and to have a lively sense of tribe and family. But to understand that is of little help when we come to explaining why a single moral type, an intense national feeling, should exist in human aggregations of tens and sometimes—as in the case of Russia and China—of hundreds of millions of persons, where individuals pass their whole lives far removed from most of their fellows, are for the most part cut off from any personal intercourse with them, and in their various groups face widely differing conditions of material living.

The study of minute political units is said to be useful because they show in embryo all the social organs that gradually develop in larger and more advanced societies; and it is supposed to be much easier to study the manner of working of such organs when they are in their rudimentary forms than when they have grown more complex. But the comparing, now so frequent, of the organization of human societies with organizations of individual animal societies has never seemed to us less apt and less instructive than in this instance. It can easily be turned against the thesis in favor of which it was invoked. We do not believe that any zoologist would try to solve problems of anatomy and physiology in the warm-blooded vertebrates by studying the lower animals. It was not, certainly, from the observation of amoebas and polyps that the circulation of the blood was discovered and that the functions of the heart, brain and lungs in man and the other higher animals were finally determined.

CHAPTER II
THE RULING CLASS

1. Among the constant facts and tendencies that are to be found in all political organisms, one is so obvious that it is apparent to the most casual eye. In all societies—from societies that are very meagerly developed and have barely attained the dawnings of civilization, down to the most advanced and powerful societies—two classes of people appear—a class that rules and a class that is ruled. The first class, always the less numerous, performs all political functions, monopolizes power and enjoys the advantages that power brings, whereas the second, the more numerous class, is directed and controlled by the first, in a manner that is now more or less legal, now more or less arbitrary and violent, and supplies the first, in appearance at least, with material means of subsistence and with the instrumentalities that are essential to the vitality of the political organism.

In practical life we all recognize the existence of this ruling class (or political class, as we have elsewhere chosen to define it).[1] We all know that, in our own country, whichever it may be, the management of public affairs is in the hands of a minority of influential persons, to which management, willingly or unwillingly, the majority defer. We know that the same thing goes on in neighboring countries, and in fact we should be put to it to conceive of a real world otherwise organized—a world in which all men would be directly subject to a single person without relationships of superiority or subordination, or in which all men would share equally in the direction of political affairs. If we reason otherwise in theory, that is due partly to inveterate habits that we follow in our thinking and partly to the exaggerated importance that we attach to two political facts that loom far larger in appearance than they are in reality.

The first of these facts—and one has only to open one's eyes to see it—is that in every political organism there is one individual

---

[1] Mosca, *Teorica dei governi e governo parlamentare*, chap. I.

who is chief among the leaders of the ruling class as a whole
and stands, as we say, at the helm of the state.   That person is
not always the person who holds supreme power according to law.
At times, alongside of the hereditary king or emperor there is a
prime minister or a major-domo who wields an actual power that
is greater than the sovereign's.   At other times, in place of the
elected president the influential politician who has procured the
president's election will govern.   Under special circumstances
there may be, instead of a single person, two or three who
discharge the functions of supreme control.

The second fact, too, is readily discernible.   Whatever the
type of political organization, pressures arising from the discontent of the masses who are governed, from the passions by
which they are swayed, exert a certain amount of influence
on the policies of the ruling, the political, class.

But the man who is at the head of the state would certainly
not be able to govern without the support of a numerous class
to enforce respect for his orders and to have them carried out;
and granting that he can make one individual, or indeed many
individuals, in the ruling class feel the weight of his power, he
certainly cannot be at odds with the class as a whole or do away
with it.   Even if that were possible, he would at once be forced
to create another class, without the support of which action on
his part would be completely paralyzed.   On the other hand,
granting that the discontent of the masses might succeed in
deposing a ruling class, inevitably, as we shall later show, there
would have to be another organized minority within the masses
themselves to discharge the functions of a ruling class.   Otherwise all organization, and the whole social structure, would be
destroyed.

2. From the point of view of scientific research the real
superiority of the concept of the ruling, or political, class lies in
the fact that the varying structure of ruling classes has a preponderant importance in determining the political type, and
also the level of civilization, of the different peoples.   According
to a manner of classifying forms of government that is still in
vogue, Turkey and Russia were both, up to a few years ago,
absolute monarchies, England and Italy were constitutional, or
limited, monarchies, and France and the United States were

classed as republics. The classification was based on the fact
that, in the first two countries mentioned, headship in the state
was hereditary and the chief was nominally omnipotent; in the
second two, his office is hereditary but his powers and prerogatives are limited; in the last two, he is elected.

That classification is obviously superficial. Absolutisms
though they were, there was little in common between the manners in which Russia and Turkey were managed politically, the
levels of civilization in the two countries and the organization of
their ruling classes being vastly different.   On the same basis, the
regime in Italy, a monarchy, is much more similar to the regime
in France, a republic, than it is to the regime in England, also a
monarchy; and there are important differences between the
political organizations of the United States and France, though
both countries are republics.

As we have already suggested, ingrained habits of thinking
have long stood, as they still stand, in the way of scientific
progress in this matter. The classification mentioned above,
which divides governments into absolute monarchies, limited
monarchies and republics, was devised by Montesquieu and was
intended to replace the classical categories of Aristotle, who
divided governments into monarchies, aristocracies and democracies. What Aristotle called a democracy was simply an
aristocracy of fairly broad membership. Aristotle himself was
in a position to observe that in every Greek state, whether
aristocratic or democratic, there was always one person or more
who had a preponderant influence. Between the day of Polybius and the day of Montesquieu, many writers perfected Aristotle's classification by introducing into it the concept of "mixed"
governments. Later on the modern democratic theory, which
had its source in Rousseau, took its stand upon the concept that
the majority of the citizens in any state can participate, and in
fact *ought* to participate, in its political life, and the doctrine of
popular sovereignty still holds sway over many minds in spite
of the fact that modern scholarship is making it increasingly
clear that democratic, monarchical and aristocratic principles
function side by side in every political organism. We shall not
stop to refute this democratic theory here, since that is the task
of this work as a whole. Besides, it would be hard to destroy in
a few pages a whole system of ideas that has become firmly rooted

in the human mind. As Las Casas aptly wrote in his life of
Christopher Columbus, it is often much harder to unlearn than
to learn.

3. We think it may be desirable, nevertheless, to reply at this
point to an objection which might very readily be made to our
point of view. If it is easy to understand that a single individual
cannot command a group without finding within the group a
minority to support him, it is rather difficult to grant, as a constant and natural fact, that minorities rule majorities, rather
than majorities minorities. But that is one of the points—so
numerous in all the other sciences—where the first impression
one has of things is contrary to what they are in reality. In
reality the dominion of an organized minority, obeying a single
impulse, over the unorganized majority is inevitable. The power
of any minority is irresistible as against each single individual in
the majority, who stands alone before the totality of the organized minority. At the same time, the minority is organized for
the very reason that it is a minority. A hundred men acting
uniformly in concert, with a common understanding, will triumph
over a thousand men who are not in accord and can therefore be
dealt with one by one. Meanwhile it will be easier for the
former to act in concert and have a mutual understanding simply
because they are a hundred and not a thousand. It follows that
the larger the political community, the smaller will the proportion
of the governing minority to the governed majority be, and the
more difficult will it be for the majority to organize for reaction
against the minority.

However, in addition to the great advantage accruing to them
from the fact of being organized, ruling minorities are usually so
constituted that the individuals who make them up are distinguished from the mass of the governed by qualities that give
them a certain material, intellectual or even moral superiority;
or else they are the heirs of individuals who possessed such
qualities. In other words, members of a ruling minority regularly have some attribute, real or apparent, which is highly
esteemed and very influential in the society in which they live.

4. In primitive societies that are still in the early stages of
organization, military valor is the quality that most readily

opens access to the ruling, or political, class. In societies of advanced civilization, war is the exceptional condition. It may be regarded as virtually normal in societies that are in the initial stages of their development; and the individuals who show the greatest ability in war easily gain supremacy over their fellows— the bravest become chiefs. The fact is constant, but the forms it may assume, in one set of circumstances or another, vary considerably.

As a rule the dominance of a warrior class over a peaceful multitude is attributed to a superposition of races, to the conquest of a relatively unwarlike group by an aggressive one. Sometimes that is actually the case—we have examples in India after the Aryan invasions, in the Roman Empire after the Germanic invasions and in Mexico after the Aztec conquest. But more often, under certain social conditions, we note the rise of a warlike ruling class in places where there is absolutely no trace of a foreign conquest. As long as a horde lives exclusively by the chase, all individuals can easily become warriors. There will of course be leaders who will rule over the tribe, but we will not find a warrior class rising to exploit, and at the same time to protect, another class that is devoted to peaceful pursuits. As the tribe emerges from the hunting stage and enters the agricultural and pastoral stage, then, along with an enormous increase in population and a greater stability in the means of exerting social influence, a more or less clean-cut division into two classes will take place, one class being devoted exclusively to agriculture, the other class to war. In this event, it is inevitable that the warrior class should little by little acquire such ascendancy over the other as to be able to oppress it with impunity.

Poland offers a characteristic example of the gradual metamorphosis of a warrior class into an absolutely dominant class. Originally the Poles had the same organization by rural villages as prevailed among all the Slavic peoples. There was no distinction between fighters and farmers—in other words, between nobles and peasants. But after the Poles came to settle on the broad plains that are watered by the Vistula and the Niemen, agriculture began to develop among them. However, the necessity of fighting with warlike neighbors continued, so that the tribal chiefs, or voivodes, gathered about themselves a certain number of picked men whose special occupation was the bearing

of arms. These warriors were distributed among the various
rural communities. They were exempt from agricultural duties,
yet they received their share of the produce of the soil, along
with the other members of the community. In early days their
position was not considered very desirable, and country dwellers
sometimes waived exemption from agricultural labor in order to
avoid going to war. But gradually as this order of things grew
stabilized, as one class became habituated to the practice of
arms and military organization while the other hardened to the
use of the plow and the spade, the warriors became nobles and
masters, and the peasants, once companions and brothers,
became villeins and serfs. Little by little the warrior lords
increased their demands to the point where the share they took
as members of the community came to include the community's
whole produce minus what was absolutely necessary for subsistence on the part of the cultivators; and when the latter
tried to escape such abuses they were constrained by force to
stay bound to the soil, their situation taking on all the characteristics of serfdom pure and simple.

In the course of this evolution, around the year 1333, King
Casimir the Great tried vainly to curb the overbearing insolence
of the warriors. When peasants came to complain of the
nobles, he contented himself with asking whether they had no
sticks and stones. Some generations later, in 1537, the nobility
forced all tradesmen in the cities to sell such real estate as they
owned, and landed property became a prerogative of nobles only.
At the same time the nobility exerted pressure upon the king to
open negotiations with Rome, to the end that thenceforward only
nobles should be admitted to holy orders in Poland. That barred
townsmen and peasants almost completely from honorific positions and stripped them of any social importance whatever.[1]

We find a parallel development in Russia. There the warriors
who formed the druzhina, or escort, of the old knezes (princes
descended from Rurik) also received a share in the produce of the
mirs (rural peasant communities) for their livelihood. Little by
little this share was increased. Since land abounded and workers
were scarce, the peasants often had an eye to their advantage and
moved about. At the end of the sixteenth century, accordingly,

[1] Mickiewicz, *Les Slaves*, vol. I, leçon XXIV, pp. 376–380; *Histoire populaire
de Pologne*, chaps. I–II.

the czar Boris Godunov empowered the nobles to hold peasants to their lands by force, so establishing serfdom. However, armed forces in Russia were never composed exclusively of nobles. The muzhiks, or peasants, went to war as common soldiers under the droujina. As early as the sixteenth century, Ivan the Terrible established the order of strelitzes which amounted practically to a standing army, and which lasted until Peter the Great replaced it with regiments organized along western European lines. In those regiments members of the old druzhina, with an intermixture of foreigners, became officers, while the muzhiks provided the entire contingent of privates.[1]

Among peoples that have recently entered the agricultural stage and are relatively civilized, it is the unvarying fact that the strictly military class is the political, or ruling, class. Sometimes the bearing of arms is reserved exclusively to that class, as happened in India and Poland. More often the members of the governed class are on occasion enrolled—always, however, as common soldiers and in the less respected divisions. So in Greece, during the war with the Medes, the citizens belonging to the richer and more influential classes formed the picked corps (the cavalry and the hoplites), the less wealthy fought as peltasts or as slingers, while the slaves, that is the laboring masses, were almost entirely barred from military service. We find analogous arrangements in republican Rome, down to the period of the Punic Wars and even as late as the day of Marius; in Latin and Germanic Europe during the Middle Ages; in Russia, as just explained, and among many other peoples. Caesar notes repeatedly that in his time the backbone of the Gallic armies was formed by cavalrymen recruited from the nobility. The Aedui, for example, could not hold out against Ariovistus after the flower of their cavalry had been killed in battle.

5. Everywhere—in Russia and Poland, in India and medieval Europe—the ruling warrior classes acquire almost exclusive ownership of the land. Land, as we have seen, is the chief source of production and wealth in countries that are not very far advanced in civilization. But as civilization progresses, revenue from land increases proportionately. With the growth of population there is, at least in certain periods, an increase in

[1] Leroy-Beaulieu, *L'Empire des tzars et les Russes*, vol. I, pp. 338 f.

rent, in the Ricardian sense of the term, largely because great
centers of consumption arise—such at all times have been the
great capitals and other large cities, ancient and modern.   Eventually, if other circumstances permit, a very important social
transformation occurs.   Wealth rather than military valor comes
to be the characteristic feature of the dominant class: the people
who rule are the rich rather than the brave.

The condition that in the main is required for this transformation is that social organization shall have concentrated and
become perfected to such an extent that the protection offered
by public authority is considerably more effective than the
protection offered by private force.   In other words, private
property must be so well protected by the practical and real
efficacy of the laws as to render the power of the proprietor
himself superfluous.   This comes about through a series of
gradual alterations in the social structure whereby a type of
political organization, which we shall call the "feudal state," is
transformed into an essentially different type, which we shall
term the "bureaucratic state."   We are to discuss these types
at some length hereafter, but we may say at once that the
evolution here referred to is as a rule greatly facilitated by progress in pacific manners and customs and by certain moral habits
which societies contract as civilization advances.

Once this transformation has taken place, wealth produces
political power just as political power has been producing wealth.
In a society already somewhat mature—where, therefore, individual power is curbed by the collective power—if the powerful
are as a rule the rich, to be rich is to become powerful.   And, in
truth, when fighting with the mailed fist is prohibited whereas
fighting with pounds and pence is sanctioned, the better posts
are inevitably won by those who are better supplied with pounds
and pence.

There are, to be sure, states of a very high level of civilization
which in theory are organized on the basis of moral principles of
such a character that they seem to preclude this overbearing
assertiveness on the part of wealth.   But this is a case—and there
are many such—where theoretical principles can have no more
than a limited application in real life.   In the United States all
powers flow directly or indirectly from popular elections, and
suffrage is equal for all men and women in all the states of the

Union. What is more, democracy prevails not only in institutions but to a certain extent also in morals. The rich ordinarily feel a certain aversion to entering public life, and the poor a certain aversion to choosing the rich for elective office. But that does not prevent a rich man from being more influential than a poor man, since he can use pressure upon the politicians who control public administration. It does not prevent elections from being carried on to the music of clinking dollars. It does not prevent whole legislatures and considerable numbers of national congressmen from feeling the influence of powerful corporations and great financiers.[1]

In China, too, down to a few years ago, though the government had not accepted the principle of popular elections, it was organized on an essentially equalitarian basis. Academic degrees gave access to public office, and degrees were conferred by examination without any apparent regard for family or wealth. According to some writers, only barbers and certain classes of boatmen, together with their children, were barred from competing for the various grades of the mandarinate.[2] But though the moneyed class in China was less numerous, less wealthy, less powerful than the moneyed class in the United States is at present, it was none the less able to modify the scrupulous application of this system to a very considerable extent. Not only was the indulgence of examiners often bought with money. The government itself sometimes sold the various academic degrees and allowed ignorant persons, often from the lowest social strata, to hold public office.[3]

In all countries of the world those other agencies for exerting social influence—personal publicity, good education, specialized training, high rank in church, public administration, and army— are always readier of access to the rich than to the poor. The rich invariably have a considerably shorter road to travel than the poor, to say nothing of the fact that the stretch of road that the rich are spared is often the roughest and most difficult.

---

[1] Jannet, *Le istituzioni politiche e sociali degli Stati Uniti d'America*, part II, chap. X f.

[2] Rousset, *À travers la Chine.*

[3] Mas y Sans, *La Chine et les puissances chrétiennes*, vol. II, pp. 332–334; Huc, *L'Empire chinois.*

6. In societies in which religious beliefs are strong and ministers of the faith form a special class a priestly aristocracy almost always arises and gains possession of a more or less important share of the wealth and the political power. Conspicuous examples of that situation would be ancient Egypt (during certain periods), Brahman India and medieval Europe. Oftentimes the priests not only perform religious functions. They possess legal and scientific knowledge and constitute the class of highest intellectual culture. Consciously or unconsciously, priestly hierarchies often show a tendency to monopolize learning and hamper the dissemination of the methods and procedures that make the acquisition of knowledge possible and easy. To that tendency may have been due, in part at least, the painfully slow diffusion of the demotic alphabet in ancient Egypt, though that alphabet was infinitely more simple than the hieroglyphic script. The Druids in Gaul were acquainted with the Greek alphabet but would not permit their rich store of sacred literature to be written down, requiring their pupils to commit it to memory at the cost of untold effort. To the same outlook may be attributed the stubborn and frequent use of dead languages that we find in ancient Chaldea, in India, and in medieval Europe. Sometimes, as was the case in India, lower classes have been explicitly forbidden to acquire knowledge of sacred books.

Specialized knowledge and really scientific culture, purged of any sacred or religious aura, become important political forces only in a highly advanced stage of civilization, and only then do they give access to membership in the ruling class to those who possess them. But in this case too, it is not so much learning in itself that has political value as the practical applications that may be made of learning to the profit of the public or the state. Sometimes all that is required is mere possession of the mechanical processes that are indispensable to the acquisition of a higher culture. This may be due to the fact that on such a basis it is easier to ascertain and measure the skill which a candidate has been able to acquire—it is easier to "mark" or grade him. So in certain periods in ancient Egypt the profession of scribe was a road to public office and power, perhaps because to have learned the hieroglyphic script was proof of long and patient study. In modern China, again, learning the numberless characters in

Chinese script has formed the basis of the mandarin's education.[1] In present-day Europe and America the class that applies the findings of modern science to war, public administration, public works and public sanitation holds a fairly important position, both socially and politically, and in our western world, as in ancient Rome, an altogether privileged position is held by lawyers. They know the complicated legislation that arises in all peoples of long-standing civilization, and they become especially powerful if their knowledge of law is coupled with the type of eloquence that chances to have a strong appeal to the taste of their contemporaries.

There are examples in abundance where we see that long-standing practice in directing the military and civil organization of a community creates and develops in the higher reaches of the ruling class a real art of governing which is something better than crude empiricism and better than anything that mere individual experience could suggest. In such circumstances aristocracies of functionaries arise, such as the Roman senate, the Venetian nobility and to a certain extent the English aristocracy. Those bodies all stirred John Stuart Mill to admiration and certainly they all three developed governments that were distinguished for carefully considered policies and for great steadfastness and sagacity in carrying them out. This art of governing is not political science, though it has, at one time or another, anticipated applications of a number of the postulates of political science. However, even if the art of governing has now and again enjoyed prestige with certain classes of persons who have long held possession of political functions, knowledge of it has never served as an ordinary criterion for admitting to public offices persons who were barred from them by social station. The degree of mastery of the art of governing that a person possesses is, moreover, apart from exceptional cases, a very difficult thing to determine if the person has given no practical demonstration that he possesses it.

7. In some countries we find hereditary castes. In such cases the governing class is explicitly restricted to a given number of

---

[1] This was true up to a few years ago, the examination of a mandarin covering only literary and historical studies—as the Chinese understood such studies, of course.

families, and birth is the one criterion that determines entry into the class or exclusion from it. Examples are exceedingly common. There is practically no country of long-standing civilization that has not had a hereditary aristocracy at one period or another in its history. We find hereditary nobilities during certain periods in China and ancient Egypt, in India, in Greece before the wars with the Medes, in ancient Rome, among the Slavs, among the Latins and Germans of the Middle Ages, in Mexico at the time of the Discovery and in Japan down to a few years ago.

In this connection two preliminary observations are in point. In the first place, all ruling classes tend to become hereditary in fact if not in law. All political forces seem to possess a quality that in physics used to be called the force of inertia. They have a tendency, that is, to remain at the point and in the state in which they find themselves. Wealth and military valor are easily maintained in certain families by moral tradition and by heredity. Qualification for important office—the habit of, and to an extent the capacity for, dealing with affairs of consequence—is much more readily acquired when one has had a certain familiarity with them from childhood. Even when academic degrees, scientific training, special aptitudes as tested by examinations and competitions, open the way to public office, there is no eliminating that special advantage in favor of certain individuals which the French call the advantage of *positions déjà prises*. In actual fact, though examinations and competitions may theoretically be open to all, the majority never have the resources for meeting the expense of long preparation, and many others are without the connections and kinships that set an individual promptly on the right road, enabling him to avoid the gropings and blunders that are inevitable when one enters an unfamiliar environment without any guidance or support.

The democratic principle of election by broad-based suffrage would seem at first glance to be in conflict with the tendency toward stability which, according to our theory, ruling classes show. But it must be noted that candidates who are successful in democratic elections are almost always the ones who possess the political forces above enumerated, which are very often hereditary. In the English, French and Italian parliaments we frequently see the sons, grandsons, brothers, nephews and sons-in-law of members and deputies, ex-members and ex-deputies.

In the second place, when we see a hereditary caste established in a country and monopolizing political power, we may be sure that such a status de jure was preceded by a similar status de facto. Before proclaiming their exclusive and hereditary right to power the families or castes in question must have held the scepter of command in a firm grasp, completely monopolizing all the political forces of that country at that period. Otherwise such a claim on their part would only have aroused the bitterest protests and provoked the bitterest struggles.

Hereditary aristocracies often come to vaunt supernatural origins, or at least origins different from, and superior to, those of the governed classes. Such claims are explained by a highly significant social fact, namely that every governing class tends to justify its actual exercise of power by resting it on some universal moral principle. This same sort of claim has come forward in our time in scientific trappings. A number of writers, developing and amplifying Darwin's theories, contend that upper classes represent a higher level in social evolution and are therefore superior to lower classes by organic structure. Gumplowicz we have already quoted. That writer goes to the point of maintaining that the divisions of populations into trade groups and professional classes in modern civilized countries are based on ethnological heterogeneousness.[1]

Now history very definitely shows the special abilities as well as the special defects—both very marked—which have been displayed by aristocracies that have either remained absolutely closed or have made entry into their circles difficult. The ancient Roman patriciate and the English and German nobilities of modern times give a ready idea of the type we refer to. Yet in dealing with this fact, and with the theories that tend to exaggerate its significance, we can always raise the same objection—that the individuals who belong to the aristocracies in question owe their special qualities not so much to the blood that flows in their veins as to their very particular upbringing, which has brought out certain intellectual and moral tendencies in them in preference to others.

[1] *Der Rassenkampf.* This notion transpires from Gumplowicz's whole volume. It is explicitly formulated in book II, chap. XXXIII.

Among all the factors that figure in social superiority, intellectual superiority is the one with which heredity has least to do. The children of men of highest mentality often have very mediocre talents. That is why hereditary aristocracies have never defended their rule on the basis of intellectual superiority alone, but rather on the basis of their superiorities in character and wealth.

It is argued, in rebuttal, that education and environment may serve to explain superiorities in strictly intellectual capacities but not differences of a moral order—will power, courage, pride, energy. The truth is that social position, family tradition, the habits of the class in which we live, contribute more than is commonly supposed to the greater or lesser development of the qualities mentioned. If we carefully observe individuals who have changed their social status, whether for better or for worse, and who consequently find themselves in environments different from the ones they have been accustomed to, it is apparent that their intellectual capacities are much less sensibly affected than their moral ones. Apart from a greater breadth of view that education and experience bring to anyone who is not altogether stupid, every individual, whether he remains a mere clerk or becomes a minister of state, whether he reaches the rank of sergeant or the rank of general, whether he is a millionaire or a beggar, abides inevitably on the intellectual level on which nature has placed him. And yet with changes of social status and wealth the proud man often becomes humble, servility changes to arrogance, an honest nature learns to lie, or at least to dissemble, under pressure of need, while the man who has an ingrained habit of lying and bluffing makes himself over and puts on an outward semblance at least of honesty and firmness of character. It is true, of course, that a man fallen from high estate often acquires powers of resignation, self-denial and resourcefulness, just as one who rises in the world sometimes gains in sentiments of justice and fairness. In short, whether a man change for the better or for the worse, he has to be exceptionally level-headed if he is to change his social status very appreciably and still keep his character unaltered. Mirabeau remarked that, for any man, any great climb on the social ladder produces a crisis that cures the ills he has and creates new ones that he never had before.[1]

[1] *Correspondance entre le comte de Mirabeau et le comte de La Marck*, vol. II, p. 228.

Courage in battle, impetuousness in attack, endurance in resistance—such are the qualities that have long and often been vaunted as a monopoly of the higher classes. Certainly there may be vast natural and—if we may say so—innate differences between one individual and another in these respects; but more than anything else traditions and environmental influences are the things that keep them high, low or just average, in any large group of human beings. We generally become indifferent to danger or, perhaps better, to a given type of danger, when the persons with whom we daily live speak of it with indifference and remain cool and imperturbable before it. Many mountaineers or sailors are by nature timid men, yet they face unmoved, the ones the dangers of the precipice, the others the perils of the storm at sea. So peoples and classes that are accustomed to warfare maintain military virtues at the highest pitch.

So true is this that even peoples and social classes which are ordinarily unaccustomed to arms acquire the military virtues rapidly when the individuals who compose them are made members of organizations in which courage and daring are traditional, when—if one may venture the metaphor—they are cast into human crucibles that are heavily charged with the sentiments that are to be infused into their fiber. Mohammed II recruited his terrible Janizaries in the main from boys who had been kidnapped among the degenerate Greeks of Byzantium. The much despised Egyptian fellah, unused for long centuries to war and accustomed to remaining meek and helpless under the lash of the oppressor, became a good soldier when Mehemet Ali placed him in Turkish or Albanian regiments. The French nobility has always enjoyed a reputation for brilliant valor, but down to the end of the eighteenth century that quality was not credited in anything like the same degree to the French bourgeoisie. However, the wars of the Republic and the Empire amply proved that nature had been uniformly lavish in her endowments of courage upon all the inhabitants of France. Proletariat and bourgeoisie both furnished good soldiers and, what is more, excellent officers, though talent for command had been considered an exclusive prerogative of the nobility. Gumplowicz's theory that differentiation in social classes depends very largely on ethnological antecedents requires proof at the very least. Many facts to the contrary readily occur to one—

among others the obvious fact that branches of the same family often belong to widely different social classes.

8. Finally, if we were to keep to the idea of those who maintain the exclusive influence of the hereditary principle in the formation of ruling classes, we should be carried to a conclusion somewhat like the one to which we were carried by the evolutionary principle: The political history of mankind ought to be much simpler than it is.   If the ruling class really belonged to a different race, or if the qualities that fit it for dominion were transmitted primarily by organic heredity, it is difficult to see how, once the class was formed, it could decline and lose its power.   The peculiar qualities of a race are exceedingly tenacious.   Keeping to the evolutionary theory, acquired capacities in the parents are inborn in their children and, as generation succeeds generation, are progressively accentuated.   The descendants of rulers, therefore, ought to become better and better fitted to rule, and the other classes ought to see their chances of challenging or supplanting them become more and more remote.   Now the most commonplace experience suffices to assure one that things do not go in that way at all.

What we see is that as soon as there is a shift in the balance of political forces—when, that is, a need is felt that capacities different from the old should assert themselves in the management of the state, when the old capacities, therefore, lose some of their importance or changes in their distribution occur—then the manner in which the ruling class is constituted changes also.   If a new source of wealth develops in a society, if the practical importance of knowledge grows, if an old religion declines or a new one is born, if a new current of ideas spreads, then, simultaneously, far-reaching dislocations occur in the ruling class.   One might say, indeed, that the whole history of civilized mankind comes down to a conflict between the tendency of dominant elements to monopolize political power and transmit possession of it by inheritance, and the tendency toward a dislocation of old forces and an insurgence of new forces; and this conflict produces an unending ferment of endosmosis and exosmosis between the upper classes and certain portions of the lower.   Ruling classes decline inevitably when they cease to find scope for the capacities through which they rose to power, when they can no longer render the social services which they once rendered, or when their talents and the services they render lose in importance in the social environment in which they live. So the Roman aristocracy declined when it was no longer the exclusive source of higher officers for the army, of administrators for the commonwealth, of governors for the provinces. So the Venetian aristocracy declined when its nobles ceased to command the galleys and no longer passed the greater part of their lives in sailing the seas and in trading and fighting.

In inorganic nature we have the example of our air, in which a tendency to immobility produced by the force of inertia is continuously in conflict with a tendency to shift about as the result of inequalities in the distribution of heat. The two tendencies, prevailing by turn in various regions on our planet, produce now calm, now wind and storm. In much the same way in human societies there prevails now the tendency that produces closed, stationary, crystallized ruling classes, now the tendency that results in a more or less rapid renovation of ruling classes.

The Oriental societies which we consider stationary have in reality not always been so, for otherwise, as we have already pointed out, they could not have made the advances in civilization of which they have left irrefutable evidence. It is much more accurate to say that we came to know them at a time when their political forces and their political classes were in a period of crystallization. The same thing occurs in what we commonly call "aging" societies, where religious beliefs, scientific knowledge, methods of producing and distributing wealth have for centuries undergone no radical alteration and have not been disturbed in their everyday course by infiltrations of foreign elements, material or intellectual. In such societies political forces are always the same, and the class that holds possession of them holds a power that is undisputed. Power is therefore perpetuated in certain families, and the inclination to immobility becomes general through all the various strata in that society.

So in India we see the caste system become thoroughly entrenched after the suppression of Buddhism. The Greeks found hereditary castes in ancient Egypt, but we know that in the periods of greatness and renaissance in Egyptian civilization political office and social status were not hereditary. We possess an Egyptian document that summarizes the life of a high army officer who lived during the period of the expulsion of the Hyksos. He had begun his career as a simple soldier. Other documents show cases in which the same individual served successively in army, civil administration and priesthood.[1]

The best-known and perhaps the most important example of a society tending toward crystallization is the period in Roman history that used to be called the Low Empire. There, after several centuries of almost complete social immobility, a division between two classes grew sharper and sharper, the one made up of great landowners and high officials, the other made up of slaves, farmers and urban plebeians. What is even more striking, public office and social position became hereditary by custom before they became hereditary by law, and the trend was rapidly generalized during the period mentioned.[2]

On the other hand it may happen in the history of a nation that commerce with foreign peoples, forced emigrations, discoveries, wars, create new poverty and new wealth, disseminate knowledge of things that were previously unknown or cause infiltrations of new moral, intellectual and religious currents. Or again—as a result of such infiltrations or through a slow process of inner growth, or from both causes—it may happen that a new learning arises, or that certain elements of an old, long forgotten learning return to favor so that new ideas and new beliefs come to the fore and upset the intellectual habits on which the obedience of the masses has been founded. The ruling class may also be vanquished and destroyed in whole or in part by foreign invasions, or, when the circumstances just mentioned arise, it may be driven from power by the advent of new social elements who are strong in fresh political forces. Then, naturally, there comes a period of renovation, or, if one prefer, of revolution, during which individual energies have free play and certain individuals, more passionate, more energetic, more intrepid or merely shrewder than others, force their way from the bottom of the social ladder to the topmost rungs.

Once such a movement has set in, it cannot be stopped immediately. The example of individuals who have started from nowhere and reached prominent positions fires new ambitions,

[1] Lenormant, Maspero, Brugsch.

[2] Marquardt, *Manuel des antiquités romaines;* Fustel de Coulanges, *Nouvelles recherches sur quelques problèmes d'histoire.*

new greeds, new energies, and this molecular rejuvenation of the
ruling class continues vigorously until a long period of social
stability slows it down again.   We need hardly mention examples
of nations in such periods of renovation.   In our age that would
be superfluous.   Rapid restocking of ruling classes is a frequent
and very striking phenomenon in countries that have been
recently colonized.   When social life begins in such environments,
there is no ready-made ruling class, and while such a class is in
process of formation, admittance to it is gained very easily.
Monopolization of land and other agencies of production is, if
not quite impossible, at any rate more difficult than elsewhere.
That is why, at least during a certain period, the Greek colonies
offered a wide outlet for all Greek energy and enterprise.   That is
why, in the United States, where the colonizing of new lands
continued through the whole nineteenth century and new industries were continually springing up, examples of men who started
with nothing and have attained fame and wealth are still frequent
—all of which helps to foster in the people of that country the
illusion that democracy is a fact.

Suppose now that a society gradually passes from its feverish
state to calm.   Since the human being's psychological tendencies
are always the same, those who belong to the ruling class will
begin to acquire a group spirit.   They will become more and
more exclusive and learn better and better the art of monopolizing
to their advantage the qualities and capacities that are essential
to acquiring power and holding it.   Then, at last, the force that
is essentially conservative appears—the force of habit.   Many
people become resigned to a lowly station, while the members of
certain privileged families or classes grow convinced that they
have almost an absolute right to high station and command.

A philanthropist would certainly be tempted to inquire whether
mankind is happier—or less unhappy—during periods of social
stability and crystallization, when everyone is almost fated to
remain in the social station to which he was born, or during the
directly opposite periods of renovation and revolution, which
permit all to aspire to the most exalted positions and some to
attain them.   Such an inquiry would be difficult.   The answer
would have to take account of many qualifications and exceptions,
and might perhaps always be influenced by the personal prefer-
ences of the observer.   We shall therefore be careful not to

venture on any answer of our own. Besides, even if we could reach an undebatable conclusion, it would have a very slight practical utility; for the sad fact is that what the philosophers and theologians call free will—in other words, spontaneous choice by individuals—has so far had, and will perhaps always have, little influence, if any at all, in hastening either the ending or the beginning of one of the historical periods mentioned.

CHAPTER III
FEUDAL AND BUREAUCRATIC SYSTEMS

1. As we have just seen, in fairly populous societies that have
attained a certain level of civilization, ruling classes do not
justify their power exclusively by de facto possession of it, but try
to find a moral and legal basis for it, representing it as the logical
and necessary consequence of doctrines and beliefs that are
generally recognized and accepted. So if a society is deeply
imbued with the Christian spirit the political class will govern by
the will of the sovereign, who, in turn, will reign because he is
God's anointed. So too in Mohammedan societies political
authority is exercised directly in the name of the caliph, or vicar,
of the Prophet, or in the name of someone who has received
investiture, tacit or explicit, from the caliph. The Chinese
mandarins ruled the state because they were supposed to be
interpreters of the will of the Son of Heaven, who had received
from heaven the mandate to govern paternally, and in accordance
with the rules of the Confucian ethic, "the people of the hundred
families." The complicated hierarchy of civil and military functionaries in the Roman Empire rested upon the will of the
emperor, who, at least down to Diocletian's time, was assumed
by a legal fiction to have received from the people a mandate to
rule the commonwealth. The powers of all lawmakers, magistrates and government officials in the United States emanate
directly or indirectly from the vote of the voters, which is held to
be the expression of the sovereign will of the whole American
people.

This legal and moral basis, or principle, on which the power of
the political class rests, is what we have elsewhere called, and
shall continue here to call, the "political formula." (Writers on
the philosophy of law generally call it the "principle of sovereignty."[1]) The political formula can hardly be the same in two

---

[1] Mosca, *Teorica dei governi e governo parlamentare*, chap. I; see also Mosca,
Le costituzioni moderne.

or more different societies; and fundamental or even notable similarities between two or more political formulas appear only where the peoples professing them have the same type of civilization (or—to use an expression which we shall shortly define— belong to the same social type). According to the level of civilization in the peoples among whom they are current, the various political formulas may be based either upon supernatural beliefs or upon concepts which, if they do not correspond to positive realities, at least appear to be rational. We shall not say that they correspond in either case to scientific truths. A conscientious observer would be obliged to confess that, if no one has ever seen the authentic document by which the Lord empowered certain privileged persons or families to rule his people on his behalf, neither can it be maintained that a popular election, however liberal the suffrage may be, is ordinarily the expression of the will of a people, or even of the will of the majority of a people.

And yet that does not mean that political formulas are mere quackeries aptly invented to trick the masses into obedience. Anyone who viewed them in that light would fall into grave error. The truth is that they answer a real need in man's social nature; and this need, so universally felt, of governing and knowing that one is governed not on the basis of mere material or intellectual force, but on the basis of a moral principle, has beyond any doubt a practical and a real importance.

Spencer wrote that the divine right of kings was the great superstition of past ages, and that the divine right of elected assemblies is the great superstition of our present age. The idea cannot be called wholly mistaken, but certainly it does not consider or exhaust all aspects of the question. It is further necessary to see whether a society can hold together without one of these "great superstitions"—whether a universal illusion is not a social force that contributes powerfully to consolidating political organization and unifying peoples or even whole civilizations.

2. Mankind is divided into social groups each of which is set apart from other groups by beliefs, sentiments, habits and interests that are peculiar to it. The individuals who belong to one such group are held together by a consciousness of common brotherhood and held apart from other groups by passions and tendencies that are more or less antagonistic and mutually

repellent. As we have already indicated, the political formula must be based upon the special beliefs and the strongest sentiments of the social group in which it is current, or at least upon the beliefs and sentiments of the particular portion of that group which holds political preeminence.

This phenomenon—the existence of social groups each of which has characteristics peculiar to itself and often presumes absolute superiority over other groups (the *boria nazionale*, the national conceit, that Vico talks about!)—has been recognized and studied by many writers, and particularly by modern scholars, in dealing with the principle of nationality. Gumplowicz, for instance, pointed to its importance in political science, or in sociology if you will. We should be quite ready to adopt the word that Gumplowicz uses to designate it—syngenism—did the term not imply, in conformity with the fundamental ideas of that writer, an almost absolute preponderance of the ethnological element, of community of blood and race, in the formation of each separate social group.[1] We do think that, in a number of primitive civilizations, not so much community of blood as a belief that such community existed—belief in a common ancestor, often arising, as Gumplowicz himself admits, after the social type had been formed—may have helped to cement group unities. But we also think that certain modern anthropological and philological doctrines have served to awaken between social groups and between fractions within one group antipathies that use racial differences as mere pretexts. Actually, moreover, in the formation of the group, or social type, many other elements besides a more or less certain racial affinity figure—for example, community of language, of religion, of interests, and the recurring relationships that result from geographical situation. It is not necessary that all these factors be present at one and the same time, for community of history—a life that is lived for centuries in common, with identical or similar experiences, engendering similar moral and intellectual habits, similar passions and memories— often becomes the chief element in the development of a conscious social type.[2]

Once such a type is formed, we get, to return to a metaphor which we have earlier used, a sort of crucible that fuses all indi-

[1] Gumplowicz, *Der Rassenkampf*, book II, chap. XXXVII.
[2] Mosca, "Fattori della nazionalità."

viduals who enter it into a single alloy. Call it suggestion, call it imitation or mimetism, call it education pure and simple, it nevertheless comes about that a man feels, believes, loves, hates, according to the environment in which he lives. With exceedingly rare exceptions, we are Christians or Jews, Mohammedans or Buddhists, Frenchmen or Italians, for the simple reason that such were the people among whom we were born and bred.[1]

3. In the early dawn of history each of the civilized peoples was virtually an oasis in a desert of barbarism, and the various civilizations, therefore, had either scant intercourse with one another or none whatever. That was the situation of ancient Egypt during the early dynasties and of China down to a day far less remote. Under these circumstances, naturally, each social type had an absolute originality that was virtually unaffected by infiltrations and influences from outside.[2] And yet, though this isolation must have contributed considerably to strengthening the tendency that every social type manifests to consolidate into a single political organism, nevertheless even in those early days that tendency prevailed only sporadically. To keep to the examples mentioned: China, in the day of Confucius, was broken up into many quasi-independent feudal states; and in Egypt the various hiqs, or viceroys, of the individual nomes often acquired full independence, and sometimes upper Egypt and lower Egypt were separate kingdoms.

Later on, in highly advanced and very complex civilizations such as the Hellenic, we see an opposite tendency coming more prominently to the fore, a tendency on the part of a social type to divide into separate, and almost always rival, political organisms. The hegemony that one Greek state or another tried to impose on the other Hellenic peoples was always a concept far removed from what we moderns think of as political unity; and the attempts of Athens and Sparta, and later on of Macedonia, to establish such a hegemony in a permanent and effective form never quite succeeded.

[1] Cf. above, chap. I, §12, and, incidentally, chap. II, §2.

[2] We are thinking here of moral and intellectual influences. Physical mixtures with neighboring barbarians must always have occurred, if only for the reason that outsiders were hunted for the purpose of procuring slaves.

The trait that is truly characteristic of many ancient peoples, and in general of civilizations that we may call primitive because foreign elements have exerted hardly any influence upon them, is the simpleness and unity of the whole system of ideas and beliefs on which a people's existence and its political organization are based. Among ancient peoples the political formula not only rested upon religion but was wholly identified with it. Their god was preeminently a national god. He was the special protector of the territory and the people. He was the fulcrum of its political organization. A people existed only as long as its god was strong enough to sustain it, and in his turn the god survived only as long as his people did.

The ancient Hebrews are the best-known example of a people organized according to the system just described. We must not assume, however, that the kingdoms of Israel and Judah were any exception in the periods in which they flourished. The role that Jehovah played in Jerusalem was played by Chemosh at Moab,[1] by Marduk (Merodach) at Babylon, by Ashur at Nineveh, by Ammon at Thebes. Just as the God of Israel commanded Saul, David and Solomon to fight to the bitter end against the Ammonites and the Philistines, so Ammon ordered the Egyptian Pharaohs to smite the barbarians to east and west and Ashur incited the sovereigns of Nineveh to exterminate all foreigners and assured them of victory. The speech that the Assyrian ambassador, Rab-shakeh, addressed to the Jews assembled on the walls of Jerusalem, illustrates the conceptions mentioned.[2] "Yield to my Lord," he argues, "for just as other gods have been powerless to save their peoples from Assyrian conquest, so will Jehovah be powerless to save you." In other words, Jehovah was a god, but he was less powerful than Ashur, since Ashur's people had conquered other peoples. The Syrians of Damascus are said to have once avoided joining battle with the Kings of Israel in the mountains because they believed that Jehovah fought better on a mountainous terrain than their god did.[3]

But little by little contacts between relatively civilized peoples became more frequent. Vast empires were founded, and these

[1] See the famous stele of Mesha, king of Moab. A translation of it may be found in Lenormant.

[2] II Kings 18:19 f.

[3] I Kings 20:28: "The Lord is God of the hills."

could not always be based upon complete assimilation and destruction of vanquished peoples. The conquerors often had to rest content with merely subduing them. In such cases the victor often found it politic to recognize and worship the god of the vanquished. The Assyrian kings who conquered Babylon paid homage to Marduk, and Cyrus seems to have done the same. Alexander the Great sacrificed to Ammon, and in general to all the deities of the peoples he conquered. The Romans admitted all conquered deities into their pantheon. At that point in history, long interludes of peace, and the lulling of national rivalries that follows upon the establishment of great political organisms, had prepared the ground for a relatively recent phenomenon—the rise of great religions which were humanitarian and universal and which, without distinction of race, language or political system, sought to extend the influence of their doctrines indiscriminately over the whole world.

4. Buddhism, Christianity and Mohammedanism are the three great humanitarian religions that have so far appeared in history.[1] Each of them possesses a complete body of doctrine, the basis being predominantly metaphysical in Buddhism and dogmatic in Christianity and Mohammedanism. Each of them claims that its doctrine contains the absolute truth and that it offers a trustworthy and infallible guide to welfare in this world and salvation in the next. Common acceptance of one of these religions constitutes a very close bond between most disparate peoples who differ widely in race and language. It gives them a common and special manner of viewing morality and life and, more than that, political customs and private habits of such a nature as to cause the formation of a real social type with conspicuous characteristics that are often so profound as to become virtually indelible. From the appearance of these great religions dates a clean-cut distinction between social type and national type that had scarcely existed before. There had once been Egyptian, Chaldean and Greek civilizations, but no Christian or Mohammedan

---

[1] The Jewish religion, parent of Christianity and Mohammedanism, has also become preponderantly humanitarian through a long process of evolution that can be traced as far back as the Prophets. Judaism, however, has never had any very wide following. There may have been humanitarian tendencies in the religion of Zoroaster, though that was just a national religion in origin.

civilization—in other words, there had never been aggregations of peoples who were different in language and race and were divided into many political organisms but were nevertheless united by beliefs, sentiments and a common culture.

Of all religions Mohammedanism is the one, perhaps, that leaves its imprint most deeply on individuals who have embraced it, or better, who have been born into a society over which it has secured control. Christianity, and Judaism too, have been and still are forms that are exceedingly well adapted to molding the soft clay of the human spirit in accordance with certain definite patterns. The influence of Buddhism is more bland, but it is still effective.

It is to be noted, however, that if these great religions, with their closely knit doctrines and their strongly organized religious hierarchies, do serve wonderfully to bind their cobelievers together in brotherhood and assimilate them to a common type, they also act as estranging forces of great potency between populations that cherish different beliefs. They create almost unbridgeable gulfs between peoples who are otherwise close kin in race and language and who live in adjoining territories or even within one country. Differences in religion have rendered any fusion between the populations inhabiting the Balkan peninsula almost impossible, and the same is true of India. In India, as is known, the religions prevailing at present are Mohammedanism and Brahamanism. The latter is not a humanitarian religion, but it is strongly organized. Minute precepts create cases of impurity at the least contact between persons of different castes. The caste, therefore, becomes a powerful estranging force, and greatly hampers any ferment of impulses toward social assimilation.

Amazing indeed is the skill that the Romans showed in assimilating subject peoples, in the face of the very considerable obstacles that arose from differences in race, language and level of civilization. They might not have succeeded so well had they encountered the resistance of hostile, exclusive and strongly organized religions. Druidism in Gaul and Britain had a very rudimentary organization, but it offered a certain amount of resistance nevertheless. The Jews allowed themselves to be killed and dispersed, but they were never assimilated. In North Africa, Rome succeeded in Latinizing the ancestors of the modern

Moors, Arabs and Kabyles and in converting them to her civilization, at least up to a certain point; but she never had to deal with the Mussulman religion, as the French and Italians of our day are obliged to do. Jugurtha and Tacfarinas could not appeal to religious passions as Abd-el-Kader and Bou-Maza have done in our time. As Karamzin so aptly remarks, the Christian religion saved Moscow from becoming wholly Asiatic under the long dominion of the Mongols. On the other hand, though the Russians in their turn are efficient assimilators, and though Finnish and Mongol blood are blended in large proportions with the Slavic in White Russia, the units of Mohammedan Tatars in Kazan, Astrakhan and the Crimea have never been absorbed. Either they have emigrated or else they have stayed on as a people apart, subject, to be sure, but sharply distinguished from the rest of the Russian people.[1] The children of the Celestial Empire have been fairly successful in assimilating the inhabitants of the southern provinces, alien by race and language, but they have not succeeded so well with the Roui-Tze, descendants of Turkish tribes who have dwelt for a thousand years or more in provinces in the northwest of China proper. These have taken on the language and the external appearance of the real Chinese, and mingle with the latter in the same cities, but they have been kept in spiritual isolation by Mohammedanism, which their fathers had embraced before passing the Great Wall. The Turkish tribes in question established themselves in the provinces of Shensi and Kansu under the Tang dynasty, on being summoned thither to check invasions by the Tibetans. In 1861 the antipathies that had always existed between the Mohammedans and their Buddhist fellow countrymen gave rise to a terrible insurrection, in which the Mohammedans waged a war of extermination against the Buddhists. After the provinces mentioned had been reduced to ghastly desolation, the civil war became localized in the Kashgar, beyond the Great Wall. It did not end until 1877, when the Mohammedan leader, Jakoub-beg, was assassinated.[2]

5. With the appearance of the great universal religions, the history of mankind becomes complicated by new factors. We have already seen that even before those religions arose, a social

---

[1] Leroy-Beaulieu, *L'Empire des tzars et les Russes.*

[2] Rousset, *À travers la Chine.*

type, in spite of its tendency toward unity, might split up into different political systems. With the advent of the great religions, this fact becomes more general and less avoidable, and the ground is prepared for the emergence of a phenomenon which, as regards Europe, is called the struggle between church and state.

The complication arises primarily from the fact that the tendency of the social type toward unity remains but is hampered by far stronger forces. The political organization still tries to justify its own existence by the tenets of the prevailing religion, but the religion, on its side, is always trying to obtain control of, and to identify itself with, political power in order to use the latter as an instrument for its own ends and propaganda.

Religion and politics are most closely united in Mohammedan countries. The head of a Mohammedan state has almost always been the high priest of one of the great Islamic sects, or else has received his investiture from the hands of a high priest. In past centuries this investiture was often an empty formality which the caliph, by that time stripped of temporal power, could not withhold from the powerful. In the period between the fall of the Abbassids of Bagdad and the rise of the great Ottoman Empire Mussulman fanaticism was less violent than it is today. Even a superficial familiarity with the history of the Mohammedan countries convinces one of that. Heirs of the Persian civilization of the age of the Sassanids, and thanks to their study of ancient Greek authors, the Mussulmans were for several centuries during the Middle Ages much less prejudiced than the Christians of the same period.[1] It is certain, moreover, that almost every great revolution in the Mohammedan world, the birth of almost every state, is accompanied and justified by a new religious schism. So it was in the Middle Ages, when the new empires of the Almoravides and the Almohades arose; and that was also the case in the nineteenth century with the insurrection of the Wahabis and the revolt led by the Mahdi of Omdurman.

In China, Buddhism lives meekly on under the protection of the state, the latter showing that it recognizes and fosters the creed as a gesture of deference toward the lower classes, which really believe in it. Down to a few years ago the Grand Lama, who is the high authority of the Buddhists in Tibet, Mongolia and

[1] Amari, *Storia dei Musulmani in Sicilia.*

certain provinces of China proper, scrupulously followed the
suggestions of the Chinese resident at Lhasa. The bonzes, who
are scattered over the greater part of China, have no centralized
organization—in a way they are the Protestants of Buddhism.
The government tolerates them and often spends a certain
amount of money on Buddhist festivals in order to humor popular
beliefs. The higher classes in China follow the agnostic positivism of Confucius, which is not clearly distinguishable from a
vague sort of deism. In Japan the same religion is tolerated, but
the government has of late been trying to rehabilitate the ancient
national cult of Shinto.

The various Christian sects have met widely varying conditions
in Europe. In Russia the czar was the head of the orthodox
religion and the church authority was practically one with the
state authority. In the eyes of a loyal Russian a good subject of
the czar had to be an orthodox Greek Catholic.[1] In Protestant
countries, too, the dominant sect often has a more or less official
character. Since the fall of the Roman empire, Catholicism has
had greater independence. In the Middle Ages it aspired to
control over lay authority in all the countries that had entered the
Catholic orbit, and there was a time when the pope could reasonably hope that a realization of the vast papal project of uniting all
Christianity—in other words a whole social type—under his more
or less direct influence was near at hand. Today the pope gets
along by compromises, lending his support to secular powers and
receiving theirs. In one country or another he is in open conflict
with them.

But a political organism, which has a population that follows
one of the universal religions, or is divided among several sects
of one of them, must have a legal and moral basis of its own on
which the ruling class may take its stand. It must, therefore, be
founded on a national feeling, on a long tradition of independence,
on historic memories, on an age-old loyalty to a dynasty—on
something, in short, that is peculiar to itself. Alongside of the
general humanitarian cult, there must somehow be a, so to say,
national cult that is more or less satisfactorily reconciled and
coordinated with the other. The duties of the two cults are often
simultaneously observed by the same individuals, for human
beings are not always strictly consistent in reconciling the various

[1] Leroy-Beaulieu, *L'Empire des tzars et les Russes*.

principles that inspire their conduct. In practice one may be a good Catholic and at the same time a good German, or a good Italian, or a good Frenchman, or a loyal subject of a Protestant sovereign, or a good citizen of a republic that makes official profession of anticlericalism. Sometimes, as frequently happened in an older Italy, one can be a good patriot and an ardent socialist at the same time, though socialism, like Catholicism, is in essence antagonistic to national particularisms. These compromises occur, however, when passions are not very keen. In point of strict consistency, the eighteenth century English were right when they thought that, since the king was the head of the Anglican Church and every good Catholic owed his prime obedience to the pope, no good Catholic could be a good Englishman.

When there is a more or less masked antagonism between a doctrine, or a creed, that aspires to universality, and the sentiments and traditions that support the particularism of a state, what is really essential is that those sentiments and traditions should be really vigorous, that they should also be bound up with many material interests and that a considerable portion of the ruling class should be strongly imbued with them and should propagate and keep them alive in the masses. If, in addition, this element in the ruling class is soundly organized, it can resist all the religious or doctrinary currents that are exerting an influence in the society that it rules. But if it is lukewarm in its sentiments, if it is feeble in moral and intellectual forces, if its organization is defective, then the religious and doctrinary currents prevail and the state ends by becoming a plaything of some one of the universal religions or doctrines—for example of Catholicism or of social democracy.

6. Before we proceed any further, it might be wise to linger briefly on the two types into which, in our opinion, all political organisms may be classified, the feudal and the bureaucratic.

This classification, it should be noted, is not based upon essential, unchanging criteria. It is not our view that there is any psychological law peculiar to either one of the two types and therefore alien to the other. It seems to us, rather, that the two types are just different manifestations, different phases, of a single constant tendency whereby human societies become less simple, or, if one will, more complicated in political organization, as they grow in size and are perfected in civilization. Level of civilization is, on the whole, more important in this regard than size, since, in actual fact, a literally huge state may once have been feudally organized. At bottom, therefore, a bureaucratic state is just a feudal state that has advanced and developed in organization and so grown more complex; and a feudal state may derive from a once bureaucratized society that has decayed in civilization and reverted to a simpler, more primitive form of political organization, perhaps falling to pieces in the process.

By "feudal state" we mean that type of political organization in which all the executive functions of society—the economic, the judicial, the administrative, the military—are exercised simultaneously by the same individuals, while at the same time the state is made up of small social aggregates, each of which possesses all the organs that are required for self-sufficiency. The Europe of the Middle Ages offers the most familiar example of this type of organization—that is why we have chosen to designate it by the term "feudal"; but as one reads the histories of other peoples or scans the accounts of travelers of our own day one readily perceives that the type is widespread. Just as the medieval baron was simultaneously owner of the land, military commander, judge and administrator of his fief, over which he enjoyed both a pure and a mixed sovereignty, so the Abyssinian ras dispensed justice, commanded the soldiery and levied taxes—or rather extorted from the farmer everything over and above the bare necessaries of subsistence. In certain periods of ancient Egypt the hiq, or local governor, saw to the upkeep of the canals, supervised agriculture, administered justice, exacted tribute, commanded his warriors. This was more especially the case during the earliest known periods and under some of the more recent dynasties. It must not be forgotten that the history of ancient Egypt covers about thirty centuries, a period long enough, in spite of the alleged immobility of the East, for a society to pass back and forth between feudalism and bureaucracy any number of times. So too the curaca of Peru, under Inca rule, was the head of his village, and in that capacity administered the collective rural property, exercised all judiciary functions and, at the request of the Son of the Sun, commanded the armed quotas that the village contributed. China also passed through a feudal period, and in Japan that type of organization lasted down to the end of the sixteenth century, its last traces not vanishing till after the revolution of 1868. Afghanistan is still feudally organized, and so was India to a great extent at the time of the European conquest. We may go so far as to say that every great society must have passed one or more times through a feudal period.

Sometimes religious functions also are exercised by the leader who has charge of other social activities. This was true of Europe in medieval times, when abbots and bishops were holders of fiefs. A feudal order may exist, furthermore, even when land, the almost exclusive source of wealth in societies of low-grade civilization, is not by law the absolute property of the governing class. Even granting that the cultivators are not legally vassals and slaves, or indeed are nominally owners of the soil they cultivate, the local leader and his satellites, having full power to exact tribute and require forced labor, will leave the workers of the land no more than is indispensable for a bare subsistence.

Even small political units, in which the production of wealth rests not upon agriculture but upon commerce and industry, sometimes show markedly feudal characteristics, exhibiting a concentration of political and economic management in the same persons that is characteristically feudal. The political heads of the medieval communes were at the same time heads of the craft and trade guilds. The merchants of Tyre and Sidon, like the merchants of Genoa and Venice, Bremen and Hamburg, managed banks, superintended the trading posts that were established in barbarian countries, commanded ships which served now as merchantmen, now as war vessels, and governed their cities. That was the case especially when the cities lived by maritime commerce, in the exercise of which anyone who commanded a vessel readily combined his functions as a merchant with political or military leadership. In other places, in Florence for example, where a large part of the municipal wealth was derived from industry and banking, the ruling class soon lost its warlike habits and therewith direction of military affairs. To that fact may have been partly due the troubled career of the commercial oligarchy in Florence after the expulsion of the Duke of Athens and down to the time of Cosimo dei Medici. The year 1325 saw the last of the cavallate, or military expeditions, in which the nobles and wealthy merchants of Florence personally participated.[1]

[1] Capponi, *Storia della Repubblica di Firenze.*

7. In the bureaucratic state not all the executive functions need to be concentrated in the bureaucracy and exercised by it. One might even declare that so far in history that has never been the case. The main characteristic of this type of social organization lies, we believe, in the fact that, wherever it exists, the central power conscripts a considerable portion of the social wealth by taxation and uses it first to maintain a military establishment and then to support a more or less extensive number of public services. The greater the number of officials who perform public duties and receive their salaries from the central government or from its local agencies, the more bureaucratic a society becomes.

In a bureaucratic state there is always a greater specialization in the functions of government than in a feudal state. The first and most elementary division of capacities is the withdrawal of administrative and judiciary powers from the military element. The bureaucratic state, furthermore, assures a far greater discipline in all grades of political, administrative and military service. To gain some conception of what this means, one has only to compare a medieval count, hedged about by armed retainers and by vassals who have been attached for centuries to his family and supported by the produce of his lands, with a modern French or Italian prefect or army general, whom a telegram can suddenly shear of authority and even of stipend. The feudal state, therefore, demands great energy and a great sense of statesmanship in the man, or men, who stand on the top rung of the social ladder, if the various social groups, which would otherwise tend to disorganization and autonomy, are to be kept organized, compact and obedient to a single impulse. So true is this that often with the death of an influential leader the power of a feudal state itself comes to an end. Only great moral unity—the presence of a sharply defined social type—can long save the political existence of a people that is feudally organized. Nothing less than Christianity was required to hold the Abyssinian tribes together amid the masses of pagans and Mohammedans that encircled them, and to preserve their autonomy for over two thousand years. But when the estranging force is feeble, or when the feudal state comes into contact with more soundly organized peoples, then such a state may very easily be absorbed and vanish in one of the frequent periodical crises to which its central power is irremediably exposed—the example of Poland comes immediately to

mind.   On the other hand, the personal qualities of the supreme
head exert relatively little influence on the destinies of a bureaucratic state.   A society that is bureaucratically organized may
retain its freedom even if it repudiates an old political formula and
adopts a new one, or even if it subjects its social type to very far-
reaching modifications.   This was the case with the Roman
Empire.   It survived the adoption of Christianity in the West
for a century and a half, and in the East for more than eleven
centuries.   So our modern nations have nearly all shifted at one
time or another from a divine-right formula to parliamentary
systems of government.

8. Bureaucratic organization need not necessarily be centralized, in the sense commonly given to that expression.   Often
bureaucratization is compatible with a very liberal provincial
autonomy, as in China, where the eighteen strictly Chinese
provinces preserved broad autonomous privileges and the capital
city of each province looked after almost all provincial affairs.[1]

States of European civilization—even the most decentralized of
them—are all bureaucratized.   As we have already indicated,
the chief characteristic of a bureaucratic organization is that its
military functions, and other public services in numbers more or
less large, are exercised by salaried employees.   Whether salaries
are paid exclusively by the central government or in part by local
bodies more or less under the control of the central government is
a detail that is not as important as it is often supposed to be.
History is not lacking in cases of very small political organisms
which have accomplished miracles of energy in every branch of
human activity with the barest rudiments of bureaucratic organization or with practically none at all.   The ancient Hellenic
cities and the Italian communes of the Middle Ages are examples
that flock to mind.   But when vast human organisms, spreading
over huge territories and comprising millions and millions of
individuals, are involved, nothing short of bureaucratic organization seems capable of uniting under a single impulse the immense
treasures of economic power and moral and intellectual energy
with which a ruling class can in a measure modify conditions
within a society and make its influence effective and powerful
beyond its own frontiers.   Under a feudal organization the

[1] Huc, Réclus, Rousset.

authority which a given member of the ruling class exerts over individuals of the subject class, few or many, may be more direct, oppressive, and arbitrary. Under a bureaucratic organization society is influenced less by the given individual leader than by the ruling class as a whole.

Egypt was bureaucratized in the golden ages of the seventeenth and eighteenth dynasties, when the civilization of the Pharaohs had one of its most lustrous periods of renascence, and the Egyptian battalions pushed their conquests from the Blue Nile to the foothills of the Caucasus. In ancient Egypt, as in China, the coinage of precious metals was unknown. Taxes therefore were collected in kind or were calculated in precious metals, which were weighed out on scales. This was no inconsiderable obstacle to the functioning of the bureaucratic system. The difficulty was overcome by a complicated and very detailed system of book-keeping. It is interesting also to note, on the psychological side, that with social conditions equal, man is always the same, even in little things, through the ages. Letters surviving from those days[1] show Egyptian officers detailing the hardships of their faraway garrisons in Syria, and functionaries who are bored in their little provincial towns soliciting the influence of their superiors to procure transfers to the gayer capital. Such letters could be drawn from the archives of almost any department in any modern European government.

The Roman empire was a highly bureaucratized state, and its sound social organism was able to spread Greco-Roman civilization and the language of Italy over large portions of the ancient world, accomplishing a most difficult task of social assimilation. Another bureaucracy was czarist Russia, which, despite a number of serious internal weaknesses, had great vitality and carried its expansion deep into the remote fastnesses of Asia.

In spite of these examples, and not a few others that might readily occur to one, we should not forget a very important fact to which we have already alluded: namely, that history shows no instance of a great society in which all human activities have been completely bureaucratized. This, perhaps, is one of the many indications of the great complexity of social laws, for a type of political organization may produce good results when applied up to a certain point, but become impracticable and harmful

---

[1] Texts and translations by Lenormant and Maspero.

when it is generalized and systematized.   Justice is quite generally bureaucratized, and so is public administration.   Napoleon I,
great bureaucratizer that he was, succeeded in bureaucratizing
education and even the Catholic priesthood.   We often see
bureaucracies building roads, canals, railways and all sorts of
public works that facilitate the production of wealth.   But
production itself we never see entirely bureaucratized.   It would
seem as though that very important branch of social activity, like
so many other branches, lends itself ill to bureaucratic regulation,
individual profit being a far more effective spur to the classes
engaged in production than any government salary could be.

What is more, we have fairly strong evidence that the extension
of bureaucratic control to the production and distribution of
wealth as a whole would be fatal.   We are not thinking here
of the economic evils of protectionism, of governmental control of
banking and finance, of the overdevelopment of public works.
We are merely pointing to a well-established fact.   In a bureaucratic system both the manager of economic production and the
individual worker are protected against arbitrary confiscations
on the part of the strong and powerful, and all private warfare
is sternly suppressed.   Human life and property are therefore
relatively secure.   Under a bureaucratic regime, the producer
pays over a fixed quota to the social organization and secures
tranquil enjoyment of the rest of his product.   This permits an
accretion of wealth, public and private, that is unknown to barbarous or primitively organized countries.   But the amount of
wealth that is absorbed and consumed by the class that fulfills
other than economic functions may become too great, either
because the demands of the military class, and of other bureaucrats, are excessive, or because the bureaucracy tries to perform
too many services, or because of wars and the debts that result
from wars.   Under these circumstances the taxes that are levied
upon the wealth-producing classes become so heavy that the
profit that an individual can earn in the field of production is
markedly reduced.   In that event production itself inevitably
falls off.   As wealth declines, emigration and higher death rates
thin out the poorer classes, and finally the exhaustion of the
entire social body ensues.   These phenomena are observable
whenever a bureaucratic state declines.   We see them in the
epoch that followed upon the maximum development of bureau-

cracy in ancient Egypt, and more strikingly still during the decay of the Roman Empire. At the end of the long reign of Ramses II, with which the decline of the third Egyptian civilization begins, taxes had become intolerable, as is attested by numbers of private documents that have been deciphered by Maspero, Lenormant and others. We know that the real reason for the decline of the Roman Empire was a falling-off in population and wealth, which in turn must have been caused in the main by the burden of taxes and the unthinking greed with which they were collected.[1] In France, too, population and wealth dwindled at the end of the long reign of the Great King. They were put into good condition again under the administration of the peace-loving Cardinal de Fleury.

9. It would take us too far afield to respond seriatim to all the theories and doctrines that diverge from our point of view concerning the classification of governmental types in human societies. Among such doctrines, however, two are so important, in view of the vogue that they are having today, that we can hardly ignore them. We allude to the closely related theories of Comte and Spencer. Large numbers of writers on the social and political sciences make the concepts of those famous sociologists the cornerstones of their reasonings and their systems.

Comte, as is well known, stressed three stages in the evolution of human intelligence, the theological, the metaphysical and the positive, with three different types of social organization corresponding to them, the military, the feudal and the industrial.

Little fault need be found with this classification of the intellectual processes of man in general. Man may, in fact, explain to himself all phenomena in the organic and inorganic universe, even social phenomena, by attributing them to supernatural beings, to the intervention of God or of gods or of spirits beneficent or maleficent, whom he takes to be the authors of victory and defeat, of abundance and famine, of good health and pestilence; and if one assumes that there was a stage in history in which man reasoned exclusively in this fashion, the stage may well be called theological. Man may also explain the same phenomena by ascribing them to prime, or first, causes which are products of his imagination or of a superficial or fanciful observa-

---

[1] Marquardt, *Organisation financière chez les Romains.*

tion of facts, as when he believed that the destinies of individuals and nations depended upon the motions and conjunctions of the planets, or that the health of the human body depended upon combinations of humors, or that the wealth of nations corresponded to the quantities of precious metals that they possessed. In this case man may well be said to be in a metaphysical, or aprioristic stage. Finally, man can give up trying to discover the prime causes of phenomena and try instead, with rigorous methods of observation, to formulate the natural laws with which phenomena conform and so enable himself to take all possible advantage of them. In this frame of mind man can be said to be in a scientific or positive stage.

Objections to Comte's system begin when he sets out to ascribe the three processes mentioned to definite historical periods and then to classify human societies by assigning them to one or another of the periods so obtained. All three intellectual processes go on in all human societies, from the maturest down to those which are still, so to speak, in the savage state. Ancient Greece gave us Hippocrates and Aristotle, and Rome Lucretius. Modern European civilization has given us physics, chemistry and political economy. It has invented the telescope and the microscope. It has tamed electricity and discovered the bacteria that cause epidemics and diseases. Yet we cannot help recognizing that in Athens as in ancient Rome, in Paris as in Berlin, in London as in New York, the majority of individuals were and are in the full midst of the theological stage, or at best in the metaphysical stage. Just as there was no time in classical antiquity when soothsayers and oracles were not consulted, or when sacrifices were not offered and omens believed, so revealed religions continue to play important roles in the lives of our contemporaries, and wherever religion weakens we witness growths of spiritualistic superstitions or of the absurd metaphysics of social democracy. On the other hand the savage who sees a fetish in a plant or a stone, or who believes that his tribe's medicine man produces rain and makes the lightning, could not live in this world if he did not possess a certain amount of soundly positive information. When he studies the habits of the animals he hunts, when he learns to identify their tracks and takes account of the direction of the wind in order to surprise and capture them, he is utilizing observations that have been accumulated and systematized by himself and his fathers, and is acting therefore in accord with the dictates of sound science.[1]

But that is not all. Comte's three intellectual processes go on simultaneously—to use his curious language, his three periods coexist—not only in one historical epoch and in one people, but also in one individual. We may say, with examples by the hundreds before our eyes, that this is the general rule and that the contrary is the exception. What Italian, in fact, has not known some God-fearing ship's captain who in religion believes in the miracles of Our Lady of Lourdes or of the Madonna of Pompeii, who in politics or in economics believes in universal suffrage or in the class struggle, but who, when it comes to running his ship, handles his tiller according to the compass and trims his sails according to the direction of the wind? All, or virtually all, physicians down to two centuries ago believed in religion and so did not deny the efficacy of prayer and votive offerings in the treatment of the sick. As regards the functioning of the different organs in the human body and the virtues of certain simples, they held various metaphysical beliefs, derived in large part from Galen or from Arab doctors. But at the same time they were not without a certain fund of scientific information that went back to Hippocrates and which, slowly enriched by the experience of many centuries, permitted rational treatments in some few cases. So prayers for victory and *Te Deums* of thanksgiving were offered in Europe to the Most High long after Gustavus Adolphus, Turenne and Montecuccoli had begun to fight wars on scientific principles. To mention one other case: When Xenophon believed that a dream was a warning from the gods he was in a full theological period. As to the shape of the earth and the composition of matter he had ideas that the geographers and chemists of our day would characterize as metaphysical. But, in leading the famous retreat of the Ten Thousand, he found it necessary to protect his main column, which was marching with the baggage train, from continuous raids by the Persian cavalry. He flanked it with two lines of light-armed troops—so guiding himself by principles which, given the arma-

---

[1] This objection to Comte's theory was seen by Comte himself, for he wrote: "This ephemeral coexistence of the three intellectual stages today is the only plausible explanation for the resistance that outdated thinkers are still offering to my law." *Système*, vol. III, p. 41.

ments then in use, a modern tactician would judge thoroughly scientific and positive. In the *Cyropaedia* Xenophon is primarily theological and metaphysical. He turns positive again in his treatise on the art of horseback riding. On this topic he draws his precepts, as any modern writer would, from study of the nature of the horse.

10. The truth is that, in this as in so many other cases, over-simplification is not well suited to the sciences that deal with the psychology of man. Man is an exceedingly complex animal, full of contradictions. He is not always considerate enough to be logical and consistent and so, even when he believes and hopes that God is going to interfere in his behalf, he is careful to keep his powder dry—careful to take advantage, in other words, both of his own and of other people's intelligence and experience. The one really valid argument that can be adduced in favor of Comte's classification is that although the three intellectual stages coexist in all human societies and can be detected in the majority of individuals who compose those societies, they may, according to the case, be very unequally distributed. A people may have an equipment of scientific knowledge that is unquestionably superior to that of another people, and in the various periods of its history it may progress or decline greatly in respect of scientific knowledge; and it is just as certain that metaphysical doctrines and supernatural beliefs generally have a stronger hold on scientifically backward nations and individuals and exert a greater influence on them. But subjected to those limitations Comte's theory comes down to something like the rather commonplace doctrine that the farther a society progresses in scientific thinking, the less room it has left for aprioristic or metaphysical thinking, and the less influence the supernatural has upon it.

"*Natio est omnium Gallorum admodum dedita religionibus* (the whole race of Gauls is extraordinarily devoted to religious rites)," wrote Caesar—a judgment that an individual belonging to a more civilized people always makes of a less civilized people.[1] It is a curious fact that if believers in revealed religions have a certain amount of scientific training they are careful not to attribute everything that happens in this world to the con-

[1] *De bello Gallico*, VI, 16.

tinuous interference of supernatural beings, as cruder peoples and more ignorant individuals usually do.

But the ideas of the father of modern sociology seem to go even wider of the mark in the matter of the parallel that he sets up between his three intellectual stages and his three types of political organization, the military, the feudal and the industrial, the first corresponding to the infancy, the second to the adolescence, the third to the maturity of human societies.

The military function, in other words the organization of an armed force for the defense of a people at home and abroad (and, for that matter, for offense too, according as human interests, prejudices and passions chance to determine) has so far been a necessity in all human societies. The greater or lesser predominance of the military element in political life depends partly upon factors which we have already examined— on whether the military element is a more or less indispensable and comprehensive political force, and whether it is more or less balanced by other political forces—and partly on other factors which we shall not fail to consider in due course. For the time being we see no necessity for the indissoluble union that Comte insists on establishing between the predominance of militarism in political life and the prevalence of the theological period in the intellectual and moral worlds. We can even go on and say that we do not consider it in any way proved that the type of organization that Comte calls military can prevail only in societies that are in the first stage of their development, or, to use the language of the modern positivists, in a state of infancy.

Hellenic society, after Alexander the Great, was evidently organized according to a pattern that any sociologist would define as military. After the Macedonian conquest the republican leagues of Greece proper had only a very limited political importance. Down to the Roman conquest they were always in the position of clients or vassals to the great Hellenized kingdoms of Egypt, Syria and, particularly, Macedonia, which were real military absolutisms based on the support of armies. Yet those were the days when Greek society was in anything but a state of infancy, or a theological period. The philosophical schools that represent the greatest effort of Hellenic thought in the direction of positive science had been formed shortly before and were flourishing at that time. The same thing may be observed in Roman society when, after Caesar, an imperial absolutism resting on the praetorian guards and the legions came to be established.

When religious beliefs are widespread and a people has ardent faith in them we inevitably get a political predominance of the priestly classes. Now those classes and the military classes are not always one and the same, nor do they always have the same sentiments and interests. The union of throne and altar that took place in Europe early in the nineteenth century, after the Holy Alliance, was due to the peculiar circumstance that both throne and altar were directly threatened by the same rationalistic and revolutionary currents. But far from constituting a general rule which might be taken as a universal law, that case is to be regarded rather as one of the many transitory phenomena that develop in history. There is no lack of examples to the contrary—the case of India, for instance, where, at one time, the Brahman caste found itself in conflict with the warrior caste. In Europe there is the celebrated struggle between papacy and empire.

Going on, we can find no justification in fact whatever for that portion of Comte's doctrine which correlates the predominance of the feudal system in political organization with the predominance of metaphysics in human thought. In Comte's system, medieval monotheism and medieval ontology represent a transition between polytheism—in other words a full-fledged theological period—and modern science, just as feudalism, which Comte regards as a defensive type of militarism, is a bridge between the military and industrial periods. "In fact," he says, "monotheism fits in with defense as well as polytheism fits in with conquest. The feudal lords formed just as complete a transition between military commanders and industrial leaders as ontology formed between theology and science."[1] Now to hold that monotheism is best adapted to defense, just as polytheism is best adapted to conquest, is to take no account whatever of large portions of the world's history—the history of the Mussulman world, for example.

We have already seen (chap. III, §6) that what is commonly called feudal organization is a relatively simple political type that is often encountered in the early stages of great human

[1] *Système*, vol. III, p. 66.

societies and appears again as great bureaucratic states degenerate. Political progress and scientific progress do not always go
hand in hand, as is shown by the history of Italy in the Renaissance. We may nevertheless grant, with reservations, that
periods of general ignorance and intellectual prostration correspond on the whole to primitive stages in political life or to
periods of political decadence and dissolution. But what we
cannot see is why such periods should be characterized by the
prevalence of metaphysical rather than theological thinking—
any more than we can see that there can necessarily be no
scientific activity during the flowering of a feudal organization.
Confucius lived in a period when China was feudally organized,
and he certainly was no metaphysician. On the other hand the
trivium and the quadrivium are unknown to the Afghans and
Abyssinians of our day—as well, for that matter, as anything
more than the very elementary forms of culture.

Comte bases his argument largely upon the example of medieval Europe, and that period undoubtedly had its great metaphysicians, as did classical antiquity. But to think of medieval
thought as a sort of bridge between ancient theology and modern
scientific thought is a mistake, just as it is a mistake to imagine
that feudalism was an organically intermediary political form
between the ancient hieratic empires and the modern state.

One has only to read a medieval writer—a writer, preferably,
who is somewhat posterior to the fall of the western Empire and
not too close to the Renaissance—to perceive at once how much
more profoundly, how much more basically theological, medieval thinking was than the thinking of antiquity. Medieval
writers and the people about them are immensely more remote,
immensely more different, from us, than the contemporaries of
Aristotle or Cicero ever were. And the feudal order developed
and flourished in the very centuries when continuous fear of
famine and pestilence, and frequent apparitions of celestial and
infernal beings tormented and utterly moronized the human
mind; when terror of the devil was a permanent mental state in
wretched souls in whom reason had languished for want of any
cultural sustenance, and to whom the marvelous and the supernatural were elements as familiar as the air they breathed.

One of the most characteristic writers of the period was the
monk Raoul Glaber (Radulfus) who wrote a chronicle that comes

down to almost the middle of the eleventh century.[1] According to that monk the ancient classical writers, Vergil included, appeared to their readers in the guise of devils. Glaber's faith is steadfast but unwarmed by brotherly love, and in it fear of the Evil One probably plays a larger role than love and worship of the good, the merciful God of the Christians. In Glaber's eyes, Satan is at all times present and has a finger in everything that happens to human beings. There is perhaps no living person who has not seen him. In spite of an energetic piety and zealous compliance with the rule of his order, Glaber himself has seen the Devil three or four times.

Not all writers of that era, to be sure, show the same derangement of the intellectual faculties, but no one is altogether immune to it. A Norman, Goffredo Malaterra, tells the story of Count Roger's conquest of Sicily from the Saracens with considerable discernment and balance of judgment, and at times he evinces a certain capacity for observing human events with an unprejudiced eye. Yet in describing a battle that was fought at Cerami between the Count and the infidels, he ascribes the victory of the Christians to the direct interposition of St. George, who fought in person in the ranks of the Normans. In proof of the miracle Malaterra records that a white flag emblazoned with a cross was seen to appear on the lance of the Christian leader and flutter in the wind.

The epidemic of demonolatry even spread to the Byzantine East. Georgius Cedrenus and the chronicler Constantine Porphyrogenitus relate that the capture of Syracuse by the Saracens was known in the Peloponnesus long before any refugees arrived, because some demons were chatting together in a wood one night and were overheard recounting the details of that disaster.

In justification of his theory Comte writes: "Noteworthy as characterizing the true spirit of Catholicism is the fact that it reduces theological life to the domain of the strictly necessary."[2] But that is failing to take account of the fact that the supernatural is "reduced to the strictly necessary" not only in Catholicism but in all monotheistic religions when they are professed by civilized peoples who possess broad scientific cultures—the modern English for instance. No such reduction occurs when

[1] Émile Gebhart, "L'État d'âme d'un moine de l'an 1000."
[2] Système, vol. III, p. 434.

monotheistic religions are professed by barbarous peoples of
low cultural levels.   In such cases the sway of the supernatural
over the minds of men may be much greater than it is among
polytheistic peoples of higher levels of civilization.

11. The third necessary correspondence that Comte sets up, the
relation between the industrial system and positive science, is
also fallacious.   We may dispense with proof of that because, in
this third section of Comte's political positivism, his ideas have
had no great resonance, being too divergent from the ideas that
are now most in vogue among our contemporaries, and not
offering sufficient leverage for justifying with a semblance of
scientific method the passions and interests that have so far
been most to the fore in our day.   Comte regarded industrialism
as a type of social organization that would be realized in a remote
future when the managerial functions of society would be
entrusted to a priesthood of positivistic scientists and to a
patriciate of bankers and businessmen, to which, it would seem,
the members of the lower classes were not to gain ready admittance.   Foreseeing that this question might arise, Comte did
not forget to write that "the priesthood will prevail upon the
proletarians to scorn any temptation to leave their own class as
contrary to the majesty of the people's function and fatal to the
righteous aspirations of the masses, who have always been
betrayed by deserters from their ranks."[1]   Another fundamental
idea of Comte's is that the entire intellectual and political movement at the end of the eighteenth century and in the first half
of the nineteenth was a revolutionary movement that resulted in
moral and political anarchy because the feudal monotheistic
system had been destroyed and nobody had been able to find
a substitute for it.   In line with this idea Comte severely condemned the parliamentary system as a manifestation of the
anarchic period (in which we are still living); and the representative function itself, whereby inferiors choose their superiors,
Comte defined as a revolutionary function.[2]

It will be more to our purpose to dwell on the second theory
mentioned (§9), that is to say, on the modification that Spencer,
and a host of modern sociologists after him, made in Comte's

[1] *Ibid.*, vol. IV, p. 83.
[2] *Ibid.*, vol. IV, chap. 5, especially pp. 368, 382, 393–94.

doctrines. Spencer divided human societies into two types, the militant (*i.e.*, military), based upon force, and the industrial, based upon contract and the free consent of the citizens. This dual classification is propounded more especially in Spencer's *Principles of Sociology*, but it is regularly assumed in most of his other writings, as well as in the works of his numerous followers.

Any classification has to be based upon distinctive traits that are clear and definite, and Spencer, in fact, does not fail to serve warning at the outset that, although "during social evolution there has habitually been a mingling of the two types [the militant and the industrial], we shall find that, alike in theory and in fact, it is possible to trace with due clearness these opposite characters which distinguish them in their respective complete developments."[1] Spencer's fundamental criterion is that the militant society is based on *status*, on "regimentation," "the members standing towards one another in successive grades of subordination,"[2] and on the supervision, therefore, and the coercion, which the governors exercise over the governed. His industrial society is based upon contract, upon the free consent of its members, in exactly the same way as a literary society, or an industrial or commercial partnership, is based on the free consent of the associated members and could not exist without such consent.

Now, for a first general objection, this classification is based upon eminently aprioristic assumptions which do not stand the test of facts. Any political organization is both voluntary and coercive at one and the same time—voluntary because it arises from the very nature of man, as was long ago noted by Aristotle, and coercive because it is a necessary fact, the human being finding himself unable to live otherwise. It is natural, therefore, and at the same time indispensable, that where there are men there should automatically be a society, and that when there is a society there should also be a state—that is to say, a minority that rules and a majority that is ruled by the ruling minority.

---

[1] *Principles of Sociology*, vol. II, chap. XVII ("The Militant Type of Society"), §547, p. 568. "The Industrial Type of Society" is discussed in chap. XVIII. Chapter XIX, "Political Retrospect and Prospect," relates to the past and future of the two types.

[2] *Ibid.*, vol. II, chap. XVII, §553.

It might be objected that, although the existence of a social organization is natural and necessary wherever human groups or multitudes form, there are states that receive the assent, or at least the tacit acquiescence, of the great majority of the individuals who belong to them, and states that do not attain that condition. We do not deny that things stand exactly that way, but still we do not see why the former should be called industrial states and the latter militant states, in the sense that Spencer attaches to the terms. The majority of a people consents to a given governmental system solely because the system is based upon religious or philosophical beliefs that are universally accepted by them. To use a language that we prefer, the amount of consent depends upon the extent to which, and the ardor with which, the class that is ruled believes in the political formula by which the ruling class justifies its rule. Now, in general, faith of that kind is certainly greater not in Spencer's industrial states but in states that Spencer classifies as militant, or which present all the characteristics that he attributes to militant states—states where an absolute and arbitrary government is based on divine right.

In the monarchies of the Near East there are often conspiracies against the persons of sovereigns, but down to a few years ago attempts to set up new forms of government were very rare. Among all the nations of modern Europe before the World War, Turkey and Russia were the ones where governmental systems were most in harmony with the political ideals of the great majority in their populations. Only small educated minorities were systematically opposed to the rule of the czar and the sultan. In all barbarous countries populations may be dissatisfied with their rulers, but ordinarily they neither conceive of better political systems nor desire any.

We can hardly agree, either, with certain applications that Spencer makes of his categories to particular cases. Spencer seems to have thought of an industrial state as a sort of democratic state, a state, at any rate, in which government is based on representation, or in which there is at least a tendency not to recognize any authority as legitimate unless it emanates from some public assembly. He says: "Such control as is required under the industrial type can be exercised only by an appointed agency for ascertaining and executing the average will; and a

representative agency is the one best fitted for doing this."[1]
He therefore classifies the Pueblo Indians of New Mexico and
Arizona with societies of the industrial type because, "sheltering
in their walled villages and fighting only when invaded, they
. . . united with their habitually industrial life a free form of
government: . . . 'the governor and his council were annually
elected by the people.' "[2]   Now Spencer could not have been
unaware how widely common the elective system was in the
republics of ancient Greece, in Rome, and even among the
ancient Germans, who chose their leaders by acclamation,
raising them on high on their shields.   Nevertheless, all those
peoples, according to Spencer's own criteria, would be classified
as militant peoples.   On the other hand, we should hardly be
able to call them industrial peoples, in Spencer's sense.   The fact
that a people participates in electoral assemblies does not mean
that it directs its government or that the class that is governed
chooses its governors.   It means merely that when the electoral
function operates under favorable social conditions it is a tool
by which certain political forces are enabled to control and
limit the activity of other political forces.

12. Spencer finds certain distinguishing characteristics in his
militant and industrial types that seem to us exceedingly vague
and indefinite.   He writes that as militarism decreases and
industrialism increases proportionately, a social organization
in which the individual exists for the benefit of the state develops
into another organization in which the state exists for the benefit
of the individual.[3]   That is a subtle distinction.   It reminds
one of the debate as to whether the brain exists for the benefit
of the rest of the body or the rest of the body for the benefit
of the brain.

Spencer elsewhere finds that the militant state is "positively
regulative," in the sense that it requires the performance of
certain acts, while the industrial state is "negatively regulative
only,"[4] since it confines itself to specifying acts that must not
be performed, and he gives his blessing to states of the negatively

[1] *Ibid.*, §566, p. 508.
[2] *Ibid.*, vol. II, chap. XVIII, §513, p. 616.
[3] *Ibid.*, chap. XVIII.
[4] *Ibid.*, §569, pp. 611–612.

regulative variety.   As a matter of fact, no social organization
has ever existed in which control is not simultaneously positive
and negative.   Furthermore, since human activity has its
limits, multiplication of negative injunctions is almost as bad,
as regards fettering individual initiative, as excessive regulation
in a positive sense.

Spencer relates to his two types of state traits that we would
explain and classify otherwise.   In ancient Peru, for instance,
public officials superintended agriculture and distributed water
(probably for purposes of regular irrigation or else in areas and
at times of extreme drought).   Spencer finds that trait characteristic of militant states.   We should think of it simply as a
phenomenon of over-bureaucratization.   Then again, Spencer,
quoting Brantôme, finds the practice of the private vendetta
still common in France in the late Middle Ages, even among the
clergy, and he regards the institution as a symptom of militancy.
We, for our part, should expect to find such phenomena as the
vendetta conspicuous in peoples among whom social authority
is weak, or recently has been weak—peoples, in other words,
who are in the period of crude and primitive organization which
we defined as feudal, or who have recently emerged from it.
Wherever the vendetta flourishes, and therefore among almost
all barbarous peoples, or peoples whose social organization has
greatly decayed, it is natural that personal courage should be a
much esteemed quality.   In fact, the same thing occurs in any
society which, for one reason or another, has had to fight many
wars of defense and offense.   It is natural that bravery and
bombast should be the attributes that confer prestige and
influence in barbarous societies, the low level of culture not
permitting aptitudes for science or for the production of wealth
to develop and to win esteem.

Spencer believes that militant societies are protectionist
societies and vice versa.   He finds in them a tendency to live
on their own economic resources with the least possible resort
to international exchange.   In our opinion that tendency is,
more than anything else, a consequence of crudeness and isolation
in primitive peoples.   In modern civilized nations it results from
popular prejudices that are exploited in the interests of a few
individuals, who are expert in the arts of serving their own
advantage at the expense of the many.   It is very probable

that the tribes which are so often mentioned by Spencer as typical of primitive industrial societies profited very little from exchange with other tribes; and in our day protectionist doctrines have, alas, no less influence in "industrial" North America than in "militant" Germany.

It would be a mistake, according to Spencer, to identify industrial societies by the degree of economic development that they attain, or militant societies by the energy they develop and the success they achieve in war. Now superficial as such criteria might be, they would have the advantage of being very simple and easily applied. But Spencer himself directly or indirectly warns that they are to be rejected. With regard to the first, he notes that "industrialism must not be confounded with industriousness" and that "the social relations which characterize the industrial type may coexist with but very moderate productive activities."[1] As regards the second, Spencer would allow one to assume that the Roman Republic was less militant than the Near Eastern empires which were subdued by Rome, and following the same reasoning, the English would be less advanced toward the industrial type than the Hindus whom they conquered in India.

Despite these objections and still others that might be urged against Spencer's classification, it cannot be denied that with its aid he glimpsed a great truth—but as through a cloud, so to speak, of misunderstanding. If we follow not so much Spencer's criteria of classification as the mass of his incidental assertions, and especially the spirit that animates his work as a whole, we cannot fail to see that by a "militant state" he means a state in which juridical defense has made little progress and by an "industrial state" another type of society in which justice and social morality are much better safeguarded.

The misunderstanding that kept Spencer from going farther than he went in the discovery of a great scientific principle lay in this: impressed by the fact that material violence has been, as it still is, one of the greatest obstacles to progress in juridical defense, he believed that war and the need of military organization were the causes of all violence. But to view the problem in that light is to confuse the cause with one of its effects. It means taking war as the sole origin of the tendency in human

[1] *Ibid.*, §562, pp. 603–604.

nature to tyrannize over one's fellows, whereas war is just one of
the many manifestations of that tendency. Now in the external
relations between people and people, that tendency can be
curbed only by the greater and greater prevalence of material
interests rightly understood. The curb operates only among
peoples that have attained high economic and scientific levels,
because it is only under highly civilized conditions that war
infallibly harms, though still in varying degrees, both victors
and vanquished. In internal relations between individual
members of one people the tendency in question can be to an
extent neutralized, as we have seen, only by a multifarious interplay of such political forces as are able to assert themselves in a
society, and by the control they are able to exercise over one
another reciprocally.

How is it that among the various ruling cliques, among the
various political forces, the section that represents material
force, in other words the army, is not always upsetting the
juridical equilibrium in its own favor and forcing its will systematically upon the state? Certainly the possibility that that
may occur is a standing danger to which all societies are exposed.
It is a danger especially to societies that are rapidly rejuvenating
their political forces or hastily overhauling their political formulas. We are, therefore, obliged to examine the relations that
obtain between military organization and juridical defense in
order to discover, if possible, the best methods for dealing with
that danger. It is a most important subject, and we shall later
go into it in some detail.

For the present we might simply remark that the foregoing
criticism of Spencer's conception of war and military power was
made from a theoretical point of view. But neither can we
approve of his doctrine in respect of a number of practical
applications that he more or less directly suggests. Of the
various forms of military organization Spencer shows a pre-
dilection for forms in which the soldier, "volunteering on
specified terms, acquires in so far the position of a free worker";
and he thinks that such an organization is best suited to a
society "where the industrial type is much developed."[1] That
means, in other terms, that those elements in a society which
have a greater inclination toward the bearing of arms ought

[1] *Ibid.*, §562, p. 603.

voluntarily to assume responsibility for military defense both at home and abroad, for a compensation which, in the military trade as in any other, would be fixed by market conditions. Now it seems to us—and so it seemed to Machiavelli and to many others after him—that, apart from special and exceptional circumstances, that is the system that yields the positively worst results among peoples of high cultural levels. It is the one that develops most readily in the military class the tendency to oppress other classes, while it deprives the latter of any chance of effective resistance and strips them of any protection.

CHAPTER IV

RULING CLASS AND SOCIAL TYPE

1. We have just seen that every social type has a tendency to concentrate into a single political organism. We must now add that the political organism, in expanding, almost always aims at spreading its own social type, and often succeeds in doing so.

We find this aspiration in remotest antiquity. It was satisfied in very early days by gross, violent and barbarous means, which were, however, effective. The Assyrians were accustomed to transplant conquered peoples. Torn by force from their native soils, these were scattered about among groups that were Assyrian in spirit and nationality, and in the end were absorbed by them.[1] Assyrian colonists were often settled in their turn in conquered territories. The Incas of Peru were likewise given to transplanting en masse the savage tribes they conquered, the more readily to tame them to Peruvian ways and assimilate them to the other subjects of the Son of the Sun. In the Middle Ages, after wiping out the Saxons in large part, Charlemagne transferred numerous colonies of Franks to their lands, and the district thus settled afterward came to be called Franconia. Some centuries later the Teutonic Knights spread the German tongue and the Christian religion from the banks of the Elbe to the mouths of the Vistula and the Niemen by similar means—that is, by decimating the native populations and settling numerous German colonies on the conquered lands. The chief inspirer and executive of this policy of far-reaching colonization was the Grand Master Hermann von Salza.

Similar methods were used on occasion by the Romans, but not as a regular policy. For example, they were never applied to the highly civilized populations of the East, and even in Gaul, Spain and Britain the empire assimilated the barbarians principally by establishing the Latin language and Roman law and

---

[1] As must have happened, in large part, to the flower of the Ten Tribes of Israel, which were transported beyond the Euphrates.

spreading Greco-Latin literature and learning—in short, by extending the benefits of an admirably organized public administration and a superior civilization.[1]

On the whole, religious propaganda and the offering of a higher level of culture are the most effective means of assimilating subject peoples. By those means Mexico, Peru and many other countries in South America took the imprint of Spanish and Portuguese civilization in the course of a few centuries, though the populations of those countries were to remain largely non-Iberian in blood.

2. But oftentimes a differing social type will survive, for some centuries at least, in spite of the fact that the hegemony or dominion of a conquering people weighs heavily upon the elements that belong to it. In the ancient Persian empire the fire-worshiping Medo-Persians were in the ascendant. Their sovereign was King of Kings and commanded all other sovereigns within his vast empire. But the subject populations, ruled by satraps or even by their old native dynasties, kept their beliefs, habits and customs intact. They did not forsake their own social type in favor of the Medo-Persian type. In the case of certain tribes, which lived in the very middle of the empire but were protected by their warlike habits and by the natural strength of their positions, subjection was more apparent than real. The fact appears very clearly from Xenophon's account of the retreat of the Ten Thousand—for instance, the stories of Syennesis, king of Cilicia, and of the march through the lands of the Karduchians, the Mosynaecians and other peoples along the south shore of the Black Sea. In spite of this the court of Susa was able to rule a huge straggling empire for almost two centuries, and from the end of the reign of Darius, son of Hystaspes, down to the invasion of Alexander the Great there were no very troublesome rebellions, except possibly in Egypt. One should note, however, that the empire crumbled at the first fairly serious shock. There was no real cohesion between the subject and the dominant peoples, nor were their social forces unified and cemented by sound administrative and military systems. The neo-Persian empire of the Sassanids was much smaller than the old, but the peoples within it were held together in common brotherhood by the teachings

[1] Mommsen, *The Provinces of the Roman Empire.*

of the Avesta. It rode out more violent storms than the old Persian empire had suffered, and more numerous ones. It lasted for more than four centuries.

We find differing social types existing side by side even in modern states. Turkish cities used to have their Greek, Armenian and Jewish quarters, and in the Balkan country Osmanli villages often adjoined Greek and Bulgarian villages. In India, Brahmans, Mohammedans, Parsees and Europeans live side by side. One peculiar thing about the Orient, indeed, is that it seems to be a sort of museum for collecting and preserving the loose ends and tags of social types that are elsewhere absorbed and vanish. This comes about either because the governments of the Orient possess fewer social forces, and therefore less power of assimilation, than European states, or else because there is more real tolerance in the East than there is among us. One need only recall how completely the many prosperous Mohammedan colonies in Sicily and Spain vanished within a century or so after losing their political dominion. More recently, in the Balkan Peninsula, the moment a country escaped from the sultan's rule, its Mohammedan population dwindled rapidly and sometimes disappeared altogether.

When a state is made up of a mixture of social types, the ruling class should be recruited almost entirely from the dominant type; and if that rule is not observed, because the dominant type is too weak either in numbers or in moral and intellectual energies, then the country may be looked upon as a sick country that stands on the brink of serious political upheavals.

This was the case in the Turkey of the sultan during the century just past. On coming into intimate contact, and into conflicts of interests, with European civilization, Turkey had to use large numbers of Greeks, Armenians and even Europeans in her ruling class. Now, as has been soundly observed, that policy provided her with some of the resources of a superior civilization; but it deprived the Turkish ruling class of much of its savage vigor, and in fact did not save the sultan from losing considerable portions of his territory. In India, the British conquerors have so far been vastly superior to the Hindus in civilization, but being few in number, they are accepting the assistance of natives in public administration, in the courts and in the army. If the share assigned to these native elements in public functions becomes so large as to make it possible to dispense with Europeans, it is doubtful whether European rule can very long endure in that country.

When a number of differing social types are mixed together in one state, a directing, if not strictly a ruling, class almost inevitably develops within the types that are in subjection. Sometimes this class is the first to be absorbed by the ruling type. The Gallic aristocracy, for instance, became rapidly Romanized. It acquired the classical and juridical culture of the Latins within a few generations and was soon clamoring for Roman citizenship, which was readily granted. So, after the battle of Kossovo, the begs of Bosnia went over to Islamism in order to save their possessions and avoid dropping to the level of the downtrodden raias. But the aristocracies in question in both these cases had no great culture and, more important still, they were not heirs to any particular memories of an ancient and glorious national past. More often, traditions of an ancient greatness, a sense of group superiority, along with an instinctive repugnance to the intruding social type, are strong enough to overcome personal interests, and then the upper strata in the vanquished classes become the most unassimilable element. Members of the noble Fanariot families in Constantinople have rarely been known to accept conversion to Islamism. The Copts of today follow professions as scribes and public clerks and seem to descend in a direct line from the lettered class which made up the aristocracy in ancient Egypt. They remain Christian, though the mass of peasants, or fellahin, have been Mohammedans for centuries. The Ghebers of today, who still maintain fire worship, seem to descend from the old Persian aristocracy. In India the highest castes have supplied fewest converts to Islamism.

3. Now we come to a social phenomenon that is less apparent to the eye but is perhaps more important. The case where several social types coexist in guises more or less masked within a single political organism may be noted in countries that present all the appearances of strong social unity. This situation arises whenever the political formula, on which the ruling class in a given society bases its dominion, is not accessible to the lower classes, or when the complex of beliefs and moral and philosophical principles that underlie the formula have not sunk deeply enough

into the consciousness of the more populous and less well educated strata of society. The same thing occurs when there is any considerable difference between the customs, culture and habits of the ruling class and those of the governed classes.

A few examples will make this clearer. In Rome and ancient Greece the slave was kept wholly outside the "city," considered as a political body, a moral community. He did not share in the national education. He was not co-interested either materially or spiritually in the welfare of the state. The Indian pariah is regarded as outside every caste. He is not allowed even to have the same gods as his oppressors. Isolated completely from the rest of the population, he represents a class of individuals that is spiritually alien to the social type within which it lives. The Hebrews, on the other hand, and other peoples of the ancient Orient, regarded the laborer and the slave, once they had been, so to say, nationalized, as sharers in the sentiments of the society to which they belonged. The idea of carefully cultivating the sentiments, beliefs and customs of the lower classes by suitable catechization was one of the great merits of Christianity and Islamism. These religions have been more or less effectively imitated in that respect by modern European nations.

As a rule it is the very ancient political formulas, complexes of beliefs and sentiments which have the sanction of the ages, that succeed in making their way into the lowest strata of human societies. On the other hand, when rapid flows of ideas agitate the higher classes, or the more active intellectual centers, which are generally located in large cities, the lower classes and the outlying districts of a state are likely to be left behind, and differing social types tend to form inside the society.

Greater or lesser spiritual unity among all social classes explains the strength or weakness that political organisms exhibit at certain moments. However grievously the governing class in Turkey may have sinned on the side of corruption, inefficiency and negligence—army, navy, and finance were completely disorganized in the domains of the Sublime Porte—nevertheless, at certain definite moments, when the Crescent seemed to be in danger, the Turkish people displayed a fierce energy that gave pause to Europe's strongest military states. The reason was that the poor nizam, ragged and barefoot, who fearlessly went to his death in a trench, the redif who left his hut at the sultan's summons, really felt the political formula which they were called upon to serve and stood ready to give their last para and even their lives to support it. The Turkish peasants in Rumelia and Anatolia believed sincerely and deeply in Islam, in the Prophet, in the sultan as the Prophet's vicar, and the beliefs for which they were asked to make the utmost sacrifices were the beliefs that ordinarily filled their lives and made up their moral and intellectual worlds.

This analysis bears on events prior to 1895, yet we cannot see that they require any great modification in the light of the events of 1912–1913, or the events connected with the World War or the rise of Kemal Atatürk. The Turkish disasters in the Balkan and World Wars were due to the disorganization and incapacity of the Turkish ruling class, intensified by thirty years of Hamidian despotism and by four years of rule by the Young Turks. But in the World War, Kut-el-Amara showed that the Turkish soldier could fight and die for the faith that was in him; and we say nothing of the tremendous Turkish uprising of 1920 that over-threw the Treaty of Sèvres, swept the Greeks from Asia Minor and set up the present Angora regime.

In spite of the talents of men like Kutuzov, Barclay de Tolly, Benningsen, Doktorov and Bagration, no one can deny that the average training and capacity of the Russian generals with whom Napoleon had to deal was decidely inferior to Austrian or Prussian standards. The famous Suvarov knew his Russian soldier well and had a way of leading him to the most daring enterprise. But Suvarov was after all a courageous leader rather than an able one. The Russian soldier was the adversary that Napoleon most feared. In the famous Moscow campaign the failure of the invading army was caused not so much by cold, hunger or desertion as by the hatred that gathered about the French and harried them from Vitebsk on—in other words, from the time they entered strictly Russian territory. It was this hatred that inspired the sinister fury of the Russians to the point of destroying all provisions along the path of the enemy and burning all towns and villages between Smolensk and Moscow. It gave Rostopchin the courage to burn Moscow itself. For the Russian muzhik God, the czar, Holy Russia, formed an integral unit in the beliefs and sentiments that he had begun to absorb on the day of his birth and which he had learned by home tradition to revere.

This same moral unity holds the secret of other successful and quasi-miraculous cases of resistance, just as lack of it yields the secret of certain shameful demonstrations of weakness. The Vendée was strong in the wars of the Revolution because nobles, priests and peasants had the same beliefs, the same desires, the same passions. Spain was strong in 1808 because the Spanish grandee and the lowliest Spanish shepherd were alike filled with hatred for the French invader (whom they regarded as a godless unbeliever), with loyalty to their sovereign, with pride in being a self-respecting, independent nation. This unanimity of sentiment, in spite of the incapacity of the Spanish generals and the utter worthlessness of the Spanish regular armies, accounts for the miracles of Saragossa and Tarragona and for the final victory that crowned the Spanish wars for independence. Never would the most ragged peasant consent, under whatever threat, to show the roads to the French. The regular Spanish army was composed largely of raw recruits and it had no experienced officers. Its ineffectualness is attested not only by French writers but by letters of the Duke of Wellington and other English officers.[1] On the other hand, Spain showed the utmost weakness during the French Legitimist invasion of 1822. At that time only a small portion of the upper classes had any comprehension of, or devotion to, the principle of constitutional monarchy which was at issue. That principle was incomprehensible to the majority of the upper classes and to the vast bulk of the nation.

The kingdom of Naples showed weakness in the years 1798 and 1799 in spite of many acts of desperate valor on the part of individuals or groups. The mass of the population, to be sure, and a majority of the middle and upper classes hated the French Jacobins and revolutionary ideas in general. They were fanatically loyal to the legitimate monarchy and still more so to the Catholic faith. However, a small minority in the upper classes, scant in number but strong in intelligence, enthusiasm and daring, despised the sentiments of their fellow countrymen and had warm sympathies for the French gospel of freedom. Trea-

---

[1] See the histories of Thiers (book XLVI, vol. XV) and Toreno, and the *Mémoires militaires* of Colonel Vigo de Roussillon.

son, therefore and, more than treason, the unending suspicion of treason, paralyzed all resistance, disorganized the regular army, which was a poor army to begin with, and diminished the effectiveness of a spontaneous popular resistance which, save for treasonable understandings, real or imagined, with the invaders, might have triumphed. As is well known, Championnet's army had halted before Capua but was invited and encouraged by the Neapolitan republicans to attack Naples. This attack would not have been made, and in any case would probably have failed, had it not been for the treasonable surrender of Castel Sant' Elmo and a rear attack on the defenders of the Capuan gate—both acts by Neapolitan republicans. Those acts explain the terrible reprisals, not only royal but popular, that followed the collapse of the ephemeral Parthenopean Republic.

4. So far we have been thinking largely of differences in religious and political beliefs between the various social strata; but disparities in intellectual cultivation and differences in language, habits and family customs also have their importance.

We are accustomed to taking for granted the distinctions that exist between the class that has received a polished literary and scientific education and the classes that have received none at all or have stopped at the first rudiments—between the "social set" that has the habits and manners of good breeding and the populous throngs that lack good breeding. We readily assume, therefore, that the same distinctions exist, equally sharp and equally thoroughgoing, in all human societies and have always existed in our own countries. That is not at all the case. In the Mohammedan East no such distinctions appear, or if they do, they are infinitely less conspicuous than they are among us.[1] In Russia the profound difference between the class called the "intelligentsia" and the muzhiks, or between those same "intellectuals" and the long-bearded merchants that were so frequently to be seen in the days of the czar, could not have existed in the age of Peter the Great, when there were no universities—the boyars of that day were almost as crude and unlettered as the peasants. Even in western Europe hardly more than two cen-

---

[1] This fact, which is attested by Renan and other writers, is obvious to anyone who has had any experience at all with Mohammedan societies and Mohammedan culture.

turies ago, disparities among the various social classes in intellectual cultivation and in public and private manners were far less striking than they are today.   Such disparities have grown more and more marked, but the trend dates from not earlier than the eighteenth and nineteenth centuries.   In France, for example, Voltaire declares,[1] that when Louis XIV actually assumed the throne, in 1660, the French nobility were rich in natural intelligence but ignorant and crude in manners.   In England, toward the end of the eighteenth century, Cobbett pointed to the difference between the farmers of the good old days—that is, when he was a boy—and those of the time when he was writing. Formerly, he says, farmers had lodged and fed all their peasants, sat with them at their great oaken boards and, after a prayer from the curate, drunk the same beer.   Then customs changed. The wage earner drew his pay and went to eat his meal alone in some tavern.   The farmer became a "gentleman," using glass bottles, ebony-handled forks, ivory-handled knives and porcelain dishes.   His sons would, if necessary, be clerks, copyists, shopboys, but in no case farmers.

A similar change has taken place during the last hundred and fifty years among the landlords, great and small, of Sicily and the district of Naples.   Their great-grandfathers may have been rich but in any case they were peasants.   Now, they may be poor but in any case they are gentlemen—they are *galantuomini* (the term *galantuomo* in the local dialects means a person of quality, of polite up-bringing).   Strange as it may seem at first glance, the trend here in question coincides with the birth and growth of that current of ideas and sentiments which generally goes by the name of democracy, and it constitutes one of the more curious contrasts between the democratic theories that are now so generally in vogue and their practical application.

Disparities in upbringing among the various social classes are likely to become more marked in bureaucratized societies.   In societies of feudal type the individual members of the ruling class are generally sprinkled about among their followers.   They live in constant contact with them and have to be, in a sense, their natural leaders.   It may seem surprising that in the Middle Ages, when the baron stood alone in the midst of his vassals and dealt with them harshly, they did not take advantage of their

[1] *Siècle de Louis XIV.*

numerical superiority to break free.   But actually that could not always have been an easy matter.   Superior as they may have been in energy and in familiarity with arms to the rest of the subject elements, the vassals were more or less bound to the lot of their lords.   But, independently of that, another consideration of very great importance must not be overlooked.   The baron knew his vassals personally.   He thought and felt as they did.   He had the same superstitions, the same habits, the same language.   He was their master, harsh sometimes and arbitrary. For all of that, he was a man whom they understood perfectly, in whose conversation they could share, at whose table, be it in a humbler station, they often sat, and with whom they sometimes got drunk.   It requires utter ignorance of the psychology of the lower classes not to see at once how many things this real familiarity, based on an identical education, or lack of education if one prefer, enables an inferior to endure and forgive.   It may be objected that as a rule the poor dislike serving the newly rich. That is true, but other elements have to be taken into account in this regard.   In the first place the man of recent wealth is likely to be envied.   Then again he is often harder and greedier than the man who has been accustomed to ease from birth.   Finally, instead of maintaining a community of habits and sentiments with the class from which he has sprung, the upstart almost always does his best to adopt the ways and manners of the higher class.   His chief ambition and concern, usually, is to make people forget his origins.

In the Middle Ages the first peasant revolts broke out not when feudalism was harshest but when the nobles had learned to associate with one another, when the courts of love—a conscious quest of good manners (the *gai saber*)—had begun to give them polish and alienate them from the rustic ways of the lonely castle. Mickiewicz makes an important observation in this connection. He finds that the Polish nobles were popular with the peasants as long as they lived in their midst.   The peasants would suffer the very bread to be snatched from their mouths that their lord might buy horses and costly weapons for hunting and for sabering Turks and Russians.   Then French education gained a foothold among the Polish nobles.   They learned how to give balls after the manner of Versailles and began spending their time in learning to dance the minuet.   From that day on peasantry and nobility became two peoples apart, and the peasants did not support the nobles with any great effectiveness in the wars they fought with foreigners late in the eighteenth century.[1]

So it was with the Celtic aristocracy in Ireland. According to Macaulay and other historians, the ancient nobility of the "O's" and the "Mc's" was very popular with the peasants, whose labors supplied the head of the clan with such luxury as his coarse and abundant table could boast and whose daughters were sometimes levied for his rustic harem. But such nobles were looked upon virtually as members of the family. They were one with the peasants, it was thought, in blood. They certainly were one with them in habits and ideas. On the other hand, the English landlord, who supplanted the Irish, was probably a gentler sort of person, and he was beyond any doubt more law-abiding and more scrupulous in his demands. All the same he was bitterly hated. He was a stranger in language, religion and habits. He lived far away, and even when he resided on his properties he had by tradition acquired the habit of keeping to himself, having no contacts whatever with his dependents except such as were strictly necessary to the relation of master and servant.

A follower of Gumplowicz might observe that in the case of Ireland the hatred that arose between landowners and peasants could be due to differences in race—to the Celt's finding himself face to face with the Saxon, to use one of O'Connell's favorite expressions. But, the fact is, the first Anglo-Norman families that settled in Ireland during the Middle Ages, for example the Talbots or Fitzgeralds, lived long in that country, ended by adopting Celtic ways, and fought in the ranks of the Irish against the English in the various insurrections.

But suppose we consider, rather, what happened in czarist Russia. There, certainly, there were no important racial differences between nobles and peasants, but there were great differences in social type and especially in manners. The cultured class, poor or rich as it may have been, had adopted European education. The rest of the population clung, as it still clings, to Asiatic ideas and customs. Tchernishevski, a Russian revolutionary of the 90's, says, referring to the possibility of a peasant revolt:

[1] *Histoire populaire de Pologne.*

Ignorant, full of gross prejudices, and blindly hating all who have forsaken primitive Russian ways [antipathy springing from differences in social type], the people would make no distinction between individuals who dressed in German styles [who had abandoned the traditional Russian costume and were dressing in western European fashion]. It would treat them all alike, deferring neither to science, nor to poetry, nor to art. It would demolish our whole civilization.[1]

5. The fact is that the human being has sentiments which, taken individually, may be imponderable, hard to analyze and harder still to define, but which in sum are very powerful and may contribute to bringing on the most important social phenomena. The person who wrote that the human being lets himself be guided by self-interest alone stated a general maxim that is almost entirely devoid of practical value, since it can tell us nothing save at the cost of exceedingly minute analyses and distinctions. Anyone who thinks that interest has to be something that can be expressed materially in terms of money and measured in pounds and pence is a person of too little heart and too little head to understand the people about him. Interest is suited in each individual to the individual's own tastes, and each individual interprets his interest in his own individual way. For many people, to satisfy their pride, their sense of personal dignity, their vanities great and small, to humor their personal caprices and rancors, is worth far more than pleasures that are purely material. We must not forget such things, especially when we set out to analyze the relations between rich and poor, between superiors and inferiors, or, in short, between different social classes. When the elementary needs of life are to an extent satisfied, what mostly contributes to creating and maintaining friction and ill feeling between the various social classes is not so much differences in the enjoyment of material pleasures as membership in two different environments. For a part of the lower classes, at least, more bitter by far than any physical privation is the existence of a higher world from which they are excluded. No law, no hereditary privilege, forbids them to enter that world. It is roped off from them by a silken thread of the subtlest fiber—a difference in education, in manners, in social habits. Only with difficulty is that thread ever broken.

[1] Leroy-Beaulieu, *L'Empire des tzars et les Russes*, vol. II, pp. 524 f.

Over and over again since very ancient times it has been written that in every city and in every state there are two hostile populations that stand ever on the alert to harm each other—the rich and the poor. Now that dictum does not appear to us to possess an unqualified, much less a universal, applicability. What we have just said may serve to explain the many exceptions and reservations that must accompany its acceptance. As a rule, the poor follow the lead of the rich, or rather the classes that are ruled follow the lead of the ruling classes, whenever they are imbued with the same opinions and beliefs and have been trained to intellectual and moral backgrounds that are not too dissimilar. The plebs, moreover, is a loyal associate of the upper classes in wars against foreigners, when the enemy belongs to a social type so alien as to arouse repugnance in rich and poor alike. So in Spain in 1808, and in the Vendée during the Revolution, peasants and nobles fought side by side, and the peasants never took advantage of the disorder, of the lawlessness, to plunder the houses of the nobles. One may doubt whether there is a single example of the poorer classes in a Christian country rising to support a Mohammedan invasion—much less of the poorer classes in a Mohammedan country rising in support of a Christian invasion.

Social democracy in central and western Europe professes indifference to the concept of nationality, and proclaims the alliance of the proletarians of all countries against the capitalists of the whole world. Those theories might have a certain practical efficacy in the event of a war between the Germans and the French, or between the Italians and the English, since all these nations belong to approximately the same social type. But if it were a question of repelling a serious Tatar or Chinese invasion, or merely a Turkish or Russian invasion, we believe that the great majority of proletarians, even in countries where they are most strongly imbued with doctrines of world-wide collectivism, would eagerly cooperate with the ruling classes.[1]

Anyone who has done any great amount of traveling must have been struck by a fact that is not without significance. Very often the poor of different countries, as well, for that matter, as the rich of different countries, more readily fraternize than the rich and

[1] In the United States, Negroes, and especially Chinese, are generally excluded from labor unions.

poor of the same country.   To be strictly exact one should note
that at the present time "cosmopolitanism" is much more
strikingly characteristic of one element in the ruling class—the
element that has the greatest wealth and the greatest leisure—
than it is of the poor.   But this cosmopolitan fraternizing arises
only so long as peoples of approximately similar customs are concerned.   If they go to faraway lands where ideas and ways are
altogether new, the rich and the poor of one country, or even of
merely neighboring countries, feel more closely drawn to each
other than to foreigners of their own class.   That is the case with
Europeans in India and China, and in general in all countries
where the civilization is markedly different from the European.
All this is just another way of saying that sooner or later a point
is reached where difference in social type as between members of
different countries becomes greater than difference in social type
as between classes in the same country.

6. Psychological and intellectual isolation on the part of the
lower classes, as well as too noticeable differences in beliefs and
education between the various social classes, give rise to social
phenomena that are very interesting to the student of the political
sciences, dangerous as they may be to the societies in which they
occur.

In the first place, as a consequence of their isolation, within
the lower classes another ruling class, or directing minority,
necessarily forms, and often this new class is antagonistic to the
class that holds possession of the legal government.[1]   When this
class of plebeian leaders is well organized it may seriously embar-
rass an official government.   In many Catholic countries the
clergy is still the only authority that exerts any moral influence
over the peasantry, and the peasants extend to the parish priest
all the confidence that they withhold from the government
official.   In other countries, where the people look upon the public
functionary and the nobleman if not exactly as enemies certainly
as utter strangers, the more resolute and aggressive of the plebeians sometimes succeed in organizing widespread and fairly
permanent associations, which levy assessments, administer a

---

[1] This phenomenon is something like the one we observed earlier in this
chapter (§2, last paragraph) in speaking of countries where differing social types,
in the strict sense of the expression, exist side by side.

special justice of their own and have their own hierarchies of officials, their own leaders, their own recognized institutions. So a real state within the state comes into being, a government that is clandestine but often more feared, better obeyed, and if not better loved certainly better understood, than the legal government.

In the second place, whenever and wherever a section of the ruling class tries to overthrow the legal government, whether because of conversion to a new political formula or for some other reason, it always seeks the support of the lower classes, and these readily follow its lead when they are hostile or indifferent to the established order. This alliance is so often struck that the plebs becomes an essential instrument in almost all upheavals and revolutions, and to the same alliance also is due the fact that we so often find men from the higher social levels leading popular movements. Yet the opposite phenomenon also appears at times. The portion of the ruling class that is holding power and resisting the revolutionary current may find its main support in the lower classes, which still cling loyally to old ideas and to the old social type. That was the situation in Spain in 1822 and down to 1830, and so it was with the Kingdom of Naples in 1799 and more or less down to 1860. In such cases there may be periods of government by an ignorant, inept and vulgar demagoguery which someone thought of defining as "the negation of God."

But the most dangerous among the consequences that may result from differences in social type between the various social classes, and from the reciprocal isolation of classes that necessarily follows in their wake, is a decline in energy in the upper classes, which grow poorer and poorer in bold and aggressive characters and richer and richer in "soft," remissive individuals. We have seen that that development is practically impossible in a state of the feudal type. In a society that is broken up into virtually independent fragments the heads of the individual groups have to be energetic, resourceful men. Their supremacy in large measure depends on their own physical or moral strength, which, moreover, they are continually exercising in struggles with their immediate neighbors. As social organization progresses and the governing class begins to reap the benefits of an improved bureaucratic machine, its superiority in culture and wealth, and especially its better organization and firmer cohesion, may compensate to some extent for the lack of individual energy; and so it may come about that considerable portions of the governing class, especially the circles that give the society its intellectual tone and direction, lose the habit of dealing with people of the lower classes and commanding them directly. This state of affairs generally enables frivolousness, and a sort of culture that is wholly abstract and conventional, to supplant a vivid sense of realities and a sound and accurate knowledge of human nature. Thinking loses virility. Sentimental and exaggeratedly humanitarian theories come to the fore, theories that proclaim the innate goodness of men, especially when they are not spoiled by civilization, or theories that uphold the absolute preferableness, in the arts of government, of gentle and persuasive means to severe authoritarian measures. People imagine, as Taine puts it, that since social life has flowed blandly and smoothly on for centuries, like an impetuous river confined within sturdy dikes, the dikes have become superfluous and can readily be dispensed with, now that the river has learned its lesson.

Tacitus described Germanic customs as eminently simple, frugal and virtuous. More than three centuries later, during the barbarian invasions, Salvian of Marseilles attributed the victories of the Goths, Vandals, Franks and other barbarians, to their moral superiority. According to Salvian, the invaders were chaste, temperate, truth-telling, whereas the Romans, and especially the upper classes among the Romans, were fornicators, drunkards and liars. In describing the manners and customs of the Germans of his day Machiavelli evidently wrote under the influence of Tacitus. In the course of the last two centuries, many philosophers have raised paeans to the holiness of savage morals and to the rustic simplicity of the plain, untutored man. It would seem therefore that there is a frequent, if not a universal, tendency in very mature civilizations, where ruling classes have acquired highly refined literary cultures, to wax enthusiastic, by a sort of antithesis, over the simple ways of savages, barbarians and peasants (the case of Arcadia!), and to clothe them with all sorts of virtues and sentiments that are as stereotyped as they are imaginary. Invariably underlying all such tendencies is the concept that was so aptly phrased by Rousseau, that man is good by nature but spoiled by society and civilization. This notion has had a very great influence on political thinking during the past hundred and fifty years.

A ruling class is the more prone to fall into errors of this kind the more closed it is, actually if not legally, to elements rising from the lower classes. In the lower classes the hard necessities of life, the unending and carking scramble for bread, the lack of literary culture, keep the primordial instincts of struggle and the unfailing ruggedness of human nature, alive. In any case, whether or not the factor of intellectual and moral isolation is reinforced by this factor of, so to say, personal isolation, certain it is that when the ruling class has degenerated in the manner described, it loses its ability to provide against its own dangers and against those of the society that has the misfortune to be guided by it. So the state crashes at the first appreciable shock from the outside foe. Those who govern are unable to deal with the least flurry; and the changes that a strong and intelligent ruling class would have carried out at a negligible cost in wealth. blood and human dignity take on the proportions of a social cataclysm.

One should note, as an example, that in the course of the nineteenth century England adopted peacefully and without violent shocks almost all the basic civil and political reforms that France paid so heavily to achieve through the great Revolution. Undeniably, the great advantage of England lay in the greater energy, the greater practical wisdom, the better political training, that her ruling class possessed down to the very end of the past century.

CHAPTER V
JURIDICAL DEFENSE

1. We might very well dispense with defining the moral sense. It is something that we all feel and understand without a definite, carefully qualified formula to describe it. Generally, however, the phrase is taken to mean that mass of sentiments by which the natural propensity of human beings to develop their activities and capacities, to satisfy their appetites and impulses, to command and enjoy, is curbed by a natural compassion for the pain or harm that other people may experience from an indulgence of that propensity. Sometimes such sentiments are carried to a point where the spiritual satisfaction one derives from procuring pleasure or advantage for another is greater than the material satisfaction one derives from providing for one's own pleasure.

When our limiting the satisfaction of our impulses at the cost of another's sacrifice rests on sentiments of affection for people who are close and dear to us, it is said to be based on "sympathy." When it is inspired solely by the respect that is due to other men, even strangers or enemies, simply because they are men, we get a sentiment that is far more delicate and not so generally felt by people—the sentiment of "justice." Idealizations and exaggerations of these moral sentiments are crystallized in the well-known formulas, "Love thy neighbor as thyself," "Do unto others as you would that they should do unto you." These maxims, however, express an aspiration to a moral perfection that can never be attained rather than a practical counsel that is applicable in real life. Save for exceptions that arise almost exclusively in connection with parental love, each individual is better qualified than anyone else to look out for himself; and if he is to look out for himself effectively he must love himself a little more than he loves others and deal with them otherwise than he deals with himself. One might well feel that all these cautions on our part were hardly required, for the fact is that, apart from some exceptional moment or some exceptional individual, people have never taken the maxims mentioned seriously.

The question as to whether the moral sense is progressive or stationary has been much debated. As is well known, Buckle, a distinguished English writer of the past century, observed that the purest and loftiest ethical principles had been known and proclaimed in remotely ancient times, and he therefore maintained that progress in human societies is almost exclusively intellectual and scientific, never moral.[1] The much followed evolutionist school of our day reaches essentially different conclusions. According to the evolutionists the moral sense can, and must, continually progress in view of the struggle for existence, which selects for survival in every society the individuals who are richest in altruistic sentiments, these being the sentiments that best serve the interests of the social body. In the struggle for existence between different societies victory regularly goes to societies in which the same altruistic sentiments are, on the average, strongest.[2]

We had better examine these two doctrines briefly, just to show that neither of them can be taken as a basis for scientific conclusions. Suppose we begin with the second, which has so far won wider acceptance.

2. We have already proved to our own satisfaction (chap. I, §13) that, in a society that has attained any degree of civilization at all, the struggle between individuals is not a struggle for existence but a struggle for preeminence. But even ignoring that, we find altogether paradoxical the principle that is proclaimed by these self-styled positivists, to the effect that within every social group those individuals who are most moral and therefore most highly endowed with altruistic sentiments are the ones who are destined to survive (in our terms, to attain the highest social rankings). All that we can grant in that regard— and we grant it very willingly—is that an individual who is particularly deficient in moral sense, and is unable to conceal his propensities sufficiently, will have to overcome greater difficulties than others because of the antipathy and repugnance that he will generally inspire. But as far as that goes, an individual who has an unusually delicate moral sense will be at a disadvantage that is

---

[1] *History of Civilization in England*, vol. I, chap. IV ("Comparison between Moral and Intellectual Laws").

[2] See Letourneau, *Évolution de la morale*, chap. I, §15.

almost as serious. In all the dealings, great or small, of life, he will find himself fighting with altogether inferior weapons. Most men will use against him tricks that he will be thoroughly familiar with but will be careful not to use; and he will certainly suffer far greater damage from that fact than the sly rascal who knows just where to stop in his crookedness will ever suffer from the ill-will that he arouses about him. Really, one may be good almost unconsciously through a natural simplicity of character, or one may be consciously good through magnanimity of purpose, high resolve, unconquerable aversion to evil, inflexible integrity of character; but certainly one could never become good from believing that by being good one could more easily realize one's aims, or achieve what is commonly called success in life. Utilitarianism interpreted in that sense, as the basis of morality, could only be, to speak quite plainly, the maneuver of a hypocrite or the dream of a fool.

It follows that, in all societies, so-called evolution, the selection of the best, ought to eventuate in a perpetuation and multiplication of individuals of average morality, who are, in literal fact, the best adapted to what is called the struggle for existence. Survival, or, as we consider it more accurate to say, preeminence, ought preferably to await those characters who, in whatever sort of social environment, represent a moral mean of the most highly refined gold. And yet the evolutionary theory does not seem to become acceptable even with that basic emendation, since it assumes in any event that the moral element is always the main factor in the success or failure of an individual in achieving the aims that he sets out to achieve in life. In practice things do not work out that way at all. To say nothing of the influence of chance, which is far greater than is commonly supposed, the possession in greater or lesser degree of certain intellectual qualities, such as readiness of perception and keenness of observation, figures very considerably in the decision as to whether a man is to reach the higher ranks in his society or is to stay in the lower. But there is the very great influence also of other qualities, which depend upon the individual's temperament, without being, strictly speaking, either intellectual or moral—such qualities as tenacity of purpose, self-confidence and, above all, *activity*. If we set out to judge whether an individual will or will not get on in life—whatever the type of society—we find that we cannot use any single criterion, to be sure, but that if we would keep an eye on the main factor, we must watch and see whether he is *active*, and whether he knows how to make good use of his activity.

Apart from brief periods of violent revolution, personal qualities are always less important, as regards attaining the highest positions in life, than birth or family. In any type of society, whether ostensibly democratic or otherwise, being born to a high station is one of the best claims a person can have to staying there. Families that have occupied the highest levels in the social scale for a number of generations often lack the qualities that are best fitted to carry a man from the bottom to the top, while they possess very different qualities in abundance. Except in unusual cases that are due to careful education, old aristocratic families are not distinguished for activity. At the same time a real refinement of the moral sense may be detected in persons who have not had to fight fierce, shady, and often degrading battles in order to reach the top. In a word, the virtues and defects that help a plebeian to force the gates of an aristocracy are something very different from the virtues and defects of aristocrats themselves.

We can accept as true only one portion of the selectionist theory. One may safely grant that, other things being equal, in a struggle between two societies that society will triumph in which the individual members are on the average better equipped in moral sense and therefore more united, more trustful of each other and more capable of self-sacrifice. But that exception hurts the evolutionary thesis as a whole more than it helps it. If, in a given society, a higher average of moral sense cannot be explained by any survival of the best individuals, then, granting that the higher average is there, it can be ascribed only to the better organization of the society—to causes, in other words, that are historical in nature and that are the worst enemies of those who try to explain social phenomena primarily by changes in the individual organism or in the individual "psyche."

3. Though Buckle's theories are not as widely at variance with our point of view as the above, we feel unable to accept them without modifying or at least supplementing them to some extent. It is of course true that in very ancient societies we find maxims and laws that denote an exquisite moral sense. In the

ancient Egyptian Book of the Dead, for instance, especially in parts of it that go back to a very remote antiquity, precepts very similar to the Ten Commandments are to be found[1]; and papyri dating from the twelfth dynasty contain moral principles that are as good as anything in Christian or Buddhist ethics. The Platonists and the Stoics in the Greco-Roman world and the Essenes in the Hebrew world represented very high levels of morality, and numerous traces of the same ethics can easily be noted in Chinese, Indian and Persian civilizations long anterior to the Christian era. But though the precepts in question go back to very remote times, they were formulated and accepted by peoples who had very ancient civilizations, and whose moral sense, therefore, had undergone a long-protracted elaboration. Indeed, if any comparison is possible between the morality of a primitive tribe and the ethical system of a relatively civilized people that has been organized for long ages in great and populous political organisms, it is the comparison that can be made between the ethical systems of a child and an adult. The former is unconscious, the latter conscious. In the former good and bad impulses are roughly sketched. In the latter we find them fully developed and mature. Child and savage alike may do evil, and great evil, but in what they do blind animal impulse will always figure more largely than calculation and premeditation; and they may even do good without ever achieving that exquisite discrimination, that deliberate sacrifice of self, of which the adult human being and the civilized human being are capable.

Making due allowances, of course, ethical feeling in the crude person stands to ethical feeling in the well-bred person much as the sense of morality in the child or the savage stands to the ethical system of the adult or the civilized man. What we call delicacy of feeling is just the intuition of a higher morality applied to a greater number of social relationships. European travelers in the interior of Africa have, in general, found the Arab adventurers who foregather there preferable to the native Negroes. That is understandable. The Arabs are heirs to an ancient civilization. Though they are perfectly capable of treachery, theft and murder, they can, when they choose, assume the manners of gentlemen. They have some conception at least of a morality that is higher, and so more like our own.

[1] Lenormant, Maspero.

But it is not only in greater refinement of moral and immoral impulses that civilized man differs from the savage. In societies of ancient culture that have for centuries enjoyed sound political organizations, the repression of immoral impulses—what some criminologists call the "inhibition" that curbs impulses—is unquestionably stronger and acquires all the force of inveterate habit. By a long and slow process of elaboration such societies gradually develop the institutions that enable a universal morality to curb the expression of individual immorality in a certain number of public and private relationships. When they are not under the sway of interests and passions, almost all individuals come to understand that a given act is not consistent with the sentiments of justice that prevail in the society in which they live. Still, the greater majority of individuals might commit that very act under stress of passion or at the bidding of an engrossing interest.

Now public opinion, religion, law, and the whole social mechanism that enforces observance of the law, are expressions of the mass conscience, which in the general case is dispassionate and disinterested as against the one, or the few, whose perception of what is just and honest is clouded at the given moment by the violence of selfish impulses. The judge is the instrument of the mass moral sense, which, case by case, curbs the passions and evil instincts of the individual and holds them in leash.

So in a highly developed civilization not only do moral instincts —and for that matter selfish passions—become more refined, more conscious, more perfect. In a society in which political organization has made great progress, moral discipline is itself unquestionably greater, and the too selfish acts that are inhibited, or obstructed, by the reciprocal surveillance and restraint of the individuals who compose the society are more numerous and more clearly defined. In every society, of course, there is a relatively small number of individuals who have tendencies that are definitely refractory to any sort of social discipline and, likewise, a certain number of individuals of superior scruples and soundly molded characters for whom any curb from without would be superfluous. But between these two extremes come the vast majority of men, who have average consciences, for whom fear of harm or punishment, and the fact that they are to be held responsible for their conduct by other people who are neither their accomplices nor their subordinates, serve as most effective means for overcoming the thousand temptations to transgress the moral law that everyday living offers.

The social mechanisms that regulate this disciplining of the moral sense constitute what we call "juridical defense" (respect for law, government by law). These mechanisms are not equally perfect in all societies. It may happen that a society that has advanced further than some other in the arts and sciences remains conspicuously inferior to that other in this respect. And it may also happen that juridical defense weakens and becomes less efficient in societies that are traversing periods of scientific and economic progress.[1] Great catastrophes, such as long wars or great revolutions, everywhere produce periods of social dissolution, when the disciplining of selfish impulses falters, when habits that have long curbed them break and when brutish instincts that have been dulled but not eradicated by long periods of peace and civilized living come to life again—for if greater culture has succeeded in veiling them it has also steeled and sharpened them.

So from time to time we see groups of adventurers from civilized countries, on coming into contact with barbarous peoples or peoples of a social type markedly different from theirs, feeling themselves loosed from ordinary moral restraints and perpetrating the sort of crimes that won infamy for the Spanish conquerors in America, and for Hastings and Clive in India. The tremendous excesses of the Thirty Years' War, or of the French Revolution and other civil wars, become explainable by reference to these same criteria.

Characteristic is the picture that Thucydides paints of the demoralization that fell upon Greece after the struggles between different cities, and the civil wars within individual cities, which took place during the Peloponnesian War. It is interesting to note that all social cataclysms that destroy moral discipline are followed by periods of relaxation in that discipline itself, so that the level of morals is reestablished but very gradually. Letourneau has well shown that intellectual progress is much more rapid among barbarians and savages than moral progress.[2] This

---

[1] In his article "Foules et sectes au point de vue criminel" Tarde expresses the opinion that of late there has been a real decline in morals in modern European society and that the decline is due to social causes.

[2] *La Sociologie d'après l'ethnographie.*

phenomenon is apparent in civilized societies as they emerge from periods of social disorganization. It is due to the fact that moral habits are established and reestablished very slowly, but it contributes to lending a semblance of truth to Buckle's doctrine, that the moral sense is absolutely stationary.

We have so far carefully avoided, it will be noted, any speculation as to the origins of the moral or altruistic instincts. For our purposes here, it is sufficient to observe that they are innate in man and necessary to social living. It will further be noted that our view is contrary to the doctrine of Rousseau, that man is good by nature but that society makes him wicked and perverse. We believe that social organization provides for the reciprocal restraint of human individuals by one another and so makes them better, not by destroying their wicked instincts, but by accustoming them to controlling their wicked instincts.

4. The chief peoples that have had histories, or are now making them, entrust the disciplining of the moral sense not to religion only but to the whole legislative system. In the early periods of all peoples the secular enactment and the religious precept go absolutely hand in hand, and the sanctions that uphold the one uphold the other also. That is the case even today in some societies. But in our time, in countries of European and Chinese civilization, secular or civil organization and religious organization are more or less distinctly separated, the religious organization becoming more effective according to the strength of the faith that it manages to inspire and maintain, whereas the secular organization bases its progress on its success in conforming to certain psychological tendencies.

It has long been debated whether the religious sanction, when taken apart from the political sanction, is more effective than the latter—whether, in other words, fear of hell is worth more in actual practice than fear of jail and the policeman. A definite answer, applicable to all the cases that might arise under the question, can hardly be given. Evidently a country in which political organization is slack and primitive while religious faith is ardent is in an essentially different situation from another country in which religious enthusiasms have deteriorated while political, administrative and judiciary systems have improved. Both religious precepts and secular laws emanate from the

collective moral sense that is indispensable to all human associations, and it is undeniable that all religions do have, as they
could hardly fail to have, some practical influence.   But there is
reason to fear, nevertheless, that the importance of religion can
easily be overestimated.   If religion were so important, it would
seem, for instance, that the moral difference between a Christian
people and an idolatrous people should be very considerable.
Now of course if we compare a civilized Christian people with a
barbarous, idolatrous people, the moral discrepancy is enormous;
but if we place side by side two peoples of the same degree of
barbarism, one of which has embraced Christianity and the other
not, it will be found that in practice their behaviors are very
much the same, or at least there is no appreciable difference
between them.   The modern Abyssinians are a living and notorious illustration of this fact.   Cardinal Massaja was a missionary
in Ethiopia for thirty-five years.   He testifies to the scant
practical influence of Christianity on the lives of the Abyssinians.[1]
If we compare the still pagan but politically well-organized
society of the age of Marcus Aurelius with the Christian but very
disorderly society that is described by Gregory of Tours, we very
much suspect that the parallel would prove to be favorable to the
former.

It is consistent with human nature that certain and speedy
punishment, however slight relatively, should be generally more
feared than a far severer punishment that is uncertain and remote.
For average consciences, at the moment when greed, lust or
vengefulness spurs them to theft, rape or murder, fear of prison
and the gallows is a more potent and, especially, a more certain
deterrent than the possibility of eternal torment.   If that is true
for great breaches of the moral law, which are committed only
in moments of violent passion, it is truer still of those petty
violations of the more obvious precepts of fairness and justice into
which human beings are misled by the daily pressures of petty
interests and little jealousies.   Is there a moral or religious law
that does not recognize that to pay one's debts is, on the whole,
a just and proper thing?   Yet one has to confess that many good
believers would fail to pay theirs, and would find a thousand
sophistries and pretenses to uphold their own consciences in
doing so, if they were not held to their obligations by public

[1] *I miei trentacinque anni di missione in Etiopia.*

disgrace and, above all, by the process server.   It takes no over-delicate conscience to understand that to pummel and beat another person is, at the very best, not a decorous thing to do; yet the habit of laying hands on one's neighbor in the moment of anger is effectively combatted in the masses only by the certainty that the man who deals a blow runs the chance of promptly receiving another in return and that the business may easily go farther than that.   As the weakest and most defenseless of human beings, women and children should be the ones most entitled to protection from the religious and moral sentiments; but we see only too regularly, alas, that in actual fact they are the most frequent victims of brutal physical assaults.   In very religious countries, where the lower classes are completely at the mercy of the higher, it is no unusual thing to see masters beating their servants or other subordinates.

Religious faith, like patriotic enthusiasms and political passions, may at moments of extraordinary exhilaration produce great currents of abnegation and self-sacrifice and spur the masses to acts and efforts which, to one considering man's ordinary nature only, seem almost superhuman.   Catholic jubilees and Protestant revivals furnish more than one example, and one might mention as characteristic the great wave of charity and brotherly love that swept over Umbria in the day of St. Francis of Assisi and a number of fleeting moments in the French Revolution and during the disturbances of '48 in Italy.

We are speaking here of collective, not individual, acts.   As regards the latter, cases where isolated individuals, or groups of individuals, give proof of extraordinary abnegation and complete self-sacrifice are not so very rare in any age, or in any civilized nation.   They come to the fore in every war and in every serious epidemic—on any occasion, in short, when it is desirable and necessary that someone suffer or face a danger in the interest of all.   On such occasions, just as a sublimation of virtue is to be seen in some individuals, so an exaggerated cowardice and self-ishness appears in others, who cast aside the mask they have been accustomed to wear the moment they are faced by a real danger and a real need of self-sacrifice.   It is equally true, of course, that just as the masses have occasional spasms of exalted abnegation and self-sacrifice, so they have feverish paroxysms of the base emotions—greed, lust for blood, panic.

But the capacity that certain sentiments have for exciting ephemeral periods of intoxication should not mislead one as to their actual efficacy in the ordinary daily lives of human beings. In moments of patriotic and religious exhilaration whole cities have been known to despoil themselves of their property in order to donate it to state or church. But no political organization can long subsist unless taxation has its compulsory aspect, and the Catholic Church itself, whenever it has been able, has made the tithes obligatory.

The patriotic, and still more the religious sentiment, and most of all the two combined in a single passion, suffice to produce general and violent insurrections, and at times they have prompted whole populations to take up arms and set out upon distant and very perilous expeditions—this was the case in the first two or three Crusades. But save in peoples who look upon war as an ordinary occupation and a normal source of gain, those two sentiments do not provide an adequate basis for sound and dependable armies that will be ready at a moment's notice wherever they are needed. Among people who normally depend upon agriculture, industry and commerce, armies of that sort are products of a sound social discipline, which inexorably forces the individual to do his duty and lend his services at certain times and in specified ways.

5. The political organization proper, the organization that establishes the character of the relations between the governing class and the governed and between the various levels and various sections of the ruling class, is the factor that contributes more than any other to determining the degree of perfection that juridical defense, or government by law, can attain in a given people. The existence of an honest government, a government that is based on integrity and justice, a government that is truly liberal in Guicciardini's sense of the term, is the best guarantee that one can have that the rights commonly known as private will be effectively upheld—in other words, that property will be protected. Guicciardini defines political liberty as "a prevalence of law and public decrees over the appetites of particular men."[1] If we take "particular men" in the sense of "individuals," meaning "single individuals," including individuals who have

[1] *Opere inedite*, vol. II, p. 169.

power in their hands, it would be difficult to find a more rigorously scientific definition.   It has, too, the virtue of being very ancient, since, unwittingly perhaps, Guicciardini was repeating the substance of an apothegm of one of the famous Seven Wise Men of Greece.   Guicciardini was certainly not an ingenuous soul.   In his *Pensieri* and *Discorsi* he often reverts to the opinion that "men in general love the good and the just whenever love of their own interest and the interests of relatives, or fear of the vengeance of others, does not mislead their understanding." These words contain a recognition of the psychological law that we have put forward as the basis of juridical defense.

A corrupt government, in which the person who commands "makes his will licit in his law"—whether in the name of God or in the name of the people does not matter—will obviously be inadequate to fulfilling its mission in regard to juridical defense. Officially it may proclaim acceptable and even lofty principles in regard to legal process.   In practice the principles will not be very strictly observed.   In the old kingdom of Naples and to an extent in czarist Russia, law enforcement by the courts, and the law itself, could be nullified by a police official.   Even equality before the law, though officially proclaimed, was more or less a farce.   To choose an ancient example, as less stirring to modern emotions, the Theodosian Code lays down[1] that the larger property owners (*potentiores possessores*) should pay their taxes through provincial governors, because, it seems, the municipal magistrates, who were generally entrusted with the collection of taxes, were too weak as compared with the landowners and too deferential towards them.   Under Arcadius, farmers who were freemen had a right, in the abstract, to hale a proprietor before the imperial courts, but such a procedure was styled an "impertinence" (*audaciam*).[2]

The extent to which relations between rulers and ruled, and between the various cliques among rulers, are inspired by principles of morality and justice, varies, of course, more or less appreciably according to the country and the period in history. Readily apparent is the difference in this respect between the government, say, of the Chinese mandarins and the government

---

[1] XI, 7, 12.
[2] Fustel de Coulanges, *Recherches sur quelques problèmes d'histoire*, pp. 100, 120.

of the Turkish pashas and viziers of the good old days—men of
the stamp of Mohammed Kuprilu, Mustapha Bairakdar, or Ali
Tebelen, who disposed offhand of questions touching the property,
persons, and lives of the raias, and sometimes of believers.
Whatever their good intentions, the Chinese mandarins were
obliged to follow the lead of bureaucratic corruption in order to
supplement their meager stipends somewhat, and they had to
refer capital sentences to Peking for review and on occasion
reversal, unless a province were subject to emergency laws.
Under Ivan the Terrible, when mass confiscations of property,
mass exterminations of whole city populations, were ordinary
occurrences in Russia, that country was ruled very differently
from the way it was under the last czars; and the czarist Russia
of the nineteenth century was, in turn, governed very differently
from England, where every arrest of an individual has to be
legalized in earnest and very promptly. The great nations of
central and western Europe have been ruled very differently
from the republics of South America. In Latin America it is
still customary for the leaders of the winning party to shoot the
leaders of the beaten party, and, not so very long ago, it was
easier to compute the thefts committed by those who held power
for any length of time in hundreds of millions than in millions.[1]

Some writers have no difficulty in explaining these variations
in the degree of excellence of political systems on the basis of
racial differences.[2] But racial defects can hardly be appealed to
in such cases. Peoples who seem backward today may at one
period or another in their history have managed to create very
advanced types of civilization, and have had political organizations in which respect for law, or juridical defense, was relatively
excellent as compared with the situation prevailing at those times
in nations which today surpass them in that regard. Even
today such peoples do not show in private relations the organic
inferiority in the moral sense that seems to be manifest in their
public affairs. The Spaniards and the Sicilians are commonly
regarded as peoples of low-grade political morality. No one
would claim that they are morally inferior to other Europeans in
their family relations, or in their personal dealings and friendships.

---

[1] For the case of Juarez-Celman, a president of the Argentine Republic, and
his accomplices, see Ebelot, "La Révolution de Buenos Ayres."

[2] We have amply discussed that view earlier in these pages, chap. I, §§10–16.

Others explain the variations in question by differences in level of civilization, and in that they are in a measure right. As we shall see hereafter, it is very difficult, if not impossible, for populous wide-spreading social units, such as the modern nations, to perfect juridical defense to any high degree unless they have attained fairly high levels of intellectual and economic development. But to be partially right is not to be wholly right. Many peoples have had periods of material and intellectual splendor and yet, as it were by a sort of fatal curse, have never been able to rid themselves of certain types of political organization that seem to be utterly unsuited to ensuring any real progress in the morality of their governing classes. The Arabian caliphates of Bagdad, Córdoba and Cairo were leaders in world civilization for some centuries. They never achieved any appreciable progress in political organization. What is commonly called civilization, therefore, is evidently a necessary prerequisite to political progress but yet not enough to provoke or explain it.

It may, indeed, be maintained that habits figure to a very large extent in determining the maximum degree of perfection or imperfection in juridical defense that a people is capable of permanently enjoying or systematically tolerating. It may be taken for granted that the modern Persians could not possibly adapt themselves in one generation, or even in many, to the system that is today in force in England; nor could the Englishmen of our day ever be brought to accept the sort of government that is provided for the subjects of the shah. We have already noted that moral habits change far more slowly than intellectual habits; yet however slowly they change, they do change, and both for the better and for the worse. Englishmen would not tolerate today a king like Richard III, a lord chancellor like Francis Bacon, a judge like Jeffreys, an army general like that John Graham of Claverhouse who commanded in Scotland, or, we may venture, a lord protector like Cromwell. So we might reasonably hope that a Barnabò Visconti or a Cesare Borgia would be impossible among the Italians of today. Polybius admired the political system of the Romans as the best of all the governments of his day. But within a few generations those same Romans had learned to accept the tyrannies of Tiberius, Caligula and Nero; while the descendants of the Greeks who had lived in the days of

Aristides, Pericles and Epaminondas submitted over long centuries to the rule of the degenerate emperors of Byzantium. Now there must be reasons why certain habits are formed in preference to other habits. Even granting, therefore, that variety in political systems is due in the main to differences in political habits, the problem of why different habits arise still remains unsolved. In a word, we are here confronted with a great psychological law which can alone explain why the moral instincts of a people are now more, now less, embodied and developed in its political constitution. And that law is only one of many manifestations of another more general law, which we set forth earlier in this chapter, and which explains the greater or lesser efficacy of moral restraints in all phases of social life.

6. The absolute preponderance of a single political force, the predominance of any over-simplified concept in the organization of the state, the strictly logical application of any single principle in all public law are the essential elements in any type of despotism, whether it be a despotism based upon divine right or a despotism based ostensibly on popular sovereignty; for they enable anyone who is in power to exploit the advantages of a superior position more thoroughly for the benefit of his own interests and passions. When the leaders of the governing class are the exclusive interpreters of the will of God or of the will of the people and exercise sovereignty in the name of those abstractions in societies that are deeply imbued with religious beliefs or with democratic fanaticism, and when no other organized social forces exist apart from those which represent the principle on which sovereignty over the nation is based, then there can be no resistance, no effective control, to restrain a natural tendency in those who stand at the head of the social order to abuse their powers.

When a governing class can permit itself anything in the name of a sovereign who can do anything, it undergoes a real moral degeneration, the degeneration that is common to all men whose acts are exempt from the restraint that the opinion and the conscience of their fellows ordinarily impose. When responsibility in subordinates in the end is one with irresponsibility and omnipotence in the man or in the little group of men standing at the head of the official hierarchy as a whole—call that man czar or sultan, or that group a Committee of Public Safety—the vices that absolutism generates in its leaders are communicated downward to the whole political structure. Anything may be ventured when one is interpreting the will, real or imaginary, of a person who thinks he has the right to bend everything to his will, but who cannot possibly see everything and who does not have free and disinterested consciences about him to control his passions and correct his mistakes.

The effects of such a system are in the highest degree deplorable, and they are swift in manifesting themselves. The Russian novelist Dostoevski lived long in a land of autocracy and spent ten years in exile in Siberia. He has described with greater veracity and feeling than anybody else among the moderns the degeneration of character that absolute power produces in men. We cannot forego a quotation:

> When a man has unlimited power over the flesh and blood of his fellow man, when a man is in a position to degrade another human being to the limits of degradation, he is unable to resist the temptation to do wrong. Tyranny is a habit. In the end it becomes a disease. The best man in the world becomes so brutalized as to be indistinguishable from a wild beast. Blood intoxicates, the spirit becomes accessible to the greatest abnormalities, and these can come to seem real joys. The possibility of such license sometimes becomes contagious in a whole people; and yet society, which despises the official hangman, does not despise the hangman who is all-powerful.

Now this type of moral intoxication has been pointed to by not a few psychiatrists of our day. It explains the excesses of those who are omnipotent. It supplies the key to the criminal follies of some of the old Roman emperors, of Ivan IV and Peter the Great, of many sultans of the East, of Robespierre, Barère, Carrier, Lebon. As is well known, some of those individuals had shown quite normal characters before achieving supreme power; they were utterly alien to the excesses in which they afterwards indulged. The failing is particularly characteristic of individuals who are not destined to supreme power by family or birth. Napoleon remarked to Dr. O'Meara at St. Helena that "no one but himself had ever done him any harm, that he had been his own worst enemy, and that schemes that were altogether his own—the expedition to Moscow and all that followed from

it—had been the sole causes of his downfall."[1] So, then, not
Napoleon's genius, not even the lucid sense he had of his own
best interests, was able, because of his despotic power, to keep
him from making mistakes in which his own fortunes foundered
and through which hundreds of thousands of human lives were
lost.

It may be objected that some absolute sovereigns have been
good, just as others have been bad, and that in continental
Europe, before the modern adoption of constitutional and parliamentary forms of government, absolutism did not produce
results that were disastrous enough to justify the view that we
have here put forward. The ready answer is that after the
Middle Ages the absolutisms that prevailed in Europe were far
from being complete, that even the authority of a Louis XIV had
powerful checks in the traditions of a day when a king was just
the first among his barons, in the long-standing privileges of the
nobility and the provinces and especially in the more or less
complete separation of church and state. In any event, human
nature is so rich and so varied that we may readily admit a thing
which, for that matter, history proves: namely, that there have
been individuals who have managed wholly to tame their passions
and to remain pure and honest even after long investiture with
absolute authority. But the good that such "lucky accidents"
have actually accomplished is not as great as is commonly supposed. In a country that is permanently accustomed to a
despotic regime, the ruling class, taken as a class, usually becomes
fawning and craven before superiors, and inevitably becomes
haughty, despotic and overbearing toward inferiors. Men,
unhappily, are so made that the more subject they are to the
caprice and the will of the persons above them, the more likely
they are to force their caprice and will upon those who are below
them and in their power.

Anyone can find examples in the private and even the family
life he sees about him to corroborate the rule which we have here
formulated. In the modern state, which is spread over a vast
territory and has extremely complicated bureaucratic and
administrative systems, the head of the state has a very slight
influence upon the ordinary life of the people, apart from a
number of important decisions, such as choice between war and

[1] O'Meara, *Napoleon in Exile*, conversation of April 6, 1817.

peace. Often, therefore, abuses will exist to which the sovereigns are personally most averse. Alexander I, Nicholas I and Alexander II of Russia were certainly very much opposed to administrative corruption, and so was Ferdinand II of Naples. Yet the practice of bribing officials persisted to the end in czarist Russia, and was never eradicated in the kingdom of Naples.[1] History shows a number of cases where the establishment of despotic government has been advantageous to peoples, at least temporarily. Cesare Borgia is said to have given Romagna a chance to catch a free breath by destroying the bandits and petty tyrants that infested that region. So Mehemet Ali gave Egypt a little peace by exterminating the Mamelukes. All that such examples show is that despotism, though the worst of all political systems, is nevertheless preferable to anarchy, the absence of any government at all.

7. Aristotle, Polybius and a number of other writers of ancient times expressed a preference for "mixed" forms of government— forms, that is, which combined traits of monarchy, aristocracy and democracy in certain proportions—so clearly intuiting the law that we have just stated. In the Greek state, the ancient monarchy, resting on its sacred character and on tradition, the aristocracy, which also represented tradition and, as a rule, ownership of land, the demos, based on money, mobile wealth, numbers, mob passions, were so many political forces, the interplay of which, so long as any one of them did not prevail to the exclusion of the others, was such as to provide a type of political organization in which due process of law was, in ordinary times, relatively secure. In Rome again, in the day when Polybius was so greatly admiring her constitution, we find the influence of great landed property in the hands of the patricians and the influence of small landed property in the hands of the plebeians tempered and balanced by the influence of money and mobile capital in the hands of the knights. We find the traditions of the great families of optimates descended from the gods holding their power in the face of popular passions and the talents and newly gotten wealth of the great plebeian families. And we find those different political forces so embodied in the various authorities, political,

[1] Leroy-Beaulieu, *L'Empire des tzars et les Russes;* Nisco, *Ferdinando II e il suo regno.*

military, administrative and judiciary, and so allying with each
other and balancing each other as to give rise to a state that was
in juridical terms the most perfect of all antiquity.

In the eighteenth century, Montesquieu studied the English
constitution and derived from it the doctrine that if a country
was to be free, power should curb power, the exercise of the three
fundamental powers that he found present in any state being
entrusted to separate political organs. Now writers on constitutional law have shown that there can be no such thing as the
absolute separation of the three powers that Montesquieu conceived and that there is no reason why the powers in question
should be three rather than any other number. But that,
probably, is not Montesquieu's main defect, which, for that
matter, comes out more prominently in the many writers who
have drawn on Montesquieu than in Montesquieu himself.
With their eyes fixed upon the master's theory, such imitators
have been inclined to stress its formal or, so to say, legalistic
aspect rather than its substantial or social aspect. They have
often forgotten that if one political institution is to be an effective
curb upon the activity of another it must represent a political
force—it must, that is, be the organized expression of a social
influence and a social authority that has some standing in the
community, as against the forces that are expressed in the political institution that is to be controlled.

That is why, in certain parliamentary monarchies, in spite of
the letter of constitutions and fundamental charters, we see heads
of states, who are supported neither by ancient traditions nor by
the all but vanishing prestige of the divine-right doctrine nor by
the influence of the bureaucracy, the army or the economically
superior classes, becoming powerless to counterbalance the influence of elective assemblies, who are supported by a belief that
they represent the totality of the citizens and actually comprise
within themselves a considerable body of capacities, interests,
ambitions and energies. That is why in those same countries the
courts are proclaimed by word of mouth to be fundamental organs
of the state, while in fact they are mere branches of a bureaucracy,
depending upon a cabinet that is loyal to the majority in the
elective chamber. So they come to lack prestige and independence and are never capable of mustering enough moral and intellectual energy to assert their own importance. For the same

reason, finally, a number of senates and upper houses have easily been relegated to subordinate positions by lower houses that are functioning at their sides.   That is because they are made up of pensioned officials, deputies and assemblymen, who have retired from militant political life, along with a few rich men whose vanities the ministries have found it expedient to flatter.   Such bodies, therefore, do not offer adequate fields either for aggressive minds or for ambitious talents.   They do not represent important social forces.

8. If a political organism is to progress in the direction of attaining greater and greater improvement in juridical defense, the prime and most essential requisite is that the secular and ecclesiastical powers shall be separated, or, better, that the principle on which the exercise of temporal authority is based shall have nothing sacred and immutable about it.   When power rests on a system of ideas and beliefs outside of which it is felt that there can be neither truth nor justice, it is almost impossible that its acts should be debated and moderated in practice.   Social progress can hardly reach a point where, in such a case, the different powers will harmonize with each other and check each other effectively enough to prevent absolute control by the individual, or individuals, who stand at the head of the social order.   The relative immobility of certain social types must be ascribed to failures in the respects here suggested.   The sacred character of the caste has for many centuries prevented any social progress in Hindu civilization.   In its beginnings that civilization must have had very brilliant possibilities.   Otherwise there would be no way to account for the great material and artistic progress which it actually did achieve.   That leads to a supposition, which seems, for that matter, to be confirmed by recent studies, that the division of the Hindu population into castes, and the isolation of the various castes, cannot always have been as thoroughgoing and extreme as we find them today.   It seems that Brahminism did not become altogether rigid, stationary and formalistic until after its victorious struggle with Buddhism in India.[1]

[1] Schuré, "La Légende de Chrisna" and "Le Bouddha et sa légende"; but especially, Sénart, "Un roi de l'Inde au troisième siècle avant notre ère: Acoka et le Bouddhisme."

Mohammedan societies are afflicted with the same weakness. The fact has been remarked by many people, but it has been stressed with the greatest penetration by Leroy-Beaulieu. The Mohammedan Tatars who dwelt in the Russian governments of Kazan, Astrakhan and the Crimea, that writer describes as prosperous, clean-living and given to trade; but he adds:

> The great vice of Islam, the real cause of its political inferiority, lies neither in its dogma nor even in its morality, but in its habit of confusing the spiritual with the temporal, the religious law with the secular law. The Koran is Bible and Code in one—it is the word of the Prophet that takes the place of law. Ordinances and customs are therefore consecrated to eternity by religion, and because of that fact alone every Mussulman civilization is necessarily stationary.[1]

To supplement that analysis, which is both keen and exact, one might add that in countries where Mohammedan populations are independent the sovereign is almost always a caliph, or vicar of the Prophet, or at least derives his authority nominally or actually from a caliph. In view of that, no believer can deny him absolute obedience without impugning the legitimacy of the caliphate's authority and initiating a religious reform. That is why, as we saw above (chap. III, §5), civil wars and revolutions among Mohammedans have as a rule taken some religious reform as their pretext, or some claim to the vicarate of the Prophet. That was the case in the conflicts between the Ommiads, the Abbassids and the Fatimids, which drenched the early history of Islam in blood. That was the case in the struggles that upset northern Africa and Spain in the eleventh and twelfth centuries, and in very recent movements that have disturbed those countries. Of course, in all such struggles, considerations of an altogether worldly character figured, along with the religious motive.

Christian peoples have managed to avoid the dangerous confusion that Leroy-Beaulieu refers to, and so, as the result of a number of favoring circumstances, they have been able to create the secular state. In the first place, the Bible luckily contains very few maxims that can be directly applied to political life. In the second place, though the Catholic Church has always aspired to a preponderant share in political power, it has never

---

[1] *L'Empire des tzars et les Russes*, vol. I, p. 86.

been able to monopolize it entirely, because of two traits, chiefly, that are basic in its structure. Celibacy has generally been required of the clergy and of monks. Therefore no real dynasties of abbots and bishops have ever been able to establish themselves. On this score the western world owes Gregory VII a great debt of gratitude. Secondly, in spite of numerous examples to the contrary supplied by the warlike Middle Ages, the ecclesiastical calling has by its very nature never been strictly compatible with the bearing of arms. The precept that exhorts the Church to abhor bloodshed has never dropped completely out of sight, and in relatively tranquil and orderly times it has always been very much to the fore. In the period between the eleventh and the fourteenth century even Guelph writers had to recognize that side by side with papal supremacy an emperor existed as a secular sovereign who functioned as the instrument and secular arm of the Church. The most complete despotisms to which Christian peoples have ever been subject arose in Byzantium and in Russia, where the secular rulers succeeded most completely in bringing ecclesiastical authority under their direct control. The English, on the other hand, are greatly indebted for their liberties to the Puritans and to other nonconformists.

9. Next after the separation of secular and ecclesiastical authority, the most essential requisites for a more or less advanced type of juridical defense are to be found in the way in which wealth is distributed in a society and in the way in which military forces are organized. Here again a distinction must be drawn between nations that are still in their feudal period and nations that have already developed a bureaucratic organization.

In the feudal state, wealth and military power are ordinarily concentrated in the hands of the ruling class—wealth consisting largely in the ownership of land, as is uniformly the case in rudimentary stages of civilization. Even in a feudal society this state of affairs presents many drawbacks, but in that type of society it never has the effects it has in more highly perfected types of social organization. The head of a feudal state will be able to wrong any one of his barons, but he will never be absolute master of them all. They have at their disposal a certain amount of public force, if one may so speak, and will always be able to exercise de facto a right of resistance which, in bureaucratic states, once it is recognized, is written into the constitutions and the code books of public law. The individual barons, in their turn, find that there is a limit to the tyranny which they can exercise over the masses of their subjects. Unreasonableness on their part may provoke a desperate unrest which may easily become rebellion. So it turns out that in all truly feudal countries the rule of the masters may be violent and arbitrary by fits and starts, but on the whole it is considerably limited by customs. The Abyssinians, for instance, and especially the Afghans, owe only a highly qualified obedience to their rases and their emirs. We have already seen (§6, above) that traditions and other remnants of a feudal system may serve to limit the authority of the head of a state. Not even in the age of Louis XIV, or of Frederick the Great, could European monarchy be compared to the political systems that were headed by the emperors of Byzantium or the shahs of Persia.

A more or less complete separation of the temporal and spiritual powers in France and Prussia must have contributed to that result. With the exception of Russia and Turkey, there has never been a country in modern Europe in which the head of the government exercised greater personal authority than did Frederick the Great in Prussia, and his father before him. The peculiar personalities of those sovereigns, the small size of the state they administered, the special circumstances that prevailed in their day in history, combined to make their administrations the real foundation of Prussian greatness.

But when the class that monopolizes wealth and arms embodies its power in a centralized bureaucracy and an irresistible standing army, we get despotism in its worst form—namely, a barbarous and primitive system of government that has the instruments of an advanced civilization at its disposal, a yoke of iron which is applied by rough and reckless hands and which is very hard to break, since it has been steeled and tempered by practiced artisans.

That an omnipotent standing army makes one of the worst forms of government is a fact so well recognized that we shall not dwell upon it here.[1] Also well known is the fact that too great a concentration of wealth in the hands of a portion of the ruling

[1] See below, chap. IX. There we consider the circumstances that make an omnipotent army possible and those that serve to limit or destroy its power.

class has brought on the ruin of relatively perfect political organisms, such as the Roman Republic. Laws and institutions that guarantee justice and protect the rights of the weak cannot possibly be effective when wealth is so distributed that we get, on the one hand, a small number of persons possessing lands and mobile capital and, on the other, a multitude of proletarians who have no resource but the labor of their hands and owe it to the rich if they do not die of hunger from one day to the next. In that state of affairs to proclaim universal suffrage, or the rights of man, or the maxim that all are equal before the law, is merely ironical; and just as ironical is it to say that every man carries a marshal's baton in his knapsack, or that he is free some day to become a capitalist himself. Even granting that some few individuals do realize those high possibilities, they will not necessarily be the best individuals, either in intelligence or in morals. They may be the most persistent, the most fortunate or, perhaps, the most crooked. Meanwhile the mass of the people will still remain just as much subject to those on high.

There is no use either in cherishing illusions as to the practical consequences of a system in which political power and control of economic production and distribution are irrevocably delegated to, or conferred upon, the same persons. In so far as the state absorbs and distributes a larger and larger portion of the public wealth, the leaders of the ruling class come to possess greater and greater facilities for influencing and commanding their subordinates, and more and more easily evade control by anybody. One of the most important reasons for the decline of the parliamentary system is the relatively huge numbers of offices, contracts for public works and other favors of an economic character which the governing class is in a position to distribute either to individuals or to groups of persons; and the drawbacks of that system are the greater in proportion as the amount of wealth that the government or local elective bodies absorb and distribute is greater, and the harder it becomes, therefore, to secure an independent position and an honest living without relying in some respect or other upon public administration. If, then, all the instruments of production pass into the hands of the government, the officials who control and apportion production become the arbiters of the fortunes and welfare of all, and we get a more powerful oligarchy, a more all-embracing "racket," than has ever been seen in a society of advanced civilization. If all moral and material advantages depend on those who hold power, there is no baseness that will not be resorted to in order to please them; just as there is no act of chicanery or violence that will not be resorted to in order to attain power, in other words, in order to belong to the number of those who hand out the cake rather than to the larger number of those who have to rest content with the slices that are doled out to them.

A society is best placed to develop a relatively perfect political organization when it contains a large class of people whose economic position is virtually independent of those who hold supreme power and who have sufficient means to be able to devote a portion of their time to perfecting their culture and acquiring that interest in the public weal—that aristocratic spirit, we are almost tempted to say—which alone can induce people to serve their country with no other satisfactions than those that come from individual pride and self-respect. In all countries that ever have been, or now are, in the lead as regards juridical defense—or liberty, as it is commonly called—such a class has been prominent. There was such a class in Rome, when Rome had a teeming plebs of small property owners who, the times being modest ones, managed to be self-sufficient and to win step by step, with amazing persistence, the rights of full citizenship. There was such a class in England in the seventeenth century, and there is one there now. England's numerous gentry, which was made up in those days chiefly of moderately rich landowners and is now chiefly made up of moderately rich businessmen, is now supplying, as it then supplied, the best elements to the ruling class. There has been and there still is such a class in the United States of America, and such a class has existed in most of the countries of central and western Europe. Where the class is inadequate to its task because of deficiencies in cultivation or in education or in wealth, parliamentary government bears its worst fruits, as would any other political system.

10. As civilization grows, the number of the moral and material influences which are capable of becoming social forces increases. For example, property in money, as the fruit of industry and commerce, comes into being alongside of real property. Education progresses. Occupations based on scientific knowledge gain

in importance.   So a new social class forms which, up to a certain
point, counterbalances the material prestige of the rich and the
moral prestige of the clergy.   Not only that.   Mutual toleration
results from advanced culture, and toleration enables different
religions and different political currents to exist side by side,
balancing and checking one another.   Specialization of public
functions enables many different influences to express themselves in government and to participate in the control of the
state.   At the same time public discussion of the acts of the
rulers becomes possible.   Freedom of the press, so-called, is a
very recent instrument of juridical defense.   It was not established in England till the end of the seventeenth century, and
not till the nineteenth century did it make its way into the constitutional and parliamentary countries of continental Europe.

And yet, in order to gain an influence proportionate to its real
importance every political force has to be organized, and before
it can be well organized, a number of factors, important among
them time and tradition, are indispensable.   That is why, in one
country or another at one time or another, we see an actual
disproportion between the importance that a class has acquired
in society and the direct influence it exerts in the government of
the country.   One thinks at once of the French bourgeoisie
before 1789, or of the English middle classes before 1832.   There
is almost always some one political force, furthermore, that
manifests an invincible tendency to overreach or absorb the
others, and so to destroy a juridical equilibrium that has gradually
been established.   That is true both of political forces of a
material character, such as wealth and military power, and of
forces of a moral character, such as the great currents of religion
or thought.   Each of such currents claims to monopolize truth
and justice, and all types of exclusivism and bigotry, whether
Christian or Mohammedan, whether sacred or rationalistic,
whether inspired by the infallibility of the pope or by the infallibility of democracy, are equally pernicious from this point of
view.   Every country, every epoch, has its own peculiar current
of ideas and beliefs, which being the strongest current, bears
down upon the political mechanism and tends to subvert it.
Quite generally the harm that has been done by weakening currents, which are going, or have gone, out of fashion, is appreciated
very well, and the deep wounds that they have inflicted on the

sense of justice are stigmatized with horror. Meantime the similar harm that the current in rising vogue has done, or is threatening to do, is not discerned or else is condoned or, at the most, feebly viewed with alarm. Men cry aloud and proclaim that liberty has been won, that the storm is over. Actually the storm has merely changed direction, or, if one may use the metaphor, merely changed shape and color.

A number of moral forces have long striven to upset the juridical equilibrium in Europe: the Church, social democracy, nationalism. In spite of its strong organization the Church may be considered the least violent and menacing of them all, and it will continue to be so unless danger of proletarian revolution forces the upper classes to turn again to religious beliefs which they have now abandoned or profess but tepidly. Among material forces, a force that is able very easily to override all the powers of the state and sometimes to violate, let alone the norms of justice and equity, the literal text of the law, is mobile wealth—it is money, or at least that portion of money which is powerfully organized. The great development of banking systems and of credit, the growth of large corporations, which often control the communication systems of vast territories and entire states, the great enlargement of public debts, have in the last hundred years created new structures, new elements of political importance, so that some of the greatest states in the Old World and the New have already had occasion to learn from experience how overbearing and how all-pervasive their influence can be.

The relative ease with which money, or mobile wealth, can be organized and the possibility of concentrating control of large amounts of money in the hands of a few individuals help to explain its growing preponderance in power. In this phenomenon we have one of the many examples of an organized minority prevailing over a disorganized majority. A very small number of individuals can control all the banks of issue in a country or all the companies engaged in transportation by land or sea. They can own and control great stock companies and industrial corporations which deal in commodities that are indispensable to national defense, such as iron and steel. They can carry out public works for which not even the finances of the richest governments would be adequate. With hundreds of millions at their disposal, such individuals possess the most varied resources for threatening or cajoling other interests however far-reaching, and for intimidating and corrupting public officials, ministries, legislative bodies, newspapers. Meantime, that portion—and undoubtedly it is the larger portion—of the national capital which is invested in the hosts and hosts of small or medium-sized industries, or scattered about in many hands in the form of savings in amounts more or less large, has no power whatever to react. Be it noted that the far larger part of the capital of banks and industrial corporations usually belongs to small and medium-sized stockholders, who not only remain completely passive but are often the first victims of their leaders, who succeed in founding great fortunes and building up powerful public influence on the losses they inflict on others.

It is difficult at the present time for real property to find the same facilities for asserting itself that money finds. Though landed property may not be very much divided, it is always divided enough to make it difficult in a large country for a small number of large landowners working in coalition to dictate to a market, or to force their will upon a government. So true is this that industrial protectionism appeared in advance of agrarian protectionism. The latter came about as a reaction to the former and as a sort of indirect compensation for the consequences of the former. A temporary monopoly may be acquired by the proprietors of lands immediately adjoining large cities that are undergoing rapid development in real estate. In such cases the same forms of corruption as are characteristic of the influence of money arise.

11. When a system of political organization is based upon a single absolute principle, so that the whole political class is organized after a single pattern, it is difficult for all social forces to participate in public life, and more difficult still for any one force to counterbalance another. That is as true when power is in the hands of elected officials who are said to be chosen by the people as it is when power is entrusted exclusively to employees who are assumed to be appointed by a prince. The checks which bureaucracy and democracy can enforce upon themselves and which are applied through the agency of other bureaucrats or elected officials are always inadequate. In practice they never wholly achieve their purposes.

The administrative history of the Roman Empire furnishes a pertinent instance of the incapacity of a centralized bureaucracy to curb itself effectively. In the beginning, both in the capital and in the municipalities, both in the colonies and in the provincial cities, there was, under the supremacy of republican or imperial Rome, what the English call self-government; that is to say, public offices were filled without salaries by a large class of well-to-do people. But beginning with the establishment of the Empire, functions in the city of Rome which until then had been delegated to aediles and censors were turned over to special salaried functionaries, and these were assisted in their work by a large personnel of employees, who also received compensation. Superintendence of the provisioning of the city was entrusted to a *praefectus annonae*, public works to *curatores viarum, aquarum, operum publicorum, riparum et alvei Tiberis*, surveillance over lighting and fires to a *praefectus vigilum* and police functions to a *praefectus urbis*. The system that had been introduced in the capital very soon spread to the municipalities, which one by one lost their administrative autonomy. Down to A.D. 80 electoral campaigning for the posts of duumvir and aedile was still very keen in some municipalities. Not a few Pompeian frescoes show candidates being recommended and eulogized. But as early as the end of the first century of the empire, a considerable diminution takes place in the authority of the *duumviri juris dicundo* and the aediles, to whom local administration of the individual cities had been entrusted, these officials being gradually replaced by employees of the empire—*juridici, correctores, curatores rerum publicarum*. Slow as the evolution may have been, by the time of Nerva and Trajan elected functionaries were periodically suspended from their posts and their duties were entrusted for specified periods to *curatores*—something like the Italian "royal commissioners" (*regi commissari*) of the present day. At the same time there was a slow growth in the inspectorial authority and directive jurisdiction of the *corrector provinciae*—in this case something equivalent to the modern French or Italian prefect. Finally, at the end of the second century, municipal autonomy was extinct almost everywhere, and a gigantic all-embracing bureaucratic network extended over the whole empire.[1]

[1] Marquardt, *Manuel des antiquités romaines*, vol. I, pp. 115, 158, 214, 225, and vol. II, pp. 187 f.

At the same time the well-to-do municipal bourgeoisie declined. That class made up the *ordo decurionum* and participated in the government of the cities. The men who held the posts of duumvir and aedile were selected from it. The office of the *curialis* involved a heavy financial responsibility, since the class of *curiales* as a whole gave bond for the payment of the whole tax laid upon a given city. This burden contributed beyond a doubt to the economic ruin of the Roman middle class. Now when fiscalism and bureaucratic centralization had created the Roman society of the Low Empire—a society made up of a very small class of large property owners and high officials and another very populous class of wretchedly poor people, who had no social importance whatever and, though freeborn, readily sank to the status of tenants—we witness the appearance of a very original institution, a new bureaucratic organ that was designed to safeguard the interests of the needy classes, and of such remnants of the small landowners as survived, and protect them from abuse by the bureaucracy. The office of *defensor civitatis* was created by Valentinian I in the year 364. This "public defender" was just an employee appointed expressly to shelter the urban plebs from the tyranny of high officials, or of the rich who made common cause with the high officials. His particular function was to see to it that the complaints of the poor were admitted to trial in accordance with the law and that their appeals reached the foot of the throne. But, in spite of the best of intentions on the part of the legislator, this effort of bureaucratic absolutism to correct and control itself can have had no very appreciable effects. The old abuses continued, and the forces that were leading the empire to its destruction continued to operate with the same potency.

The method chosen to cure the evils was not the aptest imaginable. A high official is very likely to have the points of view, the passions, the prejudices, of the class to which he belongs, and his sentiments, as well as his interests, will incline him to deport himself in such a way as to win the approval of his own class rather than the approval of another class to which he feels morally and intellectually alien and which he may already have learned to abuse and despise.

Bureaucratic absolutism in Russia had its most ancient roots in the influence of Byzantium, which made itself felt at Kiev

from the time of Vladimir the Great and his successors. It was
certainly reinforced by the terrible Mongol domination, which
supervened in the thirteenth century and was to weigh upon the
country down into the sixteenth. In Russia again, the famous
secret chancellery that was organized by the czar Alexis toward
the middle of the seventeenth century was nothing more than a
special police force that tapered directly upward to the sovereign
and was designed to keep an eye on abuses, but also on attempts
at revolt, among the high officials and the boyars who constituted,
when all was said and done, a single class. Now the "Third
Section," so deplorably famous under the last czars, stemmed in
a direct and legitimate line from this secret chancellery of Alexis.
There were periods of calm and periods of recrudescence in the
activity of the "Third Section." Many times abolished in name,
it was always retained in fact; and it appears that actually, far
from eradicating venality and corruption from the Russian
bureaucracy, it served to intensify the oppression that the
bureaucracy inflicted on the rest of the country.

In the United States, on the other hand, one sees the inability
of a democracy to control and limit itself. It cannot be denied
that the framers of the Constitution of 1787 took great care to
embody the principle of checks and balances in that document
in order to achieve a perfect equilibrium between the various
powers and the various political organs. Given the thoroughly
democratic basis of the government, the absolute lack of any
power that does not emanate directly from popular suffrage, it
is hard to believe that anything better could have been imagined.
The Senate, to begin with, has greater and more real powers than
the upper houses in Europe usually have. It actually participates in the exercise of executive power, and, expressing a still
lively sense of the independence of the separate states, it enjoys
great public prestige. But then again the president has a veto
power, and he uses it freely. He cannot be compelled to resign
by a vote of the lower house. He concentrates all governmental
responsibility in his own person for a period of four years. As an
organ of juridical defense the American presidency is far superior
to the cabinets in the parliamentary countries of Europe, since
European cabinets have less authority than the American president
and more need of kowtowing to assemblymen and politicians than
he. Since they are collective bodies, their members never feel

the pressure of personal responsibility which the American president feels. To this breadth of powers, and to the feeling of
personal responsibility that often develops with tenure in high
office, is due the fact that during the last century a number of
presidents, for example Johnson, Hayes and Cleveland, have
stood out with stubbornness and courage against the worst
excesses of the parties that elected them.

Johnson (1865–1869) came to the presidency on the death of
Lincoln. He steadfastly opposed handing over the defeated
South to pillaging by the petty Republican politicians who came
to be known as "carpetbaggers." Hayes was also a Republican.
Though he had come into power through a questionable juggling
of votes, which was upheld by a decision of the Supreme Court,
he at once put an end to the reign of plunder and terror that had
continued for eight years in the Democratic states of the South
during the double term of the greatly overestimated Grant.
Cleveland, a Democratic president elected in 1884, among other
highly meritorious acts, had the courage to retain in office a
number of Republican officials whom his partisans wished to have
dismissed—a high-minded effort to abolish the Jacksonian system
whereby the party that was victorious at the polls took over all
remunerative posts. As governor of New York State, Cleveland
had become famous through a successful fight with the Tweed
Ring that was "bossing" the aldermanic chamber of New York
City.

But this, so to say, formal perfection of mechanism in federal
and state governments has only to an extent made up for a defect
which is fundamental in the whole political and administrative
system of the American Union, and that defect has been greatly
aggravated by a tendency which began to manifest itself between
1820 and 1850 and has now become virtually countrywide. We
refer to the fact that suffrage has been made equal and universal
in almost all the American states.

In the early days of the Union the right to vote was generally
subject to a man's status as a taxpayer. Indeed in early days,
in the New England states, a Puritan system prevailed whereby
the right to vote was conferred on members of religious congre-
gations. Then the property qualification was introduced in those
states as well. High property qualifications were also required
for eligibility for election to local state legislatures and to the

governorship. Equal suffrage began to be introduced in the early nineteenth century in the western states, where everybody was a recent immigrant and a landowner. Then it was adopted for all whites in the southern states, and finally it was extended to the state of New York and to New England. This evolution was completed around 1850, under the influence of new immigrants and French democratic ideas. Negroes, as is well known, did not receive the vote until 1865. Simultaneously with the broadening of suffrage came the growth in vogue of the principles of direct election and limited tenure for judges. Again the old states of New England held out longest against this current, but they too were carried away by it in the end.[1]

As a result of this movement, a single class of electors now casts its votes in all elections. Judges in the various states were once appointed for life, and the appointments were made by the respective governors. The office of judge has now become directly elective and temporary. In this way the same electoral clique invariably chooses federal and local authorities. Governors, judges and congressmen are in the last analysis instruments of the same influences, which become the absolute and irresponsible masters of a whole country—all the more since the American politicians make a business of elections and are highly skilled in the art of manufacturing "machines" and "rings." Under this system, in other words, all the powers that should balance and supplement each other emanate from a single caucus or electoral committee.

But, it might be objected, under a system of universal suffrage all political forces and influences can be represented in the governing class in proportion to their numerical importance, and it therefore becomes impossible for a minority to monopolize power in the state to its own advantage and so to make the state an instrument of its own views and passions.

This objection reflects a theory that is still much in vogue but which we have not been accepting and in fact have been indirectly combatting all along in these pages. We had better stop, therefore, and deal with it directly.

[1] Seaman, *The American System of Government*, pp. 160–164; Jannet, *Le istituzioni politiche e sociali degli Stati Uniti d'America*, part I, chaps. II and VII. Tocqueville's worth as an observer has probably been somewhat exaggerated. He saw only the beginnings of this democratic movement and had no means of scrutinizing a fully triumphant democracy in the United States.

CHAPTER VI

SUFFRAGE AND SOCIAL FORCES

1. Many doctrines that advocate liberty and equality, as the latter terms are still commonly understood—doctrines which the eighteenth century thought out, which the nineteenth perfected and tried to apply and which the twentieth will probably dispense with or modify substantially—are summed up and given concrete form in the theory that views universal suffrage as the foundation of all sound government. It is commonly believed that the only free, equitable and legitimate government is a government that is based upon the will of the majority, the majority by its vote delegating its powers for a specified length of time to men who represent it. Down to a few generations ago—and even today in the eyes of many writers and statesmen—all flaws in representative government were attributed to incomplete or mistaken applications of the principles of representation and suffrage. Louis Blanc, Lamartine and indeed all the democratic writers in France before 1848 ascribed the alleged corruption of the July Monarchy and all the drawbacks of the French parliamentary system to interference by the monarch with the elective bodies and, especially, to limited suffrage. Similar beliefs were widely current in Italy down to thirty years ago. For instance, they formed, as they still form, the groundwork of the Mazzinian school.

A following so large, beliefs so widespread, are not to be discredited in a page or two. We shall not, therefore, attempt a systematic refutation of the theories on which universal suffrage is based.[1] We shall simply refer to some of the main considerations that most seriously undermine the foundations on which universal suffrage as an intellectual edifice rests. We deem it sufficient for our purposes here to demonstrate that the assump-

[1] Independently of the allusions we have already made to this matter in this work, we have discussed the suffrage problem in other writings, notably in *Teorica dei governi e governo parlamentare* and *Le costituzioni moderne.*

153

tion that the elected official is the mouthpiece of the majority of his electors is as a rule not consistent with the facts; and we believe that this can be proved by facts of ordinary experience and by certain practical observations that anyone can make on the manner in which elections are conducted.

What happens in other forms of government—namely, that an organized minority imposes its will on the disorganized majority —happens also and to perfection, whatever the appearances to the contrary, under the representative system.   When we say that the voters "choose" their representative, we are using a language that is very inexact.   The truth is that the representative *has himself elected* by the voters, and, if that phrase should seem too inflexible and too harsh to fit some cases, we might qualify it by saying that *his friends have him elected.*   In elections, as in all other manifestations of social life, those who have the will and, especially, the moral, intellectual and material *means* to force their will upon others take the lead over the others and command them.

The political mandate has been likened to the power of attorney that is familiar in private law.   But in private relationships, delegations of powers and capacities always presuppose that the principal has the broadest freedom in choosing his representative. Now in practice, in popular elections, that freedom of choice, though complete theoretically, necessarily becomes null, not to say ludicrous.   If each voter gave his vote to the candidate of his heart, we may be sure that in almost all cases the only result would be a wide scattering of votes.   When very many wills are involved, choice is determined by the most various criteria, almost all of them subjective, and if such wills were not coordinated and organized it would be virtually impossible for them to coincide in the spontaneous choice of one individual.   If his vote is to have any efficacy at all, therefore, each voter is forced to limit his choice to a very narrow field, in other words to a choice among the two or three persons who have some chance of succeeding; and the only ones who have any chance of succeeding are those whose candidacies are championed by groups, by committees, by *organized minorities.*   In order to simplify the situation for purposes of proof, we have assumed a uninominal ballot, where one name only is to be voted for.   But the great majority of voters will necessarily have a very limited freedom in the choice of their representative, and the influence of committees will necessarily be preponderant, whatever the system of balloting. When the list ballot is used and the voter votes for a list of candidates, it turns out that the number of candidates with some chance of succeeding is less than double the number of representatives to be elected.

How do these organized minorities form about individual candidates or groups of candidates?[1] As a rule they are based on considerations of property and taxation, on common material interests, on ties of family, class, religion, sect or political party. Whether their component personnels be good or bad, there can be no doubt that such committees—and the representatives who are now their tools, now their leaders or "bosses"—represent the organization of a considerable number of social values and forces. In practice, therefore, the representative system results not at all in government by the majority; it results in the participation of a certain number of social values in the guidance of the state, in the fact that many political forces which in an absolute state, a state ruled by a bureaucracy alone, would remain inert and without influence upon government become organized and so exert an influence on government.

2. In examining the relations between the representative system and juridical defense, a number of distinctions and observations have to be borne in mind.

The great majority of voters are passive, it is true, in the sense that they have not so much freedom to choose their representatives as a limited right to exercise an option among a number of candidates. Nevertheless, limited as it may be, that capacity has the effect of obliging candidates to try to win a weight of votes that will serve to tip the scales in their direction, so that they make every effort to flatter, wheedle and obtain the good will of the voters. In this way certain sentiments and passions of the "common herd" come to have their influence on the mental attitudes of the representatives themselves, and echoes of a widely disseminated opinion, or of any serious discontent, easily come to be heard in the highest spheres of government.

[1] For a detailed discussion of this problem see Mosca, *Le costituzioni moderne,* chap. III.

It may be objected that this influence of the majority of voters is necessarily confined to the broad lines of political policy and makes itself felt only on a very few topics of a very general character, and that within limits as narrow as that even in absolute governments the ruling classes are obliged to take account of mass sentiments. In fact the most despotic of governments has to proceed very cautiously when it comes to shocking the sentiments, convictions or prejudices of the majority of the governed, or to requiring of that majority pecuniary sacrifices to which they are not accustomed. But wariness about giving offense will be much greater when every single representative, whose vote may be useful or necessary to the executive branch of government, knows that the discontent of the masses may at almost any moment bring about the triumph of a rival. We are aware that this is a two-edged argument. The masses are not always any wiser in discerning and protecting their interests than their representatives are; and we are acquainted with regions where public discontent has created greater obstacles to desirable reforms than the mistakes of parliamentary representatives and ministries.

The representative system, furthermore, has widely different effects according as the molecular composition of the electoral body varies. If all the voters who have some influence, because of education or social position, are members of one or another of the organized minorities, and if only a mass of poor and ignorant citizens are left outside of them, it is impossible for the latter to exercise their right of option and control in any real or effective manner. In these circumstances, of the various organized minorities that are disputing the field, that one infallibly wins which spends most money or lies most persuasively.

The same thing happens if persons of ability and economic independence represent only a slender minority within the electing group and so have no way of influencing the vote of majorities directly. Then, as ordinarily happens in large cities, the majorities do not feel the moral and material influence of the "better elements." But when the "better elements" do succeed in withdrawing the majority from the influence of committees and "ward heelers" and win its vote, their control over the conduct of the organized minorities becomes effective. It follows, therefore, that the comparison of the merits and platforms of the various candidates will be relatively serious and dispassionate only when electoral forces are not entirely under the control of men who make a regular profession or trade of electioneering.

The real juridical safeguard in representative governments lies in the public discussion that takes place within representative assemblies. Into those assemblies the most disparate political forces and elements make their way, and the existence of a small independent minority is often enough to control the conduct of a large majority and, especially, to prevent the bureaucratic organization from becoming omnipotent. But when, beyond being organs of discussion and publicizing, assemblies come to concentrate all the prestige and power of legitimate authority in their own hands, as regularly happens in parliamentary governments, then in spite of the curb of public discussion the whole administrative and judiciary machine falls prey to the irresponsible and anonymous tyranny of those who win in the elections and speak in the name of the people, and we get one of the worst types of political organization that the real majority in a modern society can possibly be called upon to tolerate.[1]

In governments that are based very largely on the representative principle the referendum is in some respects a fairly effective instrument. By it the mass of likes and dislikes, enthusiasms and angers, which, when they are truly widespread and truly general, constitute what may quite plausibly be called public opinion, is enabled to react against the conduct and enterprise of the governing minority. In a referendum it is a question not of making a choice, or añ election, but of pronouncing a "yes" or a "no" upon a specific question. No single vote, therefore, is lost, and each single vote has its practical importance independently of any coordination or organization along lines of sect, party or committee. However, the democratic ideal of majority government is not realized even by the referendum. Governing is not altogether a matter of allowing or prohibiting modifications in constitutions or laws. It is quite as much a matter of managing the whole military, financial, judiciary and administrative machine, or of influencing those who manage it. Then again, even if the referendum does serve to limit the arbitrariness of the governing class, it is no less true that often it seriously hampers improvements in the political organism.

[1] See Seaman and Mosca; also Schérer, *La Démocratie et la France.*

Such improvements will always be more readily appreciated by a governing class, however selfish and corrupt it may be, than by the ill-informed majority of the governed. In many countries, for instance, if increases in taxes were to be submitted to referendum, they would always be rejected, even though they were of the most unqualified urgency and would be of the most obvious benefit to the public.

3. A question that is vigorously debated among writers on the social sciences is the extent to which the state should interfere in the various departments of social life, and more specifically in business. This problem involves, really, not one question but a group of questions, and we hope that by applying the theories that have been set forth in previous chapters we can help to dispel certain ambiguities and misconceptions which have so far hampered a clear and sound understanding of those questions, and prevented, in certain cases at least, the reaching of satisfactory conclusions.

Still very widespread is the feeling that society and the state are two separate and distinct entities, and people often go so far as to consider them antagonistic. Now it is necessary, first of all, to decide very clearly what is meant by "society" and what is meant by "state." If we keep to legal codes and concepts of administrative law, the state is certainly a distinct entity which is capable of existing in a legal sense and which represents the interests of the group as a whole and administers the public demesne. As such an entity, the state has interests, and its interests may come into conflict with the interests of private individuals and with the interests of other juridical entities. Politically speaking, however, the state is nothing more than the organization of all social forces that have a political significance. In other words, it is the sum total of all the elements in a society that are suited to exercising political functions and have the ability and the will to participate in them. In that sense, the state is the resultant of the coordination and disciplining of those elements.

That is the point of view from which the state should be looked upon by students of the social sciences. The legalistic tendency to consider political problems purely and exclusively from the standpoint not so much of law as of court practice involves an ugly and a dangerous error, which still persists in our age though it has all along hampered an adequate understanding of such problems. From our point of view there can be no antagonism between state and society. The state is to be looked upon merely as that part of society which performs the political function. Considered in this light, all questions touching interference or noninterference by the state come to assume a new aspect. Instead of asking what the limits of state activity ought to be, we try to find out what the best type of political organization is, which type, in other words, enables all the elements that have a political significance in a given society to be best utilized and specialized, best subjected to reciprocal control and to the principle of individual responsibility for the things that are done in the respective domains.

When people contrast state management with private initiative they are often merely comparing work done by a bureaucracy with work that might be done by other directing elements in society. The latter may, in fact, in some cases actually have an official status without necessarily being paid employees. In societies of our European type, however extensively bureaucratized they may be, the bureaucracy is not the state but only a part of it. When, therefore, it is said, as people commonly say, that in Italy, France or Germany the state does everything and absorbs everything, the dictum has to be taken in the sense that the French, Italian or German bureaucracies have many more functions than the bureaucracies of other countries—of England or the United States, let us say. In the same way, when we speak of the famous English "self-government," when we say that the English people "governs itself," we must not imagine, as we might be tempted to do if we kept to the literal meaning of the phrase, that on the Continent the French, the Italians, the Germans do not "govern themselves" but entrust the management of their respective political and administrative institutions to others. We must understand simply that in England certain posts are entrusted to persons who are elected by popular vote or are even appointed by the government but who in any event are chosen from among the prominent people of the various districts, who are not paid for their services and who are not transferable at will, whereas the same posts are filled in other countries in Europe by salaried employees.

4. As we have seen (chap. III, §8), state bureaucracies and the assemblies that wield supreme political power have participated and still participate, in one country or another, in the management of certain branches of economic activity, for example in banking or in the construction and maintenance of public works; but management of economic production has never been completely bureaucratized in any society that has attained even a moderately high level of prosperity and civilization. In that branch of activity management has been and still is on the whole entrusted to elements who do, to be sure, form a part of the ruling forces of society and so are real political forces, but who do not appear on the payrolls of public administration. In general the intervention in economic enterprise of elements that exercise strictly political, in other words legislative, administrative, or judiciary, control over society, has been harmful, and a large share in the pauperization that is afflicting a number of modern countries must be ascribed to that interference.[1]

In general, those who insist on limiting the activities of the state should take as their guide the very simple and very practical principle that in every branch of social activity—in education, religion, poor relief, military organization or the administration of justice—management is always necessary, and that managerial functions have to be entrusted to a special class that has the abilities required for performing them.

Now when one sets out to withdraw one of the above-mentioned functions in whole or in part from bureaucratic management, or from control by elective bodies, it must be borne in mind that there has to be present within the society a class of persons who possess the capacities, in other words have the moral and intellectual training and—let us not forget—the economic resources required for performing the new task which is to be turned over to them. It is not enough, oftentimes, that a society contain elements that are suitable for the given purpose. These elements have to be well chosen and well coordinated—otherwise the experiment may fail or result in positive harm.

---

[1] See again chap. III, §8, where we mentioned such evils as the excessive development of public works, economic protectionism, the illegal or extralegal influence exercised over political authorities by directors of banks and great corporations, and the results of governmental interference in banking.

We suspect, for instance, that that has been the real reason why the jury system has not worked so very well in many countries in continental Europe. Jurors, or "lay judges" as they have been called, represent the intervention in the administration of the penal law of social elements that are foreign to the regular magistracy. But jury panels are far too inclusive for all jurymen to be intellectually and morally equal to their tasks. Furthermore, too little distinction goes to the office of juror to bring jurymen such gratification of personal pride as to make them acquire that public spirit, that aristocratic sense, as we have called it, which is necessary to raise above the average the characters of the men to whom such delicate duties are entrusted. The same might be said of justices of the peace, citizen arbitrators and referees, charity and relief commissioners and, as regards Italy in particular, the holders of certain other offices that are entrusted to persons who are not members of the bureaucracy. It might be objected, of course, that the choices of incumbents for the offices in question are often made, more or less directly, by local elective bodies.

On the other hand, those who favor broader activities on the part of the state ought to consider the practical and positive significance of the term "state," stripping it of everything about it that in common parlance is vague, indeterminate or, we might almost say, magical and supernatural. Often in our day state ownership or control is invoked as a remedy for all the evils of private competition—for greed, for the passion for power, for the excesses of individualism or, more exactly, of selfishness. The state, it is said, is the organ of righteousness and moral progress. It ought to exalt the humble and abase the proud. Free of all vulgar preoccupations of personal interest, it ought to suppress all iniquities, provide for all material and moral needs and set mankind on the flowery pathways of justice, peace and universal harmony.[1] How much of its confidence this soaring trust would lose if, instead of thinking of the state as an abstract entity, as something foreign to the real world, one were to bear clearly in mind that in reality the state is just the concrete organization of a large number of the elements

---

[1] *Cf.* Dupont-White, *L'Individu et l'état*, p. 172: "The State is man minus passion, man at an altitude where he comes into touch with truth itself, where he associates only with God and his conscience."

that rule in a given society, that when we speak of the state's influence we mean the influence that is to be exerted by government officials and government clerks! They are all very fine fellows, to be sure, but however much they may have been improved or chastened by their sense of responsibility, by discipline or pride of office, they nevertheless possess all human capacities and all human frailties. Like all men, they have eyes they can open or shut at will and mouths that can on occasion speak, be silent or even *eat*.[1] They too can sin through pride, sloth, cupidity and vanity. They too have their sympathies and antipathies, their friendships and aversions, their passions and interests—and among their interests an interest in keeping their jobs or even in slipping into better ones if the occasion offers.

[1] [Ital. *mangiare*, to eat, take "graft"].

CHAPTER VII
CHURCHES, PARTIES AND SECTS

1. Buffon reports that if a certain number of stags are shut up in a park they will inevitably divide into two herds which will always be in conflict with each other. An instinct of very much the same sort seems to make its influence felt among men. Human beings have a natural inclination toward struggle, but it is only sporadically that the struggle assumes an individual character, that one man is at war with another. Even when he fights, man remains preeminently a social animal. Ordinarily, therefore, we see men forming into groups, each group made up of leaders and followers. The individuals who make up a group are conscious of a special brotherhood and oneness with each other and vent their pugnacious instincts on members of other groups.

This instinct of herding together and fighting with other herds is the prime basis and original foundation of the external conflicts that occur between different societies; but it also underlies the formation of all the divisions and subdivisions—all the factions, sects, parties and, in a certain sense, the churches—that arise within a given society and occasion moral and, sometimes, physical conflicts. In very small and primitive societies, where there is great moral and intellectual unity and individual members all have the same customs, the same beliefs, the same superstitions, the instinct mentioned may alone suffice to keep discordant and warlike habits alive. The Arabs and the Kabyles in Barbary share the same religious beliefs. They have the same degree and the same type of intellectual and moral culture. Yet, before the coming of the French, when they were not fighting against the infidels in Algeria and Tunis, against the Turks in Tripoli or against the sultan in Morocco, they were fighting among themselves. Each confederation of tribes stood in rivalry or at open war with its neighbor confederation. There was discord within each confederation and often "gunpowder was made to talk" between sister tribes. Within the tribe the

163

various douars were at swords' points, and often the douar was split by quarrels between the separate families.[1]

At other times, when social environments are very circumscribed, internal conflicts arise among minute sections of fairly civilized peoples. There may be no moral and intellectual differences between the enemy parties to justify such conflicts, or even if such differences exist they are used as mere pretexts. So the terms "Guelph" and "Ghibelline" supplied pretext and occasion, rather than cause, for intestine struggles in the medieval Italian communes; and the same may be said of the terms "liberal," "clerical," "radical" and "socialist," which were bandied about by the factions that used to compete for administrative posts in the little towns of southern Italy. At moments of exceptional intellectual apathy, pretexts—even the most frivolous pretexts—may occasion serious conflicts within great and highly civilized societies. In Byzantium, during and after the reign of Justinian, the city streets were often stained with blood by struggles between two parties, the Greens and the Blues (the "Prasinians" and the "Venetians"). Now those "gangs" originated in the circus, the spectators taking sides with the charioteers who raced under the two different colors. Eventually, to be sure, one faction or another at court would try to make use of the one or the other of the gangs. Now the Greens, now the Blues, enjoyed imperial favor, so that the parties came to acquire a certain political importance, without ever quite losing their status as personal "sets," or gangs. Something remotely similar went on in a number of Italian cities before 1848, when men of the younger generation would form hostile cliques and factions about the merits of some prima donna or ballet girl.

2. In small societies as in large, when the hunger for conflict finds a vent in foreign rivalries and wars it is to an extent appeased and so less readily seeks expression in civil discords or internal strife. On closely scrutinizing the nature of the political parties, the philosophical sects, the religious factions that everywhere develop within civilized societies, one sees that the pugnacious

---

[1] In Algeria and Tunis the consolidation of French rule ended the day of revolts against foreign conquerors, and all but stopped internal wars between the various tribes. The same thing, one may venture to predict, will eventually happen in Tripoli and Cyrenaica and, perhaps somewhat later, in Morocco.

instinct of herding and fighting, which is the most primitive and, so to say, the most "animal" of the instincts, is mixed with other intellectual and psychological factors that are more complex and more human. In large, highly civilized societies, which are held together not only by moral and intellectual affinities but also by strong and complicated political organizations, a much greater speculative and affective freedom is possible than in small and loosely organized societies. In a great people, therefore, political and religious conflicts are further determined by the large number of currents of ideas, beliefs and attachments that succeed in asserting themselves—by the formation of different intellectual and moral crucibles within which the convictions and sentiments of single individuals are variously fused and alloyed.

So we see Buddhism developing within Brahman society; prophetism and, later on, the various schools of the Sadducees, the Essenes and the Zealots, keeping the life of Israel in ferment; Stoicism, Manichaeism, Christianity and the cult of Mithras competing for supremacy in the Helleno-Roman world; Mazdaism —a modification of Manichaeism with a marked tendency toward communism in wealth and women—sweeping through the Persia of the Sassanids; Mohammedanism starting in Arabia and spreading rapidly into Asia, Africa and Europe. Phenomena altogether similar, though molded to the more rationalistic character of modern European civilization, are the liberalism and radicalism of the nineteenth century and, better yet, social democracy, which started almost contemporaneously with liberalism but has maintained its proselyting efficiency longer, so that it will continue to be one of the most significant historical factors in the twentieth century as it was in the nineteenth. Besides the movements we have just named, it would be easy to trace a great many other minor currents in the history of civilized peoples, doctrines which have been more or less fortunate and have had more or less widespread vogues, but which in any event have helped to feed the instincts for contention, struggle, self-sacrifice and persecution that are so deeply rooted in the hearts of men.

All these doctrines, all these currents of ideas, sentiments, convictions, seem to originate in somewhat the same way, and they all seem to present certain constant characteristics in their early beginnings. The human being—so feeble a creature in dealing with his own passions and the passions of others, often more selfish than need requires, as a rule vain, envious, petty— very rarely fails to keep two great aspirations before his eyes, two sentiments that ennoble, uplift and purify him. He seeks the truth, he loves justice; and sometimes he is able to sacrifice to those two ideals some part of the satisfaction he would other- wise give to his passions and his material interests. Far more complex and sensitive a being than the savage and the barbarian, civilized man may in some cases rise to a most delicate con- ception of these two sentiments.

At certain moments in the history of a given society, an individual rises with the conviction that he has something new to say with regard to the search for truth, or a loftier doctrine to teach with regard to the better realization of justice. Such an individual, if he has certain endowments of character, and if environment and any number of other incidental circumstances favor, is the seed that may produce a tree with branches spreading far abroad over large parts of the world.

3. History has not always preserved all the details that we might wish to have about the lives of these founders of religious and politico-social schools—the latter are in a sense religions too, though shorn of strictly theological elements. Some biographies, however, are fairly well known. The lives of Mohammed, Luther, Calvin and especially Rousseau, who left his memoirs, can be analyzed with relative adequacy.

A fundamental quality that all such people must have is, it would seem, a profound sense of their own importance or, better, a sincere belief in the efficacy of their work. If they believe in God, they will always consider themselves destined by the Omnipotent to reform religion and save humanity. Undoubt- edly it is not to such men that one should look for a perfect balance of all the intellectual and moral faculties. But neither can they be considered altogether mad—insanity is a disease that presupposes in the patient an earlier state of sanity. They are rather to be classed with so-called eccentrics, or fanatics, in the sense that they attach an exaggerated importance to certain phases of life, or of human activity, and stake their very lives and all the effort of which they are capable on one card, striving to attain their life's ideal by following unwonted paths which most people consider absurdly mistaken. But it is evident, on the other hand, that the man whose faculties are all in perfect balance, who has an exact perception of the results that he can achieve, as compared with the effort and sacrifice that will be required for achieving them, who takes a modest and sensible view of his own importance and of the real and abiding effects that his activity can have on the world in the ordinary course of human events, who calculates exactly and coldly the probabilities for and against his succeeding, will never launch out on any original and daring enterprise and will never do any very great things. If all men were normal and balanced the history of the world would be very different and, we must confess, not a little monotonous.

Indispensable in the leader of a party, in the founder of a sect or a religion, or, one might say, in any "pastor of peoples" who would make his own personality felt and force society to follow his views, is a capacity for instilling his own convictions and especially his own enthusiasms into others, a capacity for inducing many to live the sort of intellectual and moral life that he wants them to live and to make sacrifices for the ideals that he has conceived.

Not all reformers have the gift of communicating their own sentiments and passions to others. Those who lack it may have great originality of thought and feeling, but they are ineffectual in practical life and often end as prophets without believers, innovators without followers, misunderstood and ridiculed geniuses. Those who do possess it not only inspire their apostles and the masses with their enthusiasms, sometimes to the point of frenzy, but succeed in the end in awakening a sort of veneration for their persons, in becoming objects of worship, so that their least act acquires its importance, their every word is believed without discussion, their every nod is blindly obeyed. About them an aura of exaltation gathers. It is highly contagious and spurs converts to acts of daring and sacrifice that certainly could not be performed by individuals in a normal state of mind.

This explains the enormous success of certain preachers and certain teachers—the extraordinary fortune, for instance, of types so different as St. Francis of Assisi and Abelard, so unlike in many respects but so alike in the art of interesting men. It explains why Mohammed was held in such veneration by his initiates and disciples that they collected his spittle reverently and cherished the hairs of his beard as relics, and why a mere hint on his part was enough to encompass the murder of a dangerous adversary. Speaking of someone whom he considered to be a great obstacle to his designs, Mohammed would say, in the presence of some young man of the more fanatical type: "Will no one ever free me of this dog?" The disciple would rush off and commit the murder. Afterwards, naturally, Mohammed would condemn the crime, declaring that he had ordered no such thing. Any number of leaders of sects and political parties have imitated Mohammed, consciously or unconsciously, in this respect. And how many of them are doing the same thing today! Plenty of people were always ready to rush into the most hazardous undertakings at a nod from Mazzini. The various enterprises in practical communism that were launched in the course of the nineteenth century, from Owen down to Fourier and Lazzaretti, never failed to find large numbers of persons willing and eager to sacrifice their worldly goods. When one of these political or religious "founders" happens to be a fighter, as Ján Ziska was, he manages to inspire his followers with an absolute certainty of victory and hence with uncommon courage.

Nor should we expect to find an altogether exquisite moral sense presiding uniformly over all acts in the lives of these eccentrics who initiate movements of ideas and sentiments. Any such expectation would be disappointed. Absorbed in the pursuit of their visions to the exclusion of everything else, they are always ready to suffer themselves and to make others suffer so long as their ends be attained. Generally, indeed, they feel a high disdain for everyday needs and for the material and immediate interests of life, or at least they are largely indifferent to them. Even when they do not say as much in words, they censure in their hearts people who are busy at sowing, reaping and storing away the harvests. They seem to feel certain that once the Kingdom of God, or Truth or Justice, in their sense of those terms, is established, human beings will be as easily fed as are the fowl of the air or the lilies of the field. When they live in rationalistic and ostensibly more positive times, they take no account of the depletion of public resources that a mere gesture toward actuating their ideals would occasion.

There seem to be three periods through which the life of every great reformer passes.

In a first period he is conceiving his doctrine and working it out in his mind. During that stage he may be acting in good faith. He can be called a fanatic, but not as yet a cheat and a charlatan. In a second period he begins to preach, and then the need of making an impression induces him inevitably "to lay on," to overstress certain colorings, and so to become a poseur. The third period comes if he is lucky enough to be able to make a practical attempt to put his teachings into practice. Once that stage is reached, he finds himself at grips with all the imperfections and weaknesses of human nature, and he is obliged to compromise on the side of morals if he wants to succeed. All reformers agree deep down in their hearts that the end justifies the means, that if men are to be led they have to be fooled to a certain extent. So, moving on from compromise to compromise, they come to a point where the most acute psychologist would find it hard to tell exactly where their sincerity ends and acting and chicanery begin.

Father Ohrwalder was for some years a prisoner of the Mahdists and wrote an account of his experiences. At one point he describes Mohammed Ahmed, the slave trader who founded Mahdism, as a man inspired by a sincere religious zeal. At another point he makes him out a hypocrite and a charlatan. Father Ohrwalder was sharply criticized for that inconsistency. For our part we find nothing implausible about the two judgments, especially since they refer to two different periods in the Mahdi's life.

Certainly the most disparate moral elements may function simultaneously in the same individual. That was the case with Enfantin, the second high priest of Saint-Simonianism, to whom a disciple in the latter days of the movement wrote: "Others criticize you for trying to pose all the time. I agree with you in thinking that posing is in your nature. It is your mission, your gift."[1] Mohammed undeniably had a sincere and honest aspiration toward a religion that was less crude, less materialistic, than anything that had been practiced by the

---

[1] Thureau-Dangin, *Histoire de la Monarchie de Juillet*, vol. I, chap. VIII.

Arabs before his time. Nevertheless the verses of the Koran, which the archangel Gabriel communicated to him one by one, arrived at most opportune moments to free him of irksome promises that he had made or from strict observance of moral laws that he had laid down for others in earlier verses. It became important for Mohammed at one time to increase the number of his wives to seven, in order that he might strengthen certain political ties and incidentally satisfy sentimental fancies. In the Koran he had expressly limited the number of legitimate wives to four, and the precept had been proclaimed for all believers. But along came the archangel Gabriel with a most convenient verse, which authorized the apostle of God to ignore his own injunction.[1]

To simplify our task we have been implicitly assuming that the founder of every new religion or philosophical doctrine is a single individual. That is not strictly true. At times, when a reform is morally and intellectually ripe in a historical sense and finds an environment that is perfectly attuned to it, several masters may come forward simultaneously. That was the case with Protestantism, when Luther, Zwingli and Calvin began to preach almost at the same time. Sometimes the success of a first master breeds competition and plagiarism. Moseilama, for instance, and not a few others, tried to imitate Mohammed, proclaiming themselves in their turn prophets of Allah. More frequent is the case where an innovator does not succeed in developing his doctrine fully, much less in putting it into practice. Then one or a dozen continuators may arise, and Fate the Unfair may name the doctrine after one of them instead of the real founder. That seems to be happening in modern socialism, of which Marx is generally proclaimed the founder. Its first intellectual and moral parent was undoubtedly Rousseau. The master or masters who continue the work of the first founder must not be confused with the mere apostles, of whom we are about to speak.

4. About the individual who first formulates a new doctrine there always gathers a more or less populous group that receives the word directly from the master's lips and is profoundly imbued with his sentiments. Every messiah must have his

[1] Hammer-Purgstall, *Gemäldesaal.*

apostles, since, in almost all the manifestations of his moral and material activity, the human being needs society; there is no enthusiasm that does not wane, no faith that does not falter, under prolonged isolation. The school, the church, the agape, the lodge, the "regular meeting"—any grouping, whatever it chances to be called, of persons who feel and think the same way, who have the same enthusiasms, the same hates, the same loves, the same interpretation of life—intensifies, exalts and develops their sentiments and so works these into the character of each individual member that the stamp of the association is indelible upon him.

Within this directing group, as a rule, the original inspiration of the master is developed, refined, worked out, so as to become a real political, religious or philosophical system, unblemished by too many inconsistencies and contradictions, or too obvious ones. Within this group the sacred fire of propaganda is kept burning even after the first author of the doctrine has vanished; and to this nucleus, which is recruited automatically by a process of selection and segregation, the future of the new doctrine is entrusted. However exceptional the master's originality of vision, his strength of feeling, his aptitude for propaganda, those qualities are without avail if he does not succeed in founding a school before his material or spiritual death; whereas, when the breath that animates the school is healthy and vigorous, all the inadequacies and flaws which may later be detected in the work of the founder can be overlooked or corrected little by little, and the propaganda will continue active and influential.

Outside the directing nucleus comes the throng of proselytes. While this group constitutes the stronger element numerically, and supplies the church or party with its material strength and its economic basis, it is the most negligible factor intellectually and morally. A number of modern sociologists declare that the masses are conservative and "misoneistic"—chary of novelties. That means that the masses are hard to win to a new faith. However, once they are won to it, they abandon it with the greatest reluctance, and when they do drop away, the fault lies almost always with the promoting nucleus. This latter group is always the first to be affected by indifference and skepticism. The best way to make others believe is to be profoundly convinced oneself—the art of arousing passion lies in one's own

capacity for being intensely aroused.   When the priest does not
feel his faith, the congregation becomes indifferent and is ripe for
conversion to some other doctrine that finds a more zealous
minister.   If the officer is not imbued with the military spirit, if
he is not ready to give his life for the dignity of his flag, the
soldier will not die at his post.   If the sectarian is not a fanatic,
he will never sweep the crowds into rebellion.

In the case of ancient doctrines, or beliefs that have been
established for some length of time and so have acquired traditions and fixed and circumscribed fields of activity, birth generally determines the individual's acceptance of them and his
membership in the organizations that have formed around them.
In Germany or the United States, one is almost always Catholic,
Protestant or Jew, depending on the religion of the family into
which one is born.   In Spain and Italy, anyone who has any
religion left is almost always a Catholic.   But if a number of
different doctrines are still in process of formation in a country,
have active propagandas and are competing for adherents back
and forth, then the personal choice of the individual of average
intelligence depends upon a mass of circumstances, partly
accidental and partly resulting from the skill with which the
propaganda is carried on.   In France a young man becomes a
conservative or a radical according as the ideas of his father, his
teacher at school or his schoolmates chance to exercise the greater
influence over him at the moment when his ideas begin to form.
At an age when a boy's general ideas are still plastic and he is
conscious mainly of a need to be aroused emotionally, to love or
to hate something or someone, a book that comes into his hands,
a newspaper to which he has daily access, may determine the
whole trend of his after life.   For many people, political, religious
or philosophical opinions are, at bottom, very secondary matters,
especially when the first flush of youth has passed and the age of
practical occupations, of "business," comes.   So, to some
extent through indolence, to some extent through habit, partly
again through mistaken pride and respect for so-called consistency
of character, a man often ends, when no strong conflict with his
interests is involved, by keeping all his life long a doctrine that he
embraced in a moment of youthful impulse, devoting to it such
little energy and activity as the practical man is wont to set
apart for what is called "the ideal."

However, from the fact that the individual's choice of a belief or a political party may largely be determined by chance, it does not follow that chance is the main factor in the success of any given school or church. Some doctrines are well suited to making proselytes, others are less so. Whether a political or religious teaching is to win wide acceptance depends almost exclusively on three factors. In the first place it must be adapted to the given historical moment. In the second place, it must satisfy the greatest possible number of human passions, sentiments and inclinations, particularly such as are most widely diffused and most firmly rooted in the public. In the third place, it must have a well-organized directing nucleus, or "executive committee," made up of individuals who consecrate their lives to the maintenance and propagation of the spirit that animates the faith.

5. For a doctrine to be adapted to a given historical moment in a given society, it must above all correspond to the degree of maturity which the human mind has attained at that moment in that society. A monotheistic religion will easily triumph when minds have progressed sufficiently to comprehend that all natural phenomena may be ascribed to one cause, and that the force that rules the universe is one. Rationalism can be taken as the basis of successful doctrines when free inquiry and the results of the natural and historical sciences have undermined belief in revealed religions, and the conception of a God created in the image and likeness of man and intervening arbitrarily in human events has come to seem absurd to the ruling classes.

In the centuries when Christianity was spreading through the Roman Empire, almost everyone, pagans and Christians alike, believed in the supernatural and in miracles; but the pagan supernatural had become too gross and incoherent, while the Christian supernatural, besides better answering certain needs of the human spirit, was more systematic and less childish, and so was destined to triumph. Lucian was an utter skeptic, laughing at everyone—now at the pagans, now at the Christians. But he was an exception in the second century of our era. The mean intelligence of the educated public of that time was better represented by Celsus, who was a deist and believed in the supernatural and in miracles but nevertheless ridiculed the Old and the New Testaments. But since Celsus had started out on the path which is so satisfactory to rationalists and which, in fact, sixteen centuries later and under far different conditions, was to turn out so well for Voltaire, he should have seen that it would have been much easier to provoke ridicule and disgust for the disgraceful license and childish squabblings of the gods of Olympus than for the Christian histories. It is evident enough to us in our day that classical paganism had for some time been incapable of satisfying either the emotions or the intelligence of the people of that period. As Renan well observes,[1] if the Greco-Roman world had not become Christian, it would have been converted to Mithraism, or to some other Asiatic religion that was at once more mystical than classical paganism and less incoherent.

So it was with Rousseau. He emerged and prospered at a time when first humanism and the Reformation, then the progress of the exact and natural sciences, then finally Voltaire and the Encyclopaedia, had discredited the whole Christian and medieval world, so that a new rational—we do not say reasonable—explanation of political institutions was in a position to win acceptance. If we analyze the lives of Luther and Mohammed it is easy to see that at the time when they appeared Germany and Arabia were ready to welcome their doctrines.

When the human being has a certain culture and is not under any engrossing pressure of material needs, he generally manifests a tendency to rise above the ordinary preoccupations of life and interest himself in something higher than himself, something that concerns the interests of the society to which he belongs. It is much easier for a new doctrine to prosper, accordingly, in places and situations where this idealistic tendency is not able to find satisfaction in the political system in its prevailing forms, and where, therefore, a man's enthusiasms and ambitions, his love of combat, his instincts for leadership, do not find a ready outlet. Christianity would certainly not have spread so rapidly in Rome in the days of the republic, when the state could offer its citizens the excitements of election campaigns, or when it was waging its terrible duel with Carthage. But the empire brought peace. It quieted conflicts between the nations and entrusted all public functions to salaried employees. That

[1] More particularly in *Marc Aurèle*.

prepared the ground for a long period of security and political repose that rendered the new religion the best possible service. In the age just past, the consolidation of the bureaucratic state, the ending of religious wars, the growth of a cultured, well-to-do class that had no part in political functions, supplied the basis first for the liberal and then for the radical socialist movements. Nations sometimes have periods of, so to say, psychological exhaustion, when they seem to need repose. That is what we mean when we say, with less aptness of phrase, perhaps, that a people has grown old. At any rate, if a society has had no revolutions and undergone no serious political changes for some centuries, when it begins at last to emerge from its long torpor it is much more easily persuaded that the triumph of a new doctrine, the establishment of a new form of government, will mark the beginning of a new era, a new golden age, and that on its advent all men will become good and happy in a new land of Cathay. That was the characteristic illusion in France around 1789. It was to an extent the illusion in Italy in 1848.

On the other hand, after a series of disturbances and changes, the enthusiasm and faith that political innovators and political novelties have inspired tends to fall off considerably, and a vague feeling of skepticism and fatigue spreads through the masses. However, capacity for faith and enthusiasm is exhausted far less readily than might appear at first sight. Disillusionment has little effect, on the whole, upon religious doctrines that are based on the supernatural, that solve problems relating to the prime cause of the universe or that postpone realization of the ideals of happiness and justice to another life.

But strangely enough, even doctrines that are apparently more realistic and should yield their fruits in this life succeed very well in surviving the refutations of them that are supplied by experience and the facts of everyday living. After all, illusions endure because illusion is a need for almost all men, a need that they feel no less strongly than their material needs. A system of illusions, therefore, is not easily discredited until it can be replaced with a new system. As we often see, when that is not possible, not even a sequence of sufferings, of terrible trials born of experiences more terrible still, is enough to disenchant a people; or, more exactly, discouragement rather than disillusionment settles upon that people and endures as long as the generation that has personally suffered still lives. But after that, if there has been no change in the trend of ideas and in the education of sentiments, the moment social energies have somewhat revived, the same illusions produce new conflicts and new misfortunes over again. Moreover it is in the nature of men to retain favorable memories of the days during which they suffered, and of the individuals who caused their sufferings. That is the case especially when a certain length of time has elapsed. The masses always end by admiring and draping in poetic legend leaders like Napoleon, who have brought untold pain and misfortune upon them but who at the same time have satisfied their need for ennobling emotions and their fantastic craving for novelties and great things.

6. The capacity of a doctrine to satisfy the needs of the human spirit depends not only upon requirements of time and place but also upon conditions that are independent of time and place— upon basic psychological laws that must not be disregarded. In fact, this second element in the success of ambitious political and religious doctrines is an exceedingly important one.

As a general rule, if a system of ideas, beliefs, feelings, is to be accepted by great masses of human beings, it must address the loftier sentiments of the human spirit: it must promise that justice and equality will reign in this world, or in some other, or it must proclaim that the good will be rewarded and the wicked punished. At the same time it will not go far wrong if it yields some small satisfaction to the envy and rancor that are generally felt toward the powerful and the fortunate and intimates that, in this life or in some other, there will come a time when the last shall be first and the first last. It will help if some phase of the doctrine can manage to offer a refuge for good souls, gentle souls, who seek in meditation and resignation some solace from the conflicts and disappointments of life. It will be useful, also— one might even say indispensable—for the doctrine to have some means of utilizing the spirit of abnegation and sacrifice that predominates in certain individuals and of guiding it into proper channels, though the same doctrine must also leave some little elbowroom for pride and vanity.

It follows, therefore, that believers must always be "the people" or "the better people," or "progressive spirits," who speak for the vanguard of real progress. So the Christian must be enabled to think with complacency that everybody not of the Christian faith will be damned.   The Brahman must be given grounds for rejoicing that he alone is descended from the head of Brahma and has the exalted honor of reading the sacred books.   The Buddhist must be taught highly to prize the privilege he has of attaining Nirvana soonest.   The Mohammedan must recall with satisfaction that he alone is the true believer, and that all others are infidel dogs in this life and tormented dogs in the next.   The radical socialist must be convinced that all who do not think as he does are either selfish, money-spoiled bourgeois or ignorant and servile simpletons.   These are all examples of arguments that provide for one's need of esteeming one's self and one's own religion or convictions and at the same time for the need of despising and hating others.

From hatred to conflict is only a step.   In fact there is no political party or religious sect that does not envisage war— bloody or not, as the case may turn out—upon those who do not accept its dogmas.   If it eschews conflict altogether and preaches compassion and submission in all cases, that is just a sign that it is conscious of weakness and thinks it would be risking too much in undertaking a war.   In struggle, besides, all the less noble but nonetheless widespread appetites of the human heart are taken account of—love of luxury, lust for blood and women, ambition to command and to tyrannize.

Certainly no recipe can be given for founding an enduring political party or religious doctrine that will contain the exact dosages required for satisfying every human sentiment.   But one may declare with all assurance that to realize the purpose mentioned there must be a fusion, in certain amounts, of lofty sentiments and low passions, of precious metal and base metal— otherwise the alloy will not stand the wear and tear.   A doctrine that does not take sufficient account of the differing and contradictory qualities that human nature shows has little power of appeal, and it will have to be revamped in that respect if it is to gain a permanent following.   The mingling of good and evil is so inborn in human nature that a certain amount of fine metal must be present even in the alloys of which criminal gangs, secret societies and murderous sects are compounded; and a little of the base metal must enter into the complex of sentiments that inspires companies of heroes and ascetic communities that make a fetish of self-sacrifice. Too great a deficiency, therefore, of either the good or the bad elements always has the same results: it prevents any wide dissemination of the doctrine, or the special discipline, that the given sect enforces upon its members.

There have been, as there still are, organized groups of bandits that preach theft, murder and the destruction of property. But in such cases the perpetration of the criminal act is almost always colored with some specious political or religious doctrine that serves to decoy into the company some misguided person who is not wholly contemptible, whose crumb of respectability renders common turpitude more bearable to the public and introduces into the association a modicum of moral sense that is indispensable if a villainy is to succeed. Bismarck is credited with the apothegm that a man needs a little honesty to be a perfect rascal. The Sicilian Maffia, among other criminal associations, had its rules of ethics, and its members a certain sense of honor. The Maffiusi sometimes kept their word with nonmembers, and they rarely betrayed each other. It is mainly to the limitations they set to their wrongdoing that certain criminal associations owe their extraordinarily long lives. Macaulay observes that murder plots almost never succeed in England proper because English murderers lack the grain of moral sense that is essential to mutual trust. He may have been right or wrong as to the fact; the corollary he derives from it is certainly sound.

We have an example of societies of the type mentioned in the Assassins, who ravaged Syria and 'Iraq 'Arabi in the Middle Ages. The Assassins were a degenerate wing of the Ismailians, a relatively innocuous sect that had a wide following in the Mohammedan world about the year 1100. The doctrine and discipline of the sect had many points in common with present-day Freemasonry in the Latin countries.[1] The Thugs, or Stranglers, were famous in India down to the middle of the last century. Almost all travelers who have written about China speak of secret societies. Some of them are country-wide and have, or pretend to have, strictly political objectives. To the list might be added the "underground" political movements that are common today in Europe and America.

[1] Clavel, *Geschiedenis der vrijmetselarij;* Amari, *Storia dei Musulmani in Sicilia,* vol. II, pp. 119 f.; Hammer-Purgstall, *History of the Assassins.*

On the other hand, certain associations of human beings are founded upon the renunciation of every worldly vanity and pleasure, on the complete sacrifice of the member's personality, either to the advantage of the association or to the advantage of all humanity. The bonze convents in the Buddhist world and the Catholic religious orders in the West are familiar examples of this type of institution. These associations are in general recruited from among individuals who are specially fitted for their calling, either through peculiar circumstances in their personal lives or through a natural inclination toward self-sacrifice and resignation. We cannot say, however, that they are wholly exempt from worldly passions. A desire to win the admiration of the devout, the ambition of many individuals to excel within the order, and an even stronger ambition that the order shall surpass rival orders—these are all powerful motives that have contributed to the long and prosperous lives of such associations.

But in all these cases, though we see that a bit of good is always found mixed in with the evil, and that a bit of evil always sours the good, we are still confronted by the fact that such associations are still none too large. They have never embraced all the members of a great human society. In spite of all the specious justifications of crime that have been devised, sects of murderers and thieves have never been more than diseased social excrescences. They may have succeeded for a time in terrorizing, or even influencing, wide areas. They have never converted a great people to their principles. The monastery too has always been an exception, and wherever the monastic life has spread and become the habitual occupation of any considerable part of a population, the order has rapidly strayed from its original principles. The Ebionite churches of early Christian days required all the faithful to pool their earnings, and they sought to extend the monastic type over all Christian society. However, the sect led a hand-to-mouth existence and soon disappeared, for if any amount of abnegation may be obtained from a small number of chosen individuals who are trained by an apposite discipline, the same thing is not possible with a whole human mass, in which the good is necessarily mingled with the bad and needs and passions of all sorts have to be reckoned with. For that reason, if an experiment in social regeneration is to prove anything it has to be applied to an entire people, granted that one can be found to lend itself to such an experiment or can be forced to do so.

7. For all these reasons a religion with too lofty a moral system produces at the most those good, and indeed far from disparageable, results that come from a man's making an effort to attain an ideal that lies beyond his powers of attainment. But in practice such a religion must end by being observed with scant scrupulousness. The continuous conflict between religious belief and human necessity, between the thing recognized as holy and conforming with divine law and the thing that is done, and indeed has to be done, constitutes the eternal contradiction, the inevitable hypocrisy, that appears in the lives of many peoples, and by no means of Christian peoples only. A short time before Christianity became, thanks to Constantine, the official religion of the Roman Empire, the good Lactantius exclaimed:

If only the true God were honored [that is, if all men were converted to Christianity], there would be no more dissensions or wars. Men would all be united by the ties of an indissoluble love, for they would all look upon each other as brothers. No one would contrive further snares to be rid of his neighbor. Each would be content with little, and there would be no more frauds and thefts. How blessed then would be man's estate! What a golden age would dawn upon the world![1]

Such, in fact, had to be the opinion of a Christian, for he was convinced that every believer should put the precepts and spirit of his religion integrally into practice and thought it quite possible for a whole society to observe them as they were observed by those chosen spirits who, at the cost of their lives, refused to deny their faith in the face of Diocletian's persecution. But if Lactantius had lived only fifty years longer he might have perceived that no religion can of itself raise the moral level of an entire people very rapidly or to any great extent. Had he been reborn in the Middle Ages, he could have satisfied himself that by adapting itself more and more to shifting historical circumstances and to the perennial demands of the human spirit, the same religion that had supplied the martyr and was supplying

[1] Quoted by Boissier, "Le Christianisme et l'invasion des barbares," p. 351.

the missionary could just as readily supply the crusader and the inquisitor.

Mohammedans in general observe the Koran far more scrupulously than Christians observe the Gospel, but that is due not only to a blinder faith (which in turn is due to a lower scientific level) but also to the fact that the prescriptions of Mohammed are morally less lofty, and so are humanly more realizable, than the prescriptions of Jesus. Those who practice Islamism in general abstain very strictly from wine and pork, but an individual who has never tasted wine or pork feels no appreciable discomfort if he is deprived of them. For that matter, it seems that when Mussulmans have lived with Christians in countries that produce wine extensively, they have observed the precepts of the Prophet on the subject of intoxicating liquors less scrupulously. The history of the Saracens in Sicily shows not a few cases of drunkenness among Mohammedans. Ebn-El Theman, emir of Catania, was in a state of complete intoxication when he ordered the veins of his wife, a sister of the emir of Palermo, to be opened. An Arab poet, Ibn-Hamdis, sang the praises of the good wine of Syracuse, its amber color and its musklike fragrance.[1]

Adultery, again, is much rarer among adherents of Islam than among Christians, but divorce is much easier among the former and Mohammed allows a man several wives and does not prohibit relations with slaves. Believers in Islam are strongly advised to give alms to members of their faith and to be lavish with them in every sort of assistance, but they are also taught that to exterminate infidels in war and to levy tribute on them in peace are meritorious acts. At bottom, therefore, the Koran serves prescriptions to suit all tastes and, if one remains faithful to it in the letter and the spirit, one can get to paradise by any number of broad highways. Not a few Islamic doctrines, meantime, chance to conflict with some of the stronger and more deeply rooted instincts of human nature. They are the ones that least influence the conduct of Mussulmans. Mohammed, for instance, promises paradise to all who fall in a holy war. Now if every believer were to guide his conduct by that assurance in the Koran, every time a Mohammedan army found itself faced by unbelievers it ought either to conquer or to

[1] Amari, *Storia dei Musulmani in Sicilia*, vol. II, p. 531.

fall to the last man.   It cannot be denied that a certain number
of individuals do live up to the letter of the Prophet's word, but
as between defeat and death followed by eternal bliss, the
majority of Mohammedans normally elect defeat.

Buddhists, in general, are strict in observing the outward
precepts of their religion, yet in putting the spirit of the precepts
into practice they are as deft as the Christians at avoiding
embarrassment by making, to use Molière's phrase, their arrangements with Heaven.   The next to the last king of Burma was
the wise and canny Meudoume-Men.   Besides governing his
subjects well, he had an enthusiastic interest in religious and
philosophical discussion and regularly summoned to his presence
all Englishmen and Europeans of distinction who passed through
Mandalay, the capital of his dominions.   In his discourses with
them he always upheld the superiority of Buddhist ethics to the
morals preached by other religions and never failed to call the
attention of his guests to the fact that the conduct of Christians
did not always conform to the precepts of Christian doctrine.
Certainly it could have cost him no great effort to show that the
behavior of the English in wresting a portion of Burmese territory
from his predecessor was in no way consistent with the Gospel.
He, on his side, had been brought up in a bonze monastery.   He
conscientiously observed the prescriptions of Buddha.   At his
court no animal was ever slaughtered, and Europeans who stayed
there for any length of time found the vegetable diet irksome
and were obliged secretly to fill out by hunting birds' eggs in the
woods.   Not only that.   Meudoume-Men would never, for any
reason in the world, order a capital execution.   In fact, when
anybody's presence inconvenienced him too seriously, the wily
monarch would merely ask of his prime minister whether So-
and-so were still of this world.   And when, after many repetitions
of the question, the prime minister would finally answer no,
Meudoume-Men would smile contentedly.   He had violated no
precept of his religion but still had made his point: which was that
a certain human soul should begin somewhat earlier than might
normally have been expected the series of transmigrations that
leads at last, as the Buddhist faith assures, to fusion with the
universal soul.[1]

[1] Plauchut, "Un Royaume disparu."

The doctrine of the ancient Stoics was essentially virile and—except, perhaps, as regards "pose" and vanity, which were common frailties among them—made little, if any, concession to the passions, weaknesses or sentiments of men. But for that very reason the influence of Stoicism was limited to a section of the cultured classes. The pagan masses remained wholly alien to its propaganda. The Stoic school may have helped, at certain periods, to form the character of a part of the ruling class in the Roman Empire. To it, undoubtedly, a number of good emperors owed their training. But from the moment that its members no longer cluttered the steps of a throne it was completely ineffectual. Powerless to change, because its intellectual and strictly philosophical side quite overshadowed its dogmatic and emotional sides, it could not compete with Christianity for control of the Roman world, and it would have succeeded no better in competition with Judaism, Islam or Buddhism.

One could not maintain that it makes no difference whether a people embraces one religion or political doctrine or another. It would be difficult to show that the practical effects of Christianity are not different from those of Mohammedanism or socialism. In the long run a belief does give a certain bent to human sentiments, and such bents may have far-reaching consequences. But it seems certain that no belief will ever succeed in making the human being anything essentially different from what he is. To state the situation in other words, no belief will ever make men wholly good or wholly bad, wholly altruistic or wholly selfish. Some adaptation to the lower moral and emotional level that corresponds to the human average is indispensable in all religions. Those who refuse to recognize that fact make it easier, it seems to us, for people who use the relative inefficacy of religious sentiments and political doctrines as an argument to prove their absolute inefficacy. There comes to mind in this connection an opinion that has often been expressed. The bandits of southern Italy usually went about in true South Italian style, laden with scapulars and images of saints and madonnas. At the same time they were often guilty of murders and other crimes—whence the conclusion that religious beliefs had no practical influence upon them. Now, before such an inference could with justice be drawn, one would have to show that if the bandits had not

carried scapulars and madonnas they would not have committed
additional murders or acts of ferocity. If the images saved a
single human life, a single pang of sorrow, a single tear, there
would be adequate grounds for crediting them with some
influence.

8. As we have seen (§4, above), a third factor figures in the
spread and survival of any system of religious or political ideas—
namely, the organization of the directing nucleus and the means
it employs for converting the masses or holding them loyal to a
given belief or doctrine. As we also have seen, the nucleus
originates in the first instance in a spontaneous process of selection and segregation. Thereafter its cohesion is based in the
main on a phenomenon of the human spirit which we have called
"mimetism," or imitation—the tendency of an individual's
passions, sentiments and beliefs to develop in accord with the
currents that prevail in the environment in which he is morally
formed and educated. It is altogether natural that in a country
that has attained some degree of culture a certain number of
young people should have a capacity for developing enthusiasms
about what they hold to be true and ethical, about ideas which, in
semblance at least, are generous and lofty and concern the
destiny of a nation or of humanity at large.

These sentiments and the spirit of abnegation and self-sacrifice
that result from them may remain in a state of potentiality and
become atrophied, or they may enjoy a luxuriant blossoming,
according as they are cultivated or not; and the fruits they
yield differ widely according to the differing ways in which they
are cultivated.

In the son of a shopkeeper who comes into contact with no one
except the customers and clerks in his father's place of business,
the sentiments mentioned will probably never amount to very
much or even manifest themselves at all, unless the boy be one
of those rare individuals of superior type who succeed in developing all by themselves. A young man who receives a religious
training from his earliest childhood and then goes on to a Catholic
seminary may become a missionary and consecrate his whole
life to the triumph of his faith. Another, who is born into a
family that has a coat of arms, is educated in a military academy
and then becomes a lieutenant in a regiment, where he finds

comrades and superiors who are all imbued with the same sort of convictions, will think it his first and all-embracing duty to obey the orders of his sovereign all his life long and, if need be, to get himself killed for his king. Another, finally, who is born into an environment of veteran conspirators and revolutionaries, who has thrilled and shuddered from his earliest days at tales of political persecutions and riots at the barricades, and whose mind has been fed largely on the writings of Rousseau, Mazzini or Marx, will deem it his sacred duty to struggle tirelessly against oppression by organized government and will be ready to face prison and the gallows in the name of revolution. All that occurs because once the individual's environment is formed— Catholic, ecclesiastical, bureaucratic, military, revolutionary, as it may be—that individual, especially if he is a normal young man not altogether superior in intellect nor yet utterly vulgar and commonplace, will give to his sentimental and affective faculties the bent that the environment suggests to him, so that certain sentiments rather than others will develop in him—the spirit of rebellion and struggle, say, rather than the spirit of passive obedience and self-sacrifice. This training, this *dressage*, as the French call it, succeeds better with the young than with adults, with enthusiastic and impassioned temperaments better than with cold, deliberate, calculating temperaments, with docile souls better than with rebellious spirits, unless the doctrine, whether in essence or because of special historical circumstances, makes a point of cultivating and intensifying the rebellious instincts.

One condition especially is favorable, not to say indispensable, to this mimetic process—the process by which the individual is assimilated to the environment. The environment must be closed to all influences from outside, so that no sentiments, and especially no ideas, will ever get into it except such as bear the trade-mark of the environment. No book that is on the Index must ever enter the seminary. Philosophy must begin and end with St. Thomas Aquinas. When one reads one must read theology and the works of the Fathers. The tales that are offered to the child's curiosity and hunger for romance will be tales of martyrs and heroic confessors. In the military academy one will read and talk of the exploits of great captains, of the glories of one's own army and one's own dynasty. Education and training will be such as are strictly required for learning the soldier's profession and for coming to prize highly the honor of being an officer, a gentleman, a loyal champion of king and country. In the revolutionary "study hour" the talk will be all on the victories and glories of the sinless masses, on the nefarious doings of tyrants and their hirelings, on the greed and baseness of the bourgeoisie; and any book which is not written in accordance with the word and spirit of the masters will be mercilessly proscribed. Any glimmer of mental balance, any ray of light from other moral and intellectual worlds, that strays into one of these closed environments produces doubts, falterings and desertions. Real history, that earnest, objective search for facts, the discipline which teaches us to know men and appraise them independently of caste, religion or political party, which takes account of their weaknesses and virtues for what they really are, which trains and exercises the faculties of observation and the sense of reality, must be completely banned.

Now all that, at bottom, means nothing more or less than a real unbalancing of the spirit, and every environment inflicts that unbalancing upon the recruit who is drawn into its orbit. He is offered only a partial picture of life. That picture has been carefully revised, circumscribed and corrected, and the neophyte must take it as the whole and real picture of life. Certain sentiments are overstressed, certain others are minimized, and an idea of justice, honesty, duty, is presented which, if not fundamentally wrong, is certainly grossly incomplete. This thoroughgoing identification of the concept of justice and right with the given religious or political doctrine—even a morally lofty one—sometimes drives upright but violent souls to extreme fanaticism and political crimes, and may even succeed in extinguishing all gracious sentiment in a chivalrous people. According to an anecdote relating to Mohammed, a battle was being fought at Onein between the Prophet's followers and his opponents during his lifetime. In the ranks of the dissidents was one Doreid-Ben-Sana, the Bayard of his age and people. Though ninety years old, he had had himself carried to the battlefield on a litter. A young Islamite, one Rebiaa-ben-Rafii, managed to reach the spot where Doreid was and struck him with a well-aimed blow of his sword. But the weapon fell to pieces. "What a wretched sword your father gave you, boy," said the old hero. "My scimitar has a real temper. Take it,

and then go and tell your mother that you have slain Doreid
with the weapon with which he so many times defended the
liberty and good right of the Arabs, and the honor of their
women." Rebiaa took Doreid's scimitar and slew him, and then
went so far in his cynical rage as in fact to carry the message
to his mother. Less fanatical than her son about the new
religion, perhaps because she was a woman of the old school,
she seems to have received him with the contempt he deserved.[1]

And yet as we have seen (§3, above), perfectly balanced
individuals, who know and appreciate all their duties and give
to each the importance that it really has, are not likely to devote
all their lives and energies to achieving one particular and
definite thing. Mass exaggerations, or if one prefer, mass
illusions, are the things that produce great events in history
and make the world move. If a Christian could grant that
a person could be just as virtuous without baptism, or that
one could be without the faith and still save one's soul, the
Christian missionaries and martyrs would have lost their enthusiasm and Christianity would not have become the factor that
it became in human history. If the promoters of a revolution
were convinced that the status of society would not be very
much bettered the morning after their victory, if they even
suspected that there might be a chance of their making things
worse, it would be hard to sweep them in droves to the barricades.
Nations in which the critical spirit is strong, and which are
skeptical—very properly skeptical—as to the practical benefits
that any new doctrine can bring, never take the lead in great
social movements and end by being dragged along by others
whose enthusiasms are more readily aroused. The same is
true of the individuals within a nation. The more sensible
end very frequently by being swept off their feet by the more
impulsive. Not always is it the sane who lead the mad. Often
the mad force the sane to keep them company.

9. But once the heroic period of a movement is over, once
the stage of initial propaganda comes to an end, then reflection
and self-interest claim their rights again. Enthusiasm, the
spirit of sacrifice, the one-sided view, are enough to found religious
and political parties. They are not enough to spread them very

[1] Hammer-Purgstall, *Gemäldesaal*.

far abroad and assure them of a permanent existence. So the
method of recruiting the directing nucleus is modified or, better,
completed. Membership among the individuals who make up
the nucleus may still be won on purely idealistic grounds, but
the age when idealism is everything soon passes in the great
majority of human beings. They must then find something to
satisfy ambition, vanity and the craving for material pleasures.
In a word, along with a center of ideas and sentiments, one
must have a center of interests.

Here again we come upon the theory of the alloy of pure
metal with base that we formulated previously. A ruling
nucleus that is really well organized must find a place within
itself for all sorts of characters—for the man who yearns to
sacrifice himself for others and the man who wants to exploit
his neighbor for his own profit; for the man who wants to look
powerful, and the man who wants to be powerful without regard
to looks; for the man who enjoys suffering and privations and
the man who likes to enjoy the good things of life. When all
these elements are fused and disciplined into a strongly knit
system, within which every individual knows that as long as he
remains loyal to the purposes and policy of the institution his
inclinations will be gratified, and that if he rebels against it
he may be morally and even materially destroyed, we get one
of those social organisms that defy the most varied historical
vicissitudes and endure for thousands of years.

One thinks at once of the Catholic Church, which has been
and still is the most robust and typical of all such organisms.
We can only stand in rapt admiration before the complexity
and the shrewdness of its organization. The seminary student,
the novice, the sister of charity, the missionary, the preacher, the
mendicant friar, the opulent abbot, the aristocratic prior, the
rural priest, the wealthy archbishop, sometimes also the sovereign
prince, the cardinal, who takes precedence over prime ministers,
the pope, who was one of the most powerful of temporal rulers
down to a few centuries ago—all have their place, all have their
raison d'être, in the Church. Macaulay has pointed to a great
advantage that Catholicism has over Protestantism. When
an enthusiastic, unbalanced spirit arises inside the Protestant
fold, he always ends by discovering some new interpretation of
the Bible and founding one more of the many sects into which

the Reformation has split. That same individual would be utilized to perfection by Catholicism and become an element of strength rather than of dispersion. He would don a friar's robe, he would become a famous preacher, and, if he had a really original character, a truly warm heart, and if historical circumstances favored, he would become a St. Francis of Assisi or a St. Ignatius Loyola. Cogent as this example is, however, it shows only one of the countless ways in which the Catholic hierarchy manages to profit by all human aptitudes.

It is said that the celibacy rule for the clergy goes contrary to nature, and certainly for some men to be deprived of a legal family would be a very great sacrifice. But it must be remembered that only at that price can a militia that is free of all private affections and stands apart from the rest of society be obtained; and, meantime, for characters that have an inclination toward celibacy, that institution itself does not preclude certain material satisfactions. In the same way, many people believe that the Church has degenerated and lost strength and influence because it has deviated from its origins and ceased to be exclusively a handmaiden to the poor. But that too is a superficial and therefore erroneous judgment.

Perhaps nowadays, in this age of ours, when everybody is talking about the disinherited classes and is interested, or pretends to be interested, in them, it might be becoming in the Supreme Pontiff to remember a little oftener that he is the servant of the servants of God. But except for certain fleeting periods in history, the Catholic Church would not have been what it has been, and it would not have endured so long in glory and prosperity, if it had always confined itself to being an institution for the sole benefit of the poor and had been popular only among beggars. Instead, it has shrewdly found ways to enjoy the approval of both the poor and the rich. To the poor it has offered alms and consolation. The rich it has won with its splendor and with the satisfactions it has been able to provide for their vanity and pride. So well chosen has this policy proved that if the enemies of the Church have always reproached it for its luxury and worldliness, they have always, if they have been shrewd, taken care to derive as much influence and wealth from it as possible. Of late, in a number of European countries, another institution has been devoting all its energies to combating

the Catholic Church. But for its own part, it does not fail to
procure for its adherents as many personal satisfactions and
material advantages as possible.

10. Once the ruling nucleus is organized, the methods that it
uses to win the masses and keep them loyal to its doctrine may
be widely various. When no serious external obstacles, or obstacles arising from the nature of the political or religious system
itself, are encountered, both methods of propaganda that are
based upon the gradual persuasion and education of the masses
and methods that involve the resort to force yield good results.
Force, in fact, is perhaps the quickest means of establishing a
conviction or an idea, though naturally only the stronger can
use it.

In the nineteenth century it became a widespread belief that
force and persecution were powerless against doctrines that were
founded upon truth, since the future belonged to such doctrines.
They were regarded as equally useless against mistaken beliefs,
since popular good sense would attend to them on its own
account. Now, to be quite frank, it is hard to find a notion that
involves a greater superficiality of observation and a greater
inexperience of historical fact. That surely will be one of the
ideas of our time that will give posterity the heartiest laughs at
our expense. That such a theory should be preached by parties
and sects which do not as yet hold power in their hands is easily
understandable—their instincts of self-interest and self-preservation might lead them to profess such views. Stupidity begins
when it is accepted by others. "*Quid est veritas?*" asked Pilate,
and we can begin by asking what a true doctrine is and what a
false doctrine is. Scientifically speaking, all religious doctrines
are false, regardless of the number of believers they may have or
may have had. No one, certainly, will maintain that Mohammedanism, for instance, which has conquered so large a portion
of the world, is founded upon scientific truth. It is much more
accurate to say that there are doctrines that satisfy sentiments
which are widespread and very deeply rooted in the human heart
and, accordingly, have greater powers of self-propagation; and
that there are doctrines that possess the quality mentioned to a
lesser degree and therefore, though they may be more acceptable
on the intellectual side, have a far more limited appeal. If

one will, a distinction can be drawn between doctrines which it is to the interest of civilization and justice to have widely accepted, and which produce a greater sum of peace, morality and human welfare, and doctrines which have the opposite effects and which, unfortunately, are not always the ones that show the least capacity for self-propagation. We believe that social democracy threatens the future of modern civilization, yet we are obliged to recognize that it is based on the sentiment of justice, on envy and on the craving for pleasures; and those qualities are so widespread among men, especially in our day, that it would be a great mistake to deny that socialist doctrines have very great powers of self-propagation.

People always point to the case of Christianity, which triumphed in spite of persecutions, and to modern liberalism, which overcame the tyrants who tried to repress it. But these cases merely show that when persecution is badly managed it cannot do everything, and that there may be cases where pure force does not suffice to arrest a current of ideas. The exception, however, cannot serve as a basis for a general principle. If a persecution is badly managed, tardily undertaken, laxly and falteringly applied, it almost always helps to further the triumph of a doctrine; whereas a pitiless and energetic persecution, which strikes at the opposing doctrine the moment it shows its head, is the very best tool for combatting it.

Christianity was not always persecuted energetically in the Roman Empire. It had long periods of toleration, and oftentimes the persecutions themselves were only partial—they were confined, that is, to a few provinces. It did not definitely triumph, however, until an emperor who held constituted authority in his hands began to favor it. So too, liberal propaganda was not only hampered, it was also furthered, by governments from the middle of the eighteenth century down to the French Revolution. Later on it was fought intermittently and never simultaneously through all the European world. It triumphed when the governments themselves were converted to it, or else were overthrown by force, internal or from abroad.

As compared with those two doubtful examples, how many others there are to the precise contrary! Christianity itself in its early days hardly spread beyond the boundaries of the Roman Empire. It was not accepted in Persia, not only because it

met an obstacle in the Persian national religion but because it
was energetically persecuted.   Charlemagne planted Christianity
among the Saxons by fire and sword and within the space of a
generation.   The evangelization of the Roman Empire took
centuries.   A few years sufficed to carry the Gospel to many
barbarian countries, because once a king and his nobles were
converted, the people bent their necks to baptism en masse.
The cross was set up in that very summary manner in the various
Anglo-Saxon dominions, in Poland, in Russia, in the Scandinavian countries and in Lithuania.   In the seventeenth century,
the Christian religion was almost wiped out in Japan by a pitiless
and therefore effective persecution.   Buddhism was eradicated
by persecution from India, its motherland; Mazdaism from the
Persia of the Sassanids; Babism from modern Persia and the
new religion of the Taipings from China.   Thanks to persecution,
the Albigenses disappeared from southern France, and Mohammedanism and Judaism from Spain and Sicily.   The Reformation
triumphed, after all, only in countries where it was supported by
governments and, in some cases, by a victorious revolution.   The
rapid rise of Christianity itself, which is ascribed to a miracle, is
nothing as compared with the far more rapid rise of Mohammedanism.   The former spread over the territory of the Roman
Empire in three centuries.   The latter in just eighty years
expanded from Samarkand to the Pyrenees.   Christianity,
however, worked only by preaching and persuasion.   The other
showed a decided preference for the scimitar.

The fact that all political parties and religious creeds tend to
exert an influence upon those in power and, whenever they can,
to monopolize power itself, is the best proof that even if they do
not openly confess it they are convinced that to control all the
more effective forces in a social organism, and especially in a
bureaucratic state, is the best way to spread and maintain a
doctrine.

11. As regards the other means, apart from physical force,
which the various religions and political parties use to attract
the masses, maintain ascendancy over them and exploit their
credulity, we may say very largely what we said of the obligation
that founders of doctrines, and doctrines themselves, are under
to adapt themselves to a fairly low moral level.   The followers

of every political or religious system are wont carefully to list the faults of their adversaries in respect of moral practices, while claiming to be free of any reproach themselves. As a matter of fact all of them, with differences in degree to be sure, are tarred with the same brush. It is our privilege to be perfectly moral so long as we do not come into contact with other men, and especially so long as we make no pretensions to guiding them. But once we set out to direct their conduct, we are obliged to play upon all the sensitive springs of conduct that we can touch in them. We have to take advantage of all their weaknesses, and anyone who would appeal only to their generous sentiments would be easily beaten by someone else who was less scrupulous. States are not run with prayer books, said Cosimo dei Medici, the father of his country. And indeed it is very hard to lead the masses in a given direction when one is not able as need requires to flatter passions, satisfy whims and appetites and inspire fear. Of course, if a man, however wicked he might be, tried to rule a state strictly on blasphemy, that is to say by relying exclusively upon material interests and the baser sentiments, he would be just as ingenuous as the man who tried to govern with prayer books alone. If old Cosimo were alive he would not hesitate to call such a man a fool. By a sufficient display of energy, self-sacrifice, restless activity, patience and, where necessary, superior technical skill, the man at the helm of a state may feel less in need of exploiting the baser sentiments, and may place great dependence upon the generous and virtuous instincts of his subjects. But the head of a state is only a man, and so does not always possess the qualities mentioned in any eminent degree.

One notes, on close inspection, that the artifices that are used to wheedle crowds are more or less alike at all times and in all places, since the problem is always to take advantage of the same human weaknesses. All religions, even those that deny the supernatural, have their special declamatory style, and their sermons, lectures or speeches are delivered in it. All of them have their rituals and their displays of pomp to strike the fancy. Some parade with lighted candles and chant litanies. Others march behind red banners to the tune of the "Marseillaise" or the "International."

Religions and political parties alike take advantage of the vain and create ranks, offices and distinctions for them. Alike they exploit the simple, the ingenuous and those eager for self-sacrifice or for publicity, in order to create the martyr. Once the martyr has been found, they take care to keep his cult alive, since that serves very effectively to strengthen faith. Once upon a time it was a practice in monasteries to choose the silliest of the friars and accredit him as a saint, even ascribing miracles to him, all with a view to enhancing the renown of the brotherhood and hence its wealth and influence, which were straightway turned to good account by those who had directed the staging of the farce. In our day sects and political parties are highly skilled at creating the superman, the legendary hero, the "man of unquestioned honesty," who serves, in his turn, to maintain the luster of the gang and brings in wealth and power for the sly ones to use. When "my uncle the Count" reminded the Capuchin Father Provincial of the scalawag tricks that Father Christopher had played in his youth, the Father Provincial promptly replied that it was to the glory of the cloth that one who had caused scandal in the world should become quite a different person on taking the cloth.[1] A typically monkish reply, without doubt! But worse than monks are political parties and sects which conceal and excuse the worst rascalities of their adherents so long as they are loyal to the colors. For them, whoever takes the cloth becomes on the spot a quite different person.

The complex of dissimulation, artifice and stratagem that commonly goes by the name of Jesuitism is not peculiar to the followers of Loyola. Perhaps the Jesuits had the honor of lending it their name because they systematized the thing, perfected it and in a way made an art of it; but, after all, the Jesuitical spirit is just a form of the sectarian spirit carried to its ultimate implications. All religions and all parties which have set out with more or less sincere enthusiasms to lead men toward specified goals have, with more or less moderation, used methods similar to the methods of the Jesuits, and sometimes worse ones. The principle that the end justifies the means has been adopted for the triumph of all causes and all social and political systems. All parties, all cults, make it a rule to judge only that man great who fights in the party ranks—all other men are idiots or rogues. When they can do nothing more positive, they maintain obstinate silence on the merits of outsiders. All sectarians practice the

[1] Manzoni, *I promessi sposi*, chap. XIX.

art of holding to the form and letter of their word while violating it in substance. All of them know how to distort a recital of facts to their advantage. All of them know how to find simple, timid souls and how to capture their loyalty and win their assistance and their contributions for "the cause"—and for the persons who represent it and are its apostles. Unfortunately, therefore, even if the Jesuits were to disappear, Jesuitism would remain, and we have only to look about us to be convinced of that truth.

The more blatantly unscrupulous means are oftenest used in associations that are in conflict with constituted authorities and are more or less secret in character. Among the instructions that Bakunin sent out to his followers, we find this one:

> To reach the gloomy city of Pandestruction, the first requisite is a series of assassinations, a series of bold and perhaps crazy enterprises which will strike terror to the hearts of the powerful and dazzle the populace into believing in the triumph of the revolution.

Couched in cruder language, Bakunin's maxims remind one of the "Be agitated and agitate" of another great revolutionist. In the same pamphlet, *Principles of Revolution*, Bakunin goes on:

> Without recognizing any activity other than destruction, we declare that the forms in which that activity should manifest itself are variety itself: poison, dagger, knout. Revolution sanctifies everything without distinction.

Another Russian, who came to hold principles very different from Bakunin's, describes in a novel the methods by which the wily attract the ingenuous into revolutionary societies. Says Dostoevski:

> First of all the bureaucratic bait is necessary. There have to be titles—presidents, secretaries, and so on. Then comes sentimentality, which is a most effective agent, and then regard for what people may think. Fear of being alone in one's opinion and fear of passing for an antiliberal are things that have tremendous power.
>
> Then [adds another interlocutor in the dialogue] there is the trick of embroiling unsuspecting neophytes in a crime. Five comrades murder a sixth on the pretext that he is a spy. . . . Murder cements everything. There is no escape even for the most reluctant.[1]

[1] *The Possessed*, part II, chap. VI (pp. 392–393).

12. The day can hardly come when conflicts and rivalries among different religions and parties will end. That would be possible only if all the civilized world were to belong to a single social type, to a single religion, and if there were to be an end to disagreements as to the ways in which social betterment can be attained. Now a number of German writers believe that political parties are necessary as corresponding to the various tendencies that manifest themselves at different ages in the human being. Without accepting that theory we can readily observe that any new religion, any new political dogma that chances to win some measure of success, straightway breaks up into sects, under pressure of the instinct for disputing and quarreling; and these sects fight one another with the same zest and the same bitterness that the parent faith formerly displayed against rival religions and parties. The numerous schisms and heresies that are forever sprouting in Christianity, Mohammedanism and the many other religions, the divisions that keep emerging in our day within social democracy, which is still far from a triumph that it may never attain, prove how extraordinarily hard it is to achieve that unified and universal moral and intellectual world to which so many people aspire.

Even granting that such a world could be realized, it does not seem to us a desirable sort of world. So far in history, freedom to think, to observe, to judge men and things serenely and dispassionately, has been possible—always be it understood, for a few individuals—only in those societies in which numbers of different religious and political currents have been struggling for dominion. That same condition, as we have already seen (chap. V, §9), is almost indispensable for the attainment of what is commonly called "political liberty"—in other words, the highest possible degree of justice in the relations between governors and governed that is compatible with our imperfect human nature. In fact, in societies where choice among a number of religious and political currents has ceased to be possible because one such current has succeeded in gaining exclusive control, the isolated and original thinker has to be silent, and moral and intellectual monopoly is infallibly associated with political monopoly, to the advantage of a caste or of a very few social forces.

The modern Masonic doctrine in Europe is based on the belief that man tends to become physically, intellectually and morally saner and nobler, and that only ignorance and superstition, which have generated the dogmatic religons, have prevented him from following that road, which is his natural road, and driven him to persecutions, massacres and fratricidal strife. Such a view does not seem to us tenable. The revealed religions, which many people are now calling superstitions, were not taught to man by an extrahuman being. They were created by men themselves, and they have always found their nourishment and their raison d'être in human nature. They are only in part, and sometimes in very small part, responsible for struggles, massacres and persecutions. These are due more often to the passions of men than to the dogmas that religions teach. In fact, in the light of impartial history, the excuse of "the times," and of religious and political fanaticism, takes away only a small fraction of individual responsibility for outrages of every sort. Whatever the times may be, in every religion, in every doctrine, each of us can find and does find the tendency that best suits his character and temperament. Mohammedanism did not prevent Saladin from being a humane and generous soul even in dealing with infidels, any more than Christianity mitigated the ferocity of Richard the Lionhearted. That king, so celebrated for his chivalry, was responsible for the massacre of three thousand Mohammedan prisoners, taken after the strenuous defense at Acre, and it was due to the generosity of Saladin that that terrible example was not followed on a large scale by the Mohammedan army. The same religion that gave the world Simon de Monfort and Torquemada also gave the world St. Francis of Assisi and St. Theresa. The year 1793 saw the lives and feats of Marat, Robespierre and Carrier (the Conventionist Carrier, who had the children of the Vendeans drowned by the thousand at Nantes). But that same year knew Bonchamps, the leader of the loyalists in the Vendée, who, as he lay wounded on his deathbed, pleaded for the lives of four thousand republican prisoners whom his fellow soldiers were intending to shoot down—and won their release. As a matter of fact, in the course of the past century the bitterest struggles have been fought, the worst persecutions and massacres have been perpetrated, in the name of doctrines which have no basis at all in the supernatural, and which proclaim the liberty, equality and fraternity of all men.

The feeling that springs spontaneously from an unprejudiced judgment of the history of humanity is compassion for the contradictory qualities of this poor human race of ours, so rich in abnegation, so ready at times for personal sacrifice, yet whose every attempt, whether more or less successful or not at all successful, to attain moral and material betterment, is coupled with an unleashing of hates, rancors and the basest passions. A tragic destiny is that of men! Aspiring ever to pursue and achieve what they think is the good, they ever find pretexts for slaughtering and persecuting each other. Once they slaughtered and persecuted over the interpretation of a dogma, or of a passage in the Bible. Then they slaughtered and persecuted in order to inaugurate the kingdom of liberty, equality and fraternity. Today they are slaughtering and persecuting and fiendishly torturing each other in the name of other creeds. Perhaps tomorrow they will slaughter and torment each other in an effort to banish the last trace of violence and injustice from the earth!

CHAPTER VIII
REVOLUTION

1. We have just examined the ways in which the currents of ideas, sentiments, passions, that contribute to changing trends in human societies arise and assert themselves. But it is also observable that at times these currents gain the upper hand by force, replacing the individuals who are in power with other individuals who represent new principles. In societies that have attained a fairly complicated type of organization, such changes may occur on the initiative, or at any rate with the consent, of the normally ruling class, which, in ordinary cases, holds exclusive possession of arms. Then again they may be brought about by other social elements and forces, which succeed in defeating the previously ruling element. Then a phenomenon that has been rather frequent in the history of our time appears, the thing that is commonly called "revolution."

Upheavals in small states, where a bureaucratic organization does not exist or is essentially embryonic, bear only a superficial resemblance to upheavals in large states, and especially states like our modern nations. In classical antiquity when a tyrant became master of a city, or an oligarchy superseded a democracy —and often, too, when a tyranny or oligarchy was overthrown— it was always at bottom a question of one clique, more or less numerous, superseding another clique in the management of the commonwealth. When the Greek state was functioning normally the whole governing class, in other words everybody who was not a slave or a resident alien or a manual laborer, had a share in political life. When a tyrannical or oligarchical regime was established, or even a degenerate form of democracy that was called "ochlocracy," one element in the governing class usurped all power to the detriment of other elements, which were in part killed off, in part despoiled of their property and exiled. The victors, in their turn, had to fear reprisals from the vanquished, for if the latter ever succeeded in getting the upper hand again, they treated their former despoilers in the same manner.

The struggle was therefore conducted on a basis of force and cunning, with murders and surprises, and the parties to the struggle often sought the support of outsiders or of some few mercenaries. Once victorious, they usually seized the citadel and deprived all who were not of their faction of their weapons. Arms were rather costly in those days and could not easily be replaced. On rare occasions, as was the case with the coup d'état of Pelopidas and Epaminondas at Thebes, and that of Timoleon at Syracuse, someone would use a victory to establish a less sanguinary and less violent regime. But even then such a beneficent innovation would last only as long as the personal influence or the life of its author lasted. Sometimes, again, the usurping faction would succeed in keeping itself in power for more than a generation. That was the case with Pisistratus and his sons, and with the two Dionysiuses, tyrants of Syracuse. Agathocles, one of the worst tyrants known to Greek history, died an old man, and he had seized power as a youth. Poison alone seemed able to cut short his life and his rule.

The usages of the ancient Hellenic state were reborn in the Italian communes of the Middle Ages, where the political organization was very much like that of classic Greece. A faction with some nobleman at its head would seize power and banish all its enemies or murder them. In either case their property would be confiscated. Often one had to crush if one did not care to be crushed. As a rule the two richest and strongest families of the commune would contend *armata manu* for supremacy. They too, like the heads of the old Greek parties, used outside aid and mercenaries whenever they could. So the Torriani and the Visconti disputed possession of Milan, and the scene, with few variations, was repeated in smaller Italian cities. Peaces, truces, tearful reconciliations, religious repentances, were sometimes engineered by monks and honest citizens. Dino Compagni in his *Chronicles*[1] relates how he tried, and apparently with success, to reconcile the heads of the White and Black parties in Florence, bringing them together in church and inducing them, with appropriate words, to embrace each other. But such maneuvers, however well-intentioned,

[1] II, 8 (p. 99).

had only momentary effects. Worse still, they were often mere
stratagems by which the bigger rascals would get the better of
the smaller ones by striking at them when they were off their
guard and unable to defend themselves.

With the advent of the Renaissance, ways became less warlike
and open conflict rarer, but perfidy and betrayal grew still more
subtle, and long practice lifted them almost to the rank of
sciences. In some cities so-called "civilized manners" prevailed.
In Florence, for instance, the powerful drew together by kinship
and maintained a certain balance, keeping their predominance
by "stuffing the purses"—the equivalent of modern European
election lists—with the names of their henchmen. That policy
was followed, as long as Niccolò d'Uzzano was alive, by the
mercantile oligarchy that had the Albizzi at its head. It was
the policy also of Cosimo dei Medici and his colleagues, though
Cosimo was adept at using other devices on occasion.[1] Elsewhere, in Romagna and Umbria, wars that were mere struggles
between gangs and gangsters dragged on until after 1500.
In Perugia, the Oddi were driven out by the Baglioni, but came
back by surprise one night. The Baglioni fought in their
shirttails and came off best. Victorious, they turned and
exterminated each other. Oliverotto da Fermo, at the head of a
band of cutthroats, won lordship over his city by murdering
his uncle and other notables of the town, who had invited him
to a friendly dinner.

In the civil conflicts that took place in the Greek cities and in
the Italian communes, moderation and humaneness were not
useful traits of character. Power went as a rule to the quickest
and the slyest, to those who could dissemble best and had the
toughest consciences. Chance, too, played a great part in the
successful outcome of an undertaking, and many romantic
episodes are recounted in this connection. A barking dog,
a drinking bout an hour earlier or an hour later, a letter read
in time or left unopened till the next day, determined the outcome of a surprise, as when Epaminondas and Pelopidas gained
control of Thebes, and Aratus of Sicyon. It is also interesting
to note that neither the civil strife that tormented the Greek
states nor the factional wars that kept the Italian communes
in turmoil made any perceptible contributions to civilization.

[1] Capponi, *Storia della Repubblica di Firenze*, vol. II, pp. 168, 282.

Rulers changed, but whoever triumphed, society always kept the same social physiognomy. The great phenomena in history —the rise of Hellenic science and art, the emancipation of serfs, the rebirth of arts and letters at the end of the Middle Ages—developed independently of the bloody struggles that tortured Greece and Italy. At the most, these civil conflicts helped to retard the maturing of such movements, functioning in that respect like foreign wars, famines or pestilences, which impoverish and prostrate a country and so rarely fail to hamper its economic and intellectual progress.

A political science based exclusively upon observation of the historical periods to which we have referred could not help being incomplete and superficial, and those are the traits of the method embodied in Machiavelli's celebrated essay on *The Prince*. That work has been too much reviled and too much praised. In any event, whether in praise or in blame, too great an importance has been attached to it. If some observer in our day were to note the ways in which private fortunes are made and unmade on our stock exchanges, in our corporations or in our banks, he could easily write a book on the art of getting rich that would probably offer very sound advice on how to look like an honest man and yet not be one, and on how to thieve and rob and still keep clear of the criminal courts. Such a book would, one may be sure, make the precepts that the Florentine Secretary lays down in his essay look like jests for innocent babes. Even so, as we have already suggested (chap. I, §1), such a work would have nothing to do with economic science, just as the art of attaining power and holding it has nothing to do with political science. That such things have no bearing on science, in other words on the discovery of the great psychological laws that function in all the large human societies, is easily proved. Machiavelli's suggestions might have served Louis the Moor or Cesare Borgia, just as they might have served Dionysius, Agathocles and Jason of Pherae. They might have served the deys of Algiers, or Ali Tebelen, or even Mehemet Ali when he exclaimed that Egypt was up for sale on the auction block to the man who made the last bid in dollars or saber cuts.

But one can not be sure that the art taught by Machiavelli has any practical value in itself, or that even the statesmen mentioned would have derived any great profit from it. When the question of winning power and holding it is involved, knowledge of the general laws that may be deduced from a study of human psychology, or of the constant tendencies that are revealed by the human masses, does not help very much. The important thing at such times is quickly and readily to understand one's own abilities and the abilities of others, and to make good use of them. Such things vary so widely that they cannot be covered by general rules. A piece of advice may be good for one man, if he knows how to take proper advantage of it, and very bad for another. The same person acting in the same way in two apparently identical cases will fare now well now badly according to the different people with whom he happens to be dealing. Guicciardini well says: "Theory is one thing and practice another, and many understand the former without being able to put it into operation. Nor does it help much to reason by examples, since every little change in the particular case brings on great changes in the consequences."[1] Certainly Machiavelli's precepts would have been of little use to the statesmen of the Roman Republic, and they would serve the statesmen of modern Europe very badly indeed. However, to avoid any misunderstanding, we had better agree that rectitude, self-sacrifice, good faith, have never been anywhere or at any time the qualities that best serve for attaining power and holding it—nor is the situation any different today.

It need hardly be pointed out that in modern states, which are far larger in size than the ancient and have their complicated organization, their bureaucracies, their standing armies, no revolution can be achieved with a dagger thrust in somebody's back, with a well-laid ambush, with a well-planned attack on a public building. When modern revolutionists take their cue from the practices of their ancient predecessors, they fall into gross errors of anachronism. Classical reminiscences, to be sure, are not wholly useless. They fire the souls of the youthful and serve to maintain a revolutionary atmosphere. They were cleverly exploited in that sense away back in the Renaissance, for instance, in the preparation of the conspiracy of 1476, which encompassed the assassination of Galeazzo Sforza.

To kill a king may not be enough to overturn a government today, but political assassinations still help, sometimes, to inspire

[1] *Pensieri*, no. 35.

leaders of a governing class with hesitation or terror and so make them less energetic in action. Almost all political assassins lose their lives in the execution of their enterprises. Many of them become martyrs to an idea in consequence, and the veneration that is eventually paid them is one of the less honorable but not least effective means of keeping revolutionary propaganda alive.

2. Of all the ancient states, republican Rome was the one in which juridical defense was most solidly established, and in which civil strife was, therefore, least bloody and least frequent. During the protracted conflicts between patricians and plebeians there was no lack of disorders in the Forum. Sometimes daggers were drawn and, on a few occasions, gangs of troublemakers managed to seize the Capitol by surprise attacks. But for whole centuries there was no case of a faction violently usurping power and massacring or exiling its adversaries. At the time when the Gracchi were slain, the legal procedure of voting was twice interrupted by bloodshed; and later on, when the vote of the comitia to entrust command of the war in Asia to Sulla was annulled by violence, Sulla set a new example by entering the city at the head of an army. The legions had long been fighting outside of Italy, and so had become real standing armies suitable for acting as blind instruments in the hands of their generals. The civil wars that ensued were fought between regular armies, and the leader of the last army to win such a war was Octavianus Augustus. He changed the form of government permanently and founded a bureaucratic military monarchy. From then on, the regular army arrogated to itself the right to change not the form of the government but the head of the government.

In feudal Europe civil conflicts and revolutions assumed, as they quite regularly assume among peoples that are feudally organized, the character of wars between factions of barons or local leaders. So in Germany, on the election of a new emperor, the barons and the free cities would often divide into two parties that fought each other back and forth, each following the sovereign of its choice and pronouncing him legitimate. Elsewhere, as in Sicily in the period of the conflicts between the Latin and Catalan nobilities, the contending parties disputed possession of the physical person of the king, or of the prince or princess who was heir to the crown. Such possession enabled a faction to take shelter under the wing of legitimacy and proclaim its adversaries rebels and traitors. For the same reasons, the Burgundians and Armagnacs in France fought for possession of the person of king or dauphin (see below, §6). At other times the barons would align themselves under the standards of two rival dynasties, as happened in England during the Wars of the Roses. Whenever the whole of a nobility, or virtually the whole, rose unanimously against a sovereign, the revolution was soon complete, the king being easily overthrown and reduced to impotence. This latter case was not rare in any of the old feudal regimes. It was especially frequent in Scotland.

As in civil conflicts in the Greek states and the Italian communes, so in these domestic conflicts between the barons of a given kingdom, the victorious party was wont, whenever possible, to dispossess the vanquished of their fiefs and distribute these among its own followers. Assassination and especially poisoning were fairly rare; but if the vanquished did not fall on the field of battle the executioner's ax was often waiting for them. All the noble family of the Chiaramonti perished on the scaffold at Palermo; and the flower of the old English nobility was exterminated on the scaffold, or on the field of battle, during the successive victories and defeats of the two houses of York and Lancaster. In France a number of Armagnacs were assassinated. Others were lynched by Paris mobs. In his turn, John the Fearless, Duke of Burgundy, died by an assassin's hand.

As regards Mohammedan countries, one may ignore mere court intrigues that occasion the deposition and death of one sultan and the elevation of another. But if revolutions proper show a certain resemblance to the conflicts that were waged between cliques of nobles in feudal Europe, they also show traces, often, of a movement which we would nowadays call socialistic, though it usually is obscured and disguised as religious reform. The efforts of many Levantine and African sovereigns to surround themselves with regular troops serving for pay have proved fairly successful at one time or another. All the same, among most Mussulman peoples, especially among peoples that do not take to cities but lead pastoral rather than agricultural lives, a very ancient tribal organization has been preserved, and uprisings of tribal chieftains, like those of the European barons, in support of some pretender to a throne or of the claims of some new dynasty have always remained possibilities. Among the tribes themselves, furthermore, some innovator is always coming along to preach a religious reform and claim to be leading Islam back to its pristine purity. If success smiles upon the agitation of such a person, we get a religious and social revolution.

In Near Eastern countries, and in North Africa too, there is not that class struggle between capitalists and proletarians that is characteristic of modern Europe, but for hundreds and hundreds of years an undercurrent of antagonism has persisted between the poor brigand tribes of the deserts and the mountain regions and the richer tribes that inhabit the fertile plains. Hostility is still more overt between the farmers and the wealthy, unwarlike populations of the coastal cities. It can hardly be said that Islam offers no pretext for revivals of the old equalitarian spirit, the old contempt for riches and enjoyments, that we find in a number of the early Hebrew prophets—in Isaiah, for instance, and in Amos, the herdsman of Tekoa. If Mohammed did not say that it was easier for a camel to pass through the eye of a needle than for a rich man to enter the kingdom of heaven, he nonetheless loved simple ways, and among the joys of this world he prized only women and perfumes. Once eighty horsemen of the Beni-Kende, a tribe recently converted to Islamism, presented themselves before him as ambassadors, in magnificent array and clad in silken garments. Straightway he reminded them that the new religion did not admit of luxury, and they at once tore their rich raiment to shreds.[1] Omar, the second caliph, conquered many lands and endless treasure, but he ate frugally, sitting on the ground, and when he died his personal estate consisted of one tunic and three drachmas.

That makes it easier to understand how the old Arab dynasties in North Africa, during the eleventh and twelfth centuries, came to be conquered and dispossessed by the religious reform of the Almoravides, who in their turn were overthrown by a similar movement—the Reform of the Almohades, so-called. In both cases the desert and mountain tribes coaxed the reform doctrines along and used them to get the better of the wealthier

[1] Hammer-Purgstall, *Gemäldesaal*.

and more cultured populations of the Tell, or zone along the sea. Like motives may readily be detected in the growth of the Wahabi sect in Arabia and in the later fortunes of Mahdism along the upper Nile. In the old days, once the Saracens were masters of the rich lands of Syria, Persia and Egypt, they forgot the frugality of the Sahabah (the men who had known the Prophet), and some of the latter, in their old age, had occasion to be scandalized at the luxury displayed by the Ommiad caliphs of Damascus, who were to be far outdone in that respect by the Abbassid caliphs of Bagdad. It goes without saying, therefore, that in the Almoravides and Almohades, too, human nature soon triumphed over sectarian ardors. Once they found themselves in the palaces of Fez and Córdoba, they forgot the simple life that they had preached and practiced on the tablelands beyond Atlas, and adopted the refinements of Oriental ease. If the Wahabi, the Mahdist and other Mohammedan reforms did not achieve the same results, that was because they enjoyed success in far smaller measure.

3. Revolutions and violent upheavals have not been rare in China. However, it is hard for us to divine the social causes of the very ancient ones. We know that the Celestial Empire passed through a number of different economic and political phases, and that it changed from the feudal state that it once was into a bureaucratic state. The motives and forms of its rebellions must certainly have changed in accordance with those changes.

Of this much one can be sure. Whenever a dynasty had greatly declined in efficiency, when corruption of public officials overstepped the limits of endurance, when weak princes allowed women and eunuchs to rule in their places or wasted too much time in quest of the elixir of eternal life, some unruly governor, or some intrepid adventurer, would place himself at the head of insurgent bands, defeat the government troops and then, abetted by the general discontent, dispossess the old dynasty and found a new one. The new dynasty would show an improved energy for some generations. Then it too would weaken, and the old abuses would come to the fore again.

Invasions of northern barbarians and Tibetans often provoked and facilitated such overturns, and, in fact, the whole country

fell eventually under the dominion of the Mongols. Then gradually a powerful patriotic reaction ripened. (Such outbursts of
national spirit are not rare among peoples that possess ancient
civilizations. We have traces of one in ancient Egypt on the
expulsion of the Hyksos. Almost within our memory came the
uprisings in Greece and Italy in the nineteenth century.) Toward
the close of the fourteenth century of our era a group of enthusiastic and energetic men raised the standard of revolt against the
Mongols, with a bonze, one Hung Wu, at their head. It is noteworthy that the bonzes, or Buddhist monks, have always been
recruited largely from the lowest classes of the Chinese population
and, in our day at least, are held in very low esteem in all China.
On the crest of a wave of national feeling this movement swept
the country. The barbarians were driven beyond the Great
Wall and Hung Wu became the founder of the Ming dynasty,
which governed the empire down to the middle of the seventeenth
century (1644). China meantime became an almost completely
bureaucratized state.

During the nineteenth century the country had another revolution. Though it did not succeed, it is worthy of mention in
view of the analogy it offers to the revolution that had set a
bonze, Hung Wu, on the throne. A war with the English, ending
in the disadvantageous treaties of 1842 and 1844, had produced
great disorder throughout the empire. In consequence, a revolt
against the foreign dynasty of Manchu Tatars broke out in the
neighborhood of Nanking, the ancient Ming capital and the
heart of Chinese nationalism. The platform of the revolution
called for the expulsion of foreigners and the establishment of a
new religion, in which dogmas of Christianity were curiously
intermingled with, and adapted to, the philosophical ideas and
popular superstitions of the Chinese. A schoolmaster, an educated man of very low birth, a sort of fish out of water answering
to the name of Hung Hsiu Ch'üan, was the supreme chief of the
rebellion. A group of energetic, intelligent, ambitious men
gathered about him, financed his agitation and helped him both
in formulating his religious and philosophical creed and in directing his first acts of insurrection.

The Chinese bureaucratic machine had been profoundly shaken
at the time by the setbacks it had received and by the inferiority
that it had exhibited with respect to the Europeans. Supported

by public discontent, the rebels won rapid success at first.   Entering Nanking in 1853, they proclaimed the T'ai P'ing, or Era of Universal Peace, in that city—the rebels, in fact, were commonly known to Europeans as "Taipings."   At the same time Hung Hsiu Ch'üan, who certainly was no ordinary man, was exalted to the rank of Celestial Emperor and became head of a new national dynasty.   But in China too the brute force that is required for a successful revolution was to be found largely in the dregs of society.   The rank and file of the "army of universal peace" had to be recruited largely from among deserters, fugitives from justice and, in general, from the mass of vagrants and vagabonds who abound in all great cities, in China as well as in Europe. Soon the leaders found themselves powerless to control the outrages of their followers.   The Taiping bands carried pillage, desolation and slaughter everywhere.   The insurrection lost all sight of its political idea.   Lust for loot and blood gained the upper hand, and territories that fell into the hands of the rebels experienced all the horrors of real anarchy.

A new war with England and France broke out in 1860, and there was a Mohammedan revolt in the northwest.   Those misfortunes prolonged the anarchy in China for several years. But eventually the Chinese government was freed in some measure of its embarrassments and was able to dispatch forces in considerable numbers against the rebels.   By that time the latter had lost all public sympathy and otherwise found themselves in a bad way.   The early associates of Hung Hsiu Ch'üan, the only men connected with the revolt who had had a truly political outlook and broad views, had almost all lost their lives.   Nanking was invested and Hung Hsiu Ch'üan, surrounded by a haphazard group of men who stood as ready to betray him as to rob others, lost all hope of offering further resistance.   He took poison in his palace on June 30, 1864.   Masters of Nanking, the imperial troops beheaded the young son of the dead rebel leader twenty days later and stifled in blood and atrocious cruelty a revolt that had long held on only by cruelty and terror.[1]

In the Celestial Empire, as normally happens in the Mohammedan countries and to a large extent in Europe, the political idea or ideal on which the revolution had rested at the start

[1] For particulars of the Taiping insurrection, see Rousset, *À travers la Chine*, chap. XIX.

became clouded and was almost entirely lost from view the moment the period of action and realization came.

Another point of contact between the Taiping insurrection and insurrections in Europe may be seen in the fact that in China too the ground for the revolutionary movement was prepared by secret societies. The influence of clandestine organizations in fomenting popular discontents and inspiring hatred of the foreigner is apparent in that country as early as the eighteenth century. So in our day, the revolution that overthrew the Manchu dynasty was due in large part to the work of secret societies. These organizations, at any rate, survived the Taiping revolt which they had helped to stir up, and to them seem to have been due not a few murders of Europeans, which were committed in the intent of entangling the Peking government with one or another of the Western powers. As in countries that are much better known to us than China, the secret societies were joined now by ardent and disinterested patriots, now by criminals who used the bond of association to secure impunity in their crimes, and sometimes even by public officials who hoped to further their careers.

4. Noteworthy among European revolutions is the type in which a subject people rises against its oppressors. Of that type were the insurrections in Sweden against Denmark (under Gustavus Vasa), in Holland against Spain, in Spain against France (in 1808), in Greece against Turkey, in Italy against Austria, in Poland against Russia. Such insurrections are more like foreign wars, or wars between peoples, than civil wars, and they are the ones that are most likely to succeed. In our day, however, in view of our huge standing armies, if an insurgent people is to have any great probability of victory it must already enjoy a sort of semi-independence, so that a portion of its population at least is well organized in a military sense.

In Spain, in 1808, in addition to the famous guerrillas, the regular armies took an active part in support of the insurrection. In Italy, in 1848, the army of Piedmont played the principal role in the war against the foreigner; and the regular troops of Piedmont, in concert with their French allies, dealt the blows that decided the fate of the peninsula in 1859. In 1830 and 1831 again, Poland was able to hold out for almost a year against the

Russian colossus because a Polish army had previously been maintained as a part of the Russian army and it espoused the cause of nationalism. The insurrection of 1863–1864 was conducted by mere bands of irregulars. It had less significant results and was suppressed with much less effort.

To the same type of revolution belongs the American War of Independence against England. The American colonies enjoyed very broad privileges of autonomy even before 1776. When they joined in a federation and proclaimed their independence they had little difficulty in organizing an armed force, partly from the old militias of the various colonies and partly from volunteers. They were therefore able to hold off the troops that were sent by the mother country to subjugate them, until France intervened. Then they succeeded in emancipating themselves.

When the Great Rebellion broke out, in 1642, England was not yet a bureaucratic state, and Charles I had only a small standing army at his command. In the beginning Parliament had the militias of the shires on its side. The rural nobility— the Cavaliers—bore the main brunt of the conflict on the side of the king. The Cavaliers were far better practiced in the military arts and won easy victories at first; but when Cromwell was able to organize, first a regiment, and then an army of permanent disciplined troops, conflict was no longer possible. At the head of his army the Lord Protector not only defeated the Cavaliers but subdued Scotland and Ireland, put the Levelers in their places, sent the Long Parliament home with scant ceremony and became absolute master of the British Isles. The English are great lovers of constitutional privileges. Remembrance of these doings made them long distrustful of standing armies. Charles II and James II were never provided with means for maintaining permanent military forces, and every effort was made to keep the county militias in good training. William of Orange himself, greatly to his regret, was obliged to send back to the Continent the old Dutch regiments which he had led in overthrowing the last of the Stuarts.

5. Another social phenomenon of importance is the rural or peasant rebellion. Such uprisings were fairly frequent in Europe during the second half of the eighteenth century and the first

half of the nineteenth. They broke out in a number of widely separated communities. One remembers the revolts that took place in Russia early in the reign of Catherine II, on the pretext of restoring to the throne one individual or another who tried to impersonate the murdered czar, Peter III. To the Spanish rebellion of 1808, in which the entire nation took part, we have several times referred. Then there was the great insurrection in the Vendée in 1793, the Neapolitan rebellion of 1799 against the Parthenopean Republic, the Calabrian revolt against Joseph Bonaparte in 1808, and the one in the Tyrol in 1809. There have been a number of Carlist insurrections in Biscay and Navarre.

Of the rural revolt that was captained by Monmouth in the day of James II, just before the "Glorious Revolution," Macaulay observes that that uprising was made possible because at that time every English yeoman was something of a soldier. In fact, a serious insurrection by peasants is possible only in places where they have had a certain habit of handling arms, or at least where hunting or brigandage, or family and neighborhood feuds, have kept people familiar with the sound of gunfire.

Of the Russian movements mentioned, the most important was led by Pugatchev. On the whole those revolts rested on the hatred that peasants, Cossacks and all the plainsmen who were used to the freedom of the steppes felt for bureaucratic centralization, which was at that time gaining ground, and for the German employees of the government, who were looked upon as originally responsible for the bureaucracy's interference in the daily lives of the Russians. However, the revolting peasants were what we would now call "loyalist." They maintained that the true czar was in their camp, and that the czarina who held the palaces at St. Petersburg and Moscow was a usurper. Sentiments that are conservative and at the same time opposed to excessive interference by the state are characteristic, in general, of the peasant insurrection, which as a rule occurs when some triumphing party of innovation seeks to require new sacrifices in the name of civilization or progress. The Vendeans were dissatisfied with the Republic because it was persecuting their priests, and they were angered by the execution of Louis XVI. However, they did not rise en masse till March 1793, when the Convention decreed general conscription. The Neapolitan peasantry, in 1799, besides having been shocked in their habits and beliefs by new modes of thinking, had been pillaged and heavily requisitioned by the French troops. In Spain, in 1808, not only had Catholic and national sentiments been grievously offended. It was alleged and believed that the French invaders were provided with handcuffs in large numbers, which were to be used to drag out of the country all young men who were eligible for enrollment in Napoleon's armies.[1] The various Carlist insurrections in Biscay and Navarre were in large part caused by the jealousy with which those provinces cherished their old fueros, or local charters, which gave them virtual independence in local government and many immunities with respect to public burdens.

The initial leaders of rural insurrections are usually but little superior to the peasants themselves in education and social status. The famous Spanish *cabecilla* Mina was a muleteer. In Naples in 1799 Rodio was a country lawyer. Pronio and Mammone had once been farm laborers, and Nunziante, at best, had been a sergeant in the army. Andreas Hofer, who led the Tyrolese revolt in 1809, was a well-to-do tavern keeper. The initial moves in the Vendean insurrection were led by Cathelineau, a hack driver, and Stofflet, a game watchman. But if the higher classes happen to approve of the insurrectionary movement and it acquires power and weight, other leaders of a higher social status step forward very soon. In the Vendée the nobles were naturally hesitant because they better understood the difficulties of the enterprise, but the peasants went to their castles and persuaded them, or, in a sense, obliged them, to place themselves at the head of the rebellion. So Lescure, Bonchamps, La Roche-jaquelein and Charette de la Contrie, gentlemen all, were drawn into the movement. Charette was a cold, shrewd man of indomitable will and tireless energy. He at once exhibited all the talents of the perfect party leader. Instead of curbing the excesses of his followers, he let them satisfy their grudges and repay old scores with a view to compromising them and so binding them irrevocably to the cause of the rebellion. Among all leaders of rural conservative revolts, the only one to compare with him is Zumalacárreguy, a Basque, who was leader in chief

---

[1] Thiers, *Histoire du Consulat et de l'Empire.* Thiers drew most of what he wrote on the great Spanish insurrection of 1808 from Toreno.

of the first Carlist insurrection. He too had been an obscure country squire.

Conservative peasant insurrections and urban revolts that are made in the name of liberty and progress have one trait in common. However short a time they may last, there immediately comes into evidence a certain type of person, a person who seems to be enjoying the fun and to be interested in prolonging it. The initial movement may be general in character, but very soon these individuals come to stand out in the crowd. Once they have abandoned their customary occupations, they are unwilling to return to them. The instinct for struggle and adventure grows upon them. They are people, in fact, who have no talent for getting ahead very far in the ordinary course of social life but who do know how to make themselves felt under exceptional circumstances such as civil wars. Naturally they want the exception to become the rule.

After the first and grandest phase of the Vendean insurrection, which ended in the terrible rout at Savenay, the war dragged on for years and years, because about its leaders had gathered groups of resolute men who had become professional rebels and would turn to no other trade. This tendency is the more marked when revolution is a road to speedy fortune. That was the case in Naples, where Rodio and Pronio became generals overnight, and Nunziante and Mammone were made colonels. The revolutionary leaven that was left in Spain by the six years of the war for independence fermented in the long series of civil wars that ensued, and in each case at the bottom of the insurrection were a number of adventurers who were hoping for fortune and advancement. Titles and ranks were easily gained in such tumults by serving one or another of the contending parties and deserting them in time. The habit of revolution that is contracted by certain persons further helps to explain the betrayals and inconsistencies that are not rare in civil upheavals. People who begin by fighting for a principle keep on fighting and rebelling after their cause has been won. They simply feel a need for rebelling and fighting.

6. Considered as social phenomena, the revolutions that broke out in France during the nineteenth century are especially

interesting as due to very special political conditions, notably to the phenomenon of over-bureaucratization.

Not of this type was the great Revolution of 1789. That was a real collapse of the classes and political forces which had ruled in France down to that time. During the Revolution government administration and the army completely broke down, owing to inexperience in the National Assembly, to emigration and to the propaganda of the clubs. For some time they were unable to enforce respect for the decisions of any government. By July 1789, whole regiments had gone over to the cause of the Revolution. From then on, noncommissioned officers and soldiers were carefully lured into the clubs, where they received the watchword of obedience to the resolutions of the revolutionary committees rather than to the commands of their officers. The Marquis de Bouillé, commanding the Army of the East, had been unable to suppress a dangerous military insurrection at Metz. He wrote late in 1790 that, with the exception of a regiment or two, the army was "rotten," that the soldiers were disposed to follow the party of disorder or, rather, whoever paid them best, and that they were talking in such terms openly.[1] The powers, therefore, that had fallen from the hands of the king were not gathered up by any ministry that had the confidence of the Constituent Assembly. It belonged in turn to the clique, or to the man, who on the given day could get himself followed to Paris by a show of armed force, whether he were a Lafayette at the head of the National Guard or a Danton with a suburban mob armed with clubs and iron bars.

Nevertheless, apparent even in those early days were the beginnings of a tendency that was to become stronger and stronger during the first half of the nineteenth century. Leaders of insurrections always tried to become masters of the individual or individuals who impersonated the symbol, or the institution, to which France, whether because of ancient tradition or because of faith in new principles, was inclined to defer; and, once successful in that intent, they were actually masters of the country (see above, §2).

That is what the rioters of October 6, 1789, did when, obviously in obedience to a watchword, they went to Versailles and seized

[1] *Correspondance entre le comte de Mirabeau et le comte de La Marck.*

the person of the king. With the monarchy abolished, the National Convention became the goal of all surprises, such as the coup of May 31, 1793, which made the Assembly that represented all France slave to a handful of Paris guttersnipes. The provinces tried to react, but in vain, because the army remained obedient to the orders that emanated from the capital in the name of the Convention, though everybody knew that the Convention was acting under compulsion.

The same general acquiescence in everything that happened at the seat of government contributed greatly to the favorable outcome of the various coups d'état that took place under the Directory, and down to the establishment of the Napoleonic empire.

But even more characteristic, perhaps, is what occurred in 1830, then again in 1848, and finally in 1870. First of all comes a battle, more or less protracted and sometimes relatively insignificant, with the detachment of soldiers that is guarding the buildings in the capital in which are assembled the representatives of the supreme power that has previously been recognized as legitimate. The famous February Revolution of 1848, which overthrew the monarchy of Louis Philippe, cost the lives of 72 soldiers and 287 civilians, either rioters or bystanders! Next, the mob, armed or unarmed, puts sovereigns and ministers to flight, dissolves the assemblies and riotously forms a government. This government is made up of names more or less widely known to the country. The men mentioned take desks in the offices from which the former heads of the government have been wont to govern, and then, almost always with the connivance or acquiescence of the ordinary clerks, they telegraph to all France that, by the will of the victorious People, they have become masters of the country. The country, the administrative departments, the army, promptly obey. It all sounds like a story of Aladdin's wonderful lamp. When by chance or by guile that lamp fell into the hands of someone, even a mere child or an ignorant boy, at once the genii were his blind slaves and made him richer and more powerful than any sultan of the East. And no one, furthermore, ever asked how or why the precious talisman came into the boy's possession.

It may be objected that in 1830 the government had become an obedient tool of the Legitimist party, that it had given up all pretense to legality, that a large part of France was definitely opposed to the political policy which the government was following, and even that a part of the army responded feebly, or not at all, at the decisive moment.   Also, the catastrophe of 1870 might account in part for the change of government that took place in France at that time.

But no element of that sort figured in the sudden revolution of 1848.   Neither the Chambers nor the bureaucracy nor the army were sympathetic to the republican government at that time.   The majority of the departments were frankly opposed to it.   Louis Blanc himself confesses as much.   After rejecting as insulting the hypothesis that the republic had a minority in its favor, he admits[1] that a nationwide vote might have declared against a republican form of government.   And again he says, no more, no less: "Why not face the facts?   Most of the departments in February 1848, were still monarchical."[2]   Lamartine, too, in speaking of the impression that the revolution of 1848 made in France, admits that it was surrounded by an "atmosphere of uneasiness, doubt, horror and fright that had never been equaled, perhaps, in the history of mankind."   In Paris itself the National Guard had been wavering in February because it wanted to see an end put to the Guizot ministry.   However, it was manifesting a reactionary frame of mind in the following March and April.   A few hours of vacillation were nonetheless enough to drive Louis Philippe, his family and his ministers not only from Paris but from France, to abolish two chambers and to enable a provisional government—a mere list of names shouted at a tumultuous crowd that was milling about the Palais Bourbon—to assume from one moment to the next full political control over a great country—France!

Citizen Caussidière, "wanted" by the police the day before, went to police headquarters on the afternoon of February 20, 1848, at the head of a group of insurgents, his hands still smudged with gunpowder.   That evening he became chief of police, and the next day all the heads of branches in the service promised him loyal cooperation and, willing or unwilling, kept their promises.[3]   Police headquarters were, moreover, the only office where the

[1] *Histoire de la Révolution de 1848*, vol. I, p. 85.

[2] *Ibid.*, vol. II, p. 3.

[3] See the *Mémoires* of Caussidière himself.

rank and file of the personnel was changed, the old municipal
guards being dismissed and replaced by Montagnards, former
comrades in conspiracy and at the barricades of the new chief,
who afterwards uttered the famous epigram that he stood for
"order through disorder."

In the preface to his history of 1848, Louis Blanc decides that
Louis Philippe fell mainly because his sponsors were supporting
him for selfish reasons and not because of personal devotion.
According to Blanc, the "bourgeois king" had very few enemies
and many confederates but at the moment of danger failed to find
one friend. That reasoning, it seems to us, has only a very
moderate value. Not all the people who support a given form of
government have to feel a personal affection, or have a disinterested friendship, for the individual who stands at the head
of that form of government. Actually, such sentiments can be
sincerely felt only by the few persons, or the few families, who
are actually intimate with him. Political devotion to a sovereign, or even to the president of a republic, is quite another
matter. The main cause of the frequent sudden upheavals in
France was the excessive bureaucratic centralization of that
country, a situation that was made worse by the parliamentary
system itself. Public employees had grown accustomed to
frequent changes in chiefs and policies, and they had learned from
experience that much was to be gained by pleasing anyone who
was seated at the top and that much was to be lost by displeasing
such a person.

Under such a system what the great majority in the army and
the bureaucracy want—and also the great majority in that part
of the public that loves order, whether by interest or by instinct—
is just a government, not any particular government. Those,
therefore, who stand de facto at the head of the state machine
always find conservative forces ready to sustain them, and the
whole political organism moves along in about the same way
whatever the hand that sets it in motion.

Certainly, under such a system, it is easier to change the
personnel that holds supreme power, as happened in France after
1830, 1848 and 1870, than it is to change the actual political
trend of a society. For if the more radical change is the object,
governors who have emerged from the revolution itself are forced
to prevent it by the conservative elements which are their instru-

ments and at the same time their masters.   That was the case in June 1848 and in 1871.

Unquestionably, also, a strong sense of the legality and legitimacy of an earlier government would prevent submissive obedience to a new regime issuing from street rioting.   But for a feeling of that sort to rise and assert itself requires time and tradition, and for France the changes that had occurred down to 1870 were too rapid to enable any tradition to take root.   In France and in a large part of Europe, during the nineteenth century, revolutionary minorities were able to rely not only on the sympathy of the poor and unlettered masses but also, and perhaps in the main, upon the sympathies of the fairly well-educated classes.   Rightly or wrongly, young people in Europe were taught for the better part of a century that many of the most important conquests of modern life had been obtained as a consequence of the great Revolution, or by other revolutions. Given such an education, it is not to be wondered at that revolutionary attempts and successful revolutions were not viewed with any great repugnance by the majority of people, at least as long as they offered no serious menace or actual injury to material interests.[1]   Naturally, such feelings will be stronger and more widespread in countries where the de facto or legal governments themselves have issued from revolutions, so that, while condemning rebellions in general, they are obliged to glorify the one good, the one holy insurrection from which they sprang themselves.

7. One of the principal agencies by which revolutionary traditions and passions have been kept alive in many countries in Europe has been the political association, especially the secret society.   In such societies ruling groups receive their education and are trained in the arts of inflaming passions in the masses and leading them toward given ends.   When it becomes possible to write the history of the nineteenth century impartially, much space will have to be given to the effectiveness with which the Masonic lodges, for example, managed to disseminate liberal and democratic ideals, and so cause rapid and profound modifications

[1] On the effects of revolutionary education in France, see Villetard, *Insurrection du 18 mars*, chap. I.   [Pierre Mille relates that his aged mother, who had seen most of the upsets of the nineteenth century, was alarmed by the long quiet after '71.   "Quoi? Plus de révolutions? Ça a l'air louche!"   A. L.]

of intellectual trends in a great part of European society. Unless we assume an active, organized and well-managed propaganda on the part of such groups, it would be hard to explain how it has come about that certain points of view that were the property of highly exclusive coteries in a select society at the end of the eighteenth century can now be heard expressed in the remotest villages by persons and in environments that certainly have not been changed by any special education of their own.

Nevertheless, if associations, open or secret, excel as a rule in laying the intellectual and moral foundations for revolutions, the same cannot be said of them when it comes to rousing the masses to immediate action, to stirring up the armed movement at the given point on the appointed day. Under that test societies and conspiracies fail at least ten times to every time they succeed. The reason is evident. To launch a revolution it is not enough to have at one's disposal the crowd of jobless adventurers, ready for any risk, that are to be found in any great city. The cooperation of considerable elements from the public at large is also necessary. Now the masses are stirred only at times of great spiritual unrest caused by events which governments either cannot avoid or fail to avoid. Such unrest cannot be created, it can only be exploited, by revolutionary societies. The disappointment of some great hope, a sudden economic depression, a defeat suffered by a nation's army, a victorious revolution in a neighboring country—such are incidents that are well calculated to excite a multitude, provided it has previously been prepared for the shock by a revolutionary propaganda. If the rebellious group has developed a permanent organization and knows how to take advantage of such a moment, it can hope for success; but if it rushes into action without any support from exceptional circumstances, it is unfailingly and easily crushed, as happened in France in the uprisings of 1832, 1834 and 1840.

In France, Spain and Italy there are a few cities in which it is relatively easy to lead masses to the barricades. That is one of the many effects of habit and tradition. Once a population has exchanged shots with a constituted government and overthrown it, it will feel, for a generation at least, that it can make a new try any time with favorable results, unless repeated and bloody failures have chanced to undeceive it. So it is with individuals. When they have been under fire a number of times they acquire a sort of martial education and fight better and better. That is one of the reasons why the Parisian workmen fought so stubbornly in June 1848, though, as Blanc explains in his history of that episode, the habit of discipline that they had acquired in the national armories also figured in their deportment to some extent. The revolutionary elements fought even better in 1871 because, as part of the Paris National Guard, they had been carefully organized, trained and armed.

And yet, in spite of all the advantages of time, place and circumstance that a revolutionary movement may enjoy, in our day, because of our huge standing armies and the pecuniary resources and the instruments of warfare that only constituted powers are in a position to procure, no government can be overthrown by force unless the men who are in charge of it are themselves irresolute or lose their heads, or at least unless they are paralyzed by dread of assuming responsibility for a repression involving bloodshed. Eleventh-hour concessions, last-minute orders and counterorders, the falterings of those who hold legal power and are morally bound to use it—these are the real and most effective factors in the success of a revolution, and the history of the "Days of February," 1848, is highly instructive in that regard.[1] It is a fatal illusion to believe that where there is vacillation and fear of being compromised in the higher places, subordinates will be found to assume responsibility for energetic measures of their own, or even for effective execution of perplexing and contradictory orders.

We have seen that if standing armies are well handled they can become effective instruments in the hands of legal government without disturbance to the juridical equilibrium. We ought therefore to examine these complex and delicate organisms in order to see how they have come into being and how they can be kept from degenerating.

---

[1] See especially Thureau-Dangin, *Histoire de la Monarchie de Juillet*, last volume.

CHAPTER IX
STANDING ARMIES

1. We have already discussed the predominance of military classes (chap. II, §4), and we have seen that in some cases warriors have come exclusively from dominant classes, though in other cases those classes supply only generals, officers and picked corps, while a certain number of the rank and file in less esteemed divisions are recruited from lower classes.

In savage or barbarous countries, where economic production is very rudimentary, all adult males are soldiers in the rather frequent event of war. In such societies, assuming that pastoral nomadism or even an embryonic agriculture and industry exist, they are never so highly developed as to absorb human activity entirely. Sufficient time and energy are always left for adventurous raids and forays. These furnish an occupation that is not only agreeable in itself but is almost always lucrative. Among such peoples the arts of peace are regularly left to women or to slaves. The men devote themselves by preference to the chase and to warfare.

This has happened, and still happens, among all races and in all climates when the conditions described above prevail. So lived the ancient Germans, the Scyths of classical antiquity, the more recent Turkomans, and down to a few years ago the remnants of the modern American Indians. So many of the Negroes of the African interior have always lived, and the Aryan, Semitic and Mongolian tribes that have managed to conserve a de facto independence in the more inaccessible regions of Asia.

One factor favorable to the permanence of such a state of affairs is the existence of very small political organisms—a de facto autonomy on the part of each little tribe or village, which can make war a daily routine and thefts and reprisals between neighbors unending. In the long run, when even very barbarous tribes become subject to a regular government that prevents internal strife, they become peaceful. This was the case with the nomadic peoples of Asia, who were long subject to the Chinese government, and with the nomads living between the Volga and the Ural Mountains, who have long been under the Russian yoke. On the other hand, in the Germany and Italy of the Middle Ages, we see relatively civilized peoples clinging to warlike traditions because they were divided into fiefs and communes, among which the right of the mailed fist prevailed.

But as soon as great political organisms, however rudimentary and imperfect, come to be set up and, more especially, as soon as economic development has advanced somewhat and war ceases to be the most lucrative occupation, we find a special class devoting itself to the bearing of arms and making its living not so much by plundering its adversaries as by levying tribute in some form or other on the peaceful toilers of the country which it polices and defends. As we have many times remarked, production is almost exclusively agricultural when civilization and culture are at a low level, and warriors either are the owners of the land, which they force others to cultivate, or else extort heavy tribute from those who do own the land. This was the situation in the early period of Greco-Roman antiquity, when the dominant military element in the city was made up exclusively of landed proprietors, and the same phenomenon recurs more markedly still in all countries that are feudally organized. We find it, therefore, among the Latins and Germans of the Middle Ages and also among the Slavs. Among the Slavs however, it was a much later development, since they abandoned nomadic life and entered upon a permanently agricultural period at a fairly recent date. We find it, also, at one period or another, in China, Japan and India. In India it reappeared in full force during the epoch of decline and anarchy that followed the breakup of the empire of the Grand Mogul. Similar organizations may be traced in Turkey, Abyssinia, Afghanistan and in ancient Egypt in the periods of decadence that were interspersed among the various phases of that long-lived civilization. In short, we find it in all societies that have not yet issued from the early period of crude culture that appears in the history of every great nation; and we find it also in the periods of deterioration or decline, whether due to internal or external causes, by which countries that have attained a high level of civilization change and perish as social types (the Roman Empire would be an example).

2. However, as feudal states advance in civilization, a trend toward centralization, toward bureaucratic organization, sets in, since the central power is constantly trying to free itself of dependence upon the good will of the minute political organisms that make up the state—a good will that is not always prompt and freely offered. With that in view, and incidentally for the purpose of keeping the small organisms more obedient and better disciplined, the central power tries to obtain direct control of the agencies that will enable it effectively to enforce its will upon other men—control of money, in other words, and soldiers. So corps of mercenaries, directly in the service of the head of the state, come into being, and that development is so natural and so regularly recurrent that we find it, in embryo at least, in all countries that are feudally organized.

In the Abyssinia of our day, in addition to the contingents that were supplied to him by the various rases, the negus had the nucleus of an army in the guards who were attached to his person and who were maintained directly by court funds; and in the retinue of domestic attendants—butchers, hostlers, grooms, bakers, and so on—who followed the emperor everywhere and became soldiers as need required.[1]

In the Bible one notes that the core of the army of David and his successors was made up first of warriors who ate at the king's table and then of Cherethim and Pelethite mercenaries—all men so well versed in arms that they successfully dealt with the revolt of Absalom, even though that uprising was supported by a majority of the people.[2]   Renan suggests that the presence of a nucleus of foreign retainers in the service of a government was peculiar to Semitic peoples, the Semitic sense of tribe and family being so strong that native elements were unsuited to enforcing respect for the rights of the state, since they always subordinated public interests to factional or clan interests.   But that situation arises, really, wherever the social aggregate is composed of small units which are equipped with all the organs required for independent existence and are therefore easily able to rebel against the central authority.   So the medieval kings of England secured

---

[1] For an account of the organization of a Shoan army on the march (*zemeccià*), see a report presented by Antonelli to the Italian parliament and published in *Diplomatic Documents*, Dec. 17, 1889.

[2] II Sam. 15–18.

soldiers in Flanders and Brabant. The kings of France surrounded themselves with Swiss guards, the Italian lords with
hired Germans; and in this they all were bowing, at bottom, to
the same political necessities that impelled the kings of Judah to
enlist Pelethites and Cherethim and, later on, the caliphs of
Bagdad to have a Turkish guard.

Under the early republic the Romans had a citizen army that
was recruited from the dominant and well-to-do classes and was
made up of individuals who took to arms only in case of need.
Nothing less than the Roman genius for organization was
required to bring that system to such perfection as to make it
possible for the citizen army to develop without shock and almost
imperceptibly into a real standing army made up of professional
soldiers. That evolution, as is well known, began in the last
century of the republic and was already complete when the
empire was founded. As a rule, standing armies have originated
in units of native or foreign mercenaries hired by the central
power to support it against other military forces that have been
feudally organized.

As regards the practice of hiring mercenaries, it is interesting to
note that it was especially characteristic of countries that not
only were rich but derived their wealth from commerce and
industry rather than from agriculture. In such countries the
ruling classes grew unaccustomed to life in the open, which was
the best preparation for the career in arms, and found it more to
their advantage to superintend banks and factories than to go
off to wars. That was the case in Carthage, in Venice and quite
generally in the wealthier Italian communes, where the mercantile and industrial burghers soon lost the habit of fighting their
wars in person, and became more and more inclined to entrust
them to mercenaries. In Florence citizens were still fighting
in the battles on the Arbia and at Campaldino, but, as we saw
above (chap. III, §6), the latest record of a campaign conducted
wholly by citizens belongs to the year 1325. The nationality
of the mercenaries themselves may sometimes be determined by
political considerations, and perhaps by the traditional habits and
aptitudes of certain peoples; but the consideration that most commonly prevails is the plain economic consideration of the largest
results from the smallest expenditure—in other words, the desire
to have the greatest possible number of soldiers for the least

possible outlay. Therefore countries relatively poor in capital and rich in population, in which time and lives can be bought on very favorable terms, have always been the ones to furnish the largest numbers of hired troops.

When the soldier's outfit was expensive and the style of fighting required a long apprenticeship, as was the case with the medieval knight and the Greek hoplite, the mercenary career was ordinarily adopted by younger sons, or unplaced members of good families, who by choice or of necessity went seeking their fortunes outside their native lands. Xenophon's Ten Thousand originated in that way. When equipment was cheap and no very long period of training was required, mercenaries were preferably sought in poor countries where man power was plentiful and industry and capital were scarce. Down to very recently the volunteer English army was largely recruited from the poorer counties of Ireland. Machiavelli in his day noted how hard it was to raise mercenaries in the manufacturing cities in Germany. Two centuries later Voltaire remarked that of all the Germans the Saxons were least given to enlisting as soldiers, Saxony being the most industrious region in Germany. In our day, even if the Swiss federal government were to allow it, very few Swiss, probably, would be available as mercenaries, since Switzerland has become a fairly wealthy country. For their part, the European governments that once depended on Switzerland for hired guards could now probably spend their money to greater advantage right at home.

3. Native or foreign, once regularly organized mercenaries have become the preponderant force in a country, they have normally tried to force their rule upon the rest of society. Like their feudal predecessors, they have regularly taken advantage of their monopoly in the bearing of arms to levy blackmail, to live as fatly as possible at the expense of the producing population and, especially, to reduce the supreme political power to dependence on their will. The more perfect their organization and the more complete the military disorganization of the rest of the country, the more far-reaching has the influence of mercenaries been.

Pertinent examples suggest themselves. One thinks at once of the praetorian guards and the legions that toyed as they saw fit with the Roman Empire. But in general, whenever and wherever governments have built up standing armies in order to deal with feudal unruliness, or for other reasons, they have almost always found themselves at the mercy of those armies. As we saw above (chap. II, §4), in order to govern with greater absolutism and not be wholly dependent upon the contingents that were supplied by the boyars, Ivan IV of Russia organized the Strelitzes, a regularly paid force directly responsible to the sovereign. Very soon the Strelitzes were making and unmaking czars. They became virtually omnipotent in Russia, and Peter the Great was able to free himself of them only by shooting them down with grapeshot, or beheading them by the thousand. At Constantinople, again, the sultans decided to have a thoroughly loyal militia made up of men who had no countries and no families and could therefore be brought up in whole-hearted devotion to Islam and the Padishah. Such a force, they thought, would march without scruple and as need required, not only against the infidel but against the sheiks in Arabia and Kurdistan, the begs in Albania and Bosnia, and the khans of Turkistan and Tartary. So they filled their corps of Janizaries with young boys of Circassian, Greek and other Christian stocks, whom they bought or kidnaped from their families. But very soon the Janizaries became the real authority in the Osmanli empire and were creating and deposing sultans. They strangled the unfortunate Selim III, who made a first move to curb their omnipotence, and in order to get the better of them the sultan Mahmud II had to exterminate them almost to the last man.

The sultans of Constantinople might have profited by the experience of the Abbassids of Bagdad, their predecessors in the caliphate. The Abbassids, as far back as the ninth century, and perhaps earlier, had organized their Turkish guard in order to have a loyal militia that would not be raising the standard of the Fatimids or the Ommiads every other day, as their Arab troops had been in the habit of doing. By the time of Motasim, who was caliph between the years 833 and 842, the Turkish guard had become omnipotent. Turkish mercenaries were doing very much as they pleased in Bagdad and committing all sorts of outrages. Motasim's successor, Watthik by name, was deposed by the Turks and replaced by his brother Motawakkil. Then in the space of four years, 866–870, the Turkish guard made and unmade three other caliphs. The caliph Motamid took advantage of the death of their general, one Musa, to break up their power somewhat. He scattered them along the frontiers of Khurasan and Dzungaria, and counted every defeat they suffered there as a victory for himself.

In a word, history teaches that the class that bears the lance or holds the musket regularly forces its rule upon the class that handles the spade or pushes the shuttle. As society advances economic production absorbs larger and larger numbers of hands and brains, and civilized peoples come to regard the arts of peace as their customary occupations. Under these circumstances, to declare in principle that all citizens are soldiers, without providing for a sound military organization with a nucleus of generals and officers who are specialists in matters of war, means in practice that in the moment of peril there will be no soldiers at all, and that a populous country will be in danger of falling prey to a small army, national or foreign, if that army happens to be well trained and well organized. On the other hand, to entrust the bearing of arms exclusively to elements in a society that are temperamentally best suited to the military trade and voluntarily assume it—an altogether rational and obvious system which many peoples have in the past adopted —also has its numerous and serious drawbacks. If the society is unorganized or loosely organized, that system means that every village and town will have its band of armed men. The band will comprise those who feel the greatest repugnance to regular work and the greatest inclination toward adventure and violence, and sooner or later the band, or its leader, will begin to tyrannize over peaceful producers quite ignoring any rule or law. If the society is somewhat better organized, the bands taken as a whole will constitute a ruling class, which will be lords and masters of all wealth and all political influence—that was the case with medieval feudalism in western Europe and with the Polish nobility down to a century and a half ago. In a bureaucratic state, which represents the most complicated type of social organization, the standing army will absorb all the more belligerent elements, and, being readily capable of prompt obedience to a single impulse, it will have no difficulty in dictating to the rest of society.

The great modern fact is the huge standing army that is a severe custodian of the law, is obedient to the orders of a civil authority and has very little political influence, exercising indirectly at best such influence as it has. Virtually invariable as that situation is in countries of European civilization, it represents a most fortunate exception, if it is not absolutely without parallel, in human history. Only a habit of a few generations' standing, along with ignorance or forgetfulness of the past, can make such a situation seem normal to those of us who have lived at the end of the nineteenth and the beginning of the twentieth century, and so find it strange when we chance upon exceptions.

Exceptions have occurred on rare occasions in France, and more often in Spain. In Spain the standing army has at times overthrown the men in supreme power and even changed the form of government. One should remember, however, that this has happened at moments of crisis and social disorganization, and that once changing governments by violent means has become a practice, each party or social class uses the means most congenial to it and within easiest reach in order to gain the upper hand.

As a matter of fact, it has been possible to subordinate the standing army to the civil authority only through an intense and widespread development of the sentiments on which juridical defense is based, and especially through an exceptionally favorable sequence of historical circumstances. Perhaps we had better touch on these circumstances at some length at this point, but we might note at once that it is not at all impossible that different historical circumstances that are now maturing may end by weakening, or even undoing, the complex, delicate and sagely elaborated mechanism of the modern army. If that actually takes place, we may find ourselves back with a type of military organization perhaps simpler and more natural but certainly more barbarous and less suited to a high level of juridical defense.

4. The historical process by which the modern standing army developed goes back to the end of the Middle Ages. During the fifteenth century, first in France and then in other regions of Europe, centralized monarchy, parent of the modern bureau-

cratic state, gradually replaced feudal militias with standing armies. Even in those days Europe suffered relatively little from military insurrections and military tyranny. This was due largely to the fact that the substitution came about slowly and gradually. Even toward the end of the Middle Ages European armies were becoming so complicated in structure that many different social elements were represented in them and served to balance one another. At the opening of that historical period, the cavalry was in general made up of men-at-arms, who were of gentle birth and were profoundly imbued with the aristocratic and feudal spirit, but who nevertheless were in the king's pay. The infantry was a motley collection of adventurers hailing from any number of countries. Little by little a system came to prevail whereby the command of infantry regiments, and eventually of infantry companies, was entrusted to gentlemen, who differed in birth, temperament and background from their soldiers. Besides, down to the time of Louis XIV, and even after that, an old practice lingered on whereby a nobleman organized at his own expense a squadron of cavalry or a regiment or company of infantry from among the men who lived on his lands, and then hired himself out to some sovereign with his troop ready-made. It was always taken for granted that in case of need the king could call the whole nobility of the realm to arms.

The practice of leasing and hiring private regiments lasted down to the end of the eighteenth century. The traffic flourished especially in Switzerland and Germany. The La Marck regiment of German infantry was usually in service in France. Recruited preferably in the county of that name, it was always commanded by a member of the La Marck family, and the officers were appointed by the colonel. It passed on from generation to generation by inheritance. All that down to the French Revolution![1] The last general call of the whole nobility to arms took place in France early in the reign of Louis XIV. It became apparent at that time that an assemblage of twelve or fifteen thousand knights, all with different sorts of equipment, some too young and some too old, all personally courageous but untrained to fight in concerted movements, had very little value in actual practice. For much the same reasons the Polish cavalry lost most of its military importance in the eighteenth century. The

[1] *Correspondance entre le comte de Mirabeau et le comte de La Marck*, preface.

Magyar nobility was called to arms for the last time in 1809, when the French invaded Hungary. The body so formed was composed of horsemen who were individually brilliant but it showed little effectiveness in the battle at Raab, which was fought in connection with Napoleon's Wagram campaign.

Though the mixing of different social elements and different nationalities prevented the armies of the sixteenth and the first half of the seventeenth century from becoming masters of the countries they served, it was no easy matter to maintain tolerable discipline among troops made up of adventurers from everywhere and largely from the worst elements in society. The outrages committed by the German landsknechts and the Spanish miquelets became proverbial, but we have no reason to assume that the French, Swiss, Italian, Croat or Walloon regiments behaved very much better. The letters of Don Juan of Austria show what hard work, what shrewdness, what energy, that general and his officers were called upon to display in order to maintain a very relative discipline among the troops that put down the Moorish revolt in the Alpujarras, embarked on the galleys that won at Lepanto and then served in the war in Flanders. There is the story, from early in the sixteenth century, that on hearing that a Spanish army, which had gone overseas to conquer Algiers, had been defeated and all but destroyed, Cardinal Ximénez exclaimed: "God be praised! Spain is free of that many blackguards at least!" At the end of the same century, among the unattainable desires that Cervantes ascribes to the priest and the apothecary in the village where the Caballero de la Mancha was born was a hope that the soldiers who were marching from the interior to the seaboard to embark for foreign lands would not sack the homes of the peasants, their countrymen, along the road. Well known are the feats of the troops of all the countries that fought in the famous Thirty Years' War. One of the chief reasons for the aversion to standing armies that persisted so long in England was dread of the licentious ways of professional soldiers. In the reign of James II an English regiment under Colonel Kirke returned home after some years of service in Tangiers. It became notorious for its rapes and robberies. The regimental banner bore a lamb as its device, and British humor dubbed the soldiers who belonged to it "Kirke's Lambs."

In parts of Europe where medieval immunities and privileges survived down to modern times, the inhabitants of towns clung jealously to their right to man the walls and fortifications of their cities with local militiamen.   Under the Spanish domination at Palermo, for instance, though the inhabitants, apart from some few lapses, remained loyal subjects to His Catholic Majesty, only a very small number of foreign soldiers were allowed to enter the town to guard the royal palace and the castle.   The ramparts with their artillery remained in the control of the city militia made up of "the worthy guilds."   At times when a question of strengthening the royal guard in the city came up, the guilds, loud-voiced in their professions of devotion and loyalty to the king, nonetheless barricaded the streets and trained the guns of the ramparts upon the royal palace.   The revolt at Messina in 1676 was brought on in part by an attempt by Don Luís del Hoyo, the strategos, to capture by surprise the forts that were manned by the town militia.   The licentious conduct which could be taken for granted in soldiers was commonly alleged as the reason for such suspicions of the soldiery.

No better discipline was obtained until well toward the end of the seventeenth, or rather till the eighteenth century.   Then feudal and town militias disappear almost everywhere, and the era of real standing armies in the modern sense begins.   During those periods the necessity of keeping many men in arms and the difficulty of paying wages large enough to attract volunteers brought on conscription in most countries on the European continent.   That system meant that common soldiers no longer came from the adventurous and criminal classes but were recruited from among peasants and workingmen, who never thought of devoting their whole lives to military service but returned, after the few years required of them, to their ordinary occupations.   The officers continued to belong to a totally different class.   They more and more became a sort of bureaucratized nobility, combining the orderliness and conscientiousness of the civil service employee with the chivalrous spirit and the high sense of honor that were traditional in the wellborn.

Frederick II of Prussia in his time apologized for having been obliged during the Seven Years' War to make army officers of many men who were not of noble birth.   He felt a certain dislike for this new type of officer because, he said, the man who was a gentleman by birth could offer greater moral and material guarantees. If he dishonored himself as an officer, he could not turn to some other pursuit, whereas the plebeian could always find some way to get along and was therefore less interested in scrupulously living up to the standards of his rank. The founder of Prussian power was an altogether unprejudiced individual. Such reasoning on his part shows that in Germany, as elsewhere, the growth of a class of people of superior education, yet not belonging to the nobility, is a relatively recent phenomenon.

Only in England and the United States has the old system of recruiting volunteers, preferably from among the unemployable elements of the poorer classes of society, hung on, conscription being resorted to only in great crises, such as the American Civil War or the World War. In those two countries, however, and especially in the United States, standing armies have always been relatively small. In view of their geographical situation, defense against foreign foes can in large part be entrusted to a navy, while internal order is maintained partly by local militias and in larger part by strong and well-organized police forces. Class distinctions between officers and privates in the regular armies are, furthermore, much more rigorously stressed than is the case in armies on the continent of Europe. The result is that, in virtue of family connections and education, army officers retain close ties with the minority which by birth, culture and wealth stands at the peak of the social pyramid.

The corps of English officers has always maintained a highly aristocratic character. The system of purchasing rankings held on in the English army down to 1870. In his *English Constitution*, Fischel justly notes that it is not the Mutiny Act that has kept the English army from becoming a tool for coups d'état, but the fact that English officers belong by birth and sentiment to the classes that down to a few years ago were most largely represented in Parliament. The United States has followed the English tradition in all this matter. In the federal army there is a great difference in class, as well as in rank, between the commissioned officer of lowest rank and the noncommissioned officer of highest rank. In fact, between them lies an abyss that may well be compared to the gulf that separates the Negro from the white in the United States, a country where distinctions of color are of far greater moment than elsewhere.

5. The American nonprofessional militia has so far proved to be of very mediocre practical value. Washington himself remarked that if he were compelled to declare under oath whether he considered the militia useful or the reverse, he would have no hesitation in replying that it was useless.[1] American foreign wars have been fought almost exclusively by federal armies augmented by volunteer enlistments, and that was also the case in the Civil War. As regards internal disorders, one may at least wonder whether the American militia is more effective in quieting than in aggravating them. It has not been able to prevent the lynchings that are still frequent in the United States, and in dealing with strikes it has often dispersed or else come to terms. In any event, the American militia set the pattern for the European national guard, and was in a sense the parent of it. Great importance was attached to civilian militias down to a century or more ago, mainly on account of the political role which they were supposedly destined to play.[2] The idea underlying the national guard was that it would provide an armed force free of blind, unreasoning military discipline and partisanship, which would serve to protect parliamentary institutions from encroachments by an executive power supported by a standing army.

As far back as the French Revolution, Mirabeau pointed very soundly to the drawbacks of such a military body. It would, he thought, be likely to favor or suppress a revolt according to the mood it happened to be in at the moment, and so in a way come to function as an armed arbiter between constituted authority and revolution.[3] In spite of that, when the French Charter was revised in 1830, a special article provided that "the Charter and all the rights which it sanctifies shall continue to be entrusted to the patriotism and courage of the National Guard." When Garibaldi entered Naples to save the Sant' Elmo castle, whence the royal troops had theretofore held the city under their guns, he had to promise that it would always be garrisoned by the Neapolitan national guard. As regards France, to tell the truth,

---

[1] De Witt, *Histoire de Washington*, p. 104.

[2] Jannet, *Le istituzioni politiche e sociali degli Stati Uniti d'America*, part I, chap. XVII.

[3] "Aperçu de la situation de la France et des moyens de concilier la liberté publique avec l'autorité royale," in *Correspondance entre le comte de Mirabeau et le comte de La Marck*, vol. II, p. 418.

the national guard did not always prove ineffective. In 1832 and 1834, and again in June 1848, fear of socialism inspired the peace-loving Parisian burghers with spurts of courage, and the national guard helped the army to put down the rioting. But in February 1848, dissatisfied with the Guizot ministry, and not realizing that a revolution was going on, it was at first hostile to the army, then puzzled, then finally inert, and its conduct was the main cause of the fall of the July Monarchy.[1] It failed to prevent the coup d'état of December 2, 1851. In 1870–1871 socialist workers had been allowed to serve in its ranks. The elements of disorder therefore prevailed over the elements of order, and the citizen militia of Paris became the praetorian guard of the Commune. In our day, partly because the low efficiency and unsoundness of the institution are too well realized, and partly because by now every tradesman and shopkeeper has served for a time in the regular army and so has lost his enthusiasm for parades and uniforms, the national guard has been abolished in all the great countries of Europe. The fact that the national guard has lasted longest in Belgium, where the introduction of universal compulsory military service was also longest delayed, would lead one to suspect that the second of the reasons mentioned may not have been the less influential of the two.

6. On this matter of modern military organization in Europe and its relation to juridical defense, two further remarks will be in point.

As we have seen, our modern armed forces comprise two classes of people, a class of officers, usually recruited from the politically dominant ranks of society, having a special education and training and beginning service at a fairly high rank, and another class made up of privates and petty officers, who find it hard to make their way into the higher ranks. Now absurdly conventional and arbitrary as this distinction may seem to be at first glance, it has always been more or less definitely present in all great and well-organized standing armies, whatever the period or country. It prevailed at certain periods in ancient Egypt. Papyri dating back to the dynasties that won greatest glory in arms speak of chariot officers and infantry officers who

[1] Thureau-Dangin, *Histoire de la Monarchie de Juillet*, vol. VII, chap. VII.

were educated in special military academies where they were introduced to all the hardships of army life. To enter such colleges one had to pay not money, which did not then exist, but slaves and horses.[1] The same distinction was enforced to a certain extent in modern China, where the status of the military mandarin was somewhat similar to that of the modern army officer in the West. The military mandarin had to pass an examination before the military authorities of his province. He then entered the militia of one of the eighteen Chinese provinces with a relatively high rank. The examination was usually taken before the Tchang-kun, or chief, of the Tatar garrison, which was to be found, down to a few years ago, in all the strategic cities of China. After the civil wars of the middle of the nineteenth century, the various ranks of the military mandarinate came to have little importance, because they were often conferred so arbitrarily that a man who was discharged with a rather high rank in one province was often enrolled as a plain soldier in the next province, and vice versa. All the same, command of large bodies of soldiers was entrusted to governors of provinces and other civil mandarins of high rank, who won advancement only after a series of hard and thoroughgoing examinations. In China, it should be noted, as in ancient Rome, the higher civil posts were combined with high military posts.[2]

But the distinction in question was unusually strict in the Roman legions during the last centuries of the republic and the first centuries of the empire. There a line was sharply drawn between the ordinary and the so-called equestrian militias. A militiaman of the equestrian class began service as a *contubernalis* —today we would say "aide-de-camp"—to the consul, or to the commander of a legion. This cadetship opened the way to the rank of military tribune and to the other higher ranks. For long centuries, on the other hand, the man who began his career as a private in the ordinary militia could at the most become a senior centurion, or "first spear," a grade that was the marshal's baton, as it were, of the Roman rank and file. This organization assured the tenure of high ranks in the army to the same social

---

[1] Correspondence of Amon-em-ept, librarian to Ramses II (Nineteenth Dynasty), with one of his pupils, the poet Pentaur. See Maspero.

[2] Rousset, *À travers la Chine.*

class that held the high civil magistracies and which, since it possessed both wealth and political power, made up the aristocracy of ancient Rome. The distinction between the *militia equestris* and the ordinary militia was based on a law that made the nomination of military tribunes and higher officers the prerogative of the comitia. Now popular elections in ancient Rome, as today in many countries which are not in a state of latent revolution and where the elective system has been long established, almost always gave preference to the rich, or to persons whose families already enjoyed great prestige and occupied prominent positions. In the early centuries of the empire the same organization held on. Tribunes and other higher army officers were still chosen from the more conspicuous Roman families. Little by little, however, the emperors began to excuse, first senators and then knights, from military service, fearing them as potential rivals. During the period of military anarchy that supervened in the third century A.D.—the so-called era of the Thirty Tyrants—privates could become generals and even emperors.

7. Our other observation relates to one of the most widespread conceptions, or misconceptions, in the world—that military qualities are very unequally distributed among peoples, some being naturally timorous and cowardly, others daring and courageous. Of course it could never be proved that there is no truth whatever in such notions. But beyond question the more or less warlike habits of a people and the type and soundness of its military organization are the elements that contribute most, on the whole, to increasing its military prestige.

In war, as in all dangerous occupations, a certain amount of experience is required if one is to face danger calmly and coolly. When that experience is lacking it can be made up for only by those moments of frenzy that occur at rare intervals in the life of every people or by a high sense of duty and honor that can be created and kept alive in a limited class of superior individuals by a special training. In civilized countries, where the great majority of people cannot devote themselves to bloody conflicts as a regular profession, one of the goals of military organization should be to keep distributed through the masses a small minority of individuals who are familiar with such conflicts and have been so prepared by the special training mentioned that they can dominate the plain soldier, exercise a decisive influence over him and lead him to face dangers from which he would otherwise recoil. The World War showed that the soundness of an army depends very largely on the strength of the patriotic sentiments that have been instilled by long and careful education, both intellectual and moral, in individuals belonging to the ruling classes and in the masses.

The organization in question may be more or less perfect, or even completely absent, and a ruling class may be familiar with the business of arms or, for one reason or another, completely shy of it. As one scans the history of civilized peoples, therefore, it is apparent that almost all of them have had their moments of military glory and their periods of material weakness. The Hindus were conquered and despoiled time after time by Turks, Mongols, Afghans and Persians, and they submitted to a few thousand Englishmen in the eighteenth century; yet of all the Asiatic peoples they were the ones who offered the stoutest resistance to the Macedonians. The natives of Egypt have for centuries had the reputation of being cowardly fighters, yet the troops of Amasis and Thutmosis, in their day the best armies in the world, were recruited among the inhabitants of the lower valley of the Nile. From the day of Leonidas down to Alexander the Great, the Greeks were considered very valiant soldiers, and in Xenophon's time they spoke with the greatest scorn of the Syrians and the Mesopotamians. But when Islam rose, the Semitic peoples of Asia took the lead again and literally massacred the unwarlike populations that gave their obedience to Byzantium. Amari[1] seems inclined to ascribe the submissiveness that the Greeks displayed under Byzantine rule to the influence of Christianity. Now in the first place the Byzantine Empire lasted for ten centuries, and during that time it had not a few moments of extraordinary military energy. Then again, Christianity did not have any such effect on the Germans or the Slavs, and it is to be noted that the warlike spirit also revived among the Latin peoples of the West, once Roman administration had actually been obliterated and a feudal organization had emerged from anarchy. The real fact is that imperial efficiency and the Pax Romana had unaccustomed the citizens of the empire to

[1] *Storia dei Musulmani in Sicilia.*

arms, so that once the regular army was disposed of they fell
a ready prey to any invader.

The Italians of the Renaissance made wretched soldiers, being
unused to anything like real warfare. However, the Roman
legionaries had been recruited among their ancestors. They
had shown not a little valor in the day of the communes, and not
so many generations after Machiavelli's time, the Italian regiments rivaled the Spanish in steadiness at the famous affair at
Rocroi. The Neapolitans owed the very special reputation for
cowardice that they enjoyed in a day not long past rather to a
lack of cohesion and moral unity, which they displayed on a
number of occasions, than to any deficiency in personal courage.
In Spain and Russia under Napoleon I, and on other occasions
as well, Neapolitan troops gave a fairly good account of themselves. Preeminence in some special branch of warfare and in
certain definite military qualities is a very ephemeral thing
among the nations, everything depending on the civil and military
organization of the country in question. Machiavelli judged the
French cavalry the best in Europe, since, he said, the French
nobility were wholly devoted to the military calling. The
infantry of that same nation he considered very poor, "because
it was made up of the lowest rabble, and of artisans who were so
overridden by the barons in everything they did that they could
only be craven cowards." But, lo, the social and military
organization changes, and the infantry becomes the backbone of
the military power of modern France!

Muza ben Noseir, the Arab general who conquered Spain,
said, in one of his reports to his caliph, Walid I, that the Goths
(by which he meant all the Spanish) were "eagles on horseback,
lions in their castles, weak women afoot." During the Penin-
sular War Wellington deplored the unsteadiness of the Spanish
infantry in the open field, whereas behind the battlements of
Saragossa, Tarragona and other cities, the same infantry showed
extraordinary valor and stubbornness. Now we must assume
that at the time of the Arab invasion the cavalry was composed
of nobles, who were well trained in arms. As was the case later
on, in the day of Napoleon, the infantry was probably thrown
together by mass conscription and could show its native courage
only behind battlements or in fortresses, not having acquired as
yet the courage that comes from long habituation to military

life and from a well-selected personnel. That, beyond any
doubt, was the main asset of the Spanish infantry of the late
Renaissance, from the day of Ferdinand the Catholic down to
the day of Philip IV. During that period the Spanish army was
regarded as the best fighting force in all Europe.

8. In our day a reaction against large standing armies has
set in. They are blamed for withdrawing hands from factory
and field, for instilling vices in the young and for occasioning
almost unbearable expenditures of public treasure. Such plaints
come in the main, it is true, from social elements that have at all
times most conspicuously exhibited an inclination to assert themselves and to impose their will on the rest of society by force—
from those who spontaneously and by nature have the greatest
taste for the bearing of arms, and who, perhaps unconsciously,
find an obstacle to the full expression of their instincts in the
present military organization of the peace-loving, producing
masses. We allude to the subversive revolutionary elements of
our time, who count among their number the boldest, most
adventurous and most violent elements in modern societies.
But it is nonetheless true that the very pressures that have led
the different European nations to create the prevailing organization of standing armies are now tending so to broaden and extend
the application of the principles on which modern armies are
founded as to alter and denature their structure.

First in the Napoleonic wars and then, and more particularly,
in the Franco-Prussian war of 1870, victory went to the nations
that had equipped and mobilized the largest armies. Those
experiences brought the system of compulsory military service
to exaggerated extremes in almost all the continental countries
of Europe, and we have now come to the point where people
think that in case of need they can turn the whole able-bodied
populations of states of thirty, forty, seventy millions of inhabitants into armies. But to bring such an undertaking within
range of the possible, it has been necessary to curtail terms of
preliminary service, and that makes it doubtful whether con-
scripted recruits have time to acquire the habits and the special
frame of mind which should distinguish the soldier from the
rest of society, and which for technical and especially for political
reasons must not be weakened beyond a certain point. Military

expenditures for men, officers and armaments, which have to be renewed constantly, have enormously increased. It is becoming harder and harder to keep up with them, and public debts have piled up monstrously. This is one of the most serious afflictions of many modern countries, and under it some of the economically weaker nations are in danger eventually of succumbing.

In the introduction to the 1884 edition of *Das Volk in Waffen*, the late General von der Goltz expresses a favorite idea of his, that in the military history of the nations one may detect the conflict and alternating triumph of two opposite military tendencies. A first tendency is to increase masses of combatants more and more, to conquer by sheer weight of numbers. That process goes on and on until huge masses of men are led to war. Such masses are hard to handle and are always inadequately drilled, so that they come to be conquered by small armies of well-drilled professional soldiers. So specialization in the military function becomes the second tendency, which in turn leads to a renewal of mass armings.

General von der Goltz believed in the eighties that in Europe the trend toward increasing numbers of combatants had not yet reached its limit, and his prophecy was certainly valid for the World War. But the historical phenomenon which he stressed does not always unfold in regular rhythm. It at least undergoes exceptions and fluctuations, however clearly it may manifest itself in some few special cases. The Medo-Persians, according to the accounts of the Greek historians, succeeded in conquering all southwestern Asia by mobilizing enormous masses of men. The fact that Cyrus was able to keep a huge army under the colors for more than one season was the cause of the rapid decline of the kingdom of Lydia. Great units of armed men held the field for long periods of time, also, during the two sieges of Babylon that took place under Cyrus and under Darius, son of Hystaspes. Other great masses were mobilized in the expedition against the Scyths and in the campaign of Xerxes. It was during the latter that the Persian military machine began to betray its defects. Because of the very fact that they belonged to a wide-rambling state the contingents from the various peoples who made up the Persian empire came to lack the training required for unending wars. Gradually their military abilities declined. The army became a mere assemblage of disorganized mobs which could not withstand the onrush of the Greek hoplites. These were few in number but they were thoroughly trained, heavily armed and skilled in fighting in mass formations.

Certainly in its process of expansion the modern military machine has become more and more complicated, more and more delicately adjusted. To direct its functioning in time of mobilization and war has become a task that bristles with greater and greater difficulties. We may even ask ourselves whether war itself will be possible when each passing day of hostilities, what with economic losses to the country and expenditures from the exchequer, will cost every nation tens and tens of millions, and when a declaration of war will harm the interests and shock the emotions of every single family in a whole civilized population. If the moral aversions and the economic interests that are opposed to war among civilized nations are able to stave such conflicts off for as few as sixty or seventy successive years, it is doubtful whether the military and patriotic spirit upon which modern armies are based, and which alone makes possible the enormous material sacrifices that wars require, can be passed on to the rising generations.

When the decline of that spirit and prolonged peace have abolished standing armies, or reduced them to "semblances vain and subjectless," a danger will again arise that the military predominance of the West may revert to other races, other civilizations, that have had, or will have had, different developments from the European, and will meantime have appropriated European methods and instruments of destruction. If that danger seems too remote and too fanciful to some of us, no one can deny that, within the structure of European nations themselves, there will always be violent characters and timid characters—there will always be conflicts of interest, and the will to have one's own way by brute force. Now the modern organization of the standing army has so far stripped the class of persons who have natural tastes and capacities for violence of their monopoly of the military function. When that organization has been dissolved or weakened, what is to prevent small organizations of the strong, the bold, the violent, from again coming to life to oppress the weak and the peaceful? When war has ended on a large scale, will it not be revived on a small scale in quarrels between families, classes or villages?

Indeed, from the doubts we have been voicing, a conclusion which we hardly have the courage to put into words may be drawn. It is that war itself—in its present forms the root of so many evils, the parent of so many barbarities—becomes necessary every now and again if what is best in the functioning of our western societies today is not to decline and retrogress to lower types of juridical defense. Grave and terrible as this conclusion is, it is, after all, only one more consequence of our complex and contradictory human nature. In the history of the nations, good and evil are inevitably linked. The juridical and moral improvement of society goes hand in hand with expressions of the basest and most selfish passions and the most brutish instincts.

The modern organization of armies, it will be noted, runs counter to the economic principle of the division of labor and to the physiological law of the adaptability of the various bodily organs to given purposes. That shows once again how hazardous it is to set up analogies between the phenomena of the human body and the phenomena of the social body, and once again calls attention to the reservations that have to be made in regard to certain economic laws when they are applied in the field of politics. If the principle of the division of labor were to be too rigorously followed in the political field it would easily upset all juridical balance, for the whole of a society would become subject to the group that exercises not the highest function from the intellectual or moral standpoint but the most indispensable function—the function that most readily enables some men to force their will upon others—the military function, in other words.

CHAPTER X
PARLIAMENTARISM

1. In the first chapter we set forth the reasons why the constant tendencies or laws that regulate the organization of human societies can be discovered only through the study of history; and in the chapters following we tried to determine the nature and manner of functioning of some of those laws. We tried to demonstrate that in any human aggregate which has attained a certain level of civilization a ruling minority exists, and that this minority is recruited in ways that may vary but that are always based upon the possession of multiple and variable social forces—in other words, of those qualities or resources which give moral prestige and intellectual and economic preeminence to the individuals who possess them. We also tried to make it clear that every society is founded upon a complex of religious and philosophical beliefs and principles which are peculiar to it and by which it explains and justifies the type of organization that it happens to have. This gave us occasion to consider differences in social types, which are in the main due to fundamental differences in the philosophical and religious systems or political formulas that share dominion over the majority of minds in those portions of mankind that have attained a certain level of civilization.

In this connection we made two points that seem to us susceptible of scientific and practical applications of some moment. We tried to show that the highest grade of juridical defense, the greatest respect for law and morals on the part of those in power, can be obtained only through the participation of many different political forces in government and through their balancing one another. We think we showed conclusively, further, that no philosophical or religious doctrine can change human nature very radically or at all permanently, if it fails to limit its propaganda to a small number of chosen individuals, or "superior souls," and tries to educate a whole great society and govern it by imbuing it with certain principles. Of course, we do not deny that the predominance of a given doctrinary or religious outlook may have upon a people a practical influence that is very considerable.

Chapters VIII and IX applied the theories we had previously set forth to a phenomenon that is very common in modern times, revolution by violence, and to a diametrically opposite phenomenon, the modern organization of standing armies. In our opinion the standing army as at present organized prevents the element in society which would naturally monopolize military power from enforcing its will by violence upon other social forces.

A somewhat more delicate and difficult task now awaits our attention, for it would seem to be our duty, now that we have stated our theories, to see just what light they throw on the more important problems that are at present agitating the nations of European civilization. Such a study may help to clarify the nature of those problems, and even suggest the more plausible solutions that may be found for them.

2. The problems that more especially engage our interest here are three in number. We state them in the form of questions:

1. Will the dogmatic religions of our day—the different forms of Christianity in other words, manage somehow to survive the present drift toward revolution, and, especially, to resist the rationalistic movement which for some time has been tending to destroy them?

2. Will present-day forms of government by elected authorities, in particular the system of government that is commonly styled parliamentarism, be able to last very long? In case we find that such systems have to be changed, in what direction can they, or must they, be modified?

3. What is the future of our civilization to be with respect to social democracy in one form or another—that impressive current of feelings and ideas which is sweeping so many countries in Europe and the Americas and which, in one sense, is a logical consequence of their more recent history and is quite capable of modifying their future very substantially?

The first of the questions may at a casual glance seem to be the easiest to answer. Actually it is not. Many more imponderables and unforeseeables are involved in it than in the other questions, which very properly seem to be so complicated and which, for that matter, are closely related to the first.

Many people declare with all assurance that science is bound to destroy dogma; and superficially that opinion has a great deal to be said for it. There is no denying that geology, paleontology, the physical and chemical sciences and the higher criticism (which is nothing more than historical criticism itself) are opening wide breaches in the whole structure of the supernatural contained in the Old and New Testaments and in the doctrine that the early Fathers were "inspired." What is more, even if science were not impairing religious beliefs directly, a mind trained to its strict methods can, if it is dispassionate, only feel an unconquerable aversion to accepting dogmatic doctrines and statements. These it must look upon as so many gratuitous assertions.

In this connection a comment by Cherbuliez on a book issued by Behramji, a learned Brahman, is enlightening. Though he had been reared by Surat missionaries, Behramji had forsworn the religion of his fathers, without, however, becoming a Christian. Says Cherbuliez:

Hundreds of thousands of his countrymen find themselves today in the same situation. . . . In Bengal, as well as in Gujarat, Christianity is the most active of dissolvents. It is corroding and imperceptibly destroying the old idolatries. However, it does not succeed in replacing them. The altar is left empty and sits consecrated to an unrecognized god. Hindus no longer believe in the Trimurti, in the incarnation of Vishnu, in metempsychosis, but they are far from believing, either, in the Holy Trinity, in the incarnation of Jesus, in Satan, in Hell; and the Paradise to which St. Peter holds the keys has few attractions for them.[1]

This state of mind on the part of cultured Hindus is readily understandable. The Christian religion can still be practiced by a man who has been initiated into European science, because it is rooted in sentiment, not in reason. But in people who have not been born to Christianity, or have not been brought up in Christian families, no such sentiment will be active.

All the same it must not be forgotten that religious beliefs have always responded not to any demand of the reason, but to other psychological needs, and especially to the demands of human sentiment. If, in one sense, religious beliefs may be considered illusions, they endure not because they seem to be

[1] "Un voyage dans le Guzerate."

true but because men feel that they need illusion. That need is so universal and so strong, especially at certain moments in life, that we often see well-balanced, sensible individuals, people of robust intelligence who have been trained to a sound sense of realities and possess no end of scientific knowledge, paying lavish tribute to it.

Nor should we attach too great an importance to a phenomenon that we are now witnessing, particularly in Catholic countries. Christian observances are disappearing in large cities in France, in many cities in Spain and northern Italy and perhaps also in some cities in Germany and North America; and they are disappearing in those regions in the lower classes rather than in the classes that possess a certain amount of ease and education.

We must not infer from this fact that rationalistic or scientific education has made any great progress in the lower classes. A person may not only question the truth of religious doctrines—he may also be convinced that all religions are historical phenomena born of innate and profound needs of the human spirit, and that attitude may be arrived at through a realistic mental training based on comprehensive studies that has gradually accustomed the mind not to accept as true anything that is not scientifically proved. In such a case, on losing one system of illusions, the individual is left so well balanced that he will not be inclined to embrace another, and certainly not the first that comes along. But the mass of lower-class unbelievers that we have in nations of European civilization today—and also, it must be confessed, the great majority of unbelievers who are not exactly lower-class, do not arrive at rationalism over any such road. They disbelieve, and they scoff, simply because they have grown up in environments in which they have been taught to disbelieve and to scoff. Under those circumstances, the mind that rejects Christianity because it is based on the supernatural is quite ready to accept other beliefs, and beliefs that may well be cruder and more vulgar.

The workingman in Paris, Barcelona, Milan, the farm laborer in Romagna, the shopkeeper in Berlin, are at bottom no more emancipated from the ipse dixit than they would be if they went to mass, to a Protestant service or to the synagogue. Instead of believing blindly in the priest they believe blindly in the revolutionary agitator. They pride themselves on being in the vanguard of civilization, and their minds are open to all sorts of superstitions and sophistries. The moral and intellectual status which they have attained, far from being an enlightened positivism, is just a vulgar, sensuous, degrading materialism—it is "indifferentism," if one prefers to call it that. Before they go laughing at the Neapolitan loafer who believes in the liquefaction of San Gennaro's blood, such people should try to train themselves not to accept as true things that are just as absurd and certainly a great deal more harmful.

3. What religion meets today, therefore, in large portions of the European masses, is not a positivism, or an agnosticism, that is rational and, so to say, organic, but a vulgar imitative atheism. That being the situation, religious beliefs are still in a position— and will be for a time, until indifferentism has become a matter of tradition—to regain, quite as rapidly, the ground that they have so rapidly lost. It may well be that within a few generations socialist doctrines and revolutionary impulses will openly have declared their bankruptcy. It may just as well be that that result will be attained only after civil struggles and grievous moral and economic sufferings comparable not to those that followed the tiny overnight revolutions of the nineteenth century but to those which tried the generations of the great Revolution so sorely. It has often been remarked that Christianity is the religion of hard times rather than of prosperous times. People can easily get along without it when life is running along smoothly and comfortably, when the future opens smiling before us, when material pleasures abound. But people need its hopes and its comforts, and very urgently, when catastrophes or grievous disappointments are their lot, when privations and sorrows embitter today and leave the prospect of the morrow still more bitter. Christianity enjoyed a decisive triumph once before in history when the upper and middle classes of the ancient world were smitten with the appalling catastrophes and the unutterable sufferings that followed upon the final victories of the barbarians and the fall of the western Empire. Says Gaston Boissier: "The sufferings of those days [the period of the invasions] seemed destined to strike a deadly blow at Christianity. Actually they made its victory certain."[1] In a number of large cities of the

[1] "Le lendemain de l'invasion."

empire, and in Rome especially, the upper classes had been generally hostile to the new religion down to the time of St. Augustine. If, in our day, many lives are sacrificed and a large part of European wealth is squandered in social struggles, or in vain attempts to effect social reforms, it is not at all unlikely that the luxury and waste that was characteristic of the first three decades of the twentieth century will be followed by an era of depression and comparative poverty, during which Christian doctrines will again find the terrain propitious for recapturing the hearts of the masses. In France and other countries, revivals of pietism have a way of following serious epidemics or catastrophes. In 1832, for instance, a cholera epidemic very appreciably weakened an aversion to priests that the revolution of 1830 had aroused. Another religious reaction followed the terrible war year of 1870–1871. It is interesting that in both those cases the sufferings involved were very ephemeral and had been quite forgotten within a few years.

So far, in Catholic countries, the Catholic Church has enjoyed very considerable autonomy and claimed the right to interfere extensively in public affairs. Anticlerical propaganda has therefore been fostered, directly or indirectly, by all secular authorities with which the papacy has found itself in any violent conflict of interests. That was the case in France during the first years of the July Monarchy and at certain periods under the Third Republic. It was the case in Italy during and after the fall of the temporal power of the papacy. But such episodes have occurred time and again in the lives of the Catholic peoples. It would be an error to think of them as touching the essence of history, and to regard them as wars to the death, brooking neither treaty nor truce. As has very often happened in centuries past, after a position has been desperately disputed the losing party gets used to the new state of affairs and resigns itself to at least tacit acceptance. The Catholic Church has had a number of such hours of silent resignation in the course of its long history.

4. Less amenable to conciliation is the antagonism between the positive scientific method and the supernatural and dogmatic premises which underlie all religions, the Christian included, and which Catholicism has recently been stressing to a more and more marked degree. But faith is very old and science relatively new.

Certain glimmers of science were visible in ancient Egypt, in Babylon, in Brahmanic India, in China; but they were uncoordinated gleams, clouded almost always by mystery, and between them came long centuries of darkness. The scientific light that was generated by Greco-Roman civilization was stronger, but it too all but faded with the decline of the ancient world. New gleams flashed during the more splendid period of Arab civilization, which took advantage of stray rays from ancient Greece and from the Persia of the Sassanids. Those, also, were snuffed out by the progressive barbarization of the Mohammedan world.[1] But as an integrating force in a civilization, as a real contribution made by a historical period, positive science came into being in the sixteenth century. It did not get a firm hold until the eighteenth in a Europe which had inherited and was then turning to account doctrines and ideas that had been developed by many different peoples, many different civilizations. That there should have been a struggle between this new social force, which was trying to assert itself, and religion, which was trying to defend itself and, as a first step, seeking to smother its new rival in infancy, is natural and altogether understandable. Religion first tried to deny the results of science and then smote them with its anathema. Science, for its part, turned with particular zest to the task of discrediting the dogmas of religion in the eyes of the masses.

But many institutions, like many people, seem utterly incompatible yet in the end are forced to get along together somehow, since they cannot suppress each other outright. If science attacks dogma, directly or indirectly, its field at least is different from the field of religion. Scientific thought deals with the human intelligence. Faith has its basis in sentiment. Science, necessarily, is accessible only to the small number of individuals who have the ability and the opportunity to lead highly intellectual lives. Religion exerts its influence upon the masses. Any two religions, which are unavoidably obliged to refute each other and compete within the same field, are far more incompatible than science and any given religion. Sometimes, nevertheless, after long, cruel conflicts, two religions end by tolerating each other, once they become convinced that they cannot destroy

[1] Amari, *Storia dei Musulmani in Sicilia*, especially vol. III, pp. 702 f.; Renan, *Averroès et l'Averroïsme*.

each other; and today we find Catholics and Protestants, Christians and Mohammedans, Mohammedans and idolaters, living together peaceably in the same communities.

China, perhaps, offers in this regard an example that better suits our case. In China the educated governing classes subscribe to a vague sort of deism, which at bottom is rational positivism pure and simple. Rational and positive at least are the practical implications of the teachings of Confucius. Once when Kilou, a disciple of Confucius, was questioning the master on the matter of death, he obtained this reply: "You cannot find out what life is. Why should you be so anxious to know what death is?" Tze-Kong, another disciple, once asked whether the souls of the dead knew what went on in the world of the living, and Confucius answered: "You need feel no great concern, Tze-Kong, about knowing whether the souls of our ancestors are aware of what goes on among us. There is no hurry about solving that problem. Wait a while and you will see for yourself what the truth is."[1] The Chinese masses are Buddhists, or else follow Lao-tse or Mohammed. Buddhism is, in a sense, legally recognized and public authorities participate officially in its rites.

Now something of the same sort may very well come about in Europe. It seems highly improbable that any new religions will rise, let alone spread, in the western world in the near future. The various forms of Christianity will maintain their predominance, therefore, in the countries where they are now predominant. Because of its better organization and more coherent dogmatism, Catholicism will probably gain some little ground over the various Protestant sects, especially in England and the United States. In the long run, a mutual toleration may be established between the positivism, or, rather, the scientific skepticism, of the better educated and the beliefs that are held not only by the poor and unlettered masses but also by that large portion of the well-to-do classes which by sex, habit, education and temperament is more responsive to sentimental impulses.

Skeptics must understand that no social advantage is to be gained by spreading a propaganda of unbelief among those who feel a need for religious beliefs or who are too ignorant ever to succeed in developing original and personal views of their own in

[1] Rousset, À travers la Chine, chap. VI.

regard to natural and social problems. On the other hand, the leaders of the Christian, and particularly of the Catholic, movement should finally become persuaded—that persuasion, to tell the truth, seems to be rather hard to acquire—that science is now so much a part of the life of civilized humanity that it will not be easy to smother and destroy it.

However, the solutions which we have just mentioned of modern problems concerning the relations between church and state and between science and the dogmatic religions are to be thought of merely as *possible* solutions. That does not mean that they are easy ones to achieve, much less that they are the ones that will necessarily be adopted. If they are to be adopted, the parties that are now in conflict must possess great political sagacity, and, unhappily, it is not sagacity that on the whole rules human events, but passions, hatreds, fanaticisms. It should not be forgotten, either, that the democratic-socialist current today amounts virtually to another religion, which is fiercely competing with Christianity and is almost wholly incompatible with it.

Another possibility is that in the clash between the Christian and socialist currents not enough freedom and toleration will be left to allow the few individuals who are capable of retaining independence of thought in the presence of grave social and political problems, to go on living and prospering. Unfortunately, the epochs in which individuals have been permitted to express their thoughts freely, and have not been obliged to pay homage to some type of fanaticism and superstition, have been privileged epochs. They are rather exceptional in the history of mankind and as a rule they have not lasted very long. More often human societies have settled down for centuries upon some system of beliefs to which they have sacrificed all liberty of discussion and thought; or else they have cruelly tormented themselves because two different currents of doctrine and belief have been fighting for social predominance with every possible weapon. Moments of relative peace and toleration, moments when passions have been held in leash somewhat and the human mind has been able to observe and reason calmly, have been no more than blessed breathing spaces, separated by long intervals of fanatical bigotry, of savage conflict and persecution.

That any such breathing space can easily be brought to an end is proved by the many civilizations which have now declined or become static, yet which must have had their moments when thought was relatively free—otherwise they could not have attained the level of intellectual progress that they once attained. In Europe Greek civilization declined from what it was in the age of Aristotle to what it was in the Byzantine age. After the glowing scientific civilization of the early centuries of Rome—a civilization which the most cultivated modern nations did not overtake till the eighteenth and nineteenth centuries—came a decline, now slow, now rapid, to the barbarism that we find described by Gregory of Tours and Paul the Deacon, and then on to the barbarism, even more abject and degraded, that we find chronicled by Raoul Glaber.[1] As one thinks of those great eclipses of the human intelligence, one is inclined unhappily to suspect—not, of course, to prophesy—that the era in which we are now living may be followed by one in which the individual will not be free publicly to profess, or not to profess, the Christian religion, and in which spontaneous and sincere expression of thought, full independence of scientific inquiry, will be limited by the necessity of keeping intact that one of the conflicting political formulas which shall chance, after long and dogged struggles, to come off victorious.

5. Closely linked with the religious problem, as well as with the problem of social democracy, is our second question (§2), which concerns the crisis that representative, and especially parliamentary, governments are now traversing.

As is well known, new and important social forces came to the fore in Europe during the eighteenth century—forces based on the production of new wealth, on a different distribution of wealth and on the rise in Europe of an educated, prosperous middle class. But ignoring those matters for the moment, one may say that two intellectual currents were originally responsible for developments in the field of politics which brought almost all the peoples of European civilization to adopt representative forms of government, and, in not a few cases, parliamentary forms of government.

[1] See above, chap. III, §10.

The first current we shall call the liberal current. It was based on the doctrines of Montesquieu. It sought to set up a barrier against bureaucratic absolutism by means of a separation of powers. We have already seen that this theory, incomplete as it may have been, cannot be regarded as mistaken in any substantial respect.

The second current was the democratic current. Its intellectual parent was Rousseau. According to this theory, the legal basis of any sort of political power must be popular sovereignty —the mandate which those who rule receive from the majority of citizens. Not only the legitimacy of governors but their worth—their ability to satisfy the interests and ideals of the masses and to lead them toward economic, intellectual and moral betterment—depends upon their genuinely applying the premise of popular sovereignty.

Rousseau, the real parent of the doctrine of popular sovereignty and hence of modern representative democracy, expresses himself in one or two pages of the *Contrat social*[1] as decidedly opposed to any delegation of sovereignty, and therefore to representative systems. However, the democratic school, which took its cue from the principles laid down by the Genevan philosopher, was obliged to accept the principle of representation for many reasons. One of them must not be forgotten: that the practical model which liberals and democrats had before them in applying their doctrines was the English constitution of the eighteenth century. That constitution had derived the principle of representation from its feudal origins and had retained and developed it. This second current of ideas, carried to its ultimate developments and implications, has produced, along with theories of representative government, the theories of modern social democracy.

Many objections are now being urged against representative government in general, and especially against those forms of it in which the democratic ideal may be said to have been best realized, in view of a broad-based popular suffrage and the political preponderance that has been acquired by elective "lower houses." These objections are of three orders. A first group focuses upon the prattlings, the long-winded speeches, the futile bickerings, with which parliamentary assemblies largely

[1] E.g. chap. XV.

busy themselves. Another group—and we consider it better founded—is put forward chiefly by advanced socialists or anarchists. Their criticisms come down to the charge that, given the unequal distribution of wealth that prevails at present, parliaments do not represent the interests and aspirations of majorities, but the interests of wealthy ruling classes. The third group, finally, is best founded of all. It relates to the excessive interference, not so much by lower houses as political bodies as by individual members of lower houses, in the courts, in public administration, in the distribution of the large portion of the social wealth that is levied by the state in the form of duties and taxes and applied to various public services, and in the distribution of that portion, also large, of the social wealth that is concentrated in banks, in great industrial speculations and in public charities. These activities, as a rule, fail to escape the influence and supervision of modern governments in Europe.

Anyone can see that, in highly bureaucratized systems such as ours are, continuous pottering, interloping and officiousness on the part of members of lower houses must be an exceedingly baneful thing, and a special name has in fact been given to the phenomenon. The name is of fairly recent coinage but it has already had time to acquire derogatory connotations. It is the term "parliamentarism."

6. Now certain drawbacks are unavoidable in any system that is based on discussion. Assemblies will talk and they will talk. Many speeches are bound to be inane, and in many others one will more readily discern a play of petty ambitions, spites and vanities than any great devotion to public interests. New laws will often be debated and passed frivolously. Filibustering will sometimes retard urgent decisions. Epithets will often be violent and not always justified. These without a doubt are all grave defects. But they can seem disastrously grave and of capital importance only to someone who is convinced that it is possible for a country to have a political system that is exempt from the weaknesses inherent in human nature itself. The human being's ability to conceive of what is good, of absolute justice, of the best way to do one's duty, and then the great difficulties he encounters when he comes to making his conduct scrupulously conform to his high ideals, inevitably result in the

fact that no statesman and no form of government can avoid being the target of any number of criticisms, some of which, from an abstract point of view, may be quite just. But the one sound criterion for judging men as well as political systems is to compare them with others, especially with those that have preceded them and, whenever it is possible, with those that have succeeded them.

Judged by that standard, the defects of parliamentary assemblies, and the evil consequences which their control of power and their participation in power produce in all representative systems, are merest trifles as compared with the harm that would inevitably result from abolishing them or stripping them of their influence. Under the conditions that prevail at present in society, the suppression of representative assemblies would inevitably be followed by a type of regime that is commonly called "absolute." We believe it might better be termed "exclusively bureaucratic," since its chief characteristic is that it alienates from public life all political forces, all social values, except such as are represented in the bureaucracy. At the very least, it completely subordinates all other forces and values to the bureaucratic element. We are far from deeming it impossible that an ever growing disgust with "parliamentarism," and, especially, a fear of social democracy, wherever the latter assumes a menacingly revolutionary bent, may drive one people or another in modern Europe to adopt such an "absolute" or "absolutely bureaucratic" system. What we cannot admit is that such a step would be a wise one. We need give no long demonstration of that thesis in view of all that we have been saying (chap. V, §§9–10) as to the dangers and drawbacks involved in giving absolute predominance to a single political force that is not subject to any limitation or discussion whatever. That we are not dealing with a purely theoretical and doctrinaire objection, but with an objection of great practical consequence, is readily proved by recalling the experiences of a number of countries of European civilization where the representative system has functioned very imperfectly. There is the example of czarist Russia, or perhaps better still, of the old regime in France. Italians, and especially South Italians, are familiar with conditions under the old Bourbon dynasties of the south. However defective one may consider the political and social organization in the kingdom of the Two Sicilies during the last years of its existence, and however low its moral status, one should note that King Ferdinand II was a man of fair intelligence. He was energetic and devoted, after his fashion, to the well-being of his people. Morally he was far superior to the average of his subjects.[1]

People of our time have come to take for granted the advantages of a system in which all governmental acts are subject to public discussion. That alone can explain why superficial observers among our younger generations fail to realize at a glance the moral ruin that would result from the downfall of such a system. That ruin would take the form of a series of violations of juridical defense, of justice, of everything that we commonly call "liberty"; and those violations would be far more pernicious than any that can be laid to the charge of even the most dishonest of parliamentary governments, let alone of representative governments. There has been a tendency of late to criticize representative forms of government too much and too slanderously. We note, for example, in a recent pamphlet, an argument against parliamentarism that maintains that government by parliaments is dangerous because assemblies partake of the nature of mobs, in that they are easily swayed by rhetoric and oratory and so make ill-advised and reckless decisions. Now, in the first place, assemblies do not govern—they merely check and balance the men who govern, and limit their power. In the second place, an assembly of representatives is almost never a "mob," in the sense of being a haphazard, inorganic assemblage of human beings. Parliaments are customarily organized on a basis of recognized capacities and functions. They contain many men of long experience with public affairs, who are thereby safeguarded against any harm that might result to less well-balanced brains from an overardent or ravishing eloquence. Some of the drawbacks that are charged to parliaments are partly offset, furthermore, by real advantages incidental to them. Failure to act promptly, for instance, is not always an evil. Oftentimes new laws require new executive staffs, involve new outlays of money and require new sources of taxation. All that is harmful, as a rule, in modern states, where bureaucracy and devices for taxing are already overdeveloped.

[1] Memor, *La fine di un regno.*

The objections to representative systems that are commonly urged by extreme socialists and anarchists have a sound basis in an observation made above (chaps. V, §§10–11; VI, §1) and by many other writers. The wonder is that the point has not been more widely noted and more earnestly heeded. Obviously, the members of an elective chamber are almost never chosen freely and spontaneously by the majority of the voters, since voters have only a very limited freedom of choice among the very few candidates who have any chance of success. Certainly this flagrant contradiction between the fact and the theory of the law, between the juridical premise of the political mandate and its expression in practice, is the great weakness of any representative system. All the same, it can be taken as an argument of capital importance against representative systems only by those —they are still many, alas—who adopt the narrow and strictly limited interpretation that was given to the theory of popular sovereignty by Rousseau and his followers of the democratic school, who took popular sovereignty to mean that any government in any country should emanate from the numerical majority of its citizens. As we see things, the only demand that it is important, and possible, to make of a political system is that all social values shall have a part in it, and that it shall find a place for all who possess any of the qualities which determine what prestige and what influence an individual, or a class, is to have. Just as we do not combat a religion because its dogmas seem far-fetched, so long as it produces good results in the field of conduct, so the applications of a political doctrine may be acceptable so long as they result in an improvement in juridical defense, though the doctrine itself may easily be open to attack from a strictly scientific standpoint. It cannot be denied that the representative system provides a way for many different social forces to participate in the political system and, therefore, to balance and limit the influence of other social forces and the influence of bureaucracy in particular. If that were the only possible consequence, and the only possible application, of the doctrine of popular sovereignty, it would clearly be advantageous to accept it on that ground alone, however clearly we might realize that the ideas and sentiments which have produced that result have a very slim basis in scientific fact.

The fact that real and actual majorities have a limited influence on the choice of representatives does not depend altogether on the social inequalities that at present prevail. Certainly it is only natural that when inequalities exist the choice of voters should most often fall upon those who, in the particular state of inequality, occupy the highest rungs on the social ladder. But even if the social scale were to be leveled so as to become a plane —a hypothesis which we consider implausible—there would still be the inevitable predominance of organized and easily organizable minorities over disorganized majorities. The mass of voters would therefore still be forced to choose their representatives from among candidates who would be put forward by groups, or committees, and these groups would be made up of persons who by taste and by interest would be actively devoted to political life.

The soundest point, therefore, in the criticisms that for a good half century past have been leveled at representative governments is the excessive and exclusive power that is given by many of them—especially when they have degenerated into parliamentarism—to the elected representatives. The prime and real root of the evils that are being so generally lamented lies in the facts that where parliamentarism is in force the ministry directing the vast and absorbing bureaucratic machine issues from the ranks of the elected chamber, and, more serious still, the fact that prime ministers and their cabinets stay in power as long, and only as long, as it pleases the majority of the elected chamber to retain them. Because of these two facts, discussion of governmental acts in our parliaments and the control that representatives should exercise over governmental acts almost always go astray under pressure of personal ambitions and party interests. Because of the same facts, the natural desire of governors to govern well is continuously and effectively thwarted by their no less natural desire to serve their own personal interests, and the sense of professional duty in ministers and representatives is always balanced by all sorts of ambitions and vanities, justified and unjustified. Finally, the courts and the administrative departments become parts of a great electioneering agency with a corresponding cost in public money and in moral atmosphere; and a demand on the part of any important vote-getter upon the representative who needs him, or on the part of the minister who needs the representative, is often enough to silence any respect for equity and law. In a word, because of a constant, flagrant and manufactured contradiction between the duty and the interest of the man who governs, and of the man who should judge and limit governmental action, the bureaucracy and the elective elements, which should control and balance each other, end by corrupting and denaturing each other.[1]

7. Before examining the remedies which have been proposed for this state of affairs, it might be well to stop for a moment and consider what would happen if the same state of affairs were to continue unchanged for a certain length of time—if, let us say, no substantial change were to be made for a half century or more in the institutions that govern so large a part of European society, and there were to be no new upheavals violent enough to cause any considerable rearrangements in personal influences and fortunes. Now even granting such a hypothesis, dubious as it might seem to us, we must reject outright an opinion that was once embraced by many and is now accepted by few, that parliamentary institutions possess within themselves a curative property that is able automatically to heal any evils that they may be responsible for in their early, inexperienced days. We take no stock in the myth that "the cure for liberty is more liberty"—Liberty, like the famous lance of Achilles, healing the wounds that she herself inflicts. We do admit that the evils in question would change in nature somewhat by virtue of the process of stabilization or crystallization in political influences that occurs in all countries where the political system is not altered over long periods of time by foreign infiltrations or by inner ferments of ideas and passions. The scions of today's celebrities in parliament, bank and governmental positions would in fact attain with increasing ease the posts that are now occupied by their fathers, and a little world apart would come into being, a clique of influential families, into which it would be hard for newcomers to make their way. In republican Rome the

---

[1] On the drawbacks of parliamentarism, see Schérer, *La Démocratie et la France*, Prins, *La Démocratie et le régime parlementaire*, and Mosca, *Teorica dei governi*. On the evils caused by giving excessive power to elective elements, see also Seaman, *The American System of Government*.

more prominent families held the same public offices from father to son for generation after generation. In England in the eighteenth century, and in the first decades of the nine-teenth down to the Reform Bill of 1832, there were old par-liamentary families that inevitably appeared either at the head of the opposition or at the head of the cabinet. In France we see the sons, brothers and sons-in-law of politicians inheriting the constituencies that their elders have held. Now in the case we are assuming there would be an accentuation of all that. Because of the greater stability of the class that would be holding supreme political control, success would become more difficult for men of merit and of obscure birth, but at the same time things would be harder for those who emerge from the crowd and mount the first steps of reputation and political influence by flattering and whetting the lowest or maddest aspirations of the mob. Time also would pass the sponge of forgetfulness over the tainted origins of many fortunes and many influential positions, and sons born to high station would be spared the rascalities and the moral inconsistencies which their fathers had to stoop to in order to attain such station. But the contradiction between the spirit of institutions and the men who would be called upon to represent them would become more and more conspicuous, and the oli-garchy, which would be governing in the name of the people and would never be able wholly to eschew the intrigues and hypoc-risies that are inevitable in any parliamentary government, would drift farther and farther away from the sentiments and passions of the people. And by people we do not mean just the masses of peasants and workingmen, but also the populous middle classes within whose orbit so much of the economic and intellec-tual activity of a country unfolds.

So then, we should not be justified in expecting too much help from the natural effects of time. That help could not amount to very much. But looking in some other direction, it is not hard to imagine modifications in present institutions that might effectively contribute toward attenuating the evils of parliamen-tarism. No one, for instance, can fail to see how helpful it would be to increase guarantees of the independence of the courts by assuring to magistrates in all countries that real permanency of tenure which is now established in only a few, and by raising the social position and prestige of judges in fact and not merely in words. No one can fail to see how advantageous it would be to France, for instance, and not to France alone, to introduce the system that prevailed in imperial Germany, whereby all public officials of high rank were responsible for their acts to really independent administrative tribunals, and at the same time were free from the jurisdiction of ministers, and therefore of representatives. Financial control also could be better organized by increasing the independence of our auditing departments.

Unfortunately, remedies of this sort might reduce the virulence of certain symptoms of the disease, but they would not eradicate the disease itself. It would be difficult, moreover, to procure their adoption, because the elements that are in power with the sanction of popular suffrage, whence they are commonly called democratic, now tacitly oppose, now openly protest, in the name of the intangible principles of popular sovereignty, every time a question of increasing the prestige and powers of institutions that limit their omnipotence comes up. In Italy a bill guaranteeing permanency of tenure to civil employees was once brought, we remember, before the old Chamber, in the days of our personal service there. Though it had a majority in its favor, it was suddenly tabled for no apparent reason and allowed to lapse with the closure of the session. In France things went even worse. Bills were passed to force a "house cleaning" in the courts and in the departments. This simply increased the subservience of the judges to the ministers, who were themselves tools of the parliamentary majority to begin with.

A remedy which would be more radical and effective, and which has been favored by many people, would be simply to go back to the "constitutional" system of which the parliamentary system is just a transformation and, in the opinion of some, a degeneration.

To keep our language clear, we might note that "constitutional governments," as that expression is used in Europe, are governments in which prime ministers (presidents of councils of ministers, chancellors), who wield executive power, do not resign when they are defeated in a vote by the chamber of representatives, but are changed only through action by the head of the state. The typical case would be that of the old German government. A "parliamentary government," in the same technical language, is a government in which the prime minister and his cabinet are appointed by the head of the state but present their resignations whenever they lose the majority in the elective chamber. That is the almost invariable custom in England and France. In those countries, according to some writers, the cabinet is just a committee of the majority of the elective chamber. A third type of representative government prevails in the United States. It might be called the "presidential" type. In it the executive power is not changed by vote of the lower chamber. The head of the state is elected by the people for a specified term. The United States, in addition, happens to have a system of government which is not centralized.

Now, as regards Europe, a political move in the direction of a return to "constitutional" government would be fairly easy to engineer, since if one keeps to the letter of the constitutions and basic charters on which most modern European governments rest, there is no discernible difference between the parliamentary system and the constitutional system. In fact, all such documents assume the existence of constitutional systems, not of parliamentary systems. The Portuguese constitution of 1826 is the only one to distinguish between the personal sovereignty of the king (Art. 21), and the executive power, which is to be exercised by the king through his ministers (Art. 75). All other European constitutions declare merely that the head of the state exercises executive power through responsible ministers whom he appoints and recalls at will. In Italy, the constitution mentions individual ministers only, and says nothing of a cabinet or a prime minister. The functions of the latter have been determined by a series of royal decrees, the oldest of which is the Azeglio Decree of 1850 and the most important the Ricasoli Decree of March 1867. This last was abrogated a month later by Rattazzi, but its text was taken over in large part by the Depretis Decree of August 20, 1876, and by later ones.

The parliamentary form of government came into being through a series of concessions that were tacitly asked for by public opinion and tacitly granted by the heads of states. A mere change in public opinion would be enough, therefore, to effect a return to a more genuine interpretation of the principles that are codified in the various constitutions. It is erroneous to believe, as some do, that in England parliamentary government has the sanction of centuries of experience. Parliamentarism began in England only a little earlier than the middle of the eighteenth century, and it did not function in full accord with the rules which commentators now regard as correct until the nineteenth century (the reigns of Queen Victoria, and her successors). In 1783 the younger Pitt was called to the government by George III against the will of the House of Commons. In 1835 William IV tried on his own initiative to replace Lord Melbourne with Robert Peel. The king was able to maintain his position for some months.

In spite of all this, a political evolution in a "constitutional" direction would seem to be of very doubtful timeliness at present. In France and in other parliamentary countries on the European continent, the functioning of all political institutions has by now come to be linked with the assumption that the parliamentary system should function in the fact. One may question whether it was a good idea to pass directly from the absolute bureaucratic system to a parliamentary system without halting, at least for a time, in the strictly "constitutional" phase. However, events have taken that course, and one can only put up with their consequences. One very important consequence of the political theories and practices that have thus far prevailed so largely in Europe has been the fact that the elective chamber, certain that the cabinet could at any time be overthrown by an opposing vote on its part, has not paid enough attention to the need of limiting the powers and attributes of the cabinet. As a result the elective chamber has been very lavish in augmenting the resources, functions and prerogatives of the state, and has perhaps not very jealously guarded the inviolability of some of its own prerogatives since it has felt all along that the men in power would be instruments of the chamber majority in any event. The result has been that "legislation by decree," so-called, has come to be used and abused in a number of parliamentary countries.

Under these circumstances, any rapid retrogression from a parliamentary system to a "constitutional" system, in countries that are accustomed to the former, would lead to far more narrow and autocratic systems than prevail in countries in which pure constitutionalism has never been modified and all authorities have always functioned in conformity with the letter of the basic constitutions. Let us keep clear of misleading hopes and fancies. A development in that direction would, so to say, decapitate the representative chamber by stripping it of the most important of its functions, and meantime it would leave the all-absorbing bureaucratic organization intact, along with all those methods and habits of corruption whereby parliamentary governments are now able to nullify the verdicts of the ballot. The result would therefore be that, for a long time to come at least, parliaments would be deprived of all spontaneity of action and would lose all political significance, and we should be left with a system very like bureaucratic absolutism, with the vices and drawbacks of which we are already familiar. Those vices and drawbacks would be more serious, more deeply felt and far harder to bear under the new system if the cabinet that happened to inaugurate it were to issue, as it very probably would issue, from parliamentarism itself, and so be tainted with all the corruption and hypocrisy that is inherent in the parliamentary system.

8. The surest and most effective remedy for the evils of parliamentarism would be extensive and organic decentralization. That would not merely imply shifting prerogatives from central bureaucracies to provincial bureaucracies, and from national parliaments to local assemblies. It would imply transferring many of the functions that are now exercised by bureaucracies and elective bodies to the class of public-spirited citizens. In view of their education and their wealth such people are greatly superior to the average mass in ability, in independence and in social prestige. They do not seek posts in the civil service and, at present, when they do not run for parliament or when they fail of election, they take no part whatever in public life, unless they chance to belong to some provincial municipal council. Only by making constant use of such elements can the evils of parliamentarism be mitigated and a transition from a parliamentary to a constitutional system be effected without peril to public liberties.

It is a matter of common knowledge that the defects of parliamentary government in Europe almost all come down to improper interference with elections to central and local elective bodies by bureaucracies, acting mainly through prefects appointed by the ministries, and to equally improper interference with the bureaucracies by representatives elected to the national chambers.

All this gives rise to a shameful and hypocritical traffic in reciprocal indulgences and mutual favors, which is a veritable running sore in most European countries. This vicious circle can be broken neither by increasing the powers of the bureaucracy nor by enlarging the prerogatives of the elective bodies. It can be broken only by summoning new political elements, new social forces, to the service of the public weal and by perfecting juridical defense through the participation in public offices of all persons who have aptitudes for them. Such persons will not be salaried employees to be promoted or transferred at the caprice of some minister, and they will not have to depend for return to office on electioneering and on the approval of some local "machine" or some electoral busybody.

In France, Italy and certain other countries, the idea we have just set forth could be applied in every province or department by listing all people who have college or university degrees and pay a specified tax. One might regard as equivalent to higher educational degrees the rank of captain in the army, past service as a representative in parliament or as mayor of a town of not less than ten thousand inhabitants, or past service in the presidency of an industrial or agricultural association that has a specified number of members or has been working with a specified amount of capital. So a special class of volunteer unsalaried officials could be developed. Open to anyone who might acquire the qualifications mentioned, it would still have a certain homogeneousness of social status. In view of the human being's natural propensity for social distinctions, it would soon develop cohesion and group pride, and the members would be willing and eager to devote a part of their time to public business.

From the individuals belonging to such a class could be chosen, either by lot or otherwise and either for temporary or life tenures, as might seem best, referees and arbiters for petty civil cases, commissioners for voters' lists in national and local elections, and justices of the peace to deal with petty misdemeanors and other minor police cases. From the same class should come members of higher budget commissions and administrative boards, which would supplant the present administrative boards, where such exist, and which might be under the presidency of professional magistrates. The same element could, and in fact should, be represented in all councils of prefectures or provinces.

We are not, of course, proposing here to set forth in detail a complete system of reform for the political and administrative institutions of European society. We are merely suggesting the broad lines along which reforms should be developed. We are merely tracing a path which, in our opinion, it will be wise and necessary to follow.[1] We are not unaware that a number of objections might be made to the immediate application of our idea. Though they are not all of equal weight, it might be well to examine them very briefly.

It may be said that our present jury system is organized along the lines which we have proposed but that it is working out badly and discrediting itself more and more from day to day. Now one should observe, in the first place, that the charges that are brought against the jury system are probably somewhat exaggerated, in that the jury system is held to be exclusively responsible for abuses that are due rather to the general tendency of our age to be overmild in the repression of common crime. Against that tendency a strong reaction is bound sooner or later to set in. In the second place, the elements that serve on our juries are not altogether of the type we have recommended. The basis on which jury panels are made up has been greatly, too greatly, broadened, so that jury panels now contain a majority of persons who have not the intellectual training, or the moral background, required for the delicate tasks that juries are called upon to perform.

Social organisms often function badly not because the principle on which they are based is fundamentally wrong but because the principle is badly applied. Sound, unquestionably, was the principle put forward by Machiavelli that the force that is armed for the maintenance of order in a state and to protect its independence ought to be "composed of citizens who lend their services in turn, rather than of foreigners and mercenaries who make a trade of war." But while a wise and prudent application of that principle has produced our modern standing armies, a careless and unsystematic application of it would have yielded the same results that were yielded by the Florentine "ordinance," which was created at the Florentine Secretary's own suggestion, and by the national guard which functioned, or rather failed to function, in Italy down to the middle of the last century.

It may also be objected that there would be something artificial and arbitrary about our manner of designating the class of functionaries that we have proposed. We do not deny that the

[1] The idea suggested has also been developed by Turiello in his *Governo e governanti.*

criticism might seem just, at a superficial glance, for, as a matter of fact, no human institution, no law, can avoid setting more or less artificial and arbitrary limits. Arbitrary and artificial is the limit that is set by law in fixing a person's majority at twenty years, eleven months and twenty-nine days. Up to that moment a person is considered incapable of ordering his own affairs. The next morning he comes of age. Laws that fix the exact conditions under which one can vote, in countries where universal suffrage does not obtain, also set artificial and arbitrary limits. But in the matter before us, if we look somewhat deeply into it, the precise opposite seems to be the case. In our private customs and habits we always draw very considerable distinctions between people of good education and people of no education, between people who move in good society because of their economic position and people who are poor and have no social standing. If such people are all considered as on the same footing from the political point of view, it is simply because arbitrary and conventional criteria prevail all through our political systems. If anything should arouse our wonder, therefore, it is that at present people who have the requisites mentioned are, *taken as a class*, political nonentities. We say "taken as a class" intentionally. Taken as individuals, the men who now hold elective offices of any importance—members of parliaments, that is, provincial or departmental council members, mayors and city councilors in large cities—come, as things stand, almost entirely from social strata that have a certain economic ease and a certain amount of education. The trouble is that, with rare exceptions, they come from the strata mentioned by passing through a ruinous process of selection downward, which bars from positions of major importance men who will not buy votes or cannot buy them, men who are of too high a character to sacrifice dignity to ambition, or men who are too sincere and honest to throw out to left and right promises which they know they cannot keep, or can keep only by sacrificing the public welfare to private advantage.

A more real and far more serious obstacle to the practical execution of our plan would be the present economic situation in many European countries. During the eighteenth century and the first half of the nineteenth, the English gentry held almost all the offices that correspond to the ones which we would

like to see entrusted to the class that is the counterpart of the
English gentry in continental European society. The English
gentry held offices in accord with a system very much like
the one that we would introduce into continental countries,
though during past decades the system has lost a good deal of
ground across the Channel through the growing influence of
modern democratic ideas.

But England was a relatively rich country during the two
centuries mentioned and, down to a hundred years ago, specialized knowledge did not have so wide an application in the various
branches of social activity. A certain amount of wealth and a
certain social background were enough to establish the prestige
of an individual, and it was not indispensable, as it virtually is
today, that a man should have a higher education in addition to
those other assets. As things stand at present, the demands
of the times, and especially the prospect of losing their influence
unless something is done about it, may induce the members of
the wealthy class, the people who own the great fortunes, to
shake off an indolence that in many countries has become one
of their traditions and apply themselves to obtaining specialized
and higher training.

But that class has never been, and will never be, very large.
It can never fill all the positions that we have listed, and meantime the functions of the state have been broadening and broadening in Europe, so that bureaucracy today has come to absorb
a truly vast mass of activities and duties. Today we should be
at a loss to tell where one could find enough people to recruit the
class of independent honorary public servants that we refer to.
That class, therefore, has to be reinforced by another class, the
class of merely respectable, hard-working people who live in
moderate ease. However, this is the very class, in Europe at
least, that is having the greatest difficulty in holding its own,
smitten as it is, and more grievously probably than any other
class, by the heavy, pauperizing systems of taxation that prevail
today. In many countries the middle classes can hardly maintain the margin of economic well-being which is indispensable if
one is to acquire a higher education merely for reasons of personal
dignity, family standing or social usefulness. They are seeking
a higher education for strictly professional purposes, since they
are obliged to have the diplomas required for following the

so-called liberal professions. If that were all, the social harm
would perhaps be endurable; but the worst of it is that those
professions soon become overcrowded. Middle-class elements,
therefore, turn more and more to a panting search for public
office. Under the pressure of applicants, offices multiply both
in national and in local administrations, occasioning new budgetary outlays and opening new fields for bureaucracy to conquer.
So a vicious circle of reciprocal causes and effects is closed: the
impoverishment of small capitalists and holders of medium-sized
properties by an excessive burden of taxation makes it almost
necessary to increase taxes still more; and the very elements in
society that in more prosperous countries would remain independent citizens, and constitute a most effective balance to
bureaucratic influence, are themselves transformed into professional bureaucrats.

But even these economic difficulties might gradually be overcome, and a new broad-based aristocracy might be formed of a
numerous class that would contain almost all the moral and intellectual energies of a nation, and be the most available counterbalance to bureaucratic, financial and electoral oligarchies.
Unfortunately, a far more serious and intractable obstacle is
raised by the democratic philosophy which is still so much in
vogue and which recognizes no political act, no political prerogative, as legitimate unless it emanates directly or indirectly
from popular suffrage. The democratic current, as we have
seen, has been an important factor in curtailing the functions
of the English gentry during past decades and handing them
over to elective elements or to bureaucracy. Now democracy
would exert all the force that it can still muster to prevent any
evolution in the opposite direction from taking place on the
European continent. At bottom, therefore, the greatest difficulty that stands in the way of finding remedies for the evils of
parliamentarism and applying them arises wholly in the frame
of mind that prevails in the societies which are living under
parliamentary systems—in other words, in the doctrines and
opinions that are most widely accepted by them. In our quest
for such remedies we end by finding ourselves confronted with
the very order of ideas and passions in which social democracy
originates.

CHAPTER XI

COLLECTIVISM

1. In beginning our examination of social democracy, it will perhaps be advisable to consider a bit of history. In a number of religious and social movements that have eventually acquired prominence, it is hard to determine the exact share that the first founder and his early associates had in the twists that those movements developed in practice. It is often not the easiest thing in the world to verify the birth certificates of the first masters and to tell just what traits were peculiar to them at the start. The personality of Sakyamuni is draped in the vagueness and uncertainty of Buddhist legend. Perhaps we shall never know just what part Manes, the founder of Manichaeism, played in beliefs, which later on, at the end of the fifth century A.D., brought on an attempt at something like a social revolution in Persia. But when present-day socialism dawned, the world was living in a far riper intellectual period. The new doctrines, and personal recollections regarding them, were at once gathered into books, which were published in thousands of copies, and they were so well preserved for posterity that few of them probably will ever be destroyed or lost. The beginnings of the reform doctrines that are so widely current in our day are therefore well known and can be followed step by step. Going back to their not very distant origins, one can easily make sure that Voltaire and his followers, although they may have had an important part in destroying the old world, almost never referred to any new social system, or systems, that might replace the one they knew. The real parent of the sentiments, the passions, the manner of looking at social life and appraising it, that resulted practically in the birth and growth of social democracy, was Jean Jacques Rousseau (above, chap. X, §4).

It would of course be easy to find in China, in India, in the Persia of the Sassanids, in ancient Egypt, in a few Greek and Roman writers, in the prophets of Israel, in the reformers of

Mohammedanism, in the early Christian Fathers and in the heresiarchs of the Middle Ages and the beginning of the modern era, ideas, sentiments, scattered opinions and sometimes complete systems of beliefs which are amazingly similar to the doctrines of modern socialism.[1]

One of the most interesting of the ancient Chinese experiments was launched by Wang Mang, who ruled the empire about the beginning of our Christian era. Wang Mang tried to revive the ancient Chinese agrarian communities, which were something like the Russian mir. He forbade any private individual to possess more than a trin, or twelve acres of land. Better known is the evidently collectivist experiment initiated in 1069 by the minister Wang An-shih, which made the state sole proprietor of all land and all capital. Both of these efforts had been preceded by periods of discontent, and both were provoked by destructive criticism aimed at the institutions then functioning. Needless to say both of them failed lamentably. After Wang Mang's reform had come to grief, a contemporary philosopher, grievously disappointed, it would seem, wrote that "not even Yü [said to be the founder of the first Chinese dynasty] could have succeeded in reviving communal ownership of property. For everything changes. Rivers disappear from their beds, and all that time erases vanishes forever."[2]

That such anticipations of modern ideas should have been numerous is natural enough, for the sentiments on which socialism proper, as well as anarchism, so largely rests are in no sense peculiar to the generations that are at present living in Europe and America. The application of a critical, destructive spirit to the analysis of contemporary social institutions, for the purpose of supplying a basis at least ostensibly rational and systematic for demanding political recognition of the sentiments referred to, is also an ancient and altogether natural phenomenon. It may arise in any human society that has reached a certain level of maturity.

This does not mean, however, that contemporary socialism descends in a direct and unbroken moral and intellectual line

---

[1] For particulars on socialist thought in other eras and other civilizations, see Cognetti de Martiis, *Socialismo antico.*

[2] Huc, *L'Empire chinois.* See also Varigny, "Un Socialiste chinois au XI siècle"; Réclus, *Nouvelle géographie universelle,* vol. VIII, pp. 577 f.

from any of the similar doctrines which flourished in one part of the world or another in ages more or less remote and then perished, leaving more or less perceptible traces of their propaganda upon human history. The present-day movements of socialist and anarchist reform do not go back to any religious principle. They rest on purely rationalistic foundations and are a spontaneous outgrowth of the intellectual and moral conditions that prevailed in Europe in the eighteenth and nineteenth centuries.

Socialism and anarchism have a common seed in the doctrine which proclaims that man is good by nature and that society makes him bad, overlooking the fact that the structure of a society is nothing more than a resultant of the compromising and compensating and balancing that take place among the varied and very complex human instincts. Now the first to formulate the doctrine clearly, and the man who was its most famous champion, was Rousseau. In his works he not only explicitly formulates the notion that absolute justice must be the basis of all political institutions, and condemns, therefore, all sorts of political and economic inequality; he also is at no pains to conceal the feelings of rancor toward fortune's favorites, toward the rich and the powerful, which make up such a large part of the polemical baggage of socialists past and present.

Janet writes: "From Rousseau comes that hatred of property and that rage at inequalities in wealth which are such terrible assets for these modern sects."[1] It should be noted, however, that Janet, as well as other writers who soundly regard Rousseau as the intellectual parent of modern subversive theories, quotes only the well-known passage at the beginning of the second part of Rousseau's essay on inequality.[2] Viewed independently of the rest of the work, the passage is more declamatory than conclusive. It reads:

The first man who fenced in a plot of ground and then thought of saying "This is mine," and found somebody who was fool enough to believe him, was the real founder of civilized society. How many crimes, how many wars, how much slaughter, misery, horror, would have been spared the human race, had some one torn down that fence, or filled in that trench, and cried to his neighbors: "Do not heed that

[1] "Les Origines du socialisme contemporain."
[2] *Discours sur l'origine et les fondements de l'inégalité parmi les hommes.*

impostor! You are lost if you forget that the soil belongs to nobody and that its fruits belong to all."

It might be objected that in the same essay Rousseau observes that a division of lands (*leur partage*) was a necessary consequence of their cultivation. That would be recognizing, in a sense, that there can be no civilization without private property.

The most conclusive passages, we believe, come four or five pages further along. Rousseau gives a long description, after his fashion, of man's slow and gradual development from savage, animal-like living to civilized living, and notes that the more significant moments in that evolution were the discovery of metals and the discovery of agriculture. He believes, furthermore, that agriculture, and therefore private property and inequality in fortunes, preceded any social organization at all, and that there must, therefore, have been a period of anarchy when everybody was fighting everybody else and when the rich man had most to lose. At that time (allowing Rousseau to speak for himself),

alone against all, unable in view of mutual jealousies to combine with his equals against foes who stood united by a common hope of plunder, harassed by his need, the rich man conceived the shrewdest plan that has ever crept into the human mind: He would use in his own favor the very power of those who were attacking him. He would make his adversaries his defenders. He would imbue them with different principles, which would be as much in his favor as natural right had been against him.

Rousseau goes on to relate how, at the suggestion of the wealthy, human beings consented to organize a government with laws which to all appearances safeguarded the life and property of all, but which in reality were of benefit only to the powerful. Finally he concludes:

Such was, or must have been, the origin of society and of laws, which laid new impediments upon the weak man and gave new power to the rich man, which destroyed natural freedom beyond recall, crystallized the law of property and inequality forever, turned shrewd usurpation into an unimpeachable right, and for the profit of a few ambitious men subjected the whole human race for all time to toil, servitude and poverty.

No very profound knowledge of contemporary socialist and anarchist literature is required to perceive that the passages quoted contain in fully developed form the concept of the class struggle, in other words the idea that government is instituted for the benefit of a single class. They also contain in germ all the assumptions and sentiments that underlie the collectivist principle, which would abolish private ownership of land, capital and the instruments of labor in order to prevent the exploitation of one class for the benefit of another class. More logically still they lead to the anarchist principle that every sort of political organization whatsoever should be abolished in order that rulers may be deprived of all means of exploiting the ruled and of governing them by violence and fraud.

Rousseau's work on the origin of inequality among men was published in 1754. In it he planted seeds which were to find an amazingly fertile environment and enjoy a most luxuriant growth. Just a year later, in 1755, the natural implications of Rousseau's principles were developed in a book called *Code de la nature*. Though it was uncouth in form and incoherent in substance, this *Code* was long attributed to Diderot. Its actual author was Morelly. It outlined quite clearly a program for radical social reform in a collectivist direction. Morelly maintains, in the *Code*, that there should be three fundamental laws in every society: (1) There should be no private property. (2) Every citizen should be a public official. (3) Every citizen should contribute to the public welfare. Starting with these three postulates, Morelly argues that the state should feed every individual and that every individual should work for the state, and he draws a picture of a society organized according to those ideals. As a precursor and pioneer of modern collectivist ideas, Morelly is perhaps entitled to greater respect than he has had, at least from his coreligionists.

In 1776 the Abbé Mably, an enlightened aristocrat who was a fairly well-known writer in his day, reached the conclusion that private property should be abolished. The Abbé's doctrines were foreshadowed for the first time in his *Doutes proposés aux philosophes économistes*, a work published in 1768 in rejoinder to a book published the year before by Le Mercier de La Rivière, *L'Ordre naturel et essentiel des sociétés politiques*. Mably's second work on the subject of land communism was his *De la législation ou Principes des lois.* There he formulates an imaginary objection that, if a division of land were to be made, inequality would shortly be reestablished. His answer was: "It is not a question of land division, but of community of lands. It is not a question of redistributing property. Property has to be abolished." It is significant that Rousseau often accused Mably of plagiarism.

A close parallel to Proudhon's famous phrase, "Property is theft (*La propriété c'est le vol*)," first appeared in a pamphlet that was published by Brissot de Warville in 1778, under the title of *Recherches philosophiques sur la propriété et sur le vol.* There we find the words "*La propriété exclusive est un vol.*" Brissot became one of the outstanding leaders of the Girondist party during the Revolution, heading the faction called the Brissotins. He was often in trouble because of the book and the phrase.

Whether the men who directed the great revolutionary movement in France at the end of the eighteenth century were or were not tinged with socialist doctrines has long been hotly debated. Prior to 1848, Louis Blanc held that they were, and Quinet, relying principally on the memoirs of Baudot, a member of the Convention, held that they were not. It seems evident to us that socialism is a necessary consequence of pure democracy, if by democracy we mean a denial of any social superiority that is not based upon the free consent of majorities. On this point we wholly agree with Stahl, and wholly disagree with Tocqueville and others. But to say that a consequence is necessary is not to say that it is going to follow *immediately.* It is natural that a certain time should elapse between the attempt to realize absolute equality in the political field and the attempt to achieve equality in the economic field, since experience alone can teach that political equality is altogether illusory unless it leads to economic equality.

During the period between 1789 and 1793, the theories that officially prevailed in the various legislative and constituent assemblies were what socialists of today would call "individualistic" or "bourgeois." That was partly because experience was wanting and partly because socialist doctrines were still in their infancy and had not yet been carefully worked out and embodied in systems that were scientific in appearance at least. More important still, if the leaders of the active revolutionaries were soldiers, they were satisfied with changing from sergeants to generals in a few years' time; and if they were lawyers they were satisfied to save their necks from the guillotine and become "legislators," "proconsuls," "committeemen on public safety," and what not, or at the very least high government officials. Soldiers or lawyers, or just peasants, all of them were as content as could be if they could buy the private property of an émigré from the state with a fistful of fiat money. The truth is that even if "bourgeois" or "capitalist" doctrines prevailed, the instincts and passions that were then rife were of quite another color, and if war was not waged officially on wealth and private property in general, it was waged, in general with great effectiveness, on property owners and wealthy men. It would be a simple matter to mention facts and quote speeches from those days that show perfect accord with the aspirations of revolutionary socialists of half a century later and of our time.

In his newspaper, *L'Ami du peuple*, Marat wrote that Their Worthies, the grocers, the drummers, the salesclerks, were conspiring against the Revolution with the gentlemen on the Right of the Convention and with gentlemen of wealth, that they ought to be arrested as suspects, every one, and that they could be turned into first class sans-culottes, "by leaving them nothing to cover their behinds with." Cambon proposed a forced loan of a million from the rich to be secured by mortgages on the property of émigrés. A decree of September 3, 1793, confiscated all incomes over 14,000 francs a year under guise of a forced loan. There were men in the Convention who considered wealth a sin and denounced any man as a bad citizen who could not be satisfied with an income of 3,000 francs a year. The Conventionist Laplanche was sent on a mission to the Department of the Cher and reported on his work as follows to the Jacobins: "Everywhere I made terror the order of the day. Everywhere I exacted contributions from the rich and aristocratic. . . . I threw all federalists out of office, put all suspects in jail, and upheld the sans-culottes by force of arms." In the Jacobin club itself a proposal was made to confiscate all foodstuffs and distribute them among the people, and when manufacturers closed their mills, Chaumette, the attorney general, proposed that the republic take over all factories and raw materials.

Nevertheless, when the revolutionary movement was already in its decline, we find an attempt to realize absolute equality and end oppression and privilege by abolishing private property and concentrating all wealth in the hands of the state. That was the goal that the famous Caius Gracchus Babeuf set out to attain. The "Conspiracy of the Equals," which he headed, gathered in all surviving Jacobins who thought they could find in socialist ideas—which, as we have seen, were not unknown at the end of the eighteenth century—a force that might revive the Revolution, which was showing signs of petering out either into anarchy or into Caesarism.

His conspiracy frustrated, Babeuf was guillotined in 1797. A comrade of his, an Italian named Buonarroti, supplies a link between the socialists of the eighteenth century and those of the first half of the nineteenth. Buonarroti clearly expounded the doctrines of his master in a book that appeared in 1826, *De la conspiration pour l'égalité, dite de Babeuf*. It contains all the essentials of the doctrine that the state should become sole proprietor of land and capital. It is interesting that Buonarroti later became one of the founders of the Carbonari, and in fact played a leading role in all the activities of secret societies that kept France and Italy continually on edge after the fall of Napoleon's empire.

Buonarroti's book had a great influence on the intellectual training of all the revolutionary conventicles that formed in France shortly before and especially after the revolution of 1830. Then passions and thoughts began to stir in the direction of a radical reform of society, and the atmosphere for the first time became definitely socialistic. Fourier and Saint-Simon really antedate Buonarroti by a few years. Fourier had published his *Théorie des quatre movements* as early as 1808, but the *Association domestique et agricole* did not appear until 1822 and the *Nouveau monde industriel* not until 1829. Saint-Simon's *Nouveau Christianisme* came out in 1824. He died the year following. As for Saint-Simon, his last publication did in a sense come pretty close to socialism on the sentimental side, and the Saint-Simonianism that flourished after 1830 helped to prepare the ground for socialism proper. It actually anticipated many of the views which later were adopted by socialism. All the same, the thought that Saint-Simon develops in his earlier publications is too vast, too profound and too original to allow him to be mentioned outright as merely one of the many writers who heralded the rise of social democracy as we know it (below, chap. XII, §1).

During the ten or fifteen years after 1830, socialism was enriched by the publications of Pierre Leroux, Louis Blanc and Proudhon, not to mention lesser lights.[1] If one looks attentively, one can detect in the rich blossoming of reform ideas that took place in France between 1820 and 1848 all the varieties and gradations of present-day socialism. There is the "legalitarian" socialism of Fourier, and the revolutionary socialism of Blanc. Proudhon has all the seeds of modern anarchism. Buchez[2] will do for Christian socialism. If we go looking for indirect methods of propaganda, we may note a now forgotten "proletarian" novel, the *Voyage en Icarie* by Cabet, which appeared in 1840 and made a great sensation. In it Cabet imagines that he has arrived in a country where there is no private property and describes the bliss that men enjoy under such a system. About fifty years later Bellamy cut his *Looking Backward* out of virtually the same cloth. Icaria, however, was a not altogether imaginary utopia. Cabet set up his ideal state in the United States, first in Texas and later at Nauvoo, Illinois, on the Mississippi River. He died in St. Louis.

2. But suppose a close reading of socialist writers before 1848, almost all of them French, has convinced one that they left little or nothing for the Germans who followed after them to invent. Suppose we perceive that Marx did nothing but develop systematically, in a more strictly logical form and with a broader knowledge of classical economics and of Hegelian philosophy too, principles that had already been formulated by Buonarroti, Leroux, Blanc and, especially, Proudhon. Still it will be true that the socialism of today is a far more disquieting social phenomenon than the socialism of sixty years ago. It is immeasurably more widespread, for one thing. Instead of being con-

---

[1] Leroux published *De l'égalité* in 1838, *Réfutation de l'éclectisme* in 1839, *Malthus et les économistes* in 1840, *De l'humanité* in 1840. He had begun to write on a newspaper, *Le Globe*, as early as 1832. Blanc's *Organisation du travail* appeared in 1840. As for Proudhon one notes the *Mémoire sur la propriété*, 1840; the *Création de l'ordre dans l'humanité*, 1843; the *Système des contradictions économiques ou Philosophie de la misère*, 1846.

[2] *Essai d'un traité complet de philosophie au point de vue du catholicisme et du progrès.* Much of Buchez's writing appeared in a newspaper, *L'Atelier*.

fined almost entirely to the great cities of France, and more particularly to Paris, it now embraces almost the whole of Europe, and it has invaded the United States and Australia. Call it a good, call it an evil, it is at any rate common to all peoples of European civilization.

Nor has it gained any less in depth than in surface. Revolutionary instincts and noble aspirations once found an objective and an outlet in the strictly democratic movement, or in various movements for the liberation of one subject nationality or another. But now representative governments on broad-based suffrage have been introduced almost everywhere—they have even had time to result in the disappointments of parliamentarism. Italian and German national unities have for some time been virtually complete, and the Polish question seems to all intents and purposes to be settled. Now all disinterested enthusiasms are concentrated in aspirations toward substantial reforms in the prevailing social order. A time has come when many souls are athirst for justice and are welling with a hope of being able to quench the thirst very soon. No longer a lonely thinker, a solitary man of heart, would be he who "considered all the oppressions that are done under the sun: and behold the tears of such as were oppressed, and they had no comforter; and on the side of their oppressors there was power, but they had no comforter." And the author of Ecclesiastes continues: "Wherefore I praised the dead which are already dead more than the living which are yet alive. Yea, better is he than both they, which hath not yet been, who hath not seen the evil work that is done under the sun."[1] It is instructive to note that this melancholy, realistic attitude toward society is to be found in the writings of other thinkers who lived among peoples of ancient culture. It is undoubtedly the product of a refinement of moral sense, and of a lucid perception of realities, which only a long period of civilization makes possible, and then only in a few men of lofty minds and noble hearts.

With the general perception of the evil comes confidence in the possibility of promptly alleviating it. The early Christians believed in the imminent coming of the kingdom of God, which would banish all evil from the world, reward the good and punish the wicked. That faith finds its counterpart in a conviction

[1] 4:1-3.

that is now spread abroad through all strata in society, that most of the iniquities that are to be found in the world can be ascribed to the manner in which society is at present organized, and that they could be avoided if only those who hold power over society were not tools of the rich and the powerful, and would consent to interfere effectively in behalf of the oppressed.   This persuasion has now conquered many minds and is warming many hearts. There is a widespread conviction that there is a social question, that important reforms in property rights, in the family, in our whole industrial and capitalistic system, must inevitably and shortly come about, and governors and sovereigns do little else than make efforts and promises in that direction.   Now all that contributes to creating an intellectual and moral environment in which militant socialism lives, prospers and spreads abroad.

In this favoring environment two very populous political organizations have grown up about most revered masters and organizers, each of them with its aspirations, its platforms, its fairly definite and defined doctrines—two real churches, one might almost say.   The one is made up of believers in collectivism, the other of believers in anarchy.   Both, like religious communities, have a certain urge toward universality.   If they do not send out missionaries to convert the heathen, they do spread their propaganda abroad among almost all the nations of European civilization.   And in one of them more particularly— in the collectivist organization—in spite of frequent schisms and the rise of numerous heresiarchs, which are phenomena common to all organizations that are young and full of life, we see the leaders and inspirers meeting frequently in national and world councils, discussing dogma, discipline, the party's "line," and fixing norms and methods that straightway are universally accepted by masses of believers.

3. Succinctly to state the postulates of collectivism is easy enough.   They are now familiar to everybody.   In the old parliament in Germany the collectivist movement took the name "social democracy," which we regard as the designation scientifically most apt for it.   According to the doctrine most generally recognized as orthodox, the state represents the collectivity of citizens.   It is sole proprietor of all tools of production,

whether they be capital proper, machinery or land. The state is the sole director and the sole distributor of economic products. Since there are neither owners of real property nor private capitalists, everybody works for the benefit of society as a whole; and the social organism provides for all, either according to the needs of each individual, as a simpler and older formula would have it, or according to the work that the individual does, as a newer formula that is now more generally accepted contends. To be strictly accurate, followers of the first formula are known among socialists as "communists," while those who follow the other, which is much more in vogue among the many disciples of Marx, are technically styled "collectivists." As a matter of fact, many collectivists grant that communism is the ideal goal, but it has the drawback, they think, of not being immediately realizable. As will be apparent farther along, while collectivism is a concession that reformers make to the well-known frailty or, better, selfishness, of human nature, it greatly complicates the system of social regeneration which collectivists are trying to bring about and offers the greater number of sound arguments to their opponents, the communists.

The whole machine so organized is administered and directed by leaders who represent the people. The function of the leaders is to dole out to everyone the type of work for which he is best fitted, to see to it that the products of labor and social capital are not squandered or unduly exploited, and at the same time to distribute to every individual, with perfect equity and justice, the exact share that is due him either as the product of his own labor as honestly and infallibly calculated, or for his own needs, of which those in control will, with the same impartiality, furnish the exact estimate.

Suppose now we ignore the violence and the civil strife which may justly be considered indispensable to carrying out this program, and which certainly would only intensify hatreds, rancors and greeds, cleave populations into victors and vanquished, put the latter at the mercy of the former and so unleash the wickedest of human instincts. Let us go so far as to assume that the reforms mentioned have come about peacefully and by common agreement, or that revolving centuries have quenched the last echo of the fratricidal wars with which the new type of social organization has been inaugurated. Let us go on and

assume that the productivity and total wealth of society have
not been appreciably diminished by the new system, as the
economists insist and have, in our opinion, indisputably proved.
We are even ready to grant that the ethical side of the social
problem should have absolute predominance over the strictly
economic side, and that the little that is well divided should be
preferable to the much that is badly divided.

But, after conceding that much, it is our right and our duty
to ask a question on our side, and we shall call it "political,"
because it is the broadest, the most comprehensive question
imaginable; because it arises of its own accord from a comprehensive examination of every type of social relation; because its
solution should interest orthodox economists no less than
socialists, capitalists no less than workers, the rich no less than
the poor; because it is the first question, the most important
question, for all noble hearts, all unprejudiced minds which set
above every creed and every interest of party the dispassionate
search for a social adjustment that shall represent the greatest
good that it is within the power of our poor humanity to attain.
It is our right and our duty to ask whether, with the realization
of the communist (or of the collectivist) system, justice, truth,
love and reciprocal toleration among men, will hold a larger place
in the world than they now occupy; whether the strong, who will
always be at the top, will be less overbearing; whether the weak,
who will always be at the bottom, will be less overborne.   That
question we now answer decidedly with the word "no."

The late Saverio Scolari once said that it was impossible for
the student of the historical or political sciences to foresee exactly
what is going to happen in human societies in any future, near
or remote, because some part in human events will always be due
to what is called "chance," and we shall never be able to calculate
that factor in advance.   He added, however, that we are much
better able to foresee *what is never going to happen*, the negative
reasoning having a secure foundation in what we know of human
nature, which will never allow anything actually to occur that is
fundamentally repugnant to it.   This second dictum seems much
to the point in the case we now have before us, and its application should be all the easier since to a great extent we are concerned not with foreseeing what will or will not happen but
simply with noting what has happened and is happening every-

day. The much that we know from experience makes it easy to establish the nature of the little that some still consider unknown.

Communist and collectivist societies would beyond any doubt be managed by officials. Let us assume, for the best case, that in accord with the norms of social democracy, they would be elected exclusively by universal suffrage. We have already seen how political powers function when they are exclusively, or almost exclusively, in the hands of so-called "people's choices." We know that majorities have only the mere right of choosing between a few possible candidates, and that they cannot, therefore, exercise over them anything more than a spasmodic, limited and often ineffective control. We know that the selection of candidates is itself almost always the work of organized minorities who specialize by taste or vocation in politics and electioneering, or else the work of caucuses and committees whose interests are often at variance with the interests of the majority. We know the ruses that the worst of them use to nullify or falsify the verdicts of the polls to their advantage. We know the lies they tell, the promises they make and betray and the violence they do in order to win or to wheedle votes.

But communists and collectivists may object that all this happens because of the present capitalistic organization of society, because great landowners and owners of great fortunes now have a thousand means, direct or indirect, for influencing and buying the votes of the poor, and that they use them to make universal suffrage a sham and assure political dominion to themselves. To avoid those drawbacks if for nothing else, they might argue, we should change the social order radically.

Those who reason in that manner forget the most important detail in the problem. They forget that even in societies organized as they propose there would still be those who would manage the public wealth and then the great mass of those who are managed. Now the latter would have to be satisfied with the share that was allotted to them. The administrators of the social republic would also be its political heads, and they would undoubtedly be far more powerful than the ministers and millionaires we know today. If a man has the power to constrain others to a given task, and to fix the allotments of material enjoyments and moral satisfactions that will be the recompense for the performance of the task, he will always be a despot over his fellows, however much he may be curbed by laws and regulations, and he will always be able to sway their consciences and their wills to his advantage.[1]

All the lying, all the baseness, all the violence, all the fraud that we see in political life at present are used in intrigues to win votes, in order to get ahead in public office or simply in order to make money fast by unscrupulous means. Under a collectivist system everything of that sort would be aimed at controlling the administration of the collective enterprise. There would be one goal for the greedy, the shrewd and the violent, one direction for the cabals and the cliques which would form to the detriment of the gentler, the fairer, the more sincere. Such differences as there would be would all be in favor of our present society; for to destroy multiplicity of political forces, that variety of ways and means by which social importance is at present acquired, would be to destroy all independence and all possibility of reciprocal balancing and control. As things are today, the office clerk can at least laugh at the millionaire. A good workman who can earn a decent living with his own hands has nothing to fear from the politician, the department secretary, the deputy or the minister. Anyone who has a respectable position as the owner of a piece of land, as a businessman, as a member of a profession, can hold his head high before all the powers of the state and all the great landlords and financial barons in the world. Under collectivism, everyone will have to kowtow to the men in the government. They alone can dispense favor, bread, the joy or sorrow of life. One single crushing, all-embracing, all-engrossing tyranny will weigh upon all. The great of the earth will be absolute masters of everything, and the independent word of the man who fears nothing and expects nothing from them will no longer be there to curb their extravagances.

In his *Progress and Poverty* Henry George many times quotes an ancient Hindu document which held that elephants insanely proud and parasols embroidered in gold were the fruits of private ownership of the land.[2] In our day civilization is much more sophisticated than that, and life more many-sided. Wealth is producing a great deal besides elephants and parasols. But,

---

[1] See above, chap. V, §9.

[2] Book V, epigraph (p. 262), quoting Sir William Jones.

after all, the privileges that wealth confers on those who possess it come down to the fact that wealth makes the pursuit of intellectual pleasures easier and the enjoyment of material pleasures more abundant. It provides satisfactions for vanity and pride and, especially, power to manipulate the wills of others while leaving one's own independence intact. The heads of a communist or collectivist republic would control the will of others more tyrannically than ever; and since they would be able to distribute privations or favors as they chose, they would have the means to enjoy, perhaps more hypocritically but in no less abundance, all the material pleasures, all the triumphs of vanity, which are now perquisites of the powerful and the wealthy. Like these, and even more than these, they would be in a position to degrade the dignity of other men.

These criticisms, it will be noted, bear both on the postulates of communism and on the postulates of collectivism, and perhaps on the former more than on the latter; but, from the standpoint of the criticisms, collectivism is considerably worse placed than communism. If orthodox social democracy were to triumph, those in control would not only have the right to fix for everybody the *kind* of work to be done and the *place* where it was to be done but, since there would be no automatic measure of reward, they would have to specify the *return on every type of work.* That they would have far greater latitude for arbitrary decisions and favoritism is obvious. Nor would that be all. Collectivism does not allow any accumulation of private wealth in the form of industrial capital, but only in kind, in the form of commodities of pure consumption. It would certainly always be possible to distribute such commodities either gratis or for a consideration, and so electoral corruption, and the many other forms of corruption that feature bourgeois societies, would reappear.

4. The strength of the socialist and anarchist doctrines lies not so much in their positive as in their negative aspects—in their minute, pointed, merciless criticism of our present organization of society.

From the standpoint of absolute justice the distribution of wealth that has prevailed in the past, and still prevails, leaves plenty of room for many very serious criticisms in that it legitimizes great and flagrant injustices. That fact is so evident that even to state it seems quite platitudinous. One does not need the piercing keenness of Proudhon, the long algebraic demonstrations of Marx, the trenchant, savage irony of Lassalle, to prove what so readily strikes the eye of anyone who looks—even of the most superficial and untaught observer. Individual enjoyment of the good things of life has not been proportioned even to the value, let alone to the difficulty, of the work that is done to produce them. We see in economic life what we see every day in political life, in scientific life, in all fields of social activity: that success is almost never proportionate to merit. Between the service that an individual renders to society and the reward that he receives there is almost always a wide, and often a glaring, discrepancy.

To fight socialism by trying to deny, or merely to extenuate, that fact is to take one's stand on a terrain on which defeat is certain. Orthodox economists have often tried that. They have sought to show that private ownership of land and capital not only is beneficial, or even indispensable, to life in society, but also answers the absolute requirements of morality and justice. Along that line they have opened their flank to a very powerful attack. Precarious, nay hopeless, in the best case and in any age, their thesis becomes patently absurd in our day, when everybody who has eyes can see by what means great fortunes are often built up.

The whole objection that can be offered, and should be offered, to the destructive criticism of the socialists is summed up in a truth that may seem cruel. We have already stated it, but it is helpful, it is moral, to proclaim it aloud over and over again. *No social organization can be based exclusively upon the sentiment of justice*, and no social organization will ever fail to leave much to be desired from the standpoint of absolute justice. It is natural that things should be that way. In his private and public conduct no individual is ever guided exclusively by his sense of justice. He is guided by his passions and his needs. Only the man who cuts himself off from the world, who renounces all ambition for wealth, power, worldly vanity, for expressing his own personality in any way whatever, can flatter himself that his acts are inspired by a sentiment of absolute justice. The man of action, in political life or in business life, whether he be merchant or property owner, professional worker or laborer, priest of God or apostle of socialism, always tries to be a success, and his conduct, therefore, will always be a compromise, witting or unwitting, between his sense of justice and his interests. Of course, not all people compromise to the same degree or in the same ways. The type and extent of compromises depend upon the person's greater or lesser selfishness, on his sense of delicacy, on the strength of his moral convictions. These traits vary widely from individual to individual.

Human sentiments being what they are, to set out to erect a type of political organization that will correspond in all respects to the ideal of justice, which a man can conceive but can never attain, is a utopia, and the utopia becomes frankly dangerous when it succeeds in bringing a large mass of intellectual and moral energies to bear upon the achievement of an end that will never be achieved and that, on the day of its purported achievement, can mean nothing more than triumph for the worst people and distress and disappointment for the good. Burke remarked more than a century ago that any political system that assumes the existence of superhuman or heroic virtues can result only in vice and corruption.[1]

The doctors of socialism declare that all, or at least most, human imperfections, all or most of the injustices that are now being committed under the sun, do not result from ethical traits that are natural to our species but from traits that are thrust upon us by our present bourgeois organization of society. One such doctor stated explicitly in a famous book that "if we change social conditions in accord with the goals that socialism sets for itself, we shall get a radical change in human nature."[2]

---

[1] The view that the destructive side of socialist criticism derives from ascribing to our present organization of society evils and injustices that are inherent in human nature has been recognized by many writers. Schäffle alludes to it repeatedly in *Die Quintessenz des Sozialismus*. More definitely still the Italian historian of law, Icilio Vanni, wrote in 1890: "Socialism old and new, rationalistic or evolutionary as it may be, aims at bottom to realize in this poor human world an order that is absolutely just. In that it betrays its metaphysical character." In his *L'Europe politique et sociale*, Block says: "We are not unaware that injustices are worked, but they will not be eliminated by changing the organization of society. They can be done away with only by changing human nature." A number of topics in Garofalo's *La superstizione socialista* belong to this same order of ideas.

[2] Bebel, *Die Frau und der Sozialismus*.

We shall not do the reformers of today the injustice of supposing that they are trying to revive under a new form Rousseau's
old aphorism that man is born good and society makes him bad.
If one were to accept that view unconditionally, one would also
be obliged to assume that society is not the result of the natural
and spontaneous activity of human beings but was set up by
some superhuman or extrahuman will, which amused itself by
giving us laws, institutions and morals that have poisoned and
upset the innate goodness, generosity and magnanimity of the
seed of Adam. Modern socialists cannot imagine, either, that
our present social organization merely reflects the instincts of
other races, other generations of men, whose moral sense must
have been much lower than that of the present generation, so
that we, noble and enlightened as we are, feel an urgent need of
stripping ourselves, as of the shirt of Nessus, of institutions
that have been inherited from unscrupulous elders. If we were
to grant that method of applying evolutionary theories to human
societies, if we were to grant that within a few centuries selection
has considerably improved the average level of morality, we
would also have to assume that the moral progress that has
already been achieved should appreciably have diminished,
rather than increased, the defects of bourgeois organization.

Nothing of that sort has taken place. Keeping to what the
socialists themselves say, men have not become less selfish, less
hard of heart. For if the contrary were the case—if, in the eyes
of men, an atom of self-interest had not often outbalanced a
great weight of other people's interest and self-respect, if a whole
society were in large majority made up of just and compassionate
men, of upright and sincere people, as was pleasing to the Lord
of Israel and as would surely have been pleasing to Messrs. Marx
and Lassalle—all the deadly consequences of rapacious capitalism
and frantic competition which have been revealed by those
writers with such rare mastery would certainly by now have
been reduced to the lowest terms.

The world could become an Eden even under the present
bourgeois organization of society if every capitalist were to
content himself with an honest, moderate profit and did not
try to ruin his competitors, squeeze the last possible penny from
the consumer's pocket and force the last drop of sweat from the
brow of the workingman. In such an Eden, the landowner

would cultivate his fields diligently and extract from them only
the bare necessaries for his frugal subsistance. He would not
take advantage of market fluctuations in order to sell commodities of prime necessity at the highest obtainable price.
The merchant too would collect just a moderate and specified
profit on his sale, and never take advantage of the buyer's
inexperience to sell dearer, or cheat him as to the quality and
quantity of his wares. The workingman and the peasant would
toil conscientiously for their employer, doing no more and no
less than they would do for themselves, never deceiving him,
never pilfering from him, never taking a day's wages for half a
day's work. Then all of them together, instead of wasting their
surplus or their savings on ostentatious luxuries, on satisfying
vanities, on vice and good times, would seek out the wretched,
the poor, those who are not good at making a living, and spend
everything on aiding them, so that for one hand that would be
extended for help there would be ten hands ready and eager to
give it.

Henry George was certainly a man of noble heart and penetrating mind. He thought that all the evils that we ascribe to
selfishness, and to lack of fairness and brotherly consideration
in the majority of men, were due to the competitive system and
more particularly to the danger of wanting the necessaries of life
that confronts us all under the present system. Upholding that
thesis in *Progress and Poverty*, George mentions as an example
what occurs at any well-served table, where each diner, knowing
that there is food enough for all, is polite to his neighbor. No
vulgar struggle to snatch the choice morsels arises, and no one
tries to get more food than anybody else.

Now we do not think that the analogy holds. In the first
place, there are well-served boards where the behavior of guests
is not as correct as the conduct that Henry George describes.
In the second place, material appetites are necessarily limited—
as Sancho Panza pointed out, the poor man eats three times a
day and the rich man can do no better. At a well-served table,
therefore, everyone can find a way to satisfy, let us say a gar-
gantuan, hunger without pilfering his neighbor's portion. But
that is not the case when we are sitting at the allegorical banquet
of life. Then the will to get the better of others, to satisfy one's
caprices, passions, lusts, can, unhappily, be boundless and

insatiable. A man will try to have ten, a hundred, a thousand portions, so that by distributing them among others he may bend them to his will. In the struggle for preeminence, that man triumphs who can most lavishly dispense the means by which human needs and human vices are satisfied.

Even if each of us were to be assured of a minimum that would provide for the prime necessities of life, the social question would not be solved. Only the weakest and least aggressive would content themselves with that minimum, those who in any event would be least well adapted to the struggle for preeminence. The others would go on scrambling in rabid competition.

It follows that the most realistic interpretation that can at present be given to the doctrine of Rousseau is the very one that is followed by large numbers of those who are fighting in the ranks of the collectivist movement, or even among the anarchists. They believe that the natural working of selection has been profoundly disturbed and perverted by present bourgeois societies, and that that principle will be able to operate freely and exert its beneficial effects only when their programs of reform, which vary from school to school, have been carried out. But in reasoning in that fashion, they are *discounting an expectation,* and there will never be any possibility of proving in advance that it will be realized. Also, they are evidently counting on a moral progress which *they say* will be attained, in order to bring into existence a type of social organization which *assumes that that progress has already been attained,* and which in all probability would be able to function *only if that progress had been attained.* In a word, they would only be repeating on a large scale, and with more disastrous consequences, the mistake to which we primarily owe the current evils of parliamentarism.

But, if the dispassionate study of the past can tell us anything, it tells us, as we believe we have shown (chap. VII, §7), that it is difficult to modify very appreciably the mean moral level of a whole people of long-standing civilization, and that the influence that one type of social organization or another can exert in that direction is certainly far less powerful than the radicals of our day imagine. History teaches that whenever, in the course of the ages, a social organization has exerted such an influence in a beneficial way, it has done so because the individual and collective will of the men who have held power in their hands has been curbed and balanced by other men, who have occupied positions of absolute independence and have had no common interests with those whom they have had to curb and balance. It has been necessary, nay indispensable, that there should be a multiplicity of political forces, that there should be many different roads by which social importance could be acquired, and that the various political forces should each be represented in the government and in the administration of the state. Collectivism and communism, like all doctrines that are based on the passions and the blind faith of the masses, tend to destroy multiplicity of political forces. They would confine all power to individuals elected by the people, or representing them. They would abolish private wealth, which in all mature societies has supplied many individuals with a means for acquiring independence and prestige apart from the assent and consent of the rulers of the state. Both those things can only lead to a weakening of juridical defense, to what in plain language is called the tyranny of rulers over the ruled. In practice such tyranny has always resulted from oversimplified political doctrines which take no account of the complicated and difficult structure of human nature, but try to adapt the organization of society to a single, one-sided, absolute concept and establish it upon a single exclusive principle—now the will of God as interpreted by his earthly vicars and ministers, now the will of the people as expressed through those who claim to represent them.

Of course sound political doctrine may suggest legislative remedies and recommend procedures that might well lessen social injustice to a certain extent. The mechanism of juridical defense might be improved in such a way as to moderate the arrogance of those who are invested with public power. But however great the benefits that might be yielded by reforms along those lines, they would be insignificant as compared with the era of happiness, equality and universal justice which, implicitly or explicitly, the various socialist schools promise to their followers. They would be something like the few doubtful years of fair physical health which the conscientious doctor is able to guarantee his patient. A very paltry guarantee, when one thinks of the nuisance that goes with diets and a strict daily observance of medical rules! And paltry especially if it be compared with the promise of a quick and certain cure, of good health and long life that is made by the charlatan with his elixir!

It might be urged that from the moral point of view this analogy is not applicable to men who are propounding their ideas in all good faith. Besides, the physician might well show the fatuousness of the patent medicine and then be obliged to evade the challenge of the charlatan to invent a medicine that would really do what the charlatan's elixir was alleged to do. If the physician were wise he would answer that he realizes very well how many germs there are in the world, and how varied and numerous the diseases that may upset the delicate constitution of the human body; but that for that very reason he will never claim that he has a universal and infallible remedy for all diseases. Merely to think of doing so would put him on a level with the charlatan.

5. Anarchist propaganda bases its destructive criticism of present-day institutions on the same passions, the same order of observations and ideas, as collectivist propaganda, with this difference, that anarchists are as a rule more violent. Sometimes they are actually ferocious not only in their acts but in their words. We are thinking of one publication, among many others, in which an Italian anarchist advises the workers on the day of their victory to wipe out not only grown bourgeois who are captured arms in hand, but also the aged and the helpless and women and children down to two or three years—to deal with the bourgeois, in short, the way the ancient Hebrews dealt with the conquered whenever these had been expressly smitten by Jehovah's curse. The publication is so well written that its author must have been a well-educated man of fair native intelligence.

However, the anarchists differ widely from all the socialist schools in the ideals which they set out to achieve. In order to abolish, or at least considerably reduce, the injustices and inequalities they deplore in this world, the socialists would try to modify the present organization of society—very radically to be sure. The anarchists, soundly arguing that there would always be disparities of status among men under any type of social organization, that there would always be rulers and ruled, or, as they put it, exploiters and exploited, propose the destruction of all organized society. They remind one of a man who discovers that there is no prudent tenor of life that can guarantee him perfect health and so turns to suicide as a sure cure for all his troubles.

Logical and consistent followers of Rousseau, the father of them all, the adherents of anarchism maintain that since organized society is the root of all evil, only by completely disorganizing human society and going back to the state of nature can evil be eliminated. In this they are only repeating, perhaps unwittingly, a mistake of their master. The truth is that the natural state, with man as with many other animals, is not individual separation but social living, the only variation being that the society may be more or less large, more or less organized. To assume, then, that a fact so universal and so readily discernible as the fact that all men live socially can be due to the self-interest and cunning of a few schemers is a notion which we are certainly not the first to call absurd and childish. Aristotle lived twenty centuries before the Genevan philosopher, yet he had an infinitely clearer and more accurate perception of the real nature of man when he wrote that man is a political animal. But the intellectual faculties of the Greek Peripatetic were probably never ruffled either by an oversensitive pride or by literary vanity. One might even guess that the patronage of the Macedonian sovereigns, or perhaps his ability to earn his own living, saved him from the necessity of souring his disposition and ruining his digestion by hobnobbing with people who were often frivolous, sometimes spiteful and almost always of high social standing.

Rousseau came of a respectable Genevan family, and he inherited its honest and upright instincts. But because of his irresponsibility, his inability to adapt himself to modest, profitable work, and the destitution in which his father left him, he decayed morally to the point where for ten years or more he lived as a not always welcome chevalier of Madame de Warens for the support that she gave him. Awareness of the moral degradation into which he had fallen in his youth must no doubt have been one of the keenest torments to the Genevan philosopher in his maturity. Being unwilling or unable to blame himself, his father, or Madame de Warens, he blamed society. That, in our opinion, is the real psychological explanation of the fundamental idea that serves Rousseau as a basis for his whole political and social system—that man is born good and society makes him bad.

But suppose we assume that the anarchist hypothesis has come about in the fact, that the present type of social organization has been destroyed, that nations and governments have ceased to exist, and that standing armies, bureaucrats, parliaments and especially policemen and jails have been swept away. Unfortunately people would still have to live, and therefore use the land and other instruments of production. Unfortunately again, arms and weapons would still be there, and enterprising, courageous characters would be ready to use them in order to make others their servants or slaves. Given those elements, little social groups would at once form, and in them the many would toil while the few, armed and organized, would either be robbing them or protecting them from other robbers, but living on their toil in any event. In other words, we should be going back to the simple, primitive type of social organization in which each group of armed men is absolute master of some plot of ground and of those who cultivate it, so long as the group can conquer the plot of ground and hold it with its own strength. That type of society we have called "feudal." We would have happening over again exactly what happened in Europe when the collapse of Charlemagne's empire disrupted such little social organization as had survived the fall of the Roman Empire; and what happened in India when the successors of the Grand Mogul were reduced to impotence; and what will happen everywhere when a society of advanced culture, for one cause or another, internal or external, falls apart and collapses.

There can be no doubt that people who feel self-confident and strong and have nothing to lose would stand a chance to be the gainers by a revolution of that sort, for violence and personal valor would come to the top as the one political force. But it would be to the disadvantage of the immense peacable majority, perhaps ninety per cent of men, who would prefer to the rule of the mailed fist a very imperfect social justice, a little tranquility, and the certainty that they could enjoy at least some portion of the fruits of their own labor.

While most anarchists, for instance Grave,[1] believe that to

---

[1] *La Société mourante et l'anarchie.*

abolish property and laws would suffice to make all men good, others, less ingenuous, arrive at conclusions that are more or less like our own. De Gourmont wrote:

Given the absence of any law whatsoever, the ascendancy of superior people would become the only law, and their justifiable despotism would be undisputed. Despotism is necessary in order to muzzle imbeciles. The man without intelligence bites.[1]

Instead of "superior," we would say "stronger" people. Instead of "imbeciles," we would say "the weaker people." Otherwise we would agree with De Gourmont, except that we view life as a whole from a completely different standpoint.

In order not to arouse too many false hopes, one ought really to give fair warning that the blessings which the triumph of anarchy would bring us would be a few years, perhaps a few generations, in coming. If it took centuries and centuries for the world to advance from barbarism to our present level of civilization, one or two centuries at least would have to pass before it could forget its civilized ways and revert to a state of just ordinary barbarism. If the aim is to get back to a real and absolute barbarism, to the status of tribes living by hunting, fishing or nomadic agriculture, then it would take longer still— the time required for an old and thickly populated Europe to dwindle in population to a bare twentieth of what it is today. Unless, of course, in order to speed up the process, the defenders of anarchy would be willing not only to exterminate the bourgeois, and the satellites and sycophants of the bourgeois, as they say, but also to kill the great majority of people in the exploited classes over whose lot they are now shedding so many tears.

Among the novels that were published toward the end of the nineteenth century, describing what the world would be like after the triumph of the social revolution, there was one which, though popular in the Anglo-Saxon world, was not widely known on the Continent. Fantastic as the story is, it seems to come closer to reality than many more popular conceptions succeed in doing, and it is therefore more pessimistic. *Caesar's Column* was published in Chicago in 1890 by Ignatius Donnelly (Edmund Boisgilbert). It describes the triumph that the proletariat is to win over the plutocracy a few centuries hence, when a day

[1] *Entretiens politiques et littéraires*, April, 1892, p. 147.

of social justice comes to end centuries of bourgeois injustice. Caesar Lomellini, the leader of the proletarians, seizes the treasures, the wines and the women of Cabano, prince of the plutocrats, proclaims them his own and then abandons himself to orgies and cruelties. Meanwhile Europe, America and Australia are being drenched in the blood of a frightful carnage. The victorious workers annihilate the plutocrats and their satellites and consume the provisions that have accumulated. Then they turn against one another and kill until three-quarters of the world's population and all civilization have perished. The novel closes with a scene where Lomellini causes a column of human skulls and crossbones (Caesar's column) to be erected in memory of all that has happened. An inscription on it entreats all who come after, in case they feel inclined to go out and found a new civilization, to keep clear of the corruption, the iniquity, the falsehood, that caused the downfall of our present bourgeois society.

6. A doctrine common to all parties of subversion, whether anarchist or merely socialist, is the so-called doctrine of the class struggle. Developed with some fullness for the first time by Marx, it is one of the best war horses of all opponents of the present organization of society.

First of all one must point out that the doctrine is based on an incomplete, one-sided and biased examination of history, to the end of proving that the whole activity of civilized societies so far has been accounted for in efforts of ruling classes to keep themselves in power and to exploit power to their advantage, and in efforts of lower classes to throw off that yoke. Now, in the past of all peoples one finds social events of the first importance that can in no way be crowded into the narrow frame of that picture: for instance, the struggles of Greece against Persia and of Rome against Carthage, the rapid and tremendous growth of Christianity and Mohammedanism, the Crusades and even the revival of Italian nationality called the Risorgimento, which, as Angelo Messedaglia, a witty and learned economist, used to say, was much more due to the influence of poets and novelists than to economic factors. It is interesting to recall that when Hannibal marched into Italy and won a number of victories over the Romans, the masses in many Italian cities began to side with the Carthaginian general, whereas the patricians for the most part remained loyal to Rome. Such a fact is easily understandable. The poor are always more desirous of change, and they also have less political intuition, than ruling classes. In the Crusades, too, especially toward the end, love of gain was mixed in with religious fanaticism. But the presence of an economic factor in a social phenomenon does not mean that it is necessarily the main factor, much less that it actually caused the phenomenon.

Coming to civil wars, which should be especially likely to reflect struggles of class, it is noteworthy that, at this point too, the social phenomenon is described by socialists in an incomplete and therefore mistaken manner. From time to time in history one meets examples of violent uprisings by the poorer classes, or by parts of them—the helot rebellions in Sparta, the slave wars in Rome, the Jacqueries in France and the movements among peasants or miners that have broken out in Germany, England or Russia in days gone by. Such outbreaks have sometimes been occasioned by unusual and truly unbearable oppression. More frequently they have been due to governmental disturbances, with the beginnings of which the insurgents had nothing to do, but which did offer them a chance to get arms and acquire a rudimentary organization. In any event, movements in which the classes that live by manual labor have taken part all by themselves have regularly been repressed with relative ease and sometimes with brutality, and they have almost never helped to effect any permanent improvement in the condition of those classes. The only social conflicts, bloody or bloodless, that have resulted in actually modifying the organization of society and the composition of ruling classes, have been started by new influential elements, new political forces, rising within governed classes (but representing very small fractions of them numerically) and setting out to obtain a share in the government of the state which they thought was being withheld from them unjustly.

So during the fifth and fourth centuries B.C., the richer families of the Roman plebs, barred from the consulate and other prominent positions, entered upon a struggle with the old patriciate. This ended in the establishment of a broader ruling class, based on property qualifications rather than on birth alone, which became the nobility of the last centuries of the republic. So also the portion of the French Third Estate that had, in the course of the eighteenth century, acquired a wealth equal to the nobility's, and a culture and aptitude for public affairs greater than the nobility's, won access to all public offices during the years after the Revolution. If it is true that in both the cases mentioned the governed masses came to enjoy the advantages of a better juridical defense, that was because their interests happened to be in accord with the interests of the new political forces that demanded admission to the governing class. It was because, in order to attain their end, the new forces had to champion principles of social utility and social justice, the application of which, if it did help them more directly, also helped the humbler members of the nation. Certainly one cannot fail to see that the process involved in those cases is one of the many ways in which the rise of new elements to social influence comes to improve the relations between rulers and ruled and render them more equitable. But that does not mean that it has ever happened that the entire mass of the governed has in fact— whatever the law—supplanted the governing minority or stood so nearly on a par with it that the distinction between the two has come to an end. Nor will this ever happen.

Besides, it remains to be seen whether, for all the talk and preaching, there is anything real in this dividing society up into a parasite class that contributes nothing to production and social welfare and enjoys the better portion of both, and a class that does everything, produces everything and is rewarded with the bare necessaries of life and sometimes not even with that much. Not even if we isolate the phenomena involved in the production of wealth from all other social phenomena as completely as economists and their socialist adversaries sometimes do, does that theory turn out to correspond exactly to the facts. Suppose we grant that it is capital, and not the capitalist, that provides the worker with the means and opportunity for doing profitable work. Suppose we say it is the land, not the landowner, that the peasant needs. Even so, it cannot be denied that the man who knows how to get a large amount of capital into his hands and knows how to utilize it profitably for an industrial purpose and the proprietor who knows how to manage the cultivation of his lands well are rendering a real social service by increasing production and wealth, a service for which it is altogether proper that they should receive a remuneration. For if, further, we consider the social phenomenon as a whole, if we remember that the production of wealth is closely bound up with the level of civilization that a country attains, with the worth of its political and administrative organization, the charge of parasitism that is so lightly flung at the whole ruling class, made up of landowners, capitalists, businessmen, clerks, professional men—of all, in short, who do not live by manual labor, will seem supremely unjust.

In our time industry and agriculture are requiring applications of science more and more every day. Economic production has come to be based almost entirely upon exchanges among countries that are far removed from one another, and such exchanges are not possible unless people are grouped into great nations under governments that are intelligently organized. In the face of such facts it is absurd to assert that everything is produced by manual laborers and that everything ought legitimately to belong to them. It is unfair to forget the services that are rendered by the class that maintains peace and order, directs the whole political and economic movement, preserves and advances higher scientific learning and makes it possible for great masses of men to live together and cooperate. It cannot in all justice be denied that a not inconsiderable portion of economic production should be devoted to maintaining that class in all the ease that is required if it is to retain and develop its intellectual and moral leadership. For if it is certain that without the cooperation of manual laborers the directing class would be condemned to decline, and perhaps even to perish, it is nonetheless certain that without the elements that lead, manual laborers would lapse at once into a state of barbarism which would enormously diminish economic production, and their moral and material status would deteriorate very appreciably in consequence. On this point the oldest lesson in sociology, the parable of the body and its members, which Menenius Agrippa related to the Roman plebs assembled on the Sacred Mount twenty-four hundred years ago, still remains the one that is truest to reality.

A great modern liner represents the last achievements of modern industry and science. It is easy to see that it was built through the cooperation of capitalists, naval engineers and workingmen, and that it is operated through the cooperation of a number of officers and larger numbers of ordinary sailors and stokers. Would it be fair for the stokers and sailors and construction workers, taken as representing the part that manual labor has played in the building of the ship and in its operation, to claim the *whole* earnings of the liner and consider the portion that does not go to them as *stolen?* Obviously not, because if it is true that the capitalists, engineers and officers could never have built the vessel, and could not now run it without workmen and ordinary sailors, it is just as true that without the cooperation of capitalists, engineers and officers the manual workers could never have managed to build anything better than small boats for fishing or petty transport trade, from which, on the whole, they would have earned far less than from building and operating a liner. Thinking of all the various branches of social activity in some such terms, one sees that it is the combination of wealth, higher education and manual labor that produces what in sum is called civilization, and on the whole improves the condition of all.

In the higher classes there are goodly numbers of parasites or exploiters who enjoy much and consume much without rendering any real social service either in management or in execution. In those classes also there are persons who take advantage of their position in order to draw a recompense for their services that is infinitely higher than their real worth. To those elements we referred above (chap. V, §10), in speaking of social forces that are always trying to tip the juridical scales in their favor by means of their too great power; and we designated as particularly dangerous in that respect financiers, great industrialists and speculators—in general, individuals who bring great masses of private capital together into one pair of hands. However, if we look carefully at such exploitations, which are engineered in some countries by protective tariffs, and in others by banking privileges as well as protective tariffs, we have to agree that they work out to the damage both of the working classes and of the larger portion of the ruling class. The ruling class too, in its great majority, pays a high price for its weakness and ignorance, by making sacrifices that benefit only very small numbers among its members.

It can be shown that protectionism cannot help one portion of a national economy without injuring another and larger portion of it at the same time. If some few property owners and manufacturers profit by protective tariffs, others, more numerous, pay the price. Those who lose, along with the poor, are the larger number of rich and well-to-do people who live on government and industrial bonds, and people who live by trade, professional earnings or salaries. A bad banking policy on the part of a government can be of help only to certain manufacturers or politicians who obtain credit by favoritism. It does harm to all other citizens, and especially to people who have savings. A superficial examination of such facts is enough to show the absurdity of an accusation that is often leveled at the bourgeoisie as a whole, that it is knowingly responsible for certain evils and scandals. It would be far more accurate to say that the great majority in the ruling class, not out of malice but out of *ignorance*, tolerate and allow practices that are ruining them and therefore also ruining the poorer classes, whose guardianship has been entrusted not only to their probity but also to their competence and wisdom.

Parasites and exploiters exist in all social strata, just as there are those who are exploited at all levels on the economic and social ladder. A man is an exploiter when he squanders a fortune in luxury, gaming and roistering, and so dissipates the capital he has inherited; and that man is exploited who laboriously and honestly accumulates the capital that the other wastes, working much, consuming little and perhaps enjoying nothing at all. An exploiter is the politician who climbs to high offices in the state by taking advantage of the readiness of people to let themselves be duped, by flattering the conceits and vanities of the masses, by buying consciences and by using and abusing all the shortcomings and weaknesses of his fellow men. But exploited is the statesman who aims not at mere effect or applause but at the real advantage of the public and who is always ready to step down when he feels that he can no longer serve that advantage. An exploiter is the civil service employee who gets his position by cheating on examination and running crooked errands for some politician and who keeps it, does as little work as possible and gets promoted by fawning upon his superiors or betraying his oath as a public servant. Exploited, instead, is the man at the next desk who does just the opposite.

An exploiter is the soldier who vanishes in the moment of danger but comes to life when the medals or citations are being handed out. Exploited is his comrade who faces death and injury without thought of posing as a hero or asking for a soft job and a pension for life. Exploiters are those peasants and, above all, those lazy, vicious and dishonest farm hands who begin by living on their more responsible relatives, continue sponging on their comrades, whom they ask for loans and repay in chatter and bad advice, and on their employers, whom they wheedle out of a day's pay for bad work or for no work at all, and who finally end in prison or the poorhouse as parasites on society at large. Exploited are those laborers who conscientiously and quietly do their duty, who never shirk discomfort and fatigue and who live hard lives, unable to better their lot or to lay anything aside for their old age. An exploiter is the man who deliberately shuns marriage and lays snares for the honor of other men's wives. Exploited is the man who takes on the burden and responsibilities of a legally constituted family and becomes the butt of the other's intrigue. An exploiter is the scholar who wins his chair by writing a book just to please the men who are to be his judges, or pursues fame by publishing a work that will flatter the popular passion of the moment. Exploited is the scholar who sacrifices a good part of his material success in life to love of truth, and resigns himself to living on a lower plane than the one to which his ability and learning would have lifted him had he been less devoted to the truth.

Time was when the exploited were called the good, the honest, the courteous, the brave, the industrious and the temperate, and exploiters were called sinners, idlers, cowards, schemers, rascals and criminals. One may call them what one will. Perhaps it is not a bad idea to have just two expressions to synthesize the multiple categories that make up the two classes which have always existed and, alas, always will exist in the world. The important thing to remember is that although the exploited in the lower classes are more wretched, perhaps, and more to be pitied, there are a goodly number of exploited in the middle and higher classes. Otherwise there would be less of the spirit of self-sacrifice and sense of duty that are indispensable to the ruling minority if civilized living is to endure.

There are writers who have tried to "show by history" that the upper classes, as arbiters of political power, have used their power constantly to exploit the working classes. Their hypothesis, and the manner in which they develop it, would lead one to suppose that human events had for centuries upon centuries been guided by a tenacious and constant will which knew whither it wanted to go and astutely shaped its means to that destination—that events, in other words, had been guided by one continuous and sinister conspiracy of the rich against the poor. Now all that seems to be a sort of persecution mania, to use very charitable terms. A calm and dispassionate observer sees at once in studying history that events that have social significance come about partly because of passions, instincts and prejudices, which are almost always unconscious and almost never consider their practical consequences; partly because of interests, which as a rule do have some definite and immediate objective; and in part, finally, because of what men call "chance."

Contrary to what some socialist writers seem to think, Christianity was not adopted because it was a religion that promised happiness in another life and guaranteed that the powerful could quietly enjoy their wealth in this life. Modern wars have never been waged in order to increase the public debt and hence the political influence of nonproductive capital. America and Australia were not discovered in order to prepare an outlet for the teeming populations of Europe during the industrial age and so safeguard against excessive drops in wages.

It is a matter of common knowledge that by altering just a few facts a very little and saying nothing about other facts, any case of persecution mania can be made to look like the profoundest sanity. That and no other is the method that is followed by socialist writers in order to prove that the ruling classes, who have made the laws and determined the policies of states, have used their political influence to pauperize the lower classes *consciously and constantly*. They generally cite laws and provisions that may be considered detrimental to those who live by manual labor, and when they are obliged to mention a law that is obviously favorable to them, they assert, without proof, of course, that it was wrested by the wage earners by force from the greed of capitalists and landowners.

To mention a specific case: In *Das Kapital* (chap. XXVIII), Marx declares that "during the historical genesis of the capitalistic evolution, the rising bourgeoisie made use of the state in order to regulate wages, in other words, in order to keep them down to a level that was convenient for holding the worker in the desired degree of subjection." As proof of his statement, he mentions the Statute of Labourers of 1349, which fixes maximum wages, then other English statutes of the same sort from later periods and finally a French ordinance of 1350.

Now laws of that type are to be found in past centuries in other countries. Some were proclaimed in Germany at a time when the Thirty Years' War had depopulated the country. They were always enacted when, either because of long wars or plagues (1348, be it noted, was a year of the Black Death), populations had fallen off seriously and wages were rising sharply. But such provisions cannot be impartially evaluated unless they are compared with other contemporaneous, or almost contemporaneous, provisions that fixed maximum prices for bread, grain, cloth, house rent, and so on. Obviously, then, the rulers of the state could not have been thinking of systematically favoring the rise of the bourgeoisie. What they were thinking *in their ignorance* was that by passing the apposite laws they could either mitigate or prevent the serious economic disturbances that resulted from sudden and excessive rises in the prices of all sorts of commodities, including the prices of human labor.

Loria goes Marx one better. He says that there was a period when free lands were still abundant in Europe and it was to the advantage of landowners that the proletariat should not save money and so acquire the capital necessary for cultivating them. He goes on to enumerate the methods that they used to obtain that end and to keep wages low. They were, he says:

direct reductions in wages; depreciation of currency; introduction of machines that were more costly than the workers they replaced; expansion of nonproductive capital invested in stock and banking manipulations, in metal currencies and in public debts; creation of excessive numbers of useless middlemen; stimulation of over-population in order to supply competition for employed workers. . . . All these devices undoubtedly tend to limit production and so also to reduce profits. Nevertheless the proprietor class does not hesitate to resort to them, because they are a necessary condition for assuring the continuation of profit by preventing rises in wages, which would inevitably mean the end of returns on capital.[1]

[1] *Teoria*, p. 6.

Now Loria certainly never deserved the charge of being a sycophant of the capitalists, which Marx leveled at so many practitioners of economic science. It would have been useful, therefore, had he proved to us: 1. That in an epoch which cannot be very close to our own, since there were still free lands in western Europe, the ruling class had such a competent knowledge of economic science that they were able to foresee that the measures mentioned—for instance, expansion in nonproductive capital— would cause wages to fall. 2. That all those measures, among them depreciation of currency and overpopulation, could have been brought about by a voluntary decision on the part of those who held public power. While we are awaiting that proof, we permit ourselves to doubt whether even today governments or their friends have as much foresight as that, and, especially, whether they have the power to carry out all the economic manipulations that Loria credits to their ancient predecessors.

7. It remains to consider whether the great current of ideas and emotions that can be designated as a whole by the term "socialism" may not at least have had the practical effect of improving the moral, and hence the material, conditions of the majority of people, even if it is not based upon an accurate observation of the laws that regulate social life, and even if it aims at an ideal that cannot be attained until human nature has radically altered. If it has had that effect, its influence could be called beneficial, and might be compared to the influence of other great collective illusions that have helped to strengthen the fabric of society by making men better, more tolerant of each other and less impatient with the injustices of the world, and by making life less harsh, within the limits of the possible, for those who are placed on the lower rungs of the economic ladder.

The brief examination that we shall make on this important subject will, we serve notice in advance, yield a far from favorable verdict.

Books have an intellectual influence which they exert through the doctrines that they contain, and which depends upon the manner in which certain problems of life are approached and presented. But they also have what one might call a "moral" influence, and that depends upon the passions and sentiments which, deliberately or unconsciously, writers whet or attenuate.

If one sets out to examine the works of the greater sages of socialism from this moral point of view, especially the best-known socialist writers of the second half of the nineteenth century, one finds, indeed, that a spirit of peace, brotherly love, social harmony, breathes from the works, for example, of Rodbertus or of Carlo Marlo. Particularly in Henry George one notes a noble and tender compassion for the weak that is more to the fore than hatred of the strong. Among Italian socialists who stress benevolent sentiments more than hatreds, one might mention Napoleone Colajanni and Ignazio Scarabelli.[1] But books of another sort are far more numerous. To say nothing of Bakunin, in some of the most orthodox and most often republished writers—in Marx, for example, or Lassalle—the predominant sentiment is an aversion to the rich and the powerful that takes the form of unremitting irony, sarcasm and invective. In the masters this attitude is presented, now with polemical gracefulness and vivacity, now with a dialectic that is ponderous and tiresome. But the word of the masters reaches the masses largely through newspapers and pamphlets, and in being popularized is usually garbled.

In all this literature the capitalist is regarded and depicted as a man of virtually another race, another blood. The working-man is not taught to look upon him as a fellow creature whose weaknesses and virtues are the same, fundamentally, as his own but whose traits manifest themselves in somewhat different ways because his environment, temptations and life problems have been different. The workingman is taught to regard the capitalist as a rival and an enemy, as a noxious creature, an oppressor, degraded and degrading, through whose ruin alone the redemption and salvation of the working classes can be effected.

Now no movement that is as vast and complex as social democracy has become can be grounded solely upon the better instincts in human nature. It is both natural and necessary that the lower, the antisocial, the savage passions, quite as much as sentiments of justice and aspirations toward a better society, should find nourishment in such a movement. The trouble is that socialist doctrines offer the lower passions too vast and fertile a field in which to multiply and spread in a rank growth.

[1] *Sul socialismo e la lotta di classe.*

The poor man is taught that the rich man leads a merry life upon the fruit of the poor man's toil, which is stolen by means of an artificial organization of society based on violence and fraud. That belief, in minds that are not absolutely noble and pure, serves admirably to justify a spirit of rebellion, a thirst for material pleasures, a hate that curses. It fosters a vengeful spirit and an instinctive envy of natural and social superiorities which only long habituation, and the realization that they are necessary and inevitable, can render universally undisputed and accepted.

Nobili-Vitelleschi once wrote that "the keyword to the riddle that is disturbing the sleep of Europe and the world is supplied in the distinction between wealth and happiness."[1] Now an undeniable weakness in the whole socialist movement is its excessive materialization of the concept of human happiness and, therefore, of social justice. First the socialists overidealize the human being, representing him as better than he is and ascribing to the social order many or most of the vices and weaknesses that are inherent in human nature. But then they go on and express too low an opinion of their fellow men, when they believe, or pretend to believe, that wealth is the inseparable companion of pleasure, that poverty is inevitably one with suffering. To read socialist writings or listen to socialist sermons is to get the impression that individual happiness is exactly proportioned to the amount of money that one has in one's pocket. Such a system may be a useful tool of propaganda in the hands of innovators, in that it represents the injustice in present-day society as being much greater than it actually is. But it does not correspond to the facts. Luckily, things do not stand that way.

There are, to be sure, types of poverty that seem inevitably to result in pain and unhappiness. Of that sort is the extreme poverty that does not admit of providing for the most elementary human needs. Then there is the envious poverty of the man who simply cannot resign himself to the fact that others have pleasures and satisfactions of vanity that he cannot hope ever to have. Finally, there is the poverty that comes with economic catastrophes and forces a lowering in the standards of living. Conversely, the pleasures and satisfactions that come when our

[1] "Socialismo ed anarchia."

economic and social status is improved are much less intense, and especially less abiding, than the pain that results from a proportionate falling off. It would seem, therefore, that the frequent changes in fortune which lift many up and cast many down yield a net total in which suffering figures far more largely than happiness.

There is no denying that a man's ability to maintain the standard of living to which he has been accustomed, and especially a sense of security for the morrow, are conditions that are indispensable to a certain well-being. But it is no less true that many other elements, objective and subjective, figure in individual happiness. The man who has a kindly disposition and a well-balanced temperament may be far more nearly satisfied with life than another man who has more wealth than he, and a better social position. The very fact that the world generally recognizes that the former has been inadequately rewarded may, along with the inner approval that he gets from his own conscience, contribute not a little to his greater felicity.

Other doctrines, other beliefs, have found themselves confronted with the grave and tormenting problem of life, in which the just and the good often succumb while the unjust and the wicked triumph. But the solutions they have found have been different from the solutions that socialism proposes. The Stoics realized that they could not banish unhappiness from the world. They therefore taught their disciples to endure it bravely. Unable to promise everyone the enjoyment of material pleasures, they urged even those who were in a position to enjoy them lavishly to scorn them. The same scorn of material pleasures and of the joys of the flesh we find in Christianity in its early days, and in all its moments of fanaticism. Exaggeration of that tendency may lead to a sort of mysticism, which sometimes alienates noble characters, souls that are predisposed to self-sacrifice, from the world and from life. Such teachings are not only morally higher; they are also more practical than the diametrically opposite teachings of socialists in general. These latter are likely to result in a lowering, momentary at least, of some of the noblest sentiments in human nature.

Socialists are not the first to have preached equality and to have aspired to absolute justice in the world. But equality and absolute justice can be preached by urging toleration, mutual indulgence, brotherly love; and they can be preached by appealing to hatred and violence. One may bid the rich and the powerful to look upon the poor and unhappy as their brothers; and the poor and unhappy can be made to believe that the rich and powerful are their enemies. The first line was followed by Jesus, the Apostles, and St. Francis of Assisi, who said to the rich, "Give!" The second is followed by the majority of present-day socialists, who describe the pleasures of the rich as the product of the sweat of the poor man's brow and implicitly or explicitly say, "Take!" Such substantial differences in method can only lead to significant differences in practical results.

8. It will not be necessary to linger very long on the causes of the socialist current. The cause of those causes is the thing that we have been trying to combat in the whole course of this work—the intellectual attitude of our times toward doctrines that concern the organization of society, the ideas that now prevail in persons of average and sometimes of higher education as to the laws that regulate political relations. Naturally, this basic cause presents itself in a thousand forms and generates many other multifarious causes, now secondary, now direct. There is a very close connection between the moral and intellectual worlds in everything that pertains to social organization. A mistaken direction in the speculative field, therefore, a mistaken appraisal of human nature and of social tendencies in men, has the effect, in the field of practice, of placing men in false positions and so of making them more prone to compromises and wrongdoing. As a result the influence of the nobler instincts is weakened and necessarily, therefore, average levels of character and conscience are lowered.

An important factor in the progress of socialist propaganda, and one of its most direct and immediate causes, has been the broadening of suffrage, or, more exactly, universal suffrage, which has come to be more and more widely adopted in Europe in deference to the principles of the radical school and to democratic logic. Now the danger in broadbased suffrage is not so much that if proletarians get the right to drop their ballots into a box their genuine representatives may come to be in the majority in our political assemblies, as many fear or hope. After all, whatever the election system, control will always remain with the more influential classes, rather than with the more numerous classes. The danger lies rather in the fact that in order to gain an advantage over their rivals most candidates do all they can to pamper popular sentiments and prejudices. That attitude leads to promises and professions of faith that are based on the postulates of socialism. The natural result of the system is that the more honest and energetic people are alienated from public life, compromises and moral reservations become more and more the rule, while the ranks of the so-called conservatives become more and more stultified, both intellectually and morally.

Another important element in the growth of socialist parties is the revolutionary tradition that is still very vigorous in Latin countries. There the ruling classes have done their utmost to keep it alive and to perpetuate it. As Villetard has observed,[1] and as we noted above (chap. VIII, §6), in France, down to a few years ago at least, only interests were conservative. Ideas and sentiments, as inspired by private education and training, and even more by public education and propaganda, were eminently revolutionary. The same thing may be said of Italy during the fifty years preceding the World War.

It is natural for young people to feel a need of enthusiasms, of having before them a type, a model, that represents an ideal of virtue and perfection which each one seeks, as far as he can, to imitate. The model that has been set before the eyes of young people in France, and in other countries, has not been, as it could not have been, the knight who dies for his lady, his faith and his king. Much less has it been the public servant, the magistrate, the soldier, the uncompromising custodian of law and order. It has been the militant revolutionist pure and simple. It has been the champion of liberty and equality, the man who has fought tyrants and rebelled against constituted powers, who in defeat has endured their persecution intrepidly and in victory has overthrown and often supplanted them.

In view of the fact that sympathy for rebels has been so assiduously cultivated, and that our school children have been taught that everything that rebels have done has been noble and generous, it is natural that currents of sentiments and ideas in each new generation should incline toward doctrines that

[1] *Insurrection du 18 mars,* chap. I.

justify rebellion and teach its necessity. No Bastilles are left to storm. No Swiss Guards of a Charles X are left to be chased from the Louvre. Italian, Greek, Polish unities are all but achieved. The Neapolitan government that was defined as the negation of God is a memory so remote that people are even beginning to judge it impartially. In a world so free of monsters, the spirit of rebellion can only turn upon institutions that have survived old revolution, or upon the men who stand at the head of them and have often been old revolutionaries themselves.

This is all the more natural in that, partly because of the imperfections that are inseparable from any political system, partly because of their intrinsic weakness, our modern institutions have not been able to satisfy all the expectations and hopes of social regeneration that were reposed in them at the beginning. Furthermore, once the sometime conspirators and revolutionaries became statesmen and leaders of peoples, not all of them proved at all times to be free of errors and shortcomings. Under such circumstances, who can marvel that there are younger elements who think that a still more radical reform of society is possible? And who can marvel that those who hope to acquire political importance through radical reform, that a goodly portion of the noble, the active, the generous, the ambitious, in the generations now making ready to take the torch from the hands of the old, have embraced socialist doctrines? The psychological state that we have just described used to be very characteristic of the young men in European universities. It is admirably portrayed in a little book that Guglielmo Ferrero published some years ago.[1] After explaining why men of the younger generation did not believe in the ideals of their fathers and found no inspiration in them, Ferrero continues:

> There are always a certain number of individuals who need to become aroused over something that is not immediate and personal to them, something that is afar off. Their own affairs, the problems of science or of art, are not enough to take up all their spiritual activity. What is left for them except the socialist idea? It comes from far away—a trait that is always alluring. It is complex enough and vague enough, at least in certain of its aspects, to satisfy the widely differing moral needs of its many proselytes. On the one hand it brings a broad spirit of brotherhood and international feeling, which corresponds to a real

[1] *Reazione*, pp. 54 f.

modern need. On the other, it has a suggestion of scientific method that is reassuring to minds that are more or less familiar with the experimental schools. Given all that, it is no wonder that a great number of young men throw in their lot with a movement in which there may indeed be a danger of meeting some unpretentious ex-convict, or some potential second offender, but in which one will be sure never to meet a professional politician, a professional patriot, a professional grafter.

Ferrero goes on to argue that economic conditions in Italy were not such as to explain the rise of a powerful socialist movement and that, at any rate, such a movement "ought logically to find its nucleus in the working classes, not in the bourgeoisie." Then he concludes:

If a socialist movement has developed under such unfavorable conditions and in so illogical a fashion, it must be because more than any other movement it answers a moral need in a certain number of young people.

One of the maxims of Machiavelli has acquired a certain popularity among persons of erudition. The Secretary wrote that one of the best ways to save or revive an aging institution was to call it back to its first principles. In reading a history of the Mongol princes who descended from Genghis Khan, we come across another maxim that seems to run in a diametrically opposite direction to the maxim of Machiavelli, and it strikes us as being truer, since it fits in with a greater number of practical cases. According to the story, Yelui-Cutsai, prime minister to Ogdai, son of Genghis Khan, often said to his lord and master: "Your empire was conquered on horseback, but you cannot rule it from the back of a horse." No one, surely, will venture to deny the political insight of the Mongol minister, for the methods by which governments, religions or political parties are kept alive, and the sentiments and passions that have to be cultivated if they are to be kept alive, are often essentially different from the means and sentiments that have served to bring them into being.

One readily sees that a new government, a new political system, may be instituted by revolution, and one may further grant that revolutions may often be necessary. But no state can grow in strength, no system can endure, if the revolutionary atmosphere continues and if, worse still, those who are in control of power persist in fomenting revolution instead of cultivating the sentiments, passions and ideas that are directly opposed to it.

Other causes have contributed to the progress of socialism, among them the sudden fortunes that are won by many speculators, almost always dishonestly, and which are just as badly spent in purchasing improper political influence to be used in more gains or in a vulgar and showy display of luxury that offends the modest respectability of the average citizen and actually insults the poverty of the poor. The whole drift of the age is in the direction of aggravating that evil. Though equality and equal rights for all are the topics of our sermons, there has perhaps never been a time when inequalities in material advantages were so visible to the eye. Never has wealth, whatever its sources, served to open more doors, and never has it been so stupidly flaunted.

In earlier centuries, luxury and display had a, so to say, primitive something about them. One kept a large retinue of servants. One offered lavish hospitality. Sometimes one distributed food and drink to the population of a whole city. Vanity played its part, beyond any doubt, in all such devices for disposing of one's surplus, but, as things turned out, a portion of the superfluous was enjoyed by those who needed it most. In more refined epochs the bounty of the great went into patronage of artists and poets, who were encouraged and enabled to create masterpieces of art and literature that yielded exquisite intellectual pleasure not only to the owner or patron but to all who were capable of appreciating them. Modern luxury is often more selfish and less intellectual. It comes down primarily to organizing an enormous array of comforts and sensual satisfactions for those who can spend the money. Not only that, the private pleasures which it procures for the few are industriously publicized by the daily press. That again, after all, is nothing but an expression of human vanity, but the practical effect of all this modern publicity is to make pleasures which only the rich can enjoy seem greater than they really are, and so to increase the envy and appetite of those who are deprived of them.

Other factors in the growth of socialism have been stressed by many: the ill-advised warfare that has been waged on religious sentiment; the public poverty that is produced by excessive taxes; excessive public debts and too many unproductive public expenditures; the notorious dishonesty of men in power; the injustices and hypocrisies of parliamentary systems; the present arrangements in secondary and higher education that have turned the schools into factories of misfits. A leading position on this list must be reserved for the custom of using influence upon public opinion and governments to win monopolistic concessions or protective tariffs in industry and agriculture. Such things are a form of socialism, in a sense, and so it follows that any other form of socialism is justified, since a really worse one is already in vogue, in that it uses the authority of the state to serve the benefit of a few who are the richest and the detriment of all others, both poor and rich.

Neglect of the rules of hygiene, lack of good food, good water and sanitary housing, do not generate the cholera bacillus. They do weaken the human organism and lower its resistance to disease, and so help to propagate the plague once it has taken hold. In the same way, all the various factors that we have enumerated, all these various manifestations of bad public management, are not directly responsible for the intellectual germs that have caused the morbus called socialism. They have increased discontent and lowered the organic resistance of society, and so have furthered its spread. It is therefore in point to urge a stricter social hygiene upon the ruling classes, which implies their dropping old errors. Unfortunately, such advice is easy to give but hard to follow. Before it could be taken and put into practice, the ruling classes would have to develop a greater morality, a greater far-sightedness and more talent than they have been displaying in many countries of the western world.

9. Few among those who follow the movement of public life in Europe and America today fail to ask themselves sooner or later whether social democracy is or is not destined to triumph in a more or less imminent future. Many people who have no sympathy with socialist doctrines and no interest in favoring them are nevertheless inclined to answer the question in the affirmative. That is one of the results of an intellectual training that has brought a great majority of educated persons in our time to look upon the history of humanity as one continuous journey toward the realization of ideas that are now commonly

called "advanced." As for collectivists and anarchists themselves, blind confidence in the fated, inevitable, and more or less imminent triumph of their program is the common rule, and it is a great source of strength to them, serving them much as the early Christians were served by their faith in an early advent of the kingdom of God or in the future life. The primitive Christians, again, faced martyrdom intrepidly, firm in their trust in divine revelation. So the radicals of today gladly suffer annoyances, discomforts and persecutions, when by chance they are called upon to suffer a few, savoring in foretaste the joys of a certain victory that many believe to be near at hand. Many of the more enthusiastic socialist writers of the early days placed the date for the triumph of collectivism at the end of the nineteenth century, or in the early decades of the twentieth.

In view of all that we have been saying, no one will be surprised if we assert that, even granting that collectivists and anarchists may chance to be victorious and gain control of political authority in a number of countries, the carrying out of their program would continue to be *impossible;* for the postulates of collectivism, communism and anarchy never can be put into practice, any more than the ideals of the early Christians could be put into practice after the official triumph of Christianity. But it still remains to be seen just what probability there is of a triumph for social democracy. For suppose a mere attempt were made, and sustained over a number of years, to put the collectivist theories into force. Even if it did not alter the constant laws that regulate the organization of human societies, which would inevitably assert themselves in the end and triumph, it would weigh grievously on the lot of the generations on which the experiment would be made. Torn between revolution and the inevitable reactions to revolution, those generations would at the best be forced to return to a much cruder and more absolute type of government than any that we now know. There would necessarily be a deterioration in juridical defense and a real moral and material cataclysm. Centuries later such a cataclysm might be studied with interest, and perhaps even with amusement, as an unusually instructive case of social pathology; but meantime it would entail unspeakable agonies for those who would be called upon to witness it and to be its victims.

But, even when stated in those terms, the question is not one that can be answered with certainty, for many arguments can be adduced for and against the temporary triumph of the social revolution. The elements on which a prognosis has to be based vary from one European country to another, and the problem becomes still more complicated if we extend our preview to the English colonies and the United States.

Certainly it would be much harder to make a mere attempt to establish collectivism than it would be to overthrow the staunchest of the governments now existing. Under the present organization of society the two reins that any government uses in leading a nation are the bureaucracy and the standing army. As we have already seen (chap. VIII, §6), in all earlier revolutions, the great French Revolution excepted, the rider has often changed but the reins have never broken—they have continued functioning almost normally.

But if a great social revolution were to triumph, it is doubtful whether the present body of civil employees and officials could continue to function, and it is exceedingly doubtful whether the victors would find the personnel to supplant them in their own rank and file. The normal organs of government having ceased to operate, a period of anarchy would follow, of which no one could say what the outcome would be, except that it would be such an outcome that even a temporary continuation of the effort to establish collectivism would be impossible.

The present organization of society has immense powers of resistance. Just how strong they are has never, so far, been tested. The destinies of an incalculable number of people and interests are bound up with continuing the system now prevailing —bankers, merchants, manufacturers, public and private employees, holders of government bonds, savings bank depositors, property owners great and small. Such people would make up a great army. In its ranks would be many who sympathize with ideas of social equality when it is a question of something vague and faraway but who would certainly feel otherwise once they saw the execution of those principles near at hand and a threat to their personal interests imminent.

The growth within postal, telegraph and transportation departments of unions of employees that are hostile to the state might render the effect of such agencies much less dependable, but we must figure that a government might at certain moments find itself in complete control of them, and they would be very effective instruments of action. The government also could use the millions of treasure that would be lying in the public vaults, to say nothing of the millions that the banks could readily supply, or of unlimited amounts of fiat currency that could be issued. The state, finally, has the police force at its disposal, and the standing army. Proposals have been made of late to transform the army into the so-called "nation in arms," with recruiting by localities in time of peace, very short terms of training service, and so on. But unless the army has been disorganized by such concessions to the democratic spirit—if it is sound, in other words, and is resolutely used, it can deal successfully with any attempt at armed insurrection. The fact that armies might be reduced to relatively small numbers would not alter that situation.

On the other hand, account must be taken of the continuous propaganda that social democracy is carrying on in all social classes, even in groups that should be most inclined to defend the present order. This propaganda rarely makes full and thoroughgoing conversions among people of a certain age and a certain social position; but it does make many people, who ought to fight the new revolutionary current as a matter of interest or duty, doubt the justice of their own case, and in the moment of danger it might cause a large part of the forces that are appointed to arrest it to waver. Such a faltering might contribute seriously toward defeat when taken in conjunction with the slow disorganizing influence that parliamentarism is exerting upon all the organs of state. How expect steadiness in danger, or scrupulous and loyal service, from a bureaucratic machine that has grown used to the shifting policies of successive ministries, from prefects and police officials who turn every so often into vote-rustlers? What confidence can one have in men who are virtually obliged by the positions they hold not to feel any loyalty or sincere devotion to any principle or to any person, who are called upon today to fight the man whose orders they were taking yesterday—whose main concern has to be to avoid becoming embroiled with the master of today, but in such a way as not to make too great an enemy of the master of tomorrow? That is the way to train good tight-rope walkers, and

such people do very well for the routine moments of administrative life.   But they possess neither the habit of blind obedience nor the courage to take the initiative boldly and assume
grave responsibilities.   Steadiness of brain and heart is rare
enough in men who are accustomed to compromises and expe-
dients, but the quality is most essential in high officials of a
government at the extraordinary moments when revolutions
come.   Our bureaucrats will surely be found lacking in it.

What more than anything else makes any sort of prediction
difficult is the fact that the day when the revolutionary outbreak
occurs—and in our opinion it is by no means certain to come—
will not be fixed by the men who are or will be holding power in
the various countries, nor even by the leaders of social democracy.
It will be fixed by unforeseeable events—either involuntary
mistakes on the part of governments or happenings that will
profoundly shock society and throw it into spectacular ferment,
but which no one will deliberately have provoked and no one will
be able to prevent.   Events that might provoke a social revolution
would be, for instance, a disaster in a war with some foreign
power, a grave industrial and agricultural crisis or financial
bankruptcy on the part of one or more great European powers.
But there is no certainty that the occasion that will force
the revolutionary party to act will be the best imaginable
for it.   There is no telling whether, at that moment, its
forces will be in the best possible shape and the forces of its
adversaries sufficiently disorganized.   However, the longer
the favorable moment for starting the revolution is delayed in
coming, the less favorable it will be for the revolutionaries.   It
is difficult to keep up any sort of agitation in the masses for
very long when nothing concrete is being done to enable them
to see a probability of realizing the ideals propounded by the
agitation.   In France and a few other countries the habits and
traditions of armed social conflict have been preserved and are
still strong.   But if any great length of time were still to elapse,
they would be weakened, and there would be a complete lack of
leaders of the necessary experience and prestige in a position to
direct the course of a revolution.

10. In any case, suppose we grant that a violent movement is
avoided.   Suppose we grant even that the so-called "evolu-

tionary wing" succeeds in maintaining such a preponderance in the ranks of the radicals that it can prevent an armed outbreak for the present, or for generations to come. Even so, social democracy will not cease to be a violent disintegrating agency in modern society, and if the new doctrine is not subdued the order of things now prevailing will always remain in a state of instability and have to be upheld to a great extent by sheer physical force. Now physical force may suffice to prevent the outbreak of a violent catastrophe from day to day, but it cannot restore to the social body the moral unity essential for a stable order. As we have already seen (chap. VII, §10), brute force, taken all by itself, cannot suppress or even restrain a current of ideas and passions unless it is applied without scruple and without consideration, unless, that is, it is applied with a cruelty that does not falter at the number of its victims. Aside from the fact that such a use of force is undesirable, it is impossible in our day and age, our manners and morals being what they are, unless at least it is provoked by similar outrages on the part of the revolutionaries. If European civilization is forced to keep long and incessantly on the defensive against the tendencies of the various socialist schools, it will be forced by that very fact into a decline, and the decline will come whether our civilization tries to compromise, make concessions and come to terms, or adopts a policy of absolute coercion and resistance. In order to maintain the latter, it will have to abandon most of its idealism, restrict liberty of thought and adopt new types of government which will represent a real retrogression in the safeguarding of justice and in juridical defense.

Many remedies have been suggested, and certainly many among them are not to be rejected. They may increase the patient's powers of resistance, even if the best of them will not remove the cause of the malady. If national economic systems are improved, if taxes are lowered, if justice is made more equitable and effective, if all abuses that can be done away with are done away with, that certainly will be of no mean benefit to society. But social democracy aspires to absolute justice, to absolute equality, and these can never be attained. Social democracy, therefore, will certainly not disarm in consideration of such benefits. It will not pardon bourgeois society merely because bourgeois society confesses to some of its sins and does penance.　Unlike the God of the Christians, the real socialist, so far as the present economic order is concerned, wants the death of the sinner.　He does not want him to reform and live.

There is a second type of remedy on which statesmen, and some few modern sovereigns, have pinned great hopes.　It consists in applying the principle of state control to curing or reducing many of the injustices or sufferings that result from economic individualism and from the merciless competition in which property owners, manufacturers and the captains of big industry are engaged—both of which cause misery and uncertainty of the morrow for the wage-earning proletariat.　We have already expressed our opinion on this point (chap. VI, §§3–4, above).　There we said that there is not *a* social question, but *many* social questions, and that the principle of control by the state, in other words, by the bureaucracy and other organized directing groups, is to be justified or rejected case by case. Certainly there are examples where state control, used in moderation, may be welcome, as in the regulation of working hours and types of work for women and children.　There is no denying, either, that as regards charities, public assistance and mutual aid, our social organization today is inadequate.　We have no organizations intermediate between the state and the large municipality, which in Europe is an instrument of the state. Such units are too large.　Within them the individual disappears and is forgotten.　On the other hand, there is nothing intermediate between the municipality and the modern family, which has come to be reduced to the utmost simplicity, to the lowest possible terms.　Even brothers and sisters nowadays often feel no responsibility for each other.

There were such intermediate organizations in the old days in Europe, and there still are in other civilizations.　In India, for instance, in every town or village, members of the same caste, or rather of the same subdivision in the caste, assist each other. Mutual aid is customary in Mohammedan countries among members of the same tribe.　In China the family is a much more comprehensive thing than in Europe.　Descendants of the same ancestor down to the third generation ordinarily live together and are conscious of a community of interests.　In Japan, the inhabitants of the same village, or of the same quarter in a city, consider themselves obliged as a matter of course to succor a neighbor who has come upon misfortune. If his house burns down, for instance, they build him another at their common expense. In antiquity, in the Middle Ages and down to a century ago, the corporations and brotherhoods of the trades and professions performed just those functions in Italy. Such institutions impose certain obligations on their members, but they also recognize that the members have certain rights. Their main advantage is that they keep the individual, or the family, that is smitten by temporary misfortune from being left in the lurch and driven to despair. Beyond any doubt, something has to be done on that score, and perhaps it would be just as well if governments were to keep hands off, so that natural solidarities might grow up again of their own accord. The main requirement would be a long period of stability in population and in economic interests.

In western Europe, especially in large towns, the family from which assistance can be expected comes down practically to the father, the mother and *minor* children. If through some misfortune the head of the family who is working for a living chances to lose his wages for some months' time, he is certain to face poverty and despair. Now what is called "individualism" in Europe—the principle and the fact of each man for himself and God for all—has come about virtually in our time, partly because of the frequent changes of fortune that break or strain bonds of family, neighborhood or professional association, partly because of large-scale movements in population that have been due to the growth of new industrial centers, especially new cities. Great cities are inhabited in large part by floating populations. A family rarely lives in the same house for ten years in succession, and a person scarcely ever knows his next-door neighbor. Under such circumstances the most painful cases of destitution occur. Living alone in the midst of a great throng, an individual or a family can literally starve.

But what is ordinarily expected of state control is something far more than mere relief of distress. Many people want the state to influence the distribution of wealth directly. They want it to deprive the rich of their surplus through taxation and give it to the poor. This idea is being viewed with considerable sympathy even among conservatives. It is the sort of thing that appeals to our numerous "socialistoids," or "pinks,"

as they are often called—that large body of people who do not
join any collectivist or anarchist party but create the sympathetic environment in which such parties flourish and prosper.
Now the proposal in question is a truly dangerous one. Any
very wide application of it, such as striking at capital too severely,
or trying, for example, to specify the crops that shall be raised
on certain lands, would kill the goose that lays the golden egg.
It would cause a serious falling off in the production of wealth
and increase misery and discontent at all social levels. Such
a system would not give us collectivism. Social inequalities
would not disappear, and radicals would still have something
substantial to ask for. But the whole economy of so-called
bourgeois society would be seriously disturbed and its functioning
would be thoroughly disorganized. That the followers of Marx
should favor the temporary application of the system is natural
and logical enough. It would be one of those best calculated to
reduce society to a level where an experiment in collectivism
would become desirable. But it does seem strange that people
who do not accept collectivist theories should hope to combat
and neutralize them with a policy that would make the economic
situation of everybody worse, and reduce almost everybody
to looking upon collectivism as an improvement.

There are other measures which many people favor, regarding
them as very proper concessions to socialist demands. Of these
we might mention the "right to work," in other words an obligation on the part of the state to pay salaries to all the unemployed;
the compulsory breaking up of great landed properties, which
would be tantamount to forcing the introduction of small-scale
agriculture by law, even in regions where natural conditions are
not congenial to its existence; a maximum eight-hour working
day, established not by the mutual consent of workers and
employers but by statute; a minimum-wage scale, also established
by law; a single and heavily progressive income tax. Anyone
who has even a moderate knowledge of the working of economic
laws can see at a glance that the application of such provisions
would destroy private capital in the course of a few years. At
the same time, it must be confessed, the governments of not a
few European countries have gone so far in certain directions
that they can hardly reject these demands of socialists and near-
socialists, and other proposals of the same sort, without doing

grievous violence to logic and equity. If the price of bread is going to be raised artificially on the specious pretext that landowners must be guaranteed a fair profit on wheat, how can the workingman be refused a fair minimum price for his labor?

Christian socialism, and Catholic socialism in particular, are regarded by many people as tools that are well adapted to neutralizing atheistic, materialistic and revolutionary socialism. Well-intentioned efforts have been made, and are still being made, in these Christian directions, and they have not been altogether ineffective. However, we should not have unlimited faith in a flank counterattack. It is true, as we have already seen, that both Christianity and socialism take advantage of the hunger for justice and the ideal that is common to all human beings—who are nevertheless obliged to live in a world where there are many, many iniquities for which they are themselves responsible. But both Christianity and socialism depend upon other sentiments besides the hunger for justice, and such sentiments are by no means identical in the two doctrines. Their methods of propaganda and their aspirations are also essentially different, and very, very different are the intellectual settings which they require for their growth and prosperity. The basis of Christianity is faith in the supernatural, in a God who sees the tears of the poor and sorrowful, consoles them in this life and rewards them in the life to come. Socialism originates in the rationalist philosophy of the eighteenth century. It takes its stand on materialistic doctrines, which teach that all happiness lies in the satisfaction of earthly instincts and passions. Christianity and socialism are therefore two plants of a very different nature. They may well vie with each other for the sap in the ground, but they cannot possibly be grafted on each other. Vain, therefore, is the hope that a Christian shoot inserted into a socialist trunk will ever change the fruit, eliminating all its bitter flavor, its ever harmful quality, and leaving it sweet and wholesome. Christian socialism is nothing else, and can be nothing else, than a new name applied to an old thing, in other words, Christian charity. Christian charity, doubtless, is able to render great services to European society; but it could not wholly destroy atheistic and revolutionary socialism unless the world were again to be as thoroughly steeped in the Christian spirit as it was in the less tutored centuries of the Middle Ages.

11. Under the conditions that at present prevail in European civilization, the one remedy that can strike the evil at the root, cut off the supply of vital sap on which the grown tree flourishes and cause it to wither away, is of a very different order. Social democracy is more than anything else the intellectual malady of our age. To be sure, it found a propitious moral environment. It found a soil prepared by all the rancors, ambitions and greeds that necessarily resulted from a long revolutionary period and from the shiftings of fortunes that were bound up with such a period. Supremely beneficial to it has been the world's disappointment with parliamentary democracy, which set out to inaugurate a reign of justice and equality in the world, and has failed miserably to keep that promise. Nevertheless this new doctrine originates in a system of ideas which is nothing, after all, but the logical consequence of the system in which the pure democracy of the old days found its inspiration.

Belief in the possibility that government can emanate from the majority; faith in the incorruptibility of the majority; confidence that once they have been emancipated from every principle of authority that is not rooted in universal consensus, from every aristocratic, monarchical and religious superstition, men will be able to inaugurate the political system that will best serve the general interests and the interests of justice—such is the content of the body of ideas and sentiments that has combated, and is combating, Christian beliefs in the people, and is the chief obstacle to any compromise with the church. Ideas and sentiments of the same sort have produced parliamentary democracy and, as we have seen, are now preventing the application of radical remedies to parliamentarism. The same body of ideas and sentiments, finally, is sweeping us inexorably toward socialism, and ultimately toward anarchy.

There is no stopping along the road. Once experience has shown that mere political equality as embodied in universal suffrage fails to produce political equality in the fact and maintains the political preeminence of a given class and of certain social influences, it is natural and logical that a system should be contrived which will destroy disparities in private fortunes and place all who aspire to rule over society, and therefore need the votes of the people, on an equal footing. And after a somewhat riper experience has made it clear, or made it merely plausi-

ble, that not even in that way can one get a government that is a
genuine emanation of the majority will, much less absolute
justice, we will have, as the final implication of a metaphysical
concept that has vainly sought to concretize itself, a doctrine
that favors ending any sort of social organization whatever, and
therefore, anarchy.

Now democratic doctrine has rendered undeniable services
to civilization. Embodied in the representative system, for
which England set the pattern, it has contributed to important
improvements in juridical defense, which have been attained
through a system of free discussion that has been established
in many parts of Europe. But now that we have come to its
last logical implication, and men are trying to realize the principles on which it was based down to their remotest consequences,
the same doctrine is disorganizing the countries in which it
prevails and forcing them into their decline.

This would not be the first case where a society has retrogressed
from trying to carry to their logical conclusions principles,
doctrines and methods which at the start contributed to its
greatness. In the early days of the Roman Empire strong
bureaucratic organization was a great source of progress, and
thanks to it the empire was able to assimilate a large part of the
world. Later on, excessive bureaucratization became one of the
main factors in the decline of the empire. Fanaticism and blind,
exclusive faith in the Koran were the most important factors
in the rapid spread of Mohammedan civilization. As centuries
went by, they became the chief reason for the fossilization and
decadence of the Mohammedan world.

Things could not be otherwise with democracy because, at
bottom, under pseudoscientific appearances, the democratic
doctrine is altogether aprioristic. Its premises are not in the
slightest degree justified by the facts. Absolute equality has
never existed in human societies. Political power never has
been, and never will be, founded upon the explicit consent of
majorities. It always has been, and it always will be, exercised
by organized minorities, which have had, and will have, the
means, varying as the times vary, to impose their supremacy
on the multitudes. Only a wise organization of society and a
truly unprecedented number of favoring historical circum-

stances have managed to render the preeminence of a ruling class less burdensome and less abusive in our time.

Renan wrote that the Roman Empire could have arrested the spread of Christianity on one condition only—if it had consented to a positive teaching of the natural sciences. Scientific knowledge was the only thing that could, by showing that natural happenings in our world obey unchanging laws, develop a sense of reality and succeed in eradicating from the human spirit the belief in miracles and in the continuous intervention of the supernatural.[1] But at that time the natural sciences had barely reached their embryonic stage, and Christianity triumphed. In the world in which we are living, socialism will be arrested only if a realistic political science succeeds in demolishing the metaphysical and optimistic methods that prevail at present in social studies—in other words, only if discovery and demonstration of the great constant laws that manifest themselves in all human societies succeed in making visible to the eye the impossibility of realizing the democratic ideal. On this condition, and on this condition only, will the intellectual classes escape the influence of social democracy and form an invincible barrier to its triumph.

So far students of the social sciences, and more especially economists, have examined this or that postulate of socialism from the standpoint of showing its patent fallacy. That is not enough. It is something like showing that one miracle or another is false, without destroying faith in the possibility of miracles. *A whole metaphysical system must be met with a whole scientific system.* "In higher education," a distinguished scientist writes, "the theories of scientific economics and sociology must be set up in opposition to the errors of Marxism, so that youthful minds will not be left prey to chimerical fancies that are set before them as the latest results of science."[2] Wise, sound words! But they merely express a praiseworthy desire. They do not point to a remedy of swift and certain efficacy. The study of economics is an excellent thing, but it is not in itself sufficient to cleanse the public mind of the chimerical fancies

[1] This opinion is implicit in all of Renan's writings. It is developed most scientifically in *Marc Aurèle*, chap. XXI.

[2] Garofalo, *La superstizione socialista*, p. 240.

alluded to. Economic science has penetratingly investigated the laws that regulate the production and distribution of wealth. It has as yet done little with the relations of those laws to other laws that operate in the political organization of human societies. Economists have not concerned themselves with those beliefs, those collective illusions, which sometimes become general in given societies, and which form so large a part of the history of the world—as has been well said, man does not live by bread alone. As for sociology, we are inclined to think that, in the majority of its doctrines at least, it has so far not shown itself to be a mature science producing results that cannot be questioned. In the second half of the nineteenth century the democratic-socialist metaphysic had to compete only with systems that styled themselves as positive but were just as metaphysical as it was, finding even less support in the actual lives that nations have lived and being even less susceptible of practical application. As between a number of different metaphysical systems it is natural that predominance should have rested with the system that best humored the keenest and most universal passions.

Arduous, therefore, is the task which is set for political science, and it will be all the more arduous in that the truths which it will be its mission to reveal will not be generally popular, since they will shock many passions and cross many interests. It is highly probable, then, that in spite of the traditions of free discussion that distinguish our age, the propagation of these new scientific results will once more encounter the obstacles that have retarded progress in other branches of learning. There is little likelihood that the new doctrines will find much support in our governments, or in our ruling classes, which nevertheless ought to support them. Interests, whatever their nature, love propaganda, not impartial discussion. They support only the theory that serves the particular and immediate purpose, that justifies the man, that sustains the given administration or party. They have no use for the theory that can yield practical results only in the general interests of society and in a future relatively remote. If science triumphs in the end, its victory will be then as always due to the conscientiousness of honest scholars, whose duty it is, above every consideration, to seek and expound the truth.

CHAPTER XII

THEORY OF THE RULING CLASS

1. The doctrine that in all human societies which have arrived at a certain grade of development and civilization political control in the broadest sense of the term (administrative, military, religious, economic and moral leadership) is exercised always by a special class, or by an organized minority, is older than is commonly supposed even by those who support it.

The facts on which its fundamental assumptions rest are, of course, so obvious and commonplace that they could never entirely have escaped the observation of the plain man, especially one free of special theoretical bias. Vague allusions to it, fairly clear perceptions of it, may be noted here and there in some few political writers belonging to periods rather remote from ours. Machiavelli, for instance, declares that "in any city whatsoever, in whatsoever manner organized, never do more than forty or fifty persons attain positions of command."[1] But ignoring such casual allusions, one may say that the fundamental outlines of the doctrine were traced in a fairly definite and clearcut fashion a little over a hundred years ago in the writings of Saint-Simon, an author whose depth and originality have not so far been sufficiently recognized and appreciated.

Examining moral and political conditions in medieval society, and comparing them with social conditions at the beginning of the nineteenth century, Saint-Simon came to the conclusion that military and theological elements prevailed in the former, and that therefore priests and military leaders stood at the apex of the political pyramid. In the latter period, he thought, the main functions that were essential to social life were scientific and industrial in character, and so political leadership passed to men who were capable of advancing science and directing economic production. In this, not only did he implicitly assert the inherent necessity of a ruling class. He explicitly proclaimed that that class has to possess the requisites and aptitudes

[1] *Deca*, XVI.

most necessary to social leadership at a given time and in a given type of civilization.[1]

An intellectual offshoot of Saint-Simon was his pupil Auguste Comte.[2] Comte's *Système de politique positive, ou Traité de sociologie*, was published about the middle of the nineteenth century (1853). It developed, with modifications, some of the fundamental ideas of Comte's former teacher. It held that control over society was to belong in the future to a scientific aristocracy, which Comte called a scientific priesthood, and declared that such a form of government would be a necessary consequence of the "positive" stage which the human mind had attained in the nineteenth century, in contradistinction to a theological stage which had prevailed in classical antiquity and to a metaphysical stage which had prevailed in the Middle Ages. About twenty years later (1872), in his *Ancien régime*, Taine gave a masterly explanation of the origins of the great French Revolution, holding that it resulted from the need of substituting a new ruling class for an old ruling class which had lost its original capabilities of leadership and had not succeeded in acquiring the capacities that a new era demanded. A little before Comte, Marx and Engels had formulated a theory that in the past the state had always represented the class that owned the instruments of economic production, and that the same was true in their day in bourgeois society. According to the Marx-Engels doctrine, an evolutionary process in society would inevitably lead to collectivism and to the founding of a system of political and economic management in which the whole collectivity, now owner in its turn of the instruments of production, would no longer be exploited for the benefit of the minority.

So more than sixty years had passed since Saint-Simon's publications, and the first single rivulet had already branched

---

[1] See Rodriquez, *Saint-Simon et son premier écrit.* See also *Oeuvres de Saint-Simon et d'Enfantin* (in this great collection, writings of Saint-Simon are to be found in vols. XV, XVI, XVIII–XXIII, XXXVII, XXXIX). The concepts we refer to are fundamentals in Saint-Simon's doctrines and are repeated in almost all of his publications. One need hardly say that the Saint-Simonian sect, which rose and spread some years after Saint-Simon's death, ranged far from the ideas of the first master. See, in this connection, Janet, *Saint-Simon et le Saint-Simonisme.*

[2] On the influence of Saint-Simon on Comte, see Dumas, *Psychologie de deux messies positivistes*, pp. 255 f.

into a number of widely divergent currents. Toward the end of the past century, and during the early years of the present, this new vision of the political world was proclaimed and promulgated by a number of writers in a number of countries. Often they had reached the goal over separate paths and with imperfect, if any, acquaintance with each other or with their original predecessors. If this independence did, on occasion, add a touch of spontaneousness and originality to the observation of such writers, it led the doctrine on other occasions into blind alleys, or cluttered it up with irrelevancies or with easily refutable mistakes. When the history of the new doctrine of the ruling class comes to be written, it will not be hard to apportion to each writer his share of merit for contributing now good, now mediocre, now unusable materials to the rising edifice, and to determine also which materials were strictly new and which were second-hand. For the time being it will suffice to note, as a matter of record, that in 1881 Gumplowicz's *Der Rassenkampf* appeared.[1] That volume recognized the existence in every political organism of two ruling classes, one of which held governmental and military control, while the other exercised industrial, commercial and financial control. Gumplowicz explained the differentiation between the two classes and their predominance over the governed class by differing ethnic origins. In 1883 we published our *Teorica dei governi*. There we examined the inner workings of democratic systems and showed that even in democracies the need for an organized minority persists, and that in spite of appearances to the contrary, and for all of the legal principles on which government rests, this minority still retains actual and effective control of the state. In years following came the first edition of the present work, *Elementi di scienza politica*, and, among others, works by Ammon, Novikov, Rensi, Pareto and Michels.[2]

[1] Gumplowicz restated and elaborated the ideas he had expressed in *Der Rassenkampf* in his *Grundriss der Sociologie*, 1885.

[2] Earlier in these pages (chap. I, §10), we considered the doctrines of Gobineau and Lapouge regarding racial factors in the superiority of ruling classes. Ammon published *Die natürliche Auslese beim Menschen* (*Natural Selection in Human Beings*) in 1893, and in 1898 the first German edition of his *Gesellschaftsordnung* (*Social Order*). In the latter, Ammon fully develops a theory that the ruling class necessarily exists because of a natural selection that takes place in the higher social strata. As for the other writers mentioned see Novikov, *Conscience et*

Today it may be said that in the more advanced countries of Europe the idea that a ruling class necessarily exists has made its way more or less definitely into the minds of everybody who thinks, speaks or expresses opinions about historical and political phenomena. This is due to the influence of the writers mentioned. It is probably due in even greater part to an automatic enrichment of collective experience in our world, whereby the thought of one generation, when it does not fossilize into blind adoration of the teachings of the forefathers, goes a little deeper, at least, than the thought of earlier generations.

In any event, it is now a common thing to see the setbacks of one nation or another, or the catastrophes that threaten them, ascribed not so much to the ignorance of the masses or to the wickedness of men in power as to the incompetence and inadequacy of ruling classes. A logical reasoning ought therefore to lead to ascribing successes, when they are won, to the enlightened activity of the same classes. Parallel with the spreading of the attitude mentioned has come a slow erosion of optimistic conceptions of human nature. An eighteenth century product, as we have seen, this optimistic view occupied a preponderant position in European thinking during almost all the nineteenth century. It was commonly believed that once legal inequalities were destroyed, the moral and intellectual level of all social classes could be definitely raised and they would all become equally capable of managing public affairs. This point of view is obviously the only one that could furnish a moral and intellectual basis for what is commonly understood as democracy, in other words, government by numerical majorities of citizens.

2. In view of this very considerable background, one might reasonably wonder at the slight practical influence which this new doctrine has had and is still having upon the development of political institutions and upon practitioners of official and non-official science. Even those who do admit the existence of a

---

volonté sociale, 1897; Rensi, Gli "anciens régimes" e la democrazia diretta, 1902; Pareto, Les Systèmes socialistes, 1902, and Trattato di sociologia generale, 1916; and Michels, Zur Soziologie des Parteiwesens (often translated), 1911. In this book Michels proves with very sound arguments that even the great democratic and socialist parties are inevitably led by organized minorities, and often with an iron discipline.

ruling class (and not to admit it would sometimes be equivalent to denying the obvious) often fail to reason as though the fact were inevitable—they do not draw the necessary consequences from it and so do not utilize the theory as the guiding thread that must steer us as we go looking into the causes that mature and produce the effects which at times lift societies to prosperity and power and at other times engulf them in anarchy and ruin. It is of no avail to credit the ruling class for successes, or to blame it for failures, unless we scrutinize the intricate mechanism, in the operation of which the explanation for the strength or weakness of the class can be found. And in this we have already glimpsed one of the causes for the failure of the new doctrine to bear more fruit in practice.

These causes we must, therefore, go into somewhat carefully. In order to make it easier to keep them in mind, suppose we divide them into two groups: extrinsic causes, which are foreign to the essence and structure of the doctrine proper, and intrinsic causes, which are due to defects or shortcomings in the doctrine itself.

First and perhaps foremost among the extrinsic causes is the fact that, so far, all the institutions that have been functioning in Europe have been based on other doctrines, some of which are different from the doctrine we are here concerned with, and, so to say, irrelevant to it, while others are directly antithetical to it. Representative governments now prevail almost everywhere in countries of European civilization. Some of them are modeled along the lines laid down by Montesquieu, who saw the essence and guarantee of political liberty in a tripartite separation of sovereign powers. More numerous are governments that follow the principle of Rousseau, that those powers only are legitimate which represent the will of the numerical majority of citizens, while the right of suffrage is regarded as an innate right from which no individual can reasonably and properly be barred.

Now in itself the democratic system probably has greater powers of self-preservation than other systems. That is because its natural adversaries have to make a show of accepting it if they wish to avoid its consequences to a greater or lesser extent. All those who, by wealth, education, intelligence or guile, have an aptitude for leading a community of men, and a chance of doing so—in other words, all the cliques in the ruling class—have to bow to universal suffrage once it is instituted, and also, if occasion requires, cajole and fool it. On no other condition can they participate in the control of the state and reach positions from which they can best defend the interests of their particular clique. The fact, then, that the natural adversaries of democracy are obliged to pay official homage to it prevents them from openly declaring themselves followers of theories that explicitly deny the possibility of democratic government as commonly understood. And the same fact also impedes the formation of the coalitions of sentiments and interests that are necessary if a doctrine is to become an active force capable of transforming institutions—if it is to penetrate people's minds and so take hold of them as to modify the trend of a society at all appreciably. Michels has very properly stressed the point that, in countries which have representative governments, conservative parties are obliged to pay homage to democratic doctrines.[1]

Then again, a new conception in politics or religion cannot have a very great efficacy in practice until the conception that has preceded it in the public consciousness has exhausted all its powers of expansion, or, better still, has carried out, so to say, the historic mission which it was born to fulfill and which explains its more or less rapid success. The modern democratic conception is hardly more than a century and a half old. It spread like wildfire because, first in France and soon after throughout western Europe, the new ruling class at once made use of it in order to oust the nobility and clergy from their privileges and in large part to supplant them. But rapid as its progress had been, the doctrine surely had not completed its historic task at the end of the nineteenth century, and it did not begin to influence the countries in eastern Europe till very recently.

A hundred and odd years ago Saint-Simon thought that the democratic doctrine had already fulfilled its historic mission, and in an open letter to Louis XVIII he suggested that that sovereign "had better not bother with the would-be dogma of popular sovereignty, which was just a strawman that lawyers and metaphysicians had set up against the dogma of divine right—just an abstraction provoked by another abstraction," and that "the two dogmas were mere hangovers from a conflict

[1] *Parteiwesen.* See also his "La democrazia e la legge ferrea dell'oli-garchia."

already settled."[1] But in that, evidently, Saint-Simon was
making a bad guess. He was forgetting, or he may never have
realized, how exasperatingly slow history is in moving, at least as
compared with the brevity of human life. One might further
explain that Saint-Simon regarded the rule of jurists and metaphysicians as symptomatic of a period of transition between the
dominion of priests and warriors and the dominion of scientists
and businessmen. He also believed that jurists and metaphysicians had been well fitted for destroying the ancient world but
had shown themselves inept at reconstructing the modern world.

Saint-Simon thought that divine right was dead and buried
even before his time. As a matter of fact, with Charles X and
Polignac, it was still trying to hold on in France in 1830, when
Saint-Simon was already dead; and in Germany and Russia it
breasted the tide of the times well on into the twentieth century.
Meantime the metaphysic of popular sovereignty did not get a
good foothold until universal suffrage was established. That
measure was adopted in France earlier than anywhere else in
Europe, and not till 1848. So far, in all the countries that have
adopted universal suffrage more or less recently, the educated
and well-to-do classes have maintained their rule under its
aegis, though their influence has been tempered more or less by
the influence of the petty bourgeoisie and of representatives of
the interests of certain groups in the proletariat. That type of
democracy is not so very different from the sort of government
that Saint-Simon approved of and which he wanted Louis XVIII
to use his authority to inaugurate—government by businessmen,
scientists, scholars and artists. Democratic institutions may be
able to endure for some time yet if, in virtue of them, a certain
equilibrium between the various elements in the ruling class can
be maintained, if our *apparent* democracy is not fatally carried
away by logic, its worst enemy, and by the appetites of the
lower classes and their leaders, and if it does not attempt to
become *real* democracy by combining political equality with
economic and cultural equality.

3. On the main intrinsic cause for the slight success that has
so far been enjoyed by the doctrine that a ruling class necessarily exists, we have already touched very briefly.

[1] *Oeuvres de Saint-Simon et d' Enfantin*, vol. XXI, p. 211.

A doctrine is a thread by which those who are examining a given body of facts try to guide themselves in the maze which the facts seem to present at first glance; and a doctrine becomes the more useful in practice the more it facilitates and simplifies the understanding and analysis of facts. In this matter of political theory, as in so many other matters, appearances are often as satisfactory to people as the substance would be. The old classifications of the various forms of government—the classification of Aristotle, who divided governments into monarchies, aristocracies and democracies, and the classification of Montesquieu, who trisected them into despotic, monarchical and republican governments—answered that purpose well enough. Following the Stagirite and the author of the *Esprit des lois*, anyone could get his bearings in political theory by deciding in just what category the government of his own country, or the governments of neighboring or even distant countries, belonged. Once that point was settled, he could well believe himself authorized to go on and point out the values, defects and dangers of this or that form of government, and to answer any objections that might be made to it by simply applying the precepts of the master he followed, or the master's successors.

On the other hand, merely to assert that in all forms of government the real and actual power resides in a ruling minority is to dismiss the old guides without supplying new ones—it is to establish a generic truth which does not take us at once into the heart of political happenings, present or past, and which does not explain by itself why certain political organisms are strong and others weak, nor suggest ways and means of preventing their decadence or repairing their defects. To assign all credit for the prosperity of a society, or all responsibility for its political decrepitude, to its ruling class is of little help when we do not know the various ways in which ruling classes are formed and organized. It is precisely in that variety of type that the secret of their strength and weakness must be sought and found.

The comprehensive and generic demonstration that a ruling class necessarily exists has to be supplemented, therefore, with an analytical study. We must patiently seek out the constant traits that various ruling classes possess and the variable traits with which the remote causes of their integration and dissolution, which contemporaries almost always fail to notice, are

bound up.   It is a question, after all, of using the procedure that
is so much used in the natural sciences, in which no end of information that has now become an indestructible patrimony of
human knowledge is due to happy intuitions, some of which
have been confirmed, others modified, but all elaborated and
developed by successive experiments and experiences.   If it
should be objected that it is difficult, and we might add, virtually impossible, to make experiments in cases where social
phenomena are involved, one might answer that history, statistics and economics have by now gathered such a great store of
experimental data that enough are available to permit us to
begin our search.

Historians so far—following an opinion prevailing in the
public at large—have especially stressed the achievements of the
supreme heads of states, of people who stand at the vertex of
the political pyramid, and occasionally, too, the merits of the
lower strata in the pyramid, of the masses, who with their toil
and often with their blood have supplied the supreme heads
with the material means required for accomplishing the things
they accomplished.   If this new perception of the importance
of the ruling class is to gain a hold, we must, without denying
the great importance of what has been done at the vertex and
at the base of the pyramid, show that, except for the influence of
the intermediate social strata, neither of the others could have
accomplished very much of any significance and permanence,
since the type to which a political organism belongs and the
efficacy of its action depend primarily upon the manner in which
the intermediate strata are formed and function.   Once that
proof is obtained, it becomes evident that the supreme heads of
states have, in general, been able to leave enduring marks on
history only when they have managed to take the initiative in
timely reforms of ruling classes, and that the principal merit of
the lower classes has always lain in their inborn capacity for
producing from within themselves new elements that have been
able to rule them wisely.

CHAPTER XIII

TYPES OF POLITICAL ORGANIZATION

1. A glance at the various methods by which human societies, which have achieved a certain development and acquired a place in world history, have constituted themselves and have functioned furnishes perhaps the most suitable way of bringing out the importance that the ruling class has in any social organization. The anatomical differences, so to speak, that we find in such societies and the types into which the differences can be grouped correspond to the differing formations and the differing manners of functioning of their ruling classes.

An investigation something like the one we are about to make was undertaken some eighty years ago by Spencer, and after him by the members of his school. In trying to found their new science, which they called "sociology," following Comte's example, they thought it expedient to divide all political organizations into two fundamental types, the militant and the industrial. The inadequacies of that classification we noted above (chap. III, §§11–12), and we also saw that the germ of truth it contained was sterilized and lost because of a one-sided and incomplete view of the facts of which it was supposed to facilitate an analysis.

The outlook that governed the researches of the Spencerians, and the materials they used to build up the new science which they were trying to found, doubtless contributed very substantially to the barrenness of that particular classification, and in general of all corollary doctrines of Spencer and his followers. They started out on the assumption that the simplest and most primitive types of social organization, and therefore small tribes of savages or semisavages, reveal in embryonic form the various types of political organization that are to be found in peoples who have reached a certain level of civilization and have organized into political units of some magnitude. The Spencerians derived their facts, therefore, largely from the narratives of

338

travelers who had had closest contacts with the more primitive peoples.

Ignoring other objections to this method that might be made, it seems to us obvious that, as happens in the case of plants and animals, in which primitive types necessarily resemble each other because one simple cell will always be like another cell, differentiation in social organisms necessarily becomes greater in proportion as the organisms develop and grow complex. A small horde of savages, such as still wander about in the interior of Australia, will be peaceful or warlike according to the abundance or scantiness of its means of subsistence or the nature of the peoples with which it comes into contact; but political organization in such a horde will come down to the mere predominance of the strongest, most intelligent and shrewdest male, and generally of the best hunter or the best fighter—the experience of some old man or woman may well be held in a certain esteem. But it seems impossible that distinctions of class could exist in primitive social organisms of this type. Such distinctions can be based only upon a permanent differentiation in occupation.

There comes a time when the primitive stage has been definitely passed, when the subsistence of the horde is based on pastoral pursuits and even on a rudimentary agriculture. Such a horde is a tribe that includes, according to the case, various groups of huts, or even a town or a number of villages. A certain specialization of function begins to take shape, and therefore a certain order of social ranking. Even so, the political types that we meet in all such organisms, which have not passed the first phases of their development, present considerable similarities in all races and in all latitudes. Whether the tribe is still nomadic or seminomadic or already has a fixed abode, it will always have a chief who is supreme judge, military leader and priest (when the tribe has special protecting gods). But in all questions of importance this chief must consult a council of elders, and he makes no decisions without their consent. In questions of greater importance the decisions he reaches with the elders have to be approved by the assembly of all the members of the tribe—in other words, all the adults who are not slaves nor outsiders to whom the tribe has accorded its protection but whom it has not yet taken into its membership by adoption or by some other legal fiction.

That is the organization we find described in Homer.[1]   Almost identical is the organization that Tacitus met among the Germans of his day,[2] and we find the same thing in the Arab tribes of Asia or the Arabo-Berber tribes of North Africa, though in the latter, because of the prevailing Islamism, the chief has virtually lost all religious status.   Nor would any other type of organization be possible under such social conditions.   Though the chief belongs ordinarily to the richest and most influential family in the tribe, he cannot enforce obedience unless he has first come to an understanding with other members who are influential because of wealth and number of supporters or because of some special reputation for wisdom.   The mass of freemen, further, when gathered in assembly, does not take an active part in discussion, as a rule.   It limits itself to approving the proposals of the elders by applause or disapproving them by grumbling.   The leaders usually have taken the precaution of first coming to an understanding with each other, and, already skilled in the arts of mob leadership, they sometimes have apportioned the roles they are to recite beforehand.[3]

In these political organisms that are in an early stage of development, a rudimentary differentiation of classes usually begins to take form, based upon inheritance of economic and political position.   Often the position of high chief is hereditary; but, as happens today among the Arabo-Berber tribes, the son is not likely to succeed the father if he has by any chance shown himself incompetent to hold the supreme office in respect of intelligence, tact and character, and unless he is supported by large numbers of relatives and dependents and has a considerable private fortune.   So it is with the elders.   They are always esteemed for ancestral luster, but that alone is not enough to enable them to hold their political position.   In some tribes

---

[1] *Iliad* II.   This canto contains a detailed description of a council of elders and of a general assembly of warriors.   See also *Iliad* IX, and *Odyssey* II, VII.

[2] *Germania* XI: "*De minoribus rebus principes consultant, de majoribus omnes* (The leaders sit in council on minor matters; major matters are for all)."   By "all" he means all the warriors belonging to the tribe.

[3] So in the second canto of the *Iliad*.   Of the Germans Tacitus goes on to say: " . . . *Ea quoque, quorum penes plebem arbitrium est, principes praetractentur* (The leaders agree in advance on matters on which decision rests with the rank and file)."

there is no real chief because jealous elders will not tolerate one.
But there is almost always one among the elders who manages
to acquire a de facto leadership.   That seems to be the situation
today in a number of Arabo-Berber tribes in Cyrenaica.   Often
two families of influence are rivals for first place.   So originate
the cofs, or parties, that often throw the Arabo-Berber tribes
into turmoil.   And Homer relates that Antinous, son of Eupeithes
—one of the suitors—aspired to become king of Ithaca by killing
Telemachus, son of Ulysses.[1]   Of course, later on, when the
tribe has developed far enough to be a sort of nation, with some
tens of thousands of inhabitants, its political organization tends
to change; and the change occurs, in general, in the direction of a
greater   differentiation   between   social   classes.   The   elders
acquire greater influence and try to strengthen and systematize
their control over the masses.   Gallic populations of the time
of Caesar were farther advanced economically and politically
than the Germans of the time of Tacitus.   Caesar says of their
political organization: "Quite generally in Gaul the people who
count for something in numbers or prestige are of two classes
[Druids and knights].   The common people are virtually slaves.
They take no initiative of their own and are admitted to no
council."[2]   The Saxons of Charlemagne's day were certainly
farther developed socially than Tacitus's Germans.   Clearly
distinguishable among them are two classes, the nobles, or
edelings, and plain freemen, or frilings.

2. But a moment must have come—we shall probably never
know just when—when one tribe was able to absorb or subject
enough neighboring tribes to develop into a nation, create a
civilization and set up a political organization of some magnitude
and sufficiently compact to combine and coordinate individual
efforts and energies in considerable numbers, and to direct them
toward attaining common public ends, whether of war or peace.
This means that it must have been able to organize fairly large
and fairly well-disciplined armies and keep them in the field.
It may have been able to construct impressive buildings and,

[1] *Odyssey* XXII.

[2] *De bello gallico* VI, 13: "*In omni Gallia eorum hominum qui aliquo sunt
numero et honore sunt duo.   Nam plebs poene servorum habetur loco, quae nihil
audet per se, nulli adhibetur consilio.*"

more probably still, to increase the productivity of the soil by complex and carefully planned irrigation systems.

Nature could not have advanced by leaps and spurts in this development, either. The rise of the first great states must have followed long periods of gradual elaboration, during which the primitive town, which was the tribal capital, began to be a city. Progress in agriculture must have been such as to permit a relatively large number of men to live close together in a relatively small territory, and to allow political organization to become more vigorous and less rudimentary than anything described above. During this preparatory period certain arts and trades had probably advanced to some extent, and a first accumulation of capital had occurred in the form of stores of food or implements of war and peace. In that early day, writing, though still imperfect, must have begun to fix remembrances of the past and to facilitate transmission of the ideas and experience of one generation to generations following.

The first founding of a great empire that can be dated approximately by historical documents was that of the empire of Sargon I, called the Elder, king of Akkad in Chaldea, about 3000 B.C. It is possible that similar efforts may have been made a century or more earlier by the kings of Lagash and Sumer. Sargon's empire extended from the Persian Gulf to the Mediterranean and the Sinai peninsula. If it really was the most ancient of the great political organisms, it marks a decisive step in the history of human civilization. It seems to have lasted less than a century, however, falling apart into a number of rival kingdoms after the death of Naram-Sin, third in line of succession from Sargon. But the example set by that early conqueror was to find imitators, and other great empires were to rise in epochs still remote, first in lower, and later in upper, Mesopotamia. Babylonia was situated in an almost intermediate position between the upper and the lower valleys of the Euphrates and the Tigris. For sixteen centuries, the long era that elapses between Hammurabi and Nebuchadnezzar, the Babylonian empire very probably represented the greatest concentration of population, wealth and culture that the world had seen down to that time.

Perhaps some time before the day of Sargon, Menes, founder of the first Egyptian dynasty, had welded the little states, into which upper and lower Egypt had previously been subdivided, into a single state. So resulted an empire and a center of civilization which rivaled the Mesopotamian empire and were to last as long, with several periods of eclipse.

The little we know about the political organization of these two very ancient empires in Mesopotamia and Egypt indicates that at the vertex of the social pyramid stood a sovereign. He had a sacred character, offering sacrifices to the national deity in the name of the people. The deity held the guardianship of the empire. At Thebes, in Egypt, his name was Ammon, in Babylonia it was Marduk and in Nineveh, Asshur (see above, chap. III, §3). All civil and military powers were exercised in the name of the sovereign by a large body of officials, who were chosen ordinarily from the notables belonging to the race that had founded the empire. Subject peoples often kept their hereditary local leaders and preserved a certain autonomy. Sometimes they were wholly absorbed by the conquering people and blended with it. In such cases local officials were appointed and dismissed by the king directly, or rather by the court and in the court. It has been possible to establish that during the immensely long life of the Egyptian nationality the two systems replaced each other several times, according as the empire would grow stronger and more centralized for a time, or weaker and more centrifugal. The ruling class was usually made up of generals and priests, but both in Egypt and in Chaldea the priests were the repositories of all the learning of their day. They alone knew the laws, and the administration of the law devolved upon them. There were even cases where the high priests managed to replace secular powers and exercised royal authority. So in upper Egypt, in the ninth century B.C., the high priests of Amen exercised what today would be called temporal power.

As for the system of recruiting civil and military officials, it has been possible to determine that methods varied widely, especially in ancient Egypt during the three thousand years, more or less, of its history. As we have seen (chap. II, §§6, 8), there were periods when exact knowledge of hieroglyphic writing was the key that opened the doors to higher offices, whether civil or military, and there were cases where commoners attained high rank.[1] But as a rule, even if there were no really closed

---

[1] Mosca, *Teorica dei governi*, chap. II, §2.

castes in Egypt, the social hierarchy did have great stability, and a man was the child of his father rather than of his own works. In Babylonia, slaves were numerous, and almost all Egyptian documents and monuments testify to the luxury that the upper class displayed both in this life and in the next, while an intense and often forced manual labor was the normal lot of the lowly placed.

Greek writers incidentally throw a good deal of light on the social and political conditions that prevailed in the Persian empire, the last great government to flourish in the Near East before the Christian era. Greece had frequent contacts with it. It appears that birth had great importance in the constitution of the political hierarchy. Herodotus relates that the false Smerdis was able to become king by making people believe that he was the son of Cyrus. After he was murdered, seven Persian noblemen occupied the throne in turn. According to Xenophon, when the younger Cyrus died at Cunaxa, the Greek mercenaries offered the crown to Ariaeus, commander of the Persian troops that had fought with Cyrus. Ariaeus refused, on the ground that he was not noble enough, that the Persian grandees would never accept him as king. The Greeks also preserve the fact that the Persian empire was at bottom a more or less voluntary confederation of peoples of differing and more or less ancient civilizations, under the hegemony of Persia. Some peoples, such as the Armenians, the Cilicians and the citizens of Tyre, kept their autonomy and their national sovereigns. Others, such as the Lydians and the Babylonians, were governed by satraps, who were chosen from among great nobles at the Persian court of Susa. Over them the court kept strict surveillance. Almost all the subject nations paid annual tribute to the court of Susa, according to their wealth, and they furnished auxiliary troops as required. In the full midst of subject provinces, certain mountaineer populations maintained a savage de facto independence. That was the case with the Karduchians, who correspond, roughly, to the Kurds of today.[1]

In the Middle Ages, the Mohammedan state was founded largely on the pattern of the Near Eastern state. No doubt it borrowed some few details of its administrative and political

[1] Xenophon, *Anabasis.* See above, chap. IV, §2.

system from Byzantium, but to a much greater extent it followed the examples and traditions of the neo-Persian empire of the Sassanids.[1] Persian influence became preponderant especially under the Abbassid caliphs. The very title of the prime minister, "vizier," was of Persian origin. However, in spite of the stiff religious cement that was the strength of its dominant class, in spite of the fact also that at certain periods it developed a high level of culture, the Mohammedan state had innate weaknesses that inevitably produced a more or less rapid disintegration of the great political organisms which the overpowering impetuousness of the early Islamic generations had created. Almost all social and political relations in the Mussulman world were regulated by a religious code, in other words by the Koran. This, in the long run, arrested Mohammedan development. But, ignoring that, one of the most frequent causes for the rapid breaking up of the Mussulman states was the practice of allowing governors of separate provinces to conscript troops, and to collect directly the taxes that paid for them. Such a concentration of power in their hands made it easy for them to create personal followings in their armies, so that they could proclaim their independence, or at least become independent in fact, though paying a nominal deference to the caliph. This defect was noted by Averroës, one of the strongest intellects that Mohammedan civilization produced in its best days.[2]

China, too, down to a few years ago, was organized politically along the lines of the Near Eastern state, but over the course of long centuries she brought the type to a level of perfection that it attained nowhere else. This was due to the fact that Chinese civilization was based on a nonreligious, positive morality, to the great unity of culture that the Chinese peoples achieved over many centuries of common history and, finally, to the democratic system of recruiting officials, who were appointed and promoted by competitive examination. In spite of these good points, the strength of the Chinese state was almost never proportionate to its size, and the inferiority of its political machine became promptly manifest once it came into contact with modern European states. In order to conserve her independence and her ancient national spirit, Japan was obliged rapidly

---

[1] Huart, *Histoire des Arabes*, vol. I, chap. XIII.

[2] Renan, *Averroès et l'Averroïsme*, chap. II, p. 161.

to overhaul her political, administrative and military organization and conform to the models that the countries of European civilization supplied.

The organization of empires of the Near Eastern type has always proved inferior to the organization of modern states of European civilization. It was inferior to the organization of the ancient Roman Empire and, in many respects, even to the organization of the little Hellenic states of the classical period. However, the vicissitudes of the ancient empires of the Near East are gradually coming to light, as the old hieroglyphic and cuneiform inscriptions are deciphered. It would be unfair to forget that through them mankind was able to accumulate the first stores of experience and wealth that were required for making intellectual and economic progress possible. On the banks of the Tigris, the Euphrates and the Nile the groups of elders that had once ruled scattered tribes fused for the first time, and organized real ruling classes which had a chance to conceive and develop the idea that there were great interests that could be common to millions of human beings. In those classes, for the first time, a process of selection was able to operate whereby a certain number of individuals could be freed of the material cares of life. Sheltered by the organization of which they were a part from the greed and the violence of those who, in every age and in every society, are eager to get the best positions for themselves, such privileged individuals were enabled to devote their time to observing man and the world he lives in, and to elaborating the first rudiments of a morality for the family and for social groups. Those rudiments we find stated about four thousand years ago in the Code of Hammurabi, which already sanctions many of the rules that the individual has to observe if society is to endure. The ancient Egyptian Book of the Dead is in parts older than the Code of Hammurabi, some of its texts going back to the eleventh dynasty, and the most recent ones to the eighteenth (about 1400 B.C.). This collection of sacred precepts was placed in tombs, perhaps as a sacred gesture, perhaps so that the dead might have some guidance in the life to come. The texts formulate for the first time a number of moral precepts and rules of brotherly consideration that later were to become basic in the great universal religions—for example: "Feed the hungry," "Give the thirsty to drink," "Cheat not the worker of his wage,"

"Eschew falsehood," "Bear no false witness." In those empires, finally, the first trials were made in the difficult art of public administration. That art, in the last analysis, comes down to enabling a great society, with the least possible constraint, to see to it that the activity which each individual carries on spontaneously for his own advantage shall be useful to the group as a whole.

3. If European civilization has been able to create a type of political organization that is profoundly different from that of the Near Eastern empire, the fact is due in very large part to the intellectual legacy left by Greece and Rome. There are of course wide differences between a great modern European or American state and the Athenian or Spartan state, or the Roman state during the republican period; but had it not been for the writings of political thinkers of the classical age, whose minds were formed by the political institutions they could see operating before their eyes, modern Europe, and the countries that were colonized by Europeans beyond the seas, would not have adopted the political systems that distinguish them so sharply from the Asiatic empires.

Greece borrowed many elements of her civilization from the nearest of the Asiatic empires and from Egypt. The first infiltrations must have taken place during a prehistoric period, when a pre-Hellenic civilization flowered, with Crete as its center, and then vanished, leaving only vague memories of itself. But this civilization developed the rudiments of agricultural science and made other material advances. Such things may deteriorate, once they have made their way into the customs of a country, but they seem never wholly to disappear, even if the nation or civilization that first invented or adopted them is destroyed. Other infiltrations from Egypt and the Near East came in the period when a truly Hellenic culture was reawakening, in other words by the beginning of the ninth century B.C. At that time the Phoenicians were the main intermediaries between Greece, Egypt and the Near East. On this occasion the new seeds that were transplanted to the soil of Hellas bore somewhat different, and in many respects better, fruits than did the plant from which they came, especially in the respects of art, science and political organization.

The Homeric kingdom, which we find at the dawn of the second Greek civilization, was not very different from the semi-primitive type of social organization that appears in all peoples which have ascended only the first rungs of the ladder that leads to the great modern political structures. The Homeric king in many respects resembled the chief of the Arabian or Germanic tribe. His authority was primarily moral, and it had a religious aspect. He governed with the aid of a council of notables and, in weightier crises, summoned his warriors, or the freemen who belonged to the tribe, to an assembly. Yet, in a space of time that cannot be greater than three centuries, this type of political organization, which had few unusual traits about it, is transformed into the highly original Greek city of the classical era.

As for the causes of this development, it may be noted first of all that the topography of Greece hampered the formation of great empires such as were able to rise in the broad, level valleys of the Tigris, the Euphrates, the Nile and the Yellow River. The surface of the Greek peninsula is so broken that every district, every town (with the territory round about), is cut off by fairly serious natural barriers from neighboring districts. The Greek tribes, therefore, acquired relatively stable residences, and private ownership of land had become customary by the time of Homer. These two circumstances allowed agriculture to develop so that a large population was able to subsist on a small territory. A Greek city of the classical period generally lay a good day's journey from its nearest neighbor. Its territory rarely exceeded a thousand square miles. Given the agricultural development of the period, that amount of land could support thirty or forty thousand persons, including of course slaves and resident aliens. The village or primitive town became a populous city very easily. Attica had a territory of about two thousand square miles. In its heyday its population may have exceeded two hundred thousand. Syracuse and Sparta also had larger territories and populations than the normal Greek city. Now Athens, Syracuse and Sparta were the largest and strongest states of the ancient Hellenic world.[1]

The powerful organization of the ancient Greek clans also may have contributed to the different political development of Greece

[1] On the population of ancient Greece, see Beloch, *Die Bevölkerung der Griechisch-Römischen Welt*, chap. III, pp. 54–107.

as compared with the Near East. Every group of families that considered itself descended from a common ancestor retained a certain amount of political and religious autonomy in the beginning, so that the city was a sort of confederation of clans. But besides these factors, there must have been others of an intellectual and moral order which, because of the remoteness of the time and the dearth of documents, we cannot discern or analyze very exactly. These factors we are forced to define with a very generic and imperfect phrase, as products of the peculiar "genius" of the Hellenic stock and, later on, of the Italic.

In any event, the early Greek kingship eventually began to lose ground, and it had fallen into desuetude in Hellas perhaps less than a century after Homer's time. Hesiod already speaks of kings far less respectfully than Homer does. He who was called "the peasant's poet" accuses them of trafficking in justice, describes them outright as "devourers of gifts" and warmly recommends that his brother Perseus have nothing to do with them. The king either disappeared or lost his importance altogether in the council of notables. The city came to be governed by the heads of the phratries, or clans, or by groups of the oldest and most influential families, who owned the best lands and had them cultivated by slaves or by the throng of ne'er-do-wells and refugees from other countries whom every city used to accept, once an influential citizen could be found to accord them patronage. The dominant political organ, therefore, was the ancient "senate," or council of elders, in which the principal families were represented. The old assembly of all the citizens probably continued to function alongside the council of elders. But, because of a growing concentration of property and the large number of clients that the leading families could control, the council retained, for some time at least, the ascendancy that it had enjoyed in the monarchical era.

In a period that must correspond, roughly, to the seventh century B.C., progress in agriculture and an incipient commerce must have provided many of the descendants of resident aliens of long standing with the means to create independent economic positions for themselves. They began to crave admission to citizenship, that being the only way to share in the functions of government and to escape the onerous supervision of the elders. The movement must have been seconded by the poorer and obscurer families of old citizens, who also had an interest in fighting the oligarchical system which the richer and more illustrous families had instituted.

These causes are of an economic order more especially. There were others. A change in armament and military tactics occurred about this time and must have contributed to the democratization of the Greek city. War chariots had been in use in the Homeric age, when they were the arm, so to speak, that decided the outcome of a battle. Only very wealthy persons could afford chariots. But now they came to be replaced by plain cavalry, and later on by hoplites, or heavily armed infantrymen. Hoplites formed the backbone of the Greek armies during the classical period. The equipment of a hoplite, though relatively costly, was within the reach of a man of moderate income. In Draco's constitution, which antedated Solon's, participation in public office by all who are supplied with arms appears as a long-recognized right.

A period of civil conflict ensued, during which the losing parties often had to emigrate. Traces of this period are found in the poets of the age, notably in the verses of Theognis of Megara. It was at times broken by dictatorships of popular leaders, who were called "tyrants." Such conflicts generally ended in compromises of the sort that Solon effected in Athens in the early decades of the sixth century B.C., and the compromises resulted in that constitution of the Greek city-state of the classical age which was destined to have such a great significance in the political history of the world.

The bases of these compromises were in the main two: First, admission to citizenship of a certain number of descendants of old resident aliens or emancipated slaves. There was no application of this principle, however, to cases arising subsequent to the reform of the constitution. New resident aliens were, on the whole, still barred from citizenship, so that even in democratic Athens the sons of a citizen and a woman who was not of Athenian birth could not be admitted to citizenship.[1] Second, explicit recognition that sovereign power rested with the assembly of all the citizens. Over this route the citizen assembly gradually absorbed almost all the old prerogatives of the clan, which the heads of aristocratic families had formerly exercised over people

[1] Aristotle, *Constitution of Athens*, 42.

of their own blood. The council of elders lost prestige proportionately and as a rule it was transformed into a senate, which was very often a direct emanation of the assembly, the assembly having the right to determine its membership.

Classical antiquity never knew that clean-cut separation of legislative, executive and judiciary powers which, theoretically at least, is one of the outstanding characteristics of modern constitutions. Even in the period of the empire in Rome, complete separation of judiciary and administrative functions, which is a most familiar concept to us, had not been introduced.[1] The Roman praetor could exercise functions that would now be called legislative. But in classical Hellas, what would now correspond to the sovereign power par excellence, in other words the legislative power, was entrusted almost exclusively to the assembly of citizens, while what we would call executive and judiciary functions were delegated to bodies, or individuals, that were almost always elected by all the citizens, or chosen by lot from among all citizens or specified classes of citizens. Aristotle enumerates the many public offices that were considered necessary for the proper functioning of the Greek commonwealth. They busied thousands of citizens, and the incumbents were for the most part chosen by lot.[2]

Characteristic of almost all the constitutions of the Hellenic cities was temporary tenure of office, the incumbents generally being renewed at least once a year. Just as common was the rule that more than one person should exercise the given public function. This custom was designed to provide that the power of an individual should always be controlled and limited by the equal power of one or more other individuals. That was the idea of the two consuls in Rome. The principle was so conscientiously applied that, in many Greek cities, command of the army or navy in war was entrusted to a number of polemarchs or navarchs who functioned in rotation. Characteristic again of the political and administrative organization of the Greek state was the almost complete lack of what would now be called salaried officeholders. It is interesting to note that a number of judiciary and executive prerogatives which were held to be of great importance were ordinarily reserved for

[1] Hartmann, *Der Untergang der Antiken Welt*, chap. II, p. 46.
[2] *Constitution of Athens*, 42–62.

the popular assembly.   The assembly almost always retained the
right to declare war, to make peace and to apply the heavier
penalties—death or exile.   At the very least an appeal to the
popular assembly was allowed in these latter cases.

There was no standing army.   As Aristotle reports,[1] on
reaching the age of eighteen all ephebi (sons of Athenian citizens)
served a year in military training and then two more years as
armed guards on the coast and at other strategic points in Attica.
At bottom, therefore, Athens had what would now be called
"three years' service."   However, there was no permanent
body of officers.   The people merely chose, each year, five
honorable citizens over forty years of age who managed the
affairs of the corps of ephebi and superintended the commissary—
each ephebus received four obols a day for his maintenance.
Then there were two instructors in gymnastics, who taught the
manual of arms and commanded military drill.   There were no
standard regulations for discipline and no military penal code.
In times of peace at least, the ephebus was subject to the same
jurisdictions as any other citizen.   There is no indication in the
history of Athens that would lead one to suppose that the body
of ephebi had anything to do with what we would now call
police duty, the task of upholding the government or of maintaining public order.

4. Beginning with Herodotus, all the Greek writers of the
classical period recognize the existence of three forms of government—monarchy, aristocracy and democracy.   Herodotus puts
into the mouths of three of the Persian nobles who killed the
false Smerdis a dispute as to the merits and defects of the
three forms.[2]   The anecdote has little plausibility as history,
but it proves at least that as early as the middle of the fifth
century B.C., more than a century before Aristotle began to
write, the Greeks (not the Persians) were familiar with the
three categories and were exercising their critical talents in
debating the advantages and drawbacks of each type of government.   That the thinkers of classical Hellas should have stressed
the importance of the monarchical system among the possible
forms of government is readily comprehensible.   Memories

[1] *Ibid.* 42.
[2] *Histories* III.

of the Homeric monarchy were prominent in their literary tradition. There had been recent examples of tyrannies—they were especially common in the Hellenic colonies, in Magna Graecia and in Sicily. The old patriarchal monarchy itself survived in remote corners of Epirus. Traces of it lingered tenaciously on in Sparta. The Greeks, finally, were in frequent contact with barbarian peoples, who almost always had kings.

But the Hellenic state of the classical age fluctuated almost always between aristocracy and democracy. Those were the two constant tendencies that were in perpetual conflict within the Greek city-state. Aristotle, in fact, devotes a good part of his immortal *Politics* to analyzing that inevitable alternation.[1]

It is important to note that the Greek conception of aristocracy differed considerably from the Roman conception, which in turn has colored modern usage of the term. For the Greeks of the classical period, the notion of aristocracy was not inseparably bound up with the notion of hereditary power, whereby public offices descend from generation to generation in the same families. Aristocracy meant simply that offices were entrusted, exclusively or preferably, to men who stood out from the mass of other citizens through wealth or exceptional merit, whether or not they descended from ancestors who had been equally prominent. So true is this that Aristotle explicitly distinguishes aristocracy from "eugenism," which would mean government by men of families of long-standing prominence, or "men of family," pure and simple.[2] And, in fact, it happened not infrequently that some "man of family" would lead the people against an "aristocratic" party composed in the majority of men of recent fortune. That was the case with Pericles.

But as regards the conflict between aristocracy and democracy, one may say that the Greek state had an aristocratic system whenever wealth succeeded in prevailing over number among the citizens and a democratic system whenever number prevailed over wealth. Under the aristocratic system, public offices, or at least the more important public offices, when they were not actually restricted by law to citizens with specified property qualifications, paid no salaries. They were accessible only to

[1] See, especially, VI, VII, VIII.

[2] *Ibid.* III, 7, 7; VIII, 1, 7. In the latter passage Aristotle says: "For good birth is virtue and ancient wealth"—ancient in the family, that is.

people who did not have to work for a living in person and day
by day. There was no fee for attending meetings of the assembly, and these, accordingly, were unattended by the poor but
assiduously attended by the rich and their clients. When the
system was democratic, public offices were remunerative, and
attendance at the assembly entitled one to a counter, which
could be cashed.

Under aristocratic regimes, public offices were almost always
elective, because at periods of elections the wealthy combined
in more or less secret associations ("hetairies") and with plenty of
rustling by their clients they could easily manage to concentrate
their votes on their own candidates and to outvote the poor,
who had no such resources for organizing. Under democratic
regimes, public offices were generally distributed by lot among the
citizens. That system was justly regarded as absurd, even by
thinkers of ancient Greece; but after all it was the only system
whereby the influence of reputation, personal connections and
financed electioneering could be eliminated.

As we have already seen, since the poor were always more
numerous than the rich, aristocratic governments leaned heavily
on clienteles, which were kept up through the patronage that
the man of wealth bestowed on a certain number of the poor,
and through the lavishness with which those who were following
political careers showered hospitality upon the less pecunious
citizens in the mass. Aristotle expressly notes that Pericles
was not as rich as Cimon, son of Miltiades and leader of the
aristocratic party. He could not compete with Cimon on the
terrain of expenditure. He therefore made a bid to the poor by
having many posts, which had formerly carried no stipend,
paid for out of the public treasury.[1] That system, making the
proper allowances, is not exceptional even today in countries
that are democratically ruled. Well known to politicians is
the trick of offsetting the influence of private wealth by the
squandering of public wealth.

Abuse of aristocracy in the Greek state generally lay in the
direction of exaggerating the system—that is to say, in transforming aristocracy into oligarchy, in which a closed clique
jealously barred from public offices all elements that were not of
the clique, whatever their wealth or personal merit. Other

[1] *Constitution of Athens*, **27**.

frequent abuses resulted when the monopoly of public magistracies was utilized for protecting and increasing the private fortunes of the governing group and of their associates and clients. This was managed more particularly by seeing to it that judgments in civil and criminal cases were handed down by persons who were affiliated with the faction that was ruling the state, or who were loyal to it.

Vice versa, at times when poverty was self-respecting, and a majority of the poor would succeed in keeping free of clientage to the rich, abuses of democracy would readily develop. Important public offices would then be given to the men on whom the lots fell, no account being taken of their capacities and aptitudes for filling them. Since the exercise of all public functions was remunerated, the treasury was soon so overloaded that in order to meet the enormous expenditures, burdensome taxes had to be levied on the rich and well-to-do. These amounted to masked confiscations of private fortunes, and the public economy was accordingly upset. Aristotle calculates that in Athens in the day of Pericles about twenty thousand citizens were subsidized by the public treasury. This meant that virtually the entire citizenry was transformed into a class of state pensioners.[1] That was possible for a certain length of time partly because of the income which the city derived from the silver mines of Laurion, but mainly because, as Aristotle again states, the contributions that the allies paid in to Athens for the prosecution of the war against Persia were regularly misappropriated. This misappropriation was not by any means the least influential cause among the many that brought on the long and disgraceful war which was soon to break out among the Hellenes, and which came to be called the Peloponnesian War. In graver cases, some popular demagogue would kill off the rich, or else banish them, confiscate their property and divide up the loot among his partisans or among the foreign mercenaries who supported him. This would mean that the normal functioning of the constitution was suspended and that there would be a dictatorship by a leader sustained by a faction. This was called "tyranny," and the Greek writers unanimously describe it as the worst of all forms of government.[2]

[1] *Ibid.* 24.
[2] Aristotle, *Politics;* Plato, *Republic.*

One need hardly say that the normal functioning of the Hellenic state required a high level of economic prosperity and a high grade of intelligence and moral integrity in the majority of citizens. Such things are not easy to procure. In fact, this type of political organization lasted in full efficiency for less than two centuries, that is to say, from the beginning of the fifth century B.C. to the close of the fourth, a period that coincided with the maximum development of Hellenic civilization. Since there was no regular bureaucracy, and no permanent police force entrusted with the execution of the laws, the majority of citizens had to possess a strong sense of legality and the high degree of public spirit that would induce them to sacrifice their individual interests to the public interest. Such virtues therefore were inculcated and celebrated in every possible way by Greek education. That explains in large part the importance that Plato and Aristotle attach to the education of the young, and education was already regarded as one of the functions of the state in ancient Greece. It was also indispensable that a certain numerical proportion should be maintained between citizens and slaves. If the citizens were very few, the slaves were likely to rebel, as the helots often did at Sparta. On the other hand, if the population of citizens grew too large, then large numbers of them inevitably became paupers and lost interest in the maintenance of their institutions. With an eye to these difficulties, Plato, in the *Republic*, proposed the abolition of private property, and consequently of the family, at least for the ruling class. With greater practical insight, Aristotle recommended building up small property, justly noting that the door stood open to all upheavals when a few very wealthy citizens faced a host of poor ones, who had arms and votes at their disposal but no interest in defending the existing order of things.[1]

By the very character of its organic constitution, the Greek state was destined to remain a small affair, its territory never exceeding the limits of a town of moderate size. If the ancient Greeks used one word, "polis," to indicate both the state and the city, it was because they could hardly conceive of a state organized in the Hellenic manner that was bigger than one city and the immediately adjacent territory that supplied its means of subsistence. To be sure, when Alexander the Great con-

[1] *Politics*, VI, 9.

quered the Persian empire, Greek civilization spread to states of large size, such as the realms of Syria, Egypt and Macedonia. But those were great military monarchies, and their organization had nothing to do with the political type with which Plato and Aristotle deal. In those monarchies, besides, the Hellenic element was confined to a small ruling class.

Greece proper never knew a great state for the reason that the Greek city could not become one. The basis of its organization was the assembly of citizens. In order to attend regularly, one had to live in the city, or in its immediate environs. Nor could the assembly itself be too large. Otherwise the major portion of those present could not hear what the orators were saying. That is why Plato, in the *Republic*, limits the number of citizens to five thousand. In a plan he devised for an ideal constitution, Hippodamus of Miletus suggested ten thousand, and of the ten thousand only a third were to be supplied with arms and so qualified, as Aristotle observes,[1] to take part in public affairs. In the same connection Aristotle speaks of another ideal constitution that was put forward by Phaleas of Chalcedon, proposing an equal distribution of land among the citizens. The Stagirite, again with much good sense, emphasizes the difficulty of establishing such a system and especially of keeping it going afterward. Aristotle himself does not specify a number of citizens. He says that there might be as many as could hear a human voice, and not the voice of Stentor, either; and he adds that all citizens should be able to know each other, in order to judge of each others' aptitudes for public office, a thing that would be impossible if the citizens were too numerous.[2] In her best days, Athens probably had more than thirty thousand citizens, but that was an exception. Syracuse had even more than that, but at Syracuse, beginning with the fourth century B.C., the normal organization of the Greek city was no longer able to function. In the day of Aristotle, Sparta had fallen to as few as two or three thousand citizens,[3] and could arm, he thought, not more than a thousand fighters. That estimate was probably too low. Aristotle admits that in earlier periods Sparta may have had around ten thousand citizens. The number of warriors, of

[1] *Ibid.* II, 5.
[2] *Ibid.* IV, 4.
[3] *Ibid.* II, 6.

course, would always be smaller than the number of citizens. As for Athens, Beloch thinks that in 431 B.C., at the outbreak of the Peloponnesian War, the period of the city's greatest prosperity, the number of citizens must have reached 45,000, including cleruchs (Athenian colonists who lived in other cities).[1]

To compensate for the impossibility of forming a great state, while keeping the organization of the Hellenic city intact, ancient Greece attempted to apply the principle of hegemony, the supremacy of a large city over a number of smaller ones. The remedy soon showed its awkwardness and inadequacy. As happened with Athens after the battle of Aegospotami, and with Sparta after Leuctra, the subject cities reclaimed their independence the moment the dominant capital suffered a reverse. Colonies themselves increased the power of the mother city but slightly, because they too were cities and therefore so many states in themselves, retaining, if anything, a religious or merely sympathetic bond with the city in which they originated.

One may reasonably wonder that many of the fundamental concepts which later came to serve as bases for the constitutions of the great modern states of European type should first have been worked out and embodied in such tiny political organisms. To tell the truth, the concept of political liberty was not altogether alien to the peoples of the ancient East and of Egypt. But to them it meant simply that one people should not be subject to another of different race, religion and civilization, and that those who ruled a country should be men of that country and not foreigners. The concept was never interpreted in the sense that a national governmental system could be thought of as servitude from the mere fact that it was absolute and arbitrary. The Old Testament shows that the Hebrews considered themselves enslaved when they were subject to the Amalekites or Philistines, or when they were transported by Nebuchadnezzar to Babylon; but not when they had a national king, though the harsh and arbitrary government of their monarchs was very well described to the elders of Israel by Samuel.

It was in ancient Greece that, for the first time, only that people was regarded as politically free which was subject to laws that the majority of its citizens had approved, and to magistrates to whom the majority itself had delegated fixed powers for fixed

[1] Bevölkerung, and see Gomme, *The Population of Athens.*

periods. It was in Greece that, for the first time, authority was transmitted not from above downward, not from the man who stood at the apex of the political hierarchy to those who were subject to him, but from below upward, from those over whom authority was exercised to those who were to exercise it.

In other words, Hellenic civilization was the first to assert, as against the divine right of kings, the human right of peoples to govern themselves. Hellenic civilization was the first to cease looking upon the law as an emanation of the divine will, or of persons acting in the name of the divine will, and to think of it as a human and variable interpretation of a people's will. The authority that the Greek state wielded over its citizens was great. Sometimes it was disposed to regulate even the details of family life. But authority always had to be exercised in accord with norms which a majority had accepted.

As we have already seen, those fundamental concepts were adapted as far as possible to European societies of the eighteenth and nineteenth centuries, and they have helped effectively to modify European political systems. They have made their influence felt wherever there have been peoples of European origin, and today, through the intellectual contacts that the East is having with Europe and America, they are reverberating in Japan and China and among other peoples of Asiatic civilization.

CHAPTER XIV

EVOLUTION OF POLITICAL ORGANIZATION

1. The political constitution of the Italic city had many points in common with the constitution of the Greek city. This may have been due to racial affinities between the Italic and Hellenic peoples, as has often been suggested. Through the Greek colonies in Sicily and Magna Graecia, Greek civilization may have made its influence felt upon the Italic peoples in an age much more remote than the period during which those colonies were conquered by the Romans.

However that may be, in the primitive Italian city too, we find a king, a council of notables and a popular assembly. There are references in the Roman histories to the existence of the kingly office among the Etruscans and Latins at a period when Rome still had kings, or had only recently driven them out—the case of Porsena, for instance. Veii seems still to have had a king when it was captured by the Romans in 395 B.C. Then later on, at the end of the fourth century B.C., and in the early decades of the third, when the really historic period begins and the Italic populations are being forced to recognize the supremacy of Rome, we find no trace of hereditary royalty—it seems to have disappeared everywhere among them. What we do find are rivalries between aristocracy and plebs. They are in full swing. It was the general policy of Rome to favor the aristocrats in these quarrels in other cities. She very soundly reasoned that her supremacy could more safely be rested upon such elements, as more inclined to conservatism and social tranquillity. The better to attain that end, she granted citizenship quite freely to notables in the federated cities.

In a remote age Rome herself had her kings, her senate, composed of the heads of the various patrician clans that had combined in a federation to form the early city, and also her popular assembly, or comitium. Then hereditary royalty was abolished, as in Greece, and replaced by the consulate and other magistracies. These were elective, temporary and almost always "multiple," the same function being simultaneously entrusted to different persons. In Rome, too, conflicts soon arose between the old patrician citizenry, made up of members of the ancient gentes, and a new plebeian citizenry, made up largely of descendants of settlers from other places and of freed slaves. For a time, virtually two cities seem to have coexisted within the confines of the urbs, with magistracies peculiar to each. Then the two cities almost completely fused in an organization that closely resembled the Hellenic type which we have just considered. This Roman constitution, like the Greek, was designed to fit a city-state, but it was nevertheless distinguished by a number of profoundly original details.

First among them, and the most fertile in practical consequences, was a broadening of the right of citizenship, its prerogatives being subdivided in such a way that, alongside of the full-fledged citizenship, there was a partial citizenship whereby a resident could enjoy some of the prerogatives of the citizen and little by little acquire the assimilation that was necessary if he were to become equal before the law with the members of the Roman city proper. The prerogatives of the full citizen (*civis optimi juris*) were the *jus commercii*, the *jus conubii*, the *jus suffragii* and the *jus honorum*. The first bestowed enjoyment of all the private rights of the Roman citizen. The second allowed marriages with Roman citizens, male or female. The third gave the right to participate in the comitia, the fourth the right to hold public office. The first two rights were granted quite readily. They served ordinarily as a preparation for obtaining the other rights.

This device admitted of such an extension of the Roman citizenship that many persons enjoyed it who lived so far from Rome that, even having the right, they could scarcely avail themselves of the privilege of attending the comitia. In a word, Rome found a way to snap the fatal circle that had prevented the Greek city from expanding. By granting citizenship to people who lived far from Rome, she built steps, so to speak, in the abyss which, in Greece, had separated the man who was a citizen from the man who was not. In that way Rome was able to have 292,000 citizens inscribed on her rolls by 265 B.C., the year before the outbreak of the first Punic War, and despite the losses she suffered

in that war she still had 240,000 citizens in 246, in the interval
between the first and second Punic Wars. So she was in a position to recruit the many legions which enabled her to survive the
terrible trials she suffered during Hannibal's invasion of Italy.[1]
Continuing along the same lines, Rome was able little by little to
assimilate a vast territory and "make a city of the world":

Urbem fecisti quod prius orbis erat.

So sang a native poet of Romanized Gaul in the fifth century
A.D., the age that witnessed the death agony of the empire.[2]

The second original trait in the republican constitution of
ancient Rome lay in the considerably more aristocratic character
which it succeeded in maintaining as compared with the Greek.
The Roman senate eventually ceased to be an assembly of the
patresfamilias of the old clans. Its members were chosen by a
"censor" from among men who had already held high offices.
Not till a period relatively recent were the comitia centuriata
reformed in such a way as to deprive the highly propertied classes
of their preponderance in them; and quite tardily also were the
comitia tributa, in which numbers prevailed decidedly over
property, admitted to parity with the comitia centuriata. A
democratic reform of the comitia centuriata, in the direction of
removing them from the control of the propertied classes, was
carried out in the period between 241 and 218 B.C., in other words
between the end of the first Punic War and the beginning of the
second. Equalization between the plebiscites voted by the
comitia tributa and the laws voted by the comitia centuriata
is said to have been established by a certain Hortensian law of the
year 286, but authorities reserve doubts on that point. For
that matter, a good many uncertainties linger about Roman
constitutional law, perhaps because we try to find in it the clean-
cut delimitation of functions between the various organs of state
to which we have become accustomed in modern constitutions.[3]

But however the comitia were constituted, a law could not be
passed by them except in the form in which the magistrates had

---

[1] De Sanctis, *Storia dei Romani*, vol. III, p. 193.

[2] Rutilius *Itinerarium* I, 66. Claudian, a contemporary of Rutilius, uses a
similar expression, *In secundum consulatum Stiliconis*, 150–160.

[3] See, on this matter, Pacchioni, *Corso di diritto romano*, vol. I, period II,
chap. IV.

proposed it and the senate, with all its prestige, had ratified it. As for elective offices, custom rather than law prevented their being conferred on real commoners down to the last days of the republic. The military tribunate was the first step that aspirants to a political career had to mount. Down to the Punic Wars that grade was open, as a matter of practice, only to members of the equestrian order, and it seems safe to assume that the few centurions who attained the rank of military tribunes during the Punic Wars were able to meet the property qualifications of the equestrian.[1] Ferrero has soundly noted that during the period of the civil wars, except in the case of Caius Marius, who, for that matter, seems to have had equestrian origins, armies were always commanded by members of the great Roman families.[2]

Another thing: Many citizens lived so far from Rome that a law provided that a trinundinum, an interval of sixteen or seventeen (or, as others claim, of twenty-four) days had to elapse between the date of the convocation of the comitia and the date of their meeting. However the term trinundinum may be defined by modern scholars, it represented a period that was long enough for the senate to find any number of urgent cases that required its attention. This helped to multiply the functions and expand the authority of the senate, which was in a position to convene much more rapidly. Over this route the senate came to hold, by the end of the republic, virtually exclusive control of financial and foreign policy.

2. Following the day of the Gracchi—during the last century of the republic, in other words—this aristocratic organization was modified or, rather, became unable to function normally. It became manifest that a city-state, organized along the lines of the Hellenic type, could not become a world-wide political body, however much it might be tinkered with or expanded. The comitia represented the legal assemblage of the whole sovereign people in the forum of Rome. That must already have seemed pretty much of a legal fiction by the time citizenship was extended to the peoples of Italy (88 B.C.). It became a grand jest when a large part, if not an actual majority, of the

---

[1] De Sanctis, *Storia dei Romani*, vol. III, pp. 344–346.
[2] *Grandezza e decadenza di Roma*, vol. I, p. 112.

citizens were scattered over the whole Mediterranean basin, far
from Italian shores. A census taken in 28 B.C., three years
after the battle of Actium, placed the number of citizens at
4,164,000. The census of the year 8 B.C. counted 4,233,000.
The last census of which we have any information took place in
A.D. 48, under the emperor Claudius. It counted 5,894,012
citizens. Males under seventeen years of age and females were
not included in the count. The figures of the year 28 B.C., therefore, already corresponded to a population of between fourteen
and fifteen million persons, a much larger population than Italy
could then accommodate, especially if one thinks of slaves and
foreign residents.[1]

Nor was the annual alternation in public offices any longer
practicable, once the incumbents had to be absent from Italy
for years, in remote provinces where they were invested with
almost absolute power. For the same reason the armies lost
their character as annually recruited citizen militias. Gradually
they came to be more like armies of professional soldiers, who
were more closely bound to the general who commanded them
for year after year than to the state at large. It was inevitable,
therefore, that the old civitas romana should be transformed into
a political organism that would be held together and governed
by a professional bureaucracy and a standing army.

This transformation took place when, to use ordinary language,
the empire replaced the republic. One can see no prospect of an
end to the dispute as to the actual intentions that Augustus and
his confederates had when they inaugurated the new regime.
One thing is certain: They were not trying to replace the old
system with either an absolute monarchy or a limited monarchy,
as we understand those terms to-day. But it is just as certain
that the new arrangements they introduced marked a decisive
step toward transforming the old city-state into a new form of
political organization, which made far easier the task of holding
together, governing and slowly assimilating the vast dominions
that Rome had succeeded in conquering.

It is a law, and perhaps a constant law, that as political organisms are transformed, later organisms retain broad traces of
earlier organisms, especially of those immediately preceding.
The new edifice is built more or less on the ruins of the old, and,

[1] Marquardt, *De l'organisation financière chez les Romains*, part 2, p. 337 (note).

in part at least, of materials supplied by it. This law is clearly
confirmed in the case of the Augustan reform. That reform did
not deprive the comitia of legislative power at one stroke.
Those assemblies continued to be convoked from time to time.
They functioned intermittently for more than a century after the
battle of Actium. But the power of enacting laws was little by
little taken over by the senate and the emperor, and in the end
entirely. Laws approved by the comitia are still important and
numerous under Augustus. They are less frequent after his
time, and then are gradually replaced by the senatus consultum
and eventually by imperial decrees or institutes (*constitutiones
imperiales*). The last law known to have been approved by the
comitia was a lex agraria enacted under the emperor Nerva
(reigned A.D. 96–98).[1]

As for what would correspond to the executive and judiciary
powers of today, these were divided between the senate and the
emperor. The emperor was regarded as a civilian magistrate,
who concentrated many powers in his own person, but left many
others to the senate in matters that concerned the city of Rome,
Italy and the senatorial provinces. He assumed the functions
of an absolute sovereign from the first in imperial provinces.
These were looked upon as subject to military occupation. The
emperor governed at his discretion through a bureaucracy whose
directors were chosen sometimes from among the senators but
preferably from among ordinary equestrians.[2]

As always happens in the contacts and competitions that
inevitably arise between the remnants of an old system and a
new system that is better suited to the needs of an age, the offices
that were filled by appointees of the senate kept diminishing in
number. In the end few traces of them were left. In Rome
itself, beginning with the first emperors of the Julian dynasty,
much of the work done by the old honorary magistrates was
taken over by new officials who were appointed by the emperor.
Gradually the regular bureaucracy, manned by knights and even
by the emperor's freedmen, made its influence more and more felt

---

[1] Pacchioni, *Corso di diritto romano*, vol. I, period IV, chaps. IX–XI.

[2] For all this evolution of the ancient Roman city-state into a bureaucratic
empire, see Pacchioni, *op. cit.* vol. I, period IV; Hartmann, *Der Untergang der
Antiken Welt;* Ferrero, *Grandezza e decadenza di Roma*, vol. IV; Bryce, *The Holy
Roman Empire.*

throughout the empire. The senate itself came to be recruited from the higher bureaucracy and from the great families of Italy and later of the whole Roman world. In practice, after the first emperors, its authority was confined within such limits as the emperors and their creatures were pleased to draw.[1]

The empire faced a serious crisis in the second half of the third century and managed to survive it. But after that, Diocletian and Constantine had no difficulty in suppressing almost all memories and survivals of the old constitution of the city, or at least in reducing them to empty names that had no positive content. Two concepts only were salvaged from the wreck. One was that the emperor derived his authority from the people. Thanks to the lawyers, that theory hung on until Justinian's time. The jurists of that emperor's day gave the famous dictum of Ulpian, "*Quod principi placuit legis habet vigorem* (The Prince's pleasure is law)," a broad interpretation that it probably had not had at first; but in holding that the people had delegated legislative power to the sovereign in virtue of the *lex regia de imperio*, they too paid homage to the principle of popular sovereignty.[2]

The other was that every magistrate had a sharply delimited sphere of jurisdiction and should, at least theoretically, exercise his authority in accord with the law. To that principle may be due partly the fact that administration by the Roman bureaucracy was certainly more systematic, and therefore more effective, than anything that the ancient Near Eastern empires had known. Sufficient proof of that is the remarkable way in which it succeeded in spreading the language, laws, manners and customs of Rome, and in bringing almost all the civilized world of that time into moral unity.

3. The prime causes for the decline of ancient civilization and the disintegration of the Roman Empire in the West constitute perhaps the most intricate and obscure problem in history. While studies of the last century have shed much light upon them, not all the darkness has yet been dispelled.[3] The most obscure point in that great historic phenomenon still remains its beginning. Why that falling off in the supply of superior men?

[1] Pacchioni, *loc. cit.*, chap. IX.
[2] Pacchioni, *loc. cit.*, chap. XI.
[3] Ferrero, "La Ruine de la civilisation antique."

Why that artistic and literary decadence? They are already manifest in the third century A.D., when the ancient pagan ideals were outworn and the new Christian ideal had not yet spread among the educated classes.

Certainly there were many grave evils in Roman society under the Low Empire. The system of taxation was burdensome and absurd. It exhausted sources of wealth, and it fell especially upon the middle classes, in other words upon the provincial bourgeoisie that composed the decurionate of the cities and towns. The body of decurions was made up of people who could meet the higher property qualifications. It exercised functions that were somewhat similar to those of our boards of aldermen. But it also had charge of collecting direct taxes, and in case a city could not pay its assigned quota in full the decurions had to meet the deficit from their private means. The position of decurion was at first much sought after as a sign of social distinction. Eventually it became an abhorred one, and everybody tried to evade it.

The decline of the middle classes left, facing each other, an aristocracy of great landed proprietors which supplied officials to the higher bureaucracy, and a numerous pauper class which, in the capital and the larger cities, was always in turmoil and lived partly on the dole of the state and later of the Church, or else drifted along in the country in the semislavery of the tillers of the soil. Public safety was a very sketchy thing, and brigandage was rife. The historians mention one Bulla, who for a long time scoured Italy at the head of a gang of six hundred bandits. In Gaul brigandage by outlawed serfs, called bagaudae ("wanderers," "knapsackers"?) long persisted. For the rest, to see how widespread brigandage was at the time, one has only to read one of the few novels that classical antiquity bequeathed to us, the *Golden Ass* (*Metamorphoses*) of Apuleius. The rich defended themselves in these circumstances by maintaining private guards—strong-armed ruffians who were called buccelarii ("hardtack"). People of moderate or small fortunes had no way of defending themselves. They simply succumbed. Public hygiene was not advanced far enough to allow the normal increment in population to fill the gaps left by famine, pestilence, raids by barbarians and other causes of unusual mortality. As happens in all very mature civilizations where religious checks are weak, the birth rate seems to have been low. Not even by the fifth century had Christianity penetrated the rural plebs deeply enough to overcome voluntary abortions and exposures of the newborn. The latter practice was so common in antiquity that recognitions of exposed foundlings were among the commonest themes in the ancient theater.

Beginning with Diocletian's time, in order to deal with the grave depression that had fallen upon the empire about the middle of the third century, the state assumed extraordinary powers and exercised extraordinary functions of control. It presumed to discipline the whole economic sphere of life, fixing wages and the prices of crops. In order to assure continuity in what we would now call "public services," it prohibited those who were employed in them from leaving their positions and obliged the son to follow the trade his father had followed. Administration was seriously affected with a disease that is the curse of bureaucratic systems and the source of their every weakness—bribery, venality, graft. The Roman official of the Low Empire generally paid more attention to his private interests than to the public interest which he was charged to look out for. It is known from the many contemporary allusions that even at the highest levels of the bureaucratic scale nothing could be obtained without lavish gifts. When, for instance, the emperor Valens allowed the Goths to cross the Danube and settle in the territories of the empire, officials were commissioned to distribute food to them and take away their arms. But the officials were bribed with gifts. They left the barbarians their arms and appropriated the supplies. Very instructive in this connection is the report on an inquiry that was conducted in Tripolitania toward the end of the fourth century. It is digested in detail by Ammianus Marcellinus.[1]

On the other hand it must not be forgotten that no human society is without its ills, and that along with them almost always comes a natural healing force that tends to mitigate their effects. The eastern empire suffered from the same troubles as the western. It was not only able to survive them, but in the sixth century, under Justinian, and again in the eighth and ninth, under the iconoclastic emperors and the Macedonian dynasty, it had noteworthy spurts of energy. At those times it managed to save

[1] *Res gestae* XXVIII, 6, 5.

most of its territory and civilization from the barbarians who were attacking from the north, and it did the same later on against the Arabs.

An individual dies when his organs are worn out by age and are no longer able to function normally, or else when he has weakened from some cause or other and is unable to resist infection. At first sight it might seem as though old age could never affect a people or a civilization, since human generations always reproduce themselves and each new generation has all the vigor of youth. Yet something that is altogether comparable to old age or organic debilitation does manifest itself in peoples. There come times when moral bonds seem to slacken, when the religion, or the patriotic sentiment, that has been the instrument of social cohesion, loses its hold and when the natural healing force, the power to react, fails to operate. This is because the better elements in society are paralyzed, and they are paralyzed because they have turned their activity and their energies to purposes other than the things essential to the salvation of the state. The measure of this internal weakness is the relative insignificance of the external shock that produces the catastrophe. We see great peoples fall before onslaughts by peoples who were but recently their inferiors in armament, in knowledge and in discipline.

The great intrusion of the Germanic peoples upon the Roman Empire was precipitated at the end of the fourth century by the impact of the Huns. The empire in the west was called upon to meet that shock at a critical moment, when the ideas and sentiments that had constituted the moral foundations of the old classical civilization had languished and a wave of mysticism was sweeping the empire, depriving the state of all its better elements, of almost all individuals who were distinguished by loftiness of character or mind, and giving them to the Church.[1] The eastern part of the Roman world survived because, owing to its geographical position, perhaps, it had time to get past the critical moment and rally its forces. The western portion did not. It was almost wholly under the control of the barbarians by the middle of the fifth century.

It is noteworthy that toward the end of the fourth century and in the first half of the fifth, while the western empire is

[1] Mosca, *Teorica dei governi*, chap. II, §6, p. 87.

crumbling, the Church glitters with a constellation of superior men—St. Ambrose, St. Jerome, St. Augustine, St. Paulinus of Nola, Paulus Orosius, Salvian of Marseilles and others still. With the exception of Theodosius, and the unfortunate Majorian, one of the last emperors in the West, there is hardly a native Roman of any character or brains who devotes himself to the service of the state. Characteristic in this connection is an anecdote related by St. Augustine. A certain Pontitianus was attending the emperor at the circus at Trier in Germany. He went for a walk with three other officers of the imperial retinue in the gardens near the walls. They chanced to enter a monastery and began to examine a manuscript of the life of St. Anthony as written by Athanasius, archbishop of Alexandria. The reading had such an effect on them that they immediately resigned from the imperial service and entered the Church.

4. After the barbarians had settled in all the old provinces of the western empire, the process of political and civil disintegration that had begun in the third century A.D. went rapidly on. In the beginning a number of the early barbarian rulers, especially the Ostrogoth Theodoric, seem to have made an effort to retain the personnel of the old Roman civil administration as far as possible, reserving the military defense of the country to the invaders. But the new regimes could hardly adapt themselves to the complicated bureaucratic machine of the Romans. The old system presupposed an administrative experience and a legal education that the conquerors did not have. The barbarian kings, besides, found themselves obliged to reward their followers with most of the lands of the conquered. That could not fail to upset the society of the time. The upper classes of Roman origin either adapted themselves to the life and ways of the barbarians, or else disappeared into the plebs. The redistribution of land meantime must have prepared the way for the development of the great landed proprietor into the local hereditary sovereign. There is another factor also. After growing somewhat accustomed to Roman civilization and institutions, the early invaders often were replaced by others, who were completely uncivilized. So the Goths were replaced by the Lombards. It is easy to understand, therefore, that after a century or two almost nothing of the old Roman state machine should have been left, and that

the new regime should prove utterly incompetent in the long run to keep the structure of a great state sound and solid under a single government.

The new system was modeled on the institutions, and founded on the sentiments, with which the Germanic tribes had been accustomed to govern in their native homes, in other words, on the reciprocal ties of personal loyalty that bound the high chief of the warrior band to his subordinates. The ruin of the great barbarian monarchy was arrested for two or three generations by the energetic Frankish dynasty of the Heristals, and especially by Charlemagne, a truly gifted sovereign, who tried to revive the Roman tradition of unity and centralization. But after Charlemagne's death the process of disintegration went on with rapid acceleration under the pressure of new incursions by Hungarians, Normans and Saracens. By the tenth century the independence of the local chiefs as regarded the central power was virtually complete, and the system that was later to be called "feudal" was functioning in the fact.

Feudalism was not, and could not be, a reversion pure and simple to the situation that Rome had found in the western world before she conquered it—a congeries of mutually hostile tribes and small peoples. Certain intellectual advances had been made —the adoption of a common language, for instance—and especially material improvements. Such things once acquired are never entirely lost, even when the political organization that has made them possible dissolves completely. A people that has grown accustomed to living in one territory, to an agriculture based upon private property, to a certain differentiation in social classes, does not lose those characteristic habits of mind entirely, even after a long period of anarchy. Some of the materials of which the feudal edifice was built were, moreover, mere developments and continuations of institutions of the Low Empire. We know, for instance, that serfdom, the chain that bound the populous class of agricultural laborers to the soil, goes back into the Roman period. In rural districts, therefore, the new regime merely transformed the villa of the old Roman proprietor into the fortified castle of the baron.

Feudalism introduced a number of novelties—for one thing, the political supremacy of an exclusively warrior class. That left to the clergy the task of keeping such bits of culture as had survived the catastrophe of the ancient world alive. Another characteristic of the feudal system was the centralization of all administrative functions, and all social influence, in the local military leader, who at the same time was master of the land— the one instrument, virtually, for the production of wealth which still existed.

Feudalism, finally, created a new type of sovereignty that was intermediate between the central, coordinating organ of the state and the individual. Once their position had become hereditary, the more important local leaders bound lesser leaders to themselves by subgrants of land, and these lesser chiefs were tied by oaths of feudal homage and fidelity to the man who made the grant. They, therefore, had no direct relations with the head of the feudal confederation as a whole—the king. In fact, they felt obliged to fight the king if the leader to whom they were directly bound was at war with him. This, certainly, was the main cause of the long resistance which the feudal system offered to the continuous efforts of the central power to destroy it.

5. Bryce wrote that "the two great ideas which expiring antiquity bequeathed to the ages that followed were of a World-Monarchy and a World-Religion."[1] In fact, down to the fourteenth century, the memory of the old unity of all civilized and Christian peoples, guided in religious matters by the Roman pontiff, who little by little gained recognition as supreme hierarch of the universal church, and in temporal matters by the successor of the ancient Roman emperor, lingered alive and vigorous in the intellectual classes—the clergy and the doctors of the law. Unless such memories had been very much alive, we should be at a loss to explain the attempt to restore the empire that took place under Charlemagne and Pope Leo III in the year 800, or another somewhat more successful attempt that was made by Otto I of Saxony in 962.

A name and an idea may exercise a great moral influence, but they are not enough to restore a centralized, coordinated political system once that system has fallen to pieces. In order to effect such a restoration, they have to have a material organization at their disposal, and in order to have such an organization the agencies required for establishing it must be available. Such agencies

[1] *The Holy Roman Empire*, chap. VII, p. 87.

Charlemagne's successors and the Germanic emperors lacked. They had neither a sound financial organization nor a regular bureaucracy nor, finally, a standing army that was capable of enforcing obedience to imperial edicts.

In Charlemagne's day, the old Germanic band still furnished a fairly well-disciplined militia for the Frankish armies, and the local lords were not yet omnipotent. For the same reason the emperors of the House of Saxony, and the first two emperors of the House of Franconia, could count on the cooperation of the German military class, which was not yet solidly grouped about a few leaders. Imperial and regal power attained its maximum efficiency in Germany under Henry III of Franconia. That emperor managed for some time to keep a few of the principal duchies unfilled, or to have them occupied by relatives of the reigning house. He held the duchy of Franconia and, for a time, the duchy of Swabia under his personal dominion, and further retained the exclusive right to name the holders of the great ecclesiastical fiefs, bishoprics and abbacies, which were not hereditary, and which covered almost half of the territory of Germany. Henry III died an untimely death. Henry IV at that moment was a minor and he was personally weak. His struggles with the papacy permitted the higher German nobility to regain the ground it had lost.[1]

But the moment the feudal system had taken a strong hold in Germany the military base of the empire became shaky. Then the struggle between the empire and the Church gave the local sovereignties the support of a great moral force in their clash with imperial authority. The effort to reestablish the world-wide political unity of Christian peoples, which Charlemagne had made and which Otto I of Saxony had repeated, may be considered a complete and final failure with the death of Frederick II of Hohenstaufen.

But the state of semibarbarism which characterized the darkest period of the Middle Ages in central and western Europe was not to be eternal. Civilization was to rise again. The process of reabsorbing local powers into the central organ of the state had, therefore, to start anew under a different form; and, in fact, what the representative of the ancient Roman Empire had been unable to do became the task of the various national monarchies.

[1] Bryce, *The Holy Roman Empire*, chap. IX.

Meantime, from about the year 1000 on, another sort of local sovereignty had begun to rise alongside of the fief—the medieval town, the commune. The commune was a federation of guilds, neighborhood organizations and trade corporations—all the various associations of people who were neither nobles nor subject vassals—which were organized in the more troublous periods of feudal anarchy in order that those who belonged to them might enjoy a certain measure of personal security through mutual defense. The communes became powerful first in northern Italy and then in Germany and Flanders, and in those countries they were one of the greatest obstacles to the growth of the power of the Holy Roman Emperor. They achieved more modest positions in France, England, the Iberian kingdoms and southern Italy. In those countries they supported the crown against feudalism.

In general, the national monarchies claimed historical connections with the old barbarian monarchies, which the invading Germans had set up on the ruins of the ancient Roman Empire. But after the period of political dissolution that occurred under Charlemagne's first successors, they began to take shape again following geographic and linguistic lines rather than historic traditions. The France of St. Louis, for instance, did not correspond to the old territory of the Franks. In one direction it embraced ancient Septimania, which the Visigoths had formerly controlled. In the other it withdrew from Flanders, Franconia and the Rhineland, which were all Germanic territories and were eventually attracted into the orbit of the Holy Roman Empire.

Furthermore, though his title might derive officially from the titles with which the old barbarian kings had adorned their persons, the national king was at first only the head, and sometimes the nominal head, of a federation of great barons—first among them, but first among peers. Hugh Capet and Philip Augustus were looked upon in just that way in France. King John of England appears in that guise in the text of the Magna Charta, and so do the kings of Aragon in the oath which they were obliged to take before the Cortes. As is well known, the barons of Aragon, in council assembled, invited the new king to swear that he would keep all the old agreements. Before enumerating them, they repeated a declaration: "We, who one by one are your equals and all united are more than your equals, name you our king on the following conditions." And when the conditions had been read, they concluded: "And otherwise not."

More than six centuries of struggle and slow but constant ferment were needed for the feudal king to develop into the absolute king, the feudal hierarchy into a regular bureaucracy, and the army made up of the nobles in arms and their vassals into a regular standing army. During those six hundred years there were periods when feudalism was able to take advantage of critical moments that country and crown chanced to be passing through and regain some of its lost ground. But in the end victory rested with centralized monarchy. The kings little by little succeeded in gathering into their hands assemblages of material agencies that were greater than the feudal nobility could match. They also made shrewd use of the support of the communes and of powerful and constant moral forces, such as the widespread belief that reigning dynasties had been divinely appointed to rule, or a theory of the doctors of law that the king, like the ancient Roman emperor, was the sovereign will that created law and the sovereign power that enforced it.

The process by which feudal monarchy evolved into an absolute bureaucratic monarchy might be called typical or normal, since it was followed in France and in a number of other countries in Europe. Nevertheless, there were other processes which led, or might have led, to the same results. The commune of Milan, for instance, in the valley of the Po, developed first into a signoria, or tyranny, and then into a duchy. In the first half of the fifteenth century it subjected many other communes and acquired a fairly extensive territory. It might easily have become a modern national kingdom. Elsewhere great feudatories enlarged their domains and transformed them into kingdoms. That was the case with the margraves of Brandenburg, who became kings of Prussia and then emperors of Germany, and with the dukes of Savoy, who became kings of Sardinia and finally of Italy.

Economic causes seem to have exercised very little influence on the transformation of the feudal state into the bureaucratic state, and that evolution certainly is one of the events that have most profoundly modified the history of the world. Systems of economic production did not undergo any very radical changes between the fourteenth century and the seventeenth, especially if we compare them with the changes that took place after bureaucratic absolutism was founded. On the other hand, between the end of the fifteenth century and the second half of the seventeenth—in other words, during the period when the feudal system was losing ground every day and was being permanently tamed—a far-reaching revolution was taking place in military art and organization, owing to improvements in firearms and their wider and wider use. The baronial castle could easily and rapidly be battered down as soon as cannon became common weapons. The heavy cavalry had been made up of nobles, the only ones who could find time for long training, and money for the expensive knightly equipment. But cavalry ceased to be the arm that decided battles, once the arquebus had been perfected and the infantry had generally adopted it.

We saw above (chap. XIII, §3) that changes in armament had a very perceptible influence on political developments in the Hellenic city in the seventh and sixth centuries B.C. So in Japan, at the end of the sixteenth and the beginning of the seventeenth century, monarchical centralization, with the shoguns of the Tokugawa family, prevailed over feudalism shortly after the introduction of firearms, which were made known to that country by the Portuguese.[1]

6. The absolute bureaucratic state may be regarded as permanently established and fully developed in France at the beginning of the personal reign of Louis XIV—in 1661, that is. At the same time, or soon after, the strengthening of central authority and the absorption of local sovereignties became more or less completely generalized throughout Europe. The few states, such as Poland or Venice, that would not, or could not, move with the times and transform their constitutions, lost power and cohesion and disappeared before the end of the eighteenth century.

Thus the origins of absolute monarchy are relatively recent. Inside it, and under its wing, new ruling forces, new intellectual, moral and economic conditions, rapidly grew up, so that in less than a century and a half its transformation into the modern representative state became inevitable. The rapidity of that evolution strikes us as one of the most interesting phenomena in history.

[1] La Mazelière, Le Japon, vol. III.

The most important factor in the transformation was the rapid growth of a new social class, which arose and asserted its power in between the common people and the descendants of the old feudal aristocracy. The bourgeoisie, in the broad sense of the term, comprises the numerous class of people who find employment in the liberal professions, in commerce and in industry, and who combine moderate means with a technical and often a scientific education that is far superior to that of other social classes. It came into being in Europe during the eighteenth century. To be sure, even before that time the ranks of the aristocracy had not been impenetrable. A great lawyer might sometimes hope to gain admittance to it. In some of the large commercial cities powerful families of manufacturers and bankers ended by mingling with the old feudal nobility or supplanting it outright. But down to the beginning of the eighteenth century no real middle class had existed. The modest artisan class could hardly be regarded as such. In his economic and intellectual status the artisan did not differ very greatly from the man of the lowest classes.

If the elements that were best fitted to form a new social stratum were able to detach themselves from the lower classes of the population, they owe that success to the absolutist system, which guaranteed public order and relative peace and pried the nobility loose from its grip on landed property. Loss of ancient sovereign rights, and the necessity of keeping close to the courts in order to intrigue for lucrative positions, induced many noble families to leave their estates and settle in the capitals. Absence from their lands, as almost always happens, made it necessary for them in the end to rent parts of their rural properties, or even to sell them outright. From such tenants, or new owners, a rural bourgeoisie arose. At the same time this new social stratum absorbed the less wealthy and more active elements of the old nobility also and formed the class that came to be known in Russia and Germany by the very expressive term "intelligentsia."

This new middle class is sharply distinguished from the laboring classes by its scientific and literary education, by its manners and habits. On the other hand, because of its economic status, it sometimes mingles with the more well-to-do orders of society, but then again at times draws wholly apart from them. The class, as we have seen, began to be noticeable in some countries during the last decades of the seventeenth century. It developed and became influential in all central and western Europe during the eighteenth century and in the first half of the nineteenth. Its development in a way runs parallel to the development of secondary, classical and technical education, and to the growth of universities.

This class had no sooner developed its characteristic traits and acquired consciousness of its own power and importance than it perceived that it was the victim of a great injustice. It discovered that there were privileges which the nobility had retained in all absolutist˝countries, but more especially in France. We have already encountered a virtually constant law in history, that every new political edifice must to some extent be built of rubbish and remnants from the structure that it has replaced. Following that law, the absolutist system had necessarily derived almost all the elements of the new civil and military bureaucracy that began to rule the state from the nobility and the clergy, whom it had deprived of traditional territorial sovereignties. For the members of the nobility, in particular, it had reserved all the highest and most lucrative offices in government. All that seemed natural enough as long as there was only a plebs below the nobility, and as long as a traditional habit of commanding was the best and practically the only requisite for leadership. But it came to look like a hateful and harmful parasitism on society the moment education and technical preparation, in which the privileged classes generally allowed the new middle class to surpass them, became the requisites that were most in demand for exercising the higher public functions.

Now it is conceivable that the bourgeoisie might have managed, first to undermine the privileges of the nobility, and then to destroy them or reduce them to empty forms, without making any radical change in the organization of the state. This might actually have come to pass had not a new political psychology, which was profoundly different from the one that preceded it, grown up in the course of the eighteenth century. It might have come to pass had there not been a European country in which, because of its insular position, political organization had had a very different history from that of continental systems, so that by the eighteenth century it had developed a form of government that seemed, at least, to supply a practical model of a constitution capable of realizing the aspirations born of the new psychology mentioned.

Divine right, as Bossuet understood the principle at the end of the seventeenth century, meant that the people could never rebel against their rulers, however wicked they might be, and that rulers were accountable only to God for the way they exercised their power. The principle had never been interpreted in that manner by medieval writers, nor by writers after them down to the seventeenth century. St. Thomas, for instance, in the *Summa*, justifies rebellion in certain cases, and admits that peoples choose for themselves the form of government that they consider most appropriate. He shows a personal preference for a "mixed" government, in which the three forms of the Aristotelian classification, monarchy, aristocracy and democracy, are blended and balanced.

Now on the continent of Europe, religious sentiment, which alone was capable of furnishing a moral basis for the principle of divine right, had greatly weakened by the eighteenth century. All memories and survivals of the old feudal system had fallen into discredit as relics of a barbarous age. All sovereignties intermediate between the state and the individual had been destroyed. In those circumstances eighteenth century minds fed more avidly than ever on the classical political doctrines of Greece and Rome. The old concepts of liberty, equality and popular sovereignty, which classical writers had formulated with the model of the ancient Greek and Roman city before their eyes, came back into greater honor than ever. During the Renaissance, a general reshaping of the mental mold of Europe had come about in literary and artistic fields through the study of classical models. A similar reshaping came about three centuries later in the political field under the influence of the same models. This revolution in political thinking occurred before the development of historical science had enabled people in Europe clearly to perceive how greatly the constitutions of the city-states, on which the political ideas of Greek and Roman antiquity had been based, differed from anything in the modern world.

Apart from this new psychology, apart from this new vision of political life that had so profoundly penetrated the consciousness of the intellectual classes of the eighteenth century, one would be at a loss to explain the rapid success of the *Social*

Contract of Rousseau. In that book the Genevan philosopher started with the hypothesis of a state of nature, which men had abandoned as the result of a compact in which the moral and legal foundations of political association had been laid down. That hypothesis too had already come to form a part of the intellectual baggage of the eighteenth century. He went on to reach the conclusion that the only compact, or agreement, that was legitimate was one which made the law the expression of the will of the numerical majority among the associated citizens, and which entrusted the execution of the law to those who had received the mandate to execute it from that same majority for a specified length of time. This concept, as is apparent, corresponded exactly to the concept of classical democracy, with the sole difference that the ancients never admitted the bulk of their manual laborers into the management of the state. Their slaves were always barred from voting and from public office, and they were not allowed to bear arms.

But, in the eighteenth century, bureaucratic absolutism had prepared the ground for the application of these new democratic theories in one respect only: It had destroyed, or reduced to empty forms, every sovereignty that lay intermediate between the supreme power and the individual citizen. This made it possible and plausible to conceive of popular sovereignty as the sovereignty of the numerical majority, pure and simple, of the people who belonged to a country.

That had not at all been the medieval view, which as a matter of fact hung on through the sixteenth century and into the first decades of the seventeenth. The Middle Ages had conceived of popular sovereignty as the expression of the will of the hereditary and "natural" leaders of the people, such as the feudal lords, or the representatives of the communes and corporations. The political writers of the Middle Ages and even of the sixteenth and early seventeenth century merely adapted the concept of popular sovereignty, which they had inherited from classical antiquity, to conditions in the societies in which they were living. When St. Thomas, Marsilius of Padua, Hubert Languet, Buchanan, Johannes Althusius, speak of "the people" they think of it always as legitimately represented by its "natural" leaders— the barons and the heads of corporations and communes, whom they variously designate as *selecti, ephori,* and so on. The idea that each separate individual should have an equal share in the exercise of sovereignty could have arisen only after bureaucratic absolutism had broken up the old groups and destroyed all sovereign powers intermediate between the state and the individual.[1]

In all other respects—with its complex and centralized bureaucratic organization, with its standing army, with its authoritarian traditions, the absolutist system was poorly adapted to develop in such a way as to make possible any practical application of democratic principles that had been worked out on the model of the Greek and Latin city-state.

But there stood England. By the eighteenth century that country had already adopted a political system which did offer a practical model. The constitution of England seemed to demonstrate that the constitution of the absolute state could be worked over into something that was fairly consistent with the ideas that had been inherited from classical antiquity and, more important still, with the desire of the bourgeoisie to participate extensively in sovereign powers. Had that not been the case, one may doubt whether any adaptation whatever would have been possible, and whether the history of continental Europe in the eighteenth and nineteenth centuries would not have been different from the history that the three or four generations preceding ours were to witness.

7. Political institutions had had an original development in England, especially from the beginning of the seventeenth century. That development differed in substantial respects from anything that had taken place on the Continent. The feudal system had been transplanted to England by the Norman conquest, but from the very outset it showed, beyond the Channel, a number of distinctive characteristics. In the early days the conquering Normans had been, as it were, encamped in an enemy territory. They had therefore been obliged to gather in closer and better-disciplined union around the king than the

---

[1] The late Senator Ruffini has recently contended, "Guerra e riforme costituzionali," that Marsilius of Padua understood popular sovereignty in the modern sense, as sovereignty of the numerical majority of associates. This is hardly the time or the place to debate the point, but, in spite of Ruffini's great authority, we do not share his opinion.

ruling class on the Continent had ever done. Within a century and a half, more or less, the conquerors and the conquered had fused, and the high nobility had forcibly wrested Magna Charta from the king, a real two-sided agreement between the king and the baron, in which the reciprocal rights and duties of each were established.[1] In that way one of the usual feudal organizations was arrived at, which, as it came gradually to develop, came more and more to limit the powers of the crown as against the powers of parliament. And in parliament, side by side with the upper house, the House of Lords, and almost as an appendage to it, a lower house of representatives of the small county nobilities and of the municipalities soon rose, and its members were the allies and tools of the lords and the high nobility rather than of the kings.

In the second half of the fifteenth century the monarchs on the Continent were still struggling fiercely with their great vassals. In England a long civil war, called the Wars of the Roses, split the great lords into two bitterly hostile parties, which exterminated each other. When domestic peace was restored in 1485 with the advent of the Tudor dynasty, the crown found before it a higher house that was made up almost exclusively of upstarts, who had recently been elevated by the crown itself to the dignity of the peerage and had neither the material resources nor the prestige of the old barons. Meantime, no urban or rural bourgeoisie had as yet emerged in England, and the House of Commons remained a docile body that had very scant influence.

For these reasons one may say that the English crown attained the peak of its power in the sixteenth century. Giovanni Botero rightly observes in his *Relazioni universali*, published toward the end of that period, that the kings of England continued to convoke parliament regularly, but that their powers were in practice no less extensive than the powers of the kings of France, where the States-General were being convoked more and more rarely, if not falling into desuetude. These "World Reports" of Botero are a treatise on physical and political geography. The book is acute and marvelously well informed for the age in which it was written. Botero evidently drew his notes on the various countries from trustworthy sources and had an eye for distinguishing important from unimportant facts. He states

[1] Mosca, *Appunti di diritto costituzionale*, chap. V, pp. 30–31.

for instance, that the great English barons, unlike the French, had already lost all political significance. They had ceased to exercise local jurisdictions and no longer had fortified castles.[1] For that matter, the predominance of court and crown in England in the sixteenth century is generally recognized, and one indication of it is the fact that the religious changes that took place during that era in England were carried out on the initiative of Tudor monarchs—two of them queens, Mary and Elizabeth.

It may have been largely because of the ease with which the Tudors, and their courtiers and officials, could direct the political life of their country almost unopposed, that the English crown neglected to create at that time the two most essential instruments of monarchical absolutism: a standing army and a stable and regular bureaucracy. Partly for economy's sake, partly because England's insular position ensured her against foreign invasions, the kings of the Tudor family regarded as sufficient an armed militia that was recruited in each county from among its natives, individual soldiers returning to their ordinary occupations after some days of periodic drilling. Considerations of economy seem also to have dictated the policy of entrusting the civil offices of lord lieutenant, sheriff, coroner, and so on, in the provinces, to local notables. These men gladly served without stipend, because such posts lent prestige to the persons who held them and luster to their families. But there was always the chance that their loyalty might waver or become conditional on occasions when public opinion happened to be against king and court; and in the end, what the English call "self-government" became one of the main causes of the predominance of parliament over the crown.[2]

Early in the seventeenth century, in fact, the Stuarts set out to establish an absolutist system. At once opposition awakened in the House of Commons, which represented the rural and urban middle classes. Those classes had been able to emerge across the Channel (in a country that had not been pauperized by

---

[1] *Op. cit.*, part II, book I, pp. 257, 260.

[2] Self-government was tenacious in England. The prerogatives of honorary officials were first diminished in the great administrative reform of 1834. Then such offices were gradually abolished, elective councils and a paid civil service replacing them. The evolution may be considered complete by 1894. Bertolini, *Il governo locale inglese.*

foreign and civil wars, and was therefore not overburdened with taxes) some generations earlier than they did on the Continent. For religious reasons, among others, they had grown hostile to the authority of the crown. In the face of this opposition the English sovereigns found themselves without the material agencies that had given royalty the victory over feudalism on the Continent. Charles I could meet the revolting militia in the cities only with the rural militia, led by the Cavaliers. He lost the war because of his personal lack of resoluteness and because he met an antagonist of genius in Oliver Cromwell, who was the first to succeed in establishing a real standing army in England.[1] So after more than a half century of struggle, in which a king lost his head on the block, the influence of the political forces that were represented in parliament overcame once and for all the influences represented by the supporters of royalty.

This victory took the form of law in a series of acts of parliament that were duly sanctioned by the crown. Some of them, such as the Habeas Corpus Act, were designed to assure the personal freedom of all Englishmen by putting effective restraints on the arbitrariness of crown officials. Others, like the Bill of Rights of 1689 and the Act of Settlement of 1701, contained provisions of the same sort, along with new ones, whereby the crown was indirectly obligated to govern in accordance with laws approved by parliament. One need mention just one provision in the Act of Settlement, whereby no act of the government was valid unless it had been countersigned by a member of the Privy Council, who therefore became personally responsible for its legality.

This history-making provision is contained in the fourth clause of the act. It enabled absolute monarchy to develop into representative monarchy all over Europe. The Privy Council was a consulting body of high officials who assisted the king in the exercise of executive power. Toward the end of the seventeenth century meetings of the Privy Council began to be held pro forma. Finally they were allowed to lapse altogether, because it was too large a body. The Privy Council meetings were replaced by meetings of its more influential members, and

---

[1] Cromwell used his army later on to set up a military dictatorship, but once the Stuarts were restored, with Charles II, the army was dissolved. Mosca, *Appunti di diritto costituzionale*, p. 45.

these constituted what came to be called the cabinet. With the advent of the Hanoverian dynasty in 1714, the political preponderance of the elective chamber gained great momentum, because the crown began habitually to choose members of the cabinet, or shrunken Privy Council, which was entrusted with the exercise of executive power, from among outstanding personalities in the lower house majority.

By the end of the eighteenth century, therefore, the independence of the English courts had been guaranteed by the principle of life tenure. Guarantees against arbitrary arrest and imprisonment had been acquired for every Englishman. As for liberty of the press, preventive censorship was abolished in 1694. Though punishment of press offenses continued severe down to the end of the century, it became much milder after a press law had been approved in 1778, at the instance of Fox. In England, in other words, a constitutional system prevailed which, in its main outlines and in its distinctive characteristics, was very like modern representative systems. The great originality of English constitutional history, it should be noted, lies in the slow and gradual transformation of the feudal system, as recognized in the Magna Charta, into a modern representative system. That transformation was completed in the nineteenth century, without the country's having had to traverse the period of bureaucratic and military absolutism that was experienced to a greater or lesser extent by all the countries of continental Europe.

But the resemblance between the English constitution as it was in the eighteenth century and modern representative organization on a democratic basis lies more in the forms than in the substance. It is great if we think of the functioning of the principal organs of the state. It is very slight, or nonexistent, if we think of the way in which those organs were constituted, or of the political forces that they represented. Even then the English elective chamber was the preponderant power in the state, but the right to vote was granted only to a small minority of citizens, who enjoyed it either because they were owners of landed property in the rural counties, or by virtue of rights and customs which oftentimes, in the boroughs, which sometimes comprised fairly large cities, went as far back as the Middle Ages. As a result, elections of large numbers of representatives depended upon a few hundred great proprietors, who in addition often sat by hereditary right in the House of Lords.

In his *Contrat social*, which was published in 1762, Rousseau demonstrated with seemingly rigorous, not to say mathematical, logic that the only legitimate authority was an authority that was based on the consent of the numerical majority of the associated citizens. Some fifteen years before that, in his *Esprit des lois*, Montesquieu had scrutinized and, one might almost say, dissected the English constitution of the time, and he had reached the conclusion that its superiority lay in the separation and independence of the three fundamental powers of the state, which, in his opinion, were the legislative, the executive and the judiciary. Now the representative systems of the nineteenth century resulted from a blend of the ideas of the Genevan philosopher, which, furthermore, were very similar to the ideas that classical antiquity had worked out, with the ideas of the keen magistrate of Bordeaux. To make the elective chamber the organ of the preponderant political forces and have it elected by broad-based, or even universal, suffrage was enough to give the impression that the old absolute, bureaucratic state had been transformed into a system that was based on popular sovereignty as the ancients had understood it, or, better, as Rousseau and his followers understood it. If one may venture the comparison, nineteenth century constitutional systems were like suits of clothes that had been cut on the pattern of the English constitution of the Hanoverian period, but were made of a cloth that had a thread or two of principles of pure democracy.

8. The generations that lived during the nineteenth century were inclined to regard the revolution that overthrew the old absolutist regimes at the end of the eighteenth century and then, after the Napoleonic interlude, established representative systems first in France and then gradually in other countries of western and central Europe, as the greatest of social cataclysms. That point of view is very like the common optical illusion whereby objects that are close to us seem to be larger than those far away. As a matter of fact, the cataclysm which our great-great-grand-fathers witnessed, and which was followed by many smaller ones in which our grandfathers' fathers were actors and specta-tors, seems relatively insignificant if we compare it with the

great collapse of human civilization that preceded and followed the fall of the Roman Empire in the West, or with the terrible Mongol invasions of the thirteenth century that reached from China in the East to Hungary in the West and sorely tried a truly vast portion of the world. If it were possible to foresee the future at all clearly, one might venture to predict that the convulsions that were occasioned by the advent and spread of liberal institutions and the representative system will probably be considered trivial as compared with the one which may be the cause, and at the same time the effect, of their disappearance from the earth.

Among the shocks that accompanied the establishment of the representative system, the first and most violent occurred in France in the last decade of the eighteenth century. At that time in France there was one of those great and sudden displacements of wealth, to the damage of one class and the gain of other classes, which are wont to attend all serious and deep-reaching political upheavals. But in France the overturn came suddenly, and to the great majority of the people then living it was practically unforeseen. Because of the political unpreparedness of the old privileged classes and of those which aspired to supplant them, it did not find men who were capable of directing and controlling it, and the revolutionary wave dissolved the old state organization without having another one ready to replace it. Later on Napoleon was obliged to reconstruct virtually the whole state by utilizing the elements that were best adapted to the task, and he found that they were not lacking either in the old privileged classes or in the middle class that had made the revolution. But when the representative system came to be adopted in most of the other countries in Europe, its coming had been long foreseen and was socially ripe. It was possible to inaugurate it, therefore, without serious disturbances—unless we choose to regard as serious the movements that took place pretty generally throughout Europe in 1848 and 1849.

So, about the middle of the nineteenth century, roughly, a new type of political organization came into vogue. It naturally presents differing varieties, or subtypes, according to the countries that have adopted it. A form of the constitutional monarchy, for instance, was in force in Germany down to 1918.

There the executive power did not emanate from the majority
in the elective chamber. In that respect the German system
differed from the type of parliamentary monarchy, in force in
England and Belgium, in which ministries resign when they lose
their majority in the elective chamber. A parliamentary
republican state is in force in France, and a presidential republican state in the United States (see above, chap. X, §17). In the
latter country, the president is head of the state and at the same
time head of the government. We adopt the expression "modern
representative state" as covering all the many varieties of that
form of constitution.

The representative system, as we have seen, resulted from
notions and concepts that had been inherited from classical
antiquity but were adapted to the requirements of nineteenth
century society—a very different sort of society from the society
that had evolved the city-state of Greece and Rome. It was
cut to a pattern that had been worked out in England in the two
preceding centuries, almost empirically, and as the consequence
of very special circumstances in English history. Nevertheless,
the new constitutions corresponded amazingly well to the ways
of thinking and the social requirements of the age that had
adopted them. Maintaining a fairly good public order, and
supported by marvelous scientific discoveries that supplied the
means for achieving an economic progress that had not even
been dreamed of before, they went hand in hand with a material
prosperity that cannot be matched in the history of other ages
and other civilizations. Not only that: During the whole
nineteenth century they managed to maintain undisputed
throughout the world a supremacy of the peoples of European
civilization that had begun to take shape a century earlier.
The preponderance of states of European civilization over states
of Asiatic civilization became conspicuous early in the eighteenth
century, when Turkey began to give signs of weakness as compared with the rest of Europe. That country had maintained
its full offensive vigor down to the siege of Vienna in 1683. The
English conquered India in the second half of the eighteenth
century. The French might have done the same had they
realized the importance of the game that was being played in
the Orient in time. European preponderance held on unshaken
during the nineteenth century. In our day it received its first

powerful shock in the victory of Japan over Russia. The Asiatics are now beginning rapidly to understand that they can adopt the administrative and military organization of Europe and America and profit by western scientific progress, without abandoning their own type of civilization.

Now, there has been, as there could not help being, a profound and irremediable discrepancy between the theoretical assumptions of the new political system and its functioning in practice. In spite of the gradual adoption of universal suffrage, actual power has remained partly in the hands of the wealthiest classes, and in larger part still, especially in so-called democratic countries, in the hands of the middle classes. Those classes have always had the upper hand in the controlling cliques of political parties and in electioneering committees, and they have supplied in large part, the reporting and editorial staffs of the daily press, the personnel of the bureaucracies and army officers.[1]

All the same, for the very reason that a combination of bureaucratic and elective elements is inherent in the nature of the representative system, it has been possible, under that system, to utilize almost all human values in the political and administrative departments of government, and the door has been left open to all elements in the governed classes to make their way into ruling classes.

Specialization in the various political functions and cooperation and reciprocal control between bureaucratic and elective elements are two of the outstanding characteristics of the modern representative state. These traits make it possible to regard that state as the most complex and delicate type of political organization that has so far been seen in world history. From that point of view, and from others as well, it may also be claimed that there is an almost perfect harmony between the present political system and the level of civilization that has been attained in the century that saw it come into being and grow to maturity. That civilization may perhaps have shown itself inferior to some of its predecessors as regards the finer perfections of artistic and literary forms, as regards depth of philosophical thought and religious sentiment, as regards appreciation of the importance of certain great moral problems. But it has shown itself far superior to all others in its wise organization of economic and scientific

[1] Ostrogorski, *La Démocratie et l'organisation des partis politiques.*

production and in its exact knowledge and shrewd exploitation of the forces of nature. There can be no question that the political system now prevailing has won over the spontaneous energies and wills of individual human beings the same victory which the complex of institutions, instruments, knowledge and aptitudes that form the culture and the strength of our generations has won over the forces of nature.

Certainly, it was possible yesterday, and it is possible today, for the special interests of small organized minorities to prevail over the collective interest, paralyzing the activity of those whose duty it is to safeguard the latter. But we must realize that the state machine has grown so powerful and become so perfected that never before in Europe or in the world has such a mass of economic resources and individual activities been seen to converge upon the attainment of collective purposes—the World War has recently supplied a terrible but irrefutable proof of that. If it be objected that some ancient cities, and perhaps some of the medieval communes, on occasion exerted no less effort in proportion to their size, the answer is that the smaller the organism, the easier it is to coordinate the activities of the cells that compose it. Athens, Sparta and certain medieval communes that were large for their day had territories and populations a hundredth the size of the average modern state. Rome only, at the time of her Punic Wars, and again during the first two centuries of the empire, when she was successfully extending her language and civilization over all of western Europe, obtained results which are comparable in magnitude to the results that the political organizations of our day obtain, or which in some respects may be of greater magnitude.

But every human organism, whether individual or social, the modern representative state included, bears within itself the germs which, if they ripen, may bring on its decline and destruction. Let us mention here just a few such germs of decay, the main ones, that is, which already can be clearly seen at work.

Apparent at this moment in many countries in Europe is a considerable economic decline of the middle class, the prosperity of which made the advent of the representative system possible. If the economic decline of that class should continue for a whole generation, an intellectual decline in all our countries would inevitably follow. According to Aristotle, a certain distribution of moderate property ownership was an indispensable requisite for the proper functioning of the Greek city. So the existence of a moderately well-to-do middle class is necessary today for the normal livelihood of the modern representative system. So true is this that in countries and regions where such a class is not very well developed, or is without the requisites for maintaining its prestige and influence, the modern representative system has yielded its worst results.[1] If the decline in question should be accelerated, or merely continue, the forms of our present organization might be observed for some time still, but really we would have either a plutocratic dictatorship, or else a bureaucratico-military dictatorship, or else a demagogic dictatorship by a few experts in mob leadership, who would know the arts of wheedling the masses and of satisfying their envies and their predatory instincts in every possible way, to the certain damage of the general interest. Worse still, there might be a combination of two of these dictatorships, or indeed of all three. It is interesting to note that this danger was clearly perceived by Rousseau: "Taking the term in its strictest sense," he wrote, "there has never been a real democracy and there never will be. It is against the natural order that the great number should rule and the small number be ruled."[2]

This danger would seem to be all the greater in that it is linked with another, which is a logical consequence of the system of ideas that has supplied the moral and intellectual basis for the representative system. We allude here to the frame of mind, so widely prevalent hitherto, that has made the introduction of universal suffrage almost inevitable. During the first decades of representative government the bourgeoisie was disposed to compromise with the dogma of popular sovereignty on which the representative system had been founded, and adopted varieties of restricted suffrage almost everywhere. But later on, swayed more by force of logic than by any upthrust that came from the lower strata of society, and constrained especially by the necessity of seeming to be consistent with the principles which it had proclaimed and in the name of which it had fought

---

[1] See above, chap. V, §9.

[2] *Contrat social*, book III, chap. IV. The passage is a typical example of the perception of the necessity of a ruling class to which we referred above (chap. XII, §1). It did not escape Michels, *Parteiwesen*, part II, chap. III.

and overthrown absolutism, the bourgeoisie adopted universal suffrage. Universal suffrage came first in the United States, then in France, in 1848, and after that in all other countries that were governed by representative systems.

Now never have the many, especially if they were poor and ignorant, ruled the few, especially if they were fairly rich and intelligent. The so-called dictatorship of the proletariat, therefore, could never be anything more than the dictatorship of a very restricted class exercised in the name of the proletariat. Perhaps some perception of that truth may have penetrated more or less clearly into the consciousness, or subconsciousness, of the ruling classes and inclined them to accept universal suffrage without very much resistance. But once everybody has acquired the right to vote, it is inevitable that a clique should detach itself from the middle classes and, in the race to reach the better posts, try to seek leverage in the instincts and appetites of the more populous classes, telling them that political equality means almost nothing unless it goes hand in hand with economic equality and that the former may very well serve as an instrument for obtaining the latter.

That has come about and is still coming about all the more easily, in that the bourgeoisie has been, in a sense, the prisoner not only of its democratic principles but also of its liberal principles. Liberalism takes it to be an axiomatic truth that every belief, every opinion, has the right to be preached and propagated without hindrance. Certainly liberalism and democracy are not the same thing, but they have a certain common foundation in an intellectual and emotional current which started in the eighteenth century on the basis of an optimistic conception of human nature or, rather, of the sentiments and ideas that *ought to prevail* in associations of human beings. Just as democracy, therefore, has to admit that the best government is the government that emanates from the consent of the numerical majority of citizens, so liberalism has to believe that the good sense of the people is enough to distinguish truth from error and to treat harmful or antisocial ideas as they deserve. Our ruling classes have molded their conduct to fit those principles, and it is not to be wondered at, therefore, that in many countries a new doctrine, indeed a new religion, is being widely proclaimed and has widely spread. From a theoretical standpoint this doctrine could be presumed to be unfitted for reconstructing a better, and especially a more moral, system of social and political organization than we have at present, and practical experience has shown it to be so.   Certainly it could not be better fitted for destroying the present system.

To all this we must add the great complexity of the modern economic system and the resulting specialization in activities that is required for the production and distribution of the commodities and services that are most essential to the daily life of society as a whole and therefore of the state.   If we realize that under these circumstances it is possible for small minorities to cause the most serious disturbances in the whole social system simply by folding their arms, we are in a position to gain some slight conception of the destructive force of the elements which are at present corroding the framework of our political and social structure and threatening its existence.[1]

[1] Mosca, "Feudalismo funzionale," "Il pericolo dello Stato moderno," and "Feudalismo e Sindacalismo."   Also, *Appunti di diritto costituzionale,* pp. 164–165: and see chap. XVII below.

CHAPTER XV

PRINCIPLES AND TENDENCIES
IN RULING CLASSES

1. In his dialogue on the Laws, which was one of his last, Plato wrote that monarchy and democracy are the two fundamental forms of government, and that from them all others derive through more or less happy combinations. In the first lines of the *Prince* Machiavelli wrote that "all states, all dominions which have held or do hold empire over men have been and are republics or monarchies." Thus he too recognizes two fundamental forms of government, one in which sovereign power is exercised in the name of an individual and another in which it is exercised in the name of the people.

If that concept is properly interpreted and supplemented, it may be accepted even today. For, really, in any form of political organization, authority is either transmitted from above downward in the political or social scale, or from below upward. Either the choice of the lower official is left to the one above him, till we reach the supreme head, who chooses his immediate collaborators—the case of the typical absolute monarchy; or else the authority of the governor derives from the governed, as was the case in ancient Greece and in republican Rome.

The two systems may be fused and balanced in various ways, as happens in representative governments today. The present form of government in the United States would be a good example. There the president is chosen by the citizens as a whole, and he in turn appoints all the principal officials of the executive branch of the federal government and the magistrates of the Supreme Court.

The type of political organization in which authority is transmitted from the top of the political ladder to officials below Plato calls "monarchical." It might more accurately be styled "autocratic," because a monarch, in the broad sense of the term, is just the head of a state, and there is always such a head, what-

394

ever the political system.   It is more difficult to choose the word
that is exactly suited to Plato's second type.   Following his
example, one might call it "democratic."   We consider it more
satisfactory to call it "liberal," for by "democracy" today we
commonly mean a form of government in which all citizens have
an equal share in the creation of the sovereign power.   That has
not always been the case in the past in systems in which "the
people" chose their governors, because "the people" often
meant a restricted aristocracy.   One need only recall what
happened under the constitutions of Greece and Rome.   Some
of them were unquestionably "liberal."   In many medieval
communes only men who were enrolled in the major trade guilds
were full-fledged citizens.   The designation "liberal" seems to us
all the more appropriate in that it has become the custom to
regard as "free" peoples those whose rulers, according to law at
least, must be chosen by all, or even by a part, of the governed,
and whose law must be an emanation of the general will.   In
autocratic systems, the law either has something immutable and
sacred about it or else it is an expression of the autocrat's will
or, rather, of the will of those who act in his name.

Conversely, the term "democratic" seems more suitable for
the tendency which aims to replenish the ruling class with
elements deriving from the lower classes, and which is always at
work, openly or latently and with greater or lesser intensity, in
all political organisms.   "Aristocratic" we would call the
opposite tendency, which also is constant and varies in intensity,
and which aims to stabilize social control and political power
in the descendants of the class that happens to hold possession
of it at the given historical moment.

At first glance it might seem that the predominance of what we
call the "autocratic" principle should go with what we call the
"aristocratic" tendency; and that the opposite principle which
we call "liberal" should go with the tendency that we call
"democratic."   Examining a number of types of political
organizations, one might conclude that a certain affinity does
exist between autocracy and aristocracy on the one hand, and
between liberalism and democracy on the other.   That, nevertheless, would be a rule that is subject to a great many exceptions.
It would be easy to find examples of autocracies that have not
recognized the existence of classes on which birth conferred legal

privileges. The Chinese empire, during long periods of its history, might be mentioned in that regard. It would be easier still to find examples of elective systems in which the electing group has been made up entirely of hereditary ruling classes. That was the case in Venice and in the Polish republic.

In any event, though it is difficult to find a political system which can be shown to have absolutely precluded one of the two principles or one of the two tendencies, it is certain that a strong predominance of autocracy or liberalism, or of the aristocratic tendency or the democratic, supplies a fundamental and trustworthy criterion for determining the type to which the constitution of a given people, at a given time, belongs.

2. Beyond any doubt, autocracy formed the basis of the first great human aggregations. All the ancient empires of Asia and Egypt were organized autocratically, and so was the neo-Persian empire of the Sassanids. The Arab caliphates gave lavish recognition to the autocratic principle. The first four caliphs were chosen by the Mussulman community or, more exactly, by the more influential members of the Mussulman community, who were assumed to represent it. Afterward the caliphate became hereditary and remained an appanage of certain families. Nevertheless, however absolute the Mussulman sovereign may have been, he could not change the fundamental law. That was contained in the Koran, or else could be inferred from the tradition transmitted by the early interpreters of the Koran.

Down to a few years ago the governments of Japan and China were autocratic, as was the old government in Turkey, which might be considered an Asiatic country from the nature of its civilization. As regards Europe, the government of the Roman Empire after Diocletian's time, and the government of the Byzantine Empire, may be called autocratic. Under Ivan the Terrible, Peter the Great and Alexander III, and during the early days of Nicholas II, Russia was governed by a pure autocracy. As we have seen, even in western Europe as our great modern state developed, the intermediate sovereignties that had grown up under the feudal system collapsed, and that gave rise to autocratic governments, which later evolved into our modern representative systems. In the Americas, finally, the two great states which the Europeans found in existence on the new continent,

Mexico and Peru, were organized autocratically.   In Mexico, to
be sure, the Spanish conquerors found one republic of a sort.
The state of Tlaxcala seems to have been ruled by a council of
tribal chiefs.   It struck an alliance with Cortez and provided him
with a base of operation for his conflict with the Aztec empire.[1]

A political system that has been so widely recurring and so
long enduring among peoples of the most widely various civilizations, who often have had no contacts material or intellectual
with one another, must somehow correspond to the political
nature of man.   The artificial or exceptional thing never shows
such great tenacity.   In fact, whether the supreme head, who
stands at the vertex of the political pyramid, exercises his
authority in the name of God or of the gods, or receives it from
the people or from those who presume to represent the people,
autocracy supplies a political formula, a principle of authority, a
justification of power, that is simple, clear and readily comprehensible to everybody.   There can be no human organization
without rankings and subordinations.   Any sort of hierarchy
necessarily requires that some should command and others
obey.   And since it is in the nature of the human being that many
men should love to command and that almost all men can be
brought to obey, an institution that gives those who are at the
top a way of justifying their authority and at the same time
helps to persuade those who are at the bottom to submit is
likely to be a useful institution.

But a very sound objection might be raised against autocracy.
Autocracy, one might say, may be a system that is well adapted
to forming great political organisms—such as the ancient empires
of Mesopotamia and Persia and in more recent times those of
China, Turkey and Russia—and to assure their existence for
indefinitely long periods.   But it does not allow the peoples that
have adopted it, and especially their ruling classes, to attain all
of the moral and intellectual development of which civilized
mankind is capable.   The art and thought of Greece and Rome
were on the whole superior to the art and thought of the Near
Eastern empires.   Not one of the Asiatic civilizations, ancient
or recent, has had an intellectual life intense enough to bear
comparison with what we find in the great nations of central
and western Europe, or in nineteenth century America.   But the

---

[1] De Solis, *Historia de la conquista de México.*

resplendent age of Athens lasted about a century and a half. It
opened with the battle of Plataea, which took place in 479 B.C.,
and extended, at the latest, down to the Lamian war, which
began in 323 B.C. Rome could begin to be considered a great
state and a center of culture by the end of the second Punic War,
around 203 B.C. But civil conflict was beginning as early as
133 B.C., with Tiberius Gracchus; and in 31 B.C., after a century
of almost continuous tumults, proscriptions and domestic
struggles, the ancient city-state was reorganized into the empire
of Augustus.

Among the great modern nations, England and the United
States have lasted longest with governments based on liberal
principles. But we have seen that England was fighting absolutism down to 1689, while the birth date of the United States can
be fixed as 1783. In power, wealth and intellectual worth the
England of 1689 was a very different country from the England
of today; and it is well known that virtually down to the middle
of the nineteenth century the great North American republic
was a largely agricultural country, sober, self-contained, attached
to old traditions, and very far from the opulence and world
importance that it has attained in our time. It would seem,
therefore, as though the liberal principle were likely to prevail
at those exceptional periods in the lives of the peoples when some
of the noblest faculties of man are able to show themselves in
all their intensity and energy, and when seeds are ripening that
will shortly produce considerable increases in political power and
economic prosperity. But it also would seem as though those
periods, which mark some of the most important milestones on
the road of civilization, were followed by other periods during
which human societies feel, as it were, an overpowering need for
a long sleep. This they find in the political field by slowing down
to an autocracy that is more or less masked and more or less
well-adapted to the level of development and culture that they
have attained.

The autocratic system naturally assumes the existence of an
autocrat—of a man, that is, who personifies the institution in the
name of which all who are invested with any part or particle of
public authority act. Now autocracy may be hereditary, in
which case we get a combination of the autocratic principle with
the aristocratic tendency; or it may be elective, in which case

we get a combination of the autocratic principle with the democratic tendency. However, autocrats who secure life tenure invariably tend to make their positions hereditary. As happened in Rome under the empire, the autocrat who has received his mandate nominally from the people is actually created, now by the ruling classes (or rather by that group in the ruling classes which has the most effective means of imposing its will upon other groups and classes), now by a clique of high officials who hold the levers by which the machine of state is guided. The most effective and certain instruments for using power have always been money and, better than money, soldiers. In autocratic governments the successor to the throne has often been chosen by the men with the state treasury and the armed forces of the state at their command, especially that portion of the armed forces stationed in the capital as a guard for the sovereign, for the court and for the central organs of government (see above, chap. IX, §3).

When inheritance is so well regulated that there can be no doubt as to the heir to the throne, the hereditary principle certainly has the advantage of automatically assuring the stability and continuity of power, and of avoiding the situation where each accession supplies a ready pretext for civil wars and court intrigues for or against a number of pretenders. From this point of view the system that has been adopted by the European monarchies, whereby the legal family has always been, and still is, monogamous, and succession always falls to the first-born male child, has yielded better results than the systems that have been used in Near Eastern monarchies. In the East the right of succession has never been regulated in such clear and definite terms, and there has always been the assumption that the reigning sovereign was at liberty to change it. This, naturally, has opened the door to intrigues by the favorite sultana, by high officials and even by menials in the court personnel who have daily access to the sovereign. For example, eunuchs in the personal service of the sultan often had great influence in the court at Constantinople; and eunuchs appear not rarely in the history of China in periods of decline in one dynasty or another.

Autocratic dynasties often originate with some strong and energetic individual who attains supreme power and then manages to acquire prestige with the ruling class, and also with the masses, weaving such an intricate network of interests and loyalties among high officials as to make it seem wise and natural that the succession should be transmitted to his descendants. In China new dynasties have as a rule been founded by energetic and lucky adventurers who have led victorious revolts and overthrown earlier dynasties. The dynasty of the Tokugawa shoguns originated in just that way in Japan. In India during the first decades of the sixteenth century a Turk, one Baber, placed himself at the head of a great band of adventurers, also Turks, and succeeded in founding the empire of the Grand Mogul. Such things have occurred in Europe more rarely. Napoleon did not succeed in handing on his throne to the King of Rome. The son of Oliver Cromwell held the post of Lord Protector for less than a year. The case of Gustavus Vasa might be cited as a western illustration of the general rule. Son of a Swedish nobleman, but reduced to becoming a shepherd and then a miner in the Dalecarlia in his youth, Vasa headed a revolt of his countrymen against the Danes and became the founder of a dynasty which reigned in Sweden from the first decades of the sixteenth century down to the coming of the Bernadottes, also adventurers. The more frequent case in Europe is the dynasty that is small and weak at first but little by little strengthens its position and expands through the consistent efforts of a number of generations. Examples would be the Capets, the house of Savoy, the Hohenzollerns and perhaps even the Hapsburgs.

There is little likelihood that the person designated by birth to hold the difficult post of supreme head of a great state will have the qualifications required for filling it effectively. Heredity, family tradition and education may contribute greatly toward enabling a hereditary sovereign to develop the outward demeanor and to learn the formalities that go best with the station that he is to occupy. Such things undoubtedly have their importance, since every bodily movement and every word of a sovereign may attract the attention of a whole people. But they are not enough to make up for deficiencies in more substantial qualities—capacity for work, energy, will to rule, knowledge of men and, also, a certain affective insensibility that is very helpful to rulers. They must not be too greatly stirred by the sufferings of others. They must know how to repress pangs and impulses of the heart and must sedulously avoid those critical moments when the human soul is irresistibly impelled to speak its innermost feelings and thoughts. There is the saying of Louis XI of France, "*Qui nescit dissimulare nescit regnare.*" Yet some malicious critic might feel that that sovereign would have done better to rest content with practicing the precept, as he did, without formulating it so neatly and handing it down to history. "*N'ayez jamais d'attachment pour personne,*" Louis XIV wrote with his own hand in the advice he penned for his nephew Philip, who was going off to be king in Spain.[1]

The deficiencies mentioned are compensated for in the great majority of cases by dividing the functions of autocracy between two individuals. The titular autocrat is given the representative, decorative part of the office, while the actual power is wielded by another person, who is called now major-domo, now prime minister, now vizier. Often, again, the task of governing is committed not to a single person but to a council made up of a small group of notables. Such were the councils of ministers that assisted European monarchs under the old regime, such the Tsong-li-yamen in China, the divan in Turkey, the Ba-ku-fu in the Japan of the Tokugawas.[2] But ordinarily in such groups there is one individual who couples a greater capacity for work with a stronger and firmer will to rule and who, therefore, comes to overshadow the others. When the titular prince reigns and the prime minister governs, and circumstances require a radical change in policy, the change can be affected by changing ministers and leaving the dynasty and the reigning sovereign as they were. That advantage, of course, involves a danger too. The de facto sovereign, the man who is actually governing, may try to retain his power for life and even pass it along to his children. That happened in France in the days of the Merovingian mayors of the palace. It has taken place repeatedly in Japan where, long before the shogunate of the Tokugawas was instituted, the power of the mikado had become nominal and was exercised in reality by the head of one or another of the great feudal families—the Tairas, the Minamotos, the Hojos, or the Ashikagas.[3]

It is not easy to formulate a theory as to how and when this dividing of autocratic power becomes necessary. It is inevitable,

[1] Michels, *Parteiwesen*, p. 365.

[2] La Mazelière, *Le Japon*, vol. III, book VI.

[3] *Ibid.*, vol. II, book II.

certainly, when the autocratic dynasty has aged and deteriorated, so that the legal autocrat remains shut up in his palace
amid enervating sensual pleasures, loses all contact with his
nobles and people and forgets the art of making the wheels of
the state machine go round. But in Europe especially there
have been many examples of descendants of old dynasties who
have managed to run the governments of their states effectively.
One thinks of Charles V and Philip II of Spain, Louis XIV of
France, Victor Amadeus II of Savoy, Peter the Great of Russia
and Frederick the Great of Prussia. Studying one by one such
characters, or others that might be mentioned, we can make out
that, among widely differing personal traits, they have had two
fundamental qualities in common, namely, a great capacity for
sustained physical and intellectual exertion and a strong will to
rule.

One might surmise offhand, that in the beginning the choice
of the autocrat coadjutor who exercises actual power should rest
with the titular autocrat, and that the former must first have
succeeded in winning the confidence of the latter. As time goes
on, however, a strong character is likely to acquire such ascendancy over a weaker character that the latter will not dare to
recall what was once freely conceded. In that case the manda-
tory who was voluntarily chosen may become the guardian who
has to be endured. The first and most pressing task of the vice-
gerent is to fill all high positions with persons bound to him by
ties of family, gratitude or, better still, complicity in questionable
acts or actual crimes. He can then count on the fidelity of the
clique that comes into frequent contact with the ruler and
sedulously keep him away from anybody who does not belong
to the clique.

The formation of a clique, perhaps of two or three dozens of
persons, or even as many as a hundred, according to the case, who
monopolize the management of the state and occupy the more
important offices, sometimes in rotation, is a thing that occurs in
all autocracies and, in fact, in all forms of government. What
varies is the criterion by which this group, which makes up the
highest stratum of the ruling class, is selected; for the criteria
will be different according as the system is autocratic or liberal,
or as the democratic or aristocratic tendency prevails. But in
all cases and in all systems, there is one criterion that never

varies, and it is always of great importance: Those who already belong to the clique have to be satisfied. In normal times, when it is a question of securing one of the positions that involve actual control over part of the forces of a state, and so over the fates of many individuals, the consent, or at least the tacit approval and acquiescence of those who are already in similar posts, is almost always necessary. Rightly enough the proverb says that one cannot enter paradise over the veto of the saints.

In countries where the autocratic principle and the aristocratic tendency jointly prevail, the group mentioned is usually made up of members of the highest nobility, who are appointed by birth to occupy the more important offices and exercise the more important functions of state. In such cases the court is usually the arena in which rivalries between the great families for pre-eminence in the realm unfold. So it was in France in the days of the conflict between the counts of Armagnac and the dukes of Burgundy, in Sicily during the latter half of the fourteenth century, and in Spain under the weakling Charles II. But when the titular sovereign has talent and strength of will, he sometimes succeeds in breaking the ring of aristocratic cliques that serve him—or, more often, rule him—and he snaps it by elevating to the highest positions persons who are of ordinary birth, who owe him everything and who therefore are loyal and effective instruments of his policies. The two outstanding ministers of Louis XIV were Colbert and Louvois. They did not belong to the high French nobility. Peter the Great of Russia often appointed adventurers of foreign origin to important offices, or even Russians of humble extraction. In the Near Eastern autocracies, cases where persons of very humble origin first attained high office and then supreme power were not unheard-of. One might mention Basil the Macedonian, who became emperor at Byzantium in the ninth century, and a certain Nadir who became shah of Persia in the eighteenth century.

Basil the Macedonian died in 886. He was the son of a peasant. He got his start through his skill at managing horses. Becoming squire to one of the court nobles, he succeeded, by his wits and tireless energy, in making himself first the favorite and then the colleague of the emperor Michael III. When Michael was thinking of getting rid of him, he got rid of Michael by murdering him, and succeeded in taking his place on the throne. Apart from the craft and crime by which he made his way in the world, he may be considered one of the best emperors Byzantium ever had. Nadir was the son of a Turkoman tribal chief. He began life as leader of a band of brigands. After many adventures he entered the service of Tahmasp II, shah of Persia in the Safawid dynasty. Finally he deposed Tahmasp and had an infant son of the latter proclaimed shah, becoming his guardian. Soon after that he had both the father and the son killed and he himself was proclaimed shah. That was in 1736. Energetic, exceedingly cruel, he enhanced the prestige of Persia abroad and succeeded in taking Delhi, capital of the Grand Mogul's empire. He is said to have won booty at Delhi to the value of half a billion dollars. He was assassinated in his turn in 1747. Basil and the shah Nadir would both have been magnificent materials for Machiavelli's *Prince*. Agathocles and Cesare Borgia seem tame in comparison.

Needless to say, in such exceptional careers extraordinary good fortune plays a large part, along with unusual mental gifts and, especially, a faculty for taking advantage of every propitious circumstance that will lift one a bit higher. This faculty comes down, more than anything else, to knowing how to make oneself useful, or shall we say necessary, to those who already are where one wants to be, and then in playing to all their qualities, good and bad.

3. Below the highest stratum in the ruling class there is always, even in autocratic systems, another that is much more numerous and comprises all the capacities for leadership in the country. Without such a class any sort of social organization would be impossible. The higher stratum would not in itself be sufficient for leading and directing the activities of the masses. In the last analysis, therefore, the stability of any political organism depends on the level of morality, intelligence and activity that this second stratum has attained; and this soundness is commonly the greater in proportion as a sense of the collective interests of nation or class succeeds in exerting pressure on the individual ambitions or greeds of the members of this class. Any intellectual or moral deficiencies in this second stratum, accordingly, represent a graver danger to the political structure, and one that is harder to repair, than the presence of similar

deficiencies in the few dozen persons who control the workings of the state machine. To use a comparison: The strength of an army depends primarily on the intellectual and moral value of the officers who come into direct contact with the soldiers, beginning with the colonel and ending with the second lieutenant. If, by some improbable accident, all the generals and staff officers of an army were to disappear at one stroke, the army would sustain a very serious shock, but it would still be on its feet and the lost leaders could be replaced in a few months' time by promoting the better regimental commanders and raising other officers, from among the more competent, to the staff. But if all the officers who actually lead the soldiers were to disappear the army would dissolve before they could possibly be replaced. The higher stratum in the ruling class corresponds to the generals and staff, the second stratum to the officers who personally lead the soldiers under fire.

In primitive autocratic systems, and in the more ancient ones in general, this second stratum in the ruling class was almost always made up of priests and warriors, the two groups of persons who had the material forces of the society at their disposal, exercised intellectual and moral leadership and, as consequence rather than as cause of that leadership, were economically pre-eminent. Under social conditions of that sort, it was natural that autocracy in government should be combined with a prevalence of the aristocratic tendency. But as time goes on, in countries where class differentiation rests originally on invasions by foreign peoples, the conquering and conquered races fuse completely. The level of civilization rises. Wealth and culture therefore increase, and technical preparation becomes necessary for the satisfactory performance of public duties. Aristocratic autocracies therefore almost always develop into more or less bureaucratic autocracies. That was the case with the Roman Empire, especially after Diocletian, with the Byzantine Empire, with the Chinese Empire, at least during the last centuries of its existence, with Russia after Peter the Great, with the principal European states in the eighteenth century and, with certain reservations, with Japan after the creation of the Tokugawa shogunate. As is well known, after Iyeyasu, who reigned in Japan from 1598 to 1616, had founded the shogunate of the Tokugawas, the power of the daimios, or great barons, was greatly curtailed.[1]   All the regimes mentioned may be considered bureaucratic autocracies.

Before an autocracy can begin to bureaucratize a great state, the political organization must be so strong that it can regularly levy on the income of private individuals a portion that is large enough to pay the salaries of public officials and defray the expenses of a permanent armed force.   But then, as is often the case with social phenomena, a series of actions and reactions follow.   Once bureaucratization is well advanced, it in turn enhances the coercive efficiency of the state machine and so enables the ruling class, and especially the leading group in it, to exercise greater and greater influence over the governed masses and to direct the efforts of the governed more and more efficiently toward the purposes that their governors wish to achieve.   In other words, a bureaucratized autocracy is a perfected autocracy and it has all the advantages and disadvantages of that perfection.

Among the advantages, one may mention the possibility of assigning the various functions of leadership to specialists and the possibility of opening all doors to talents that are forging upward from the lower strata in society, and therefore of making room for personal merit.   So homage is paid to a principle of distributive justice that has always had a grip on the hearts of men and is especially cogent in our time, a feeling that there should be an exact and almost mathematical correspondence between the service an individual renders to society and the position which he comes to hold in the social ranking.

But, as Ferrero well notes,[2] personal merit is one of the things that the passions and interests of men best manage to counterfeit. In autocratic systems, where success depends upon the judgment of one person, or of a few persons, intrigue may be enough to produce the counterfeit semblance of personal merit.   In liberal systems, especially when the democratic tendency is also prevalent and the regard and active sympathy of many people are necessary if one is to get on in the world, intrigue has to be coupled with a good dose of charlatanry.   At any rate, quite aside from such a prejudicial and, if one will, such an over-pessimistic objection, it is certain that the judgment of a person's merits and aptitudes will always be more or less subjective, and

---

[1] La Mazelière, *Le Japon*, vol. III, book VI.

[2] *Memorie e confessioni di un sovrano deposto*, p. 29.

that, therefore, each judge will in all good faith give a candidate
a higher rating for intellectual and moral qualities which he
likes or happens to possess himself.   That is one of the chief
reasons for the blind conservatism, the utter incapacity to correct
one's faults and weaknesses, that is so frequent in exclusively
bureaucratic regimes.

The example of China is apt to this point.   In China the
higher mandarinate was made up of educated persons, but they
were educated in the old traditional culture of the country.
In the second half of the nineteenth century the mandarinate
strenuously opposed a new method of recruiting public employees
based on knowledge of European languages and European
sciences.   In Japan, on the other hand, the men who led the
great reform of 1868 grasped the necessity of acquiring European
culture at once.   These men came almost all from the samurai
class.   They were educated people, but they were not scholars
and scientists by profession.

To avoid distortions in judgments on merit, it is not enough
that the higher officials on whom the choice and advancement of
the lower functionaries depend should be individuals of great
intelligence.   They have to be generous and noble of heart.
Sometimes the person who is endowed with the rarest and loftiest
qualities of mind prefers people of mediocre or second-rate
talents.   They give him less cause for jealousy and they better
supplement his own capacities, for the mediocre man does things
that the first-rate one cannot do, or scorns to do.   Furthermore,
the mediocre man is almost always flattering and smooth: he is
without, or at least is better able to dissimulate, a certain youthful
cocksureness frequently encountered in men of green age and
lively talents—a sort of presumptuousness, real or apparent,
typical of those men who seem to see at a glance things that
other men, even old and experienced ones, either do not see at all
or see very tardily.

Suppose, then, that in our distrust of human impartiality
we try to replace choice and appointment by superiors with
automatic rules of advancement.   Such rules can be based
only upon the principle of seniority.   In this case, unfailingly,
the lazy and the diligent, the intelligent and the stupid, get along
equally well.   The public employee knows perfectly well that
it will not help him to do any more or any better than others.

He will therefore do the minimum that is indispensable if he is not to lose his position or his promotion. In such circumstances the bureaucratic career tends to become the refuge of the talentless, or of people who absolutely need to have salaried positions in order to provide for their daily wants. If an intelligent man does happen to stray into the bureaucracy, he devotes only a part of his activity and his talent to his office, and often it is not the best part.

Though a bureaucracy may be legally open to all social classes, in fact it will always be recruited from the middle class, in other words from the second stratum of the ruling class. For one thing, those who are born into the second stratum find it easier to secure the education that is required of them, and in their family background they develop a practical sense of the best ways of getting started in the bureaucratic career and of advancing in it. How helpful the guidance and influence of a father, of an influential relative or of family friends can be, one can easily imagine. For this reason it can in general be said that in a purely autocratic system, or in systems that combine autocracy and liberalism, the moral level of the bureaucracy is the moral level of the ruling class. That level will be higher when the ruling class has deep-rooted traditions of probity and honor because it has been formed and disciplined over long periods of time, and has devoted itself for many generations to the service of the state, now in civil, now in military capacities. The level will be lower when the ruling class is of more recent date and stems either from rustling, bustling and lucky adventurers, or from families of peasants and shopkeepers who have acquired, at best, the first rudiments of manners and education. Even if such people have developed a certain competence, they are still often without a spark of idealism and retain an inveterate and sordid greed for large, and even for petty gains.

In cases such as these bureaucratic organization yields its worst results. One notes brazen favoritism in superiors, base servility in subalterns and, in superiors and subalterns both, a tendency to exchange for favors of any sort such influence as their positions put at their disposal. In the more serious cases, bargaining turns into outright sale, and then we get a system of pecuniary corruption which disrupts and paralyzes every state activity once it has become common in the higher and lower grades of the bureaucratic scale.

Another defect common to bureaucracies, even when their moral level is high, is a disposition to believe in their own infallibility. Bureaucrats are by nature exceedingly loath to accept criticisms and suggestions from persons who are not of their calling, and even from those who are.

4. As we have seen (§2 above), the liberal principle has had a more brilliant record than the autocratic principle, but it is certainly a shorter record and it is less widespread over the world's surface and through history. To the examples of liberal countries, ancient and modern, that we have mentioned, one might add Poland, Holland, the Hanseatic cities, Genoa, Florence, Switzerland—places all where liberal regimes have lasted, in one era or another, for considerable lengths of time. Finally there is Venice, where a system that was liberal, in the sense that we attach to the term, and at the same time oligarchical, prevailed for a good thousand years. But almost all the other states just mentioned, apart from some few cantons in Switzerland, were governed by aristocracies of more or less limited membership. In Poland, the country where the liberal system was applied over a considerable territory, aristocracy degenerated very soon into turbulent anarchy.

Looking for the essential characteristics of the system which we call "liberal," one may say that in such systems the law is based upon the consent of the majority of citizens, though only a small fraction of the inhabitants may be citizens; and then that the officials who apply the law are named directly or indirectly by their subordinates, that their posts are temporary and that they are personally responsible for the lawfulness of their acts. In the great liberal states, in general, citizens do not exercise legislative power personally. They delegate it to assemblies which are directly or indirectly named by them, and the work of the elective officials is supplemented and coordinated by the work of a bureaucracy proper. Furthermore, in cases where the liberal principle prevails, the state customarily recognizes certain limits to its powers in its relations to individual citizens and to associations of citizens. Such limits were not entirely unknown to classical Greece and ancient Rome. They are almost always recognized in modern constitutions. They relate to such things as freedom of worship, of the press, of education, of assembly and of speech. They guarantee personal liberty, private property and inviolability of domicile.

In states where the liberal principle prevails we also find the two strata of the ruling class which we found in autocratic systems, the first very small, the second much more extensive and deeper reaching. The elective system, in fact, does not preclude the formation of more or less closed cliques which compete for the highest offices in the state, each of them tapering up to some aspirant to the highest office—it may be the presidency of a republic or the presidency of a council of ministers. These parties correspond to the court cliques in autocracies, from among which the immediate coadjutors of the supreme head of the state are chosen. The methods used are of course different. In order to reach high station in an autocracy it is sufficient to have the support of one or more persons, and that is secured by exploiting all their passions, good and bad. In liberal systems one has to steer the inclinations of at least the whole second stratum of the ruling class, which, if it does not in itself constitute the electorate, at least supplies the general staffs of leaders who form the opinions and determine the conduct of the electing body. From within it come the committees that direct political groupings, the speakers who address assemblies and meetings, the men who make and publish the newspapers and, finally, that small number of persons who are capable of forming opinions of their own as to people and events of the day, and therefore exercise great influence on the many who are not capable of having opinions of their own and are ready, perhaps without knowing it, always to follow the opinions of others.

The results which applications of the liberal principle yield vary according as the electorate, with which rests the choice of those who are to occupy the highest public offices, varies from narrowly exclusive to broadly inclusive.

In the former case, a large part of the ruling class, or of those who have the requisites for belonging to it, are kept out. This exclusion makes a liberal system look very much like masked autocratic rule by a narrowly limited class of people—at times by a few powerful or virtually omnipotent families. That was the case in Poland in the decades just preceding the partition of that country. Furthermore, when the electorate is narrowly limited, almost all the voters are or may be regarded as eligible for office. In fact, almost all of them do become candidates. In other words they are offered for judgment but without there being a sufficient number of judges.

Something of the sort happens in elective chambers in countries with parliamentary governments. There the frequency of cabinet crises and the difficulty of forming new ministries depend, to an extent at least, on the fact that large numbers of deputies want to be ministers or undersecretaries of state. The candidates being too many, judges become too scarce, for judges should be men who share none of the interests that are at issue.

As a rule, therefore, in narrowly limited electorates, either a single clique forms, made up of those already in office and of their associates or partisans, or else there are two cliques, one of which is in power, while the other offers a spiteful and systematic opposition. The few who hold aloof from both cliques ordinarily are left isolated and are ignored. They can exert an effective influence only at critical moments, when a series of startling scandals or serious failures makes the fall of the clique that is in power probable or inevitable.

In the second case—in other words, in systems where everybody, or almost everybody, can vote—the chief task of the various party organizations into which the ruling class is divided is to win the votes of the more numerous classes, which are necessarily the poorest and most ignorant. These classes ordinarily live in submission to a government which often they do not care for, and the aims and workings of which more often still they do not understand. Their first, their natural, their most spontaneous desire is to be governed as little as possible, or to make as few sacrifices as possible for the state. Their second desire, which develops more especially with the exercise of suffrage, is to profit by government in order to better their economic situation, and to vent the repressed resentments and envies which often—not always—the man who is below feels for the man who is above, especially for the man who is his immediate superior.

When success in the struggle between the different groups in the ruling class depends upon the support and sympathy of the masses, the group that has the less effective means of influence at its disposal will unfailingly avail itself of the two desires mentioned, especially of resentments and envies, in order to draw the lower strata of society along with it. Connected with the group, now as a matter of sentiment, now as a matter of interest, are individuals who were born in the less favored classes but have managed by special talent and energy, or by exceptional cunning, to climb out of them. Michels has examined with great acumen the contribution to the management and organization of the socialist parties in the various countries that has been made by elements deriving from the middle classes and by elements issuing from the working classes themselves, and the rivalries and competitions that often arise between those two categories in the socialist general staffs.[1]

Whatever their origins, the methods that are used by the people who aim to monopolize and exploit the sympathy of the masses always have been the same. They come down to pointing out, with exaggerations of course, the selfishness, the stupidity, the material enjoyments of the rich and the powerful; to denouncing their vices and wrongdoings, real and imaginary; and to promising to satisfy a common and widespread sense of rough-hewn justice which would like to see abolished every social distinction based upon advantage of birth and at the same time would like to see an absolutely equal distribution of pleasures and pains.

Often enough the parties against which this demagogic propaganda is directed use exactly the same means to combat it. Whenever they think they can profit by doing so, they too make promises which they will never be able to keep. They too flatter the masses, play to their crudest instincts and exploit and foment all their prejudices and greeds. A despicable competition, in which those who deliberately deceive lower their intellectual level to a par with those they deceive, while morally they stoop even lower!

The oldest example of demagogic eloquence is the speech that Homer puts into the mouth of Thersites, a man who was in the habit of baiting leaders of the Greeks.[2] He accuses Agamemnon of waxing rich on the labors and perils of the common

[1] *Parteiwesen*, part IV.
[2] *Iliad* II.

soldiers and of passing his time amid the allurements of beautiful slave girls. Then he incites the Greeks to a sort of military strike, urging them to leave their leader to his own resources, that he may come to realize how much he owes to the sufferings of the soldiers. Unsurpassable models of demagogic eloquence are the speeches ascribed to Caius Marius by Sallust[1] and a speech that Machiavelli has an unknown workingman deliver on the occasion of rioting by the wool carders in Florence.[2] Modern demagogues almost always fall short of these classic models, in which all the arguments that can be advanced against those who owe wealth or high position to birth are set forth in such masterly fashion as to arouse deep echoes in the hearts of all the disinherited.

All in all, then, the liberal principle finds conditions for its application most favorable when the electorate is made up in the majority of the second stratum of the ruling class, which forms the backbone of all great political organizations. When it is sufficiently large, no very great proportion of the voters can aspire to candidacies, and the candidates therefore can find judges in them and not rivals or accomplices. At the same time, when the electorate is fairly limited, success does not depend on paying homage to the beliefs and sentiments of the more ignorant classes. Only under such circumstances can one of the chief assumptions of the liberal system be made, we do not say complete, but not wholly illusory—namely, that those who represent shall be responsible to the represented.

Another advantage, presumed or real, of the liberal principle, is that the acts of rulers can be publicly discussed, either in political assemblies and administrative councils or in the daily press and in periodicals. But if this last and very effective means of control is really to enlighten public opinion, the newspapers must not be organs of political or financial cliques nor blind instruments of faction. If they are, the public should know about it and be in a position to take due account of the fact.

5. The democratic tendency—the tendency to replenish ruling classes from below—is constantly at work with greater or lesser intensity in all human societies. At times the rejuvenation

---

[1] *Bellum Jugurthinum* III, 75.

[2] *Storie fiorentine* III.

comes about in rapid or violent ways. More often, in fact normally, it takes place through a slow and gradual infiltration of elements from the lower into the higher classes.

In the past, violent renovations not infrequently came about as a result of foreign invasions. A conquering people would settle on the territory of the conquered and, without destroying the old inhabitants or driving them out, force its rule upon them. That happened in western Europe after the fall of the Roman Empire, in the Persia of the Sassanids after the Arab invasion, in England after the victory of William the Conqueror, in India after the invasion of the Mohammedans, in China after the invasion of the Mongols and again, later on, after the invasion of the Manchu Tatars. In such cases, remnants of the old native aristocracies have almost always crept into the new aristocracies of foreign origin. In the examples mentioned, also, the conquest by foreigners was usually facilitated by an incipient domestic decline. The indigenous ruling class had either weakened or disintegrated, or else had become alienated spiritually from the rest of the population.

In times more recent, violent and far-reaching renovations of old political classes have sometimes come about through internal upheavals. These would be "revolutions" proper. They occur when a wide breach opens between a people's official political organization and its customs, ideas and sentiments, and when many elements which would be competent to participate in government are artificially held in a subordinate status. The classic example of that situation would be the French Revolution. Another example is developing before our eyes in Russia today.

But cases where violent crises radically alter the criteria of selection for ruling classes, and change or modify their composition profoundly in the course of a few years, may be regarded as exceptional. They are characteristic of a few particular periods in history. Such overturns sometimes give a vigorous impetus to intellectual, moral and material progress. At other times they have been the beginnings, or else the results, of periods of decay and disintegration in civilizations. Even in normal times, one can almost always observe that a slow and gradual renewal of the ruling class is going on through infiltrations into the higher strata of society of elements emerging from the lower.

But this tendency, which we have decided to call democratic, sometimes is outstanding in a civilization and operates in a more effective and rapid manner. At other times it proceeds covertly and therefore more blandly, because of the thousand obstacles that laws, habits and customs put in its way.

As we have seen (chap. II, §8), the democratic tendency is more likely to prevail in unsettled times, when new manners of thinking and feeling are undermining the old concepts on which the structure of social rankings has been based, when scientific and technical progress have created new ways of making money or produced changes in military organization, or even when a shock from outside has forced a nation to rally all the energies and capacities which, in quiet times, would have remained in a potential state. Revolutions and long wars give many new men a chance to assert themselves and make use of their talents. Had there been no French Revolution, Napoleon Bonaparte would probably have lived to be a good colonel of artillery, and had it not been for the wars of the Revolution and the Empire, some of his marshals would certainly have remained lieutenants. In general, changes in religion, new movements in philosophy and political thinking, invention of new weapons or new instruments of warfare, application of new discoveries to economic production and corresponding increases in economic production, are all elements that favor rapid translations and interchanges of the molecules that make up the various social strata. Such changes and interchanges come about more readily in new countries, where natural resources have not been very much exploited and still abound, permitting energetic and enterprising men to attain wealth and reputation with ease, or at least with less difficulty. The examples of Australia and the different countries in the Americas are apt to this point.

If it is confined within moderate limits, the democratic tendency is in a sense indispensable to what is called "progress" in human societies. If all aristocracies had remained steadfastly closed and stationary, the world would never have changed, and mankind would have stopped developing at the stage that it had attained at the time of the Homeric monarchies, or the old Near Eastern empires. The struggle between those who are at the top and those who are born at the bottom but aspire to climb has been, is and will ever be the ferment that forces individuals and classes to widen their horizons and seek the new roads that have brought the world to the degree of civilization that it attained in the nineteenth century. That high level of civilization made it possible to create in the political field the great modern representative state, which, as we have seen (chap. XIV, §8), is of all political organisms the one that has succeeded in coordinating the largest sum of individual energies and activities and applying them to purposes that are related to the collective interest.

When the democratic tendency does not exert too great an influence, to the exclusion of other tendencies, it represents a conservative force. It enables ruling classes to be continually replenished through the admission of new elements who have inborn talents for leadership and a will to lead, and so prevents that exhaustion of aristocracies of birth which usually paves the way for great social cataclysms. Nevertheless, beginning with the end of the eighteenth century and continuing through the nineteenth, the dogma of human equality, modernized to accord with modern ways of thinking, has been taking on new vigor, and it has been deemed possible to make a complete application of it on this earth. Many people have believed and still believe, and not a few have feigned to believe and still feign to believe, that every advantage due to birth can, in time and by appropriate changes in our social system, be eliminated, and that the future will see human associations in which there will be an exact correspondence between the service a person renders to society and the rung he occupies on the social ladder.

The notion that in an ideally organized state there would be absolute correspondence between the service rendered by an individual to society and the rank he comes to occupy in it was clearly formulated for the first time by Saint-Simon. He presses the doctrine in many of his works under one form or another. Later on the same concept became one of the tenets of the Saint-Simonian school, which in other respects ranged far afield from the master's teachings.[1] This aspiration has never, perhaps, been so widely held and so clearly formulated as it is today, but it would be absurd to imagine that it was first conceived in Saint-Simon's time, or even a little less than two centuries ago. It has been the moral basis of every attack that

[1] *Oeuvres*, and see Bernardo Mosca, "Il pensiero di Saint-Simon considerato dopo un secolo."

has ever aimed at renewing or rejuvenating ruling classes. Whenever an effort has been made to remove the barriers that have separated an aristocracy, hereditary by law or in fact, from the rest of society, the appeal has always been to the claims of individual merit as against the privileges of birth, now in the name of religion, now in the name of the natural equality of all men or at least of all citizens. In this respect, the democracies of Greece and Rome, the Ciompi (wool carders) of Florence, the Anabaptists of Münster—without, to be sure, having the Bill of Rights at their fingers' tips—thought and acted like the French reformers of the eighteenth century and like the communists of today. Wat Tyler was the leader of a famous rebellion of the English peasants against the lords which broke out in 1381. Some years before, while the insurrection was brewing, a priest named John Ball wrote the often quoted couplet that exactly expresses this attitude:

> When Adam delved and Eve span
> Who was then the gentleman?

But every time the democratic movement has triumphed, in part or in full, we have invariably seen the aristocratic tendency come to life again through efforts of the very men who had fought it and sometimes had proclaimed its suppression. In Rome, after forcing the doors that barred their access to high office, the rich plebeians fused with the old patriciate and formed a new nobility to which access by outsiders was legally permitted though in practice it was left very difficult. In Florence an oligarchy of "fat proletarians" supplanted the noble families whose political influence they had seen fit to destroy by the famous "ordinances of justice." In France the bourgeoisie of the nineteenth century in part replaced the nobility of the old regime. Everywhere, the moment the old barrier has been cast down a new one has been raised in its place, perhaps lower at times and less bristling with brambles and thorns, but high enough and hard enough to cross to offer fairly serious obstacles to anyone disposed to leap over it. Everywhere, those who have reached the top rungs on the social ladder have set up defenses for themselves and their children against those who also wished to climb.[1]

---

[1] Mosca, "Il principio aristocratico ed il democratico nel passato e nello avvenire."

It will be said that all that is a necessary product of private property, which makes wealth hereditary and smooths the road for those who inherit it to attain power and stay there. In that objection there is certainly a large element of truth—we do not say the whole truth, because the cultural level and the family connections of a parent can be passed on in part to his children, even when the family has no patrimony proper. But few people realize today that in a collectivist state the drawback mentioned, for which private property is at present held responsible, will not disappear. It will simply present itself in a graver form. As we have already demonstrated (chap. XI, §3) (and as is now happening in Russia), the governors of a state that is organized along collectivist lines will have far greater resources and means of action than have the rich and powerful of today. The rulers of a collectivist state pile economic power on political power and so, controlling the lots of all individuals and all families, have a thousand ways of distributing rewards and punishments. It would be strange indeed if they did not take advantage of such a strategic position to give their children a start in life.

In order to abolish privileges of birth entirely, it would be necessary to go one step farther, to abolish the family, recognize a vagrant Venus and drop humanity to the level of the lowest animalism. It is interesting that in the *Republic* Plato proposed abolishing the family as an almost necessary consequence of the abolition of private property. He seems to have been inclined, however, to confine the two abolitions to his ruling class—the class of philosophers and warriors. He was not in favor of what would now be called "free love." He envisaged temporary unions, in which choice of the temporary mate was to be made by his philosophers. He further arranged that the children born of such unions should not know their parents, or be known by them, since the state should form one single family. A similar system is expounded and defended in Campanella's *City of the Sun.* Campanella also wanted to abolish private property and the family.

But we do not think that even provisions as radical as these would suffice to establish in the world an absolute justice that will never be realized, but which will always be appealed to by those who are trying to upset the system of social rankings that prevails in a given country at a given time. The Catholic clergy have not been allowed to have legal children. But whenever they have come to wield great economic and political power, nepotism has arisen in the Church. And we may well imagine that if nephews as well as sons were to be suppressed the human being would still find among his fellow men some whom he would love and protect in preference to others.

It is not so certain, meantime, that it would be altogether beneficial to the collectivity to have every advantage of birth eliminated in the struggle for membership in the ruling class and for high position in the social hierarchy. If all individuals could participate in the scramble on an equal footing, struggle would be intensified to the point of frenzy. This would entail an enormous expenditure of energy for strictly personal ends, with no corresponding benefit to the social organism, at least in the majority of cases.[1] On the other hand, it may very well be that certain intellectual and, especially, moral qualities, which are necessary to a ruling class if it is to maintain its prestige and function properly, are useful also to society, yet require, if they are to develop and exert their influence, that the same families should hold fairly high social positions for a number of generations.

6. In this twentieth century of ours, there are few people indeed who do not make public profession of an enthusiastic support of democracy. It might seem superfluous, therefore, to linger very long on the evils and disadvantages of an excessive predominance of the aristocratic tendency or of stabilizing political power and social influence in certain families. Yet just such stabilization is a common trait in civilizations that have disappeared, and in civilizations that have remained outside the sphere of present-day European progress. Social stabilization has been considerably weakened in the West but it is far from being a thing of the past. The aristocratic spirit is not entirely dead among us, and probably will never die. Now that tendency has its dangers and disadvantages.

When a people has long been ruled by a closed or semiclosed aristocracy, almost inevitably a group spirit, a sense of caste, arises and asserts itself, so that the members of the aristocracy

[1] Mosca, *op. cit.*

come to think of themselves as infinitely superior to the rest of men. This pride often goes hand in hand with a certain frivolousness of spirit and an excessive attention to external forms. Those who are at the top are likely to feel that everything is automatically due to them, without their having any definite obligations toward those who do not belong to their caste. They look upon outsiders as in a way created to be blind instruments of their aims, passions and caprices. That state of mind comes easily to the human being. It is amazing, sometimes, to note how quickly people who have managed to climb to high position from humble origins come to consider themselves superior to the rest of mankind.

This manner of thinking and feeling develops spontaneously in individuals who are destined to occupy conspicuous positions from the day of their birth and who enjoy many privileges and receive much adulation from their earliest childhood. But it prevents them in general from understanding, and therefore from sympathizing with, the sorrows and tribulations of those who live on the lower rungs of the social ladder; and they are equally insensitive to the toils and efforts of those who have managed to climb a rung or two on the ladder by their own achievement. Exaggeration of the aristocratic spirit, moreover, brings people to avoid contacts with the lower strata of society. They are at no pains to make any close study of them, and are left in complete ignorance of real psychological conditions in the lower classes. Those conditions are sometimes portrayed to them in literature, especially in novels, as something very close to the primitive simplicity and goodness of man, and then again as something that takes directly after the brutes. Whatever their inner process, both exaggerations have the one result of depriving the ruling classes of any influence whatever on mental and sentimental developments in the masses, and so of unfitting the ruling classes for managing them.

Rarely in history do we find examples of hereditary upper classes that have been conscious, as they should properly be, of their intellectual and moral superiorities, and yet have been spontaneously and equally conscious of the obligations toward the lower classes which those superiorities lay upon them. More rarely still among individuals belonging to hereditary ruling classes has there been any widespread distribution of the sentiments of real brotherhood and oneness of man that have been the foundation and the glory of the great world religions, Buddhism, Christianity and Islam—sentiments, in other words, which enable the man of high station to recognize and sincerely feel that the lowliest human being is also an integral part of the common humanity to which they both belong. This feeling, after all, is the one sound element that lies embedded in that great conglomerate of dreams and falsehoods which is going about today under the name of "democracy."

The most insidious enemy of all aristocracies of birth is, undoubtedly, idleness. Idleness generates softness and sensuality, stimulates frivolousness of mind and creates an aspiration to a life of pleasures unaccompanied by duties. When there is no daily pressure from an obligation to do a set task, and when the habit of work has not been formed in early years, it is hard to escape the traps of that deadly enemy. Yet aristocracies that cannot defend themselves adequately from idleness decline rapidly. They may succeed in retaining their ranks and offices nominally for some time, but when such functions are actually exercised by subalterns, the subalterns soon become the actual masters. It can only turn out that the man who acts, and knows how to act, will eventually succeed in commanding.

Exemption from physical labor, the assurance of being able to live and retain one's social position without a corresponding and compelling need of attending to an onerous daily occupation, may in certain cases yield results that are excellent from the standpoint of the collective interest. The fact that a certain number of people have been in that position has been one of the main factors in the intellectual and moral progress of mankind. The Spanish critic Unamuno once wrote a witty and very learned eulogy on laziness. In it he tried to show that the world owes much to the loafer, for had there not been among our ancestors a certain number of people who did not have to work with their hands, and who had at their disposal all the time there was, neither science, nor art, nor morality would have come into being.[1]

Unamuno's thesis is a daring one, and it contains a considerable amount of truth. But the question might be stated in a better form. In the case in point, what the uninitiate calls laziness—

---

[1] "En defensa de la haraganería."

and the uninitiate may belong to the upper classes as well as to the lower—is often very far from being any such thing. It may be the noblest form of human labor. It may be a form of labor that envisages no immediate utility to the individual who devotes himself to it, or even to any other specified individuals. It may simply seek to discover the laws that regulate the universe of which we are part, or to learn what the development of human thought and human institutions has been. It may have no other motive than a disinterested passion for widening to some extent the confines of the known at the expense of the unknown. It may have no other end in view than to clarify somewhat, within the limits of the possible, those grave and tormenting problems that try the souls and minds of men, and to endow men with the characteristic truths that lift them above the status of the animals. Now those impulses have expressed themselves most readily, and have had the best chance to develop, in people who have belonged to ruling classes—classes which have been so firmly established in their rule that some of their members could be exempted from the material cares of life and from the worries that go with defending one's social position from day to day. Under any other conditions these same impulses would not have asserted themselves at all. We are obliged to admit that science and social morality originated in aristocracies, and that even today they normally find their most consistent practitioners in aristocracies.

It would be untrue and unfair to maintain that a disinterested passion for knowledge is not to be found in individuals belonging to the lower strata of society. Modern civilized nations are products of a very ancient culture, and their social classes have undergone so many upheavals and so many amalgamations that it is not surprising that most aristocratic instincts should sometimes appear in individuals of low status, who may have inherited them from remote ancestors. One of the happiest applications of the democratic tendency would lie in enabling such individuals to develop their superior qualities. That, however, is not an easy thing to do, and we do not believe that compulsory elementary education will alone be sufficient to accomplish it.

It might be objected that we owe great discoveries in the scientific field, and great pronouncements in morals, to men who

have been endowed with what is commonly called "genius"—
men, that is, who have had exceptional capacities of mind or
heart and exceptional strength of will—and that genius is rarely
hereditary. This is true. But genius more often reveals
itself in individuals who belong to peoples and classes that
have shown high average levels of intelligence, and it is a fact
of common observation that intellectual qualities which are
above the average, though not necessarily extraordinary, are
readily transmitted from parents to children. It is not far-
fetched to imagine that in the beginning, the upper classes, on
whatever basis they may have been constituted, attracted many
of the more intelligent individuals into their membership, and
that when such classes are not hermetically sealed they are continuously replenished with intelligent elements deriving from
the lower strata of society.

The selective process that goes on in the higher social classes,
whereby their average intelligence becomes higher and stays
higher than that of the lower classes, has been the subject
of careful investigation by Ammon.[1] That scholar soundly
attaches great importance to the fact that marriages almost
always take place between individuals of the same class, largely
because of the aversion that women of the higher classes manifest
for marrying men of a class, and therefore of an education,
inferior to their own. In this matter we must be on our guard
against a wrong appraisal into which we often fall because of the
European custom of transmitting names from father to son.
As a result of that custom the only visible ancestor is the one
whose name is transmitted. From the physiological standpoint,
any number of other ancestors have no less right to be taken
into account. An individual always has two parents, one male
and one female. He has 2 ancestors in the first generation, 4
in the second, 8 in the third, and 1,024 in the tenth. The intellectual and moral type of a family of ancient lineage is to be
ascribed, therefore, rather to sustained eugenic crossings than
to some particular remote ancestor, who gave the present
generation not more than, say, a thousand and twenty-fourth
part of its blood.

The phenomenon of family inheritance is more striking still
in the regard of moral qualities. Home training has a great

[1] *Gesellschaftsordnung*, chaps. XX–XXI.

influence on the development of moral traits, and especially the indirect training that comes from the environment within which one is born and lives. Ancientness of lineage has at all times and everywhere been prized, and the fact that a family has for long generations been able to maintain a high social position. There is a profound reason for that. It is comparatively easy to get to the top when time and fortune favor and an individual has a certain amount of intelligence, hustle, perseverance and, especially, a great and unwavering desire to get there. But in human affairs stability is artificial and change natural. Constant watchfulness and an alert and abiding energy are necessary to preserve through the centuries and over a long series of generations what a distant ancestor acquired—now by merits, now by a stroke of luck, now indeed by an unscrupulous performance.

Families that have long been able to survive that test are usually families in which the majority of individual members, at least, have been able to maintain a sense of restraint and proportion and to resist the temptation to yield to impulsive desires that might at once have been satisfied. They must have been people, in other words, who knew the art of commanding themselves and who practiced it. That art is harder to learn and practice than the art of commanding others, which in its turn is harder to learn and practice than the art of obeying. The Greek historians relate that Dionysius the Elder, tyrant of Syracuse, was once harshly rebuking a son of his for running away with the wife of a citizen. He pointed out that when he was young he would never have done such a thing. "Yes, but you were not born the son of a king," the youth replied. Whereupon the father: "And your sons will not be kings, if you do not change your ways!"

So, automatically, a selective process goes on whereby families that lack the virtues mentioned soon lapse into obscurity and lose the rank they once acquired. If that process of selection is to go on, the ruling class must have a certain stability and not be renewed every generation. That necessity, perhaps, accounts for the tenacious persistence of the aristocratic tendency in the instincts of men. At any rate, it constitutes its soundest justification.

Undoubtedly, one of the strongest and longest-lived organisms that history has any knowledge of is the Catholic Church. The

Church has always admitted individuals from all social classes into its clergy, and on occasion it has brought men from the lowest strata of society to the most eminent post in the ecclesiastical hierarchy. One thinks at once of Popes Gregory VII, Sixtus V, Pius X. Now the principle of celibacy for priests has prevented a real hereditary aristocracy from developing within the Church. Nevertheless there have in the past been great families that almost always had some member in the sacred college, and the majority of popes and cardinals have long come, and are still coming, from the upper and middle classes. Perhaps one of the greatest difficulties with which Catholicism has had to contend in recent years lies in the fact that the old aristocracy, and the higher middle classes in many countries, are no longer sending a sufficiently large number of men into the ranks of the clergy.

If a rule could be deduced from this example, and from other examples that might easily be mentioned, one might say that penetration into the upper classes by elements coming from the lower is helpful when it takes place in due proportion and under such conditions that the newcomers at once assimilate the best qualities of the old members. It is harmful when the old members are, so to say, absorbed and assimilated by the newcomers. In that event an aristocracy is not replenished. It turns plebs.

One of the most essential traits in ruling classes is, or should be, honesty in its relations with subordinates. The lie is a defense that is commonly used by the lower against the higher, by the weak against the strong. It becomes doubly repugnant and cowardly when the strong use it to the harm of the weak. It strips the man in command of all title to respect and renders him despicable in the eyes of the subordinate. Simply because men so often resort to lying, the person who abstains from it acquires great prestige. Now abhorrence of falsehood is a a quality which is ordinarily acquired by a long, careful and, one might say, traditional moral training. It is only natural, therefore, that it should be more characteristic of ruling classes, in the development of which the element of inheritance plays a preponderant part.

Another important and almost indispensable requisite in ruling classes, even in relatively peaceful and commercial ages, is personal courage. Men as a rule shun danger and fear death, and they admire those who can risk their lives intrepidly in case of need. When such risks are not undertaken irresponsibly or frivolously they presuppose great strength of will and self-control, which last, perhaps, of all the moral qualities is the one that exacts the greatest respect and deference. When a detailed history of the many ruling classes comes to be written, and we are able to see just how they arose, flourished and decayed, we believe that it will be shown that ruling classes which have had military origins and traditions have been the strongest and that they have, in general, lasted longer than those which have had only industrial or plutocratic backgrounds. Even today, in western and central Europe, one of the best defenses of the ruling class lies in the personal courage that army officers coming from the ruling classes have in general displayed before their soldiers.

The Venetian aristocracy might seem, at first glance, to offer an example to the contrary. That group managed to stay in power for centuries and yet was made up of merchants and bankers. However, Venetian noblemen often commanded the ships and fleets and sometimes, down to the second half of the seventeenth century, even the armies of the Serenissima. They lost touch completely with military life in the eighteenth century. Then, significantly, the republic was in full decline.

To look upon ruling classes as economically unproductive is to succumb to an absurd preconception. In maintaining order and keeping the social structure united they create the conditions under which productive labor can best be prosecuted, and ordinarily they supply production with its technical and administrative personnel. All the same, it is in point to ask, in this regard, whether a ruling class of recent origin contents itself, in the distribution of wealth, with a smaller share than suffices for a ruling class of ancient date, in which, therefore, the aristocratic tendency predominates. That is another way of asking whether democracy is more economical for a society than aristocracy.

Ruling classes, whether democratic or aristocratic, which keep in power by systematically favoring the interests of private individuals or small organized minorities at the expense of the public are always the most costly. There is little to choose between the tendencies in that regard. But otherwise the question is hard to answer, and the answer, moreover, varies widely according to the times and peoples that happen to be considered. In general, the great are more given to flaunting a blatant luxury in barbarous countries, or in countries that have recently grown rich, and something of the sort happens with individuals in ruling classes. It is a matter of common observation that those who most distinguish themselves by an insensate squandering of the fruits of human toil are the ones who have most recently attained the peaks of wealth and power. But that much granted, one must not overlook a consideration that is often overlooked—namely, that in the distribution of the economic production of a country among the various social classes, the class that rules politically has to be allowed a sufficient share to enable it to give its children a long, careful and therefore expensive education and to maintain a dignified standard of living. It must have a large enough share, in a word, to spare it from showing too great an attachment to petty earnings, to small savings and in general to those economies which sometimes lower a man in the eyes of his fellows more than any amount of bad conduct.

7. In his dialogue on the Laws Plato sets forth the thought of his maturer years, and it is significant that he there maintains that the best form of government is one in which autocracy and democracy are fused and balanced. As we have already seen, aristocracy and democracy were, for Plato, the two typical forms of government. In his *Politics*, Aristotle gives an objective description of his three fundamental forms of government, monarchy, aristocracy and democracy, and then goes on to show his preference for a modified aristocracy or, better still, for a modified democracy, in which not even the working classes, let alone slaves and metics, would be admitted to public office.[1] Almost two centuries later, Polybius considered the political organization of Rome the best, because he thought that the three fundamental types of Aristotle found simultaneous application in it.[2] About a century after Polybius, Cicero set forth a somewhat similar view in *De Republica*, and more than twelve centuries after Cicero, at a time when political science

[1] *Politics* III, 3, and VI–VII.
[2] *Histories* VI.

was beginning to show signs of new life, St. Thomas also expressed a preference for mixed governments.[1] Montesquieu freed himself of Aristotle's classification and divided governments into despotic, monarchical and republican. His preference lay with a modified monarchy, in which the three fundamental powers, the legislative, executive and judiciary, were entrusted to separate organs, all independent of one another. In that, evidently, Montesquieu was groping toward the concept of a necessary balance between the various political forces and influences. One might add that Cavour, too, declared that in politics he was a believer in the *juste milieu*, which would involve balance and mutual control between the many political forces or doctrines.[2]

All these great thinkers or statesmen, then, would seem to have had one common feeling: that the soundness of political institutions depends upon an appropriate fusing and balancing of the differing but constant principles and tendencies which are at work in all political organisms. It would be premature in the present state of political science to attempt to formulate a law, but some such hypothesis as the following might be ventured: that violent political upheavals, such as occurred at the fall of the Roman Empire and are today occurring in Russia, entailing unutterable suffering for large portions of humanity and interrupting the progress of civilization for long years and perhaps centuries, arise primarily from the virtually absolute predominance of one of the two principles, or one of the two tendencies, that we have been studying; whereas the stability of states, the infrequency of such catastrophes, depends on a proper balancing of the two principles, the two tendencies.

This hypothesis could be corroborated by historical experiences in considerable numbers. But it rests primarily upon the assumption that only the opposition—one might almost say only the competition—of these contrary principles and

---

[1] After describing the various forms of government, St. Thomas says, *Summa* II, *quaestio* XCV, *Art.* IV: "*Est etiam aliquod regimen ex istis commixtum quod est optimum: et secundum hoc sumitur lex quam majores natu simul cum plebe sanxerunt.* (There is a certain form of government that is a mixture of these, and it is the best. In this form, that law is adopted which the elders along with the plebs have approved.)"

[2] Ruffini, *La giovinezza del Conte di Cavour.*

tendencies can prevent an overaccentuation of the vices that are congenital to each of them.

This conclusion would correspond very closely to the old doctrine of the golden mean, which judged mixed governments best. In fact, we would only be reviving that doctrine, though on the basis of the more exact and profound knowledge that our times have attained as to the natural laws that influence and control the political organization of society. To be sure, there would still be the difficulty of determining just where the golden mean lies, and that difficulty would be so great that each of us could feel quite free to locate it as best suits his passions and interests.

But one practical method has occurred to us for helping well-meaning persons, whose exclusive aim is the general welfare and prosperity quite apart from any personal interest, or any systematic preconception. It would be to watch for—so to say—atmospheric changes in the times and in the peoples who live about us.

When, for instance, a glacial calm prevails, when we can feel no breath of political discussion blowing, when everybody is raising hymns of praise to some great restorer of order and peace, then we may rest assured that the autocratic principle is prevailing too strongly over the liberal, and vice versa when everybody is cursing tyrants and championing liberty. So too, when the novelists and poets are vaunting the glories of great families and uttering imprecations upon the common herd, we may safely consider that the aristocratic tendency is becoming too strong; and when a wild wind of social equality is howling and all men are voicing their tenderness for the interests of the humble, it is evident that the democratic tendency is strongly on the upgrade and approaching the danger point. To put the matter in two words, it is just a question of following a rule that is the opposite of the one that climbers have consciously or unconsciously followed at all times in all countries. If we do that, the little nucleus of sound minds and choice spirits that keep mankind from going to the dogs every other generation may on occasion be able to render a service to its contemporaries, and especially to the children of its contemporaries. For in political life, the mistakes of one generation are almost always paid for by the generation that follows.

CHAPTER XVI

RULING CLASS AND INDIVIDUAL

1. There is a close connection between the intellectual and moral worth of the second and larger stratum of the ruling class and the intellectual and moral worth of the man who is actually at the head of the political organization and the small group of persons who directly assist him. The men who occupy higher posts are more or less imbued with the ideas, sentiments, passions and, therefore, policies of the social strata which come just below them, the strata with which they are in continuous and immediate contact and without which they could not govern.

But the history of human societies is very complicated, and very diverse are the material, moral and intellectual factors that help to determine its development. Cases, therefore, are not rare where ruling classes show themselves capable of sound organization and are fairly rich in members who are energetic and devoted to the public welfare, but yet have at their heads, even at critical junctures, mediocre and sometimes corrupt leaders, so that they find themselves in the position of having to put up with those foolish kings of whom the Bible speaks as scourges that God sends upon the peoples to chastise them.

There are many reasons for this, but the chief one is that in choosing its supreme leaders a political class is in a sense the prisoner of the ideas and principles which it has adopted in regard to leadership. Those ideas and principles result from its whole history and from the level of intellectual maturity that it has attained. It cannot, therefore, change them from one day to the next. Such, for instance, are the hereditary principle and the elective principle—the elective principle, when electoral mechanisms have become crystallized and are convenient tools in the hands of little cliques of politicians, who use them to get into power and to remain there as long as possible.

When a civilization or a nation has a vital and energetic ruling class, the harm that is done by the silliness or even dishonesty of its supreme leaders is far less serious than might be expected. Some historians have tried to rehabilitate Caligula, Claudius and Nero. We, for our part, believe that the first two probably, and the third certainly, were not, as regards their personal qualities, fit men to stand at the head of a political organism as important as the Roman Empire. Of course the great Roman families that were in direct contact with the court had much to endure from the eccentricities and villainies of those rulers and of the men who were their immediate tools. But the rest of the Roman world went on during their reigns enjoying the Pax Romana and absorbing the culture that a fairly wise and orderly administration was successfully spreading through the provinces. It is notorious that George III of England was a man of little brains. He reigned from 1760 to 1820, and in the course of that long period he had several attacks of insanity, during which the Prince of Wales assumed the regency. When he was in his right mind he evinced a most unfortunate obstinacy of disposition. The influence of his royal will undoubtedly made itself felt at times to the harm of the public interest. In spite of that, during his reign England won the Napoleonic Wars, laid the firm foundations of her world empire and became absolute mistress of the seas. The conquest of Canada, and consequently of all the vast territories to the north of the United States, extending from the Atlantic to the Pacific, took place during the Seven Years' War, that is, between 1756 and 1763. The English conquest of India may be said to have begun in earnest with the battle of Plassey, which Clive won in 1757. It was carried on to a successful conclusion during the latter part of the eighteenth century and the first decades of the nineteenth. During the reign of George III, to be sure, England lost the war with her American colonies and the colonies themselves, but it is very doubtful whether what is now the United States could long have been held under foreign sovereignty.

If one were disposed to probe this matter more deeply, one could easily show that the most lasting and effective work of the great heads of states whose deeds have come down in history has been very largely their success in transforming ruling classes by improving the methods by which they were recruited and by perfecting their organization. Even then one reservation might perhaps be still in point—that at times the work credited to great rulers had been launched and carried forward by predecessors.

Historians have long debated, and the debate is far from ended, as to what the real intentions of Augustus were. All agree, however, that he successfully transformed the old republican system into another that better suited the needs of the times, and that he revived the old Roman ruling class, which had been decimated by almost a century of civil warfare, by introducing new elements into it. This idea of Augustus was taken up later on by Vespasian, who raised representatives from many of the more illustrious families of Italy to senatorial rank.

In France the organization of the absolutist bureaucratic state chiefly resulted from the constant and assiduous work of Richelieu, Mazarin and Louis XIV and his ministers Louvois and Colbert. All of them little by little managed to build up a sound and efficient administration, a financial system consistent with the requirements of the times and a strong standing army. In eastern Europe, the development of an old and feeble Muscovy into the empire of the czars that has weighed so heavily in the destinies of Europe and Asia came about through the successive reorganizations of the ruling class that were effected by Ivan the Terrible, Peter the Great and Catherine II.[1] Alexander the Great could not have conquered Persia and spread Hellenic culture over so great a portion of the Asiatic world had Philip of Macedon, his father, not reorganized Macedonia completely and succeeded in building up the Macedonian army. Much the same might be said of Frederick the Great and his immediate predecessor in Prussia.

To cap the proof with the counterproof, one could show, conversely, that when chance or despair has brought a superior man to the head of an actually collapsing political organization, his efforts have rarely availed to save the state or to retard its fall very appreciably. The unhappy emperor Majorian, who ruled the declining Roman Empire of the West from 457 to 461, was an energetic man and a lofty soul. To his good intentions historians unanimously pay tribute. He did not succeed in delaying the fall of the Roman Empire in the west even for a

[1] For the reforms of Ivan IV, see Waliszewski, *Ivan the Terrible*, part III, chap. II. Peter the Great and Catherine II are also the subjects of books by the same writer.

year. The Byzantine Empire was in a position to be reinvigorated by the Isaurian dynasty in the eighth century, and to acquire new vitality in the ninth and tenth under the Macedonian dynasty, because its ruling classes still retained, during those periods, very considerable resources in intellectual power and patriotism, and the subject peoples were still able to supply large revenues to the public treasury and numerous soldiers to the army. At the end of the fourteenth century Byzantine civilization was so run down that contemporary chroniclers could say that Manuel IV would have saved the empire had it still been possible for anyone to save it. Some generations later the gallant leadership and heroic death of the last emperor, Constantine Dragases, retarded the fall of the capital and the demise of the state only for a few weeks.[1]

2. People might admit that there is a fairly close connection between the moral and intellectual qualities of the ruling clique in a state—the supreme head and his immediate associates— and the moral and intellectual qualities of the ruling class as a whole; but they would be loath to grant that connections are equally close between the ruling class as a whole and the great masses of the governed. In our opinion this second relationship is more certain and less varying than the other. Many contingent factors show their influence in the choice of a particular individual for a high position, and they operate at given moments only. Such would be the prevalence of this or that political doctrine, or the way the few men who already occupy high positions happen to feel about this or that person. Always in the offing is the element that may be called "chance," which is merely another name for the unforeseeable. Among such factors one might also place birth. Now those factors operate much more effectively in determining who shall attain the foremost position in a state than in determining the criteria that are to serve as the basis for the great and continuous selective process from which the ruling class as a whole results.

In our day one often hears it said that "the people" are naturally good and virtuous and that the ruling class is vicious

---

[1] The tendency nowadays is to speak better of the Byzantine Empire than was once the case: see Diehl, *Histoire de l'empire byzantin*, and *Byzance: grandeur et décadence;* also Schlumberger, *L'épopée byzantine à la fin du dixième siècle.*

and corrupt.   One could not deny that such assertions sometimes wear an appearance of truth.   But those who make them
almost never take account of the fact that it is easy for a man
to preserve certain virtues when it is materially impossible for
him to acquire certain vices.   Tyranny cannot be practiced by
the weak.   Luxury, mad extravagance and excessive indulgence
in pleasures are beyond the reach of the poor.   If, therefore,
an exact comparison is to be drawn between the moral levels
of two different social classes, one has to observe the morals
and moral tendencies of those who succeed in rising from the
lower class and entering the higher.   Only if they and their
children are really better than their new class associates could
one, with any assurance, claim moral superiority for the class
that is ruled over the class that rules.   An investigation of this
character does not seem, on the whole, to yield results that
are at all favorable to the new arrivals.

It may be objected that only the worst types in the lower
classes succeed in getting ahead and climbing into the ruling
classes.   But that view represents an incomplete, confused and
therefore inaccurate conception of the criteria that regulate
the struggle for social preeminence.   To those criteria one must
look for the chief reason why "one tribe ruleth and another
languisheth."   Undoubtedly there are qualities which those who
succeed in climbing from the bottom to the top are at all times
and in all places obliged to possess, and which their descendants
also must retain to a certain degree, if they do not wish to fall
back to the status of their grandfathers or forefathers.   Among
such qualities are the capacity for hard work and a constant
determination to rise in the world and to cling to one's place
at the top when one gets there.   But there are other qualities,
which vary greatly according to times and places, since they
correspond to the needs and natures of the various epochs and
to the tendencies of the various peoples.   In general, in every
society, circumstances being equal, success is reserved for individuals who possess in eminent degree the endowments which,
in that society at that particular time, are most widely diffused
and most highly esteemed.

If one is to recognize and appreciate the value of an intellectual or moral quality in one's fellows, one must to some extent
possess it one's self.   That rule we think we can infer from

our own experience in life, and anyone can establish the truth of it for himself, if he will simply look about him. In order to feel the charm of a great artist we must possess a certain amount of artistic sense ourselves, and so if we are sincerely to admire great courage, or great uprightness, we must ourselves be in a measure courageous and upright. It is not possible to grasp the noblest qualities of human intelligence and character if they are totally foreign to our natures. Conversely, where slyness, intrigue and charlatanry are the common rule and highly prized, the slyest man, the best intriguer, the most perfect charlatan, will, other things being equal, make a great success. If the majority believe that deceit is the royal road to fortune, those who excel in the art of deception will most often be the ones to make their mark.

In all countries, at all times, the man who would get ahead must have a certain amount of ability—he must possess an aptitude for making use of his talents. He must have the knack of claiming the attention, and sometimes the admiration, of his fellows—he must be able to convince them of his superiority. Possession of this particular aptitude for advertising oneself has become much more important, as a means to success, than it was down to a few centuries ago. The important thing nowadays is to have the good will and the protection of the daily newspapers that have the largest circulations. More than four centuries have passed since Machiavelli wrote in the *Prince:* "Everyone sees what you seem to be—few know what you are." Today it has become infinitely easier to "seem," since the great majority of people form their opinions about politicians, scholars and scientists from what the newspapers say of them.

But the kind of ability that is required for success varies considerably according to times and places. We know that there is a white magic and a black, a white magic that is based on the higher qualities of mind and character, and a black that is based upon the lower. Probably white magic has never really been very effective in any country, or in any position, unless it has been mixed with a little of the black, or at the very least, with the art of displaying the best sides of one's character and intelligence, and keeping the worse sides in the dark. But the respective dosages in the mixture may vary widely from one nation to another, and within the same nation from age to age.

They vary because when black magic comes to be too much used in a given social environment, public taste rebels and the individual who relies on the mixture is then disqualified, much as a gambler is disqualified when he cheats at cards. Evidently, in an environment that is highly refined in its tastes, those who best know the arts of white magic will be more likely to get to the front. The contrary will be the rule in environments where the arts of black magic are more common and so more tolerated.

As we study the history of the peoples, we see that many of them have long undergone and are still undergoing foreign dominations, or have been governed by aristocracies of foreign origin for long periods. That was the case with Russia, where the first empire was founded by a group of Scandinavian adventurers. After Ivan IV, and especially under Peter the Great, foreign elements in goodly numbers entered the ruling class of the country. After Alexander the Great had destroyed Persian dominion in Egypt, Egypt formed an independent kingdom under the Ptolemies, who introduced Hellenic culture. During that period the Egyptian ruling class was of Hellenic or Hellenized origin. Conquered later by the Romans and governed by the Byzantines after the fall of the western empire, Egypt was one of the most turbulent countries in the world during the fifth and sixth centuries. Then in the seventh century the country was conquered by the Arabs, and deferred first to the Ommiad caliphs of Damascus, and then to the Abbassides of Bagdad. Toward the middle of the tenth century Egypt regained its autonomy, because it was conquered by a Berber army which came from Tunisia and set up the Fatimid caliphate under a Berber dynasty, with its seat at Cairo. The Berber dynasty weakening little by little, and the population of Berber origin mixing with the natives, Egypt was annexed, toward the end of the twelfth century, by Saladin's empire. After the death of that sultan, Egypt was almost continually governed by the generals of mercenary armies of foreign origin, mainly Circassian, until in the sixteenth century it was conquered by the Turks. The Turks, however, promptly handed the government of Egypt back to the beys of the Mamelukes, a militia also of Circassian origin. The Mamelukes were first defeated by Bonaparte and then exterminated by Mehemet Ali, the first khedive, a man of Albanian origin. Today in Egypt, upper-class families are in the main of Turkish, Circassian and Albanian descent.

As for India, it seems certain that long before the first Mohammedan conquest (A.D. 1000), the country had suffered invasions from barbarians to the north. These are supposed to have been ancestors of some of the more warlike populations. They assiduously avoided any intermixture with natives. That was the case with the Rajputs, who nevertheless embraced the Brahman religion and culture. On the other hand, the more recent conquerors of Turkish or Afghan origin did not adopt any native religion. They had already become converts to Islamism before they entered the country. The last Turkish conquest was led by Baber, who laid the foundations of the empire of the Grand Mogul at the beginning of the sixteenth century. Since the territory is so vast and conditions vary so widely from one section to another, populations of ancient Hindu origin and of Brahman culture have also founded large states in relatively recent times, as, for example, the great federation of the Mahrattas. This state was well organized from a military point of view. But almost the whole of the great valley of the Ganges, and a large part of central and southern India, were governed by Mohammedan sovereigns at the time of the English conquest, and the dominant class was Mohammedan and in the main of foreign ancestry.

Not a few examples serve to show that as long as a dominant class of foreign origin keeps fairly pure in blood, the state retains its strength and the country its prosperity, but that, as the class begins to fuse and confuse with indigenous elements, the political structure weakens and the nation falls into anarchy or comes under a new foreign dominion. Now when such facts are continually repeated and endure through long revolving centuries, they seem to show that the indigenous elements in the nations in question did not possess the aptitudes and virtues required for developing a native ruling class worthy to rule, and that if they did at one time possess such virtues, as Egypt and India at one time certainly did, they subsequently lost them. We have already remarked that it is harder to command than it is to obey. When a nation or a race does not possess elements that are fitted for command, or when those elements wither away or fail to develop because they are stifled by the general intellectual and moral mediocrity about them, then that people or that race is destined to fall under foreign rule, or under ruling elements of foreign origin.

All this emphasizes the great practical importance of the doctrine which we have been setting forth in this work. It should serve to call attention to the fundamental importance of the problems that relate to the growth, composition and organization of ruling classes. The old and obsolete classifications of Aristotle and Montesquieu put a common label on bottles that held most widely differing contents. For example Athens, present-day Switzerland and the United States could be classified simply as democracies. Ancient Rome and Venice, or Argentina and Brazil, could be placed among republics. Our new doctrine of ruling classes is not yet able to devise labels for the various types of ruling class. It simply bids us examine the contents of our bottles and investigate and analyze the criteria that prevail in the constitution of the ruling classes on which the strength or weakness of our states depend, and in which the faithful image of the political virtues and defects of every nation and every race can be detected.

The method is certainly hard to use. It demands an earnestness and objectivity of observation, an experience with political life and a knowledge of history that are infinitely greater than anything demanded by the old methods. But unquestionably it keeps one closer to positive facts, and if it is used with discretion and with adequate preparation it is capable of leading to sounder results. It is, finally, more consistent than the old method with the level of intellectual ripeness that the better-educated elements in our rising generations have now attained.

3. But even our new method will not be able to do all that it is capable of doing until certain residua of eighteenth and nineteenth century manners of thinking, certain preconceptions that balk, or at least hamper and disturb, its effective application to the study of political problems, are abandoned. The greatest obstacle to the acceptance of an idea or method that comes a step closer to the truth lies in the presence in the human mind of another less perfect idea or method to which it has grown accustomed.

Now one of the doctrines that are widely popular today, and are making a correct view of the political world difficult, is the doctrine commonly called "historical materialism." That doctrine is not only an article of faith for the exceedingly numerous followers of Marx. It has also influenced to a greater or lesser extent many who are not altogether adherents of Marxian ideas. The greatest danger that lies in the wide acceptance of the theory, and in the great intellectual and moral influence which it exerts, lies in the modicum of truth that it contains. In science, as in life in general, the most dangerous falsehoods are the falsehoods that are mixed with a certain amount of truth. The truth helps to mask and color them in such a way as to make them plausible.

Historical materialism may be summed up in two propositions, which constitute its fundamental axioms, or assumptions. On these rest the proofs of all the theorems deriving from it.

The first assumption is that the whole political, juridical and religious organization of a society is uniformly subordinated to the prevailing type of economic production, and to the character of the relations that that type creates between labor and the owners of the instruments of production. From this it would follow that any change in the system of economic production should necessarily bring on a change in the form of government, in the legislation regulating relations between individuals and between individuals and the state, and even in those religious and political concepts which constitute the moral foundations of the state organization, such as the concept of the divine right of kings and the concept of popular sovereignty. The economic factor would, in other words, be the sole and exclusive cause of all the material, intellectual and moral changes that occur in human societies, and all other factors should be regarded not as factors but as mere effects and consequences of the economic factor.

The second assumption is in a sense a postulate of the first. It maintains that every economic period contains seeds which, slowly maturing, make the advent of the successive periods necessary, with a consequent transformation of the whole social structure, political, religious and legislative. From this it would follow that during the present bourgeois period, in view

of a progressive concentration of wealth in a very few hands
that is taking place, economic and social conditions are being
prepared which make collectivism unavoidable and predestined.
When this last phase of historical evolution has been reached,
every inequality that is based upon social institutions will vanish
forever, any control and exploitation visited by one class upon
other classes will be rendered impossible, and a new system will
be inaugurated, which will be based not on individual selfishness
but on universal brotherhood.

These doctrines were already hinted at in the *Communist
Manifesto* which was published by Marx and Engels in 1848.
They were further elaborated in the preface to the *Kritik der
politischen Ökonomie,* which Marx issued in 1859. They form
the skeleton, so to speak, of the first volume of *Das Kapital,*
published in 1867, since they are either intermittently enunciated,
or else taken for granted, throughout the course of that work.
Some of Marx's fundamental ideas are not altogether original.
They may be found set forth, with less orderliness and definiteness to be sure, in the publications of a number of earlier writers
of more or less socialistic tendencies, and especially, in mixture
with many mystico-transcendental notions, in the works of Pierre
Leroux. Leroux wrote his *Egalité* in 1838, and his *Humanité*
in 1840. He too looked upon communism and absolute equality
as the inevitable conclusion of the whole historical evolution of
mankind. He thought of the nineteenth century as representing a
transitional period between a world of inequality, which was coming to an end, and a world of equality, which was about to dawn.

As regards the former of the two assumptions, it is to be
observed first of all that many historical examples might be
adduced to show that very important changes have occurred
in human societies—changes that have radically altered political
constitutions and sometimes the political formulas on which
those constitutions were based—without any simultaneous or
approximately simultaneous modifications in systems of economic
production, and in the relations between labor and the owners of
the instruments of production. The Roman Republic was
transformed into the empire of Augustus and his successors—
in our terms, the classical city-state became a political organism
of the bureaucratic type—without the slightest change in systems
of production and without any alteration in the laws regulating

the ownership and distribution of wealth. The only change that did take place, and it was certainly not a general one, was a change in the persons who owned the property. After the second civil war especially, a great deal of private property was confiscated and distributed among the soldiers of the triumvirs.[1] The triumph of Christianity wrought a great intellectual and moral revolution in the ancient world. Many fundamental ideas, many sentiments and, in consequence, many institutions were changed by the new religion—one has only to think of matrimony and other family relationships. But it does not appear, indeed it may positively be denied, that any particular changes occurred in the fourth and fifth centuries A.D. in the relations between manual labor and those who possessed the tools of economic production—chief among them at that time was land.

It is hard to think of an upheaval of a whole society that is comparable in extent and significance to the fall of the Roman Empire in the West, to the collapse of the splendid civilization of antiquity over so large a part of Europe. One might possibly liken to it the catastrophe that has fallen upon Russia in our day. The Russian disaster will almost certainly have less abiding and less far-reaching effects, but the immediate effects have been more intense, since they developed in a very few years. One may regard as roughly accurate an epigrammatic statement made by Guglielmo Ferrero, that Russia completed in four years a task of social disintegration for which the ancient civilization of Europe required four centuries. Yet, as regards Rome, it is clear enough that the system of economic production remained identical before and after the barbarian invasions. Rural serfdom was not brought about by the barbarian invasions. It was already a generalized institution under the Low Empire. We might, indeed, mention the economic exhaustion of Roman society in that period as one of the factors in the fall of the western empire. That poverty was due to a falling off in production and, accordingly, in national wealth. But an attentive examination of the phenomenon shows that the general impoverishment was a consequence, rather than a cause, of the political decline, since a bad financial administration was largely responsible for it. During this period the Roman middle classes suffered virtual

[1] Ferrero, *Grandezza e decadenza di Roma*, vol. III ("Da Cesare ad Augusto").

ruin. That was due not only to increased taxation but also to the fact that the decurions, who made up the well-to-do bourgeoisie in the towns in the provinces, were responsible in their own property for payment in full of the taxes levied upon the town as a whole.

Turning from antiquity to times less remote, one sees that in Italy toward the end of the thirteenth and during the fourteenth century, the communes quite generally developed into tyrannies without any appreciable modifications in systems of production, and consequently in the relations between the working classes and the owners of land and capital. In the same way, during the seventeenth century, the modern absolute state was established in France and a middle class began to form, without any important change taking place simultaneously in systems of production and in the economic relations deriving from them. Serfdom had disappeared almost everywhere by that time. Only a few traces of it remained, and they hung on till the French Revolution.

Nor can we believe that there has been any perfect synchronism between the rise of modern large-scale industry and the adoption of systems of representative government, with a consequent spread of liberal, democratic and socialistic ideas. Beginnings of large-scale industry appear in England during the second half of the eighteenth century, when parliamentary government had been functioning for about half a century; but the ruling class still stood on its old aristocratic foundations. In France, Germany and the United States, and in all western Europe, large-scale industry, and the great concentrations of capital and working populations that resulted from it, came in general after 1830. The application of steam to land and sea transportation did not begin to spread, and coal did not acquire its prime importance as a material factor in production, till that time. All that can be granted in this regard is that the large factory, with the great agglomerations of manual workers that it has necessitated, has contributed considerably to the development and popularization of communistic ideas, which had long since been enunciated and which were, after all, only natural corollaries to the democratic ideas that had already been formulated by Rousseau.[1]

[1] Chap. XI, §1, above.

This is not to deny that a prevailing system of economic production, with the special relations that it sets up between labor and those who direct production and own its instruments, is *one of the factors* that most largely influence changes in the political organization of a society, and that that factor has its necessary repercussions upon the ideas that serve as moral foundations for political systems. The error of historical materialism lies in holding that the economic factor is the *only* factor worthy of consideration as cause, and that all other factors have to be regarded as effects. Every great manifestation of human activity in the social field is at the same time both cause and effect of the changes that occur in manifestations of the same activity—cause, because every modification in it influences other manifestations, and effect, because it feels the influence of modifications in them. A rather crude comparison may serve to make the point clearer. No one would deny that, if the brain is diseased, the entire human organism ceases to be in its normal state. But the same thing might be said of the digestive system, of the respiratory system and of any essential organ in the body. It would therefore be a fallacy to conclude that *all* diseases were brain diseases, or diseases of any other particular organ. It is evident that the individual's health depends on the proper functioning of *all* his organs.

No one has ever claimed that changes in political systems have been solely due to the changes that changes in armaments, tactics and recruiting systems have in the past occasioned in military systems. Nevertheless, we have already seen (chaps. XIII, §3; XIV, §5) the political effects that resulted in the Greek city from the substitution of hoplites for the old war chariots and cavalry as the decisive arm in the military establishment; and we have observed that the final victory of royalty over feudalism, which was won in the period between the middle of the fifteenth and the middle of the seventeenth century, was largely due to an increasing use of firearms and to continuous improvements in them. Careful examination of the history of the last century of the Roman Republic would bring out political consequences that followed changes in the recruiting system for the legions. The reform by Marius was carried out in 107 B.C. Marius enlisted men without property and sons of freedmen in the army. Except under most unusual circumstances, for instance toward the end of the second Punic War, such people had been barred from military service. A few years earlier, in 123 B.C., a lex militaris, moved by Caius Gracchus, put the costs of the soldier's equipment and armament upon the state. Before that, each man had had to provide his own equipment out of his own purse. This reform made it possible for even the poorest man to serve in the army. The two reforms taken together help very considerably to explain why, during the last sixty years of the republic, the soldiers became blind instruments in the hands of their leaders, on the strength of promises that were made and kept of bonuses and of distributions of the lands which were often confiscated from political adversaries. Freedmen and slaves were also enrolled in the army during the second triumvirate. Now the old republican state could not have survived if arms had ever been granted to the lower strata of the population.[1] When it becomes possible to write the history of the nineteenth and twentieth centuries in some sereneness of mind, it will be easy to see the political effects that resulted from the extension of compulsory military service to all citizens. First introduced by the French Revolution, that measure was later adopted and improved upon, first by Prussia and then by the other Continental countries.

It seems altogether absurd to regard as mere effects, and never as dignified, respectable causes, the political doctrines and religious beliefs which constitute the moral foundations of state organisms. Penetrating deep down into the consciousness of ruling classes and masses alike, they legitimize and discipline command and justify obedience, and they create those special intellectual and moral atmospheres which contribute so greatly toward determining historical circumstances and so toward directing the course of human events. Apart from Christianity and the power it acquired over the minds of both masses and ruling classes, and apart from a tenacious remembrance of the unity that the civilized world had achieved under Rome, there could be no explaining the age-long struggle between papacy and empire which was one of the outstanding events in medieval history. Had it not been for Mohammed and the Koran, the great Mussulman state would never have come into being; yet that state has played, and still plays, an important part

[1] Ferrero and Barbagallo, *Roma antica*, vol. I, pp. 251, 272.

in the history of the world, and it has introduced a special type of civilization wherever it has been able to get a foothold and survive. Had we not inherited from our distant forebears, Greek and Latin, the concept of political liberty and the doctrine of popular sovereignty, which was later modified and adapted to a new age by Rousseau and other political writers of the eighteenth century, the modern representative state would not have been heard of, and political organization in Europe in the nineteenth century would not have been so profoundly differentiated from organization in the eighteenth. If the development of political thought is followed through the various periods of history, one easily sees that the political circumstances of a writer's day do greatly influence his manner of feeling and thinking and therefore his theories, but that his theories in their turn help very considerably to influence the political views of successive generations and so to determine new circumstances. Many examples could be adduced to this point, and, this, after all, is just one more of the many cases that one meets in the social sciences where what is an effect at one moment becomes a determining cause at another moment.[1]

It is useless to argue whether moral forces have outweighed material forces to a greater extent than material forces have used the moral in their own service. As we have already shown (chap. VII, §9), every moral force tries, as soon as it can, to acquire cohesion by creating an underpinning of interests vested in its favor, and every material force tries to justify itself by leaning upon some concept of an intellectual and moral order. In India the populations of Aryan race subdued the aborigines of Dravidian race and pushed them down into the lower strata of society. They must have had them there for some centuries before the writers of the Vedas began to teach that the Brahmans had issued from the head of Brahma, the Kshatriyas from the arms of Brahma, and the lowest castes, the Vaisyas and Sudras, from the legs and feet of the god. Christianity began as a purely moral and intellectual force, yet scarcely had it gained an important following when it became a material force as well: It acquired wealth, it found ways to exert pressure upon the public powers and, finally, its bishops and abbots became actual sovereigns. In Mohammedanism the religious conception took

[1] Mosca, "Principio aristocratico . . . ," p. 4.

on body at once, with the exercise of sovereign power, but had it not been for the disinterested and sincere conversion of its early followers, that would not have been possible. Modern collectivism itself was also born as a purely intellectual and moral force. Today it is trying, wherever it can, and as far as it can, to create a whole network of material interests which serve marvelously to keep the rank and file faithful and to remunerate the ruling class that has grown up within it. Even the purely material influences of plutocracy try to put on sheep's clothing today. They subsidize newspapers of a conspicuously democratic tinge to Right and Left. They exert pressure upon electioneering committees. They bow their heads to the baptism of popular sovereignty, and they often send their representatives to parliaments to sit on the benches of the most advanced parties.

The truth is that the great factors in human history are so complex and so intertwined that any single-track doctrine which tries to set up one among them as the principal one, "ever moving and never moved," necessarily leads to erroneous conclusions and false applications, especially when it undertakes to explain the whole past and present of humanity by following one method and looking at them from a single point of view. Worse still befalls when one sets out to predict the future in the same way.

As we have already suggested, the second of the assumptions on which historical materialism rests may be regarded as an implication of the first, and it therefore loses its significance when the first has been disposed of. Nevertheless, one might point out that to assert generically that every historical period contains the germs which will eventually flower and transform it into the epoch immediately following is to state a truth so obvious that it may be regarded as a platitude. It is, at any rate, one of the commonplace assumptions of modern historical science. But the fact is, Marx insists that the only seeds that flower and produce are seeds of an economic nature. We believe, instead, that they are much more numerous and much more diversified. Marx's view of the historical phenomenon is so limited that it would in itself be sufficient to make one reject the thesis, which is one of the fundamentals in Marxist doctrine, that our present bourgeois period is ripening the seeds that will make the advent of collectivism inevitable—or, accord-

ing to some, has already ripened them. But quite apart from
that consideration, it is now certain that the concentration of
wealth and of the instruments of production in a very few hands,
which should have preceded their collectivization and made it
easy for the countless hordes in the proletarian phalanx to
expropriate the handful of proprietors, had not taken place
before the World War and had not even moved in the direction
of doing so. If the war has recently impaired the situation of
the middle classes everywhere to a greater or lesser extent, that
has been due to other causes, which were in no sense foreseen
by historical materialism. And again, if the organization of
the bourgeois state has today been destroyed in a number of
countries, and in others is hanging on only by a thread, that
is happening not because of the concentration of wealth in a
few hands, but for quite different reasons. To them we have
already referred in the course of this book, and to them we shall
again turn shortly.

The conclusion of the second assumption of historical materialism, and indeed of the doctrine as a whole, seems to us utterly
fantastic—namely, that once collectivism is established, it
will be the beginning of an era of universal equality and justice,
during which the state will no longer be the organ of a class and
the exploiter and the exploited will be no more. We shall not
stop to refute that utopia once again. This whole work is a
refutation of it. One should note, however, that that view is a
natural and necessary consequence of the optimistic conception
of human nature which originated in the eighteenth century and
which has not yet completed, though it is coming pretty close
to completing, its historical cycle. According to that idea,
man is born good, and society, or, better, social institutions,
make him bad. If, therefore, we change institutions, the seed
of Adam will be, as it were, freed of a choking ring of iron, and
be able to express all their natural goodness. Evidently,
if one is going to reason in that fashion one will go on and reason
that private property is the prime and sole cause of human
selfishness. Aristotle argued much more soundly, in his day,
that selfishness is the cause that makes private property inevitable. Combatting the communistic theories of Plato, the
Stagirite declares that private property is indispensable if the
individual is expected to produce and therefore provide for his

own needs and the needs of his family and city.[1] The justification that St. Thomas offers for private property in the *Summa* is almost identical. We do not believe there could be a better one, as long as the human being loves himself and his own family more than he loves strangers.

Beginning with Morelly, Mably and Babeuf, and coming down to Louis Blanc, Proudhon and Lassalle, most writers who have tried to sketch a complete plan for human regeneration have included in their programs, now a partial and gradual, now a complete and immediate, inauguration of communism and abolition of private property. These results were regarded, of course, as desirable results, which were to be achieved by the majority will because they were desirable. Following, roughly, some hints of Pierre Leroux, Marx simplifies all that. He dispenses with the individual will and has the desired results achieved by the fatal course of history. Without any doubt at all his method has its advantages. If a reform is inevitable, there is not much that one can do about it. It cannot be criticized and demolished, the way one can criticize and demolish a fundamental reform that rests upon the authority, or the desire, of a mere individual. Not only that. Among all the arguments in favor of a doctrine, the most convincing will always be the one that represents its triumph as inevitable in a more or less immediate future.

4. Another notion that has troubled the minds of people who have pondered political problems since the day when Plato wrote his dialogues is that "the best people" ought to be the ones to govern a country. The consequence of that aspiration has been, and perhaps still is, that good souls go looking for a political system that will make the concept a reality, or at least point the way to doing so. During the last decades of the eighteenth century and the first half of the nineteenth and, indeed, for a decade or two longer, that yearning has been intensified because it has found nourishment in the optimistic conception of human nature to which we have so often alluded. That opinion made it easy to imagine that if one could change institutions all the less noble instincts that ravage our poor humanity would automatically be suppressed or become atrophied.

[1] *Politics* II, 1–2.

In order to determine just how much truth and error there may be in that outlook, we ought first to decide just what sort of people deserve to be called "the best."

Evidently, in ordinary language, the word "best," as the superlative of the adjective "good," should serve to designate persons who are distinguished from the average of men by exceptional "goodness." The "best" on that basis would be the most altruistic people, those who are most inclined to sacrifice themselves for others rather than to sacrifice others to themselves, those who in life give much and receive little, those who are—to use a phrase of Dora Melegari—*faiseurs de joie* rather than *faiseurs de peines*. They would be people in whom the instinct to surmount or remove any obstacle to the satisfaction of their passions or interests is better restrained and controlled than it is in the average run of men.

But surely it must have become apparent by this day and age that "goodness," taken in such a literal sense, is a quality that is of great service to others but of very little service, as a rule, to those who possess it. At best, it does fairly little harm to people who are born to a social position, or who by chance achieve a social position, that is so high as to cure all temptation in any one who might be inclined to take advantage of them. But even in such a case, the individual to whom the adjective "good" might legitimately be applied must be able to renounce the prospect of rising as high in the social scale as he might be entitled to rise in view of his other qualities. For to rise in the social scale, even in calm and normal times, the prime requisite, beyond any question, is a capacity for hard work; but the requisite next in importance is ambition, a firm resolve to get on in the world, to outstrip one's fellows. Now those traits hardly go with extreme sensitiveness or, to be quite frank, with "goodness" either. For "goodness" cannot remain indifferent to the hurts of those who must be thrust behind if one is to step ahead of them; and when goodness is deep and sincere, one is loath to appraise the merits, rights, and feelings of others at an infinitely less value than one's own.

It may seem strange at first glance that, in general, people should insist that their rulers have the loftiest and most delicate moral qualities and think much of the public interest and little of their own, but that when they themselves are in question, and especially when they are trying to get ahead and reach the highest positions, they are at no pains whatever to observe the precepts which they insist should be the unfailing guides of their superiors. As a matter of fact, all that we can justly ask of our superiors is that they should not fall below the average moral level of the society they govern, that they should harmonize their interests *to a certain extent* with the public interest and that they should not do anything that is too base, too cheap, too repulsive—anything, in short, that would disqualify the man who does it in the environment in which he lives.

But the expression "best," when applied to political life, may also mean, and indeed ordinarily does mean, that the "best" man is the man who possesses the requisites that make him best fitted to govern his fellow men. Understood in that sense, the adjective may always be applied to ruling classes in normal times, because the fact that they are ruling classes shows that, at the given time, in the given country, they contain the individuals who are best fitted to govern—and such fitness by no means implies that they are the "best" individuals intellectually, much less the "best" individuals morally. For if one is to govern men, more useful than a sense of justice—and much more useful than altruism, or even than extent of knowledge or broadness of view—are perspicacity, a ready intuition of individual and mass psychology, strength of will and, especially, confidence in oneself. With good reason did Machiavelli put into the mouth of Cosimo dei Medici the much quoted remark, that states are not ruled with prayer-books (chap. VII, §11, above).

In our day the distinction between the statesman and the politician is beginning to make its way into the plain man's thinking. The statesman is a man who, by the breadth of his knowledge and the depth of his insight, acquires a clear and accurate awareness of the needs of the society in which he lives, and who knows how to find the best means for leading that society with the least possible shock and suffering to the goal which it should, or at least can, attain. Statesmen in that sense were Cavour and Bismarck. A statesman was Stolypin, the Russian minister of 1906, who saw that in Russia, what with a growth in population and a necessary intensification of agriculture, a system of collective property without division among the peasants could not last, and who therefore put forward measures which would have created a class of private peasant landowners and a true rural bourgeoisie in Russia in about half a century. It was not Stolypin's fault if the measures that he promoted did not have time to show their full effects. He died a premature death in 1911, murdered by fanatical idiots.

The politician, on the other hand, is a man who has the qualifications that are required for reaching the highest posts in the governmental system and knows how to stay there. It is a great good fortune for a people when it can find leaders who combine the eminent and rare qualities of the statesman with the secondary qualities of the politician; and it is no mean stroke of luck for a nation when its politicians have at their elbows statesmen by whose views they can profit.

In the conclusion of his dialogue on the Laws, reinforcing a contention that may be regarded as fundamental in his political system, Plato says that a city cannot be governed well as long as its kings, or governors, are not philosophers, or as long as its philosophers are not kings. By philosophers he seems to have meant wise men, men who possess the knowledge that is necessary for the statesman and who are at the same time above all low and vulgar passions.

Now, on a few occasions, heredity or chance has brought a philosopher, in Plato's sense of the term, to headship in a state; and not always has the philosopher come down in history as a model of the good ruler. Marcus Aurelius was the real type of the emperor-philosopher. He was born, to begin with, on the steps to a throne. He was a good man, but not a fool, and so, as his *Meditations* reveal, the exercise of power gave him on the whole an unflattering idea of human nature. He was also a man of action to an extent. He led his armies in person in a number of wars, and in fact died while conducting a campaign on the Danube. In spite of all that, it is doubtful whether his virtues always stood the public interest in good stead. The very historians who favor him accuse him of maintaining unfit persons in the governments of the provinces. Discipline in the army had been considerably improved by Trajan. It began again to slacken under the rule of Marcus Aurelius. During his reign, also, a serious mutiny occurred in the legions in Asia, which proclaimed one Avidius Cassius emperor. Cassius would have become a very dangerous competitor had not one of his centurions murdered him.

There is little likelihood, moreover, that in normal times the philosopher, as Plato conceived of him, would win out in the struggle for preeminence among the many who are scrambling for high station. In many cases real wisdom does not excite ambition, but smothers it. Then again lofty qualities of character and mind do not draw philosophers toward high office, but turn them away, especially when the qualities of the philosopher are not blended with the qualities of the politician, and the individual has not enough practical sense to temper the former, at least momentarily, and bring the others into action. Manzoni's Don Ferrante was a scholar who "liked neither to command nor to obey." He was not a philosopher exactly—not the "wise man," according to Plato's definition. He belonged to something of the same family, however, because "he passed long hours in his study," had a library full of books and spent his time reading them. He was, perhaps, what we would now call an "intellectual." Persons who are really given to meditation, and enjoy it, sometimes adapt themselves fairly well to commanding, and they will obey when it is absolutely necessary. As a rule they do not care much either for commanding or obeying.

As we have already suggested, therefore, we can afford to be satisfied if the politicians who are in power do not fall below the average for the ruling class in their brains and in their morals. When the intellectual and moral level of the ruling class is high enough for its members to understand and appreciate the ideas of thinkers who study political problems intensively, it is not necessary for the latter to attain power in order to have their programs carried out. The intellectual pressure that the ruling class as a whole exerts—what is commonly called "public opinion"—will force the politicians to suit their policies more or less to the views of those who represent the best that the political intelligence of a people can produce.

What we have taken away from Plato's coupling of the highest qualities of mind and character, as regards the political field, we must hasten to restore as regards many departments of life that are extraneous to politics. The physicist Galileo Ferraris thought that no great scientific discovery was possible as long

as the experimenter was trying to obtain practical results—
when, that is, instead of being interested in mere knowledge,
he was trying to wrest from nature some secret that would
enable a great industry to turn out a product at less cost.   The
maxim which Galileo Ferraris thought was applicable to the
natural sciences, applies, we believe, especially to the social
sciences.   In the social sciences it is impossible to find the
truth unless good qualities of intelligence are cemented and
unified by good qualities of character, unless the thinker is
able to strip himself of every partisan passion, every interest,
every fear.

5. The fact that, as a rule, those who occupy high office are
almost never the "best" in an absolute sense, but rather individuals who possess the qualities that are best suited to directing
and dominating men, shows how hard, and indeed how impossible,
it is under ordinary circumstances to apply absolute justice,
as man is able to conceive of that ideal, to a political system.
But to achieve absolute justice has been the dream of noble
spirits and lofty minds from Plato on.   We might even say that
it has been a convenient pretext for many ambitious and more
or less vulgar men to use in trying to replace those who are at
the top.

Absolute justice in a political system can only mean that the
success of every individual, the rank he occupies in the political
scale, should correspond exactly with the actual utility of the
service which he has rendered, or is rendering, to society.   At
bottom, it is a question of applying a concept which was definitely
formulated for the first time by Saint-Simon (chap. XII, §1,
above) and which furnished the famous formula in which the
Saint-Simonians summed up their program: "To each according
to his ability, to each ability according to its results."

Now a number of objections to this doctrine occur to one.
In the first place, how are we to evaluate accurately, and with
a certain promptness, the exact worth of the service which an
individual has rendered, or is rendering, to the society of which
he is a part?   We say "promptness" because if the evaluation is
to come a century later, or even a decade or two later, whether
it is to bring reward or punishment does not matter much.
The man to whom it will be owing will already be in his grave, or

at least in an advanced old age. Not only that. However great our good will, merits or mistakes of a political nature are, from the largest to the smallest, the mistakes that bring their consequences after the longest lapses of time. Only in fairly distant perspective, as a rule, can we judge calmly and with relative sureness as to whether the policy of an official, the vote of a chamber, the decision made by a cabinet at some grave moment, has been, or has not been, to the best interests of a country. As a matter of fact, men almost never wait as long as that to judge such acts, but for that very reason their judgment is often influenced by passions or interests, or artfully diverted by the wiles of intrigue and charlatanry.

But suppose time and the passing of generations have snuffed out interests and stifled passions. Suppose the wiles of intriguers and charlatans have gone the way of the interests and passions. Suppose there are no more crowds to applaud because they are trained to applaud, and no more writers or newspapers to extol or disparage in bad faith. Even then, men are so constituted for the most part that they do not succeed in being objective and impartial, even in the solitude of their studies. As we have seen (chaps. I, §18; XII, §3), historical research always yields more or less uncertain results when we are trying to judge of great personalities in the past, whereas its inferences and conclusions are much less uncertain when we are reconstructing and interpreting the institutions, the ideas, the achievements of great civilizations. Now that uncertainty is largely due to the emotional habits of writers. Many a scholar cannot express his admiration for one great personality who lived twenty centuries before our time without disparaging some other personality of the same ripeness of age. Many a historian, writing in the twentieth century, cannot manage to exalt Caesar without taking a fling at poor Cicero. All of which would go to show that even when personal interests and greeds have fallen silent, antipathies and sympathies, in the classical sense of those terms (in other words affinities or disaffinities of mind or of temperament) are enough to make men unjust toward other men who vanished from the earth centuries and centuries before their time.

Evidently, therefore, to establish an exact and unerring relationship between merit and success, between the works of each individual and the reward or punishment that is due him, would be a superhuman task within the competence only of an omniscient and omnipotent being, who could look behind the veils that hide all consciences, who had none of our ignorance, none of our weaknesses, none of our passions. For that reason, perhaps, almost all the great religions, beginning with the religion of the ancient Egyptians, have deferred final judgment on a man's work to the end of his earthly life, and have then handed the judging along to the gods, or to God.

A certain equivalence between service rendered and recompense received might be found in the free contracts that are made in private life. But that equivalence is not founded upon a moral principle such as is desired for political life. It is simply a question of demand and supply, or of the relative needs of the two contracting parties, whereby the service is rated higher when it is much in demand, and the recompense is lower when the supply of work to be done is scant and the supply of service is overabundant. This purely economic equivalence does not, as the moral equivalence would require, take account of the sacrifice that the service has cost, and it ceases functioning altogether when the services are rendered not to definite individuals or groups of individuals but to collectivities as wholes. It is a common impression that great scientific discoveries, whether in the field of the natural sciences or of the social, have not invested their discoverers with high office in the state, or lifted them to the summits of wealth, or supplied them with the "gilded parasols and the elephants mad with pride" which, according to the ancient authors of India, awaited the powerful on earth (above, chap. XI, §3). On the other hand, practical applications of discoveries have almost always enriched inventors and given them influence and power. Truly, it should be one of the duties of those who govern, at least in countries of ancient and sound cultural traditions, to give moral and material recompense to scientists like Copernicus, Galileo, Volta, or Champollion, who have made discoveries that are useful to all mankind but cannot be directly exploited by private industry. Sometimes, in fact, rulers have performed that duty more or less satisfactorily, though usually when performance of it could be profitable to them as corresponding to the wishes of an enlightened public opinion.

But even if there is never to be an absolute justice in this world until humanity comes really to be molded to the image and likeness of God, there has been, there is and there will always be a relative justice in societies that are fairly well organized. There will always be, in other words, a sum of laws, habits, norms, all varying according to times and peoples, which are laid down and enforced by public opinion, and in accordance with which what we have called the struggle for preeminence— the effort of every individual to better and to conserve his own social position—will be regulated.

The coexistence of an absolute justice and a relative justice has been recognized since classical antiquity, which had learned to distinguish "civil right (*jus civile*)" founded on law, from "natural right (*jus naturale*)" based on reason and the human being's natural sense of equity. Seneca analyzed slavery as an institution that was consistent with civil right but contrary to natural right. That relative justice varies from place to place and time to time has also been pointed out repeatedly. One thinks at once of the *Pensées* of Pascal.

According to relative justice, a certain amount of work is almost always necessary to achieve success—work that corresponds to a real and actual service rendered to society. But work always has to be reinforced to a certain extent by "ability," that is to say, by the art of winning recognition. And of course a little of what is commonly called "luck" will not come amiss— those unforeseeable circumstances which help or seriously harm a man, especially at certain moments. One might add that in all places at all times the best luck, or the worst, is often to be born the child of one's father and one's mother.

There are many who deny, or try to reduce to very low terms, the part that luck plays in the success of individuals and of groups. They should read, or reread, the *Thoughts* of Guicciardini, who very soundly remarks: "Those who attribute everything to wisdom and virtue, and rule out the power of fortune as far as they can, at least have to confess that it is very important for a man to stumble upon an age, or to be born in an age, when the virtues or qualities on which he prides himself are held in high esteem."[1] The truth is that men who have not had all the success they hoped for in life are willing enough to lay the

---

[1] *Pensieri*, nos. 30–31.

blame on luck, while those who have succeeded beyond their expectations are prone to give all the credit to themselves.

But the game of life, after all, is not so different from an ordinary game of cards, where winning depends now on blind chance, now on the skill of the player, now on the mistakes of the adversary. The game of cards would become plain fraud if the cards could be changed or manipulated. So in the great game that every man plays in life, violating the established rules, or cheating, should never be permitted. That society will always be a wretched and disorderly affair in which it is tacitly conceded that the player who is sly enough can give an occasional nudge to fortune. With regard to the impossibility of realizing absolute justice in this world and the necessity for observing the norms of a relative justice, Gina Lombroso-Ferrero has written a number of pages that are full of acute reflections.[1] She argues, among other things, that a high grade of social perfection could be reached in our societies if the struggle to achieve high position were carried on in frank conformity with what she calls accepted standards, instead of unavowable standards.

Often, and very often in our day, those who know best how to emphasize, and do loudest emphasize, the sometimes blatant contradictions that appear between absolute justice and the relative justice sanctioned by law and custom, are people who hold bad cards and would like to have better ones and therefore propose stopping the game and having a new shuffle and a new deal. Ordinarily they are not displeased if the new shuffle and the new deal are entrusted to them. Truly altruistic individuals, who sincerely abhor lying and cheating, end by becoming persuaded from their experience with life that absolute justice is impossible of attainment and that therefore true and conscious sincerity and goodness necessarily have to be coupled with generosity, which knows how to give without hope of any return.

6. Will progress in political science some day enable mankind to eliminate, or even to attenuate or make rarer, those great catastrophes which, from time to time, interrupt the course of civilization and thrust peoples that have won glorious places

[1] *The Soul of Woman*, p. 245.

in history back into barbarism, be it a relative and temporary barbarism? That is a most serious question. From the practical standpoint it may be the most important of all the questions with which political science is called upon to deal.

Before one can hope to make any useful contribution toward the solution of it, the problem itself has to be stated in its exact terms. The catastrophes mentioned are commonly said to occur when a nation has "aged." Death comes, therefore, as a natural consequence of that "age." Now, as we have been at some pains to show (chap. I, §14), to speak of the "old age," or of the "death," of a people or a civilization is to use a metaphor that fails to give an exact picture of what actually takes place. An individual grows old—inevitably, alas! An individual dies when his vital resources are exhausted, or when some infecton, or a violent cause, halts or impedes the functioning of some organ that is essential to the continuance of life. But physical aging is not conceivable in a society. Each new generation is born young. Nor is the physical death of a society possible. For a society to die, one whole generation at least would have to abstain from procreation. René Worms has dealt in masterly fashion with the question of old age and death in peoples:

> To be sure there are thinkers who declare that states, like individuals, are fatedly condemned to disappear some day or other. So far, no sound proof has ever been given of any such necessity, and, for our part, we do not believe in it. Quite to the contrary, we judge that peoples are able to renew their composition by procreation, a thing that individuals cannot do, and that therefore they may look forward to a literal immortality.[1]

It would not be difficult to mention cases of peoples that have disappeared without leaving any descent. The aborigines of Tasmania vanished in that way. The aborigines of Australia are fast disappearing. Few descendants of the Guanches of the Canary Islands still survive. Many native tribes in the Americas are extinct and others are dwindling in population. But those peoples were, or are, small groups, living by hunting and fishing. Colonization by the whites deprives them of their means of sustenance, and on coming into contact with the whites

[1] *Philosophie des sciences sociales*, vol. III, p. 305.

they are too backward in civilization to adapt themselves at once to agricultural livelihoods, or adopt the white man's methods of production.   In Mexico and Peru the native populations were practicing agriculture at the time the Europeans arrived.   They were much more numerous, therefore, and they were not exterminated.   In the United States, too, it seems, Indian tribes that have been able to turn to agriculture show no tendencies toward dying out.

Very different is the situation with peoples that have long since reached the agricultural stage, have organized into orderly, powerful and thickly populated nations and created or developed civilizations.   In such cases, anything that could be called physical death—the elimination of a race through lack of descent —has perhaps never occurred.   Once a people has reached that stage of culture, it may lose its original physiognomy, it may be absorbed by other peoples, by other civilizations, it may change its religion and sometimes its language—it may, in a word, undergo a comprehensive intellectual and moral metamorphosis; yet it continues to survive physically.   Against this thesis one might urge the example of the Britons, who had long been practicing agriculture at the time when their country was invaded and occupied in large part by the Angles and Saxons. But in the first place, a primitive Celtic lineage still survives in the north of Scotland, in Wales and also in French Brittany, whither some of the Britons emigrated under Saxon pressure. In the second place, if the Celts lost their language over the major part of Great Britain, they were by no means exterminated.   They were simply absorbed by the invaders of Germanic race.   Studies of such problems often yield vague or uncertain results, but it really seems as though the population in the western counties of England, and in a large part of Scotland, had remained basically Celtic.

History is full of such transformations and survivals.   The descendants of the ancient Gauls and the ancient Iberians survived underneath the crust of Latin civilization that came to give them a new outward shape.   The descendants of the ancient peoples of Mesopotamia and Syria survived, even though they adopted the language and religion of the Arabs, who conquered them in the seventh century.   That was the case too in Egypt, where the modern and so-called Arab population still retains, in the mass, the physical traits of its real ancestors, who created the civilization of the Pharaohs and preserved it for forty-odd centuries. Modern Italians are still, in the main, descendants of the ancient Italic peoples, and in the veins of the modern Greeks, however much their blood may be mixed with other bloods, the blood of the Hellenes who knew Pericles and Aristotle still flows, and so does the blood of the Byzantines of the ninth and tenth centuries.

But suppose we ignore that type of survival, and also the case where a people is assimilated by a domination of foreign origin that brings in a higher culture—the case of the Gauls, the Iberians, and the many other more or less barbarous peoples whom the genius of ancient Rome successfully welded into a single state. Then, evidently, there is still a sense in which a people that has been able to create a civilization of its own and maintain it through long centuries can be said to have died. And the death may be attributed more especially to two causes, which undermine and corrode the inner mechanism of the nation and bring it to such a pass that the least shock from outside is enough to kill it.

These two causes seem almost inevitably to go together. Nations die when their ruling classes are incapable of reorganizing in such a way as to meet the needs of changing times by drawing from the lower and deeper strata of society new elements that serve to give them new blood and new life. Then again, as we have already seen (chap. XIV, §3), nations are also marked for death when they suffer a dwindling of those moral forces which hold them together and make it possible for a considerable mass of individual efforts to be concentrated, disciplined and directed toward purposes related to the collective interest. In a word, old age, the forerunner of death, comes upon political organisms when the ideas and sentiments which make them capable of the collective effort that is required, if they are to maintain their group personality, lose influence and prestige without being replaced by others.

An instinctive fear of that eventuality explains the blind attachment to tradition, to ancestral customs and examples, that lay at the bottom of the religions and the political psychologies of all the great nations of antiquity, beginning with the old civilizations of Mesopotamia and Egypt and coming down to Rome. The same attachment was very strong, down to a few generations ago, in Japan and China; and in spite of appearances to the contrary, it is far from being unknown to modern nations of European civilization, especially to the peoples of Anglo-Saxon stock. The national soul seems instinctively to feel that if it is not to die it must hold faithful to certain principles, certain fundamental and characteristic ideas, which impregnate all the atoms that unite to form its organic being. It seems to feel that only on that condition can it conserve its personality, maintain its social structure intact and keep each stone in its composition from losing the cement that binds it to the others. That instinct underlies the ancient Christian persecutions, and the old religious wars. For the historical events that have helped most to modify the complexes of sentiments and beliefs that were peculiar to the old nations were the rise and spread of the great world religions, which seek to embrace all humanity and blend it in a universal brotherhood, yet impress upon their believers a special intellectual and moral stamp. In fact, there are three special types of civilization that correspond to the three great world religions, Buddhism, Christianity and Islam.[1]

Unfortunately, or perhaps fortunately, an excessive and exclusive cult of the past is likely to result in fossilization, and for a nation to be allowed to remain stationary with impunity, all other nations have to be equally fossilized. China and Japan tried to relax into immobility during the seventeenth and eighteenth centuries and part of the nineteenth. In order to keep influences from Europe out of China the emperor Yung Cheng, who reigned between 1723 and 1735, drove out the missionaries. Japan had preceded him on that road. As early as 1639 an edict of the shogun Yemitsu prohibited commerce with foreigners with very few exceptions and made it subject to very severe penalties. Neither nation succeeded entirely even at home, but in any event they both underwent brusque awakenings from outside. China had to begin opening her doors after the so-called Opium War with England, which broke out in 1839. Japan did the same when Commodore Perry, with his American squadron, appeared off her shores in 1853.

Complete immobility in a human society is an artificial thing, whereas continuous change in ideas, sentiments and customs,

---

[1] That fact, we may note in passing, is another argument against historical materialism.

which cannot help having its repercussions upon political organization, is natural. To prevent change, it would be necessary to
destroy all influences from the spirit of observation and inquiry,
from the growth and spread of knowledge, from accumulating
experience; for such influences make it inevitable that new
manners of thinking should mature, and new manners of feeling,
and these necessarily corrode faith in ancestral teachings and
weaken the traditional concepts that form the foundations of the
political structure of the forefathers.

It was not at all likely that a Greek living in the days of Plato
and Aristotle could still believe in the gods as the childish anthro-
pomorphism of Homer conceived them. Much less could he
admit that the gods were accustomed to lending their counsel and
their aid to those hereditary chiefs of the cities whom the greatest
poet in Greece had been wont to call "shepherds of peoples." It
would have been hard to convince a French contemporary of
Voltaire that Louis XV had received his mandate to govern
France from God. And one may doubt whether a Chinese, or a
Japanese, who attends a European or an American university
today goes home with a very firm conviction that the books of
Confucius contain a perfect and complete expression of human
wisdom.

Things being as they are, there is only one way to avoid what is
called the death of a state or a nation, one of those periods of
acute crisis, that is, which sometimes cause or enable a type of
civilization to disappear, to the unutterable woe of the generations that witness them. That way is to provide for a slow but
continuous modification of ruling classes, for a slow but continuous assimilation by them of new elements of moral cohesion that
will gradually supplant the old. In this case, probably, as in
others, the best results in practice are obtained by a sound balance
between two different and opposite natural tendencies, between
the drift toward conservatism and the urge for innovation. In
other words, a political organism a nation, a civilization, can,
literally speaking, be *immortal*, provided it learns how to *transform itself continually without falling apart*.

A truly remarkable example of adaptation to necessary contacts
with foreign peoples, without any abandonment of the special
traditions and sentiments which form the core of the national
soul, has been supplied during the last fifty or sixty years by

Japan. That country has found a way to transform itself radically without falling apart. It is interesting that during the period in question Japan has been governed in practice by a limited aristocracy, made up of the most intelligent men in the country. Of course there is still the chance that, gradually, as other European concepts percolate into the lower strata of the Japanese population, the country will have to face one of those unavoidable conflicts between old and new ways of thinking and feeling that pave the way for crises of the sort we have been considering.

7. If the death of peoples, the complete ruin of political organisms, those lasting and violent social crises that interrupt the course of civilization and throw men back toward the brutes, were in any real sense avoidable, the development and recognition of a real political science might certainly contribute considerably toward avoiding them.

In the past more than one of the crises mentioned have been retarded for very considerable periods by mere political empiricism, when the latter was not led astray by false doctrines and when it was illumined by flashes of genius. Augustus, Trajan, and perhaps Diocletian too, retarded the breakup of the Roman Empire in the West. France would not have been reorganized as well or as promptly after the Revolution had she not had a Napoleon Bonaparte to take the lead. One must also bear in mind that sometimes to retard a great crisis may amount to avoiding it for a long time. Byzantine civilization managed to survive the catastrophe that overtook the western Roman Empire in the fifth century, and was able to live on for nearly a thousand years longer.

But better than empiricism, better than the saving intuition of genius, will be an exact knowledge of the laws that regulate the social nature of man. Such knowledge, if it does nothing else, will at least help people to distinguish between things that may happen and things that cannot and never will happen, and so it may help to keep many generous intentions and much good will from being unprofitably and even perniciously wasted, in efforts to attain levels of social perfection that are now and will be forever unattainable. Such knowledge also will enable us to apply to political life the same method that the human mind has learned to use practically in trying to master the other forces of nature. That method comes down to an attentive observation and understanding of their manner of working, and then to learning how to control and utilize them without doing brutal violence to them. It would be doing brutish violence to a natural law to sow grain in the northern hemisphere in July and expect a harvest in January. In all the branches of his activity, man has been able to master material nature only by observing her and adapting himself to her ways. He must follow the same method if he wishes to correct to his advantage the consequences that follow from his own political nature.

As we have seen (chap. I, §§16–19), the nineteenth century, and the early decades of the twentieth, have already developed, thanks to progress in historical research and in the descriptive social sciences, such a mass of verified data, such a wealth of scientific materials, that the generations that are now living may be able to do a thing that was impossible for earlier generations— they may, that is, be able to create a truly scientific politics. Even if they should succeed, it would still be very hard to imagine just when such a science would be able to become an active factor in social life, and serve to coordinate and modify the other factors that have figured so largely in determining the course of human events.[1] Before a mere system of ideas can become an active force in political life, it must first have obtained a strong hold on the minds of at least a majority in the ruling class, and thoroughly remodeled them. It must, that is, have come to control and determine the manner of thinking, and therefore of feeling, of those whose opinion counts as public opinion. Now truly scientific ideas are the least adapted of all ideas to doing things like that. They are not at all *adaptable*. They lend themselves little, if at all, to any stirring of the passions of the day, or to any direct satisfying of the interests of the moment.

[1] As to the other factors referred to, see above, chap. XI, §6 (pp. 305–306).

CHAPTER XVII

FUTURE OF REPRESENTATIVE GOVERNMENT

1. A hundred years generally offer a sufficient length of time for the psychology, customs and institutions of a nation or a civilization to change appreciably. An age, therefore, is often named after the century to which it corresponds. And yet, if we set out to specify the year in which those changes become clearly perceptible, in which we are able to say that one age has ended and another begun, the age and the century rarely correspond exactly. Between the end of one historical period and the beginning of another there are periods of compromise, of so-called transition, that are more or less arduous and are sometimes accompanied by violent crises.

If we choose to fix on a definite moment when the age corresponding to the eighteenth century ends, the year most plausibly indicated would be the celebrated year of 1789, and not the year 1800. If we were to do the same for the next period, one might say that a new era opened in the year 1815 and ended about a hundred years later, in 1914. The period of twenty-six years that elapsed between 1789 and 1815 would be one of those parentheses, marked by violent crises, that often, though not always, accompany great transformations in human societies. The character of that period was apparent to the Italian poet Manzoni as early as 1821. In his famous ode on the death of Napoleon, "The Fifth of May," he writes, speaking of Napoleon's career:

"He pronounced his name. Two ages facing each other in arms turned toward him, hushed, as though waiting on the approach of Destiny. He called for silence and took a throne in their midst as arbiter."[1]

> Ei si nomò: due secoli
> L'un contro l'altro armato
> Sommessi a lui si volsero
> Come aspettando il Fato.
> Ei fe' silenzio, ed arbitro
> S'assise in mezzo a lor.

If we were to examine the political character of the nineteenth century in Europe, we should have to consider events between 1815 and 1914, this last year again corresponding to the opening of a new parenthesis that will close at some later moment with the beginning of a new age which will take the name of our twentieth century.

Today we find ourselves at a historical moment that may be decisive for the future of our civilization.   It would perhaps be wise, therefore, for the present generation, especially the younger members of it, to withdraw within themselves for a moment or two before they go into action and make what the Church calls an "examination of conscience."   It is quite possible that the people who are living today, especially the younger among us, might refuse to submit to such an examination, on the ground that anything wrong that is to be found with their consciences would be the fault of the three generations that have preceded us. In this case, we could only reply that, for better or for worse, we have received an inheritance from our fathers which we shall not be allowed to renounce.   At the very least, therefore, we might as well have an inventory of it.

2. During the nineteenth century the nations of European civilization made an effort to carry out in the political field the program that had been sketched as an ideal by the preceding century.   That program may be summed up in three fundamental concepts, expressed in three magic words: liberty, equality, fraternity.

We have already seen that the concept of liberty, in the sense in which the word is used in the political field, was inherited by modern Europeans from the ancient Greeks and Romans.   Confusedly and imperfectly grasped in the Middle Ages, and much more clearly and accurately in the Renaissance and after, this concept was popularized by Rousseau and other writers of his day and interpreted to conform with conditions in eighteenth century society.[1]   But there could be no development of the absolute bureaucratic state of the eighteenth century into a city-state,

---

[1] On the different historical phases of the concept of popular sovereignty, which, during the Middle Ages and in modern times down to the French Revolution, was often identified with the concept of political liberty, see Crosa, *Sulla sovranità popolare.*

such as Athens and Sparta had been, and Rome too in the age of Fabricius and Atilius Regulus. The concept that had been inherited from the ancients, therefore, had to undergo some further adaptation, and an attempt was made to do that by borrowing as a model the type of constitution that was already functioning in England in the eighteenth century. The advantages of that constitution had been brilliantly set forth by another celebrated writer, Montesquieu.

So instead of the assemblies of classical Greece and the comitia of Rome, in which all citizens could take part, and in which laws were approved and appointments to all public offices made, there came to be parliaments, almost always consisting of two houses, moral rather than legal ascendancy being given to the house that originated more directly in popular suffrage. These parliaments were entrusted with lawmaking, with the voting of taxes and budgets and with general control over the whole administration of the state. Departing in another respect from the examples of classical antiquity, the elective system was not extended to the administrative organization of the state or, in general, to the judiciary. The functions which the European state was exercising at the end of the eighteenth century were very important, and highly technical knowledge was almost always indispensable for the men who directly exercised them. That made it necessary that they should be entrusted, not to elective and temporary officials, as was the practice in the ancient city-state, but to permanent professional employees, who were generally chosen by competitive examination, or appointed at will by the men who occupied the higher posts in each department of the public service. The appointive system prevails very widely in the United States, where the bureaucracy does not enjoy the guarantees of permanent tenure which it has won in almost all the countries of Europe. American officials are generally dismissed and replaced by new appointees when the party in power changes. Even in the New World the American system presents many drawbacks, along with many advantages. It would not work in Europe for two reasons. A higher grade of preparation is required of a public employee in Europe. More than that, once a man has lost a position, it is not as easy for him to get a new one as it is in America.

The bureaucratic structure that had been built up by the absolutist governments, far from being demolished, was gradually expanded and strengthened by the new functions which the state kept taking on during the nineteenth century. In fact, two of the fundamental powers of modern governments, the executive power and the judiciary power, came ultimately to be vested in bureaucracy. As for safeguarding against any excesses on the part of bureaucracy, it seemed sufficient to entrust to parliaments control over income and expenditure and the right to audit and criticize the state administration as a whole; and, in countries governed by parliamentary systems, to put the various branches of the bureaucratic machine in charge of men who came largely from the membership of the elective chamber itself, and who therefore issued indirectly from popular suffrage.

In almost all countries of European civilization, military systems underwent enormous developments and very considerable modifications. But of all the departments of state they retained most completely, throughout the whole history of the modern representative system, and quite generally, the features which the old absolutist systems had stamped upon them. Compulsory military service has been adopted almost everywhere, and it has been extended to all classes of citizens. It is now possible, in case of war, for a country to mobilize its whole able-bodied population. The privileges which a monopoly of the higher military rankings conferred upon the old nobility have been abolished, though traces of them have hung on in a number of European armies down to very recent dates. Purchase of officers' commissions, which tended to confine the supply of officers to the richer classes, was not abolished in England till 1871, in Germany not till 1914. In Germany certain regiments would not accept officers who were not of noble birth, and down to the outbreak of the World War—in fact, whatever the law—Jews could not become army officers.

But the modern armed force has retained its strictly autocratic organization. Military advancement has remained dependent on the judgment of those who hold the higher ranks, and the old distinctions between officers and privates has persisted, with varying vigor but always to a very considerable degree. Officers are as a rule military men by profession. They come from the upper and middle classes, to which they are bound by ties of origin, education and upbringing. Privates are almost always recruited by compulsory conscription and, therefore, the great majority have the ways of thinking and feeling of the working and peasant classes.

This distinction forms the basis of military discipline and organization. Combined with the better general and military education of the officers, it makes the privates, ordinarily, dependable instruments in their hands. To this fact, more than to anything else, is due the remarkable success that modern European society has had in trusting its proletarians with arms without having had to face the danger that the proletarians would use them to seize power. To the same distinction is again due the fact that the army has almost everywhere been a conservative force, an element of social order and stability.

Public opinion today is in general not fully awake to the *political* importance of this modern military system. There would be no very general alarm in a number of democratic countries, if it were to be radically altered, for instance, by shortening terms of military service and replacing them with so-called premilitary training. During the last great war, the physical and moral strength of the human being was at times so overtaxed that in almost all the European armies there were moments when discipline grew lax and military organization showed grave symptoms of breaking down. In Russia, the moment the first revolution broke out, the supremely idiotic Russian bourgeoisie hastened to destroy its own army with the famous "Prikaz Number One," whereby officers were stripped of authority over their soldiers. Very wisely, instead, the Bolshevist government set out to create its own army, organizing it under an iron discipline. It is now trying by every possible means to build up a corps of officers, who will be bound to the present rulers of Russia by ties of training and interest.

But in modern Europe, and in all countries of European civilization in general, the conception of political liberty has not been applied solely by instituting representative government. Almost everywhere the latter has been supplemented to a greater or lesser extent by a series of institutions that assure individuals and groups of individuals not a few effective guarantees as against holders of public power. In countries that have so far rightly been reputed free, private property cannot be violated arbitrarily.

A citizen cannot be arrested and condemned unless specified rules are observed. Each person can follow the religion of his choice without forfeiture of his civil and political rights. The press cannot be subjected to censorship and is free to discuss and criticize acts of government. Finally, if they conform with certain rules, citizens can meet to engage in discussions of a political character, and they can form associations for the attainment of moral, political or professional ends.

These liberties, and others like them, may be looked upon as real limitations which the state has imposed upon its own sovereign powers in its relations to individual citizens. They are largely imitations of laws that England had adopted at the end of the seventeenth century, after the "Glorious Revolution," or even at later dates. They are necessary complements to representative systems, which would function very badly if all free political activity on the part of individuals were suppressed, and if individuals were not fairly well protected against arbitrary acts on the part of the executive and judiciary powers. At the same time, those liberties find their maximum guarantee in the existence of the representative system, which provides that legislative power, which alone has the right to remove or restrict them, should emanate from the same political forces that are interested in conserving them.[1]

Far harder to put into practice has been the concept of equality, for equality is contrary to the nature of things, and is also less real, less concrete, than liberty in the sense just mentioned.

Naturally, the class privileges that still remained at the end of the eighteenth century were abolished as a matter of law at that time, since it was to the interest of the bourgeoisie to abolish them. All citizens were solemnly proclaimed equal before the law. But little could be done with natural inequalities, or with those artificial inequalities, so to speak, which result from family inheritance—disparities in wealth, upbringing and education, for instance.

Now equality ought to imply the disappearance of social classes as one of its necessary implications, and equality has in fact been officially proclaimed. But the gap between the various social classes in ways of thinking, in manners of feeling and in tastes and inclinations has perhaps never been more marked than it is in

---

[1] Mosca, *Appunti di diritto costituzionale*, §17, pp. 152 f.

twentieth century European society; and never, perhaps, have classes been less comprehensible to each other. That is not due altogether to inequalities in wealth. The intelligence and the psychology of a man of the lower middle class, who has managed to win a university degree or even a secondary school diploma, are almost always closer to those of a millionaire than to those of a workingman, though from an economic standpoint a man of the lower middle class stands closer to the workingman than he does to the millionaire. All that is a result of progress in culture, in what Italians call "civility," whereby those who devote themselves to intellectual pursuits, and sometimes to the refinements of leisure, necessarily become more and more differentiated from the social strata that are devoted exclusively to manual pursuits and are fitted for no other.

In the course of the nineteenth century and the early decades of the twentieth, as guarantee and tangible proof of equality, the European and American middle classes granted the vote to all citizens, including the illiterate, who in some countries still form a considerable percentage of the population. Universal suffrage confers the right to participate in equal measure in the choice of members of elective chambers. As we have already indicated (chap. XII, §2), this concession was primarily a consequence of the doctrines that prevailed in the ruling classes as part of the intellectual legacy of the eighteenth century to the nineteenth. In view of these, the only government that could be looked upon as legitimate was a government based on popular sovereignty, which in turn was interpreted as the sovereignty of the numerical majority of the members of the social unit. The gift of the vote to all adult citizens therefore became indipensable, if the minority that really held political control was to avoid charges of inconsistency and to continue to govern with a clear conscience.

But, as early as the day of Aristotle, when the majority of manual laborers were still excluded from citizenship and therefore from suffrage, people were aware of the difficulty of reconciling political equality, which gave the poor predominance over the rich, with economic inequality. It is not surprising, then, that the European and American ruling classes should have found themselves facing the same difficulty after granting universal suffrage. They were able to meet that difficulty with relative ease before the World War, and to overcome it up to a certain point. That was due partly to the political unpreparedness of the masses, which, in many countries, readily allowed themselves to be regimented within the framework of bourgeois parties. But it was also due in part to the great powers of resistance that the modern state has; and in larger part still to the great economic prosperity that prevailed in the second half of the nineteenth century and which even increased during the twenty or thirty years prior to 1914. Prosperity made it possible in many countries to grant very considerable concessions of an economic nature to the more populous classes, without preventing increases in private savings, without impairing the inviolability of private property too seriously and without laying unbearable burdens upon large and moderate fortunes. Among these concessions one might mention shorter working hours, insurance against old age, illness, unemployment and accidents, and restrictions on labor by women and children. Such provisions are all acceptable when they are not carried too far, and when industry, agriculture and public finance are able to carry them. Unfortunately they almost always serve to justify creating large bureaucracies, which regularly become drags and nuisances. The best and the most welcome of all these concessions was a rapid raising of wages, which was made possible by increased production in industry and agriculture, especially in the last decades before 1914.

As matters turned out, these improvements in the status of the lower classes were of no little service to agitators too, for they could boast of wresting them from the bourgeoisie through their organization of labor and through the activity of their representatives in parliament. In such claims, as all economists know, there is a small amount of truth and a large amount of falsehood. Certainly improved economic conditions have on the whole made the laboring classes less prone to resort to desperate and violent acts.

Hollower than the realization of equality, if not altogether devoid of content, has been the realization of fraternity.

Long before the philosophers of the eighteenth and nineteenth centuries thought of advocating fraternity, or brotherly love, between all human beings, the principle had been proclaimed and preached by a number of thinkers of antiquity. The ancients on the whole thought of brotherliness as a virtue to be practiced among members of one nation, or one city. Only a few writers, such as Seneca, who lived in one of the most cultured periods that classical antiquity knew, believed that brotherhood should be extended to all humanity.   The doctrine won no great following, in general, among the Greeks and Romans.   Universal brotherly love also figured in the programs of the three great world religions, Buddhism, Christianity and Mohammedanism.   In those religions, again, only members of the faith were commonly regarded as brothers, and even among comrades in the faith the practice of fraternity was far from perfect.

Now rivalries and conflicts of interest are unavoidable in the struggle for social preeminence.   But apart from that, for the principle of brotherhood to become a fact, the human being should need only to love his fellow man, whether the latter were close or remote, and whether or not he spoke the same language, followed the same religion or accepted the same political doctrine. He should never need to hate him.   Unhappily, the human being's need for hating has at no time seemed very close to disappearing from his nature (chap. VII, §§1–6).

This being the basic state of the human psyche, it is not at all strange that the sense of universal brotherhood should have been very feeble during the nineteenth century and at the beginning of the twentieth, and should be feeble still.   The failure to make equality a fact must have helped to impede any strengthening of it, for that disappointment has intensified rivalries between the rich and the poor, the powerful and the helpless, the happy and the unhappy.   A certain gross materialism prevailed very widely down to a few years ago, and a reaction against it has set in only very recently, and that, too, only among the more cultivated classes.   All such circumstances could not fail to stimulate, not love, but hatred between nations, between classes, and between individuals, by inflaming the lust for worldly goods and withholding all consolation from those who are defeated in the battle of life.

3. In spite of all that, when our remote posterity come to look back upon the work of our times dispassionately, we believe that they will admit that the historical period which takes its name from the nineteenth century was one of the greatest and most magnificent of all the eras that humanity has traversed.   During that period, no longer penned in within boundaries it could not cross, human thought obtained results that far surpassed the

intellectual legacy that had been transmitted to the nineteenth
century by the civilization of earlier ages, whether in the field of
the natural sciences or in the fields of history and the social
sciences.   During the last century and a half the human being
has had many more instruments of observation at his disposal,
and newer and more efficient ones, than ever before.   Never
before has he had such a wealth of accurate information on
natural and social phenomena.   Never before has he been in a
position to have such an accurate and detailed knowledge of the
laws that govern the world he lives in, or of the laws that regulate
his own instincts and conduct.   Never has he better known, or
been able better to know, himself and the universe of which he
is part.

The consequences that have followed the application of this
knowledge to progress in all departments of material living are
evident to the eye.   Today human labor can accomplish ten
times more, with the same effort, than it could a hundred years
ago.   Progress in facilities of communication, in agriculture, in
industrial procedures, has made it possible to exchange products,
services and information between remotely separated countries,
and this has produced, and distributed proportionately through
all social classes, a well-being that is without precedent in the
history of mankind.

Our political system must necessarily have made its contribution to all these scientific and economic achievements.   Confining
oneself to the political field, one has to admit the great benefits
which constitute the undying glory of the nineteenth century as a
result of the very illusions that guided it.   To be sure, majority
government and absolute political equality, two of the mottos
that the century inscribed on its banners, were not achieved,
because they could not be achieved, and the same may be said
of fraternity.   But the ranks of the ruling classes have been held
open.   The barriers that kept individuals of the lower classes
from entering the higher have been either removed or lowered,
and the development of the old absolutist state into the modern
representative state has made it possible for almost all political
forces, almost all social values, to participate in the political
management of society.

This development, it should be noted, has divided the political
class into two distinct branches, one issuing from popular suffrage,

and the other from bureaucratic appointment.   This has not only permitted a better utilization of individual capacities; it has also made it possible to distribute the sovereign functions, or powers, of the state, and that distribution, whenever social conditions are such as to make it effective, constitutes the chief virtue of representative systems.   It is the chief reason why they have given better results than any of the many others that have so far been applied to great political organizations.[1]   Rousseau set himself an unattainable goal when he tried to show that the only form of legitimate government was one that was founded upon the express consent of the majority of citizens.   Montesquieu stated a much more practical and profound idea when he maintained that if a nation is to be free, in other words governed according to law and not according to the arbitrary will of its rulers, it must have a political organization in which authority arrests and limits authority, and in which, therefore, no individual and no assembly has the power to make laws and at the same time the power to apply them.   To make that doctrine complete, one need add that a controlling and limiting political institution can be effective only when it represents a section of the political class that is different from the section represented by the institution to be limited and controlled.

If, again, we take due account of the individual liberties that protect the citizen from possible arbitrary acts on the part of any or all of the powers of the state, especially of liberty of the press, which, along with liberty of parliamentary debate, serves to call public attention to all possible abuses on the part of those who govern, one readily sees the great superiority of the representative system.   That system has permitted the establishment of a strong state, which has been able to canalize immense sums of individual energies toward purposes related to the collective interest.   At the same time it has not trampled on those energies or suppressed them.   It has left them with sufficient vitality to achieve remarkable results in other fields, notably in the scientific, literary and economic fields.   If, therefore, the nations of European civilization have succeeded in maintaining their primacy in the world during the age that is now closing, the fact has been due in large part to the beneficent effects of their political system.

[1] As regards the social conditions that are required for the proper functioning of the representative system, see above, chaps. V, §9; X, §8.

In order not to carry this causal relation too far, it might be more accurate to think of a number of different causes functioning simultaneously, the action of the one being supplemented by the action of the others. Then we would say that representative systems were able to function regularly during the nineteenth century in the majority of countries of European civilization because cultural and economic conditions in those countries were such as to enable them to function in that manner. That would be another of the many cases where the effect becomes cause and the cause effect.

As we have seen, the military and administrative superiority of the European countries over countries of Asiatic civilization had become apparent as early as the eighteenth century, when the absolutist bureaucratic system still prevailed. The peace treaties of Carlowitz and Passarowitz were concluded in 1699 and 1718 respectively, and after them Turkey ceased to constitute a serious menace to Europe. In the second half of the eighteenth century, the English conquest of India was already far advanced, and it may not have been by mere chance that it was effected by the European country that had been the first to adopt the representative system. The predominance of European over Asiatic countries became more and more marked and remained unshaken throughout the nineteenth century. In 1904 Japan succeeded in defeating Russia. It is significant that by that time Japan too had adopted the European military and administrative systems. That victory gave the Asiatics grounds for hoping that their civilization was on the road to an early recovery, and the hope has grown very considerably since the World War, which left large portions of Europe exhausted and revealed many weak spots in its organization.

Even before 1914 a shrewd observer could have seen that the center of gravity in European civilization was tending to shift towards the Americas. The United States, Canada, Brazil and Argentina, not to mention other American countries, have vast territories at their disposal and great natural resources that are only partially exploited. In the future they can support populations at least four times as large as those they have today. But down to the eve of the World War, those countries still needed capital and man power in order to develop their resources. If Europe might have supplied the capital, China, Japan and a number of other Asiatic countries would have been able, and perhaps willing, to supply the man power. But immigrants of yellow race do not fuse with the American populations within a visible period of time, as Europeans do. That fact seemed to imply a danger at which the American countries were, as they still are, very properly alarmed. At any rate, any danger of an ascendancy of the New World over the Old can still hardly be regarded as pressing. For one thing, the artistic and scientific culture of a number of European countries is still considerably superior to the general level of culture in the Americas. But then again, a number of European countries have begun to reclaim equatorial and southern Africa to their own advantage. There too there are vast territories of rich potentialities which are inhabited by primitive peoples, who can be easily governed for some time to come. They will therefore, in all likelihood, eventually be able to furnish the raw materials of which an over-populated Europe is sorely in need.

4. Like all political systems, the representative system also developed, during the historical period that corresponds to the nineteenth century, the seeds which were, as they still are, preparing either its gradual transformation or its swift dissolution. We have already seen (chap. XVI, §6) that only by slow and continuous transformations of their political systems can peoples avoid periods of rapid disintegration accompanied by violent crises that bring untold suffering to the generations that have to undergo them and almost always set them back on the road of civilization.

Undoubtedly the most important of those seeds has been, and still is, the patent contradiction between one of the chief objectives which the century set for itself and the results that have been achieved. Western and central Europe have so far had forms of government which have guaranteed a fair amount of individual liberty, provided a fair amount of restraint on arbitrary action by rulers and produced a very high grade of material prosperity. But the principle of equality has not been realized, nor have majorities been given actual control in the various countries. At the very most, the masses have been wheedled at election times with promises of this or that material advantage, which has often been more apparent than real. When such promises have actually been kept, they have not seldom resulted in harm to national economies and, therefore, to the interests of the lower classes themselves.   A typical example of this sort of concession has been the eight-hour day.   Such a limit on working hours may be endurable in a very rich country.   It can only be fatal to a poor country.   The ruling classes in a number of European countries were stupid enough and cowardly enough to accept the eight-hour day after the World War, when the nations had been terribly impoverished and it was urgent to intensify labor and production.

It is readily understandable that in European society, under such psychological and material circumstances, a strong political movement should have grown up within the bourgeoisie itself, composed partly of idealists and partly of ambitious politicians, who have aspired, as they still aspire, to realize equality and bring the masses into actual participation in the management of the state.   It is also understandable that that movement should have won adherents among elements in the working classes that have succeeded in acquiring enough education to lift them above the level of their birth.   It is understandable, finally, that the thinkers in the movement should at once have leaped to the conclusion that neither absolute justice nor real equality can be established in this world unless private property is abolished.

But what at first sight is not so easy to understand is that during the nineteenth century, and into the twentieth, the European bourgeoisie should have offered such feeble and spasmodic resistance to the spread of socialist doctrines, and to the organization of the political forces that have embraced those doctrines.   That has come about for a number of reasons.   In the first place, there has been a widespread deference to the liberal principle that the good sense of the public can be depended upon to distinguish between truth and error and to discover what is realizable and what is not realizable in the real world.   Then again a vague sense of optimism prevailed, with few interruptions, all through the western world down to the very end of the nineteenth century.   Confidence in the reasonableness and goodness of the human being, and in the ability of the schoolmaster eventually to educate the masses, remained unshaken.   It was the common belief that the world was moving toward an era of universal concord and happiness.   The bourgeois mind itself was until very recently imbued with many of the principles that form the intellectual substructure of socialism. Slave to its own preconceptions, therefore, the European bourgeoisie has fought socialism all along with its right hand tied and its left hand far from free. Instead of fighting socialism openly, many countries in Europe came to terms with the movement, accepting compromises that were sometimes, nay almost always, undignified and harmful.

The consequences of that weakness have been aggravated by a number of other circumstances. Of all the various versions of the socialist gospel, the version that has been canonized and universally adopted has been the one that promises the certain triumph of the doctrine and meantime deliberately fans feelings of class hatred. Those are the feelings that are best calculated to undermine the structure of a nation or civilization and destroy it. As we have seen (chap. XI, §7), a pernicious and effective propaganda of destructive hate between the social classes is developed in the pages of Marx's *Kapital*. It is also certain that to promote that hatred was one of the purposes that Marx set himself in his writings. The correspondence between Marx and Lassalle is replete with sentences of which the following is typical: "The thing to do now is instill poison wherever possible *(Gift infiltrieren wo immer ist nun ratsam).*"[1] If it be argued that perhaps one in a thousand of all the many socialists have read and comprehended Marx's works, one can answer that from Marx's new gospel a brief catechism has been carefully extracted which anyone can easily commit to memory. Today there is hardly a factory worker who does not believe, or at least has not been told over and over again, that the wealth of his employer, or of the shareholders who have supplied capital for his factory, has been amassed by depriving workingmen of some of the wages that were due them, and in not a few countries there is hardly a farmhand to whom the same good tidings have not been brought.

One of the commonest sophisms of socialist propaganda is that class hatred is not produced by socialist doctrines, but is a natural consequence of the inequalities and injustices that prevail in society. The answer is that social inequalities and injustices have always existed, whereas class hatreds have been intermittent

---

[1] *Briefwechsel zwischen Lassalle und Marx*, p. 170. For further interesting details see Luzio, *Carlo Alberto e Mazzini*.

in the past, or at least have never been as strong as they are today
as a result of socialist propaganda.

Socialism and the more extreme wings of socialism are dangerous largely because of the state of mind that they create and
maintain in the masses, and because of their actual organizations, which are more or less strong according to the country.

But another and perhaps a graver danger confronts our modern
society. It lies not in a mental state that can be modified but in
the very nature of the economic organization which modern
society has adopted. Not only that. Modern society cannot
abandon that organization without abandoning the larger share
of its prosperity, and without ceasing to satisfy many needs that
have only recently come to be felt as needs but which are already
to be classed among the indispensables.

Division of labor and specialization in production have been
carried to extreme lengths in western societies. Without rail-
roads, steamships, postal systems, telephones and telegraphs,
supplies of fuel and other raw materials, not one of our great cities
could live for more than a month; and within a few months the
greatest of our nations would find itself unable to feed more than
a small percentage of its population. Never before has the
material life of each single individual been so directly dependent
upon the perfect functioning of the whole social mechanism as it is
today. Now the functioning of each part in the mechanism is
entrusted to a particular group of persons and the normal life of
society as a whole comes, therefore, to depend upon the good will
of each of its groups.

This state of affairs is becoming very hard to change, and of it
has come the syndicalist peril—the danger, that is, that a small
group may impose its will upon the rest of society. Today it
would not be strictly necessary to conform to the letter of the
apologue of Menenius Agrippa—it would not be necessary for all
the members to combine against the stomach or, better, against
the directing brain. If any single member, any single essential
organ, should stop doing its duty, the brain and all the nervous
centers that depend on it would be paralyzed.

Every group of persons that is engaged in a special function has
a certain homogeneousness of spirit, education and, especially,
interests. It is only natural, therefore, that it should try to
organize in a trade or professional union, or syndicate, under

leaders of its own, and that once the unions are organized they should immediately perceive their power and the profit they can derive from exercising it. What is commonly called "syndicalism" has become, therefore, a graver danger for the modern state than feudalism ever was for the medieval state. During the Middle Ages, society, and therefore the state, was very primitively organized. Each fraction of society was all but sufficient unto itself. It had at its disposal all the organs that it needed for subsisting. The opposition of the part against the whole arose along local lines. A powerful baron, or a great city, or a league of barons and cities, could now and again dictate to the emperor or the king. Today the opposition of the part to the whole has a functional basis. A powerful labor union or, a fortiori, a league of labor unions can impose its will upon the state.

In order to obviate this danger, it is necessary to prevent, at all costs, the rise of new sovereignties intermediate between the individual and the state. That was what happened in the Middle Ages, when the vassal gave his direct obedience to the baron and not to the king. In other words, it is absolutely indispensable that the heads of our present governments should at all times receive greater obedience from the members of the unions than the heads of the unions themselves receive. Devotion to the national interests must always be stronger than devotion to class interests. Unfortunately, one of the major weaknesses of present-day European society—another of the seeds of dissolution in the modern representative system—lies in a relaxation of those forces of moral cohesion which alone are capable of uniting in a consensus of sentiments and ideas all the atoms that make up a people, and which, therefore, constitute the cement without which any political edifice totters and collapses.

The fundamental doctrine of the old religion aimed at uniting all the citizens of a given nation, and all Christian nations, in brotherhood with each other. But especially during the last two centuries religion has lost much of its prestige and practical efficacy. There are a number of causes for that. Outstanding among them, particularly in the Latin countries, has been the irreligion of the ruling classes, who are now perceiving, too late, that the emancipation of the lower classes from what were too lightly called "outmoded superstitions" has thrust them into the clutches of a gross and crass materialism and opened the road to

far worse superstitions.[1] It was thought that once the religious
bond had been weakened it could be replaced by faith in the three
great principles of the century, liberty, equality, fraternity; and
that the application of those principles would inaugurate a new
era of peace and universal justice in the world. But socialist
propaganda had no difficulty in demonstrating that this liberal
faith had no foundation in fact, that democracy, however generous, did not prevent power from remaining in the hands of the
bourgeoisie, which, according to socialist doctrines, will always be
separated from the humbler classes in society by an incurable
conflict of interests.

Patriotism, therefore, has been left as the chief factor of moral
and intellectual cohesion within the various countries of Europe.
Patriotism, too, has generally been combated by socialism as an
invention that the ruling classes have devised to prevent the
union of the proletarians of all the world against the bourgeoisie
of all the world which had been foretold by Marx. But having
deeper roots than religion in the souls of the modern nations
today, patriotism has offered sturdier resistance to the attacks of
its adversaries. Patriotism is grounded in the sense of common
interests that binds together people who live in the same country,
and in the oneness of sentiments and ideas that almost inevitably
arises among people who speak the same language, have the same
background, share common glories and meet the same fortunes
and misfortunes. It satisfies, finally, a yearning of the human
soul to love the group to which it belongs above all other groups.

It would be hazardous, and perhaps inconsistent with the facts,
to assert that the middle classes in Europe have had any clear or
definite awareness of the great moral obstacle that patriotism
offers to the progress of socialism. But it is certain, nevertheless, that, beginning with the early years of the twentieth century,
a powerful awakening of patriotic feeling was observable in the
educated youth of almost all the European countries. Unfortunately, love of country, and a natural desire that one's country
should make its influence more and more felt in the world, often
goes hand in hand with diffidence toward other countries and
sometimes with hatred of them. The overexcitation of these
patriotic sentiments undoubtedly helped to create the moral and
intellectual atmosphere that brought on the World War.

[1] See chap. XI, §3.

5. The grave and far-reaching consequences of the World War, during which each of the contending nations strained its capacities to the utmost, are now too familiar to need minute description.[1] At the end of 1918 all the belligerent states were burdened with enormous public debts. Most of the money represented by the debts had been applied to purposes of war and were therefore unproductive from an economic standpoint. Much wealth had gone abroad to neutral countries, or to nations that had entered the conflict very tardily. In the countries that had borne the major weight of the war private capital also had shrunk considerably. It was therefore inevitable that the period of prosperity that had preceded 1914 should be succeeded by a period of relative poverty, which in less wealthy countries, and especially in the defeated and therefore worse-treated countries, reached the point of acute misery.

The economic disaster was reinforced by the moral disaster that resulted from the changed distribution of what little wealth was still left. In the belligerent nations, and to a considerable though lesser extent in neutral countries, while large proportions of the population were markedly impoverished, a certain minority found opportunities to make unexpected and handsome gains in the war. Now nothing is more demoralizing to people than to see sudden wealth acquired through no special merit, side by side with sudden impoverishment that is not due to any fault. That spectacle offends the sense of justice and overstimulates sentiments of envy and greed. Many individuals who had lived honest, respectable lives down to the great cataclysm turned to a dishonest scrambling for wealth, since they were resolved to be counted among the newly rich at any cost, rather than to suffer the hardships of the newly poor.

But what helped most of all to shake the stability of the political organization of Europe, and to disturb the equilibrium between social classes, was the impoverishment of the middle class, of that portion of the bourgeoisie that lives on small savings, on moderate holdings of real estate and, especially, by its intellectual labors. We have already seen (chap. XIV, §6) that the rise of such a class was one of the factors in the creation of the conditions that are required for the proper functioning of the representative

[1] One still remembers the effective pictures drawn by Keynes in *The Economic Consequences of the Peace* and by Nitti in *L'Europa senza pace.*

system.   It is only natural, therefore, that the economic decline
of that class should make it difficult for the representative system
to go on functioning, and if the decline continues, an intellectual
and moral decline will necessarily ensue.

In all countries that played sustained roles in the World War,
the state machine was called upon to undertake such hard work
and so much of it, it was called upon to repress or to crush so
many private passions, sentiments and interests, that it is not to
be wondered at that its gearings should at certain moments have
shown signs of deteriorating and of failing to function.   At the
point where the state machine was weakest, in Russia, that is,
the wear and tear was so great that the machine flew to pieces
outright; but it is evident that it needs more or less rest and
repairing in all countries.

In almost all countries, these causes, and other secondary ones,
have made it more or less difficult for the prewar political system
to go on functioning.   Especially in countries that were more
distressed than others by the common misfortunes, the idea has
arisen that the present crisis can be solved, and ought to be
solved, by some profound and radical change in the institutions
that have been inherited from the last century, and that it is
and should be the duty of the new generation, of the young men
who fought the war, to effect that transformation by dismantling
the political structures reared by their fathers, and building them
over according to new and better patterns.

Now, if one examines the present economic, intellectual and
moral situation in European society and takes into account the
various currents of ideas, sentiments and interests that are
stirring within it, one finds but three possible solutions of a
radical nature for the present political crisis.   One of them has
already been resorted to in Russia—the "dictatorship of the
proletariat," so-called, with its corresponding experiment in
communism.   The second would be a return to old-fashioned
bureaucratic absolutism.   The third would be syndicalism, in
other words, a replacement of individual representation by class
representation in legislative assemblies.

In view of the Russian experiment the results of the dictatorship of the proletariat are now sufficiently familiar, and they are
such that many fervent and long-standing admirers of Marx are

today more or less openly opposed to any immediate realization
of the master's program.

The disagreement between Marxists who favor an immediate
and violent realization of the program commonly attributed to
their master, and Marxists who favor a slow and gradual application of it, has of late become sharply marked. Those who belong
to the more violent faction have taken the name of "communists." The others have kept the old name—"socialists." A
more scientific criterion for distinguishing the terms "socialism"
and "communism" would be to call socialism a system under
which the community pays each worker according to the value or
efficiency of the work he does. Under communism, each worker
would receive an income according to his needs.[1] This criterion
is the one that Lenin himself adopted. He asserted that in a first
phase his system would be socialistic, whereas communism would
be attained in a second phase, when society should have become
completely free of any remnants of bourgeois morality—or,
rather, immorality.[2] The men who are today governing the
former empire of the czars are themselves trying to moderate the
realization of the Marxian program.

It is inevitable that a new bourgeoisie should eventually emerge
in Russia from the ranks of the very men who carried the revolution through, and that private property should be reestablished in
substance if not in form. Nevertheless it proved impossible,
during the first period of the revolution, to avoid an attempt to
establish pure communism in that country. That attempt, as is
well known, brought on a rapid and complete disorganization of
every sort of production, and want and famine came in its wake.
Nor can we believe that if communism were to triumph in other
parts of Europe it would be possible to avoid a similar experiment, which would inevitably yield the same results, and perhaps
worse ones. Less fortunate than Russia, western Europe is
overpopulated and in continual need, even in normal times, of
certain raw materials that are indispensable to daily living, and
these can be supplied only by America or other parts of the world.

These results are of an economic nature. As for moral results,
the dictatorship of the proletariat, in whatever country, would

---

[1] See chap. XI, §3 (p. 282).

[2] Lenin, *State and Revolution*.

have consequences far more disastrous.[1]   In Russia, in the name
of that dictatorship, the old ruling class has been all but exterminated and replaced by another that is certainly shrewder and
more energetic, and perhaps even more intelligent.   Morally,
alas, it can only be regarded as inferior.   In order to hold its own
in the face of the general discontent, in order to deal with the
desperation of all who are not members of it, and to make up
for others of its deficiencies, the new Russian ruling class has
had to govern tyrannically, override all scruples and enforce
obedience by sheer terror.   One can say more than that.   In
Russia, for better or for worse, it has been possible to find another
ruling class to supersede the old.   In western Europe that
would be virtually impossible.   Communism would immediately
resolve, or, better, dissolve, into complete anarchy.   In Russia,
the old bourgeoisie has been replaced after a fashion by the
Jewish petty bourgeoisie and by other more or less allogeneous
elements such as Letts, Armenians and Mohammedan Tatars.
The individuals composing each of those elements have long been
bound to each other by comradeships of race, language and
religion, and by the petty persecutions and disabilities which they
suffered in common under the government of the czars.   The
present rulers of Russia can therefore count on their loyalty.
Such minorities, however—minorities differing in race and religion
from the rest of the population—hardly exist in western Europe,
and such as there are are so situated that they would greatly fear
the advent of communism.   The new ruling class, therefore,
would have to be recruited from the more violent elements in the
plebs and the less reputable portions of the old bourgeoisie.
These people would be incompetent on the intellectual side and
they would almost certainly be lacking in that minimum of
morality that has to regulate relations between people who are
committing a great villainy in common, if their villainy is to
achieve any abiding success.

An experiment in so-called "moderate socialism," which would
allow private property to exist provisorily and nominally but
would subject it to such burdens and limitations as to deprive it
of significance, would have even less chance of lasting in western
Europe than a downright and thoroughgoing dictatorship of the
proletariat.   Such a system would always be open to violent

[1] See chap. XI, §§3–6.

attack by the regular communists, without having the prestige and strength to suppress them, and it would not have at its disposal the margin of wealth that would be indispensable to cover the wastage inevitably incident to any attempt to apply a moderate form of socialism. Because of its failures and the disappointments it would occasion, it would either degenerate rapidly into pure communism, or merely lead to a development of the present political and economic system into a bureaucratic and military dictatorship.

Such a development would correspond to the second of the solutions of the present crisis in the representative system that we mentioned above. It might for the moment have its advantages for one or another of the European countries, though it would itself present very serious drawbacks if it were to be adopted as a permanent solution. Down to 1914, elective elements played an important and effective part in the exercise of sovereign power in all countries that are governed according to one or another of the representative systems. Under the solution in question such elements would vanish from public life, or be reduced to fulfilling secondary or merely decorative functions, leaving the civil and military bureaucracy with a de facto authority that would be virtually unbalanced and uncontrolled.

The bureaucratic system here in question would not be like any of the various forms of representative government. It would resemble neither the parliamentary form, which prevails in England and France, nor the presidential form, which is functioning in the United States, nor the strictly constitutional form which existed in Germany prior to 1918. It would be a sort of "Caesarism," such as prevailed in France during the First Empire, and, in more moderate form, during the Second Empire down to 1868. Under those forms of government parliament had purely decorative functions. This new Caesarism, furthermore, might even try to find a legal basis for itself in a popular referendum, or plebiscite, as the two Napoleonic Caesarisms did.

As we have seen, the participation of the elective element is very important in the modern state, and the great superiority and the main strength of modern political systems lie in the ingenious balancing that they admit of between the liberal principle and the autocratic principle, the former represented by parliaments and local councils, the latter by permanent bureaucracies. We have also seen that this joint participation is essential if all political forces and capacities are to make themselves felt in public life, and if all sovereign powers are to exercise the reciprocal control and limitation that is the indispensable condition of political liberty.   On any other basis liberty becomes a mere word devoid of any practical significance.   Liberty of the press and, in general, all personal liberties—in other words, all the safeguards that the citizen has against arbitrary conduct on the part of the public official—would be insufficiently guaranteed once elective elements came to have little or no weight on the scales of public power.

In such a case we would be going back to the old absolutist system, disguised perhaps under a mask of popular sovereignty, which our fathers fought so strenuously to destroy, which our younger generations have not experienced and of the character of which they have not the remotest idea.   Now the effects of such a system would be infinitely more serious today than they could ever have been a century and a half or two centuries ago, because the prerogatives of the state have increased enormously in the meantime, and with them the amount of wealth which the state absorbs and distributes.   The absolutism of rulers would therefore no longer find, as it once found, and indeed still finds in crude and primitive political organizations, a natural curb and limit in the scarcity of means that are at the disposal of a government. Today, in view of the great perfection and comprehensive development of the state machine, a bureaucracy that possesses an unlimited and uncontrolled power can easily shatter all individual and collective resistance, suppress every initiative on the part of elements not belonging to it and so exhaust the whole social body by sucking all vital energies from it.

We need not spend many words in describing the dangers of the third radical solution for the present crisis in the parliamentary system—the syndicalist, or unionist, solution.   A chamber possessing sovereign powers and participating in lawmaking as the legal mouthpiece of class syndicates would supply the best possible basis for the organization of sovereignty intermediate between the individual and the state, which is perhaps the most serious threat to society that we confront at the present moment in our political life.   By means of their representatives, the unions themselves can carry on a most effective activity within the state and against the state, and paralyze every effort of the state to free itself of their tutelage.

It would be naive to imagine that the coexistence of another chamber, or even of two other chambers, formed under the old system of individual representation and from elements not belonging to the unions, would be sufficient to counterbalance the influence of the third chamber elected by the unions. It should by now be apparent that the effectiveness of a given political organ—the importance it assumes in the actual management of the state—is not related primarily to the legal powers which the fundamental constitution confers upon it, but derives from the prestige which it enjoys in public opinion, and especially from the number and efficacy of the social forces, interests, ideas and sentiments which find their expression in it. That is the reason why, so far, parliamentary chambers that have depended directly on popular suffrage have in general exercised a greater influence than houses that have been constituted on different principles, though very often the latter counted among their members larger numbers of technical capacities and greater personal values. In view of the importance that separate classes have acquired in the economic life of every civilized country today, it is not far-fetched to assume that the syndicalist chamber would easily prevail over others—all the more so if we consider that the more populous syndicates could, by marshaling a compact and disciplined vote, exert great influence upon elections to chambers constituted on the present basis of individual representation.

We must not imagine that, in a chamber made up of representatives of syndicates, the better-educated elements, such as the representatives of magistrates and scholars, or of lawyers and engineers, would be likely to have the controlling influence. The predominant influence from the outset would probably rest with the representatives of railway men, seamen, stevedores and, in England and Germany, miners. The strength of a union would lie not in the education or cultivation of its members but in their numbers, and especially in the material indispensability of the function that they fulfill in the daily life of the people. In that regard the work done by a railwayman or a baker is certainly more indispensable than the work done by a professor or a lawyer. On that basis, furthermore, if the more unlettered and larger unions, all more or less imbued with Marxist doctrines and carefully trained to believe in the necessity of the so-called "class struggle," should succeed in working together, they would be able to seize control of the state outright. Having done that, they would in all probability and in the long run, begin to quarrel with each other, and the economic disorganization that would result would end in political anarchy.[1]

6. It follows, therefore, that the only three possible radical solutions of the crisis which the representative system is now traversing would lead the European countries to adopt a less perfect, and, one might say, a more primitive, political system than the one they now have. The adoption of any one of the three would be symptomatic of a political decline which, as usual, would become simultaneously cause and effect of a general decline in civilization. Certainly no one would try to maintain that the representative system cannot be improved upon very considerably, or that in time it could not be replaced with something different and better. Quite to the contrary, if Europe is able to overcome the difficulties with which she is struggling at present, it is altogether probable that in the course of another century, or even within half that time, new ideas, new sentiments, new needs will automatically prepare the ground for other political systems that may be far preferable to any now existing.

Unfortunately, the moral and economic results of the World War have, at this critical moment, made it difficult for the institutions that were in force down to 1914 to go on functioning properly. For them to keep their vitality unimpaired, they needed, as they still need, a continuation of the period of relative peace and general prosperity which the world enjoyed during the last decades of the nineteenth century and the first years of the twentieth. The war did not create the germs of dissolution from which the representative system is now suffering. Like any other system it contained those germs within itself and still contains them. The war simply rendered them more virulent. Today they are threatening to kill the representative system before the

---

[1] See Mosca, speeches delivered in the Italian Chamber of Deputies, Mar. 7, 1919, and in the Senate, Mar. 31, 1920, and Nov. 27, 1922; also "Feudalismo funzionale," "Il pericolo dello stato moderno" and "Feudalismo e sindicalismo;" See also above, chap. XIV, §8.

healing forces which are at work within every society, unless it is
altogether effete, have time to develop the elements required for
creating a new type of political organization that will be better
than the one now in force.   In other words, the old house is
threatening to fall before the materials for building the new one
are ready.   If the collapse were to come, our peoples would be
obliged to take refuge either in the ruins of a still older structure
that has been unoccupied for two or three generations, or else in a
hurriedly improvised shack.

Fifty years ago the author of this volume opened his career as
a writer with a book which was a book of his youth but which he
still does not disown.[1]   In it he sought to lay bare some of the
untruths that lie imbedded in certain assumptions of the representative system, and some of the defects of parliamentarism.
Today advancing years have made him more cautious in judgment and, he might venture to say, more balanced.   His conclusions at any rate are deeply pondered.   As he looks closely and
dispassionately at the conditions that prevail in many European
nations and especially in his own country, Italy, he feels impelled
to urge the rising generation to restore and conserve the political
system which it inherited from its fathers.

That task, evidently, is not an easy one.   Before it can even
be essayed, Europe has to be rehabilitated economically, and the
condition of the European middle class has to be improved.
Without the cooperation of such a class no form of representative
government is, in the long run, possible.   In the way of that
rehabilitation stand the still living hatreds between the various
social classes in Europe, and the still livelier hatreds between the
different European countries, hatreds which the war terribly
stimulated and which have not yet died down.   The first
requisite, therefore, would be that all the European peoples
should at last work into their minds and into their hearts the
firm conviction that they have many common and supreme
interests to safeguard, that they are bound to each other by a
close-knit fabric of intellectual, sentimental and economic relations and that they have so many psychological and cultural
affinities that suffering, humiliation and decay for any one of
them must mean suffering, humiliation and decay for them
all.

[1] Mosca, *Teorica dei governi.*

To restore the representative system by no means implies that that system should not be modified or changed in one respect or another, especially in certain countries.   In our opinion, one of the most important changes would concern legislation on the press.   Ways can surely be found to maintain freedom for scientific investigation and for honest criticism of acts of government, and at the same time to place restraints on the corruption of minds that are, and will forever remain, minds of children.   That corruption has so far been freely practiced in our European countries.   A first step in that direction would be to adopt the principle that responsibility for offenses of the press, like responsibility for any other crime, should rest with those who actually commit them, in other words, with the writers.   A number of European countries have a legal monstrosity that permits a man who writes in a newspaper or periodical to evade penal responsibility for what he writes as long as he is willing to remain anonymous or unknown.   In such cases the penalty goes to the publisher's agent, who is known in technical language as the "responsible manager."[1]   In honest criticism of acts of government we mean to include criticism that is based on fundamental differences in political ideas and principles, provided it does not stoop to defaming insult, to deliberate and brazen falsehood and to slander.

Another difficulty which requires urgent attention in several, if not all, countries of Europe, arises in connection with freedom of assembly and association.   Present laws are so vague and indefinite that they permit a strong authoritarian government to suppress any sort of association by police force.   At the same time they do not offer a weak and timid government any effective legal defense against the organization of elements that are opposed to the existing order and aim to suppress the state itself by violent seizure of its organs.

We have not mentioned limitation of suffrage among the resorts that might be best calculated to ensure the duration of the representative system.   We regard the granting of universal suffrage as a mistake and mistakes are not more frequent in public life than they are in private life.   At the same time one could not go back on it without committing a second mistake which might have unforeseeable consequences of a very serious nature.

[1] Mosca, *Appunti di diritto costituzionale*, pp. 167–168.

Brief periods of strong government, where the state exercises many powers and great authority, may prove of actual benefit in some European countries, as helping to restore or provide conditions that will enable the representative system to function normally in a near future. In Rome, in the best days of the republic, brief periods of dictatorship were not infrequent.

But if the present crisis that is threatening our political systems and the social structure itself is to be surmounted, the ruling class must rid itself of many of its prejudices and change its psychological attitude. It must become aware that it is a ruling class, and so gain a clear conception of its rights and its duties. It will never be able to do that unless it can raise the level of its political competence and understanding, which have so far been woefully defective in the most highly civilized countries in Europe, and in some countries altogether lacking. Then only will it learn how to appraise the conduct of its leaders soundly, and so gradually regain in the eyes of the masses the prestige that it has in large part lost. It must be able to see a little beyond its immediate interests and no longer squander most of its energies in the pursuit of objectives that are of advantage to certain individuals only, or to the little cliques that are grouped about certain individuals. It must be persuaded once and for all that the situation that confronts us today is such that, in order to be worthy of belonging to the chosen minority to which the lot of every country is entrusted, it is not enough to have won a university degree, or to have managed a commercial or industrial enterprise successfully, or even to have risked one's life in the trenches. Long study and great devotion are also necessary.

Every generation produces a certain number of generous spirits who are capable of loving all that is, or seems to be, noble and beautiful, and of devoting large parts of their activity to improving the society in which they live, or at least to saving it from getting worse. Such individuals make up a small moral and intellectual aristocracy, which keeps humanity from rotting in the slough of selfishness and material appetites. To such aristocracies the world primarily owes the fact that many nations have been able to rise from barbarism and have never relapsed into it. Rarely do members of such aristocracies attain the outstanding positions in political life, but they render a perhaps more effective service to the world by molding the minds and guiding the sentiments of their contemporaries, so that in the end they succeed in forcing their programs upon those who rule the state.

We cannot suppose that there will be any lack or deficiency of such generous souls in the generations that are now rising. But it has happened more than once in the long course of human history that the efforts and sacrifices of such people have not availed to save a nation or a civilization from decline and ruin. That has occurred, we believe, largely because the "best" people have had no clear and definite perception of the needs of their times, and therefore of the means best calculated to achieve social salvation. Let us hope that that clear perception will not be wanting today in the nobler elements among our youth, and that it may so enlighten their minds and quicken their hearts that they can think and act in peace as resolutely and courageously as they fought in war.

INDEX AND BIBLIOGRAPHY

A